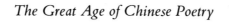

The Great Age of Chinese Poetry

盛 唐 詩

THE GREAT AGE OF CHINESE POETRY

The High T'ang

STEPHEN OWEN

New Haven and London, Yale University Press

Published with assistance from
the Frederick W. Hilles Publication Fund
of Yale University.

Designed by Sally Harris
and set in Monophoto Bembo type by
Asco Trade Typesetting Ltd., Hong Kong.
Printed in the United States of America by
Vail-Ballou Press, Binghamton, N.Y.

Library of Congress Cataloging in Publication Data

Owen, Stephen.
   The great age of Chinese poetry.

  Bibliography: p.
  Includes index.
   1. Chinese poetry—T'ang dynasty, 618–907—
History and criticism.   I. Title.
PL2321.094   895.1′13   80–141
ISBN 0-300-02367-7

1 2 3 4 5 6 7 8 9 10

Contents

Acknowledgments

Stolen evenings and weekends, even well-protected summers, cannot provide the time necessary for a project of this magnitude. My thanks, therefore, go first of all to the Morse Fellowship of Yale University for its financial support during the academic year 1976–77, allowing me (with an extra summer) sixteen uninterrupted months to do research for this volume. My thanks also go to the Moore Fund of Yale for helping to defray the considerable costs of printing this volume with Chinese characters and the texts of the poems.

Of my many friends and colleagues who have commented on parts of the manuscript, I would like especially to thank Hugh Stimson, Hans Frankel, Maureen Robertson, and Marsha Wagner. I should also thank my students, who have for several years been reading and commenting on the various chapters. Many thanks to Wen-tao Cheng for his calligraphy in this volume and to Ch'ung-ho Frankel, who inadvertently was not acknowledged for her calligraphy for *Poetry of the Early T'ang*.

I would like to dedicate the book to my parents, George and Deha Owen, for their many years of love and support.

Chronology of Rulers
(with important reign titles)

Chung-tsung 中宗	705–710
Jui-tsung 睿宗	710–712
Hsüan-tsung 玄宗	712–756
K'ai-yüan Reign 開元	713–741
T'ien-pao Reign 天寶	742–755
Su-tsung 肅宗	756–762
T'ai-tsung 代宗	762–779
Ta-li Reign 大歷	766–779
Te-tsung 德宗	779–805

Introduction

Chinese critics usually designated the periods of literary history by reigns, by dynasties, or by dynastic subdivisions such as "Early," "Middle," and "Late." When they looked back on the T'ang, however, a new term, originally from the vegetative cycle, intruded between the "Early T'ang" and "Mid-T'ang." This term reveals the extent to which wonder overcame the literary historian's usual sobriety: as in the poetry of no other dynasty, there is a "High T'ang" 盛唐, a "T'ang in Full Flower." To later readers, this era, centered in the reign of Hsüan-tsung, possessed a unique aura of splendor and greatness, was a moment when cultural efflorescence and literary genius happily coincided. Their awe was justified: the work of at least three major poets and of a dozen nearly great shed a light that no reader could ignore. But that very radiance also obscured the literary-historical realities of the period: a complex process of continuous change was perceived as a single sunburst of genius and variety that vanished almost as quickly as it appeared, leaving later ages to struggle for its afterglow.

Appearing in the ninth century, growing through the Sung, and firmly rooted in the minds of all born later was the conviction that the High T'ang had been the apogee of all Chinese poetry. Later poets lamented their own dimness in face of its luminosity; they imitated it slavishly, revolted against it violently, declared they would ignore it and write spontaneously according to the dictates of their inner natures; but in the history of Chinese poetry it remained the fixed center that defined the positions of all later poets.

Any serious understanding of the period and its poetry demands that we put aside the myth of radiance. Wang Wei's poems contain an allegory of a mountain temple whose natural beauty existed to lead the pilgrim to

xii   *Introduction*

a truth behind the seductive surface (p. 42); in a similar way, the myth of
the golden age of poetry is not the goal itself, but an enticement to enter
the age and comprehend its true nature. If we are content simply to con-
template it from afar, we cannot appreciate its full dynamism and variety:
the internal relationships between the poets are distorted; the age's roots in
past poetry are severed; and a series of reductive, platitudinous attributes
are allowed to characterize the period style.

The tenacity of the myth of the golden age of poetry demands caution
in three important areas. First, the period must not be identified with the
two poets who dominated it for later readers: Li Po and Tu Fu. Literary
history cannot comprehend the fullness of major talent; more modestly, it
seeks to set that talent in its essential contexts. If we set aside the High T'ang
myth, we realize how uncharacteristic of the period Li Po and Tu Fu were.
Later readers tended to complacency about the stature of Li Po and Tu Fu:
they were viewed not only as the height of poetry but also as the two
antithetical norms of the poetic personality. But the context of contemporary poetry casts Li Po and Tu Fu in a very different light, and in that
light can be seen the nature and degree of their originality. Later readers
would often link Wang Wei and Meng Hao-jan for their shared interest in
the theme of reclusion. A contemporary poetic context reveals how far
apart the two men were—in training, in sensibility, and in the nature of
their poetic talents. Our goal thus becomes not to define the age by its
major talents, but rather to use the true norms of the age to understand its
greatest poets.

The second caution lies in the general problem of period style. From
the point of view of conservative literary historians, there is the illusion
that a period style is a fully coherent entity with conveniently fixed dates.
Others distrust any period labels and see in them something inimical to the
true appreciation of poetry. Period styles are real: no sensitive reader of
Chinese or English poetry can escape that historical sense of language, style,
and literary context which is a natural and pleasurable part of the reading
process. But period styles are shapeless, multifaceted, and permeable en-
tities that do not submit to easy definition. They are most comprehensible
at their boundaries: new ideas, influential poets, or rediscoveries can contribute to a general change in poetry over the course of a few years. These
boundaries are highly permeable: there the roots of a new style and the
continuities of an older one are clearest. The shape that High T'ang poetry
took roughly between 715 and 725 was clearly an outgrowth of the Early
T'ang style; at the same time, the changes then taking place were grounded
in the dissatisfactions of many Early T'ang poets with the poetry of their
own age. At its other boundary, the High T'ang style lingered on after the
death of its last major talent, Tu Fu. The real break into the Mid-T'ang did

not occur until the renewed interest in *fu-ku* 復古 in the early 790s.[1] But that boundary is far from absolute: conservative poets continued to write border poems in the style of Wang Ch'ang-ling, while the radical innovators fashioned a new poetry with their eyes set on Li Po and Tu Fu.

The third and most serious danger of the High T'ang myth is the collapse of its internal chronology into a moment of glittering variety. The variety of High T'ang poetry is indeed partially a function of the differences between individual poets, but it is also in part a result of the changes in the literary situation over the course of seventy years. A poet who reached his maturity in the 720s had a very different view of poetry and his poetic past than a poet who matured in the 740s. In the 720s poetry was a polished craft that could, theoretically, aspire to deep moral and cultural significance. Moreover, that there had been no unquestionably major poet for centuries left ample room for genius. The poet maturing in the 740s faced a heritage of twenty years of creative magnificence. Thus, Tu Fu stands in the shadow of his immediate predecessors in a way that the earlier Meng Hao-jan never did.

In addition to its purely descriptive responsibilities, literary history is a study of poetic norms and the processes of change. Rather than try to define the period style by a new series of attributes, I shall instead establish several general areas of concern to follow through this study. These areas of concern loosely distinguish the High T'ang from its predecessors and successors, but at the same time they admit the many individual responses that give the period its variety.

The High T'ang was dominated by a phenomenon that we will call "capital poetry," a direct descendant of the court poetry of the preceding century. Capital poetry was never a monolithic entity, but it possessed an amazing tenacity, coherence, and continuity of literary values. Capital poetry refers to the norms of social and occasional poetry practiced and appreciated by the upper circle of capital society. Members of the great eighth-century clans figure prominently among its practitioners and recipients, and it was largely through them that a poet would become "famous in the age." In capital poetry we find the strongest interest in regulated verse forms (though other forms could be demanded by an occasion); we find a special interest in Buddhist and eremitic themes, as the great topics of social renunciation were domesticated to the bucolic yearnings of the great; and we find a powerful sense of generic and subgeneric decorum, though less rigidly limited than the decorum of court poetry. Like court poetry, capital poetry was conceived less as an independent "art," than as a social practice, and there was a web of personal and poetic relationships linking the court poets of Chung-tsung's reign to the imperially favored poets of the *Yü-lan shih* 御覽詩, an early-ninth-century anthology. This web of social relationships appears clearly in the exchanges of occasional poetry that inevitably constitute a large part of the poetic corpus of the capital poets.

In spite of the social prestige and influence of the capital poets, the greatest poetry of the age was written by outsiders, with the notable exception of Wang Wei. Wang Wei was at once the apogee of capital poetry and its transfiguration: he was the poet who worked within the rules to go beyond them. Li Po and Tu Fu may have dominated the imaginations of readers from the ninth century onward, but during the second half of the eighth century itself, Wang Wei's was the lingering poetic voice that haunted the poems of lesser men. The other great names of High T'ang poetry—Meng Hao-jan, Kao Shih, Wang Ch'ang-ling, Li Po, Ts'en Shen, Tu Fu, Wei Ying-wu—all worked to some degree outside the world of capital poetry, because of social rank, historical circumstance, or personal disposition. Some aspired to capital poetry; some rejected it; but it was the background against which they became poets with truly individual voices.

In this lies one partial explanation for High T'ang greatness: never before and never afterward in the history of Chinese poetry was there a single, unified aesthetic norm beside which poets could still attain the full latitude of individual talent. The age of court poetry possessed a unified poetic norm, but that norm too rigidly circumscribed poetic identity. Even as gifted a poet as Yü Hsin was held in chains by its strict rhetorical rules. On the other hand, in the ninth century and afterward there were many aesthetic norms, and no single one could carry the full authority of social sanction.

Related to this balance of a unified aesthetic norm with individual talent were changes taking place in the very concept of poetry. It was a period of transition between a view of poetry as a social gesture, represented by capital poetry with its roots in the tradition of court poetry, and poetry as an art with cultural and personal dimensions that transcended social occasion. High T'ang occasional poets spoke with one eye on posterity and one eye on the poem's recipient. Chinese occasional poetry is alive and well even today, but after the High T'ang, major poets increasingly looked to posterity with both eyes. Poets began to prepare and edit their own collections, and each occasional poem came to rest more comfortably in the full context of the poetic tradition. The slow transmutation of Chinese poetry into a self-conscious art form did not prevent the creation of poems as great as any in the High T'ang, but we sense in High T'ang poetry deeper roots in the fleshly world of historical and social circumstance. Furthermore, the strong commitment to poetic craft that was the legacy of court poetry enabled genuinely minor poets to create more than a few great poems. For contrast, one need only compare the minor poets of the Sung, who are all too often genuinely unreadable, producing a doggerel that observes no aesthetic standards but rhyme. Occasional poetry had ceased to be an integral part of social intercourse, and become an amusing, aesthetic pastime.

One particularly significant event during the High T'ang was the "rediscovery" of the poetic past and the attendant excitement this brought to poets. Poets of the sixth and seventh centuries were not unaware of their poetic past, but more often than not thought it only a quaint artifact; the social demands of the poetic present were far more acute. Celebrating an imperial visit to an aristocratic villa, Sung Chih-wen would never have thought to write in the style of T'ao Ch'ien simply because it attracted him or because he thought it a style on which to base great poetry. But High T'ang poets drew styles and poets out of the past in rapid succession, making them the silent heroes of a whole decade or a single poem. Juan Chi, T'ao Ch'ien, Ssu-ma Hsiang-ju, Yü Hsin, Hsieh Ling-yün, and others rose and fell with the passing decades. This excitement in the rediscovery of the poetic past continued through the Mid-T'ang, but during later centuries the literary past became a familiar part of contemporary poetry, a series of styles to draw upon, to imitate, or to recombine. Familiarity bred not contempt but limitation, and the literary past became a true burden rather than a means for liberation.

The first decades of the High T'ang soon became themselves a burdensome literary past. Already in the 750s poets were turning wistful eyes back to the K'ai-yüan and early T'ien-pao reigns, first as a period of lost cultural and social splendor, but soon as a vanished literary glory as well. The myth of the High T'ang began almost immediately after the An Lu-shan Rebellion, the event that marks the end of the T'ien-pao and literary glory. The myth was built consciously by poets like Tu Fu and Wei Ying-wu and unconsciously by the melancholy conservatism of the later capital poets. Mid-T'ang poets stood in its shadow no less than the later capital poets, but they differed from their immediate predecessors by creating the first of a long succession of creative reinterpretations of High T'ang greatness.

I have tried to keep this work as self-contained as possible, but it builds on *The Poetry of the Early T'ang* (New Haven: Yale, 1977), and the two books should, ideally, be read in sequence. The format used is basically the same as that of *The Poetry of the Early T'ang*. Poems are referred to by their numbers in *Tōdai no shihen*. Where available, I used critical texts; elsewhere, I made choices among the earliest texts.

PART ONE

The Beginning of the High T'ang and the First–Generation Poets

I

Early T'ang and High T'ang

During the seventh and eighth centuries, major and fundamental changes occurred in Chinese poetry (*shih* 詩). In the early seventh century, poetry was primarily a stylized form of social discourse practiced mainly in court circles. By the end of the eighth century, poetry, while retaining its function as social discourse, had also become a conscious art form serving a variety of ends and practiced by a wide range of literate Chinese. Never in traditional China was poetry an autotelic "pure art" in the Western sense: it was bound both to occasion and to concepts of poetry as the expression of inner nature or as a vehicle for the enduring principles of the civilization. But during the course of these two centuries, poetry was transformed from a minor diversion to an art that fully embodied these private, social, and cultural values.

The court poetry of the Early T'ang rigidly circumscribed the occasions for composition, the topics, the diction, and the structure of poetry. It was a poetry to be enjoyed most at the time of composition, and its quality depended on the fulfillment of clear standards of judgment. But the history of Early T'ang poetry is primarily a history of the breakdown of that old world of poetry, which was threatened both by prose polemics against it and by an increasing individuality in the poets themselves. Major changes, however, awaited the second and third decades of the eighth century, the beginning of the High T'ang.

The High T'ang began in mute rebellion against the Early T'ang. There were no manifestos, no denunciations of the preceding age; in fact, the first generation of High T'ang poets rarely acknowledged even the existence of their Early T'ang predecessors, preferring to look past them to more remote ancestors. Rebellion is a form of close relationship, however, and despite all the changes in High T'ang poetry, its paternity is unmistakable: its poetic tradition was of the Early T'ang. High T'ang regulated verse (*lü-shih* 律詩) had its origins in Early T'ang court poetry; the High T'ang *ku-feng* 古風 came directly from the Early T'ang poet Ch'en Tzu-ang 陳子昂 and the opposition poetics of the seventh century.[1] The heptasyllabic songs of the High T'ang retained many of the topics, modal associations, and conventions of diction of the heptasyllabic songs popular in Empress Wu's reign.[2] The conventions of a *yung-wu* 詠物 topic (an "object" or "phenomenon"), the common consolations in parting poems, and the formal structure of a journey through a landscape all had their roots in the poetry of the Early T'ang.

On the other hand, during the second and third decades of the eighth century, the Early T'ang style was radically modified, and genuinely new elements were introduced. The nature of these changes was in part determined by a deep dissatisfaction with Early T'ang poetry, particularly with the constricting formality of court poetry. The same dissatisfaction with the court poet's art had been one important aspect of the Early T'ang itself, but the antithetical impulse had largely been lost in sterile polemics.

Through the early decades of the eighth century, this antithetical impulse found a new freedom of concrete poetic expression. If the Early T'ang poet was bound by decorum, the High T'ang poet was fascinated by the lack of decorum—both in stylistic convention and thematically in the exaggerated gestures of the eccentric. If the court poet was committed to aristocratic society and its ambience, the High T'ang poet turned his interest to lower social types and their life, finding in them a true aristocracy of the spirit. If the court poet proudly held to mannered formality, the High T'ang poet would love what was plain and straightforward. If the Early T'ang poet disdained the showiness of bold metaphors and stylistic tours de force, then the High T'ang poet delighted in them. If the Early T'ang poet saw poetry as essentially a social phenomenon, then the High T'ang poet was drawn to private values and themes of reclusion, even in social poetry.

The liberation that High T'ang poets found in the antithetical impulse was neither constant nor universal, but that impulse helps to explain the multiple, often contradictory directions that High T'ang poetry took. Particularly in the early decades of the High T'ang, the new poetry was unified by its negative relationship to the Early T'ang: the stern moralizing of the *fu-ku* sentiment (pp. 8–9) and an interest in popular songs (anathema to *fu-ku*) could stand side by side as gestures against the aristocratic decorum of court poetry. The best High T'ang poets possessed the full technical range of the court poet—and court poetry was a complex craft with considerable range—but High T'ang poets were also able to ignore or modify details of that craft, producing a virtuosity and control that no court poet possessed.

Parallel to the changes in forms, themes, and the conception of poetry, a profound change took place in the social basis of poetry. During the Early T'ang the center of poetic composition had been the imperial court and the lesser courts of imperial princes and princesses. During the first half of the seventh century, poets were often members of the old literary families of the Southern Dynasties, and there was a strong continuity in poetic training as well as a conservatism in approved practice. This tradition was supported by members of the royal family and their favorites, on whom poets depended for appreciation and advancement.

During the late seventh and early eighth centuries, a series of events changed the situation dramatically. In 680 poetic composition was introduced into the *chin-shih* examination.[3] The *chin-shih* examination was designed specifically to bring into the government candidates for office who were not scions of the great capital families. The latter had privileges and prerogatives that ensured the continuity of their power and participation in the central government, though they also made extensive use of the *chin-shih* examination. But the *chin-shih* examination was primarily perceived as an avenue for minor gentry and collateral branches of great clans to establish themselves in the central government. The introduction of poetry into the *chin-shih* examination was a strong inducement for the spread of interest in poetic craft.

Through the examination and their own whims, Empress Wu and her various favorites promoted poets of relatively humble birth; two such poets, Chang Yüeh and Chang Chiu-ling, became ministers in Hsüan-tsung's reign, and they continued to support poets from lesser families. As critical appreciation and the patronage that accompanied it passed from the old literary families of the court, new and less rigid standards of taste were applied to poetry. Most of the poets famous in the K'ai-yüan Reign (713–41) enjoyed the patronage of Chang Yüeh or Chang Chiu-ling, and the two ministers' keen judgment played an important role in the evolution of the High T'ang style.

The final deathblow to the old social order of poetry was Hsüan-tsung's edict of 722 directed against the large entourages of the imperial princes. This edict closed off the principal source of patronage for court poetry and the previous route to poetic fame in the capital. All these new conditions changed not only the social class from which poets were drawn; they also changed the milieu in which most poetry was composed.

The development away from the aristocratic world of Early T'ang poetry appeared most strongly in five areas.

1. The Tradition of Exile Poetry

The nature and development of T'ang poetry cannot be understood apart from its ties to occasion. In the modern West, poetry is conceived not as a private or social activity that is an integrated part of a multifaceted life, but rather as an exclusive vocation: it is precisely "what poets do." A few

T'ang poets, such as Li Po and Li Ho, remotely approach such an occupational definition of poetry, and much of their work was in nonoccasional forms such as *yüeh-fu*. But most T'ang poets conceived their art quite differently: it was what a literate person did *in a certain situation or on a certain kind of occasion*. This meant that without a motivating occasion conventionally associated with poetry, a person usually did not write. The occasion might be social or private, an event or an internal mood, but the poem was conceived as a response to some life situation that was external and prior to the world of poetry. The autonomous literarity of the Western tradition is alien here: though he longed for the honor of posterity, Tu Fu did not sit down to write "the great Chinese lyric" as Milton or Keats sat down to write the "English epic." In later dynasties the occasions that might be commemorated in poetry became so numerous that they covered most aspects of life, but during the Southern Dynasties and Early T'ang, legitimate occasions for poetry were extremely limited, mostly to public and social situations. One occasion, however, did demand intensely personal poetry and permit violation and rejection of the decorum demanded by court poetry—exile.

Presumably the audience of exile poetry was still that of the capital, but in this case the audience would expect the poet to write on subjects avoided in the capital: the poet's moral values, his doubts, the intensity of his suffering, his hatred of public service. From Wang Po and Lu Chao-lin in their Szechwanese exiles, to Sung Chih-wen and Shen Ch'üan-ch'i exiled to the far south, to Wang Wei's exile of the mid-720s, it was the poetry of exile more than of any other occasion that fostered the private poetic voice and grew into the great personal lyrics of the High T'ang. Exiles and nonexiles alike turned to the tradition of exile poetry to express their private intensities, and it was in this tradition that the greatest personal poetry in all Chinese literature was written—the later poetry of Tu Fu.

2. Eremitism and the T'ao Ch'ien Revival

When the poets of the eighth century searched their poetic past for a writer whose values were exactly opposed to those of court poetry, they found in the georgic poet T'ao Ch'ien (365–427) a figure whose literary gifts and poetic personality answered all their needs. T'ao's simple diction opposed the court poet's artifice and refinement; T'ao's rebellious freedom opposed the court poet's obsequiousness; T'ao's emphasis on writing poetry for purely personal pleasure provided an alternative to the social necessity that motivated the court poem. T'ao Ch'ien was the perfect model of the free and individual poet.

Most High T'ang poets either served the state or wished to do so:

the disdain for office expressed by many famous poets was sporadic, and rarely accompanied by the conviction of action when an attractive opportunity for service was offered. The audience for poetry, those who conferred or withheld fame, was made up primarily of public officials. For complex reasons shared by most high civilizations, these poets and their audience were drawn to the antithesis of their public selves, to themes of eremitism and spontaneous, unconventional behavior. T'ao Ch'ien provided the model for a poetry that could be more than a gesture of social conformity. (Though there was great conformity in the rejection of conformity.) Though reinterpreted and often misinterpreted, T'ao was the idol of an entire generation. Poems were written in his praise; his themes were used; lines of his poetry were reworked; and his unmistakable stylistic traits appeared everywhere. Of all the models from the literary past, his was the most potent and enduring alternative to court poetry.

3. Informal Occasional Poetry

There was a great range in the formality of a social occasion: when the grand old statesman Chang Yüeh left the capital for a frontier post, the parting banquet Hsüan-tsung held for him demanded poetry of a style very different than a farewell by Meng Hao-jan to one of his friends in Hsiang-yang.[4] Even in the Early T'ang, the more informal the occasion, the more freedom displayed by poets in modifying courtly poetic decorum. By the second and third decades of the eighth century, the informal occasional poem had become the norm. The reasons for this lay not so much in the decrease of court occasional poetry as in the spread of poem exchanges between friends of approximately equal rank. Many poets would never be required to compose a poem at a court outing, and though a degree of formality was requisite in poems to high officials, the scrupulous aesthetic standards of a court arbiter like Shang-kuan Wan-erh would not be applied to such poems.[5]

The liberation of informal occasional poetry from courtly standards was only relative: it still had deep roots in court poetics. Informal occasional poetry was usually written in regulated verse, whose distinctive diction, structural conventions, and careful craft grew out of court poetry. The informal occasional poetry of the High T'ang often possesses an attractive balance between the expressive directness of the new age and the formal restraint of the regulated genres. However, that balance grew out of the literary historical changes occuring through the period, and it was not the conscious creation of any individual poet. It was a shared mode that enabled many otherwise mediocre poets to produce memorable anthology pieces.

Although regulated forms were the norm for informal occasional poetry, other genres also came to be used. For a greater degree of seriousness,
especially when writing to high officials, a highly ornamented version of
"old style poetry," *ku-shih* 古詩, was considered proper, often following
the model of occasional poetry in the *Wen-hsüan* 文選. Toward the middle of the eighth century, even heptasyllabic songs came to be used on
some informal occasions. The strict proprieties that bound certain genres
to certain topics or occasions loosened considerably throughout the course
of the first half of the eighth century, and they became only norms rather
than requirements of poetic taste.

4. The *Ku-feng* 古風

The poetry associated with *fu-ku* remained the most overt form of opposition to courtly poetics. *Fu-ku* "return to antiquity," was a sentiment that
had been gaining force for the preceding three centuries. *Fu-ku* opposed
contemporary literature primarily on ethical grounds, but *fu-ku* writings
gradually came to possess their own aesthetic appeal. Not only did poems
in the various *fu-ku* forms avoid the rhetorical devices of court poetry, their
very style carried the implicit message of rejection of courtly poetics and,
later, of the poetics of capital poetry. *Fu-ku* poetry encompassed a broad
range of distinct styles—from didactic poetry, to ornate topical allegory,
to a consciously "unpoetic" archaism that aspired to the authority of classical prose. But the most common of the High T'ang *fu-ku* styles was often
called the *ku-feng*, the "ancient mode." Although this term was not applied
consistently in the eighth century itself, we will regularly use *ku-feng* to
refer to a style modeled loosely on the *shih* of the late Han, Wei, and Chin
periods. Experiments in the *ku-feng* during the Early T'ang culminated in
the *Kan-yü* 感遇 of Ch'en Tzu-ang. In the High T'ang, the *ku-feng* lost
some of its polemical associations and became simply one subgenre among
many. *Ku-feng* appear in the collections of most High T'ang poets, but
none made it the center of their poetic oeuvre as Ch'en Tzu-ang had. Its
moral authority and literary historical priority often caused *ku-feng* to be
placed at the beginning of collections, as in the series by Li Po specifically
entitled *Ku-feng*.

The *ku-feng* had its own themes, its own turns of phrase, and its particular modal associations. True metaphor and allegory appeared most
commonly here and were linked with the implications of moral seriousness
carried by all *fu-ku* forms. And through its association with the *Yung-huai*
詠懷 of the Wei poet Juan Chi, the *ku-feng* became the appropriate vehicle
for hidden topical commentary, a means to express socially or politically
dangerous feelings and opinions. The majority of *ku-feng*, however, were

not topical: despite its mild archaism, the form also served for intense emotional effusions and philosophical meditations that were not tied to occasion.

5. *Yüeh-fu* 樂府

During the Early T'ang, *yüeh-fu* (poems written under old song titles) had been confined to a very limited range of stock themes: the abandoned woman, the soldier on the frontiers, the "bravo" (*yu-hsia* 遊俠), and several other conventional figures in stock situations. Though most *yüeh-fu* could trace their origins to folk poetry, Early T'ang *yüeh-fu* had been one of the most mannered forms of poetry. Through the first half of the eighth century, many poets continued to write *yüeh-fu* in the Early T'ang style, often with a genius of craft that far excelled that of their seventh-century predecessors. Modifications of courtly rhetoric, similar to those in occasional poetry, produced an effective tension between emotionally intense situations and the detached eyes of the poetic craftsman.

The heptasyllabic song (sometimes technically a *yüeh-fu*, sometimes not) was an allied form that had achieved great popularity in the later seventh and early eighth centuries. These songs were often long, sensuously descriptive mood pieces associated with the theme of impermanence. But the form also permitted exercise of the speculative imagination to a degree found in no other genre. Such flights of fancy pointed strongly to the character of the imagining poet, and poets and readers alike tended to see in such poems the expression of a specific character type. In the early eighth century the most common persona assumed in such songs was that of the carefree young nobleman who disdained social convention, and the song form took on associations of wild behavior and free spirit. Making use of its imaginative freedom and its implications of the poet's spiritual freedom, Li Po built his reputation on his work in the song form. In the mid-eighth century the range of the heptasyllabic song increased greatly, and it came to admit *yung-wu*, narrative poems, and occasional pieces.

Though these older *yüeh-fu* and song forms were transformed into vital parts of the High T'ang poetic repertoire, *yüeh-fu* developed in two new directions that had no roots in the Early T'ang past. First, Chinese lyrics were written to the music brought back from Central Asia in the early eighth century, and new tune titles were added to the *yüeh-fu*. (Among the older titles, some still had music, while others probably did not.) Other attempts to capture the manner of popular song were assimilated to *yüeh-fu*, often under old tune titles. Literary recreations of soldiers' songs, drinking songs, boatmen's songs, and love songs were written in this form.

Finally, because *yüeh-fu* was originally a Han poetic form often con-

taining social criticism, it became associated with *fu-ku*. Toward the middle
of the eighth century some poets, most notably Tu Fu, tried to recapture
some of the rough irregularity and reformist goals that they felt belonged
to *yüeh-fu* in its original state. Though several of Tu Fu's most famous
poems represent this mode of *yüeh-fu*, it was only a minor current during
the High T'ang, bearing fruit finally in the Mid-T'ang with the "New
Yüeh-fu" of Po Chü-yi and Yüan Chen.

2

The Poets of Transition

The early years of Hsüan-tsung's reign, from 712 until the closing of the salons of the imperial princes in 722, saw no major poet at his creative peak. Of the last great court poets, Sung Chih-wen was granted permission to commit suicide in 712, while Shen Ch'üan-ch'i and Li Chiao died probably in 714. The politically prominent and poetically gifted Kuo Chen 郭震 died in 713: his few surviving poems are remarkable achievements for their time, almost every one anticipating the best of the High T'ang.[1] In those few short years the world of poetry lost its most famous names, but during this same period several of the future luminaries of the High T'ang were beginning their careers: young Wang Wei was achieving renown for his precosity in aristocratic circles, while the elder Meng Hao-jan produced a few, sporadic masterpieces. The poets most active during this period have survived mainly in fragments. The moribund tradition of conservative court poetry was enjoying its last flicker in the salon of Li Fan, prince of Ch'i. At the same time the new style of the transition was developing under the patronage of an eminent but unaristocratic political figure, Chang Yüeh.

Chang Yüeh 張説 (667–730) rose from a relatively humble background during Empress Wu's reign to eventually become one of Hsüan-tsung's great ministers. His collected works survive in twenty-five *chüan* and contain 352 poems, making it the largest body of poetry centered in the transition period. Chang Yüeh's political prestige and the powers of patronage his prestige commanded made his literary tastes influential in the early K'ai-yüan Reign. Chang's political abilities entirely overshadow his modest poetic talents, but his taste in poetry was progressive and played an important role in the formation of the High T'ang style.

In addition to several anecdotes that provide indications of Chang's poetic preferences, there is one passage from his own hand which suggests new aesthetic values: his praise of the Early T'ang poet Fu Chia-mo was a characteristically High T'ang appreciation of the affective force of poetic talent, and it also deprecated the decorous timidity of public poetry: "Like a lone peak, a sheer slope, a mile-high cliff from which dense clouds swell, from which both thunder and lightning emerge. Truly terrifying—if displayed in the halls of government it would cause shock."[2] The qualities Chang admired in Fu Chia-mo's poetry were far from the graceful competence of court poetry. The fascination with awesome power and the sense of poetic values beyond the social world (the "halls of government") were new. Fu Chia-mo's one extant poem partially confirms Chang's estimation,[3] but more important were the implications of such a point of view for younger literary men seeking advancement through their poetic talents.

Chang Yüeh's own work contains a large number of technically competent but utterly uninspired court poems. He lacked the keen sense of craft, the gift for ornament, and the intuitive mastery of parallelism that went into the best court poetry. An ungainly plainness that maimed his court poetry became a positive value in his private poetry, especially in his poems in the exile tradition, written at the provincial posts to which he was demoted early in Hsüan-tsung's reign. The Ming critic Hu Chen-heng 胡震亨 (probably quoting an unnamed source) succinctly evaluated Chang Yüeh's minor talent: "In his poetry Chang Yüeh wrote just as he pleased and usually clumsily, but there is a clear-headed aliveness in his work."[4]

Chang Yüeh usually did not strive for the appearance of spontaneity —what Hu meant by saying he wrote "just as he pleased"—and in most of his work he remained entirely within the scope of Early T'ang poetics. The appealing plainness that characterized his work was more a function of his limitations than a conscious application of a new style. Lacking the court poet's ability to give a topic a formal, rhetorical amplification, he wrote with a pleasing, almost discursive unity of argument. Uninterested in or incapable of the subtleties of craft, Chang became a more thoughtful poet. On a few occasions his directness produced great poems, most written when he was in "exile," serving in his provincial posts. And in a very few cases we can indeed see a poet who wrote "just as he pleased": the uncomfortable mask of the Early T'ang rhetorician fell away completely, and a poetic voice emerged that had not been heard since Wang Chi:

Composition in Drunkenness   醉中作

I'm drunk—my joy is boundless—   醉後樂無極
In every way better than not being drunk: 彌勝未醉時
Each time I move it's a dance,   動容皆是舞
Each time I speak it's a poem.   出語總是詩
              [04771]

Such a celebration of the self and of its authentic impulses released by wine were taboo in the social world of Early T'ang poetry.[5]

More significant than Chang Yüeh's own work was his support for younger poets. His most famous protégé was Chang Chiu-ling (chapter 3). Chang Yüeh's patronage of poets was in the tradition of the aristocratic patrons of the Early T'ang: it was a mark of power and importance. But because of the relative obscurity of his own family background, Chang Yüeh probably took special delight in retaining members of the great clans in his entourage. Among these was a T'ai-yüan Wang, Wang Han 王翰 (*chin-shih* 710–died, 726), a notorious drinker, huntsman, horseman, and womanizer who served in Chang Yüeh's government and followed the elder statesman through his shifting political fortunes.

The riotous young aristocrat was a fixed character type, and it may have been the association of proud insouciance with nobility of birth that led to the affectation of such behavior by later, less wellborn figures, most notably Li Po. In his own day Wang Han was a more famous poet than Chang Yüeh, but only fourteen of Wang's poems survive. Several of these are the sensual heptasyllabic songs so popular in the first decades of the eighth century. From Wang Han the song style and the figure of the wild, insouciant poet can be traced to a somewhat later poet, Ts'ui Hao, who served Chang Chiu-ling as Wang Han served Chang Yüeh. Finally, the form and the persona were taken up and transformed by a poet of very dubious background who clung fiercely to the role of the proud and fallen aristocrat—Li Po.

Wang Han's "Liang-chou Songs" 涼州詞 (07557–58) have become minor classics of frontier poetry, but they are also among the best examples of how Early T'ang conventions were modified in the High T'ang. The first poem of the pair is closer to the High T'ang style, but the transformation of Early T'ang convention is more significant in the second poem:[6]

In Ch'in the season of birds and flowers surely is over now,	秦中花鳥已應闌
Here past the frontiers the wind and sand still are bitter cold.	塞外風沙猶自寒
By night we listened to nomad flutes play "Break Willow Branch, Farewell,"	夜聽胡茄折楊柳

It made a man's bold spirit fail,
    think back upon Ch'ang-an.
                    [07558]
	教人氣盡憶長安

One of the most common *topoi* in frontier *yüeh-fu* was to note that spring was already passing in the Chinese heartland while it was still winter on the frontier.[7] In the Early T'ang such a commonplace was the crude material for ornamental embellishment or witty variation. What separates Wang Han's treatment from an Early T'ang treatment is its disarming simplicity; the commonplace is treated as a commonplace. Attention is drawn away from ornamental craft and directed instead to a mood and a set literary situation.

When a reader of the 720s read the third line, he knew immediately the effect of the flute song on the soldiers. But the poem resists the temptation to vary or thwart expectations: it states simply that they "think back upon Ch'ang-an," and the neutrality of the statement conceals the intensity of longing the readers know the soldiers must feel. By using poetic convention as convention and avoiding ornament, Wang Han simultaneously lowered the social level of the poem and transformed "convention" into "universal." This poetry is willfully naïve: it pretends to represent the thoughts of the soldiers in some authentic form. And in the decades that followed, the quest for authenticity, for a poetry that escaped the artifice of craft, was to become an abiding concern, both in poetry about the self and in poetry on universal types, like the frontier soldier.

Wang Wan 王灣 (*chin-shih* 712–13) was another Wang though of a less eminent branch of the clan. Wang Wan lived well into the High T'ang, but he was already a famous poet during the transition period. "Reaching the Foot of Pei-ku Mountain" (or "Mood of the Southland") is the most important of his ten extant poems and probably one of the earliest. The poem exists in two versions, of which the middle couplets are virtually identical but the opening and closing couplets are completely different. The ways in which the two versions differ are themselves interesting: "Mood of the Southland" is closer to the mid-eighth-century style, while the version translated below is closer to the rhetorical structure of Early T'ang poetics and probably earlier.[8]

Reaching the Foot of Pei-ku Mountain   次北固山下

Path for a wanderer past the blue mountains,   客路青山外
A boat moving on before the green waters.   行舟綠水前
High waters level, the two shores wide,   潮平兩岸闊
Wind holds steady, a single sail far.   風正一帆懸
Now sun born from sea in the last of the night,   海日生殘夜
Spring comes to the river in the year before.   江春入舊年
And where shall letters from home reach me?   鄉書何處達
Migrating geese, toward the edge of Lo-yang.   歸雁洛陽邊
                        [05527]

In the aesthetics of regulated verse, the parallel couplets were of central importance; the opening and closing couplets were often no more than frames. T'ang readers had little sense of the textual integrity of poems that we observe so religiously: singers and anthologists felt free to revise lines, extract quatrains from regulated verses or longer poems, or change titles. The reputation of this poem rested on its third couplet, greatly admired by Chang Yüeh and many later readers. The energy of the couplet lay in the sixth line, with its seeming paradox: the spring, which begins legally on New Year's Day, comes early in the south and thus appears "last year." Unlike the simple cleverness of Early T'ang wit, this line truly defers comprehension, startles the reader, and forces him to consider the couplet more deeply. As he stops to consider the parallel relationships, the reader may find an analogous paradox in the preceding line: hints of sunlight diffuse through the water *before* sunrise and create a "sunlight at night." It is a daring couplet that offers a fresh perception of the relation between the inadequate words of human time and the more subtle gradations of nature's time. In terms of craft, the couplet is even more arresting by its perfect and difficult parallelism. Though the couplet demands subtle thought, the demand itself is not made subtly. If Wang Han's conscious naïvete appealed to one facet of the new High T'ang aesthetics, Wang Wan's sophisticated boldness of craft appealed to another.

The region south of the lower Yangtze (which we will call the Southeast for its directional relation to T'ang Ch'ang-an rather than for its modern geographical position) played an important role in the development of the High T'ang style. Although court poetry had its origins in courts of the Southern Dynasties, by the eighth century that formal style was firmly associated with Ch'ang-an in the Northwest. Through a directional symmetry that appeared often in eighth century poetry, the Southeast became the world antithetical to that of court poetry: it provided settings for the isolation of exile poetry, the grand scenery for private excursions in the mountains, the languid, sensual life-style associated with the region, and the lower-class personae of southeastern *yüeh-fu*, the "Songs of Wu."

The Southeast was probably most significant as a unifying geographic "mode," combining a variety of themes, topics, and moods. But the popularity of the southeastern mode in the capital grew out of many fine poems written in and about the region by poets who lived, toured, or served there. Meng Hao-jan, Li Po, Ch'u Kuang-hsi, Ts'ui Kuo-fu, and Chi-wu Ch'ien all produced some of their finest works in the Southeast. Later, during the political upheavals of the later eighth century, the Southeast truly became a safe haven and a center for poetic composition that rivalled the capital.

During the transition period, southeasterners may also have played a role in the creation of the High T'ang style. The *Old T'ang History* lists a group of southeastern poets famous in the Shen-lung Reign of Chung-tsung (705–706): Pao Jung 包融, Ho Chih-chang 賀知章, Chang Jo-hsü 張若虛, Wan Ch'i-jung 萬齊融, Ho Chao 賀朝, and Hsing Chü 邢巨.[9] "All were literary men of Wu and Yüeh, brilliant in their writing, whose fame was spread in the capital."[10] Elsewhere the first three of these men are grouped with the famous eccentric and calligrapher Chang Hsü 張旭 as the "Four Literary Men of Wu."[11] These laconic notices indicate a contemporary interest in and awareness of the Southeast as a literary region separate from the capital. But very little of the work of these men survives and nothing datable to the second decade of the eighth century.

Ho Chih-chang enjoyed the patronage of both Chang Yüeh and Chang Chiu-ling and became one of the most renowned eccentrics of the High T'ang. He was one of Tu Fu's "Eight Immortals of the Winecup" and singled out Li Po's genius when the stiffer members of Wang Wei's group discreetly avoided mentioning him. Quatrains figure prominently in the works of Ho and the other southeasterners. The T'ang quatrain, with its roots in the *yüeh-fu* of the Southern Dynasties, was often associated with elements of the southeastern geographical mode and particularly with its popular songs. Quatrain vignettes frequently treated aspects of lower-class life in the region—boating songs, lotus-picking songs, love songs, and so on—and this may have been the form for which southeastern poets became famous in the early eighth century. In almost all such quatrains poets assumed the persona of the southeasterner, and many used colloquial phrases associated with Wu dialect in the *yüeh-fu* of the Southern Dynasties (e.g., 05448 遮渠不道是吳兒).

The southeastern literary mode could be translated into other forms, such as the heptasyllabic song, which was already very popular in the capital. Chang Jo-hsü accomplished this in his famous "Spring River Flowers Moon Night" 春江花月夜, which evoked the languid ambience of a Yangtze riverscape by night.[12] But the fragments of early-eighth-century poetry by southeasterners are not numerous enough to draw secure conclusions about their impact on capital taste.[13]

The heptasyllabic song had enjoyed several decades of popularity before the transition period, but its associations of sensual indecorum or spontaneous eccentricity gave it continued appeal in the High T'ang. One of the most famous poets of the heptasyllabic song was Liu Hsi-yi 劉希夷. Though Liu's creative life is usually dated in the 670s, it is more likely that he was active during the transition period or shortly before.[14] By all its dubious accounts, Liu's life was brief and tempestuous: he was known as a musician and a rake, and there was even a story that his uncle, Sung Chih-wen, had him murdered because he refused to let Sung steal the sixth couplet from the song below.[15] Liu remains at best a famous name to which several famous songs are attributed. The following piece, also attributed to Sung Chih-wen, can be taken as representative of the heptasyllabic song style as it was practiced in the first decades of the eighth century.

Song for White Hair   白頭吟

East of the walls of Lo-yang
    the flowers of peach and plum,   洛陽城東桃李花
Flying here, flying away,
    into whose yard falling now?   飛來飛去落誰家
And the young girls of Lo-yang
    grieve for their loveliness,   洛陽女兒惜顏色
Walking they meet the fallen flowers
    and sigh their long-drawn sighs.   行逢落花長歎息
This year as the flowers fall
    their loveliness is changing.   今年花落顏色改
Next year when the flowers bloom,
    who will still be here?   明年花開復誰在
For I have seen cypress and pine
    smashed apart to kindling,   己見松柏摧爲薪
And heard that fields of mulberries
    have changed into the sea.   更聞桑田變成海
Those of the past will never again
    be east of Lo-yang's walls,   古人無復洛城東
But people today still must face
    the winds that bring down flowers.   今人還對落花風
Every year, year after year,
    the flowers are always alike;   年年歲歲花相似
Year after year, every year,
    the people are not the same.   歲歲年年人不同
I send these words to boys in their prime,
    youths with glowing faces.   寄言全盛紅顏子
Have pity on one already dying,
    a white-haired old man.   須憐半死白頭翁
The white hair of the old man
    is truly worth your pity—   此翁白頭眞可憐
A while ago his face glowed too,
    a handsome young man.   伊昔紅顏美少年
You princelings, young noblemen
    beneath the flowering trees,   公子王孫芳樹下
Clear singing, exquisite dancing
    before the falling flowers,   清歌妙舞落花前
The Chamberlain's pool terrace,
    patterned as rich brocade,   光祿池臺文錦繡
And tower and hall of General Liang
    bear murals of the gods.   將軍樓閣畫神仙
Then one morning lie down sick,
    no one knows your name,   一朝臥病無相識
And the pleasures of the springtime
    linger beside another.   三春行樂在誰邊

Eyebrows gracefully curving—
    how long can they endure?
In an instant crane-white hair,
    tangled all like silk.
Look now to where from ancient days
    were lands of song and dancing.
Now nothing more than the brown of dusk
    and the lament of sparrows.

宛轉蛾眉能幾時

須臾鶴髮亂如絲

但看舊來歌舞地

惟有黃昏鳥雀悲

[04335]

This effusive lament for the impermanence of things grew out of the treatment of the capital theme in the heptasyllabic songs of the 670s. Indeed, the similarities between Liu's most famous songs and pieces like Wang Po's "Looking Down from the High Terrace" may have been one reason why the dating of Liu in the 670s has not been seriously questioned.[16] The earlier songs, however, were richly descriptive, while Liu's song is a fluid evocation of the theme built out of redundant clichés. It possesses all the charm of popular songs everywhere: it appeals to readers but for reasons that do not admit close scrutiny. In the context of a poetic world where mannered formality and sparseness of diction were mandatory, its bathetic repetitiousness could create the illusion of spontaneity and authenticity of emotion. Like many of the truly popular lyrics of the early nineteenth century in England, the illusion of delicate sensibility fades with time. But the poem was immensely popular, often anthologized and widely imitated. Its echoes can be heard in many later poems by poets who had a firmer control of their art.

3

The Social Context

The ornamental rhetoric of court poetry had developed in the aristocratic milieu of the Southern Dynasties courts, but originally its use had suggested only sophistication in poetic craft and not deference or distinction in rank. The style of poems exchanged between equals did not differ greatly from that of poems to superiors, and private poetry like Yü Hsin's might be no less mannered than public poetry. Most social occasions in Early T'ang poetry involved significant distinctions of rank between the poet and the person for whom the poem was written. Thus, the ornamental rhetoric of the poetic craft gradually became associated with those differences in rank: most poems were directed "upward," and the level of style was determined by the "highest" member of the audience: one of the imperial family, a noble, a favorite, a high official.

As courtly rhetoric shifted from a qualitative feature (sophistication) to a level of style associated with the social rank of the recipient, private poetry and informal occasional poetry were liberated to develop in new stylistic directions. In fact, distinctions in levels of style were probably widened to clarify the gradations in social formality that became so important in T'ang poetry. Aware that the message of "familiarity" would be carried by his style, a poet might intensify the linguistic gestures associated with "natural" expression when writing to a close friend. Conversely, to demonstrate his respect for a superior, a poet could exaggerate the mannerisms of courtly rhetoric, including a generous admixture of classical phrases. Because highly formal poems constitute only a small minority of extant occasional poems, we will necessarily be more interested in the differences within informal occasional poetry. But we must not forget the full range of social gradations in style and the silent message of rank relationships carried by all T'ang occasional poems.

During the K'ai-yüan Reign (713–41) the social context of poetry can be divided into roughly four areas, each with its own proprieties of diction and topic: the imperial court and its formal occasions; the courts of imperial princes until 722; the entourages of important political figures, especially Chang Chiu-ling; and occasions involving poets of approximately the same status or in which friendship transcended distinction in rank. The rest of· this study will largely concern poetry from the fourth category, but this chapter briefly outlines the more formal situations for poetic composition.

Poetry from the salons of the imperial princes and princesses faithfully carried on the conservative court poetic traditions of the last decades of the Early T'ang. Until Hsüan-tsung's edict of 722 against the large entourages of the princes, the princes' patronage was no less important than it had been in earlier reigns. During the Early T'ang it was through the princely courts that many poets had risen to fame and imperial favor, and a well-born young poet of the early K'ai-yüan had no reason to doubt the continuity of this route to success. Furthermore, considering the political instability of the preceding generations, there was some reason to hope that an imperial prince might himself become emperor at any time. Thus, an established older poet who was presently out of favor in the imperial court or a hopeful young man of good family could expect a congenial atmosphere at a court like that of Li Fan 李範, prince of Ch'i 岐王.

Before 722, Li Fan was the greatest patron of the reign. In addition to several minor figures associated primarily with his court, distinguished poets from earlier reigns, like Yen Chao-yin 閻朝隱, found support there. Yen had risen to fame under Empress Wu and had been one of Chung-tsung's favorite court poets. In the same salon were some promising younger poets, notably Wang Wei and Ts'ui Hao. In his juvenalia Wang Wei had already shown the ability to produce highly individual poetry, but in the conservative atmosphere of Li Fan's court, Wang turned out gracious banquet poems utterly indistinguishable from the best works of Chung-tsung's court (p. 29). If there was any difference with the court poetry of earlier reigns, it was in the scope of Li Fan's celebrations: Hsüan-tsung's constraints on the princes even before 722 reduced them to more intimate occasions, and we find many poems on topics such as the performances of singing girls.

Literary activity in the imperial court continued, though with a different emphasis than in Chung-tsung's reign. Two of Chung-tsung's favorite poets, Su T'ing 蘇頲 and Li Yi 李乂, dominated court composition. The fundamental rules of court poetry stayed the same, but greater emphasis was placed on the imperial theme and the augustness of imperial acts.[1] Hsüan-tsung was a stronger personality than Chung-tsung, and his self-image was reflected in the poetic tributes from his courtiers. Furthermore, most of Hsüan-tsung's court poets were also functioning members of the government, in contrast to the small circle of Chung-tsung's favorites, whose primary qualifications were their literary talents. It was among the true "poet-officials" like Chang Yüeh and Chang Chiu-ling that the imperial theme was particularly strong. In other poets of the court (particularly among those later associated with the aristocratic faction of Li Lin-fu), the older, celebratory traditions of court poetry rested uneasily beside the new, imperial dignity. Hsü An-chen 徐安貞, for example, displayed a far sterner countenance when writing a court poem in honor of Chang Yüeh (05760) than when accompanying the emperor on a pleasure excursion to the Warmsprings Villa (05751). But even when Hsüan-tsung's court poets sought to be purely celebratory, their work lacked the smooth beauty of Early T'ang court poetry.

During T'ai-tsung's reign poetry had been a pleasurable pastime of the court: not only were great outings celebrated, the emperor and his poets would amuse themselves with *yung-wu* and other set topics of Southern Dynasties poetry. Like many emperors from northern military families, T'ai-tsung was drawn by the spell of southern culture. The ornamental rhetoric of such poetry was still largely an attribute of sophistication in craft and not of the gravity of the occasion. T'ai-tsung and his poets may have evinced a certain unease about the frivolity of the pastime, but a few allusions to the sage rulers of antiquity and an infrequent burst of spontaneous didacticism seem to have eased their consciences. During the reigns of Empress Wu and Chung-tsung, poetry had become more a formal celebration of the great occasions of the court, sometimes with vast numbers of participants all dutifully producing variations on the imperially designated topic. But poetry was still a pleasure, and a particularly close bond linked Chung-tsung and his small entourage of Auxiliary Scholars from the *Hsiu-wen kuan*.[2] By the reign of Hsüan-tsung, court poetry had become ceremonial, a task to be endured by emperor and courtier alike. All the sparkle of wit and grace was lost in its periphrastic stateliness and the implicit moralizing of the imperial theme. Yet poetry had not died entirely as a court amusement: as the old literary offices such as the *Chi-hsien tien* 集賢殿 (successor to the literary offices of former reigns) lapsed into ceremonial tedium, Hsüan-tsung established a new academy for poets and professional entertainers to amuse him on his outings with his court ladies. This was the Han-lin Academy 翰林院, and appointment to it was by imperial whim, bypassing the usual qualifying procedures of the official bureaucracy. A few years after Chang Chiu-ling offered his last turgid commemoration of a grand court outing, the Han-lin academician Li Po was to write light, sensual songs celebrating the beauty of the emperor's ladies in the seclusion of the parks of the inner court.

The power of the T'ang aristocracy had certainly not been broken during the K'ai-yüan, but it had been forced to share power and offices with "lowborn" figures such as Chang Yüeh and Chang Chiu-ling. Whatever economic and social realities lay behind the rise of such men to power, the spiritual authority of these "lowborn" officials and, to some degree, even of officials from the great clans rested on ideas of public morality and the meritocracy of virtue sanctioned in the Confucian classics. They saw themselves as representing the ethical traditions of statecraft, and it was in these terms that they were addressed by poets.

Poets had always written to and for the great ministers, but the high officials of the K'ai-yüan seemed to embody values different from those of the corrupt Changs and aristocratic Weis of Empress Wu's and Chung-tsung's courts. As the imperial theme had been supplanting sensual celebration in the poetry of Hsüan-tsung's imperial court, in public poems to great officials an austere public morality was mandatory. Even eremitic themes were acceptable, if expressed with the proper formality and moral dimensions.

Chang Chiu-ling 張九齡 (678–740) was by far the most important of the nonaristocratic patrons of letters in the K'ai-yüan. Chang was from a locally prominent family of the hinterlands of modern Kwangtung, and like many other "lowborn" officials of the K'ai-yüan, entered the central government during the reign of Empress Wu. Passing the *chin-shih* examination of 702, Chang Chiu-ling had mastered the requisite craft of court poetry with enough grace to have his work praised by none other than Shen Ch'üan-ch'i. It was only with his later rise to high position that his poetry became more seriously concerned with public values and the imperial dignity. In later ages the T'ang examination in poetry often seemed a frivolity indicative of a laxness in the due concern for administrative capability; but it should be remembered that in Empress Wu's reign it was a bold step towards meritocracy, an avenue of advancement theoretically not tied to family status.

The three-year mourning period that followed the death of Chang's father carried him safely past the purges that occurred with the transition to Chung-tsung's reign. Chang continued for some years in middle-level posts until 722, when Chang Yüeh became minister. From that time until Chang Yüeh's death in 730, Chang Chiu-ling's fortunes rose and fell with those of Chang Yüeh. After his patron's death, however, Chang Chiu-ling rose steadily, becoming minister himself in 734.

Like Chang Yüeh, Chang Chiu-ling gathered an entourage of literary men around him, but this entourage was distinguished by the presence of many of the finest poets of the eighth century. Wang Wei applied to Chang for a position and received one; Meng Hao-jan came north from Hsiang-yang, formed ties with the group around Chang Chiu-ling, and tried unsuccessfully to pass the *chin-shih* examination. Although failure excluded him from good office in the central government, Meng was later appointed to Chang Chiu-ling's staff after Chang's demotion to a provincial military command. Wang Ch'ang-ling, probably Ch'u Kuang-hsi, and a number of other poets were also associated with Chang's government. Later ages considered Chang Chiu-ling an exemplary "virtuous minister," but even in 734 there seems to have been a special feeling that Chang's appointment promised moral government and the possibility of advancement on the basis of merit alone. Writing to Chang for a position, Wang Wei spoke not with the formality of most such occasional poems to a high official, but rather with a simple dignity achieved through the archaic mode of *fu-ku* (05785):

Indirectly I've heard of a great and good man	側聞大君子
Who cares not of the faction a man may have known.	安問黨與讐
Nor does he barter the vessels of state	所不賣公器
In his constant plans for the common weal.	動為蒼生謀

Through the distorting conventions of historical hagiography it is impossible to judge the true administrative gifts of the men Chang Chiu-ling brought into office, but Chang's eye for literary talent is a verifiable talent of the minister. In most cases recognition is a contributing factor to literary genius. Those of Chang's entourage who achieved literary fame did so only after their association with him, and it seems that Chang's support was a significant aid in their growing reputations.

For all its renown, Chang Chiu-ling's period in power was brief: in 737 the aristocratic faction gained the upper hand, and Chang was demoted to governor of Ching-chou. With Chang's fall, most of his appointees were also sent off to provincial posts. Finally, in the spring of 740, Chang Chiu-ling returned to his home in the far South and died.

Chang Chiu-ling participated competently in the formal occasions of the court and in the poetic intercourse of upper officialdom. He lacked technical versatility, however, and usually avoided certain genres and subgenres, including *yüeh-fu*, quatrains, and most forms of heptasyllabic verse. Though he did not explicitly acknowledge his debt, Chang's principal model in less formal composition was Ch'en Tzu-ang, an outlander like Chang himself. Chang's poetry in the direct tradition of Ch'en Tzu-ang includes some of his works best known in later dynasties.

The most egregious example of Ch'en's influence appears in Chang's *Kan-yü* 感遇 (02965–76). Like Ch'en Tzu-ang's *Kan-yü*, Chang's *Kan-yü* are moral allegories and treatments of the *hsien-jen shih-chih* theme, but they lack the stark imagination and intellectual complexity of the earlier series. In the same tradition are Chang's *tsa-shih* 雜詩 (02960–64). These two series, along with a few other poems, have led many literary historians to consider Chang Chiu-ling an important link in the tradition of *fu-ku* poetry. The legacy of Ch'en Tzu-ang and the impulses to public morality in Chang's court poetry may indeed suggest that Chang saw himself in that tradition, but taken as a whole, Chang's oeuvre is more complacent and conservative than that of the great *fu-ku* poets.

The deepest and most successful aspect of Ch'en Tzu-ang's legacy to Chang was in Chang's personal poetry, most of which was written late in Chang's life while he was serving in the provinces. This work possessed an intellectual heaviness that appealed to later critics, who found in it a seriousness and moral authenticity touching many Confucian values. The critic and poet-monk Chiao-jan praised this intellectual quality in a poem "On Reading the 'Ch'ü-chiang Collection'" (44792):

Proper in form, fullness of strength,	體正力已全
Subtle comprehension of Nature's inner laws.	理精識何妙

The qualities Chiao-jan admired were also stressed by later critics: Chang's poetry was seen to possess *hsing-chi* 興寄, a term with strong *fu-ku* resonance through its use by Ch'en Tzu-ang. *Hsing-chi* combines the idea of "deeper significance" with moral authenticity in expression: the poem as a whole, and particularly the physical world described in it, are read as a vehicle for intense personal and moral sentiment. Above all, the poem is not an artifact of craft; the text has a transparence through which one reads the character and state of mind of the historical poet. Thus, in Yao Tzu-yen's 姚子顏 unofficial biography of Chang Chiu-ling we read: "The Way of his poetry [*feng-ya* 風雅] is based on the dominance of 'deeper significance' [*hsing-chi*]—not a single line in a single poem lacks it."[3] Ssu-k'ung T'u 司空圖 translated this essentially Confucian interest in ethical seriousness into the modal poetics of the Late T'ang; he describes Chang's poetry as *shen-yü* 沈鬱, a brooding gloom that suggests richness and depth of feeling.[4] This term too had Confucian overtones through its original association with the Han intellectual Yang Hsiung.

The responses of these critics are of interest not only for the specific case of Chang Chiu-ling, but also as representing one aspect of reading poetry in the T'ang. A poem was seen as generating a mood that combined with the reader's biographical understanding of the poet to create a unified sense of the poet's identity. Poetry's function was to permit comprehension of the poet, both his inner nature and its incarnation in a specific response to a life situation. This was not the only mode of reading in the T'ang, and it was engaged more in some kinds of poems than in others; moreover, it was a historical phenomenon, appearing rarely in seventh-century comments on poetry and becoming increasingly frequent in the High T'ang. Because some poets, like Li Po, came to use poetry as a means to project a self-conscious mask, it is often necessary to dissociate the persona from the complex human being with his own complex motives for generating the persona. For this reason one should avoid a simpleminded biographical criticism that easily identifies poet and persona. On the other hand, it should be recognized that poets and readers alike might *presume* a poem to be an authentic expression of the poet's inner nature. And this presumption partially explains why poetry played such an important role in social relationships—as a qualification for office in the examination, as an introduction, as a petition for office, or as a complaint seeking redress of wrongs. Through the poem a person could be known.

As a whole, Chang Chiu-ling's oeuvre is more varied than the responses of early critics would suggest. At moments in his work we can see the mastery of courtly craft that won him the praise of Shen Ch'üan-ch'i, couplets like (03132):

Wind through eaves fells the down of birds, 簷風落鳥毳
Leaves by the window dangle spider threads. 窗葉掛蟲絲

Hsing-chi and *shen-yü*, the qualities admired by Chang's T'ang readership, appear primarily in his later poetry in the exile tradition, written when he was serving in the provinces. There he was the meditative poet who took his vantage point—the traditional "high place"—gazed out over the scene, described what he saw, and drew associations to the events and problems of his life.

Climbing a Tall Building on an Autumn Evening: 秋晚登樓望南
  I Gaze to Where the South River Touches the 江入始興郡路
  Shih-hsing Road

Streaming rivulets draw back, sandflats emerge, 潦收沙衍出
Frost comes down, the sky's vault, crystalline. 霜降天宇晶
Hunched at the railing, I gaze long and far, 伏檻一長眺
Path and ford draw many emotions of distant places. 津途多遠情
Longing comes from beyond the rivers and mountains; 思來江山外
Where my gaze breaks off, clouds and mists arise. 望盡煙雲生
A rolling flood where nothing is distinct— 滔滔不自辨
Oh, what is accomplished from all this constant toil? 役役且何成
I came here, wind shaking my frail white locks, 我來颯衰鬢
No one could say it shook ribbons of high office. 孰云飄華纓
A stabled horse suffering cramped restraints, 櫪馬苦踡跼
A caged bird longing for faraway journeys. 籠禽念遠征
The year grows ever darker toward its close. 歲陰向晼晚
At the end of day, a pointless restlessness. 日夕空屏營
All living creatures value fulfilling their natures, 物生貴得性
The bonds upon my body grow from recent fame. 身累由近名
I look back, find I'm truly right now— 內顧覺今是
But when will ease come for sorrow at what is past? 追歎何時平
[02949]

As the poet in "exile" stares at the landscape before him, each element in his vision signifies, metonymically or metaphorically, some aspect of his present situation or seems to offer a hidden resolution of his troubles. Paths and fords lead his thoughts if not his body toward the capital; the rolling river in spate reminds him of the world's turmoil and the futile toiling of his life. Clouds and mists exist only to block his vision to the far places he longs to be. The fluttering of his white hair in the wind reminds him of his age and the absence of the "ribbons of office."

Chang Chiu-ling was a conservative poet, blending the Early T'ang and High T'ang styles. He used the tripartite form in its most basic state, with none of its High T'ang refinements. But though his work lacked the bravado, the complexity, and the descriptive genius of the major High T'ang poets, it did represent the height of one very compelling mood, deepened because the author was Chang Chiu-ling, the "virtuous minister" of the glorious K'ai-yüan.

Our judgment of the social scope of poetry is necessarily conditioned by the limits of what survives. We know next to nothing of regional poetry, of poetry by the literate (?) class of "clerks" (*li* 吏), or of folk poetry or popular urban poetry, except insofar as upper-class poets practiced it. The social scope of extant poetry may indeed reflect accurately the social scope of composition, but it may also indicate no more than the power of the capital upper class to conserve their own poetry.

Judging by what does survive, it seems that the social scope of poetry broadened in the K'ai-yüan, but not by much. We find that more poets were writing from a wider spectrum of the official hierarchy, but they still represented a very small and homogeneous group: many were from the great families of the capital, and most knew each other. There were also a handful of southeasterners, who fitted smoothly into capital society and formed friendships with members of the great clans. Later in the K'ai-yüan, outsiders to this closely knit group begin to appear, poets like Kao Shih, Li Po, and Wu Yün. But the rise of these men to fame was more a pheno-menon of the T'ien-pao Reign, when poetic taste became more diverse and poetic activity, more widespread. From the T'ien-pao on we find a true broadening of poetic activity throughout gentry society. The tradition of capital poetry retained its aura of nobility and elegance, but there were numerous groups of poets, larger and more open to new talent. In contrast, if we examine the works of poets famous in the K'ai-yüan, we find them linked to one another by poem exchanges and stronger bonds of friendship. At the center of this group was one poet acquainted with virtually everyone practicing poetry in the capital—Wang Wei.

4

王維

Wang Wei
The Artifice of Simplicity

Wang Wei, your brother, was the most revered man of letters in all the world. He served throughout the former reign, and his fame was great among the treasures of the age. High he soared among Chou's Odes; deeply he reverenced the Songs of Ch'u. In all his works the humors of the cosmos were in harmony, and the rules of musicality were correct in his noble rhymes. The waterfall sent his lush imagination leaping into the sky; scattering clouds spread his innermost emotions with them.

> Emperor Tai-tsung to Wang Chin in 763, on the presentation of Wang Wei's collected works to the throne

Now, late in life, I love only stillness;
The affairs of the world touch not my heart.
I look within, there find no great plans,
Know nothing more than return to the forests of home.

> Wang Wei, "Answering Magistrate Chang"　　　　　　[05922]

It is an important and nearly universal attribute of high civilization that those who have attained wealth and power are fascinated by the prospect of renouncing what they once coveted so greatly. In the eighth century there began in earnest a peculiarly intense relationship between the high official and the recluse or eccentric, a relationship that was to continue in many forms throughout the remaining centuries of traditional Chinese civilization.

As an individual phenomenon, the conflict between the attractions of public and private life had been a long established theme in the literary tradition. But only in the High T'ang did a fascination with rejection of public service become a pervasive theme in upper-class literary life. During the Eastern Han, Chang Heng may have written a "Return to the Fields"

27

fu, but imperial recognition came for his *fu* on the capitals. Early in the T'ang, T'ai-tsung still preferred a Shang-kuan Yi to a Wang Chi. But by the mid-eighth century we find the emperor Tai-tsung extravagantly praising the poetry of Wang Wei, the greater part of which concerned the renunciation of court and the public life. Wang Wei's own life and work enacts this same contradiction between social position and personal values.

The precise dates of Wang Wei's life are the subject of much scholarly debate. He was born either in 699 or 701 and died in 759 or 761. The major biographical sources are in conflict, but the dates 699 to 761 are the most plausible. Though Wang Wei's father and grandfather were never more than middle-level officials, they were members of the powerful T'ai-yüan Wang clan, and thus it is impossible to say to what extent their rank in the central government reflected their actual local power or their national social prestige. Wang Wei's mother was a Po-ling Ts'ui, another old and prominent clan. Thus, in terms of social prestige, Wang Wei's background was the highest of the major High T'ang poets, and it should be no surprise that he found a warm welcome in the courts of the T'ang princes.

During his teens Wang went to the capital, ostensibly to take the preliminary examination, but more likely to obtain the patronage of an imperial prince. This had long been one accepted course by which a young man of good family sought advancement, and young Wang Wei could not have known that the powers of the princes and the old patterns of poetic advancement were to be irrevocably changed. After four rulers in a single decade, no one could foresee that Hsüan-tsung was to exert firm control over his imperial family and to reign for over forty years.

Wang Wei's collection contains a small number of juvenalia, datable from text notes probably written by Wang Chin or Wang Wei himself. The inclusion of juvenalia is an unusual feature in T'ang collections; in the case of Wang Wei they may have served to validate the biographical convention of literary precosity or perhaps to represent the works for which Wang achieved youthful fame in the capital. It is possible these juvenalia were revised later in Wang's life, but some few are indeed juvenile, while others represent the heptasyllabic song style popular in the early eighth century. Several of the juvenalia, however, rank among Wang Wei's best-known works. One such poem was written at age seventeen in Ch'ang-an; the occasion was the Double Ninth Festival, when it was customary to climb some high place and think on absent friends and relations.

On the Double Ninth: Remembering My Brothers   九月九日憶山東兄弟
   East of the Mountains

Alone in a strange land,   獨在異鄉爲異客
   and I here, a stranger,

Each time this holiday comes
   I long doubly for my kin,
And know that brothers far away
   are climbing someplace high,
Decking themselves with dogwood twigs,
   short one person.
       [06137]

每逢佳節倍思親

遙知兄弟登高處

徧插茱萸少一人

The word repetition in the first line and the clever play on strangenesses, doublings, and absences show a firm mastery of the court poet's rhetorical craft (cf. 03512–13, 03764). But young Wang Wei already infused rhetorical play with something deeper, a psychological seriousness and speculative capability that belong firmly in the High T'ang.

    Wang Wei passed the preliminary examination in 717, becoming a candidate from the capital prefecture, a position of prestige with a relative certainty of success in the *chin-shih* examination. This latter he passed in 721. During this period Wang Wei enjoyed the patronage of several imperial princes, most notably Li Fan. The surviving anecdotes concerning Wang's relations with Li Fan are all of dubious authenticity, but they do suggest that he was famous as a musician in addition to his poetic reputation. Wang Wei was also, of course, a painter, and though we know little of his musical interests after this period, his reputation as a painter grew and endured. Few critics of his poetry or painting fail to cite the couplet (05864):

I erred in this life, becoming a poet.   宿世謬詞客
In some life before I'm sure I was a painter.   前身應畫師

And though Wang admits his true vocation in this life, most of those who have written on his poetry have found something of the painter's eye in his work.

    It was probably in the court of Li Fan that Wang Wei met Ts'ui Hao, a lifelong friend, and their names were paired as two of the most famous poets of the day. Together with the older poets of Li Fan's court, they celebrated the prince's outings in the old court style, and with far more grace than the emperor's poets dared summon.

His Majesty Lends the Prince of Ch'i His Chiu-   勅借岐王九成宮
   ch'eng Palace that My Prince May Escape the   避暑應教
   Heat: To My Prince's Command

The Imperial Prince withdraws afar   帝子遠辭丹鳳闕
   from the Gates of Rose Phoenix,
A Royal missive lends him this distant   天書遙借翠微宮
   palace of azure mists.
Outside its windows clouds and fog   隔窗雲霧生衣上
   rise from our very robes,

Roll up the curtains; its streams and hills 　　卷幔山泉入鏡中
　　enter into a mirror.
By its woodlands the sounds of water 　　　　林下水聲喧語笑
　　drown out our laughter and chatter,
From its cliffs bright colors of trees 　　　　巖間樹色隱房櫳
　　shade the latticework.
It's by no means certain that homes of gods 　仙家未必能勝此
　　are any finer than this,
So why did pipe-playing Wang-tzu Ch'iao 　　何事吹笙向碧空
　　head off to the emerald sky?
　　　　　　[06057]

The fourth line probably refers to the reflection in a lake or pool (cf. 05060.4), but it may suggest the framing space of the window. The closing comparison to the dwellings of the immortals was a virtual requirement in the old court poetic style: since joys even superior to those of the immortals can be found in this palace on earth, why seek apotheosis like Wang-tzu Ch'iao?

After passing the metropolitan examination, Wang Wei received a minor position in the Music Office, perhaps because of his abilities as a musician. Soon thereafter Wang became involved in political difficulties the true origins of which are not altogether clear: he was accused of having permitted a musician to perform a dance that must have been taboo, but possibly this was no more than a pretext for dismissal. Wang's difficulties probably stemmed from his associations with the princes at a time when Hsüan-tsung had decided to curb the constant threat they presented to the throne.

Whatever the true causes, Wang Wei was demoted to a low post in Chi-chou in modern Shantung. On his journey east Wang turned to the great tradition of exile poetry and produced the first datable examples of the controlled, austere style for which he was to become famous. The relatively unornamented diction of these poems followed the exile poetry of Tu Shen-yen, Shen Ch'üan-ch'i, Sung Chih-wen, and Chang Yüeh, but Wang Wei's exile poems went far beyond mere simplicity of diction: their depth and complexity revealed the hand of a major poet.

One of the many elements that constitute the greatness of these poems is a serious interest in perception: how things are seen, how the physical world controls how things are seen, and how the forms of perception have inner significance. In the following poem from the Chi-chou journey, the poet is scarcely present at all: his function is to move and see. But the succession of scenes and their implied viewpoints enact a pattern basic to the human experience of journeys.

Crossing the Yellow River to Ch'ing-ho 　　　渡河到清河作

Drift by boat upon the Great River, 　　　　汎舟大河裏

Massed waters touching the sky's very edge. 積水窮天涯
Sky and waves suddenly split apart— 天波忽開拆
The million houses of a district capital. 郡邑千萬家
And further on, see walls and market, 行復見城市
Then clearly appears mulberry, hemp. 宛然有桑麻
I look back toward my homeland— 迴瞻舊鄉國
Vast floods stretching to the clouds. 淼漫連雲霞

[05848]

Two points in space define a journey: a starting point and a destination. Whichever point draws the traveler's eyes reveals a state of mind that need be expressed only in describing the direction of vision. Similarly, when the poet's eyes shift from destination toward home, the act defines a sudden change of heart.

But vision is not free: what the poet sees is determined by the indifferent features of topography, which here assume a dramatic and protean form in the riverscape. With its power to conceal or expose, the riverscape possesses the corollary power to create interest and longing in the human mind: it controls visual absence and loss, the necessary stimuli of desire. The riverscape creates expectant interest in what lies hidden ahead on the far bank, then dissipates that interest in revelation. His curiosity sated, the poet looks back and meets a second dramatic revelation, in this case not of a place but of a loss of place. The poem is intensely visual, but no reader could call it descriptive; the focus of interest lies not on what is seen but on the interior life of the perceiving poet. But beyond the interior concerns of the occasional lyric, there is a more general interest in the relativity of perception and in the relationship between perception and human response.

As in Wang Han's poem, the simplicity of diction thwarts the average reader's interest in ornamental craft and demands that the reader look more deeply to the significance implicit in the structure of representation. Like Wang Han, Wang Wei strives for a kind of authenticity—not the authenticity of universal responses achieved through typological convention, but an authenticity of unmediated perception. By making the poem represent what is seen more than the poet in the act of seeing, the poet would have the reader's eyes repeat the experience of the poet's eyes and thus share directly his inner responses. Objective closure becomes a means to avoid the direct statement of emotion, to make the reader experience what the poet felt when he turned his head to look home and saw only vast stretches of the river.

The ornamental craft over which Wang had such perfect mastery was avoided even more intensely in his later poetry; Wang Wei's style achieved an austere simplicity that became the touchstone of his individual poetic voice. Again the poet gazes over a broad stretch of water:

South Cottage   南垞

A light boat goes off to south cottage;   輕舟南垞去
North cottage, hard to reach over vast waters.   北垞淼難即
Look at men's houses on the other bank—   隔浦望人家
So far away we cannot recognize them.   遙遙不相識
                                      [06087]

Like other quatrains from the *Wang Stream Collection*, "South Cottage" is
animated by a mask of naïvete and understatement built upon the kind of
structural genius seen in the preceding poem. Wang Wei also learned to
draw in unobtrusive echoes from earlier poetry: the last couplet here unmistakably echoes several famous Early T'ang poems suggesting isolation
and anonymity in both a positive and a negative sense (02612.7; 02762.15).
The enigmatic value of the last line shows greater poetic maturity than the
easily identifiable moods of "Crossing the Yellow River to Ch'ing-ho,"
but Wang's interest in the relativity of perception remains constant. Distance prevents the poet from recognizing men he probably knows (the
cottage is on his estate) and grants him an anonymity that may be the negative value of loneliness or the positive value of reclusion.

Wang Wei returned from his Chi-chou exile sometime during the
mid 720s. Little is known of his life between his return and 734, when Chang
Chiu-ling became minister and promoted Wang to a responsible position
in the government. Some scholars have suggested that it was during this
period that Wang purchased the Wang Stream Estate, formerly owned by
Sung Chih-wen. Whether Wang acquired the estate at this time or later in
the 740s, he loved it dearly and celebrated its beauty in the *Wang Stream
Collection* 輞川集, a small series of quatrains written by Wang together
with his friend P'ei Ti (06078–97; 06169–88). For partings, banquets, and
yung-wu series, small collections of one or more scrolls (*chüan* 卷) were
common, but the form of the *Wang Stream Collection* was something new.[1]
The two poets took turns treating a series of set topics, points of interest on
the estate that together constituted a programmatic journey through the
landscape.[2] By the second half of the eighth century the collection had
become an immense success and a model for many subsequent quatrain
series, including one by the Mid-T'ang poet Han Yü (10840–60). In aesthetic sensibility and intellectual interests, few T'ang poets were as far apart
as Wang Wei and Han Yü; Han's uncharacteristically meek submission to
the model of the *Wang Stream Collection* suggests something of its compelling influence.

In 734 Wang Wei petitioned the new minister, Chang Chiu-ling, for
a post. Chang's circle was filled with men bearing surnames like Wang,
P'ei 裴, Ts'ui 崔, and Wei 韋—the great families of the capital. Wang Wei's

close friends and supporters came largely from these families, and it was a group in which he could be comfortable. During this period Wang again turned his talents to the court and formal banquet poems requisite when accompanying the great court figures on their outings. But Wang was neither a courtier-poet nor a member of the court literary establishment; rather he held a political post, Omissioner of the Right.

When Chang Chiu-ling fell from power in 737 and was exiled to Ching-chou, Wang's genuine distress occasioned several poetic consolations for his patron. As a member of Chang's party, Wang Wei had reason to be concerned for his own position: a few months after Chang's fall, he was ordered away from the capital on a mission to the northwestern frontier, where he served as regional censor. Several occasional poems on frontier themes and probably several of his border *yüeh-fu* date from this period. Some of Wang's border poems, such as "Army Song" 從軍行 (05782), are among the finest of their kind, but they belong to the tradition of the mannered frontier *yüeh-fu* of the Southern Dynasties. The conservatism of Wang's literary training is apparent in the contrast between these poems and contemporary border songs by Kao Shih and others, poems that began a more spirited style that was to culminate a decade later in the work of Ts'en Shen.

Arriving at the Frontier on a Mission   使至塞上

With a single coach I'll visit the frontiers,   單車欲問邊
And of client kingdoms, pass by Chü-yen.   屬國過居延
Voyaging tumbleweed leaves the passes of Han,   征蓬出漢塞
A homebound goose enters Tartar skies.   歸雁入胡天
Great desert: one column of smoke stands straight;   大漠孤煙直
Long river: the setting sun hangs round.   長河落日圓
At Hsiao ramparts I met a mounted messenger—   蕭關逢侯騎
"The Grand Marshall is now at Mount Yen-jan."   都護在燕然
[05984]

Like many famous T'ang poems, including the Wang Wan poem quoted earlier, this piece is remembered for a single couplet, the third, whose balanced geometry of forms represents one characteristic of Wang Wei's descriptive art. But surrounding the memorable couplet is a highly conservative poem. The last line closely echoes the closing of a frontier *yüeh-fu* by the Liang poet Wu Yün 吳均.[3] For all Wang Wei's undeniable originality, his work was more deeply rooted in the Early T'ang than that of any other major High T'ang poet.

Wang Wei's stay in the Northwest was brief: General Ts'ui Hsi-yi, in whose camp Wang was stationed, died soon after Wang's arrival, and in 738 or 739 the poet returned to Ch'ang-an. A year later he was sent off to the provinces again, this time to take charge of the preliminary examinations in the South. Another of Wang's friends and sponsors, P'ei Yao-ch'ing, posted Wang back to the central government, but probably because of his associations with Chang Chiu-ling, he held a post that was low for one of his age and background. From 742 until 755, when the capital fell to the rebel army, Wang held a succession of such posts, perhaps no more than sinecures. During the 740s and early 750s the poet probably spent most of his time at his estate, enjoying the fellowship of his many friends and writing poems for them on how his gates were always closed to visitors.

Like many other officials left behind in Hsüan-tsung's unseemly flight from Ch'ang-an, Wang Wei fell captive to An Lu-shan's army and was given the undesired honor of an office in the rebel government. Wang is said to have tried desperately to avoid complicity with the rebels by taking drugs to simulate incapacitating sickness. When the capitals were retaken, he was imprisoned by T'ang forces on the charge of treason. Conveniently, Wang Wei's brother Wang Chin was then serving in the Bureau of Justice and managed to have the charges against his brother dropped: the extenuating evidence was a poem that Wang had given to P'ei Ti while imprisoned by the rebels, a poem that obliquely expressed the poet's loyalty to the T'ang house (06149). Beyond this short expression of distress—and the motives for its fabrication after the fact are overwhelming—Wang Wei's poetic silence on the An Lu-shan Rebellion is remarkable. The fact that Wang spent most of the rebellion in An Lu-shan's prison is sufficient to explain why he never wrote vehement attacks on the rebel occupation as Tu Fu did, but his silence after his release is perhaps best explained by the proprieties of poetic topic that Wang Wei usually followed: the rebellion and its devastation simply would not come to mind in the kind of private meditation and social exchange that dominated his last poems.

Restored to good position in the central government by Su-tsung, Wang Wei held a series of high posts until his death, probably in 761. During his last years Wang is said to have become increasingly devout as a Buddhist layman, leading an austere and simple life. His last great poems have a quality all their own: even Wang's masterful descriptive powers were abandoned, and there remained a starkness of style that avoided any hint of artful craft.

Villa on Chung-nan Mountain   終南別業

In middle age I grew truly to love the Way,   中歲頗好道
Now late, my home lies at South Mountain's edge.   晚家南山陲
When the mood comes, I always go alone,   興來每獨往
I know all about its wonders, without motive, alone.   勝事空自知
I'll walk to the place where the waters end   行到水窮處

Or sit and watch times when the clouds rise.   坐看雲起時
Maybe I'll run into an old man of the woods—   偶然值林叟
We'll laugh, chat, no hour that we have to be home. 談笑無還期
[05968]

A concern with time appeared powerfully in Wang Wei's later poetry. Various aspects of spontaneous action were measured against actions planned or done with fixed purpose and fixed times. Wang's interest in the organization of space, which can be seen in "Crossing the Yellow River to Ch'ing-ho," became an analogous interest in the organization of time by will and hidden motives. The paradoxical "goal of spontaneity" appeared in an equally paradoxical art that sought to be artless.

    Another aspect of Wang's concern with time was his interest in life changes, usually as part of a process of renunciation and growing freedom. More than most poets, Wang Wei saw his own life and those of others as processes of becoming. From his early years he foresaw the deepening wisdow, religiousness, and abandonment of worldly ties in old age, and the poet fulfilled his prophecy for himself. The opening of the preceding poem is a variation on a set opening trope that recurs through Wang's poetry:

Now, late in life, I love only stillness,   晚年惟好靜
The affairs of the world touch not my heart.   萬事不關心
[05922]

In my youth understanding was shallow,   少年識事淺
Drove myself to study to grasp profit, fame.   強學干名利
. . . .
Now in winter's clarity I see the far mountains, 清冬見遠山
Massed snows, a frozen blue-green   積雪凝蒼翠
And sparkling white, emerge from eastern forests, 皓然出東林
Stirring in me desire to leave this world.   發我遺世意
[05786]

Late I learned that pure and true law,   晚知清淨理
Daily grow more distant from the crowds of men. 日與人羣疎
[05841]

My youth is not worth speaking of—   少年不足言
I saw the Way when years were already long.   識道年已長
[05842]

Wang had seen similar processes in the lives of others as early as his Chichou exile (05853–54). The lament for passing youth and hair growing white had little place in Wang Wei's poetry: for him old age was a visionary state, and in his private poetry he celebrated each stage by which it drew nearer.

It is difficult to know which poets were considered the greatest contemporaries by K'ai-yüan and T'ien-pao readers. Critical and prefactory
tropes such as "the most famous of the age" were applied generously to a
wide range of indisputably minor poets, and even when these laudatory
evaluations are not mere politeness, they involve more disturbing unknowns
such as "precisely when" and "to what audience." The K'ai-yüan and T'ien-
pao clearly had no stable canon of contemporary writers, but a few figures
stood out, most notably Wang Wei and Wang Ch'ang-ling. Particularly
in the last decade of his life and the two decades following his death, Wang
Wei has a strong claim to having been considered the greatest poet of the
day. His late prestige with the imperial family was surely one factor in the
admiration of his younger contemporaries, but he was also the central social
figure in the world of poetry; his acquaintance with other contemporary
poets was broad and his influence tremendous. The capital poets of the later eighth century reused and misused the style he perfected until it became
tedious. Gradually, in the last decades of the later eighth century, interest
in other K'ai-yüan and T'ien-pao poets, such as Wang Ch'ang-ling and Li
Po, began to challenge Wang Wei's dominance, and when the great Mid-
T'ang writers reevaluated their High T'ang past, Li Po and Tu Fu were
raised to the pre-eminence they have held ever since. Wang Wei came to
be ranked just below Li and Tu, and though he was occasionally criticized
and his position challenged, his reputation remained relatively stable, with
none of the fluctuations in popularity that other High T'ang poets suffered.

Wang Wei's collected works were presented to the throne in 763 in
an edition prepared by his brother Wang Chin, then minister. Wang Chin
claimed that the collection represented only a small proportion of Wang
Wei's entire output, the greater part of which had been lost in the rebellion.
The presence of an authorized edition in the imperial library so soon after
the poet's death is one factor responsible for the relative stability of the text.
Textual problems do exist, but these are minimal in comparison to the collections of some other poets, like Meng Hao-jan. A few interpolations have
been identified, but on the whole, Wang's collection is a secure one.

The image of Wang Wei that has endured since the T'ang has been of
a meditative poet, a private poet, and a landscape poet. This image is to
some degree justified, because Wang Wei saw himself in similar terms. But
at the same time Wang Wei was one of the most social and urbane of
T'ang poets. There is great variety both in his poetry and in the facets of
of his personality. He could abandon the strong poetic identity that perme-
ates his reclusive poetry to write the most gifted and graceful court poetry
since Sung Chih-wen and Shen Ch'üan-ch'i. When he was innovative, he
could work either through the traditions of his predecessors or deliberately
take new departures. During his Chi-chou exile he created major poetry

out of a base of Early T'ang exile poetry, but he also could boldly modify elements of the *Ch'u-tz'u* for a new kind of poetry in the exile tradition. The poet who concealed interior processes of thought and emotion beneath a descriptive surface also hid the theme of exile beneath the description of a shamanistic performance near Chi-chou. The model was the "Nine Songs" of the *Ch'u-tz'u*: the accepted interpretation of these poems in the T'ang was that Ch'ü Yüan had composed them as revisions of popular shamanistic performances he had seen in his exile. When Wang Wei wrote such a poem, it carried a silent literary-historical context, a tacit assumption of the role of Ch'ü Yüan in his unjust exile. The two songs are not veiled satire or metaphorical complaints; rather, they evoke exile out of the famous poetry of the past.

Second Song for the Worship of the Goddess at Yü Mountain: "Bidding the Goddess Farewell"	魚山神女祠歌二首之二 送神曲
In a swirl they come forward and bow there before the hall,	紛進拜兮堂前
Eyes filled with love-longing toward the sacred mats like jade.	目眷眷兮瓊筵
She came but did not speak, Her will was not made known,	來不語兮意不傳
And She is the evening rain, makes the empty mountains somber.	作暮雨兮愁空山
The pipes grieve in shrillness,	悲急管
Flurried strings throb with longing,	思繁絃
The carriage of the goddess is about to turn majestically.	靈之駕兮儼欲旋
In a flash clouds draw back, the rain ceases,	倏雲收兮雨歇
And green stand the mountains amid water's splashing flow.	山青青兮水潺湲
[05906]	

In this case, the use of *Ch'u-tz'u* meter echoes specific source texts, but Wang also followed in the footsteps of Sung Chih-wen by using *Ch'u-tz'u* meter for personal poetry.[4] But Wang complicated the expressively emotional mode associated with the meter, forcing it to work at curious cross-purposes to the quiet surface of the poems.

A Song on Gazing at Chung-nan Mountain: For Hsü of the Secretariat	贈徐中書望終南山歌
One evening you came out from the Secretariat,	晚下兮紫微
Sad how affairs in this world of dust go so often awry.	悵塵事兮多違

You halted your horse   駐馬兮雙樹
  by a two-trunked sāla tree,
Gazed on green mountains,   望青山兮不歸
  did not go home.
              [05902]

    In much of Wang Wei's poetry there is a law of repression: the uni-
versal feeling of homesickness, the literary historical context of grief in
exile, or the modal associations of a meter will tell the reader that some
deeper significance or intense emotion lies beneath the poem's placid surface. The song above and other seemingly simple poems are fed by the
energy of that repression.
    In addition to *Ch'u-tz'u* meter, Wang Wei experimented with the six-
character line (06125–31) and achieved perhaps the greatest success of any
Chinese poet in that awkward meter. On at least one occasion Wang followed T'ao Ch'ien's characteristic use of the tetrasyllabic line, for associations of simple primitive dignity (05772).
    Beyond metrical experimentation, Wang Wei possessed a wider the-
matic and stylistic range than any T'ang poet before him, perhaps wider
than any earlier Chinese poet. He could treat border themes and the semi-
erotic themes of palace poetry with genius (05776–80). In the tradition of
temple visiting poems, Wang sometimes followed his Early T'ang predecessors, but he also used the abstruse terminology of Buddhism in several
poems (05796, 05798–99, 05760–61, 06038) and demonstrated a Buddhist
learning far greater than any of his immediate predecessors. He could write
playfully joking poems, including a semicolloquial piece that may represent
an attempt at dialect poetry (05805). In short, Wang Wei was a High T'ang
poet not only in developing a truly individual poetic voice, but also in his
degree of mastery over traditional poems and in his powers of innovation.
    Wang Wei's most significant contribution to the development of a
genre probably lay in his treatment of the quatrain. All literary forms are,
to some degree, oriented toward closure; regulated verse (*lü-shih*) is a partial exception because so much of the reader's attention is directed to the
aesthetics of the middle couplets. But of all genres, the quatrain had always
been the most dependent on closure for success. Wang Wei could use the
pointed, epigrammatic closure of the Early T'ang quatrain, though he preferred the imagistic closure that was popular in the High T'ang (e.g., 06075).
But Wang also developed another form of closure that carried the quatrain
even farther away from epigram: Wang's quatrains often ended in enigmatic understatement—a statement, a question, or an image that was so
simple or seemed so incomplete that the reader was compelled to look beneath it for the importance expected in quatrain closure.
    The success of this new form of closure depended entirely on generic

expectations, and Wang Wei manipulated those expectations, teasing the reader to look for profundity beneath a mask of simplicity. The distrust of surfaces, the disjunction between appearance and reality, and the hiddenness of meaning had not been prominent features of the poetry of the preceding two and a half centuries: court poetry was a poetry of surfaces—what was said was indeed what was meant. Court poetry's metaphors permitted easy substitutions—the court for Heaven, courtiers for immortals.

The rule of repression in the realm of emotional response became a rule of hiddenness in the cognitive realm. The hiddenness of truth did have deep roots in the philosophical tradition; in contrast to the West, in the Chinese tradition truth usually lay not behind a mask of orphic complexity but rather behind a mask of guileless simplicity. To draw on this philosophical tradition was to alter entirely the way in which poetry was read: what was said was no longer necessarily all that was meant, and the surface mood might not be the real mood. Particularly in the *Wang Stream Collection*, we find poems that are visually complete but intellectually incomplete, which tease the reader to decipher some hidden truth.[5]

Rapids by the Luan Trees	欒家瀨
The moaning of wind in autumn rain,	颯颯秋雨中
Swift water trickling over stones.	淺淺石溜瀉
Leaping waves strike one another—	跳波自相濺
A white egret startles up, comes down again.	白鷺驚復下
[06090]	

Even in less enigmatic quatrains, there is often a strange uncertainty about the full significance of Wang's flat statements.

Look Down from the High Terrace: Seeing Off Reminder Li	臨高臺送黎拾遺
I say goodbye, looking down from this high terrace	相送臨高臺
Where stream and plain stretch in endless distances.	川原杳何極
At sunset the birds return in flight	日暮飛鳥還
And travelers go on and away, never ceasing.	行人去不息
[06108]	

The reader knows that the movements of men and birds constitute a ground for comparison, but there is no clue whether the travelers are like the birds, moving off to where they belong, or unlike the homing birds, moving on and on in the constant toil of human life. At the time of composition, the circumstances of occasion may have provided the clue, but the popularity of the poem in later centuries suggests that the relationship was more interesting in uncertainty. The poem signals "analogy" to the reader and then blocks the reader from defining the analogy.

Wang Wei's public poetry was not always mere graciousness, nor was it always written to command. In a poem to encourage the emperor to perform the state sacrifices on Mount Hua (05830), Wang wrote in a style entirely different than his court poetry or his reclusive poetry. He began by praising the mountain in cosmic terms and modulated to the theme of imperial glory with a public dignity more characteristic of Tu Fu or Han Yü than the manner usually associated with Wang Wei. If Wang's inclination to private experience was a more fertile source for his poetry, his public values were also strong, and the genuine conflict between them gave real force to Wang's gestures of renunciation.

Conflict generated natural pressures on structural conventions and proprieties such as unity of response. Even in the High T'ang a shift of resolution midway through the course of a poem was unusual; it occurs in Wang Wei as the enactment of conflict between public and private values, between family obligation and the desire to withdraw.

Offhand Composition III   偶然作六首之三

At day's evening I see the T'ai-hang Mountains.   日夕見太行
I fall into brooding that I cannot go.   沉吟未能去
"Well, tell me then, why is that so?"   問君何以然
The web of the world has snared me.   世網嬰我故
My little sister grows taller each day,   小妹日成長
My brothers have not yet married,   兄弟未有娶
The family's poor, my salary low,   家貧祿既薄
And our savings, not what they once were.   儲蓄非有素
So often I have longed to fly away,   幾迴欲奮飛
But I hesitated, looked back again.   踟躕復相顧
The site of Sun Teng's Whistling Terrace,   孫登長嘯臺
Still out there somewhere among pine and bamboo.   松竹有遺處
No, I'm not all that far from it—   相去詎幾許
Old friends are already on their way.   故人在中路
Daily the stains of desire fade away,   愛染日已薄
Meditation's stillness grows daily more firm.   禪寂日已固
Suddenly I resolve to go!   忽乎吾將行
Why wait till my years are approaching their end?   寧俟歲將暮
                        [05861]

The value conflict between social obligation and private inclinations to freedom were as much a part of the intellectual interests of the age as they were a central concern of Wang Wei. But in Wang Wei's poetry this conflict is part of a much larger pattern of renunciation. It is not simply a stable state of conflict: there is a primary value, usually a social one, and the dominant movement is one of negation. This central act of negation occurs in literary terms, in intellectual terms, and in terms of the poet's self-image.

The literary gesture of negation lay in renouncing those kinds of poetry associated with public social life and the court. In the work of many other High T'ang poets the same impulse took the form of an antithetical movement, finding in eccentricity a conscious violation of poetic decorum and restraint. Li Po and a wide number of minor poets chose this path of opposition in gestures of wild spontaneity, but in Wang Wei's case, the movement was one of negation rather than antithesis.[6] Wang's characteristic eremitic poetry is austere, written in a language stripped of ornament, a language of basic words (05980):

The river flows out beyond Heaven and Earth,	江流天地外
The mountain's color, between Being and Nonbeing.	山色有無中

In contrast to poets like Li Po, Wang Wei had been deeply trained in the craft and rhetoric of court poetry. Wang was unable to oppose the feigned wonder and excitement of court poetry with a show of spontaneous wonder and excitement; instead, Wang opposed the danger of falseness of feeling by its true negation—absence of feeling. If genuine feeling is to be present, it must be hidden, only implied, spared the manipulative self-consciousness implicit in overt expression.

The restraint and stylistic control of the court poet's training appeared clearly in Wang Wei's best personal poetry, particularly in his descriptive art. But Wang used that control against the tradition it grew out of, against artifice.

Returning to Mount Sung	歸嵩山作
A clear stream lined by long tracts of brush,	清川帶長薄
There horse and coach go rumbling away.	車馬去閒閒
The flowing waters seem to have purpose,	流水如有意
And birds of evening join to turn home.	暮禽相與還
Grass-grown walls look down on an ancient ford,	荒城臨古渡
As setting sunlight fills the autumn mountains,	落日滿秋山
And far, far beneath the heights of Mount Sung,	迢遞嵩高下
I return and close my gate.	歸來且閉關

[05969]

Return was one of the most compelling themes in the poetry of Wang Wei and that of his contemporaries, return to what is basic and natural. High T'ang poets knew the place they were leaving in their various "returns"— the artificial world of capital society with its dangers, frustrations, and humiliations, as well as its poetry. However, the goals of their "returns," their definitions of "the natural," were often quite different.

In Wang Wei's poetry the object of a return was usually a form of stillness and inaction: the poet chose to cut himself off from the world rather than to show his disdain for society's decorum by acting as he pleased.

Wạng Wei's version of freedom was a "freedom from" rather than a "freedom to." As in the preceding poem, return to stillness was often indicated in the closure of a poem by a gesture that symbolized renunciation of human society and the end of discourse—shutting a gate:

In eastern marshes, the beauty of spring's plants,　　　　東皋春草色
In deep sorrow I shut my wicker gate.　　　　　　　　　惆悵掩柴扉
　　　　　　　　　　　[05970]

And he who is still—tell me why it is so　　　　　　　　靜者亦何事
That his briar gate is closed in broad daylight?　　　　荆扉乘晝關
　　　　　　　　　　　[05976]

Shutting a gate is simply one of many final gestures of renunciation in Wang Wei's poetry. It may be a refusal to go home, thereby rejecting the social structure of time (05968; 05981); sometimes it is an explicitly Buddhist gesture towards asceticism and self-negation:

At sunset by the curve of a deserted pool　　　　　　　薄暮空潭曲
I sit in meditation, mastering　　　　　　　　　　　　安禪制毒龍
　　　the poison dragon of passion.
　　　　　　　　　　　[05958]

If you would learn escape from sickness and old age,　　欲知除老病
For you there is only the discipline of Non-Life.　　　惟有學無生
　　　　　　　　　　　[05987]

　　　The Buddhist allegory "Climbing Pien-chüeh Temple" 登辨覺寺 illustrates the progress of the soul from the illusion of the physical world to the extinction of self in Nirvana. The beauty of the temple landscape serves only to draw the deluded soul onward along the right path: it is the "City of Illusion" of Buddhist parable, a hollow thing of outward sensual attraction that entices the weary and unenlightened soul towards enlightenment.

A bamboo path leads through the First Stage　　　　　　竹徑從初地
Where the City of Illusion appears from Lotus Peak.　　蓮峯出化城
Up in its windows all Ch'u is encompassed,　　　　　　愿中三楚盡
Above its forests Nine Rivers lies level.　　　　　　　林上九江平
Pliant grasses accepted for sitting in meditation,　　輭草承趺坐
Tall pines echo with sutra chanting.　　　　　　　　　長松響梵聲
Then dwelling in void, beyond the Clouds of Law,　　　空居法雲外
Observe the World, attain Non-Life.　　　　　　　　　觀世得無生
　　　　　　　　　　　[05961]

The visually present landscape of a temple-visiting poem is superimposed on an allegorical landscape, structured to lead the passive soul to transcendence. Lured up the mountain by the illusory natural and architectural beauty, the soul attains a vantage point that disorders its habitual perspective.

Grasses yield softly to the contemplative body as the soul and the eyes of the poem are drawn upward with the sounds of sutra chanting, past the pines and clouds, past the final stage of the Clouds of Law (Dharma), to transcendence. And in the notion that the beauty of temple and landscape exist only to overcome the illusion of beauty, we find an emblem for a rigorous poetic craft that exists to overcome craft.

As a progress to silence, isolation, or nothingness, the poem is an act of regression, a return. But the poem need not regress as far as these anterior states of Chinese cosmogony. A poem might return only as far as some earlier kind of poetry—regression of language (05837)—or to some primal activity such as farming (05797). One of the most interesting of such poems moves back to both the primal activity, farming, and to the primal poetry, the ritual hymns of Chou in the *Shih-ching*. The poem echoed is *Shih* 290, which begins:

They clear away grass, clear away bushes,	載芟載柞
In their plowing the earth is laid open,	其耕澤澤
A thousand pairs of plowmen turn up roots	千耦其耘
In the marshes, on the path-banks.	徂隰徂畛
Here the master, here the eldest,	侯主侯伯
Here the younger sons, their children,	侯亞侯旅
Here strong helpers, here the servants	侯彊侯以
In multitudes eating in the fields.	有嗿其饁
The men think lovingly on their wives,	思媚其婦
The wives rely upon their husbands.	有依其士
And sharp are their ploughshares	有略其耜
As they set to work on the south acres.	俶載南畝

Wang Wei uses this vision of primitive agrarian harmony in his characteristically enigmatic fashion:

An Evening Under Newly Cleared Skies	新晴晚望
Under clearing skies the plains stretch broad,	新晴原野廣
No dirt in the air as far as eyes see.	極目無氛垢
A city gate looks down upon a ford,	郭門臨渡頭
Village trees reach to the mouth of a stream.	村樹連溪口
Silvery waters bright beyond the fields,	白水明田外
Green peaks emerge behind near mountains.	碧峯出山後
These are farming months—no one takes their ease,	農月無閒人
All the family is at work on the south acres.	傾家事南畝

[05845]

Wang Wei's poem begins in stillness and clarity as the eye moves over the static relationships of the landscape and out to the edge of its broadened field of vision. In this still and harmonious world emptied of movement and human presence, Wang Wei shifts abruptly in closure to mankind, which is "not at ease." Though not at ease, mankind has its own harmony, doing what is proper in the season. It is a strange poem and lists the business of humanity as yet another "item" in the tranquil landscape. The natural is identified with the primal, and mankind is put in its proper place, in the ancient and eternal labors of farming.

After renouncing the complexities of capital society and its poetry, the poet "returns" to a primal, natural state—to the stillness behind a closed door or to the religious stillness of enlightenment or to the primitive world of earlier poetry. Sometimes a poem will end in action, as in the preceding poem, or even in the eccentric version of the natural that was favored by Wang's contemporaries—but such natural action must come from a ground of stillness.

Dwelling in Ease at Wang Stream: To P'ei Ti	輞川閒居贈裴秀才迪
Chill mountains growing ever more azure,	寒山轉蒼翠
Autumn waters daily rush by.	秋水日潺湲
I lean on a staff outside my wicker gate,	倚杖柴門外
Face to the wind, hear cicadas of evening.	臨風聽暮蟬
At the river crossing the last of setting sun,	渡頭餘落日
A lone column of smoke rises from a village.	墟里上孤煙
Once again I meet old Chieh-yü drunk,	復值接輿醉
And we sing crazy songs before the five willows.	狂歌五柳前

[05914]

Chieh-yü was the legendary "madman of Ch'u," the representative example of the eccentric whose seeming madness concealed true wisdom. Five willows echoes the "Master of Five Willows," a fictional biography by T'ao Ch'ien describing the ideal recluse. As the preceding poem integrated human activity into the natural world, here the still and tranquil scene reduces wild madness to a gentle and decorous lunacy in the landscape.

On an intellectual level the act of negation in Wang Wei's poetry was inextricably bound up with Wang Wei's Buddhism. Many critics have pointed out Wang's obsessive use of terms like *k'ung* 空 ("emptiness," "the Void," Śunyata, "in vain") that have meaning both in the secular poetic tradition and in Buddhist thought. Wang knew at least a few sutras well, drew terms from them, and alluded to them. But no matter how devout a Buddhist, Wang Wei was a poet and not a Buddhist thinker; religion played a significant role in his poetry, but the poetic tradition and the concept of poetry it presumed excluded the possibility of a truly religious or devotional poetry. Not until the early ninth century did the scope of poetry broaden enough to admit a discursive and meditative treatment of religious values; this can be found in some of the poems of Po Chü-yi. But for a

body of poetry whose primary orientation was religious, one must go outside the secular poetic tradition to the collections of Han-shan and Wang
Fan-chih.

A third theme developed out of the twin themes of negation and return: this was unselfconsciousness. In one form it involved a negation of
the will that projected into the future and manipulated it. Or in social terms
it was a negation of motivated behavior, of treating one's fellow man in
such a way as to advance or confirm one's social position.

Unselfconsciousness and its opposition to social privilege appear clearly
in the closing of the following poem. The closure uses two allusions to the
Taoist text *Lieh-tzu*. The first story concerns Lao-tzu's rebuke to Yang Chu
for allowing himself to appear so grand that others paid him deference.
Yang Chu mended his ways, and when he returned to the inn where he had
been staying, the innkeeper and guests, previously respectful, now ignored
him and even squabbled to take possession of the mat he was sitting on. The
second story tells of a man who was fond of seagulls, and when he would
visit them on the shore, they approached him without fear. His father then
urged him to trap them by taking advantage of their trust, but the next time
the man returned to the shore—this time with a motive—the gulls sensed
it and fled.

Written after Long Rains at My Villa by Wang Stream	積雨輞川莊作
Long rains in deserted forests, smoking fires burn slowly,	積雨空林煙火遲
Steaming greens, boiling millet, the men take their meals on the eastern acreage.	蒸藜炊黍餉東菑
Over the mists of watery fields a white egret flies.	漠漠水田飛白鷺
In the shade of a summer wood a yellow oriole warbling.	陰陰夏木囀黃鸝
Here in the mountains practice stillness, watch flowers that bloom for a day,	山中習靜觀朝槿
Beneath the pines fast in purity and harvest dewy mallows.	松下清齋折露葵
An old man of wilderness long ago ceased squabbling for the mat,	野老與人爭席罷
So why should the seagulls ever suspect him any more?	海鷗何事更相疑

[06072]

The theme of unselfconsciousness appeared early in Wang Wei's poetry in a poem on T'ao Ch'ien's "Peach Blossom Spring," from the year
717 (05880). Wang reinterpreted the story in the retelling, emphasizing the
unselfconsciousness of the fisherman when he found the utopian village.

But once the fisherman was received by the villagers and had settled for the night, verbs of thinking, longing, planning, and remembering filled the poem. Once the fisherman "wanted" to go home and "wanted" to return to Peach Blossom Spring again, of course he was unable to find the way. Wang Wei's reinterpretation of the fable was the first of a long series of poems retelling the story in later centuries.

Negation of will is related to the negation of self, a theme with both Taoist and Buddhist dimensions. In much of his descriptive poetry, the speaking poet became an eye passing over the landscape and isolating significant elements. As in any literary form, the disappearance of the poetic artificer was an unattainable goal: Wang Wei's powerful organizing consciousness mediated between the world seen and the representation. But that manipulative consciousness tried to negate its presence by hiding from the surface of the poem, and by creating enigma to thwart the reader's impulse to find simple meaning. The conventions of poetic structure demanded personal response in the closure: Wang Wei would often give his "response" in a gesture of renunciation, a response that denied further response, further acts, or further emotions.

Such quintessentially negative gestures may not be true for the greater part of Wang Wei's poetry, but they do appear in most of the poems for which Wang was later admired, poems that embodied his poetic identity. Often Wang described a world of objects in static relationships or harmonious movement and then, at the end, positioned himself in that world (05982):

A fire on shore, a lone boat spending the night,	岸火孤舟宿
Fishermen's houses, there evening birds return.	漁家夕鳥還
Vast and empty, heaven and earth grow dark—	寂寥天地暮
The heart is as calm as the broad stream.	心與廣川閒

These lines work through traditional poetic associations: the single fire of the boatmen suggests loneliness; the return of the birds calls to mind personal return and homesickness; the sunset evokes melacholy. In "Crossing the Yellow River to Ch'ing-ho," the poet structured the visual scenes dramatically to create an interior narrative. In this poem, written also on the journey to Chi-chou, the poet tried to overcome the interiority of the scene by the objective eye that reduced these fragments of the world and its own conciousness (*hsin* 心 "heart"/"mind") to a series of "items" in the calm scene. The consciousness moves through the world with the steadiness of the river, passing things and not fixing on them.

Wang Wei's independence and originality did not preclude a base of Early T'ang convention in much of his work. How close he stands to seventh-century compositional technique can be appreciated only by contrast to a later T'ang treatment. To cite one telling example, after a poem in praise of the capital region, Wang closed with a shift to the figure of Ssu-ma Hsiang-ju, the Han *fu* writer, excluded from the delights of capital society and sick in Mao-ling, near the capital.

Sightseeing on a Winter Day 冬日游覽

I walked forth from the city's eastern gate	步出城東門
And let my gaze sweep a thousand miles.	試騁千里目
Green mountains stretched behind azure forests,	青山橫蒼林
The crimson sun was a ball on the level land.	赤日團平陸
North of the Wei, sight sped to Han-tan,	渭北走邯鄲
And to East of the Passes, out of Han-ku.	關東出函谷
A thousand directions converge on the land of Ch'in,	秦地萬方會
Satraps of the Nine Regions come to court.	來朝九州牧
As the cock crows in Hsien-yang City,	鷄鳴咸陽中
Caps and awnings go on in succession.	冠蓋相追逐
The minister visits the nobility,	丞相過列侯
Lords banquet the royal chamberlain.	羣公饌光祿
Now Hsiang-ju is old and sick	相如方老病
And returns alone to Mao-ling for night.	獨歸茂陵宿

[05829]

The poem is a High T'ang transformation of the seventh-century song on the capital, best represented by Lu Chao-lin's "Ch'ang-an: *ku-yi*" (02762) and by Lo Pin-wang's "The Imperial Capital" (04148).[7] The closing shift from the glory of the capital region to the figure of the suffering outsider was an irresistible instinct of Early T'ang poetic convention. Lu Chao-lin's poem had closed with Yang Hsiung, the Han intellectual who had become the medieval exemplary recluse; Lo Pin-wang's poem closed with Chia Yi, the Han political writer whose talents were unappreciated. The structural convention was compelling; Wang Wei asserted his identity through the conventions of closure, through his choice of Ssu-ma Hsiang-ju as the outsider and emblem for himself. Hsiang-ju was the Han figure who would most strongly represent the true poet.

About a century later Li Shang-yin echoed the closing of the poem above (and of another poem by Wang, 06026) in a quatrain in which he, like Wang Wei, assumed the role of Ssu-ma Hsiang-ju.

To Secretary Ling-hu 寄令狐郎中

From Mount Sung's clouds, from the trees of Ch'in, long have I dwelt apart.	嵩雲秦樹久離居
A carp-form letter-case came from afar, in it a single letter.	雙鯉迢迢一紙書

Oh, ask no more of those who once were
   guests in the garden of Liang—
At Mao-ling in the autumn rain,
   sick Hsiang-ju.
     [29160]

休問梁園舊賓客

茂陵秋雨病相如

    The pathos in the figure of the outsider was achieved in the Early T'ang poems by an abrupt closing shift away from a lengthy praise of the capital's delights. Wang Wei may have abbreviated the rhetorical praise of the capital, but the technique was essentially the same. Li Shang-yin was able to concentrate on the figure in isolation and to represent the intense pathos of his condition without a long rhetorical contrast. The conventional antithesis of joyful communality survives only as an echo, as Ssu-ma Hsiang-ju's former happiness as a "guest in the Garden of Liang." Indeed, the antithetical joy survives only as something "not to be spoken of," and that negative imperative points to the isolated poet for whom memory is pain. The structural convention of Early T'ang poetry had not disappeared entirely, but it had been transformed almost beyond recognition.

    Among the major High T'ang poets, only Tu Fu surpassed Wang Wei in the seriousness of his use of the literary past.[8] Wang's use of early poetry has already been seen in the closure of his poems on renunciation and return. Despite his conscious primitivism in echoing the *Shih-ching* and *Ch'u-tz'u*, Wang generally avoided the ethical *fu-ku* associations of those early poems. From the tradition of the pentasyllabic *shih*, Wang often borrowed elements from the poetry of Ts'ao Chih, Pao Chao, Hsieh Ling-yün, Hsieh T'iao, and Yü Hsin. But no poet or group of poems exerted as powerful an appeal for Wang as the poetry of T'ao Ch'ien.

    During the centuries that followed his death, T'ao Ch'ien's influence was slight. Poets echoed lines and phrases from his work, but he was not considered a major poet. The *Chin History* classified him as an exemplary recluse rather than as a man of letters, while Chung Jung's 鍾嶸 *Shih-p'in* 詩品 ranked his work only in the second level of excellence. But T'ao's poetry was particularly well represented in the *Wen-hsüan*, which may have been one factor in his increasing popularity during the eighth century. The major exception to sixth-century and seventh-century indifference to T'ao was the Early T'ang poet Wang Chi 王績: few poets were as exclusively devoted to a single predecessor as Wang Chi was to T'ao Ch'ien, but even in that case T'ao served primarily as a model of personality rather than as a true literary model. The T'ao Ch'ien revival that took place in the 720s and 730s established T'ao's pre-eminence in Six Dynasties poetry, a position never challenged in later dynasties. The T'ao Ch'ien revival began in the works of a few poets and soon spread to the wider circle of capital poets. In part this phenomenon reflects Tao's genuine appeal to the new High

T'ang taste, but in part it also seems that the T'ao Ch'ien persona was merely fashionable. If the note dating Wang Wei's "Peach Blossom Spring" to 717 is correct, then that poem was one of the earliest monuments to the new interest in T'ao Ch'ien. Wang Wei and Ch'u Kuang-hsi were the poets most strongly under T'ao's spell, and it was probably from them that interest spread to other members of their circle.

At times Wang Wei simply imitated T'ao Ch'ien's style, as in one of his "Offhand Compositions" (05862), written specifically in T'ao's praise. However, the more serious use of T'ao's poetry lay in integrating T'ao's casual simplicity with the sophistication and craft of the eighth-century capital poet. This Wang Wei accomplished to perfection, and the two antithetical voices seem to merge as one.

To P'ei Ti   贈裴十迪

The scenery is lovely in the evening of the day,   風景日夕佳
As here with you I write new poems   與君賦新詩
And, calm, gaze into the distant sky,   澹然望遠空
Our chins resting on our *ju-yi* staffs.   如意方支頤
The spring wind stirs all the plants,   春風動百草
Orchid and iris grow by my hedge.   蘭蕙生我籬
Through a haze the sun warms the bed chamber   曖曖日暖閨
And a farmer comes to bring me word: 田家來致詞
Joyously spring returns to the marshes,   欣欣春還皋
Waters rise, full and churning, by the banks.   澹澹水生陂
And though peach and plum haven't blossomed,   桃李雖未開
Buds and leaflings fill their branches.   荑萼滿其枝
Sir, get your walking stick ready to go home—   請君理還策
I tell you, it's time for farming soon.   敢告將農時
                              [05797]

Some of the echoes of T'ao's poetry here are identifiable textual references, while others are simply turns of phrase. Wang Wei's fascination with T'ao's manner did not lead to subordination to the older poet: T'ao's characteristic celebration of the free and joyful self must be tied to the order of the natural world, the scene at hand that was the central concern of court poet's descriptive art. T'ao might describe an agrarian scene, but the primary emphasis lay on the poet. The High T'ang poet cannot resist halting the movement of the poem now and again to focus on some picturesque, static scene. The thematic development is also Wang Wei's own— from poetry to contemplative stillness to natural action.

Wang Wei's first line would remind every educated reader of the seventh line of T'ao's "Drinking Wine: V": "Mountain air is lovely in the evening of the day" 山氣日夕佳. Later, when Wang Wei speaks of his hedge, the reader must think back to T'ao Ch'ien's famous hedge in the fifth line of the same poem. Wang has orchid and iris growing by his hedge, while T'ao "picks chrysanthemums" by his. But T'ao does not lack orchid and iris: in poem XVII of the "Drinking Wine" series, they grow in his front yard. To ensure that his readers hear T'ao Ch'ien's famous hedge echoing behind his own, Wang uses the personal pronoun *wo* 我, "my." During the age of court poetry, personal pronouns had been gradually driven from poetic diction, but T'ao used them often. In the hands of a T'ang poet, an informal pronoun like *wo* suggested "natural language" and a certain archaic directness. The second line of Wang's poem echoes the second poem of T'ao's "Moving House" series:

In spring and autumn are many lovely days,   春秋多佳日
I climb a high place and write new poems.   登高賦新詩

One could continue to extract fragments of T'ao Ch'ien's work from the remainder of Wang Wei's poem, but our primary concern is with the significance of these echoes. Wang Wei's poem is a fine work with its own integrity and not simply a pastiche of phrases from T'ao Ch'ien. Their function is essentially modal: as the *ku-feng* carried with it implicit messages of political concern and moral rectitude, so the style of T'ao Ch'ien possessed an aura of honest simplicity and basic agrarian values. On the one hand, Wang Wei is not making allusion to the full contexts of specific poems by T'ao; on the other hand, he is not simply repeating the T'ao Ch'ien manner as Wang Chi did. Rather, Wang Wei is using the T'ao Ch'ien mode to give an added dimension to a poem that also carries his own personal voice.

Of those now considered major High T'ang poets, Wang Wei was not only the most prominent in his own time, he was also the earliest to attain prominence. Meng Hao-jan was an older poet, and a few of his better works antedate the early 720s when Wang Wei began to produce major poetry. But Wang Wei early became an influential figure in capital poetry, while Meng Hao-jan was at best considered an interesting provincial with a moderate gift for poetry. When Meng Hao-jan met Wang Wei in the capital in approximately 734, Wang Wei was the established poet. Meng's chronological priority has tempted at least one critic to see the influence of Meng upon Wang Wei's work, but if there was much interchange, the influence would probably have gone in the other direction. Wang Wei was socially superior and better known; writing to Wang, Meng paid him the most telling gesture of deference: he wrote in Wang Wei's distinctive poetic voice and not his own.[9]

Other hints in the two collections tend to confirm Wang's poetic, if not chronological, priority; for instance, on his journey to Chi-chou in the early 720s, Wang wrote (05846):

In a strange land, cut off from companions, 他鄉絕儔侶
A lone wanderer grows closer to his servant boy. 孤客親僮僕

It is highly unlikely that Wang would have known Meng Hao-jan's poetry at this stage. In an undatable poem by Meng, but a poem presumed to be from his later years, we read (07795):

Gradually I grow farther from flesh and blood 漸與骨肉遠
And become ever closer to my servant boy. 轉於僮僕親

One line is clearly borrowed from the other, and we can be reasonably certain that it was Meng who borrowed from Wang. Meng Hao-jan is the greatest of Wang's early contemporaries, but the scope of Wang's work is broader, his style more clearly individual, his intellectual concerns more serious, and the quality of his work consistently greater than that of Meng Hao-jan.

High T'ang writers usually thought of contemporary poetry in terms of couplets rather than whole poems. Wang Wei was a master of the parallel couplet. The distinctive aspects of his couplet art were imitated: geometrical balance of forms, plain words for grand scenes, an unmatched clarity and restraint. Even when his couplets are in the general style of his lesser contemporaries, he was the superior craftsman. When he wrote of Wang Wei's art, Tu Fu spoke of his couplets (11577):

Most known, those fine couplets that fill the entire world. 最傳秀句寰區滿

The individual aspects of his couplet style were one of Wang's major contributions to T'ang poetry: he replaced the dense, ingenious couplets of Early T'ang poetry with a purity and simplicity of style that was extremely compelling. He stripped away the visual complexities of what he called "the realm of vision" (*yen-chieh* 眼界 06035), leaving a world of simple forms and elements in meaningful relationships. But the purity and simplicity of his style was not the spontaneous "natural language" that other poets sought: though it opposed the artifice of poetic craft, it was itself a highly sophisticated manifestation of that same craft. In this we have the emblem of the paradox that echoes in every aspect of Wang Wei's poetry—the craft that tries to overcome craft, the artifice of simplicity. Later critics saw only the simplicity, the poet of nature and reclusion; but in his own time he was, in the words of a friend, "of this age, the master craftsman of poetry" 當代詩匠 (06199).

5

The First Generation
Capital Poets of the K'ai-yüan

Wang Wei's liberation from the more restrictive aspects of Early T'ang poetics was not an isolated phenomenon; he was one member of a whole new generation of poets who passed the metropolitan examination in the 720s and early 730s. Many of these men became close friends, and their extensive poem exchanges mark the spread of poetry as a normal part of social intercourse among officials of the central government and the great families of the capital. The term *poet* here is a misnomer of convenience: poetry was an activity practiced and enjoyed by many members of the capital elite, and those men we call "capital poets" were simply the most famous, the most interested, and the most capable in this pursuit. Drawn together by their poetic avocation, these men formed a more closely knit group within the larger realm of capital society. Furthermore, as poetry was still considered a means for an outsider to win recognition in the capital, it is not surprising to find several provincials in this group: these men had conformed to capital taste and had been accepted for their poetic accomplishments.

The primary bond between these men was social.[1] Though they shared certain poetic interests and aesthetic values, they espoused no allegiance to an individual master or theory of poetry and were far from the true "literary groups" that began in the ninth century. The shared elements of their poetics were subordinate to their friendship and position in capital society. Several came from the great capital families, and all had ties with those families. Many were associated with Chang Chiu-ling's government and had to leave the capital in 737 when Chang fell. Few ever achieved high political office, with the notable exception of Wang Wei in his last years.

The preferred themes of these poets were quietism and reclusion; their preferred genre, pentasyllabic regulated verse. As might be expected, occasional poetry was most common, and they preferred a relatively unornamented style, but one more elegant than Wang Wei at his most austere.

They also shared with Wang Wei an interest in the rough sincerity of T'ao Ch'ien. However, these characteristics are far from universal; among the capital poets were acknowledged masters of the heptasyllabic song and quatrain: Ts'ui Hao, Li Ch'i, and Wang Ch'ang-ling.

What gives the capital poets their loose coherence as a group is the contrast to those of their contemporaries who developed poetic voices in relative isolation. Those outsiders lacked the capital poets' common bond of literary training and constant exercise of their art in the demanding circles of the capital elite. As a result, the outsiders often developed strongly individual styles. For example, the southeasterner Ts'ui Kuo-fu spent much of his life in the capital, but had little contact with the capital poets. This social separateness is reflected in the idiosyncracy of his poetry, much of which assumes the self-conscious pose of the southeasterner. Kao Shih and Li Po are the most famous of the true outsiders: they developed entirely individual poetic idioms in the K'ai-yüan with virtually no contact with capital poets.

Between the capital poets and these true outsiders were a number of poets with tangential relation to the capital group. Meng Hao-jan is the most prominent. Meng developed as a poet early, in the relative isolation of his native Hsiang-yang, and he never resided in the capital for any extended period of time. His poetic interests, however, were consonant with those of the capital poets, his contacts with them were frequent, and he received support and encouragement from them. Ch'ang Chien represents another kind of poet on the fringes of the capital group. Unlike Meng Hao-jan, Ch'ang Chien probably did learn poetry in the company of the young intellectuals of the capital: he passed the metropolitan examination in 727 when the new K'ai-yüan style was being perfected. But Ch'ang spent the rest of his life in provincial posts, largely cut off from poetic intercourse with his contemporaries. Thus, we find in his work a basis of capital convention, but developed in a highly personal way.

The capital poets formed their social ties and shared poetic interests during the K'ai-yüan Reign (713–41), but their work continued through the T'ien-pao (742–55) and, in many cases, later. Indeed, many were at the height of their poetic powers during the T'ien-pao. Early in the T'ien-pao, however, interest in new kinds of poetry began to appear in some circles of the capital; in particular, the flamboyant, imaginative style of Li Po cast its allure over many readers and younger poets. The capital poets generally ignored Li Po and other outsiders, holding to the decorous and balanced style that had won them fame.

A change in generations had occurred: between 735 and the early 740s very few younger poets and appeared to join the circle of capital poets. The new poets of the early 740s confronted a whole galaxy of established masters, both capital poets and outsiders. Their various responses to their talented predecessors defined the second generation of the High T'ang.

Wang Wei, Wang Ch'ang-ling, Ch'u Kuang-hsi, Lu Hsiang, and Ts'ui Hao formed the core of the first generation of capital poets. As major figures with independent poetic identities, Wang Wei and Wang Ch'ang-ling are treated separately. Of the lesser poets, Ch'u Kuang-hsi was the most independent; though much of his work was conventional, he developed an individual poetic voice in one kind of poetry: bucolic in the tradition of T'ao Ch'ien. The other capital poets are best distinguished not by strong poetic identities but by interest and excellence in certain themes and subgenres. They spoke the collective voice of the group and the age, and the characteristics of genre and subgenre were far stronger than the characteristics of the individual poet. The style of a parting poem by Ts'ui Hao will be far closer to a parting poem by Lu Hsiang than to one of Ts'ui Hao's heptasyllabic songs.

K'ai-yüan readers and critics honored genius in the performance of convention as much as they honored originality. Later readers honored individuality, a coherent poetic identity that they could perceive through a poet's work. As a result, whatever their contemporary reputations, poets with individual voices have generally survived better than masters of the shared style. During the K'ai-yüan, Lu Hsiang and Ch'u Kuang-hsi probably enjoyed equal fame; Ch'u, the more individual poet, has a large corpus of poems extant; Lu has only twenty-eight poems, including several of doubtful attribution.

Lu Hsiang 盧象 can be taken as representative of many capital poets of the K'ai-yüan: admired and influential in his own time, today he has been virtually forgotten. Lu became acquainted with Wang Wei as early as 719 or 720, and the two men served together in the Chang Chiu-ling government. Lu was also one of Meng Hao-jan's earliest admirers and supporters.

In the *Ho-yüeh ying-ling chi* Yin Fan praised Lu Hsiang's poetry highly (though without the superlatives accorded to some other poets): his work was "decorous but not flat, possessing the grand style, attaining the manner of the *Kuo-feng* [in the *Shih-ching*]."[2] Yin Fan's modal categories of style are difficult to define, but the description of Lu's style represents one aspect of the shared capital poetics. "Decorous" (*ya*) is the antithesis of "low" (*su* 俗, "popular," "vulgar") and suggests emotional restraint, graceful diction, and the avoidance of certain "low" themes and words. The flatness that Lu escapes is the danger that besets a too decorous style.[3] This balance of verve and restraint reflects the High T'ang sense of the *Kuo-feng*, at once plain and grand.

A preface to Lu Hsiang's works by the great Mid-T'ang writer Liu Yü-hsi 劉禹錫 suggests that Lu was still admired early in the ninth century.[4] But during the course of the ninth century, Lu's poetry was forgotten, and like so many other capital poets of the K'ai-yüan, he did not figure prominently in the great anthologies of the Early Sung. Lu Hsiang's few extant poems reveal not only the mastery for which he was admired but also the lack of strong poetic personality that caused his works to be forgotten.

With Wang Wei's "Stopping by Recluse Ts'ui's Forest Pavilion"	同王維過崔處士林亭
Hidden by bamboo hear now and again a well-pulley turning,	映竹時聞轉轆轤
But at his window see only webs of spiders.	當窗只見網蜘蛛
Our host rests ever aloof, and does not plead sickness—	主人非病常高臥
In a circling wall of tangled growth one aging man of learning.	環堵蒙籠一老儒
[05732]	

The occasional works of the K'ai-yüan capital poets had deep roots in court poetry and the occasional poetry of the Early T'ang. Play on the contrary evidence of presence and absence, which appears in the first couplet of this poem, passed from court poetry into the conventions of High T'ang poems on visiting recluses. Ts'ui Hsing-tsung, at one time Ommissioner of the Right and himself capable of gracious court poetry (e.g., 06195), had been living in retirement for ten years when this poem was written. Lu's poem is one of a series of quatrains by Wang Wei, Wang Chin, P'ei Ti, and Ts'ui himself, all treating different aspects of reclusion. Ts'ui's social status is unknown; he may well have been one of the great Ts'ui clan of the capital, living a life of leisure in his "rustic" villa. Whatever Ts'ui's rank, this is a social poem that possesses all the gracious courtesy of a court poem or formal occasional poem of Chung-tsung's reign. What has changed are the values, and these have indeed been dramatically inverted. Instead of receiving praise as an immortal who dwells among the stars, this kind host receives praise for his rusticity and the integrity of the recluse. (Ts'ui does not even stoop to the mendacity of a polite fiction, unwilling to offer the conventional excuse of illness for refusing to serve.)

Tsu Yung 祖詠 was another early member of the capital group, a close friend of Wang Wei and a client of Chang Yüeh. Tsu passed the metropolitan examination in 724 or 725, then held several minor offices before retiring to private life. The forty-six poems that constitute Tsu Yung's surviving corpus are primarily occasional pieces in pentasyllabic regulated verse. Like Lu Hsiang, Tsu lacks a strong poetic personality, but in Tsu's case Yin Fan notes the deficiency, a lack of "impelling spirit" or "energy" (*ch'i* 氣), for which Tsu compensated by an excellent "tone" (*tiao* 調). In effect, this means grace and competence without identity: "energy" was strongly associated with force of personality manifest in poems.

Changes in values, new poetic devices, and a new aesthetic sensibility marked the capital poets' departure from Early T'ang poetics, but still the continuities were strong, and nowhere stronger than in the very conception of poetry. Like court poetry, capital poetry was a social phenomenon, learned by practice and poetic exchange. Poets of later ages also followed contemporary trends, but they saw their work in the context of the entire poetic past. The poetic past defined the materials with which they worked; it was an immense vocabulary of moods, styles, and themes, each with strong literary historical dimensions. One image could evoke Tu Fu; another turn of phrase could call to mind Po Chü-yi.

To the capital poets of the K'ai-yüan, the compositions of friends more perfectly defined poetry than any private experience of the literary past; the need to speak the shared poetic language far transcended any desire for personal innovation or a "return to antiquity." T'ao Ch'ien was deeply admired, but he was not the towering figure of genius that Tu Fu was to become for later poets. As in court poetry, there existed a body of themes, antitheses, stylistic devices, and structural patterns that enabled a competent practicioner to produce fluent, attractive poems. We find this conventional fluency throughout the T'ang, but from the later eighth century onward, elements of conventional styles were sorted into literary historical "sets," each with strong associations of a given period or a given poet. In this way inescapable echoes of past poetry gradually permeated all levels of the poetic language. Though the K'ai-yüan possessed a wide range of subgeneric "sets," there were only two important period sets—those of the *ku-feng* and court poetry—and one set associated with an individual poet—T'ao Ch'ien. The shared style of the lesser capital poets showed as little sense of literary history as it did of individuation. As Lu's Hsiang's poem illustrated the quatrain, the following poem by Tsu Yung shows a successful treatment of the pentasyllabic regulated verse. The similarity to Wang Wei is marked, but it is Wang Wei without Wang's genius.

The Su Family Villa   蘇氏別業

Your villa lies in a secluded spot, where   別業居幽處
Whenever I come, reclusion fills my heart.   到來生隱心

The South Mountains face its doors and windows, 南山當戶牖
The Feng's waters reflect its gardens and groves. 灃水映園林
Its roof, covered by snows through the winter, 屋覆經冬雪
Its yard, darkened by shade before evening. 庭昏未夕陰
In the empty stillness beyond the realm of men 寥寥人境外
I sit in peace, listen to the birds of spring. 閒坐聽春禽

[06270]

If the capital poets' conception of the nature of poetry remained close to that of the Early T'ang, their aesthetic values were changing as quickly as their intellectual values. Tsu Yung's most famous poem was "Looking at the Last of the Snow on Chung-nan Mountain". The occasion for the poem has been preserved in an anecdote that provides a fascinating glimpse of the conflict between High T'ang aesthetics and the aesthetics of formal poetry from the Early T'ang:

An important official gave out the topic for composition, "Looking at the Last of the Snow on Chung-nan Mountain." Tsu Yung wrote:

The northside ridge of Chung-nan rises grandly, 終南陰嶺秀
Drifts of snow at the edge of drifting clouds. 積雪浮雲端
Beyond the woods the color of clear sky bright, 林表明霽色
And in the city, increasing the evening cold. 城中增暮寒

[06291]

When these four lines were received by the official, someone rebuked Tsu Yung, and he answered, "That's all I had to say."[5]

The "rebuke" may have been because the set topic required eight lines, or perhaps because Tsu ended a quatrain with a parallel couplet. Tsu's reply, "That's all I had to say" (*yi-chin* 意盡, "meaning exhausted," "intention exhausted"), suggests two different things: either the poet's inspiration had failed him midway through the poem ("That's all I could say") or that he had made his point ("That's what I had to say"). A set topic from an important official, perhaps an examiner, required the formality of court poetry, and according to those rhetorical rules, Tsu Yung's quatrain was a grotesquely deformed thing. Tsu's closure with a roughly parallel couplet gave a strong sense of incompleteness, as though he had stopped speaking in the middle of a sentence. The only possible explanation was that the poet was incapable of continuing—"That's all I could say." On the other hand, in the context of the new aesthetics of the capital poets, "the point has been made"—"That's what I had to say." The same incompleteness makes the closure suggestive, and the growing chill in the city takes on a mysterious significance.[6]

Tsu Yung's ambiguous reply admits his failure before the formal demands of composition to a set topic; at the same time it ridicules the man who rebuked him for his failure to understand the beauty of the quatrain. The aesthetic sensibility of the High T'ang was to prove victorious in later ages, and the deformed fragment that earned Tsu Yung a rebuke was to become a minor classic.

Though no more individual than Lu Hsiang or Tsu Yung, Chi-wu Ch'ien 綦毋潛 was perhaps the finest stylist among the minor figures. Twenty-six of his poems survive, including some of dubious authenticity. With his sharp ear for fine couplets and the subtleties of style, Yin Fan praised Chi-wu Ch'ien as the finest poet from the middle Yangtze region in many centuries. The regional boundaries of Yin Fan's praise were probably a device to accord Chi-wu superlative praise among many other superlative poets. Indeed, the best of Chi-wu Ch'ien's poetry shows the heights to which the shared, virtually anonymous style of the capital poets could rise.

Sailing on Jo-yeh Creek in Spring   春泛若耶溪

Seclusion on my mind never ceasing,   幽意無斷絶
From here I'll follow whatever I meet: 此去隨所偶
Evening breezes blow my moving boat   晚風吹行舟
On a path of flowers into the creek mouth.   花路入溪口
At night's edge I turn with the western ravine,   際夜轉西壑
Across mountains gaze on the Southern Dipper.   隔山望南斗
Mist over pools flies billowing, rolling,   潭煙飛溶溶
And the moon of the forest lowers behind me.   林月低向後
Life's problems and deeds have swollen now to flood, 生事且瀰漫
My wish—to grow old, my fishing pole in hand.   願爲持竿叟
                    [06417]

This is the oldest thematic pattern in Chinese landscape poetry: the poet moves through the landscape, attaining enlightenment or understanding the futility of public life. Here Chi-wu Ch'ien handles the traditional formula without deviation, amplifying it perfectly in the tripartite form. Nevertheless, the poem is unmistakably a creation of the K'ai-yüan capital poets. From Wang Wei's "Peach Blossom Spring" (05880) Chi-wu Ch'ien borrowed impersonal narration to emphasize passivity, and the theme of Peach Blossom Spring lies only thinly veiled beneath the surface of line four. However, instead of a stable utopian community, Chi-wu Ch'ien continues on the water, crossing the boundary into night, and facing the billowing mists that are an emblem of the flux of the world, the "swelling flood." The resolution comes in the image of the fisherman, who like the "Fisherman" of the *Ch'u-tz'u*, moves with the processes of change and craves no illusory stability.

The stylistic sophistication of the capital poets can be seen in the contrast between this poem and Chang Chiu-ling's roughly contemporary "Climbing a Tall Building on an Autumn Evening" (pp. 25–26). Though

Chang's visual itinerary is a physical journey in Chi-wu Ch'ien's poem, the themes of the two poems are remarkably similar. But Chang Chiu-ling's poem seems heavy, discontinuous, and old-fashioned compared to Chi-wu Ch'ien's poem: Chang's style evoked a seriousness that had a special appeal to T'ang readers, but the fluid unity in Chi-wu Ch'ien represented a more sophisticated, if less personal art.

Lu Hsiang, Tsu Yung, and Chi-wu Ch'ien were only three of many poets writing in the shared style, only a handful of whose works are extant. They included a number of Wang's, Ts'ui's, Wei's, and P'ei's. Among these, P'ei Ti 裴迪 deserves brief mention. P'ei was Wang Wei's closest friend and his collaborator. Apart from his twenty quatrains in the *Wang Stream Collection*, less than ten of P'ei's poems are extant. These include three interesting temple-visiting poems (06164, 06166, 06167), but none show the quality of the *Wang Stream Collection* poems. There P'ei was scarcely distinguishable from Wang Wei, even in the technique of enigmatic, understated closure.

Striped Apricot Lodge   文杏館

Far, far Striped Apricot Lodge,   迢迢文杏館
Each day I climb there more often.   躋攀日已屢
South Ridge and North Lake—   南嶺與北湖
I look ahead, then I look behind.   前看復回顧
              [06171]

Wang's individual voice grew out of the shared style of capital poetry, and the appeal of his work was such that other poets easily fell into Wang's personal variation of the style, especially when writing with him. This was a natural phenomenon when a minor poet wrote with a major one, but P'ei's half of the *Wang Stream Collection* is remarkable in the perfection of his unconscious assimilation to Wang Wei's style. Some critics have found P'ei's quatrains inferior, but this may be no more than an expectation of genius from Wang and mediocrity from P'ei. In fact, the quatrains are so perfectly matched that the collection proceeds with superlative ease, without the least disjunctive note.

The occasional and eremitic poems above represent the norm of capital poetry. Only Wang Wei achieved greatness through this mode; the bland fluidity of the shared style became in Wang Wei's poetry the austere veil for an intellectual passion. However, variation from the norm usually produced more interesting poetry. On the one hand, outsiders like Meng Hao-jan and Ch'ang Chien created a more vital and compelling nature poetry than that of the capital poets. On the other hand, poets like Wang Ch'ang-ling and Li Ch'i remained within the social sphere of capital poetry but experimented with new topics and modes. Ts'ui Hao, one of the earliest members of the group, transformed the heptasyllabic song of

the Early T'ang to suit the new High T'ang sense of aesthetics. And Ch'u
Kuang-hsi, the most individual poet of the group apart from the two
Wangs, created his own rugged bucolic poetry on the model of T'ao Ch'ien.

崔顥

TS'UI HAO

Ts'ui Hao began his career as a court poet, serving with Wang Wei in the
court of Li Fan in the late 710s or early 720s. The two poets were linked
as the rising stars of poetry in the 720s. Ts'ui Hao may or may not have
been connected with the great Ts'ui clan of the capital, but he assumed
the role of the dissolute young nobleman, both in his poetry and—if we
can believe the anecdotes told about him—in his behavior. He shocked
eighth-century society by marrying and divorcing a number of wives in
close succession. He was also reputed to have offended Li Yung   , one
of the grand old men of letters in the K'ai-yüan and the son of the *Wen-
hsüan* scholar Li Shan 李善: poems were often presented at introductions,
and Ts'ui Hao offered up to Li Yung a poem using a female persona. The
horrified Li Yung refused to see Ts'ui, saying, "This child lacks all manners." True or not, the anecdote reveals the essential decorum of T'ang
occasional poetry. Ts'ui Hao's violation of manners did not lie in writing
such poetry, but in presenting it to a distinguished personage. Furthermore,
Ts'ui could hardly have been unaware of this decorum, and the episode
suggests a prank rather than a *faux pas*. However unruly Ts'ui's youth may
have been, Yin Fan claimed that Ts'ui sobered his style in later years. Ts'ui
died in 753, before the rebellion.

Though a friend of many poets in the group, Ts'ui Hao had little
interest in the gracious pentasyllabic poetry of reclusion. Consonant with
his typological role as the rake, Ts'ui preferred *yüeh-fu* and the heptasyllabic
song. Much of his work was essentially conservative, particularly in his
use of the song style of the first decades of the eighth century; among these
are several songs on the splendor of the capital, distinguished by their
quality if not by their originality (e.g., 06225). But Ts'ui also composed
several shorter songs in which he curtailed the form's tendencies toward
repetitious sentimentality. These short songs link the early-eighth-century
song to the wilder, more dramatic and imaginative songs of the T'ien-pao.
Li Po in particular was attracted by Ts'ui Hao's work.

These short songs frequently concentrated on a single scene or fragment
of narrative, and in this they parallel the development of the quatrain
vignette by other capital poets.

A Girl on a Stream   川上女

A girl on the stream,   川上女

Brightly made up this evening;

The sun is sinking past green isles
    as she plies the light oars.

The sandbar long and flowers are full,
    there she turns her boat,

And with the darkness waves are rising,
    winds blast stronger still.

She tells herself that Heng-t'ang
    is not so far away.

On the dark green river without companion
    she goes alone this night.

She goes alone and touching her heart
    is sorrow without end.

        [06229]

晚妝鮮

日落青渚試輕榿

汀長花滿正迴船

暮來浪起風轉緊

自言此去橫塘近

綠江無伴夜獨行

獨行心緒愁無盡

From Wang Wei's enigmatic closure to this maiden's inexplicable sorrow, the new K'ai-yüan poets explored the poetic power of concealment. "A Girl on a Stream" belongs directly in the tradition of Liu Hsi-yi's "Song for White Hair," and comparison reveals how much poets had learned in the intervening decades. Beside Liu's earlier song, Ts'ui's song is the essence of dramatic concision. Liu elaborated each fluttering flower and fading beauty as richly as convention and the reader's patience would allow. Moreover, every reader knew what a "Song for White Hair" should say, and Liu's song fulfilled their every expectation. Ts'ui's short song is more ambiguous and undefined: it begins with a languid southern boating scene, but soon develops into an unexpected and uneasy vision of a helpless lady in wild and violent surroundings.

In Ts'ui Hao's longer songs, themes were developed in the Early T'ang pattern, but Ts'ui did add some innovations in the technique of framing. For example, a very lovely but conventional meditation on the rise and fall of dynasties, the wheel of fortune, and youth versus age was given new vigor by a highly original frame: a youth meets an old man who recounts his life as the scion of a great Southern Dynasties clan, how he grew up in splendor, endured the collapse of the South, and escaped to live in poverty (06227). Even granting the old man's claim to one hundred and five years, the dates do not correlate, and the frame is clearly a fiction. In the poetic tradition the theme of the dynastic cycle demanded a symmetrical, almost abstract treatment, but Ts'ui's frame reveals a contrary narrative impulse. Also, the elegiac tone of the poem is an early example of the nostalgic vision of the Southern Dynasties that developed in the eighth century.

The strict propriety associating topic, genre, and subgenre relaxed during the first half of the eighth century, and the scope of some new genres like heptasyllabic regulated verse grew dramatically. Ts'ui Hao carried his fascination with the unregulated (or loosely regulated) heptasyllabic song toward heptasyllabic regulated verse, writing "Yellow Crane Tower" 黃鶴樓, one of the most famous poems of the age. "Yellow Crane Tower" begins as an unregulated, heptasyllabic song, then in the third couplet shifts to strict regulation. But even in regulation the dominant inspiration is the heptasyllabic song style, and the poem is far more reminiscent of Wang Po's "The Tower of the Prince of T'eng" (03444) than of earlier heptasyllabic regulated verses.

The poem is based on an anecdote about a tavern keeper whose establishment was frequented by an old man who never paid his bill. The tavern keeper never importuned the old man for his debts, and after half a year, the old man came in, took an orange peel, and painted a crane on the tavern wall. Whenever the guests of the tavern sang, the crane would begin to dance, and the tavern keeper grew rich from the curious customers attracted by the prodigy. After ten years the old man returned, summoned his crane from the wall, and flew off into the sky on its back. In commemoration of the event the tavern keeper built Yellow Crane Tower.

That man of old has already ridden white clouds away,	昔人已乘白雲去
And here in this land there remains only Yellow Crane Tower.	此地空餘黃鶴樓
The yellow crane, once it has gone, will never come again,	黃鶴一去不復返
But white clouds of a thousand years go aimlessly on and on.	白雲千載空悠悠
Clear and bright in the sunlit stream the trees of Han-yang,	晴川歷歷漢陽樹
Springtime's grasses, lush and green, all over Parrot Isle.	春草萋萋鸚鵡洲
Sun's setting, the passes to home— where can they be?	日暮鄉關何處是
Beside this river of misty waves it makes a man sad.	煙波江上使人愁

[06244]

Li Po imitated "Yellow Crane Tower" in his famous "Climbing Phoenix Terrace at Chin-ling" (08569). According to anecdote, even the supremely confident Li Po felt depressed at his inability to equal Ts'ui's poem.[7] Not only in Ts'ui's own time but in later centuries as well, this poem has held a tremendous appeal for Chinese readers. That appeal can be best explained in terms of certain aspects of Chinese aesthetics, an interest in a poem's "energy" and mood. Impermanence and change were compelling themes in their own right, constituted of elements found here: the irrevocable loss of past magic and wonder, nature's luminous indifference and continuity, and the utter isolation of the individual. But the "energy" of the poem came at least in part from the generic characteristics. Much as Wang Wei used the modal associations of the Ch'u song style, the heptasyllabic song style that Ts'ui used here had strong associations of authenticity and intensity of emotion. Yet the poem refrains from any direct expression of emotion until the brilliantly understated last line. Li Po, for one, could not resist the appeal of Ts'ui's closure and borrowed the final hemistich verbatim. Through genre as well as through theme and diction, High T'ang poets learned concealment, learned the energy generated by "seeing through" the text to something deeper, more complex, and often opposite to the surface text.

儲光義

CH'U KUANG-HSI

His poetry lies in the tradition of T'ao Ch'ien; his simplicity and directness give a sense of the classical style of the *Odes*. He can take his place beside Wang Wei and Meng Hao-jan without embarrassment. [*Bibliography of the Ssu-k'u Ch'üan-shu*]

Wang Wei may have been the earliest figure in the T'ao Ch'ien revival, and his reinterpretation of T'ao's poetry may have been the most profound, but no High T'ang poet has been more strongly linked to the T'ao Ch'ien mode than Ch'u Kuang-hsi. Unlike the Early T'ang poet Wang Chi, Ch'u did not try to relive T'ao in his life and the entire corpus of his work; rather, Ch'u's fame rests largely on a small group of superlative georgic poems in the T'ao Ch'ien tradition. Ch'u Kuang-hsi was an important social figure in capital poetry who knew and corresponded with most of the first-generation poets, but in the normative occasional mode of capital poetry he was at best mediocre and at worst awkward. It is probably extravagant to say that his work can "take its place" beside that of Wang and Meng, but in his georgic and bucolic poetry in the tradition of T'ao Ch'ien, Ch'u rose briefly to greatness.

Despite his importance and a large corpus of over two hundred and twenty poems, little is known about Ch'u Kuang-hsi's life. The bulk of his writings, once comprising seventy *chüan*, has been lost; there is no extensive biography, and the preface to his works by Ku K'uang is of little use. From his own testimony (06472) and that of the "Bibliographical Treatise" in the *New T'ang History* (under Pao Jung), we know he was a native of Kiangsu.[8] Ch'u passed the *chin-shih* examination in 726, in the same year as Ts'ui Kuo-fu and Chi-wu Ch'ien. Although there is no supporting biographical data, he may have been connected with the Chang

Chiu-ling government; this is suggested by his return to Kiangsu in 737, the year Chang fell from power.[9] Later in the T'ien-pao, Ch'u held a low-level position in the censorate, but fell captive to An Lu-shan's forces and was compelled to take office by them. After the recapture of the capital, Ch'u was imprisoned, then pardoned; however, as he lacked Wang Wei's important family connections, his transgressions were not entirely forgiven, and he was exiled to Kwangtung, where he died.

Ch'u Kuang-hsi occupied an anomalous position among the capital poets. On the one hand, Yin Fan treated him as a representative of southeastern poetry in the *Tan-yang chi* 丹陽集, but on the other hand, he was one of the many literary southeasterners who came to serve the central government during the K'ai-yüan, and one of a much smaller number who became part of the social group of poets around Wang Wei. Ch'u was clearly accepted and appreciated by the group, but his work lacked the polish of poets born into capital society. Social exigencies demanded that Ch'u produce a kind of poetry for which he had little talent, and if the resulting occasional poetry is tedious, he should not be judged harshly for it. His collection contains many long formal pieces, often dating from the early 750s: in these he suffered the double disability of being a mediocre practitioner of an already outdated style. Ch'u's "Climbing the Pagoda of the Temple of Compassionate Mercy with Several Gentlemen" (06560), when compared to poems on the same occasion by Tu Fu and Ts'en Shen, seems stiff and old-fashioned beside the imaginative vigor of the younger poets' T'ien-pao style (pp. 177–78). With a few fine exceptions, Ch'u Kuang-hsi's regulated verses are no more successful.

During the eighth century native southeasterners often worked more confidently in the "old style" forms, and there Ch'u found a congenial style.[10] As the southeastern poet Meng Chiao was to find a receptive audience for his "old style" poetry in the *fu-ku* sentiment of the late eighth century, so Ch'u Kuang-hsi found a receptive capital audience through the incipient T'ao Ch'ien revival. His relaxed, often discursive "old style" poems made up the greater part of Ch'u's poems anthologized in the *Ho-yüeh ying-ling chi*, and significantly, none of his poems were included in the *Kuo-hsiu chi*, an anthology with a marked preference for regulated forms. The dates of most of these "old style" poems are uncertain: a few date from the mid-730s, but he probably composed them throughout his life.

The "old style" poetry of T'ao Ch'ien served as an open model for much of Ch'u's best work.[11] Ch'u most closely approached T'ao Ch'ien in his poetry on farming. Representative pieces here include "Farm Life" 田家即事 (06503); the first and third of the series "Ten Poems to Wang Wei's 'Offhand Compositions'" 同王十三維偶然作十首 (06504, 06506); "Four Poems on Farm Life: Answering Ts'ui's 'East Marsh Compositions'"

田家即事答崔二東皋作四首 (06552–55); and the "Eight Various Responses to Farm Life" 田家雜興八首 (06515–22). The final poem of the last series is particularly reminiscent of T'ao Ch'ien, but the occasional invitation in the closure is characteristic of the T'ang.

I've planted over a hundred mulberries,	種桑百餘樹
I've planted thirty acres of millet.	種黍三十畝
So I've plenty of food and clothing	衣食既有餘
And can now and again meet relatives, friends.	時時會親友
In summer we have the sesame rice,	夏來菰米飯
In autumn, chrysanthemum wine.	秋至菊花酒
My wife shall greet them cheerfully,	孺人喜逢迎
My children know to scurry away.	稚子解趨走
Then at sunset we relax in the garden,	日暮閒園裏
Under willow and elm's spreading shade.	團團蔭榆柳
Staggering drunk they go home at night,	酩酊乘夜歸
As chill winds blow through my window.	涼風吹戶牖
I gaze on the River of Stars so clear,	清淺望河漢
Watch the Dipper rise and sink.	低昂看北斗
"We've a couple of jugs not opened yet—	數甕猶未開
Shall we drink them tomorrow morning?"	明朝能飲否

[06522]

Wang Wei's powerful sense of craftsmanship is entirely absent here; Ch'u feels none of Wang Wei's temptation to interrupt the easy narrative flow with parallel couplets describing static scenes. Instead, the narrative impulse is dominant, and the form it takes is vignette. The art of vignette, a brief sketch of a significant human situation, had assumed an important role in the works of many capital poets, particularly in the poetry of Wang Ch'ang-ling, Ts'ui Hao, and Li Ch'i. But the gift for vignette was probably the defining element of Ch'u Kuang-hsi's genius, and it was applied to diverse forms, from the first-person convivial vignette inspired by T'ao Ch'ien, to the discursive vignettes on bucolic types, to quatrain vignettes.

   Like that of T'ao Ch'ien before him, Ch'u's poetry possessed a strong ethical strain that was a natural part of the poetic philosophy of agrarian Taoism. The celebration in the preceding poem was predicated on plenty. More commonly an explicit moral or philosophical message was included. In the following poem the Buddhist compassion for all living things appears in the Confucian disguise of Mencius's "compassionate heart."

Farm Life	田家即事
Leaves of the cattails daily grow longer,	蒲葉日已長
Flowers of apricot daily more moist:	杏花日已滋
An old farmer has to watch for these—	老農要看此
Crucial not to miss Heaven's seasons.	貴不違天時

Greeting the dawn, I rise to feed my oxen,   迎晨起飯牛
Hitch the pair to plow my eastern fields.   雙駕耕東菑
Earthworms are turned up from the soil,   蚯蚓土中出
And the field crows fly along after me;   田烏隨我飛
A flock joins in, wildly pecking, cawing,   羣合亂啄噪
Sad cries, as though telling of their hunger.   嗷嗷如道飢
My heart is filled with compassion,   我心多惻隱
I look on these, for both feel pain.   顧此兩傷悲
So I give out food to the crows of the field   撥食與田烏
And turn home at sunset, my basket empty.   日暮空筐歸
My family will chide me more than ever now,   親戚更相誚
But this heart of mine will never change.   我心終不移
                              [06503]

Here vignette approaches verse parable. Though the theme would have been alien to T'ao Ch'ien's poetry, the rustic persona, the style, and numerous verbal echoes all derive from T'ao. It is difficult to determine the extent to which T'ao Ch'ien's own style was a reaction against the highly ornate style of Chin poetry, but in such poems of Ch'u Kuang-hsi there was a willful artlessness that went beyond the decorum of simplicity in reclusive capital poetry.

Ch'u's impulse to narrative vignette appeared even more strongly in a group of poems on specific bucolic topics: "The Woodcutter" 樵父詞 (06445); "The Herdboy" 牧童詞 (06447); "Picking Lotus" 采蓮詞 (06448); "Picking Water Chestnuts" 采菱詞 (06449); "Shooting Pheasants" 射雉詞 (06450); and "The Fierce Tiger" 猛虎詞 (06451). Ch'u showed little interest in these rural scenes for themselves; rather, they embodied philosophical and moral values.[12]

The Fisherman   漁父詞

The fish of the marsh love singing waters,   澤魚好鳴水
The fish of the creek love to be higher upstream. 溪魚好上流
So now, with no luck at the fish weir,   漁梁不得意
He goes down to the islet, to sink the hook.   下渚潛垂鈎
Tangles of watergrass often block his oars,   亂荇時礙枻
A new growth of reeds conceals his boat.   新蘆復隱舟
Calmly he broods on the course of things,   靜言念終始
Sits at rest, observes floating and sinking.   安坐看沈浮
His white hair rising with the wind,   素髮隨風揚
His mind drifting on, afar with the clouds.   遠心與雲遊
In the surging waves he turns back to far shores, 逆浪還極浦
With the appointed tide goes down to Ts'ang-chou: 信潮下滄州
He goes not as slave to the physical man,   非爲徇形役
His joy is in passive halting, drifting on.   所樂在行休
                              [06446]

Throughout the poem are terms that refer both to the physical scene and to abstract concepts: "floating and sinking," "halting, drifting on" are antithetical pairs referring to activity and quiescence, service and private life, but they also are part of the fishing scene. The abstract patterns of natural principle are incarnate in the rustic scene. Even the philosophical fish do not follow poetic convention by loving the "deepest pool," but rather yearn for the "source," from stagnant marshes back to flowing waters and from there farther back upstream.

    The heaviness of Ch'u's philosophical treatment may be contrasted to the following treatment of the same theme by Ch'u's contemporary Kao Shih. If Ch'u's poem represents an impulse to primitive truth and authenticity by artlessness, Kao's song represents the sophistication of the High T'ang vignette and its dramatic concealment.

The Song of the Fisherman	漁父歌
By twisting shoreline and deep pool an old man of the mountains,	曲岸深潭一山叟
Eyes' movement halted watching the hook, the hand does not move.	駐眼看鉤不移手
Here, a worldly man who seeks to know the fisherman's name,	世人欲得知姓名
Asks him, waits long—the old man won't open his lips.	良久問他不開口
A rainhat of young bamboo skins, a coat of lotus leaves,	筍皮笠子荷葉衣
Nothing busying his mind, he keeps to the fishing jetty.	心無所營守釣磯
I suppose that single boat of his has no fixed resting place—	料得孤舟無定止
Where will he go this evening, his fishing pole in hand?	日暮持竿何處歸

[10384]

The fisherman's complete freedom is here embodied in the poem itself rather than in the physical scene observed in the poem. The absolute barrier that separates the fisherman's nature from that of ordinary men is enacted by the fisherman's silence: the "worldly man" and the equally worldly reader can only see him from outside. There is no communication, no attempt to expose a state of mind that cannot be exposed in the limited language of the world. But if it cannot be exposed, at least it can be indicated —by silence and a mask of opaque actions that seem to conceal a truth. Both Kao's song and Ch'u's poem close with the fisherman going off into endless movement, movement that symbolizes the passive drifting with change advocated by the primal "Fisherman" of the *Ch'u-tz'u*. Ch'u makes the principle explicit; Kao lacks Ch'u's comfortable omniscience and closes with a question. The reader may guess at the fisherman's nature, but it is ultimately unknowable.

Closely related to Ch'u Kuang-hsi's georgic and bucolic poems are his true *ku-feng*, including poetry on immortals and on the *hsien-jen shih-chih* theme. In addition to poems with conventional *ku-feng* titles—"Imitations of the Ancient Style" 效古 (06483–84) and "Unclassified Poems" 雜詩 (06485–86)—there are five occasional *ku-feng*, "Visiting Mao Mountain" 遊茅山五首 (06471–75), and most of the "Ten Poems to Wang Wei's 'Offhand Compositions'" (06504–13).

Ch'u's *ku-feng* are less distinctive than his georgic and bucolic poetry, but in most of his occasional poetry, Ch'u's personality fades entirely into the collective style of the capital poets. The control and narrative unity of the vignettes is lost in a babble of disparate voices.

Drifting on East Creek of Mao Mountain   泛茅山東溪

In clear dawn I climbed an immortal's peak.   清晨登仙峯
The peak was far, my journey did not reach its end.   峯遠行未極
Lake and river lay clear in the new light,   江海霽初景
Grasses and trees were filled with fresh color.   草木含新色
And I gave myself to Heaven's harmony,   而我任天和
Now moving, now halting as I pleased,   此時聊動息
And gazed at my home among white clouds,   望鄉白雲裏
Or set oars in movement beside clear creeks.   發棹清溪側
Pine and cypress grow deep in the mountains,   松柏生深山
Unconsciously their natures are straight and true. 無心自貞直
[06469]

The poem is not a bad one, but it is a pastiche of styles and betrays a lack of a controlling poetic identity. In Chinese the first couplet has a compelling energy, but it probably derives from an even better opening by Meng Hao-jan (06469):

At dawn I wandered to visit a famous mountain,   朝遊訪名山
The mountain was far, set in blue mists of sky.   山遠在空翠

Both couplets derive from Hsieh Ling-yün's (*Wh* 25.35a):

At autumn's end I sought a famous mountain,   杪秋尋遠山
The mountain was far, I couldn't get close to it.   山遠行不近

The third couplet echoes Wang Wei's (05862):

T'ao Ch'ien gave himself to Heaven's purity.   陶潛任天眞

And Ch'u's closure echoes the closure of a Sung Chih-wen poem on a pine tree (03189):

Its whole life long, a nature straight and alone.   一生自孤直

Priority is uncertain in the parallel lines by Meng and Wang, and even if they are borrowings, it does not demean Ch'u's poem: this was a natural part of T'ang compositional technique. However, they do represent a pastiche of styles, successfully joined, but not unified by an individual voice. Ch'u opened with the energetic discursiveness of Meng Hao-jan at his best, continued with a stiff descriptive couplet followed by the "spontaneous' style associated with T'ao Ch'ien, and closed with a touch of *ku-feng*. Sometimes, as here, Ch'u succeeded in using the voices of others (e.g., 06632), but nowhere outside of his georgic and bucolic poetry did he retain a fully individual poetic voice.

Ch'u's greatest success in the shared style of the capital poets was in the quatrain. There he could apply his gift for vignette, with a result quite different from his discursive bucolic vignettes. He evoked scenes from the life of the capital and the Southeast, and though they are in the shared style, they are among the finest of their kind.

The Roads of Ch'ang-an   長安道

He cracked his whip passing the tavern,   鳴鞭過酒家
Robed in finery, roamed to courtesans' gates,   袨服遊倡門
And his fortune, a million, gone in a moment,   百萬一時盡
His true feelings inside, not even a hint.   含情無片言
                    [06648]

Westward I went a thousand miles   西行一千里
Till evening's blackness grew in cold trees,   暝色生寒樹
And in darkness I heard the songs and the piping,   暗聞歌吹聲
And knew that this was the road to Ch'ang-an.   知是長安路
                    [06649]

Among the quatrain vignettes were four poems on Wang Chao-chün, whose legend was becoming popular among High T'ang poets, When Wang Chao-chün became a member of the imperial harem, she failed to bribe the court painter Mao Yen-shou, and he took his revenge by misrepresenting her beauty. Misled by Mao's portrait, the emperor neglected Wang, but eventually the error was discovered, and she became the emperor's favorite. For his crime Mao was banished to Central Asia, where he convinced the Great Khan to demand Wang Chao-chün in a treaty of marriage alliance with the Han. Reasons of state compelled the emperor to part with her. Here versions of the legend diverge: either she drowned herself at the river that formed the boundary between the two states, or she lived to a ripe and miserable old age in the court of the Khan. Ch'u favored the second version of the legend.

Wang Chao-chün (third of four)   明妃曲四首之三

At sunset the wind shakes the sand,
    snow flies wildly,   日暮驚沙亂雪飛
Those beside her urge the lady
    to change her robes of gauze.   傍人相勸易羅衣
They force her out to the forehalls
    to watch the songs and dances   強來前殿看歌舞
And together wait for the Great Khan
    to return from the hunt of night.   共待單于夜獵歸
             [06660]

Among his contemporaries, only Wang Ch'ang-ling surpassed Ch'u Kuang-hsi in the ability to paint a dramatic, visual scene in swift strokes. We see the helpless court lady, robed in frail gauze, shivering in the blizzard, as she watches barbaric dancing and awaits the return of the Great Khan with his torch-bearing outriders.

The quatrain vignette was a legacy of "palace poetry," but the K'ai-yüan poets perfected the form, adding dramatic energy and stark contrasts. The form became immensely popular in the late eighth and ninth centuries, but the famous quatrain vignettes of the High T'ang remained the norm for other poets. The success of poets in the quatrain vignette probably influenced the development of short songs like Ts'ui Hao's "A Girl by a Stream": Ts'ui used the devices of the quatrain—the quick shifts, the unexpected juxtapositions—to evoke the pathos of a fragile beauty in wild and violent surroundings, a figure similar to Chu's Wang Chao-chün in the quatrain above.

6

孟浩然

Meng Hao-jan
The Freedom Beyond Decorum

I love the Master, Meng Hao-jan,
A free spirit known the whole world through.
In the flush of youth he spurned the cap and carriage,
And rests now, white-haired with age, among clouds and pines.
Drunk in moonlight, often "smitten by the sage,"
Or led astray by flowers he does not serve his lord.
The highest mountain—how can I look to climb it?
I can do no more than kneel to his pure fragrance.

Li Po, "To Meng Hao-jan"

[08153]

Searching to find their values manifest in human form, poets and readers of every age have created heroes; yet those complex and contradictory mortals who are forced into the hero's role inevitably suffer simplification and distortion at the hands of their greatest admirers. The image of Meng Hao-jan that emerges from his own poetry is protean: Meng was a frustrated officeseeker, an enthusiastic traveler, a convivial friend, and an easygoing country gentleman. He enjoyed the society of intellectuals in the capital; he delighted in the grandeur of the Southeast's landscapes; and above all he loved the provincial life at his family estate near Hsiang-yang, meeting with his many friends and visiting local spots of scenic and historic interest. But Li Po and others wanted a proud recluse, a 'free spirit" who would disdain "the cap and carriage" of office, an eccentric who would spend his days "smitten by the sage" of moderately priced wine. Li Po's poem of praise echoes Meng Hao-jan's own poetry throughout, as if to prove that the figure in the poem is indeed Meng Hao-jan.[1] Ultimately Li's sketch is no more than the icon of the eccentric recluse reduced to his essential attributes; it is the projection of Li's own values and those of his age. But the reasons for Meng's transformation into a saint of reclusion are as much a part of the true face of the poet as his original poetic identity.

Few reliable facts are known about Meng Hao-jan's life. Around the handful of datable events, several scholars have woven travelogue narratives from the evidence of Meng's poems.[2] Their labors have amplified the meager biographical data, but much remains tentative and uncertain. Meng was born around 689, probably into a landowning family of Hsiang-chou, and spent much of his life on the family estate just southeast of Hsiang-yang. Meng loved the region deeply, and later poets and critics always associated the locale with Meng.

Meng Hao-jan was the eldest of the major High T'ang poets, about a decade senior to Wang Wei and Li Po. A few of Meng's poems are datable to the first two decades of the eighth century, and it is clear that Meng developed a personal style in relative isolation from the evolving trends in capital poetry.

Meng Hao-jan could have spent a life of comfortable ease in his native Hsiang-yang, but three times he traveled north to the capitals, seeking patronage and employment. In 718 Meng went to the eastern capital at Lo-yang, where Hsüan-tsung had taken up temporary residence; later, in 723 and again in the early 730s, he journeyed to Ch'ang-an, taking the *chin-shih* examination on the second of those trips. The attempts to gain patronage were failures, and Meng did not pass the examination, but in Ch'ang-an Meng made the acquaintance of the major literary figures of the day: Wang Wei, Wang Ch'ang-ling, and Chang Chiu-ling. Following his second trip to Ch'ang-an, and perhaps on other occasions, Meng toured the lower Yangtze region, where he wrote some of his finest poetry.

In 737, Chang Chiu-ling was demoted to prefect of Ching-chou, south of Hsiang-yang, and he invited Meng Hao-jan to join his entourage. While Meng had sought a position in the capital government, he seems to have been less pleased to serve on the provincial staff of a disgraced minister in failing health. Ill at ease in Chang's service, Meng returned to Hsiang-yang in the spring of 738. In 740, after a visit from Wang Ch'ang-ling, Meng died after a long illness. From his extant poems it appears that he did other traveling in his life, but these journeys cannot be dated.

The classical formulation of the nature of the Chinese lyric is that "poetry articulates intention" (詩言志, *Shu-ching*, II, i, 24; "Great Preface" of the *Shih-ching*); "intention," that which one's mind is fixed on, grows out of an interior response to some particular event or experience of the world. If the formulation were "poetry articulates natural principle" (a possible Chinese rendering of the Western association of poetry and truth), one could expect a certain consistency in the philosophical position espoused by a single poet. However, "intention" is conditional upon psychological realities and particular experiences of the world, and its contingency accounts for the contradictory variety of responses that are found in the works of a Chinese poet.

The poetic personality of Meng Hao-jan that emerges behind the stereotype of the recluse is even more various in its responses than the lyric norm. The negative impulses in much of Wang Wei's work defined a strong and unified poetic personality; Meng Hao-jan was less obsessed, his responses more dependent on his mood and the occasion. He was the easygoing country gentleman who desired office in the central goverment, but not so much that it would seriously upset his disposition. He enjoyed visiting landscapes and recluse friends, but not enough to become a true recluse himself. He loved his farm at the foot of Hsien Mountain, but not so much that he would hold to it with the single-minded determination of a T'ao Ch'ien. To his friends in the capital he would be staunch in his dedication to literary study and state service (07608):

My family ever honored Confucian custom,	家世重儒風
· ·	
I labored constantly day and night	畫夜常自強
Achieving some skill in poetic composition,	詞賦頗亦工
But a grown man should establish himself at thirty,	三十既成立
And I, alas, have met with no success.	嗟吁命不通

On the other hand, when visiting a Buddhist monk, he would conclude (07623):

All my life I have yearned for true reclusion,	平生慕眞隱
Days on end sought wonders beyond this world:	累日探靈異
Here old peasants enter their fields at dawn,	野老朝入田
And mountain monks return to their temples at night.	山僧暮歸寺
Clear sounds come from pine-shaded springs,	松泉多清響
Mossy walls filled with ancient truths.	苔壁饒古意
I will lodge on this mountain forever,	願言投此山
I and the world are done with each other.	身世兩相棄

Sick in Lo-yang, Meng wanted to go home to his farm and spend his days in georgic bliss (07764):

I too love the pleasures of T'ao Ch'ien—	我愛陶家趣
In orchards and gardens, no worldly cares.	林園無俗情
Spring's thunder splits all plants into life,	春雷百卉坼
At Cold Food Festival all the neighborhood is pure.	寒食四鄰清

These various roles came easily to Meng, but he took greater pleasure in such speculative visions of himself than in a single-minded enactment of a specific role. Often these speculative roles were true "intention," set in the future as the poet longed to be something other than what he already was; but Meng also wrote in sleek self-satisfaction, delighting in a present performance of an attractive role. His poetic identity does not lie in any single role or unifying obsession; rather, it lies in the protean freedom and joy of his transformations.

Meng Hao-jan often appeared as an exemplary recluse in occasional poems addressed to him; however, the K'ai-yüan poets used the figure of the recluse indiscriminately as a form of compliment. Furthermore, when the recipient of a poem was out of office (as Meng was his entire life, except for a few months), praise of the virtues of reclusion was mandatory. Thus, when Wang Wei said farewell to Meng after Meng's examination failure, the encouragement to reclusion was clearly a form of consolation:

Close your gate fast, yearn not to leave.	杜門不欲出
Keep yourself far from worldly cares ever,	久與世情疏
Take this as the best policy—	以此爲長策
I urge you, go home to your old cottage.	勸君歸舊廬
Sing drunkenly of wine taken in field-huts,	醉歌田舍酒
Chuckle, reading the books of ancients.	笑讀古人書
This is right for a whole lifetime—	好是一生事
Don't suffer writing a "Master Emptiness."	無勞獻子虛

[05951]

"Master Emptiness" 子虛賦 was the *fu* of Ssu-ma Hsiang-ju that won him fame in the court of Han Wu-ti. Wang Wei is, of course, playing on the title, suggesting the vanity of public fame.

Wang Wei's poem above is the typical High T'ang occasional poem, its values conditional upon the social situation. Li Po's "To Meng Hao-jan" was something different, not social politeness or consolation, but enthusiastic admiration of a personality type, the perfect recluse. It was not Meng Hao-jan's poetry that most interested his contemporaries, but his personality as they perceived it; the poems were the access to that personality. By the time Wang Shih-yüan 王士源 wrote the preface to Meng Hao-jan's collected works in the mid-740s, Li Po's version of Meng Hao-jan's personality seems to have been widely accepted. Wang did not even mention Meng Hao-jan's brief service on Chang Chiu-ling's staff or the poet's two unsuccessful bids for office. Wang included an anecdote on how a couplet by Meng was admired by Wang Wei and Chang Chiu-ling when Meng was in the capital, but Wang did not say why Meng happened to be there. Wang Shih-yüan wanted an exemplary recluse, and Meng Hao-jan was shaped to fit the mold:

Meng Hao-jan was a man of culture who did not serve the state, writing instead as his inclinations dictated. Thus he was sometimes a bit "slow." [In social poetry one was supposed to respond "swift as an echo."] He did not act so as to give himself a fine appearance, but rather he always sought the true and honest; thus, he may seem rather wild. He traveled, but not for personal gain, wanting only to do as he pleased. As a result, he was always poor.

This image was echoed by Yin Fan, and continued unchanged thereafter.

Meng Hao-jan's contemporaries clearly admired his poetry, but judging from scattered comments and the weight given his poetry in anthologies, Meng was ranked no higher than a dozen of his contemporaries. As T'ao Ch'ien was in his own time, Meng Hao-jan was a recluse who wrote poetry rather than a genius of the poetic art; he was not "of this age, the master craftsman of poetry." Comments treating Meng Hao-jan specifically in terms of the literary tradition began to appear only in the 760s, when Tu Fu praised his poetry as surpassing even the work of Pao Chao and Hsieh T'iao (10616). The evaluative components of such praise are critical commonplaces, but the earlier poets used in such comparisons are of great importance: they define the tradition to which a poet's work seems to belong. Tu Fu had placed Meng Hao-jan not in the tradition of T'ao Ch'ien, but in the tradition of fifth-century poetry, with its richly descriptive couplets and interest in landscape. Tu Fu's interpretation of Meng Hao-jan's poetry also corresponded to Wang Shih-yüan observation that Meng's "writing did not follow antiquity."

P'i Jih-hsiu 皮日休 (833?–83) was the first writer to accord Meng Hao-jan the position he now holds in the canon of High T'ang poetry, a place with Wang Wei and just behind Tu Fu and Li Po:

At their best the literary works of Hsüan-tsung's reign came up to the level of poetry written during the Chien-an. Those who have deliberated such matters consider Li Po and Tu Fu to have been the greatest. But among the others only Meng Hao-jan of my native region may stand beside them and not be ashamed.[3]

Despite P'i Jih-hsiu's exaggeration from local pride, most later critics allowed Meng Hao-jan a position beside that of Wang Wei. However, there were dissenters, like the cantankerous Su Shih, who is reputed to have said that while Meng's "tone" was lofty, he was short on talent: "like a maker of wine for monks—no real substance in the stuff."[4] But Su's was a minority evaluation, and the very limpidity that he mocked was the stylistic quality in Meng's poetry most prized by later critics.

Several collections of Meng Hao-jan's poetry were in circulation soon after his death. The "Bibliography" of the *New T'ang History* mentions an edition by Meng's younger brother, but the editions we have were probably based on the edition of Wang Shih-yüan. According to Wang, Meng Hao-jan did not keep a complete set of his poems, and Wang had to gather texts from a variety of sources.[5] In 750 Wei T'ao 韋滔 sent a recopied and enlarged edition, based on Wang Shih-yüan's, to the Imperial Library. Despite this early work on the collection, the texts of Meng Hao-jan's poems are among the poorest in the T'ang, and modern editions differ substantially.

Meng Hao-jan was the most limited of the major T'ang poets; this is true generically, thematically, and stylistically. He wrote every few heptasyllabic poems (five *ku-shih* and four regulated), and his quatrains make up a far smaller proportion of his collection than they do in those of other eighth-century and ninth-century poets. Virtually all of Meng's poems were occasional; he had no *ku-feng* and only a few *yüeh-fu, yung-wu,* (poems on "things"), and private meditative poems. The limited subgeneric range of Meng's poetry partially accounts for a general stylistic homogeneity in his work. He did vary the formality of his style to correspond with the formality of the occasion, and he did mix occasional styles, but there was little creative use of styles from other subgenres or from past poets. Within his restricted scope, however, Meng Hao-jan was a master.

A superficial similarity between the poetry of Wang Wei and Meng Hao-jan has led some critics and anthologists to link the two poets; however, their shared interest in eremitism and landscape description conceals fundamental differences of temperament and poetic personality. Their relationship to contemporary poetry also was different. The austerity of Wang Wei's poetry was an act of renunciation born of deeply negative impulse; in literary-historical terms that negative impulse was directed against the glittering rhetoric and mannered formality of public poetry, which Wang had been forced to master as a youth. Wang was a master craftsman in that public mode, but when allowed the freedom of private poetry and informal poetry, he stripped away the surface traces of courtly ornament with a thoroughness that betrays profound hostility beneath his mask of dispassionate impersonality.

Meng Hao-jan was a provincial, and this greatly influenced his conception of the poetic art. In his youth as in his adulthood, he belonged to a world in which poetry was a pleasure and not a social compulsion. Poetry might serve as a means for a provincial to enter capital society and the central government, but Meng seems never to have appreciated the extent to which the restrictive formal style was necessary. He was poorly trained in that formal style, and his failures in the examination and obtaining patronage suggest the great difference between private poetic talent and the remunerative appreciation accorded to mastery of craft. Because he was not fully aware of the difference, he never felt the fundamental opposition between the formal and informal styles, and Wang Wei's negative impulse is absent in his poetry. Meng either did not understand or willfully ignored the decorum of capital poetry, and as a result he went beyond the decorum of the Early T'ang tradition as Wang Wei could never do. The negative poet was bound to what he opposed. Beneath the surface repudiation of ornamental rhetoric, Wang Wei's style possessed a control that was an inescapable manifestation of the court poet's training; that control is absent in Meng Hao-jan. On the other hand, in his aversion to ornament, Wang Wei was compelled to reject the rich, dense beauty of the courtly descriptive art; Meng Hao-jan did not feel that revulsion and was capable of a lush complexity that led Tu Fu and some later critics to filiate him to poets of the Southern Dynasties.

The capital poet, listening for the tripartite form and a harmony of diction, could not but have been surprised to hear Meng Hao-jan ramble from topic to topic, from mood to mood. Midway through a poem, the capital poet would hear lines signaling closure, only to find Meng Hao-jan continuing with an extended descriptive passage. He unified these disparate elements by an asymmetrical but pleasing poetic personality, rather than by the older structures of poetic order. He moved from scene to narrative to meditation and back to scene again, creating a full and balanced portrayal of an experience. In a formal situation such as an examination or a poem presented to a superior, his style would seem to have an untrained and ungainly rusticity, but to the new sensibility of the High T'ang, to the capital poets, his very rambling was the emblem of freedom.

Seeking the Monk Chan on Fragrance Mountain　尋香山湛上人

At dawn I wandered to visit a famous mountain.	朝游訪名山
The mountain was far, set in blue mists of sky,	山遠在空翠
Its swelling vapors covered a hundred miles,	氛氳亙百里
And I just arrived as the sun went down.	日入行始至
I heard a bell's sound at valley's mouth,	谷口聞鐘聲
By wood's edge recognized incense in air.	林端識香氣
So staff in hand, I sought my old friend,	杖策尋故人
Ungirthing my saddle, halted my mount for a while.	解鞍暫停騎
By the gate of stone a sheer ravine falls off sharply,	石門殊壑險
And the path through bamboo grew darker, deeper.	篁逕轉森邃
Dharma's companion rejoices meeting me,	法侶欣相逢
In speculative discussion we do not sleep.	清談曉不寐
All my life I have yearned for true reclusion,	平生慕真隱
Days on end sought wonders beyond this world:	累日探靈異
Here old peasants enter their fields at dawn,	野老朝入田
And mountain monks return to their temples at night.	山僧夜歸寺
Clear sounds come from pine-shaded springs,	松泉多清響

Mossy walls filled with ancient truths.
I will lodge on this mountain forever—
I and the world are done with each other.
                    [07623]

苔壁饒古意
願言投此山
身世兩相棄

Meng's poem is beautifully unified, but its unity is not that of the poetic tradition—except in the theme of enlightenment attained by visiting a temple. On his conservative side, the K'ai-yüan reader still saw the poetic "art" as a set of rules; the freedom to ignore the rules lay not in the domain of art itself but in the personality behind the poem. Thus, it should not be surprising that contemporary readers looked beyond Meng's poetic "art" (attractive only in details of his couplet craft) to a personality behind the poem, a personality they tried to normalize as an exemplary recluse. In the K'ai-yüan the concept of poetry as pure craft was waning, and a focus of interest on the poet's personality (exemplified in the K'ai-yüan reading of Meng Hao-jan and T'ao Ch'ien) was a necessary stage as poetry progressed to something beyond craft; this stage had deep roots in the critical tradition, in the idea that "poetry articulates intention" and thus refers primarily to the identity and state of mind of the poet. The next stage was to be when the personality that transcended poetic craft defined himself as a creative poet; this demanded a new and more autonomous concept of poetry that went beyond an idea of poetry as craft or as a subordinate extension of personality. This stage was to appear in the work of Li Po.

"Lack of design" (*wang-chi* 忘機) was an important concept for Chinese quietist thinkers and appeared in various forms in the K'ai-yüan poetry of reclusion, as in Wang Wei's concern with unselfconsciousness. Absence of motive and premeditation were essential elements in the iconography of the perfect recluse, as in Wang Shih-yüan's description of Meng: "He did not act so as to give himself a fine appearance, but rather he always sought the true and honest." Note that the antithesis of "the true and honest" is not falsehood per se, but inauthenticity and ulterior motivation, behavior tainted by conscious purpose.

The preceding poem did conclude with a proper closing response as the poet "articulated his intention" filled with enthusiasm for life at the temple. But in many other poems Meng refused that inner conclusion. It was through such features as his rambling structure and refusal to draw a conclusion that the sense of a wild, free personality was conveyed to contemporary readers; these features enacted an authenticity and "lack of design" quite apart from the themes of his poetry. Meng Hao-jan would often conclude the description of an excursion by saying "and then I went home": this was not the grand, symbolic gesture of negation as in Wang Wei's poetry—it was simply what Meng Hao-jan did next. With his cult of spontaneous action and celebration of the accidental, the Sung reader would have been less excited by Meng Hao-jan's casualness; indeed, interest in Meng as an exemplary recluse all but disappeared in the Sung. The eighth-century reader, with his strong sense of rhetorical order, would have felt Meng Hao-jan's casualness far more acutely. And especially in closure the eighth-century reader expected some strong burst of emotion, some vow to reclusion, some new knowledge ("now I understand" 始知), some subtly symbolic gesture, scene, or object. Meng Hao-jan might provide it—but also might not.

If Wang Wei manipulated the expectations of readers, Meng Hao-jan often thwarted them. It is uncertain whether Meng Hao-jan fully realized how his poetry appeared in the context of contemporary poetic convention, but it is clear that Meng's admirers were attracted to a sense of freedom in his work; reading the man through the poetry, they concluded he was "wild" and "did as he pleased." Compared to the work of many later poets, Meng Hao-jan's poetry is mellow indeed; the fiercely independent eccentric of Li Po's praise poem appears only in the restrictive context of K'ai-yüan social poetry.

Gathering Firewood   採樵作

I went deep in the mountains to gather firewood.   採樵入深山
In the mountains' depths were stream after stream.   山深水重疊
Where a bridge had fallen, a recumbent log was clasped,   橋崩臥查擁
Where the road dropped sheer, hanging vines were held.   路險垂藤接
By sunset companions had grown fewer,   日落伴將稀
And a mountain wind brushed my burlap robes.   山風拂薜衣
A long song, my light staff over my shoulder,   長歌負輕策
I gazed into mist of wild plains and went home.   平野望煙歸
                          [07644]

"Return" here is simply "what happened." The unity of the poem is neither that of the older poetic rhetoric nor of the intellectual structure of experience or the landscape. Instead of attaining enlightenment, penetrating the vanity of the world, or making a vow to reclusion, Meng Hao-jan simply turns around and goes home.

By ignorance or strength of personality, Meng Hao-jan worked outside the decorum of capital poetry: in the poem above the dense craft of the second couplet does not "properly" belong with the discursive simplicity of the third couplet. But Meng's freedom was not simply negative: it permitted him to integrate experience in new ways that seemed to reflect an order of "natural" perception. Again the reader was directed to the authentic expression of personal experience. Usually Meng Hao-jan's

poems have an asymmetrical beauty, from the accidental sequence of
events in the preceding poem to the associative unity of "Seeking the
Monk Chan on Fragrance Mountain."

Another kind of unity that appeared with particular force in Meng
Hao-jan's poetry was unity of process. More than almost any poet before
him, Meng could describe a landscape changing through time, showing
a sensitive awareness of subtle gradations in light and movement. Sunrise
was one of his best topics, as in "Setting Out Early from Yü-p'u Pool":

Dawnlight in east, earliest radiance,	東旭早光茫
Birds of isles have startled awake with a din.	渚禽已驚聒
Still lying abed, I hear at the Yü-p'u mouth	臥聞漁浦口
The sounds of oars being plied in the dark.	橈聲暗相撥
Then the sun comes out. I can tell the weather	日出氣象分
And know how broad is my river road.	始知江路闊
Fair ladies, by habit rising late,	美人常晏起
Watch their reflections, toy with drifting bubbles.	照影弄流沫
We are wary of startling gibbons drinking by streams,	飲水畏驚猿
Or sometimes see otters offering fish.	祭魚時見獺
Traveling by boat I feel no sorrow,	舟行自無悶
And still less in this clear scene's open expanse.	況值晴景豁

[07646]

The gradual illumination of the landscape as the sun rises correlates with
the poet's state of mind, and the breadth of the river scene generates a
corresponding expansiveness of mood. Though the basic pattern of scene
and response is still present, the poem has the sequential unity of experience
rather than the artificial unity of rhetorical amplification. The most brilliant
of Meng Hao-jan's dawn poems is "On P'eng-li Lake Gazing at Lu
Mountain" (07631) where the gradual illumination of Lu Mountain, abode
of recluses, enlightens the poet and stirs the expected desire to be a recluse
himself. But the poet of authenticity does not stop with the moment of
vision in which he knows he must "change his life": he adds that at the
moment he is on a mission (for Chang Chiu-ling?) and that he really
can't stay, but he promises to return and join the hermits of the mountain.

Not only was Meng Hao-jan a master in describing natural processes,
he knew how to arrange such descriptions for the most dramatic effect,
as in the following poem on watching the tidal bore on the Ch'ien-t'ang
River.

Climbing to Camphor Pavilion with Yen of Ch'ien- t'ang to Watch the Tidal Bore	與顏錢塘登樟亭望潮作

For a hundred miles the sound of thunder rolls,	百里雷聲震
The playing strings stop music for a while.	鳴絃暫輟彈

Out from the office a line of riders comes,   府中連騎出
To await by the river a view of the tide.   江上待潮觀
Lit by the sun, fall's clouds turn round,   照日秋雲迴
The Po Sea's breadth floats the skies.   浮天渤澥寬
Uprearing billows come onward like snow,   驚濤來似雪
And all the guests shiver, sensing the cold.   一坐凛生寒
                          [07734]

The most famous description of the Chien-t'ang bore was in the "Seven Stimuli" (*Ch'i-fa* 七發) by Mei Sheng 枚乘 in the second century B.C. The *fu* poet was necessarily more concerned with process than any *shih* poet could be, and Mei's dazzling account of the progress of the tide is extensive and minute. But within the more compressed scope of the *shih*, Meng Hao-jan structures the description for dramatic effect: first, an abrupt crash like thunder signals the oncoming tide; then the music stops, and a line of riders gallops forth. Not until line 4 does Meng mention the tidal bore. After a brief description, the poem closes as abruptly as it began, with a shiver from the sightseers. The poem is far more artificed than Meng Hao-jan's most characteristic work, however, and seems to show the dramatic techniques of capital poetry, especially in the suggestive image of the last line.

    The unities generated by the inner order of experience were not always as asymmetrical as in some of the preceding poems: the unities of experience could fuse scene, theme, and gesture as few earlier poets could do.

Evening View from a Boat   舟中晚望

I set my sails and gaze southeast   挂席東南望
To green mountains and river kingdoms far.   青山水國遙
Here prows and sterns cross in struggle for gain, 舳艫爭利涉
Coming and going at the will of wind and tide.   來往任風潮
You ask me where do I go now—   問我今何適
To T'ien-t'ai Mountain to visit the Bridge of Stone. 天臺訪石橋
I sit and watch rose clouds turn evening—   坐看霞色晚
They seem to be markers of Redwall Mountain.   疑是赤城標
                          [07770]

Direction is important in this poem: the poet has a fixed line of gaze and travel, in contrast to other men who move back and forth without apparent direction, men whose only goal is profit and thus live in constant insecurity, trusting themselves to the wind and tide. The poet's journey is linear, and the empty spot in the vector of his southeastward movement is the North-west, Ch'ang-an and the public life it represented. Away from those insecurities, the poet orients himself to something fixed and secure—a stone bridge and a mountain. The fixety and security were also spiritual, for T'ien-t'ai and the rose-colored clouds were both associated with immortality. As the poet gazes in anticipation, the red clouds of evening become a mirage of Redwall Mountain near T'ien-t'ai, whose "summit"/ "marker" 標 draws the poet onward.

Among the K'ai-yüan capital poets the technical proprieties of regulated verse forms had become fixed, and one can begin to speak of true "genres" like *lü-shih*, even though the genre was less rigid than it was to become in the later eighth century. There is a technical interest in the Meng Hao-jan poem above: though it possesses the correct tone pattern of a *lü-shih*, neither of the middle couplets are parallel, as the *lü-shih* demands. The interlocutor of line 5 appeared often in K'ai-yüan poetry, but it was appropriate only in nonregulated forms. The poem is not a "hybrid" form, but rather a relaxation of the rules of regulated craft on an occasion when they were not necessary. Similar irregularities, often in middle couplet parallelism, appear frequently in Meng Hao-jan's regulated poems. Meng's technical freedom may be a function of his provinciality and his seniority to the capital poets, but it is also an expression of informality against a craft associated with social performance.

In the preceding poem the rose-colored clouds underwent a visionary transformation into Redwall Mountain. Though Meng Hao-jan was a gentler poet than Li Po, in many ways his work foreshadowed that of Li: in the unity of experience (more intelligible to Western readers than older forms of rhetorical unity), in the ultimate reference to the personality of the poet, and in the visionary eye that imbued something real or imagined with an otherworldly aura, an epiphany of the imagination.

On a Visit to T'ien-t'ai Mountain	尋天臺山作
I love the Master of Ultimate One,	吾愛太一子
He feeds on rose cloud, rests high on Redwall.	飡霞臥赤城
I will go seek the Peak of Flowers,	欲尋華頂去
Not shrinking from Evil Creek's name.	不憚惡溪名
I rest my horse, lodge the night among clouds,	歇馬憑雲宿
Raise sails to cleave the lake in passage,	揚帆截海行
Then high, high amid the azure mists	高高翠微裏
Afar I see the Bridge of Stone stretch before me.	遙見石梁橫

[07729]

Meng Hao-jan recites the place names of the T'ien-t'ai Range almost magically. If Meng Hao-jan's representation of the inner experience of a journey is less psychologically complex than Wang Wei's "Crossing the Yellow River to Ch'ing-ho," Meng compensates by the intensity with which he looks to his unattained and visionary goal.

The decorum of capital poetry and court poetry preferred sedate openings that stated the general setting or theme. Though such an opening appears in the preceding poem, Meng's opening couplets were often bold and startling, frequently inverting conventions of poetic order. Sunset was a conventional marker of poetic closure; if a poem was about night, then the poem should begin at night. But Meng might begin a poem with the world turning suddenly black (07629)

The evening sun crosses the western ridge,	夕陽度西嶺
The crowd of valleys turn pitch dark instantly.	羣壑倏己暝

As in the poem on the tidal bore of the Ch'ien-t'ang, Meng Hao-jan was drawn to the energy and interest generated by abruptness. The parting poet should follow the route of the traveler's boat and close with its passage over the horizon; Meng would begin such a poem (07617):

A swift wind blows on the wanderer's sail,	疾風吹征帆
In an instant it sinks into emptiness.	倏爾向空沒

Time is boldly compressed as the strong wind blows the sail out of sight in a moment. A poem on taking up lodging for the night had its own decorum, a resolution in security or in a pervasive feeling of isolation and melancholy. Meng Hao-jan began such a poem abruptly, with a strange sense of urgency and menace (07774):

At sunset my horse moves swiftly,	日暮馬行疾
The town, gone to weeds, few dwell there.	城荒人住稀

Similarly, sententiae were often placed in the closure as part of the response; Meng Hao-jan placed them in the opening, where their effect was entirely different. On Hsien Mountain near Meng's home was Yang Hu's stele, the "monument of tears," where all visitors were to weep in memory of the good magistrate Yang:

Climbing Hsien Mountain with Others	與諸子登峴山
In human affairs there is succession, loss,	人事有代謝
Men come and go, forming past and present.	往來成古今
Rivers and mountain keep traces of their glory,	江山留勝迹
Our generation also climbs here for the view.	我輩復登臨
The water sinks, runs shallow by Fishweir,	水落魚梁淺
The sky cold, Yün-meng Marsh far.	天寒夢澤深
Yang Hu's stele yet endures;	羊公碑尚在
Once read, the tears soak our robes too.	讀罷淚沾襟
[07727]	

The aphorism here is not the eternal truth that sums up an experience; rather it is an opening proposition that must be modified by what the poet sees. The landscape here is not one of indifferent nature, but a landscape pregnant with history, with the "traces" of great men of the past. There is Fishweir, where the recluse P'ang Te-kung lived, and the famous Yün-meng Marsh, which calls to mind the ancient kings and poets of the state of Ch'u. Continuity does exist in human memory, as each generation and "our generation also" remembers and recognizes the great men of the past. In this context, the tears at Yang Hu's stele take on a special meaning: they are less a sign of loss than a gesture of continuity, a remembrance that has occurred before, occurs now, and will occur again. The recognition of mortality in the opening aphorism paradoxically is transformed into a kind of immortality.[6]

If Meng Hao-jan sought an independent identity in much of his poetry, his independence was achieved through a style and form that was not entirely alien to capital poetry. In contrast, a poet like Li Po seems to have worked in a mode so alien to the capital poets that they could not fully appreciate his talents. Meng Hao-jan stood half within the poetics of capital poetry and half outside it. This may have been what Yin Fan was referring to when he said of Meng's poetry: "He half followed the Way of decorum, yet cut away entirely the common style" 半遵雅道，全削凡體 Many readers were attracted to the independence that "cut away the common style" and projected the personality of the wild, eccentric recluse. But the other aspect of Meng's talent, the half that "followed the Way of decorum," was a craftsmanship in the parallel couplet that attracted capital readers for the modal quality of "lucidity," *ch'ing* 清. *Ch'ing* was implicit in Tu Fu's comparison of Meng's poetry to that of Hsieh T'iao, a poet with whom *ch'ing* was always associated. Tu Fu refers explicitly to Meng Hao-jan's *ch'ing* in another line (11574):

Line after line of lucid poems, all worth passing on.   清詩句句盡堪傳

Chinese modal concepts do not fare well in translation; "lucidity," *ch'ing*, usually refers to an elegantly simple style describing situations with clear, distinct sensations, neither too intense nor too faint. Wang Shih-yüan cited the following couplet as an example of Meng's *ch'ing*, a couplet that supposedly dazzled Wang Wei and Chang Chiu-ling when Meng met them in the capital:

Faint clouds pale the river of stars,   微雲淡河漢
Sparse raindrops drip the pawlonia trees.   疎雨滴梧桐

The paleness is created by a film of cloud that dims the starlight. An indefinite, but synasthetically appropriate relationship exists between these pale points of light and the droplets slowly falling from the trees.

Such minor details of Meng Hao-jan's poetic art touched the existing interests of contemporary readers and exemplified the K'ai-yüan style to later readers; however, it was only a detail of Meng's art and rarely sustained through an entire poem. Such couplets would appear beside couplets that were chatty or boldly abrupt, or written with the gnarled density of the couplet from "Gathering Firewood":

Where a bridge had fallen, a recumbent log was clasped.	橋崩臥查擁
Where the road dropped sheer, hanging vines were held.	路險垂藤接

If Meng succeeded in unifying his stylistic variety by his personality, he observed the modal unities of the capital style no more than he observed the norms of poetic structure.

Whatever his descriptive talents, Meng Hao-jan was primarily a poet of interior experience. In Wang Wei's poetry the enigmatic closing image usually referred to some hidden significance in the world itself or in the limiting nature of perception. In contrast, Meng Hao-jan's mysterious closing images usually served as a modal evocation of the poet's state of mind.

Year's End, Returning to My Southern Mountains	歲暮歸南山
I've ceased my petitions to palace gates,	北闕休上書
I go back to a poor cottage in southern hills.	南山歸弊廬
No talent—my wise prince has cast me from him,	不才明主棄
Often sick now, old friends growing fewer.	多病故人疎
This whitening hair hurries on old age,	白髮催年老
As spring's green force presses in a new year.	青陽逼歲除
In constant depression I cannot sleep—	永懷愁不寐
Pines and moonlight in the empty window at night.	松月夜窗虛

[07767]

Before Meng Hao-jan, few T'ang poets were able to create effective poetry without recourse to the descriptive couplet, yet this poem was to become one of Meng's most famous. Meng Hao-jan's work was the beginning of a poetry about the self, and it was certainly this element that attracted Li Po to Meng.

The poem above was the occasion of the most famous anecdote told about Meng Hao-jan, an anecdote that is almost certainly apocryphal, but nevertheless has become a part of the Meng Hao-jan legend. Wishing to introduce Meng Hao-jan to the emperor, Wang Wei hid the old poet under a bed in a room the emperor was about to enter. Meng Hao-jan emerged into the surprised imperial presence, and Hsüan-tsung asked him to recite one of his poems. Meng recited the preceding poem, and instead of pitying the old poet, Hsüan-tsung was irritated at what he felt was a slander. After all, Meng had never applied to him for a post, so how could His Majesty be accused of having cast the poet off? At this sign of disfavor, Meng Hao-jan left the capital in disgrace.

The quatrain was not Meng Hao-jan's preferred form, and he did not devote the attention to it that Wang Wei and Wang Ch'ang-ling did. Though several of Meng's quatrains are among the most famous in the T'ang, they lack Meng's boldness, energy, and descriptive talents. The following two quatrains are Meng's most famous.

Spending the Night on the Chien-te River   宿建德江

I move the boat on to moor by a misty isle, 移舟泊煙渚
At sunset a traveler's sorrow strikes anew: 日暮客愁新
The wilderness vast, heaven low upon the trees, 野曠天低樹
The river clear, and the moon, near the person. 江清月近人
       [07855]

Spring Dawn   春曉

Sleeping in spring, unaware of the dawn, 春眠不覺曉
Then everywhere I hear birds singing.   處處聞啼鳥
Last night, the sound of wind and the rain— 夜來風雨聲
Flowers have fallen, I wonder how many. 花落知多少
      [07848]

The second poem here is perhaps the finest and most famous example of a form that became very popular in the High T'ang—drawing inferences from limited evidence, often using senses other than the expected ones. This is a poem of sounds, and the poet infers the dawn and the fall of the flowers from what he hears and has heard the night before. The poem almost resembles Wang Wei's work in its interest in problems of cognition. In the first couplet the poet can verify what he has inferred from the bird-calls simply by opening his eyes; by going to the window he can know that flowers were brought down by last night's rain. But the question of "how many" flowers have fallen cannot be answered.

Though Meng Hao-jan was familiar with earlier poetry, he did not have Wang Wei's or Tu Fu's strong sense of the power of the poetic past. Living as he did at the height of the T'ao Ch'ien revival, T'ao's poetry attracted him, but only in isolated cases. In some poems Meng referred to T'ao specifically (e.g., 07605); in other poems he loosely adopted T'ao Ch'ien's manner; but usually Meng used T'ao Ch'ien as he used other poets, grafting echoes of T'ao's work into poems that were entirely Meng Hao-jan's own (e.g., 07686.1).

Unlike Wang Wei, Meng Hao-jan did not seriously try to recreate past styles. He usually borrowed phrases out of context, and when he did echo the original context, it was often playfully. "Boating on Yeh Creek" offers an excellent example of such playfulness. The seventh line is taken almost verbatim from Wang Chi's famous "View of the Wilds" (02612), where it represents a melancholy estrangement between figures in an autumn scene. The eighth line is taken verbatim from the tenth of the Nineteen Old Poems, where it is applied to the loving glances exchanged between the Herdboy and Weaving Girl stars.

Last sunlight, some clear radiance left,   落景餘清暉
My light oars play among the creek's islets.   輕橈弄溪渚
I love the water creatures in these clear depths,   泓澄愛水物
And take my ease looking down into the current.   臨泛何容與
A white-haired old man, dangling a fishing line,   白首垂釣翁
Freshly made-up, a girl washing gauze.   新粧浣紗女
They look at each other, seem to know each other,   相看似相識
With longing glances they can't get to speak.   脈脈不得語
                           [07630]

The archetypal figure of the aloof and disinterested old fisherman is not behaving as he is supposed to. Meng playfully applies these grand lines of human isolation and love-longing to the amorous glances exchanged between the lusty old fisherman (the poet?) and a washer girl. This is a comic inversion of the use of past poetry in the closure for authority, one of Wang Wei's favorite techniques. It is no subtle reworking of past poetry —the lines are famous and quoted almost verbatim; rather, their grand seriousness makes them humorous in an incongruous situation.

Anecdotes and poem exchanges provide some idea of Meng Hao-jan's social relations to the contemporary capital poets, but his poetic relations with them are more complex. The similarities between Meng Hao-jan's poetry and the shared style of the capital poets may have been accidental, one reason for their interest in Meng's work. That interest on the part of the capital poets was responsible for the fame Meng achieved. On the other hand, some elements of Meng's work seem to have been learned from the sophisticated craft of capital poetry: interest in T'ao Ch'ien, enigmatic closure, and dramatic juxtaposition. But Meng Hao-jan had an individual poetic voice, and he did not change it in poems addressed to Ts'ui Kuo-fu, Chi-wu Ch'ien, Chang Tzu-yung, and Wang Ch'ang-ling. Writing to Chang Chiu-ling, Meng tended to an awkward formality, but such formality was a function of Chang's high office and prestige. In one clear case, however, Meng was drawn to speak in another poet's voice:

Parting From Wang Wei　　　　　　　　　　　　　留別王維

In utter stillness what times are these?　　　　　寂寞竟何時
Every morning I return alone in vain.　　　　　　朝朝空自歸
I go off to seek plants of fragrance　　　　　　　欲尋芳草去
And regret I shall stray from a dear friend.　　　惜與故人違
Qf men in power, on whom can I depend?　　　　當路誰相假
True friends are known to be few in this age.　　知音世所稀
I ought only to hold to that utter stillness,　　　祇應守寂寞
Go home and shut the gate of my garden.　　　　還掩故園扉
　　　　　　　　　[07698]

Wang Wei's distinctive poetic voice is unmistakable here, though Meng's use of it is awkward to the point of parody. That Meng adopted Wang's voice was a mark of the power, prestige, and attraction of Wang Wei's poetry, but in denying himself the freedom of his own style, Meng Hao-jan did not know quite what to say, and Wang's austere plainness became merely an exaggerated flatness.

Though Meng Hao-jan's best poetry can stand beside the best of Wang Wei, Meng was less consistently a major poet. His inspiration was fickle and often abandoned him to mediocrity. Even at his most characteristic, Meng Hao-jan's poetic identity is more elusive than that of Wang Wei—an energy or a mood—and one can understand why contemporary readers saw in it not a greatness of poetic art, but the authentic expression of a free personality.

常建

CH'ANG CHIEN

Ch'ang Chien is perhaps the outstanding example of an early-eighth-century poet who possessed the unrealized seeds of greatness. Like Meng Hao-jan, Ch'ang Chien shared many poetic interests with the capital poets but moved toward a personal version of the shared style. Ch'ang passed the metropolitan examination in 727 and probably become acquainted with at least some of the young capital poets (Wang Ch'ang-ling did visit him later in his life); at the very least, he must have been acquainted with their work. But Ch'ang Chien was to become a solitary poet, spending the rest of his life in a minor provincial office and later in provincial retirement. His poem exchange with Wang Ch'ang-ling is the only concrete evidence of contact with the larger world of poetry. Information on his life is meager, and much of it is contradicted by the poems themselves.

Yet this obscure figure was and remains a strangely attractive poet. Yin Fan placed Ch'ang first in the *Ho-yüeh ying-ling chi*, and Ch'ang's poems in that anthology are second in number only to the selection from

Wang Ch'ang-ling's works. To Yin Fan, Ch'ang Chien represented the unrecognized genius, a man whose great talents were hidden in the provinces and thus wasted. Ch'ang was not a prolific poet: his collected poems seem to have survived intact, but they make up only one *chüan*.

Ch'ang Chien is often considered a reclusive poet, and some of his works in this mode have all the control and restraint of the best capital poets. His most frequently anthologized poem is a minor classic of reclusive poetry.

Written on the Meditation Garden Behind Broken Mountain Temple	題破山寺後禪院

At clear dawn entering the ancient temple,	清晨入古寺
First sunlight shines high in the forest.	初日照高林
A bamboo path leads to a hidden spot,	竹逕通幽處
A meditation chamber deep in the flowering trees.	禪房花木深
The mountain light cheers the natures of birds,	山光悦鳥性
Reflections in pool void the hearts of men.	潭影空人心
All nature's sounds here grow silent,	萬籟此都寂
All that remains are the notes of temple bells.	但餘鐘磬音

[06891]

Like Meng Hao-jan, on a private occasion Ch'ang felt free to violate the requisite middle couplet parallelism of the *lü-shih*. But on the whole, this poem belongs entirely to the shared style of capital poetry.

In his other poetry, however, Ch'ang Chien showed greater independence; for example, the following passage has a dreamy luminosity entirely different from the sparseness of a Wang Wei or energy of a Meng Hao-jan (06878):

Evening shines in azure mountain depths,	夕映翠山深
A last radiance here, at Dragonhole:	餘暉在龍窟
A tiny boat, my thoughts as in Ts'ang-lang,	扁舟滄浪意
I rock in pale waters, sunk in reflections of flowers,	澹澹花影沒
Then drift west and into the color of sky,	西浮入天色
Gaze south and confront the towers of cloud.	南望對雲闕

Ts'ang-lang was where the "Fisherman" of the *Ch'u-tz'u* floated, passively responding to the conditions of the world around him.

There is an immense variety and originality in Ch'ang Chien's small collection. In frontier poetry his "Lament at the Grave of General Wang" (06887) is a minor classic. Ch'ang was also interested in *fu-ku* poetry and wrote a moving lament for T'ai-kung's late meeting with Chou Wen-wang (06885), one of the exemplary stories of a man of talent being recognized by his ruler and raised to high position. Ch'ang treated several unusual topics in his poetry: he wrote on the primitive tribesmen of the south

(06884), on meeting the "Hairy Girl," an immortal (06883), and a strange and moving poem on encountering a corpse (06875). More than anything else by Ch'ang, the opening of this latter poem suggests the genius that Ch'ang did not fully develop:

By the River Han I met an old man,　　　　　　　　漢上逢老翁
At the broad stream's mouth, a stiff corpse,　　　　江口為僵屍
His white hair mired in the brown mud,　　　　　　白髮沾黃泥
His abandoned bones, the perch of ravens.　　　　　遺骸集烏鴟
All craft and cunning forgotten now,　　　　　　　機巧自此忘
Where does the bright soul make its way?　　　　　精魄今何之
The wind blows on his fishing pole, snaps it,　　　風吹釣竿折
How can it now take the leaping fish?　　　　　　　魚躍安能施

7

王昌齡　李頎

Wang Ch'ang-ling and Li Ch'i
New Interests in Capital Poetry

During the K'ai-yüan Reign the poets Wang Ch'ang-ling, Kao Shih, and Wang Chih-huan were equally famous. In those days before the rebellion the three often traveled around together. One cold day it was about to snow, and the three poets went into a tavern, ordered wine, and had been drinking a while, when all of a sudden a group of ten or so musicians from the Imperial Ensemble came up the stairs for a party. The three poets left their seats and concealed themselves, huddling behind a brazier to watch what would happen. A moment later four lovely singing girls followed the musicians into the room. These girls were a delight to the eye, voluptuously beautiful, the very height of charm. Soon they began to play the most famous songs of the age, whereupon Wang Ch'ang-ling and the others made this agreement: "Each has gained renown for his poetry, and yet we still have not established which is foremost among us. Let's now listen in secret to what these musicians sing, and whichever of us has the most poems set to music will be the master." Soon one of the musicians set the tempo and sang:

Cold rains stretch to the river, by night entering Wu,	寒雨連江夜入吳
At daybreak bid traveler farewell, loneliness in Ch'u's mountains.	平明送客楚山孤
If friends and kin in Lo-yang should ask you how I am—	洛陽親友如相問
In a vase of whitest jade a heart like a sheet of ice.	一片冰心在玉壺

Wang Ch'ang-ling made a mark on the wall: "One quatrain for me." Then another musician sang:

I open the trunk, tears soak my breast,	開篋淚霑臆
I see letters you sent me long ago.	見君前日書
The terrace of night lies in utter silence—	夜臺何寂寞
Yang Hsiung the recluse lives here still.	猶是子雲居

Kao Shih made a mark on the wall: "One quatrain for me." Then another musician sang [of the Imperial Consort Pan Chieh-yü, who had lost the emperor's favor to the Chao sisters]:

Broom in her hand at break of day, golden halls open wide,   奉帚平明金殿開
She struggles to hold her moon-disk fan, both waver to and   強將團扇共徘徊
 fro.
Her face white as jade no rival to the color of winter's crows   玉顏不及寒鴉色
That come now, still lit by the beams from the Palace of   猶帶昭陽日影來
 Shining Favor.

Wang Ch'ang-ling made another mark on the wall: "*Two* quatrains for me." Wang Chih-huan had been a famous poet for many years, so he said to his companions: "These fellows are a poor excuse for musicians, and the songs they are singing are your common village verses—they have no place beside the truly great songs that a connoisseur of music would recognize." Then he pointed to the most beautiful of the singing girls and said: "Let's wait and see what *she* sings— if it's not one of my poems, I'll never dare enter into competition with you again; but if it *is* my poem, then you have to pay your respects to me as the true master." So saying he laughed and waited her turn. In a few moments this lady with the lovely coiffure raised her voice in song:

Yellow sands rise far away on high among white clouds,   黃沙遠上白雲間
Silhouette of a lonely fortress on a thousand-foot mountain.   一片孤城萬仞山
Why should this nomad flute be playing wrath at the   羌笛何須怨楊柳
 "leaves" of willow,
Since the wind of spring will never cross Jade Gate Barrier?   春風不度玉門關

Wang Chih-huan danced with glee and roared with laughter: "Peasants! Wasn't I right?" Of course, the musicians had had no idea what was happening, and they went over to the poets: "And what do you gentlemen find so amusing?" Wang Ch'ang-ling and his companions told their tale, and the musicians hurried to pay their respects to the poets. "Our mortal eyes did not recognize the gods. Please grace us with your presence at our party." The poets joined them and drank the whole day through."
   [from the *Chi-yi chi*, an early-ninth-century collection of anecdotes]

  The first song sung by the musicians was Wang Ch'ang-ling's "At Lotus Hall: Sending Off Hsin Chien" (06821). When he wrote the quatrain, Wang was speaking about himself to someone he knew, someone who understood certain things and felt a certain way about him; moreover, Wang was speaking to Hsin in a specific place at a specific moment in time, a unique moment that was the focus of the infinite contingencies of human lives and weather. The rain that came in the evening may have stirred a certain mood in the two men, and Wang's poetic description of the rain

may have complicated and deepened that mood, but it was a real rain
that soaked clothing and filled the streams. As one human speaking to
another, there was no doubt in the mind either of speaker or listener precisely
who would find himself the next day in the solitude of Ch'u's mountains:
in the occasional context the poem's indefinite "traveler" became the very
definite "you, Hsin Chien." And when the poet spoke of himself as "a
heart like a sheet of ice, " the line was heard against certain historical truths
about Wang's life at that moment; its meaning was inextricable from how
Wang felt about himself and how Hsin felt about him. Like any statement,
its meaning was contingent upon the context of a real situation. But when
those same four lines were sung by an imperial musician to an audience
of his colleagues and singing girls, what was the poem about? Suppose
the listener did not know when the poem was written, or under what
circumstances, or even by whom. The structure of meaning in the poem
changes radically: a moving interpretation of a specific situation becomes
a fragmentary representation of something hidden and inaccessible. The
affirmation of icy purity and rectitude is surrounded by mystery, and that
mystery becomes part of the significance and power of the poem.

There is probably no historical truth in the anecdote translated above;
the dating of the poem and the lives of the poets makes such a meeting
highly unlikely, if not impossible. The poetry competition was a fictional
frame in which to set some very famous quatrains. But setting aside questions of historical validity, the anecdote tells much about the presentation
of certain kinds of poetry. Not all poets and not all poetic genres were
associated with song performance; a long *p'ai-lü* by Tu Fu would have
made a decidedly dull (and probably incomprehensible) song. But quatrains
were often sung, especially quatrains on *yüeh-fu* and quasi-*yüeh-fu* themes
(e.g., historical vignettes like Wang Chao-chün). The musical treatment
of the quatrain was closely related to the development of the "song-lyric"
(*tz'u* 詞) in the late eighth and early ninth centuries. These songs were
not "popular" in the sense that they had true mass appeal, but they were
the entertainment of the educated urban classes and those who catered to
them, musicians and singing girls. Many of the tunes used for such quatrains had been recent importations from Central Asia and thus were
particularly appropriate for poetry on frontier subjects.

The use of contemporary quatrains as songs for entertainment represented a fundamental change in the attitude toward poetry. Older
poetry was read and chanted both as a literary experience and as a means
to learn composition. As a literary experience, the lives of the authors and
the specific circumstances of composition were of primary interest: poems
were more strongly a peculiar form of historical representation than a
statement of universal truth. Ch'en Tzu-ang probably would not have

recited a Juan Chi poem to apply to a T'ang political situation; rather, Juan Chi's poems would be truly *about* the Wei. In its analogical function, Juan Chi's poetry might provide Ch'en Tzu-ang an example of *how* to write about a T'ang political situation, perhaps echoing earlier poems by Juan Chi. The major exception was the *Shih-ching*: though an individual *Shih* usually had a topical interpretation, many also carried general or universal referents. Thus, a poem like "A Deer Cries Out" (*Shih* 161) could be performed as a convivial expression of friendship: it was a *repeatable* literary experience.

Contemporary poetry was still largely an "event ' rather than a text. Modern poetry was thought of as something to compose or to be heard at composition rather than as something to be read in books in the privacy of one's library: a poem was primarily an act of the moment for the moment. Though composition was still the center of the experience of poetry, in the K'ai-yüan contemporary poems were more widely circulated, read, and repeated. But as with earlier poetry, when a reader read a poem by Meng Hao-jan, he did not experience an elation parallel to Meng's own or grasp a higher truth; rather, the reader conceptualized what he read as "knowing" Meng Hao-jan and Meng's experience of higher truth. The occasional poem was in essence one person speaking to another, and this mode had potent implications for the way in which poetry was read.

The *yüeh-fu* was the form most strongly divorced from occasion, though they too were often used in occasional situations. *Yüeh-fu* was a literary experience that was *repeatable* in a way that occasional poetry was not. *Yüeh-fu*'s referents were general; it was not bound to the circumstances of its composition; and usually the personality and biography of the author were not the primary contexts for understanding. It was a form with whose fictional personae the reader could identify by the various forms of transference that occur in fictional modes. A millenium-long tradition of topical interpretations for famous *yüeh-fu* and other fictional poetry attests to the resistance of many readers to this kind of reading and their need for the security of historical anchoring.

The quatrain song became a significant means by which occasional poems moved toward the general referents of *yüeh-fu*. The first two quatrains in the anecdote above were both occasional poems; in song form the particularities of composition cease to be the relevant context in which the poem is "read," and the poems become universal statements of parting or longing. Such transformations often appeared in the change from an occasional title to a song title; for example, Wang Wei's "Sending Off Yüan on a Mission to An-hsi" 送元二使安西 became "The Song of the City by the Wei" 渭城曲 or "The Song of Yang Pass" 陽關曲. Occasion and the kind of reading it generated never left T'ang poetry, but the quatrain song was the manifestation of a new mode of reading, which in turn became an integral part of the way poets thought about their work. The occasional poem might have universal and therefore repeatable dimensions; the poet began to see himself as speaking to all people present and future, as well as to the person standing before him. Poets could expect that posterity would find not only the historical poet in poems but universal applications to their own experience as well. And as the eighth century progressed, the idea of "literary creation" achieved ever grander dimensions and came to be thought of again, as it had been before in the centuries after the Han, as the corollary of the larger cosmic processes of Creation.

In the High T'ang, most major poets and more than a few minor ones produced famous quatrains, but Wang Ch'ang-ling is generally acknowledged as the High T'ang master of the quatrain. Moreover, Wang's poems were strongly associated with music and song, as in the anecdote above. Quatrains make up about half of Wang's regular collection and a sizable part of the large addenda to his collection. Of the sixteen Wang Ch'ang-ling poems anthologized in the *Ho-yüeh ying-ling chi*, only three are quatrains, and this suggests that Wang's contemporary fame did not rest entirely on that form. But in the slightly later *Kuo-hsiu chi*, three of Wang's five poems are quatrains, and by the ninth century Wang Ch'ang-ling had become the poet of the quatrain.

Little is known of Wang Ch'ang-ling's life. The modern scholar Wen I-to gave the date 698 for Wang's birth, and most literary historians have followed him.[1] But that date is highly tentative. Wang Ch'ang-ling came from the capital region, and if we are to believe Yin Fan, he was connected with the T'ai-yüan Wang clan, from which Wang Wei came. Wang passed the examination in 727 and later served in the Chang Chiu-ling government. After Chang's fall in 737, Wang was exiled to a minor post in the south and subsequently experienced the familiar oscillations in political fortunes without ever rising to high office. In 757 Wang was executed by a provincial governor for unknown reasons.

Despite Wang Ch'ang-ling's great popularity in the T'ang, the early textual history of his collection is obscure. There is no T'ang preface to his works, and the large proportion of his poems also preserved in the major T'ang and Sung anthologies might suggest that present editions are based on a collection reconstituted in the Sung from anthology sources. A larger collection seems also to have been in circulation in the Sung, and this may have been the source of the large addenda that makes up almost a third of Wang's one hundred and ninety poems. Numerous textual variants in his works were often the result of wide representation in anthologies. Wang also wrote one or more critical works on style and the technical aspects of verse, the *Shih-ko* 詩格 and the *Shih-chung mi-chih*

詩中密旨 (which may have been part of the *Shih-ko*). Genuine critical material has been preserved in the *Bunkyō hifuron* 文鏡密府論, and there are Chinese editions of the *Shih-ko* and *Shih-chung mi-chih*. It is difficult to say, however, to what extent this material represents Wang Ch'ang-ling's own work and to what extend it is an accretion of T'ang critical material under Wang's prestigious name.

Wang Ch'ang-ling was a master of frontier poetry, and this has led many scholars to assume that Wang actually spent time in military service on the frontier.[2] The most reliable evidence, however, suggests that Wang Ch'ang-ling's Central Asia was a combination of the poetic tradition and his own imagination. Had Wang Ch'ang-ling ever actually served on the frontier, there should be at least a few occasional poems from the region or some reference to the experience in his later occasional poetry. But Wang's occasional poetry suggests that he went only as far north as Ching-chou, about 300 kilometers northwest of Ch'ang-an, just inside the frontier region, but far short of the distant Central Asian locations mentioned in Wang's poetry. All of Wang's frontier poems are either *yüeh-fu* or in the *yüeh-fu* manner, and this was one of the few forms in which T'ang poets used patently fictional personae. There is no more reason to suppose that Wang Ch'ang-ling served on frontier campaigns than to suppose that he was a lady in the imperial harem, a theme of which he wrote with equal skill. Indeed, Wang Ch'ang-ling's importance in High T'ang poetry comes in part from his interest in fictional modes and the freedom they permitted. Moreover, the immense popularity of his work attests to a contemporary thirst for nonoccasional poetry, particularly frontier poetry and palace poetry.

Biographical and prefatory convention generously applied the epithet "most famous poet of the day." But if we look to the frequency of anecdotal reference, anthologizing, critical comment, as well as to the seriousness of critical comment, it is clear that Wang Ch'ang-ling was Wang Wei's most serious competitor as the most famous contemporary poet in the K'ai-yüan and T'ien-pao. Like Wang Wei, Wang Ch'ang-ling was a capital poet of good family and thus possessed all the social legitimacy that a poet like Li Po lacked. Contemporaries probably felt that such stability and legitimacy were requisite for serious literary endeavor. In the *Ho-yüeh ying-ling chi* Yin Fan granted to Li Po a certain faddish interest, but he evaluated the work of Wang Ch'ang-ling with the authoritative formulae of *fu-ku* literary history: "After the Ts'ao's, after Liu Chen, after the Lu brothers and the Hsiehs, for four hundred years all true affective power and strength [*feng-ku*] disappeared. But now we have Wang Ch'ang-ling of the T'ai-yüan Wangs." Wang Ch'ang-ling was not in the tradition of *fu-ku* poetry, even in its broadest interpretation. Yin Fan probably used *fu-ku* formulae because they were the only available model of serious literary historical evaluation. "After 'major poets' from the great clans of the past, now we in the T'ang have our own great poet from our own great clan, the T'ai-yüan Wangs." The quality that linked Wang Ch'ang-ling's poetry to the masters of the past was *feng-ku* 風骨, literally "wind and bone." *Feng-ku* is a difficult term that meant different things in different contexts at different times. Roughly, the *ku*, "strength" (bones), referred to the inner structure and meaning of a poem, while *feng*, "affective power," was the ability to move or sway people unconsciouly, like the "wind." *Feng* often carried the implication of moral and political persuasion, but this sense was probably absent in the application to Wang Ch'ang-ling's poetry above.

Wang Ch'ang-ling was not a master craftsman of the parallel couplet: it is significant that in Yin Fan's introduction to the selection of Wang Ch'ang-ling's poetry very few of the many exemplary couplets and passages quoted were parallel. Wang usually avoided the stylistic decorum and balanced amplification of capital eremitic poetry. Even excluding his interest in fictional personae, Wang did not develop the function of poetry as an extension and expression of the poet's personality. And in Wang Ch'ang-ling one rarely finds the serious intellectual concerns that played such an important role in the poetry of Wang Wei. Instead, Wang Ch'ang-ling sought a poetry that in a few quick strokes could evoke a mood, a figure, an emotionally fraught situation. He was the master of the evocative image, the dramatic gesture, and the suggestive scene.

T'ang categories of mood were holistic, aesthetic impressions, seemingly immediate but actually trained literary responses to some integral of qualities in a work—the theme, the fixed associations of images, the style, the associations of tonal euphony and sound value, and sometimes the quality of personality expressed. Since the categories were holistic impressions, they are not easily broken down into the specific components that generated the impression. If there is no way to describe adequately Chinese model categories, they can at least be learned by habit of association gained from reading traditional modal characterizations of poems and couplets. But though they remain intangible, these modal distinctions were among the most important ways in which eighth- and ninth-century poets thought about their art. The category of "lucidity," *ch'ing*, has appeared in connection with the poetry of Meng Hao-jan, but there were many others, for example, "manly and resolute pathos," *pei-chuang* 悲壯; "lofty and ancient," *kao-ku* 高古.

Categories of mood were applied to all kinds of poetry; a poetry whose primary purpose was to evoke a mood became something more specific. Seeking immediacy of response, a poetry of mood had to transcend recognizable structural patterns, to substitute mystery for coherent propositions. A poetry of mood would avoid not only the older forms of rhetorical amplification but the more logically constructed scenes and narratives of K'ai-yüan poetry as well. The unity and value of a poem lay in its affect, and that affect would strive for the prerational. Contrast Chang Yüeh, writing several decades before Wang Ch'ang-ling, on hearing temple bells at night; he closes (04568):

Now truly I understand that at last we are on the edge of   信知本際空
    Nothingness,
Yet hollow illusions of life and death linger.[3]   徒掛生滅想

Experience is rationalized into a meditation on the illusoriness of existence; hearing the music from an unseen source was a lesson to which he responded with the formalized conclusion "now I understand. . . ." Hearing flute music by night, Wang Ch'ang-ling drew no such conclusions; rather, he was fascinated by music's affective power itself, its ability to evoke a series of moods that he in turn tried to evoke in his poem. Response became an immediate outburst of emotion rather than a disjunctive conclusion from contemplation.

Hearing a Flute on the River   江中聞笛

A flute speaks complaint to the river moon,   橫笛怨江月
Where can my small boat find the music's source?   扁舟何處尋
Notes stretching long, beyond Ch'u mountains,   聲長楚山外
Melody circling the depths of Tartar passes.   曲繞胡關深
Ten thousand miles apart these are,   相去萬餘里
Yet a mind is carried that far tonight.   遙傳此夜心
A desolate vastness, the shore turns cold,   寥寥浦漵寒
The echoes die only in hidden forests.   響盡唯幽林
I wonder who that man might be   不知誰家子
Playing again the songs of Han-tan.   復奏邯鄲音
We water voyagers all huddle round our oars,   水客皆擁棹
As sky's frost falls then, filling hearts: 空霜遂盈襟
A lean horse galloping, eyes on the north,   羸馬望北走
And exiles grieving for songs of the Southeast.   遷人悲越吟
Oh, when shall the border grasses turn white,   何當邊草白
And our standards and banners be north of Lung Fort?   旌節隴城陰
                       [06725]

We know the general situation: someone is playing the songs of the frontier on a southern river. But many elements of the poem—the fading of the echoes in the forests, the image of the lean horse galloping northward— are visually unrelated fragments whose presence is primarily for the mood they evoke.

Fragmentation of the implied physical scene provided the ground on which a unity of mood could be asserted. In extreme cases, Wang Ch'ang-ling's evocative fragmentation violated even the presumptive unities of time and weather. The following poem is a meteorological prodigy: mist, rain, frost, bright moonlight, and a pervasive darkness that hides the flying geese dwell together comfortably only in the melancholy mood evoked.

Autumn Evening on the Great Lake   太湖秋夕

Spend the night on water, mist and rain chill,   水宿煙雨寒
Over Lake Tung-t'ing the frost comes down faintly.   洞庭霜落微
The moon is bright, the boat shifts on and away,   月明移舟去
As in night's stillness the soul returns from dream.   夜靜魂夢歸
I sense the wind pass over the lake in darkness,   暗覺海風度
And through its moaning hear wild geese in their flight.   蕭蕭聞雁飛
                              [06726]

The fragmentation of visual and logical unity for a unity of mood had great appeal to T'ang readers. Through the eighth and ninth centuries modal distinctions became increasingly subtle, and representational fragmentation, more daring. Ultimately these aesthetic values became one important component of the song-lyric, "*tz'u.*"

The impulse to modal poetry also appears in Wang Ch'ang-ling's treatment of several traditional forms. The following extract is a modal opening for a narrative in the *yüeh-fu* manner.

Written to Serve as the Reply of My Host at Fu-feng   代扶風主人答

The breath of killing hangs motionless, not drifting on,   殺氣凝不流
The winds are mournful, moonglitter cold,   風悲月彩寒
Dust swells in the distance all around,   浮埃起四邊
And the traveler is lost and joyless.   遊子迷不歡
As ever I lodge for the night at Fu-feng,   依然宿扶風
Here buy some wine to ease my spirit,   沽酒聊自寬
But I cannot control this heart of mine,   寸心亦未理
Can't tap with my sword hilt and boldly sing.   長鋏誰能彈
My host now joins me in a drink;   主人就我飲
Facing me he's filled with sorrow,   對我還慨然
Weeping first a few tracks of tears,   便泣數行淚
Then singing to me "Hardships of Travel."   因歌行路難
                              [06694]

The rest of the poem consists of the host's narrative of his sufferings and experiences on campaign, closing with a ringing praise of the present age and counsel that the poet not be so gloomy. The conventions of the narrative section and the device of putting such a narrative in the mouth of an interlocutor belong comfortably in the *yüeh-fu* tradition. But that conventional narrative is transformed and colored by the affective intensity of the opening.

The priority of mood and immediacy of response precluded more complex intellectual problems. In much of his work Wang Ch'ang-ling was the easiest of the major High T'ang poets. T'ang and later readers took great delight in the perfect expression of a stock situation, in the intelligible gesture that incarnated a certain character type. Many of Wang's most famous poems are such poems of surfaces, hiding no deeper meaning. They are true mood pieces vividly constructed of scene and gesture.

Song by the Walls   城傍曲

Autumn winds cry through mulberry branches,   秋風鳴桑條
The grasses are white, fox and hare exult.   草白狐兔驕
He returns from his dinner at Han-tan,   邯鄲飯來酒未消
   the wine not gone from his blood,
North of the wall in Levelplain County,   城北原平掣皂鵰
   the great hawk held on his arm.
In the empty fortress he shoots and kills   射殺空營兩騰虎
   a pair of leaping tigers
And turns around to the halfmoon,   迴身却月佩弓弰
   the bow tip strung at his waist.
    [06741]

The feat of transfixing two tigers with one arrow and the brave insouciance of the last line incarnate the heroism of the stock Han-tan knight—half soldier, half dangerous bravo. The poem does not question or complicate the stock figure; it celebrates him.

Often there is some element of mystery in the scene that produces the mood. In the poem above the reader knows a poetic association between the full moon and a bent bow, and he can carry the analogy to a half moon and a strung bow. But the association is mystery for the sake of mystery, with no deeper significance. A sense of mystery is often created by visual and logical fragmentation, as in 'Hearing a Flute on the River." Hiddenness in Wang Ch'ang-ling's poetry is rarely in the deeper significance of the poem, as was the case in Wang Wei's work; what is hidden is rather the basic situation or proposition. Complexity often takes the shape of an ambiguity of mood.

Wang Ch'ang-ling's modal and propositional ambiguity appears most clearly in a few poems that are like optical illusions, changing what they say according to the expectations of the reader.

Campaign Song 從軍行

Long clouds from the Sea of Kokonor 青海長雲暗雪山
    darken the Mountain of Snows,
From this lone fortress gaze far away to Jade Gate Barrier: 孤城遙望玉門關
Yellow sands, a hundred battles 黃沙百戰穿金甲
    have pierced our coats of mail—
If we do not smash Kroraina we never shall go home. 不破樓蘭終不還
          [06781]

The problem lies in whether the last line is a heroic vow of self-sacrifice
by the soldiers to serve the emperor and accomplish their mission or a
complaint against a condition imposed upon them, an expression of a
hopeless yearning to return home. There is no sublety in this ambiguity:
the alternatives are the two most common resolutions of frontier poetry.

    Fragmentation was Wang Ch'ang-ling's most common technique to
create mystery. Often Wang used the common poetic device of indirect
evidence, but the bits of evidence would be contradictory or insufficient
to arrive at the conventional situation expected by the reader. Such a poem
could become a series of evocative fragments that teased the reader with
a world he could not fully apprehend.

Dawn Song 朝來曲

Moon past its zenith, bridle-pendants stirring, ringing, 月晟鳴珂動
Flowers reach to springtime of a finely wrought door. 花連繡戶春
A coiling dragon: the mirror on a stand of jade 盤龍玉臺鏡
Awaits only she who will paint her eyebrows. 唯待畫眉人
          [06764]

In the first half of the eighth century the full range of stock situations of
boudoir poetry was in the process of formation, and it is difficult to say
the extent to which the conventions in their final form are applicable here.
From the movement of the bridle-pendants we know there is a rider,
a man. Stock situations will have this man either leaving the brothels in
the early morning or, less commonly, leaving his wife on the way to court.
Two stock situations may come into play in the second couplet: postcoital
lassitude and the beginning of the toilette early in the morning as an indication of the desire to attract a husband or lover.

    We have the fragments of many potential situations. Is this the wife,
whose husband is off at the brothels, neglecting her toilette in despair?
Or does it imply that this same wife begin her toilette very early (in which
case the waiting implies that she will come soon) in order to entice her
husband away from the company of singing girls. Or is the woman the
courtesan trying to attract a lover or neglecting her toilette in postcoital

languor? Or is this a simple domestic scene, the husband setting off for dawn court and the lady beginning her toilette for the following evening? Given the conventions of boudoir poetry, the images of the poem are highly suggestive, but they point the reader to a solution he cannot find.

Literary characterization inevitably begins with typology, a fixed vocabulary of stereotypes in conventional situations. In its later forms, Chinese prose fiction managed to break out of strict typology by individuation, but Chinese poetry took another path to complicate the portrayal of human character. The fixed typology of "characters" was retained, but limitations and complications were added to the evidence that revealed them. This is another manifestation of Wang Ch'ang-ling's individual version of the general High T'ang interest in hiddenness.

The use of indirect evidence to reveal inner states of emotion had been part of boudoir poetry since the fifth century; there was a High T'ang revival of the form with many new complications. In some cases, as in the preceding poem, the reader was blocked from discovering the precise nature of an emotional intensity he presumed was there. In other cases, as in Ch'u Kuang-hsi's poem on Wang Chao-chün, the situation and emotion are known from a background story, and the "evidence" itself carries the interest in dramatic contrasts. In still other cases, the concern with illusory surfaces concealing hidden truths is brought into the theme of the poem itself. In the following poem no reader wonders how the lady feels: the concealing disjunction between lush surfaces and inner emotion is exposed. The poem is from a series by Wang on Pan Chieh-yü, one of the most famous of the "deserted consorts." Pan had been the favorite of Han Ch'eng-ti and was sequestered in Ch'ang-hsin Palace when the two Chao sisters supplanted her in the imperial favor.

An Autumn Song for Ch'ang-hsin Palace (first of five)   長信秋詞五首之一

By the golden well the autumn leaves   金井梧桐秋葉黃
   on pawlonia turn yellow,
The beaded curtain is not rolled up—last night's frost.   珠簾不捲夜來霜
Censer for her robes, pillow of jade lack all loveliness.   熏籠玉枕無顏色
She lies, listens to the clear dripping   臥聽南宮清漏長
   of the water-clock stretch on.
     [06794]

As often in boudoir poetry, there is a fascination here in the contrast between rich surroundings and personal unhappiness. The precious censer and the pillow of jade lose their value and beauty because their inner meaning has changed; they were not really precious in themselves, but only as marks of imperial favor. Together the reader and the lady see behind the glittering surfaces. In the end the lady lies awake through the night, hopelessly awaiting a royal visit, and conscious of passing time that carries her into the chill isolation and old age associated with autumn.

In composing a poetry of mood and in reading a poem for mood, intellectual complexity was unnecessary; the connotative value of words was more important than their denotative value; linear structure was subordinate to cumulative affect; and the particulars of a scene were significant primarily in their modal associations. Reading for mood, a later reader could share completely in the experience of an occasional poem. Thus, when the musician in the opening anecdote sang Wang Ch'ang-ling's occasional poem, it could be a universally shared literary experience through the poetics of mood.

Li Ch'i represents an even greater divergence from the norms of capital poetry than Wang Ch'ang-ling. Li Ch'i was socially intimate with Wang Wei, Wang Ch'ang-ling, and other capital poets, but he was also an eccentric recluse and alchemist whose poetic interests inclined to the wild T'ien-pao style. Though there is no direct evidence in his poetry, the influence of Li Po seems likely. Li Ch'i may have been the youngest of the first-generation capital poets—he passed the examination in 735 and most of his datable work comes from the T'ien-pao—and this would support the possibility of Li Po's influence. Li Ch'i alone in the social circle of the capital poets wrote in the new T'ien-pao style that developed with the introduction of Li Po's poetry to the capital in the early 740s.

Regulated genres, including quatrains, occupy a smaller proportion of Li Ch'i's extant works than they do in most poets. The blandness and anonymity of his regulated poetry reveal most clearly his association with the capital poets. The following *p'ai-lü* is a lovely and moving work, but it could have been written by any minor capital poet: it shares the conventions of landscape and monastery poetry behind which lie the descriptive and structural norms of Early T'ang poetry.

Spending the Night in the High Stone Hall of Fragrance 宿香山寺石樓
   Mountain Temple

I spent the night midway up an azure slope,	夜宿翠微半
From highest chambers heard streams in darkness;	高樓聞暗泉
There fishing boats wore their distant fires	漁舟帶遠火
And mountain chimes issued from lonely mists.	山磬發孤煙
Halls stand mighty past cloud-covered pines,	殿壯雲松外
And the gates lie clear by the river of stars.	門清河漢邊
Peaks and ridges, lower than my pillow and mat,	峯巒低枕席
A world here that links Heaven and man.	世界接人天
Dark and dusky flowers appear in the fog,	靄靄花出霧
Glimmering stars cast their light on the stream.	輝輝星映川

But now eastern groves fill with dawn's orioles,   東林曙鶯滿
Unwillingly I soon must turn back home.   惆悵欲言旋
                              [06393]

Contrast the following "old-style" poem by Tu Fu, written when Tu
was detained in the rebel-held capital; the tradition behind the two poems
is the same, yet Tu Fu's private vision of the temple at night is an imaginative
blindness that liberates the spirit from the ugly realities exposed by the dawn.

In the Chambers of Reverend Tsan at the Temple of   大雲寺贊公房四首之三
    Great Clouds (third of four)

Lamplight cast on sleeplessness,   燈影照無睡
The mind clear, knowing wondrous scents.   心清聞妙香
The halls loom high in depths of night,   夜深殿突兀
And wind rattles the metal chimes.   風動金琅璫
The black of sky closes the gardens of spring,   天黑閉春院
On earth's cool clarity hidden fragrance settles.   地清棲暗芳
Far in the sky the Chain of Jades breaks   玉繩迴斷絕
Past the roof's iron phoenix whirling in dark flight.   鐵鳳森翔翔
Sanscrit chants intoned, often reach the outside,   梵放時出寺
Bell's aftertones still shake my bed.   鐘殘仍殷牀
When day breaks on the vast and fertile plain,   明朝在沃野
It will hurt to see sand's brown and dust of horses.   苦見塵沙黃
                              [10544]

    Heptasyllabic "old-style" poems, including heptasyllabic songs, occu-
py a much larger proportion of Li Ch'i's collection than is usual—thirty-
five out of one hundred and twenty-four poems. It was from this group
that post-T'ang anthologists selected most of the pieces they considered
representative of Li Ch'i's work. Most of Li Ch'i's heptasyllabic songs
used traditional material associated with the form—*yüeh-fu* themes and
yung-wu—but Li Ch'i also followed the T'ien-pao fashion of using the
form in occasional poetry. This use of the heptasyllabic songs antedated
the T'ien-pao, but it became common only in that reign. Li Ch'i's heptasyllabic songs manifest the T'ien-pao fascination with the exotica, with
shifting extremes, and with the intrusion of the supernatural into the
human world.
    The poem on music is a good index of the fictional imagination in
Chinese poetry. As music is basically a nonrepresentational art, the poet
who sought to describe a musical performance was compelled to resort
to modal corellatives, scenes whose mood corresponded to the mood of
the music. Shen Ch'üan-ch'i's "Thunder-rumble Song" was one of the
first typically T'ang treatments of a musical performance, and it has a
verve rare in K'ai-yüan poems on the theme.[4] Wang Ch'ang-ling's "Hearing

a Flute on the River" was a subdued work in which the mood evoked was closely tied to frontier poetry and the incongruity of its performance in the South. In the following poem Li Ch'i begins with such conventional associations, but soon the music becomes a series of imaginary scenes in the mind of the poet, and these scenes show a speculative freedom that goes far beyond the fixed associations of the musical genre.

Hearing Tung T'ing-lan Play the Nomad Pipe Songs: I Tell About It in This Piece Playfully Sent to Grand Secretary Fang Kuan	聽董大彈胡笳聲 兼語弄寄房給事
Long ago the lady Ts'ai Yen composed songs for the nomad pipes,	蔡女昔造胡笳聲
A full suite consisting of stanzas eight and ten:	一彈一十有八拍
Here the tears of nomads fall onto the frontier grasses,	胡人落淚向邊草
And the heart of the Chinese envoy breaks facing the homeward traveler.	漢使斷腸對歸客
Some ancient outpost swollen with weeds, its beacon fires cold,	古戍蒼蒼烽火寒
A vastness of steppelands sunk in gloom, where snow flies white.	大荒陰沈飛雪白
First he strikes the note *shang*, then the *chüeh*, then *yü*,	先拂商弦後角羽
And autumn leaves in the circling wastes tremble, rattle, break loose.	四郊秋葉驚摵摵
You, Master Tung, Have reached that godlike vision—	董夫子　通神明
Deep in the mountains, lurking and listening, there come the sprites and goblins.	深山竊聽來妖精
It may be fast, it may be slow with the movement of his hand,	言遲更速皆應手
It seems to turn back, it seems to go as though with a heart of its own.	將往復旋如有情
In empty mountain all species of birds scatter, then gather again,	空山百鳥散還合
Clouds drifting for a thousand miles, the shadow and the brightness.	萬里浮雲陰且晴
The bitter cry in the night when the fledgling goose loses the flock,	嘶酸雛雁失羣夜
The shattering voice of the nomad child longing for his mother.	斷絕胡兒戀母聲
The rivers still their waves, And birds too cease their songs; A tribe of Uchu nomads, their homeland far away,	川爲靜其波 鳥亦罷其鳴 烏珠部落家鄉遠

Dust and sand around Lhasa,
   from which bitter wailing rises. 邏娑沙塵哀怨生

The dark and somber tune changes,
   suddenly gusting and spattering, 幽陰變調忽飄灑

A steady wind blows the forest,
   rain sends tiles crashing, 長風吹林雨墮瓦

Cascades leap in the howling gale,
   fly to the tips of the trees, 迸泉颯颯飛木末

Deer in the wilderness cry out
   and run beside the hall. 野鹿呦呦走堂下

The bastions of Ch'ang-an
   touch the palace's east wall, 長安城連東掖垣

And the Pool of Phoenixes faces
   the blue-chain-patterned gate. 鳳凰池對青瑣門

A great genius who cast from him
   all glory and all fame, 高才脫略名與利

You at whom evening of day I hope to see
   come to me lute in arm. 日夕望君抱琴至

[06366]

When heptasyllabic songs were used as occasional poems, it was appropriate to append a brief section carrying the occasional message. The 'palace's east wall (gate)'' was a kenning for the Chancellory, of which Fang Kuan was the grand secretary. The "Pool of Phoenixes" stood for the Secretariat, where presumably Li Ch'i was employed. The last couplet suggests either that Fang Kuan or Li Ch'i himself hopes for a visit from Tung T'ing-lan. The traditions of the heptasyllabic song were not always amenable to the social occasions of T'ang poetry, and often, as here, the occasional message hangs incongruously at the end of an otherwise unified poem.

   A fascination with personality—often the eccentric personality— pervades both Li Ch'i's pentasyllabic and heptasyllabic "old-style" verse. In such character sketches, Li Ch'i most closely approaches the work of Li Po, whose character sketch "To Meng Hao-jan" has appeared earlier. If Wang Ch'ang-ling complicated character typology by indirection of the evidence revealing character, many other poets paradoxically sought the individual in a stereotype—the eccentric.

   The character sketch became the form in which to present the eccentric. In the High T'ang the character sketch was closely related to Wei and Chin poetry on exemplary figures, such as two poem series by T'ao Ch'ien on ancient worthies, the *Yung p'in-shih* 詠貧士 and the *Yung san-lang* 詠三良. During the age of court poetry this form fell into relative disuse; it was at best a dully homiletic poetry. During his exile in the mid-720s Wang Wei was one of the first High T'ang poets to rehabilitate the form, writing three biographical sketches on local worthies of Chi-chou (05853–55). But Wang Wei never fully developed the form, and one of his few later character sketches was addressed to Li Ch'i, perhaps suggesting Li Ch'i's association with the form (05788). The character sketch was also closely related to the purely typological poetry also developing in the K'ai-yüan; for example, Ch'u Kuang-hsi's series on bucolic types. Though he clearly preferred the character sketch, Li Ch'i did write one such typological poem, "The Fisherman," and this was singled out for special praise by Yin Fan (06295; see also Ch'u Kuang-hsi's and Kao Shih's versions, pp. 66–67.)

Though the High T'ang eccentric was a stereotype with an iconography of appropriate actions, eccentricity was implicitly individuation from the social norm. The eccentric was defined by what he did and his attitude. One might visit the recluse, not find him in, and experience the recluse through his surroundings. But there was no substitute for the human presence of the eccentric.

In the following poem the great calligrapher Chang Hsü does not simply inhabit a landscape poem—he acts. His actions may now seem more comic than eccentric, but they were the kinds of actions associated with eccentricity, just as there were fixed gestures that signified elegance, sensitivity, or resignation.

To Chang Hsü 贈張旭

Master Chang has an inborn craving for wine, 張公性嗜酒
Free and easy, no care for the world's business. 豁達無所營
Snow-white hair, total master of cursive and script, 皓首窮草隸
Named by the age "Genius of Great Lake." 時稱太湖精
Bareheaded he rests on his folding chair, 露頂據胡牀
Gives forth three or four long bellows, 長叫三五聲
And as his mood comes, daubs ink on white walls, 興來灑素壁
Waving his brush like a shooting star. 揮筆如流星
Round his low cottage the winds moan, 下舍風蕭條
Winter grasses fill his yard. 寒草滿戶庭
Do you wonder about his possessions? 問家何所有
To him things of this life are floating weeds. 生事如浮萍
In his left hand he nibbles a crab claw, 左手持蟹螯
In his right holds alchemical tracts, 右手持丹經
And he stares wide-eyed at the river of stars, 瞪目視宵漢
Then none can tell if he's drunk or sober. 不知醉與醒
His guest all come, take their proper seats 諸賓且方坐
As the dawn sun looks down on eastern walls: 旭日臨東城
He serves Yangtze fish wrapped in lotus leaves, 荷葉裹江魚
In white bowls heaps the sweet-scented rice. 白甌貯香秔

Petty salary is beneath his concern,   微祿心不屑
His spirit roams free to the world's confines.   放神於八紘
For those of the age who don't recognize him—   時人不識者
This is the immortal—Master An-ch'i.   即是安期生
                                   [06300]

The Early T'ang court poet effaced himself in his poem; the objects of his praise were defined by the social position they held and the appurtenances of that position. By the end of the K'ai-yüan the new interest in the individual had largely supplanted the older social values. It was just a short step from character sketches by Li Ch'i and Li Po, from the attempt to portary "the individual," to the poet who sought to *be* "the individual" —Li Po.

8

李白

Li Po
A New Concept of Genius

A hundred poems per gallon of wine—
    that's Li Po,
Who sleeps in the taverns
    of the market of Ch'ang-an.
The Son of Heaven summoned him, and he
    couldn't stagger on the boat,
Said, "Your servant is indeed
    an immortal in his wine."

from Tu Fu, "Eight Drinking Immortals" [10520]

In four lines Tu Fu succinctly enumerated the essential elements of the accepted image of Li Po, an image that Li himself labored to project: he writes quickly and voluminously; he drinks heavily; he does as he pleases and shows a cheerful disregard for custom and authority; and he is an immortal, different from ordinary men and privileged to act differently. No other T'ang poet, including Tu Fu, devoted so much of his energy to describing and projecting his identity, signaling to the reader his uniqueness both as a poet and as a personality.

Beside his pre-eminence as a poet, Li Po left this one great legacy to future poets: an interest in personal and poetic identity. Mere excellence was no longer sufficient; the poet had to be both excellent and unique. Thus, later critics admonished aspiring poets to imitate Tu Fu rather than Li Po: in their eyes the two poets were equal in stature, but Tu Fu's genius seemed somehow more imitable than that of Li Po. The rationale for directing young poets away from the model of Li Po was that Li's art was perfectly natural, uncontrollable, almost divinely inspired. But the real reason that Li Po was inimitable was that Li Po's poetry primarily concerned Li Po: its goal was to embody a unique personality, either through the persona of the poem or through an implied creator behind the poem. Imitation necessarily failed, because it contradicted the very reason for the style's existence.

From the very beginning of his career, Li Po was indeed very different from other poets. In the late 710s a young T'ai-yüan Wang named Wang Wei was being introduced into the courts of the T'ang princes. Playing the traditional role of the precocious young poet, he dazzled them with his faultless mastery of the courtly style. This Wang Wei was already developing a private dimension in his poetry, but his gestures of personal identity were bound negatively to that shining world for which his family background and literary training had prepared him. At about the same time, far to the west in Szechwan, a poet of much the same age but of a far more questionable background had gone to visit a recluse on Tai-t'ien Mountain and not found him in:

A dog barks amid the sound of waters,   犬吠水聲中
Peach blossoms dark, bearing dew.   桃花帶露濃
Where trees are thickest, sometimes see a deer,   樹深時見鹿
And when noon strikes the ravine, hear no bell.   溪午不聞鐘
Bamboo of wilderness split through blue haze,   野竹分青靄
A cascade in flight, hung from an emerald peak.   飛泉挂碧峯
But no one knows where you've gone—   無人知所去
Disappointed, I linger among these few pines.   愁倚兩三松
                    [08680]

Young Li Po has a good grasp of the rules of tonal balance, and like another young Szechwanese poet before him, he aims for certain conventionally "poetic" effects, such as using the verb "splits" (*fen* 分) to describe a disruption in visual continuity.[1] The verb "hung" (*kua* 挂) is a permissible, if somewhat inelegant variation on the more common "suspended" (*hsüan* 懸) applied to a cascade (cf. 03744.2). With a few important reservations, the aristocrats of the capital would probably have found this an adequate performance.

The shortcomings that conservative readers would have found in Li Po's poem would have been traced to Li's poetic education, which was quite different than that of young Wang Wei. Li violates basic decorum by crowding his short poem with too many trees and at least two streams. A more serious "fault" would have been found in Li's opening couplet; it upsets the balance that should exist between the parts of a poem. This is not the "proper" way to begin a poem; any capital-trained poet would know that a poem should begin with the general scene or an indication of the occasion. Li's abrupt "barking ' unbalances the poem and focuses too much attention on a first line that is simple but aggressively brilliant; the rest of the poem trails limply behind its brilliance. When one visits a hermit, of course, it is entirely proper to find some evidence of the hermit's presence in the landscape, but "barking" is simply too noisy, and, if it must be included, it should be placed where the "evidence trope" belongs, in the middle couplets, where its ingenuity can be muted by a parallel.

This was a poet who surprised his readers and violated their sense of poetic order and decorum. Poets had always taken pride in writing "surprising" lines, as much as their readers had enjoyed being surprised, but such delights occurred within clearly defined boundaries of taste. Many centuries of literary experience had created these boundaries to preserve the balance and unity of a poem. But Li Po stepped outside of these boundaries and found readers that loved his effrontery. The dog's barking heard through the splash of the stream was only moderately "strange"; as Li Po himself pushed back ever farther the boundaries of poetic decorum, he found that he had to go to ever greater lengths to achieve the "strangeness" that became his trademark. Writing of Li Po's "Hard Roads to Shu" in 753, Yin Fan was to call it "strangeness on top of strangeness" (奇之又奇).

Li Po's poem on visiting the hermit was marked by other "faults": it was utterly lacking in allusions, ornamentation, and elegant variation. The ability to use allusions and ornament gracefully was a matter of study. A line like "A dog barks amid the sound of waters" was too plain, too direct. The young poet had talent but he was unpolished and untutored: this was the verdict of one of the greatest patrons and court poets of the early K'ai-yüan, Su T'ing, recently banished from court and demoted to governor of Yi-chou in Szechwan. In a letter, Li Po proudly recounted his meeting with Su T'ing and Su's verdict on his work: 'The lad has a wealth of natural talent and practices constantly. If only he broadens himself with learning, he could be the equal of Ssu-ma Hsiang-ju. Though his mastery of style is yet imperfect, I see in him the potential for greatness."[2]

If such a meeting did occur, it must have had a profound effect on the young poet. Su T'ing was one of the foremost literary and political figures of the day; Li Po was an unknown whose social background was, at best, dubious. Li claimed descent from Li Kao, the fifth-century ruler of a semi-barbarian kingdom in northwest China. In itself this claim would have been little to boast of, but it happened that the T'ang royal house claimed descent from the same prince and, through him, to the ill-fated Han general Li Kuang. Thus, Li Po could have the effrontery to refer to members of the royal clan as "cousins."

It is important to remember that because Li Po's family was not well known and was based far in the provinces, accounts of his family background probably came from the poet himself. It surely was Li Po who informed his biographers that his family had been banished to Central Asia and had only recently returned to China and "resumed" their surname Li. All this has the marks of a genealogy created for convenience, and Li Po's family is suspected of having Iranian or Turkish origins.[3] Li Po's father seems to have been neither landowner nor official, and he may well have been a merchant. Meng Hao-jan may be considered an outsider to the circle of capital poets because he was of a regional landholding family and had only indirect relations with the higher levels of capital society. But Li Po was a true outsider, a man with no connections whatsoever, a man who would have to rely solely on his native talent to succeed in the capital.

The background of Li Po's family may have been murky in reality and glorious in the imagination, but in his upbringing Li Po was a native of Szechwan. T'ang poetry had none of the strong regional divisions that we find in later dynasties: the major regional distinction was between the areas around the two capitals and everywhere else. But two sections were beginning to develop regional poetic identities: the Southeast and Szechwan. The situation in Szechwan was peculiar: on the one hand, it possessed a brilliant literary past, having produced the most famous *fu* writers of the Han, Yang Hsiung and Ssu-ma Hsiang-ju. On the other hand, Szechwan had played no significant role in the history of *shih* poetry, the dominant poetic form in the T'ang. Thus, it was quite natural that a poet from Szechwan, like Ch'en Tzu-ang several decades before Li Po, would associate himself with the literary past when his work was rejected by the literary arbiters of the court. He could recall that in the past being from Szechwan had been an asset to a literary career and not a rustic liability: *fu-ku* opposition to court poetry was a natural response.

Both of the great Szechwanese poets, Ssu-ma Hsiang-ju and Ch'en Tzu-ang, became important models for Li Po. During his youth Ch'en Tzu-ang was reputed to have been a rash bravo who didn't begin literary study until his late teens; similarly, Li Po boasted that in his teens he had been a master swordsman and had killed several men. Another anecdote about Ch'en Tzu-ang is that when he first arrived in the capital, he bought and smashed a very expensive lute to attract the attention of capital residents to his poetry; Li Po told proudly of his ability to toss away a fortune on a whim. Together the two poets were acting and boasting in the context of a set of values that differed radically from the values of the aristocratic court poet, the serene recluse, or the Confucian moralist. This set of values was related to the figure of the "bravo" or "knight-errant," but more generally, it involved expansive, generous behavior and exaggerated gestures associated with spontaneous violation of social norms of behavior.[4]

Generosity and rash violence had aristocratic associations in the stereotype of the young nobleman. In the K'ai-yüan, the spontaneous and eccentric genius was becoming a popular figure, represented by men like Chang Hsü. The combination of the two types was not necessarily associated with Szechwan, but anecdotes about Ch'en Tzu-ang, Li Po, and others do suggest that Szechwanese were often associated with some variation on these values. It may have been that Szechwan was in fact a less stable region than central China, and that violent behavior or the boasting menace of violent, unpredictable behavior was an asset there. Whether or not he was assuming a conscious pose is impossible to tell, but Li Po did identify himself strongly with these values, and they were the values of an outsider.

As the most eminent example of the rash, eccentric Szechwanese literary figure, Ch'en Tzu-ang was a model for Li Po, and in Li Po's *Ku-feng*, Ch'en's poetic model was also important. But Ch'en's importance to Li Po as a poet was overshadowed by the example of Ssu-ma Hsiang-ju, who became virtually an obsession in Li Po's work. During the T'ang, Ssu-ma Hsiang-ju had a double image. On the one hand, Ssu-ma Hsiang-ju was the figure of popular legend who eloped with Cho Wen-chün and kept a tavern with her in Ch'eng-tu until her wealthy father relented and provided the couple with an income; he was the empathetic poet who wrote the *Ch'ang-men fu* on behalf of the abandoned imperial consort A-ch'iao, through which she regained imperial favor; he was the fickle husband who left Cho Wen-chün for another woman and to whom Cho wrote "The Song of White Hair" 白頭吟 as a reproach.

On the other hand, Ssu-ma Hsiang-ju was the most famous *fu* poet of the Han: his works overwhelmed readers with their verbal exuberance and speculative imagination. Important in the T'ang image of Ssu-ma Hsiang-ju as a poet were comments preserved in the *Miscellany of the Western Capital* 西京雜記; these are now considered spurious, but they would have been thought genuine in the T'ang. In the *Miscellany* Ssu-ma Hsiang-ju is quoted as having said, "The consciousness (*hsin* 心, "heart"/"mind") of the *fu* poet encompasses the entire universe; this is accomplished within—it cannot be formulated and passed on."[5] This was a grand and cosmic conception of the nature of literary art, with parallels in Ts'ao P'i's *Lun-wen* and Lu Chi's *Wen-fu*; the poet's consciousness was linked in a sympathetic resonance with the order of the universe, and that order was embodied in the literary art. Such a view of literature differed sharply from the *fu-ku* view of art as an expression of cultural order and social morality, but like *fu-ku*, it provided for poetry some first principle, some reason for being, which was singularly lacking in court poetry and its successor, capital poetry. Another comment from the *Miscellany* attributed to Yang Hsiung is even more important: "Ssu-ma Hsiang-ju's *fu* do not seem to come from the human world. This is precisely because he had attained the ultimate in 'divine transformation.'"[6] Both comments from the *Miscellany* point to the transcendent nature of art and the artist. To be, in Su T'ing's words, "the equal of Ssu-ma Hsiang-ju" meant to be a cosmic genius.

Originally associated with Ssu-ma Hsiang-ju, such a lofty conception of poetry and the poet was to become an essential part of Li Po's self-image. It was a self-image that unified Li's fascination with the cult of immortality and his vocation as a poet. Su T'ing had told him he was to be "the equal of Ssu-ma Hsiang-ju," and when Li Po arrived in the capital, the famous Ho Chih-chang called him a "banished immortal," an immortal who had misbehaved in Heaven and had been punished by spending a lifetime on Earth. In Ch'en Tzu-ang the heroic, eccentric Szechwanese persona had been at odds with his stern moral posture as a *fu-ku* poet and had eventually succumbed to it. But Li Po had found a concept of poetry that could comfortably accommodate his Szechwanese persona: he possessed a divine nature that legitimized wild eccentricity in both poetry and behavior. He was, as later critics called him, the "poet immortal," who could violate the rules because he was beyond them; he saw his talent, like that of Ssu-ma Hsiang-ju, as not of "the human world." Out of this heady liberation from everyday humanity came Li Po's multiple guises: the wild drinker, the womanizer, the man who cheerfully disregards authority and social decorum, the poet who dashes off verses without thinking, the spontaneous genius.

Li Po was born in 701. His exact birthplace is uncertain, but it may have been in a semi-Sinicized region of Central Asia. Early in Li's childhood the family moved to Szechwan. If we are to believe the stories Li Po told of his youth—and we should be very wary of them—he had already acquired a certain amount of local fame as a poet and recluse by the time he left Szechwan in the mid-720s. Then Li went traveling down the Yangtze, visiting famous spots and trying to make connections with various notables. The most noteworthy figure that Li Po met during this period was the Taoist master Ssu-ma Ch'eng-chen.

By 730 Li Po had ceased his wanderings and settled in An-lu, north of the Yangtze in modern Hupei. A few years later he married the daughter of a local family whose ancestor Hsü Yü-shih had been a minister during Kao-tsung's reign. By 730 the family's influence was, at best, only local. Li Po possessed an overweening desire to provide himself with an illustrious background and aura of nobility, and to accomplish this he clearly was not unwilling to shade or bend the truth. This admonishes us to regard all Li Po's comments on himself and his relatives with a certain skepticism, but it also suggests how necessary such family background was for recognition and social advancement; it is most comprehensible in the context of an unspoken social prominence in the backgrounds of many more reserved poets.

Thus, Li Po married the daughter of a locally prominent family whose ancestor had once been minister: the way Li Po himself recounted the episode, he had just finished touring the famous Yün-meng Marsh, celebrated by his "countryman, Ssu-ma Hsiang-ju," when "I was summoned by the family of Minister Hsü, who gave me to wife his granddaughter, and I rested from my travels there."[7] In fact, Hsü Yü-shih had been long dead, and it is extremely unlikely that any "granddaughter" of his could have been under sixty. In the same letter Li makes the anomalous and mendacious claim that his family was originally from Chin-ling, the former capital of the Southern Dynasties; he further claims that on his travels through the South, every time he saw a nobleman down on his luck, he would give away a fortune to help him. This gesture presumably represented his feeling of commiseration with men of aristocratic birth who "like himself" had come down in the world.

The truth was that An-chou was an undistinguished country town and that Li Po was an obscure person whose greatest hope of advancement lay in convincing others of his grand vision of himself. Basing himself in An-chou, Li made a number of side trips. The most interesting was a short trip to Hsiang-yang, where he met Meng Hao-jan and the influential Han Chao-tsung. To Meng Hao-jan, Li addressed the ecstatic praise poem quoted earlier, but the old poet seems to have paid Li little attention. There is also a story that Li affronted Han Chao-tsung on introduction by not paying the governor the proper respects; Li is supposed to have compensated for his rudeness by the quip "Wine makes its own manners." A similar story about Meng Hao-jan and Han Chao-tsung casts suspicion on the incident, but even if the Li Po version did occur, Li gained nothing from his wit.

In the late 730s or first years of the 740s, Li Po left An-chou to resume his wanderings, probably hoping to build a reputation. His fortunes changed when he met the Taoist master Wu Yün on Mount T'ai. Wu was sufficiently impressed by Li Po to arrange an introduction for Li when Wu was summoned to the court in 742. Li managed either to impress or amuse Hsüantsung, and he was given a post in the Han-lin Academy. The Han-lin was a special bureau outside the usual government table of organization; entrance was by imperial appointment only, and many of its members were in close and frequent attendance on the emperor. The Han-lin's function and composition changed greatly through the course of Hsüan-tsung's reign, but it contained everything from classical scholars and literary men to diviners, doctors, and entertainers. Thus, in a very short time, Li Po found himself close to the emperor, having completely circumvented the usual channels of family, official patronage, and the *chin-shih* examination. Li Po's function in the Han-lin Academy seems to have been to draft imperial documents, but he also probably wrote poems to be sung at inner court occasions when members of the imperial harem, notably Yang Kuei-fei, were present.

If Li's inner court poems are genuine, their style is very different from the ornamental style of court banquet poetry, which was reserved for more formal court occasions. In honor of Yang Kuei-fei and the peonies planted in the palace garden, Li Po was supposed to have composed three songs to the *ch'ing-p'ing* melody. These were sung to the imperial couple by Li Kuei-nien, the emperor's chief musician. The following is the first of the series:

Clouds call to mind her robes,　　　　　　　　　雲想衣裳花想容
　　the flowers recall her face.
Spring breezes brush the railing,　　　　　　　　春風拂檻露華濃
　　dew full on the blossoms.
If you don't see her in gods' abode,　　　　　　　若非羣玉山頭見
　　on the mountain Hoard of Jade,
You can surely meet her in moonlight,　　　　　　會向瑤臺月下逢
　　there on the Terrace of Jasper.
　　　　　　　　　[08019]

The wine, Li Kuei-nien's singing, and Yang Kuei-fei's plump body may have made this very stimulating for Hsüan-tsung, but taken purely as a piece of poetry, the song is rather light fare. It elaborates the idea that "Yang Kuei-fei is like a flower and a goddess." Few compliments to female beauty are more platitudinous.

Numerous delightful anecdotes survive concerning Li Po's period in court: they tell of his habitual drinking, his eccentricity, and his lack of ceremonial respect when appearing before the emperor. Here it is impossible to separate fact from fiction. A certain amount of insouciance was not only permitted to someone in Li Po's position, it was positively admired. Li Po's reputation as an "interesting person" certainly was an important factor in Hsüan-tsung's fondness for him, and had Li become suddenly obsequious or staunchly moralistic, it is likely that he would have found himself quickly out of favor. Both in and out of court, Li Po's erratic behavior was part of his chosen role, but it was not, as some biographers have seen it, an indication of a genuine disdain for position. Li wanted recognition: he showed no unwillingness to come to court and complained bitterly when he was forced to leave it. Wildness was expected of him, but he did nothing deliberately to provoke the emperor. However, T'ang readers took the same delight in indiscretion that the emperor did, and anecdotes of Li Po's behavior were embellished and exaggerated.

One famous anecdote was told first by Li's friend and first editor Wei Hao 魏顥: Li had been drinking at a nobleman's house when he was summoned to court to draft an edict; Li arrived at the palace half drunk and dashed off the edict without a draft. This basic story, in all its credible modesty, reappeared, altered and embellished, in several later sources: the emperor was "testing" Li Po's poetic ability; the powerful eunuch Kao Li-shih was commanded to remove the poet's slippers; and so forth. Our rich sources for Li Po the legend overwhelm our meager sources for Li Po the mortal man, and Li's own comments contribute far more to the former than to the latter. But for the literary scholar the legend is ultimately far more important than the man, for much of Li Po's poetry was dedicated to the service and glorification of the legendary image.

The imperial favor that Li Po enjoyed rested on very insecure foundations: someone appointed on imperial whim could be dismissed on imperial whim. In 744 Li was either dismissed from court or was driven to resign by the pressure of his enemies. One should remember that Li Po was virtually unknown in the literary world of the capital until 742, and that in all he spent less than three years in court and in the capital. As a Han-lin functionary, he was outside the vast web of social relations that bound together literary men in the bureaucracy. Clearly Li Po attracted the interest and admiration of many literary men, young and old, but like his position in court, his popularity rested on foundations less stable than those of Wang Wei or Wang Ch'ang-ling.

Leaving Chang-an, Li Po went east, first to Lo-yang and then downriver to Pien-chou. It was on this trip that Li met Kao Shih and young Tu Fu. For ten years Li wandered from place to place, living off his reputation as a poet and eccentric.

When the An Lu-shan Rebellion broke out in 755, Li Po was in the Southeast, and he wisely stayed there, safely out of harm's way. True to character, he began to claim that he had foreseen the rebellion and had tried to prevent it. It was not long, however, before Li Po found himself in trouble: after Hsüan-tsung abdicated, Su-tsung deputed his brother, the prince of Yung, to take command of the lower Yangtze region. The prince had plans of his own and soon organized a military force that he thought sufficient to set up an independent state in the region. On his way down the Yangtze to take Yang-chou, the prince picked up Li Po and kept him on board as the literary adornment of his tiny court. At Yang-chou the prince's army was routed, and Li Po escaped in the general flight. The extent of Li Po's treason is unclear: Li himself claimed that he had been a prisoner and had escaped before the expedition reached Yang-chou; however, Li also wrote poems for the expedition that pretend, at least, that it was under the command of the central government. It is possible that Li was naïve enough to believe this, but more likely it was the polite fiction of a prisoner or collaborator.

Soon after the prince of Yung's army was destroyed early in 757, Li was arrested and imprisoned at Hsün-yang. Later he was given a conditional release, and he resumed his wanderings, constantly petitioning for the imperial pardon that he finally received in 759. He spent his last years traveling through the Yangtze region, vainly hoping to procure a post in the new government. In 762 the poet died, having entrusted his writings to a friend, the great calligrapher Li Yang-ping 李陽冰.

One of Li's earliest works had been an exuberant, visionary *fu* on the P'eng, the Great Bird described in the first chapter of the *Chuang-tzu*. The P'eng was a poetic and philosophical symbol of a greatness that transcended the limits of mortal understanding. The bird appeared again in Li Po's deathbed poem as a metaphor for the poet. The vital exuberance of the Great Bird in the youthful *fu* was gone, and in its place appeared a bitter pride:

The Great Bird flies/	大鵬飛兮振八裔
shakes world's edge with wingbeats,	
Then broken midsky/	中天摧兮力不濟
his might cannot save him.	
His aura will linger still/	餘風激兮萬世
myriad ages,	
He roamed to Fu-sang/	遊扶桑兮掛左袂
there caught his left sleeve.	
If you, born later, comprehend this,	後人得之傳此
pass it on—	
Now Confucius has perished,	仲尼亡乎誰爲出涕
who is there to weep for it?	
[08147]	

In this Ch'u song the Fu-sang was the mythical tree that grew at the eastern limit of the world; there the cosmic poet, whose encompassing consciousness circled the universe, brushed his sleeve on passing.

It is difficult to follow the growth of Li Po's poetic reputation through his lifetime and through the latter part of the eighth century. Li had his devotees during the T'ien-pao, but no one thought of him as a major poet, much less *the* major poet of the T'ien-pao, as he was later considered. Li's poetry was well represented in the *Ho-yüeh ying-ling chi* of 753, but Yin Fan did not accord to him the superlative evaluations that he generously applied to several other poets. In the *Kuo-hsiu chi*, mainly concerned with tonal and sound values in poetry, Li Po was not represented at all; the *Kuo-hsiu chi* was compiled in the late 750s or early 760s and represents the postrebellion shift in capital taste away from the bolder style of the T'ien-pao.

There was little mention or imitation of Li Po's poetry during the decades immediately following his death. Then, in the last two decades of the eighth century, some interest revived in his work, particularly in the Southeast. By the early ninth century the writers around Han Yü and Po Chü-yi considered both Li Po and Tu Fu the greatest and most exemplary poets of the High T'ang. Since that time Li Po's shared pre-eminence with Tu Fu has been virtually unquestioned, and relative evaluation of the two poets has grown into a popular critical pastime, particularly in the twentieth century.

As with the works of Meng Hao-jan, there are serious textual problems in Li Po's poetry. Shortly after Li's death there were two editions of his works in circulation, the *Ts'ao-t'ang chi* 草堂集, edited by Li Yang-ping, and the older *Li Han-lin chi* 李翰林集, edited by Wei Hao. We know virtually nothing of the history of these two editions until they came together in Sung printed editions. The two collections probably differed both in the texts and in the poems included. Sung editions also claimed to have found a number of "lost" poems. The greatest virtue of Chinese editorial policy was also its greatest vice: every poem with every variant was included. In the case of variants, editors were forced to make choices, but in most cases their choices were determined by a single source text. In the case of whole poems, the patently spurious would usually be included beside the indisputably genuine. In addition to poems that may be spurious, Li Po's collection also contains different versions of the same poem, sometimes under the same title and sometimes with a different title. These may represent different drafts, differences between the first two editions, versions taken from anthologies, or modification of poems for singing. As a result, many scholars have been understandably skeptical about Li Po's collection as a whole. The famous nineteenth-century scholar and poet Kung Tzu-chen 龔自珍 went so far as to admit only 122 of Li's over 1100 poems as genuine.[8] The situation is probably not as bad as Kung Tzu-chen believed, but one should exercise caution with poems whose authenticity is in doubt.[9]

Yüeh-fu and "songs" (*ko-hsing* 歌行) make up about one-fifth of Li Po's collection in its present form. The "songs" are mostly written in the *yüeh-fu* manner, but they differ from traditional *yüeh-fu* in two ways: first, the "songs" were not written to traditional *yüeh-fu* titles (though some *yüeh-fu* were not either); second, the songs tend to be more occasional than the *yüeh-fu*. The second distinction is not hard and fast, but it is probably the more significant in the T'ang perception of genres. During the T'ang, Li Po was best known for his *yüeh-fu* and songs: not only were they the most widely anthologized of his works, they also occurred in anecdotes and comments about his poetry far in excess of their proportions in his present collection.

Li Po's contemporaries found his *yüeh-fu* and songs new and exciting, and readers of Chinese poetry have always felt their uniqueness. We know very little about how individual poems were read, classified, and evaluated in the eighth century, but in the following progression of comments, we can see something of the changes in taste that were occurring in the first half of the century.

Both poems are equally matched in craftsmanship, but Shen Ch'üan-ch'i's last couplet goes:

> This humble courtier would carve rotting stuff,
> And is ashamed to perceive the timber of Camphor Terrace.

In my opinion, the energy of his lines comes to a stop in this. But Sung Chih-wen's poem closes:

> I do not grieve that the bright moon is gone,
> For the pearl that shines by night comes in its stead.

This ends his poem on the upbeat.
> [The court lady Shang-kuan Wan-erh, giving her judgment at a poetry competition in 709]

At his leisure Meng Hao-jan visited the Imperial Library and under an autumn moon and the recently cleared skies, a poetry party was held there. Meng wrote a couplet that went:

> Faint clouds pale the river of stars,
> Sparse raindrops drip the pawlonia trees.

All the party sighed at its perfect lucidity.

> [Meng Hao-jan appearing before Chang Chiu-ling and Wang Wei in the early 730s: from Wang Shih-yüan's preface]

When he [Li Po] was in Ch'ang-an [ca. 742] the director of the Imperial Library, Ho Chih-chang, named him the "banished immortal," and when he read Li's "Song of the Roosting Crows," Ho said, "This poem could make gods and ghosts weep."
> [Fan Ch'uan-cheng's tomb inscription for Li Po]

Shang-kuan Wan-erh's comments looked first to the formal requirements of craft and then to the decorum of the positive ending: poems were not described but rather judged in relation to some knowable standard of taste. Description and evaluation exist in about equal proportions in the response to Meng Hao-jan's couplet: the couplet was *ch'ing-chüeh* (清絶), "perfect lucidity," understood in terms of the mood it created, however elusive that mood might be to define. But when the response to a poem was that it could "make gods and ghosts weep," we are confronting new literary values that are different in kind from the two earlier comments. Such a comment was directed to the affective power of the poem, not in a category of mood but in degree: it tried to account for something that seemed to transcend the usual limits of literature. The "sigh" accorded to Meng Hao-jan's couplet was an affective recognition of great talent, but it remained essentially within the decorous boundaries of poetry. To speak of "making gods and ghosts weep" was a recognition of genius, and genius demanded a response more than the merely human. Ho's praise of "Song of the Roosting Crows" was not unique: in Li Ch'i's song, Tung T'ing-lan's music had drawn the minor divinities of the landscape to listen from their hiding places. T'ien-pao readers sought, and Li Po proudly provided, genius that went beyond the old boundaries of art.

After Li Po became known in the literary world of the capital, the capital poets politely avoided mentioning either Li or his work: their aesthetics were more conservative. But Li Po did capture the imaginations of readers outside that social web of poets: old eccentrics, like Ho Chih-chang, and impressionable younger poets, like Ts'en Shen and Tu Fu. As Ho Chih-chang's praise of "Song of the Roosting Crows" represented literary values different from those of the capital poets, so the song itself was altogether different from the restrained austerity of a Wang Wei.

Song of the Roosting Crows	烏棲曲
The time when the crows are roosting on the terrace of Ku-su	姑蘇臺上烏棲時
Is when, in the Wu king's palace, Hsi Shih is growing drunk.	吳王宮裏醉西施
The songs of Wu and dances of Ch'u— their pleasure had not reached its height,	吳歌楚舞歡未畢
As the green hills were about to swallow a half side of the sun.	青山欲啣半邊日
From waterclock more and more drips away, from the basin of gold with its silver arrow,	銀箭金壺漏水多
And they rise and they watch the autumn moon sink down in the river's waves,	起看秋月墜江波
As in the east the sun grows higher, what shall their joy be then?	東方漸高奈樂何

[07929]

Every contemporary reader knew the legend, knew that while the king of Wu was carousing with his lovely consort Hsi Shih, his kingdom was about to fall to the forces of Yüeh.[10]

To a reader of the early 740s there would have been many things new and startling about this poem. First, Li Po possessed a capability that relatively few Chinese poets before him had in any great degree—a fictional

imagination. In contemporary poetry the quatrain vignettes of Wang
Ch'ang-ling and Ch'u Kuang-hsi were closest to Li's "Song of the Roosting
Crows," but they may postdate it. To treat a historical theme, most poets
before the 740s would turn to the *huai-ku*, a meditation occasioned by a
visit to an ancient site. The *huai-ku* might indeed contain a few lines of
speculation on what the site had been like in the past, but the center of the
poem was inevitably the poet's present: what *he* saw, what *he* felt, and
(reducing the imaginative act to a mental process) what *he* imagined.

   To write fictional poetry in the seventh century, a poet had to use the
stylized components of the traditional *yüeh-fu* themes. Beginning in the
last decade of the seventh century, there was an ever-increasing interest in
the fictional imagination and a growing freedom in the way poets used it.
It appeared in some of the visionary allegories of Ch'en Tzu-ang's *Kan-yü*
and in the heptasyllabic songs of the early eighth century. Later it appeared
in Wang Wei's youthful "Ballad of Peach Blossom Spring" (05880) and in
poetry on music. But the dreamlike fragments of "Song of the Roosting
Crows" went beyond any of Li's predecessors. Wang Wei's treatment of
the Hsi Shih legend offers a striking contrast:

Voluptuous beauty is valued the world over,	豔色天下重
So how could Hsi Shih stay long unknown?	西施寧久微
One morning, just a girl by the streams of Yüeh,	朝爲越溪女
That evening, a consort on the palace of Wu.	暮作吳宮妃
When poor she was thought no different from others,	賤日豈殊衆
When great, they realized how rare she was.	貴來方悟稀

[from 05851]

The exemplary, typological aspects of the legend, which play no role in
Li Po's poem, dominate Wang Wei's treatment. Wang Wei's exposition
is supremely rhetorical: thesis ("Voluptuous beauty ..."); specific example
("So how could Hsi Shih ..."); amplification of example in antithesis of
conditions before and after recognition (second and third couplets). In
contrast, Li Po presents fragments of a scene through the course of a night.

   A second new feature that may account for the popularity and appeal
of "Song of the Roosting Crows" is the tension between the simple, sensual
surface and its more complicated, tragic significance in terms of the Hsi Shih
legend. The royal couple's ignorance of their impending doom is represented
by a similar ignorance in the surface of the poem. It is we, the readers, who
bring tragedy to the poem. Li Po does not resolve this tension in the poem;
he does not step in to moralize, and he even resists the temptation to give
a scene of the aftermath of their fall. Instead, Li undermines the simplicity
of the royal couple's pleasure through hints that only the readers can
understand. Time is passing, and things are coming to their ends: the
waterclock is dripping out, the sun is being swallowed by the mountains,

the season is autumn, the moon is sinking into the river, and the rising sun will bring a revelation of their future.

The audience knows important elements of a narrative plot of which the protagonists are ignorant. This device is basic to drama; it forcibly calls attention to the difference between illusion and reality. It played no role in the touching gestures of the quatrain vignettes of Wang Ch'ang-ling and Ch'u Kuang-hsi, but it dominates every line of Li Po's poem. If it appeared at all in earlier Chinese poetry, it was exceedingly rare, and its impact on contemporary readers must have been tremendous. Its affective power was such that it was not appropriate to comment on the poem's technical decorum or mood. It was a poem that could "make gods and ghosts weep."

Aside From Li Po's "Song of the Roosting Crows," the poem that made the greatest impression on his contemporaries was Li's "Hard Roads to Shu" 蜀道難 (07926). There had never been anything like it in Chinese poetry. Yin Fan called it a "strangeness on top of strangeness" and filiated it to the *Ch'u-tz'u* tradition. The filiation was appropriate for several reasons: first, the visual imagination was at its height in the *Ch'u-tz'u*, with its visionary flights through the cosmos, its demonic scenes, and its gods and goddesses. Second, the ritual pattern of the "Summons to the Soul" 招魂 lay just beneath the surface of "Hard Roads to Shu": as the shaman sought to persuade the soul to return to its body by vivid descriptions of the terrors that awaited in all directions, so the poet-speaker of "Hard Roads to Shu" tried to persuade the traveler to return east by hyperbolic descriptions of the horrors of the mountainous Szechwanese landscape.

It was quite proper to close an emotional poem with a decorous groan or sigh, but Li Po *began* "Hard Roads to Shu" with a most indecorous Szechwanese shriek:

Yi-hsü-hsi!!!! Sheer!! High!!!	噫吁嚱危乎高哉
The roads to Shu are hard,	蜀道之難難於上
harder than climbing the blue sky.	清天

The poem continues with hyperbolic description in wildly irregular meter, using syntactic forms that would have been considered rambling even for good prose:

Above are the high marks of peaks that	上有六龍回日之
make the six dragons turn back the sun.	高標

Nor does the poet-speaker refrain from directly addressing the audience as the traveler:

This place is so dangerous.	其險也若此
You, you poor traveler on a journey	嗟爾遠道之人
from faraway parts,	胡爲乎來哉
why on earth have you come?	

This was more lively entertainment than most readers of *yüeh-fu* were accustomed to.

Li Po clearly delighted in whatever would shock the supremely shockable sensibilities of his contemporaries. The bravo was a common enough topic in *yüeh-fu*: his courage was praised, or his life was lamented if he spent it in unrewarded service. The bravo's values were in conflict with those of the capital elite, and poets were usually careful not to point up the contradiction. Li Po not only emphasized the difference between the two sets of values (07932):

Never in his entire life
  did he read a single word

〔邊城兒〕生年
不讀一字書

he even placed the scholar at a disadvantage by comparison:

Men of learning fall short of the bravos—
White-haired they will draw their curtains,
  teach their disciples,
  and what good will it do them?

儒生不及遊俠人
白首下帷復何益

To lament "time's swift passage" was one of the oldest and most common of *yüeh-fu* topics, but Li Po would shout wildly at the charioteer of the sun and boast that he would transcend common mortality:

The Sun Rises and Sets

日出入行

The sun comes up from its nook in the east,
Seems to rise from beneath the earth,
Passes on through Heaven,
  sets once again in the western sea,
And where, oh, where, can its team of six dragons
  ever find any rest?
Its daily beginnings and endings,
  since ancient times never resting.
And man is not made of its Primal Stuff—
  how can he linger beside it long?
Plants feel no thanks for their flowering in spring's wind,
Nor do trees hate losing their leaves
  under autumn skies:
Who wields the whip that drives along
  four seasons of changes—
The rise and the ending of all things
  is just the way things are.

日出東方隈
似從地底來
歷天又入海
六龍所舍安在哉
其始與終古不息
人非元氣安得與
之久徘徊
草不謝榮於春風
木不怨落於秋天
誰揮鞭策驅四運
萬物興歇皆息然

Hsi-ho! Hsi-ho!
Why must you always drown yourself
  in those wild and reckless waves?
What power had Lu-yang

羲和　羲和
汝奚汨沒於荒淫之波
魯陽何德

That he halted your course by shaking his spear? 駐景揮戈
This perverts the Path of things, 逆道違天
   errs from Heaven's will—
So many lies and deceits! 矯誣實多
I'll wrap this Mighty Mudball of a world 吾將囊括大塊
   all up in a bag
And be wild and free like Chaos itself! 浩然與溟涬同科
          [07950]

The hysterical protagonist that appears in many of Li Po's *yüeh-fu* was not without antecedents: similar railing appeared in some of Lu Chao-lin's work, especially at the close of his "Hard Traveling (02761), and earlier in some of Pao Chao's *yüeh-fu*.

    When the poet renounced impermanence to leap off into the infinite, such wildness was to be expected in the free exercise of the protean mind; but even in the more modest *carpe diem* response to impermanence, the poet-protagonist projected a frenzied intensity. Li Po's *yüeh-fu* are studded with golden goblets sloshing with wine, with singing, dancing, and eating. The most famous of such poems is "Bring in the Wine" 將進酒:

Look there! 君不見
   The waters of the Yellow River, 黃河之水天上來
   coming down from Heaven,
   rush in their flow to the sea, 奔流到海不復回
   never turn back again.
Look there! 君不見
   Bright in the mirrors of mighty halls 高堂明鏡悲白髮
   a grieving for white hair,
   this morning blue-black strands of silk, 朝如青絲暮成雪
   now turned to snow with evening.
For satisfaction in this life 人生得意須盡歡
   taste pleasure to the limit,
And never let a goblet of gold 莫使金樽空對月
   face the bright moon empty.
Heaven bred in me talents, 天生我材必有用
   and they must be put to use.
I toss away a thousand in gold, 千金散盡還復來
   it comes right back to me.
So boil a sheep, 烹羊宰牛且為樂
   butcher an ox,
      make merry for a while,
And when you sit yourself to drink, always 會須一飲三百杯
   down three hundred cups.
   Hey, Master Ts'en, 岑夫子
   Ho, Tan-ch'iu, 丹邱生

Bring in the wine!　　　　　　　　　　　　　　　將進酒
　Keep the cups coming!　　　　　　　　　　　　杯莫停
And I, I'll sing you a song,　　　　　　　　　　　與君歌一曲
You bend me your ears and listen—　　　　　　　請君爲我傾耳聽
The bells and the drums, the tastiest morsels,　　鐘鼓饌玉不足貴
　　it's not these that I love—
All I want is to stay dead drunk　　　　　　　　但願長醉不復醒
　　and never sober up.
The sages and worthies of ancient days　　　　　古來聖賢皆寂寞
　　now lie silent forever,
And only the greatest drinkers　　　　　　　　　惟有飲者留其名
　　have a fame that lingers on!
Once long ago　　　　　　　　　　　　　　　　陳王昔時宴平樂
　　the prince of Ch'en
　　　held a party at P'ing-lo Lodge.
A gallon of wine cost ten thousand cash,　　　　斗酒十千恣歡謔
　　all the joy and laughter they pleased.
　　　So you, my host,　　　　　　　　　　　　主人何爲言少錢
How can you tell me you're short on cash?
Go right out!　　　　　　　　　　　　　　　　徑須沽取對君酌
　　Buy us some wine!
　　　And I'll do the pouring for you!
Then take my dappled horse,　　　　　　　　　五花馬
　Take my furs worth a fortune,　　　　　　　　千金裘
Just call the boy to get them,　　　　　　　　呼兒將出換美酒
　　and trade them for lovely wine,
And here together we'll melt the sorrows　　　　與爾同銷萬古愁
　　of all eternity!
　　　[07931]

The Chinese poetic tradition had no lack of *carpe diem* poems and drinking poems, but there never had been a poem before that spoke to its audience with such violent energy: it was one thing to say, "Man should drink to forget the troubles of this world and mortality"; it was something else altogether to say, "Drink with me and don't be stingy with your money." But the poet's seeming mania swallows this grand violation of social taboo.

The exuberance of the poem had another aspect: it shifted the center of interest away from the idea itself—which, all things considered, was a rather dull commonplace—and directed it toward the poet-speaker. Even more than in Meng Hao-jan, the traditional theme is only a form through which a personality can emerge. As we will discuss later, this concern with creating and defining an identity was even more characteristic of Li Po's non-*yüeh-fu* poetry.

In many of Li Po's less frenetic *yüeh-fu* there was a similar interest in

the implicit protagonist rather than in the surface statements of the poem itself. As the preceding poem tried to project the frenzy of the drinker, so the following poem tries to recreate the dreamlike disorientation of the lover. This technique of fragmentation to represent the distraught consciousness of the poet became an essential part of mid-ninth-century poetics.

Yearning	長相思
Endless yearning	長相思
Here in Ch'ang-an,	在長安
Where the cricket spinners cry autumn	絡緯秋啼金井闌
by the rail of the golden well,	
Where flecks of frost blow chill,	微霜淒淒簟色寒
and the bedmat's color, cold.	
No light from the lonely lantern,	孤燈不明思欲絕
the longing almost broken—	
Then roll up the curtain, gaze on the moon,	卷帷望月空長嘆
heave the sigh that does no good.	
A lady lovely like the flowers,	美人如花隔雲端
beyond that wall of clouds,	
And above, the blue dark of heavens high,	上有青冥之高天
And below, the waves of pale waters.	下有淥水之波瀾
Endless the sky, far the journey,	天長路遠魂飛苦
the fleet soul suffers in flight,	
And in its dreams can't touch its goal	夢魂不到關山難
through the fastness of barrier mountains—	
Then endless yearning	長相思
Crushes a man's heart.	摧心肝
[07939]	

The theme of "longing for someone" (*yu so ssu* 有所思) was one of the oldest in the *yüeh-fu* tradition. The theme had certain requisite components, and Li Po included most of them: autumn, the frost, cries of crickets or cicadas, the chill of bedclothes, opening the curtain and seeing the moon, always followed by mountains, clouds, or waters that block the lover from the person for whom he or she longs. The remarkable thing about "Yearning" is that Li Po combines all these well-worn elements into something entirely new: they become a series of fragments of sight and thought that pass deliriously through the consciousness of the lover. As a result, the poem possesses an immediacy and affective power that few earlier treatments of the theme have. But to succeed as it does, the poem presumes the reader's knowledge of the conventional associations of these images. It is a modal poem, but the mood it generates is to be the same as the mood of the speaker: it tries to make the reader identify with the speaker, to see the world through his eyes and feel the world through his heart.

The thematic scope of Li Po's *yüeh-fu* covers much the same range as earlier *yüeh-fu*: themes of love-longing and the hardships of military service figure prominently, but there are also poems on bravos, on immortals, laments for the impermanence of things, convivial poems, poems celebrating the beauties or hardships of certain regions, poems on the sufferings of the common people and many other subjects. As in "Yearning," Li Po often made use of the conventional components of these themes, but within these limits Li Po's *yüeh-fu* represent an immense variety in their manner. If in "Yearning" Li Po treated the theme of love-longing from inside the lover, he could also treat the theme from an entirely external perspective, as in the famous "Bitterness on the Stairs of Jade" 玉階怨 (08005): there the reader can see the lady's actions and gestures, but no explicit reference is made to the emotional turmoil that the readers knows is in her heart. Though Li Po lacked the stylistic mastery and subtlety of the capital poets, he more than compensated by an innovative virtuosity that none of his contemporaries (excepting Tu Fu) could equal. Indeed, the originality and variety of Li Po's work is such that it is very difficult to isolate features that are true for more than a handful of poems.

Most of Li's *yüeh-fu* translated above use irregular metrical patterns; while such forms did occur earlier in the T'ang, Li Po used them far more often than any of his predecessors or contemporaries. Early T'ang *yüeh-fu* were predominantly pentasyllabic, and those were metrically indistinguishable from any other form of poetry. Heptasyllabic and irregular *yüeh-fu* became more frequent early in the eighth century with the popularity of the heptasyllabic song, itself often slightly irregular. Such irregular songs and *yüeh-fu* were written on a heptasyllabic base with a few trisyllabic and, less commonly, pentasyllabic lines constituting the metrical variation. But no earlier poets dared the extreme irregularity that can be found in many of Li Po's best-known *yüeh-fu*: at his wildest, Li used lines of length up to twelve syllables and often ignored poetic caesura for prose rhythms and *fu* rhythms. As many of the earliest Han *yüeh-fu* were highly irregular, the irregularity of Li Po's poems had an element of primitivism. But a more important effect in the case of Li Po's *yüeh-fu* was a sense of freedom, a willingness to transcend common metrical rules with the same ease that he transcended thematic and modal proprieties.

In his willingness to experiment, Li Po sometimes tried his hand at the conservative *yüeh-fu* modes of the Southern Dynasties and Early T'ang. "Bitterness on the Stairs of Jade" was such a poem, a brilliant exercise in Southern Dynasties "palace poetry" combined with the High T'ang quatrain vignette. Several poems in Li Po's famous series "By the Passes" 塞下曲 (07997–08002) clearly were attempts to capture the manner of Early T'ang frontier *yüeh-fu*. Li Po's peculiar "failure" to approximate his model marks how greatly poetry had changed in the preceding decades. It was the curse of Li Po's genius that he could not efface his poetic personality enough to truly write in the Early T'ang style. For example, the third poem of "By the Passes" begins:

Our fine steeds are like the whirlwind, 　　　　　駿馬似風飇
Cracking whips emerge from the Wei River Bridge. 　鳴鞭出渭橋

The reader familiar with the conventions of Early T'ang poetry would immediately see here the set opening formula: the imperial army marching out of the capital. The ornamentation is also Early T'ang: the "whips" are synecdoche for the riders, and "emerge" is the properly elegant word in the proper position in the line. "Cracking whips," however, verges on violent indecorum, and the comparison of the first line is too original, too bold, and too direct. The courtly dignity for which Li was striving was lost amid the protean energy of horses "like whirlwinds" and the snapping of whips. But it was precisely this sensuous energy that made Li Po's poetry a delight for the next millenium, during which only the most devoted antiquarian would read an Early T'ang *yüeh-fu*.

Like many of his contemporaries, Li Po was a master of the quatrain vignette, often written as *yüeh-fu* in the southern manner. There Li often captured a sensuous immediacy that was both compelling and memorable. Meng Hao-jan had written often of his native Hsiang-yang, but when Li Po wrote of Hsiang-yang, he sounded more native than the native. Li mentioned local songs like "Shining Hooves-of-Bronze" and famous local figures like the Chin governor Shan Chien, the greatest drinker in Hsiang-yang's history.

Hsiang-yang Songs (first of four) 　　　　　　　　襄陽曲四首之一

In Hsiang-yang's places of delight 　　　　　　　襄陽行樂處
They dance and sing "Shining Hooves of Bronze." 　歌舞白銅鞮
The river walls turn back clear waters; 　　　　　江城回淥水
Flowers and moonlight make you lose your way. 　　花月使人迷
　　　　　　　　　[08006]

Meng Hao-jan and every visitor to Hsiang-yang had to mention the "monument of tears," erected for the virtuous magistrate Yang Hu: the visitor to Hsien Mountain nearby was supposed to read the stele and weep at the memory of Yang Hu's virtue. Li Po bowed to the convention obliquely and negatively; characteristically, he used the norm in such a way as to differentiate himself from everyone else:

So let's get drunk at the Hsi family's pool, 　　　　且醉習家池
Rather than viewing the monument of tears 　　　　莫看墮淚碑

When drunk Lord Shan goes to get on his horse, 　　　　　山公欲上馬
The children of Hsiang-yang die with laughter. 　　　　　笑殺襄陽兒
[08009]

Evoking the young gallant of Ch'ang-an, Li might begin in the evocative manner of Ch'u Kuang-hsi's "The Roads of Ch'ang-an," but he closes with a sensual laugh rather than a conventional image of the sadness of the flesh:

Ballad of Youth (second of two) 　　　　　　　　　　少年行二首之二

A young man of Five Barrows suburb 　　　　　　　　五陵年少金市東
　　east of the Golden Market,
Silver saddle and white horse 　　　　　　　　　　　銀鞍白馬度春風
　　cross through wind of spring.
When fallen flowers are trampled all under, 　　　　　落花踏盡遊何處
　　where is it he will roam?
With a laugh he enters the tavern 　　　　　　　　　笑入胡姬酒肆中
　　of a lovely Turkish wench.
[08045]

Because Li Po occasionally mentioned some aspect of everyday life that most poets ignored, some modern critics have found "realism" in his work. In fact, nothing could be further from the truth; his are idealized situations, conventional figures in a schematized scene often (as in the quatrain vignettes of his contemporaries) performing the one significant gesture that epitomizes their existence. The following poem is not included in the *yüeh-fu*, but it is an excellent example of Li Po's vignette technique:

The Girls of Yüeh (third of five) 　　　　　　　　　越女詞五首之三

A girl picking lotus on Jo-yeh Creek 　　　　　　　　耶溪採蓮女
Sees the boatman return, singing a rowing song. 　　　見客棹歌回
With a giggle she hides in the lotus flowers 　　　　　笑入荷花去
And, pretending shyness, won't come out. 　　　　　　佯羞不出來
[08827]

Such poetry represents genius, but it is the genius of a man who can capture a fantasy, rather than that of a keen observer of the physical world.

　　The division between the *yüeh-fu* and the "songs" in Li Po's collection probably represents the work of an editor rather than that of the poet, perhaps even of a Sung editor. Despite the tendency of the songs to be more occasional than the *yüeh-fu*, the two forms are quite close. Just how close can be seen in the long "Hsiang-yang Song" 襄陽歌 (08072) in the "songs" section: part of it consists of sections from the four "Hsiang-yang Melodies" 襄陽曲 (08006–9) included in the *yüeh-fu*. Given the free textual variation in T'ang poem titles (and especially in generic terms such as *song* and *melody*), one can see just how arbitrary the division between the two sections is.

Among the "songs" are two of Li Po's most famous series, the "Autumn Banks Songs" 秋浦歌 (08100–08116) and the "Heng-chiang Lyrics" 橫江詞 (08087–92). In many ways these two series are touchstones of Li Po's genius: they seem pellucidly simple, and yet they bear the indelible stamp of Li Po's poetic personality. Behind the various personae of these poems, the manipulating figure of Li Po the poet is exposed; the reader confronts patent insincerity and the ironic distance of the playful poet toying with his creations.

In the first of the "Heng-chiang Lyrics," Li Po plays the southern rustic whose blustering awe at the storm is viewed with a condescending smile by the reader and the poet behind the poem.

Everyone says that Heng-chiang's great,	人道橫江好
I say that Heng-chiang's awful—	儂道橫江惡
Three days of steady wind blows the mountains over,	一風三日吹倒山
And white waves higher than Wa-kuan Tower.	白浪高於瓦官閣
[08087]	

Note the characteristic act of differentiation in the first couplet, in which the poet opposes his opinion to that of everyone else. But Li Po is striking a pose in this poem that neither he nor anyone else is supposed to believe: the poem is not so much about the persona as it is about the poet's power to invent and play a persona.

As the series moves forward, Li Po invents new versions of himself, versions that redeem the ridiculous figure of the first poem and at the same time show the poet's power over all roles. In the fifth poem:

In front of Heng-chiang Station the ferry master meets me,	橫江館前津吏迎
Faces me, points east where clouds are rising from the sea.	向余東指海雲生
Mister, why on earth would you want to cross today?	郎今欲渡緣何事
With wind and waves like this we just can't go.	如此風波不可行
[08091]	

In this swift vignette we see the worried ferry master pointing at the coming storm in the background. But the real center of the poem is the hidden persona of the poet, hair blowing in the gale, mountainous waves rising all around, heroically facing the coming storm. But the ironic distance of the poet from his pose is not absent here either.

The sixth and final poem of the series represents the ultimate transformation and apotheosis of the poet's persona:

Ring around the moon, wind from heaven, fog unopening.	月暈天風霧不開

The sea's leviathans crush eastward;　　　　　　海鯨東蹙百川迴
 rivers run back in their courses.
Waves shaken rise together,　　　　　　　　　　驚波一起三山動
 Three Mountains moves.
My lord, cross not the river,　　　　　　　　　　公無渡河歸去來
 turn back home.
   [08092]

"My lord, cross not the river" 公無渡河 was a *yüeh-fu* title based on the following legend: a ferry master in Korea once saw an old madman, his white hair flying loose and carrying a jug, try to cross a river during a storm. The old man's wife came running after him, trying to prevent his embarking, but before she could get him to turn back, he fell into the stormy waters and drowned. Then she took a harp and played the song "My Lord, Cross Not the River," after which she jumped into the stormy waters herself.

The rustic persona of the first poem of the series, indicated by the southern first-person pronoun *nung* 儂, was transformed into a foolish but brave "mister," *lang* 郎 in the fifth poem. In the last poem he has become the mysterious and tragic "My lord," *kung* 公, and "awful" Heng-chiang has been transformed into a vast panorama of tempest, filled with river-reversing leviathans and ominous portents in the heavens. But the context of the series as a whole makes it clear that even this last version of the persona is a pose, something "made" by the poet. The series is not really "about" crossing the river; the real center of interest lies in the creative poet, in his absolute mastery over his art, and in his power to manipulate and transform. At his best, Li Po was usually writing about his favorite subject—Li Po.

A series of fifty-nine poems entitled *Ku-feng* 古風 was placed first in the earliest printed editions of Li Po's poetry and had probably been first in at least one of the original editions. *Ku-feng* means something like "ancient manner," though *feng*, literally "wind," also indicated the affective power of moral influence. We do not know whether the title *Ku-feng*, the grouping of the poems as a series, and their placement at the head of the collection represents the work of Li Po or an editor. One hint that the poems of the series may have originally been untitled comes from the inclusion of the ninth poem of the series in the *Ho-yüeh ying-ling chi* under the title *Yung-huai* 詠懷, "singing my feelings." Though *Yung-huai* had originally been the title of Juan Chi's famous poem series, by the T'ang it was also a sub-generic term, and it would have been natural for Yin Fan to affix it to an untitled poem. Whether the series title was Li Po's or an editor's, the *Ku-feng* are, of course, *ku-feng* in the subgeneric sense we have been using the term: *fu-ku* poetry in the style of the Chien-an, Wei, and Chin.

With the exception of the first poem and perhaps the last, there is no apparent order in the arrangement of the *Ku-feng*. The first poem of the series is a *fu-ku* set piece, a versified lament for the decline of literature which presents the *fu-ku* version of literary history and closes with a praise of the T'ang for its restoration of ancient values. The final poem is a lament for the decline of the Way. Again, we do not know if this framing was the choice of Li Po or of an editor. Within the frame, the poems themselves are a miscellaneous lot, and there is no reason to suppose that they were composed at the same time; however, attempts to *prove* that the *Ku-feng* were composed at different times have been based on extremely tenuous topical interpretations and should not be credited.

Li Po's *Ku-feng* are strongly in the tradition of Ch'en Tzu-ang's *Kan-yü*; a number of *Ku-feng* are clearly imitations of individual *Kan-yü*, insofar as Li Po was capable of imitation. The *Ku-feng* cover approximately the same thematic range as the *Kan-yü*, and the topics are treated in the accepted High T'ang *ku-feng* style that grew out of the *Kan-yü*: there are poems on the *hsien-jen shih-chih* theme, poems on immortals, exemplary historical poems, frontier poems, and *yung-wu* allegories. Even if the poems were not conceived as a series, they are something of a tribute to Ch'en Tzu-ang. Li Po was playing the Szechwanese poet in the accepted mode, and it is interesting to note that the three most famous *fu-ku* poem series of the seventh and eighth centuries were all by men from outlying provinces: the *Kan-yü* of Ch'en Tzu-ang and Chang Chiu-ling, and the *Ku-feng* of Li Po.

As might be expected, Li Po was weakest in the stiffly formal allegories and strongest in those topics that allowed his imagination free rein. Historical poems and poetry on immortals served his genius particularly well: both concerned an unseen world. The theme of a ruler's frenzied quest for immortality appeared first in one of Ch'en Tzu-ang's *Kan-yü*, a poem on the peripatetic Chou King Mu (04372). The theme was indeed a very old one and appeared in early Taoist texts and romance; in *fu-ku* poetry it required a moral judgment that could only be negative. In two *Ku-feng* (07867, 07912) Li Po treated the figure of Ch'in Shih-huang and his legendary passion for immortality; the First Emperor became a powerful figure of demonic but futile frenzy. Early in the ninth century, Li Ho was to take Li Po's Ch'in Shih-huang and transform him into an obsessed titan, at war with time and change (20685). The second of Li Po's versions of Ch'in Shih-huang, the forty-eighth poem of the series, was based on a legend that the First Emperor wanted a bridge built over the Eastern Ocean so that he could travel to the place where the sun rose; to build his bridge the First Emperor had a wizard animate the boulders of eleven mountains and drive them with a whip to the sea's edge.

Ch'in's emperor set hand on his jeweled sword,	秦皇按寶劍
Crimson in rage, he let his godlike power thunder.	赫怒震威神
He chased the sun in journey to sea's west edge,	逐日巡海右

Made stones gallop to frame a ford over deeps.　　　　　驅石架滄津
He summoned laborers, emptied all the land　　　　　　微卒空九寓
To make his bridge, the suffering of thousands.　　　　作橋傷萬人
He sought only elixir from isles of the gods;　　　　　但求蓬島藥
He cared nothing for springtime's farming.　　　　　　豈思農扈春
Their strength was used up, not enough for the deed.　力盡功不贍
Now a thousand years later it still causes pain.　　　　千載爲悲辛

[07912]

From the last line it is possible that some topical point was intended. The last line comes from the *Kan-yü* (04376), where it does indicate topical interpretation: it causes pain because some present abuse repeats an abuse in the past. But far beyond any topical interpretation, no reader can miss Li Po's genuine fascination with the demonic figure of Ch'in Shih-huang.

　　Like the *yüeh-fu*, the *Ku-feng* allowed Li Po scope for his fictional imagination. One distinguishing mark of Li Po's talent is that he was more convincing when he described an encounter with an immortal or a flight through the heavens than when he described some social occasion at which he was actually present. He was most at ease in his imagination, and there is a clarity in his mind's eye, as in the nineteenth poem of the series, where the poet looks down from an aerial perspective and sees the forces of An Lu-shan massing in the distance:

Westward I climbed to Lotus Blossom Peak,　　　　　西上蓮花山
Far in the distance I saw the bright star:　　　　　　迢迢見明星
In her pale hand she held a lotus,　　　　　　　　　素手把芙蓉
Stepping in emptiness, pacing pure ether.　　　　　　虛步躡太清
Her rainbow robes trailed broad sashes,　　　　　　霓裳曳廣帶
Then, fluttering in wind, she rose up to Heaven.　　　飄拂昇天行
She invited me to climb Cloud Terrace Peak,　　　　　邀我登雲臺
On high to salute Wei Shu-ch'ing, the immortal.　　　高揖衛叔卿
Then, in a blur she went off with him,　　　　　　　恍恍與之去
Riding their swans over Purple Darkness.　　　　　　駕鴻凌紫冥
I looked back down on the Lo-yang rivers:　　　　　　俯視洛陽川
Far and wide Tartar troops were speeding,　　　　　茫茫走胡兵
And flowing blood mired the wild grasses　　　　　　流血塗野草
Where wolves and jackals all wore official's caps.　　豺狼盡冠纓

[07883]

　　Toward the end of Li Po's collection in its present form, there are a number of other *ku-feng* poems that were not included in the *Ku-feng* series. These have the more common titles of T'ang *ku-feng*: *chiao-ku* 效古 (08694–95), *ni-ku* 擬古 (08696–707), *kan-hsing* 感興 ("responding to stir-rings" 08708–13), *kan-yü* 感遇 (08718–21), and *yü-yen* 寓言 ("parables" 08714–16). These poems may represent later gleanings, perhaps spurious, that one or both of the first editors didn't possess, or they may represent Li Po's *ku-feng* poems that originally did have titles.

The remainder of Li Po's collection contains the usual range of private and occasional poetry: here Li shows a slight aversion to regulated forms. In one of the anecdotal elaborations of Li Po's period in court, the emperor was supposed to have summoned Li to test his poetic abilities because His Majesty knew that Li was "weak on tonal rules."[11] Compared to most of the collections of his contemporaries, Li's collection has a somewhat larger proportion of private poems to occasional poems. Within Li's considerable corpus of occasional poetry, there are many careless pieces and many fine poems marred by weak sections. The free and easy manner in which Li Po took such pride claimed its toll: Li's favorite images and phrases were repeated time and again, and the most hackneyed clichés flow smoothly past the reader, who scarcely notices them. The dividing line between poems that seem spontaneously natural and those that are merely facile is often difficult to draw.

At times Li Po could be as formal and ornate as he could be simple, though he lacked the grace to write such poetry well. Even in his most imaginative descriptions his vocabulary was relatively simple. Similarly, except in his formal pieces, Li usually avoided periphrasis, and his syntax was unusually direct. His work abounded with what seem to have been colloquialisms and colloquial phrasings. Padded, prosaic lines often served functions that ordinary poetic diction would treat in two or three characters (e.g., 08231. 21).

Contemporary aristocratic taste might have frowned on Li Po's lack of craftsmanship, but the smoothness and simplicity of his style gave his work enduring appeal. Perhaps the most important characteristic of Li Po's style was simplifying and limiting the relationship between lines and between couplets. Li Po's contemporaries generally conceived of the couplet as the basic unit of thought; as a result, their poetry often tended to extreme parataxis. Li Po retained the line as the basic grammatical unit (though he did use enjambment), but in his poetry the thought crossed the gap between lines and couplets with easy continuity. Much of the energy and directness that readers feel in Li Po's poetry arises from his weakening of the barrier between couplets. At their best, the capital poets sought to complicate the relations between parts of a line, between the lines of a couplet, and between the couplets in a poem; Li Po sought to simplify these relations and make them immediately understandable.

Li Po was interested in projecting energy and lack of restraint in other ways than style. All the various roles he assumed in his poetry—the immortal, the bravo, the drinker, and the eccentric—were all models of behavior that lay outside the twin roles of scholar-official and serene recluse.

The implicit message beneath much of Li Po's occasional poetry was a refusal to assume the role of an "ordinary" poet; instead, he assumed roles that other poets had looked on longingly, but from a distance. Through these roles, Li was saying that he was "different from" other poets, and Li's "different from" meant "better than." Born and raised an outsider to the capital-centered world of poetry, Li Po placed a new value on his separateness: instead of being merely alien, he was alien because he was superior. As the poet without legitimate social background, he was the poet who had to "invent himself," not only in his boastful letters, but in a poetry largely concerned with creating and defining Li Po. Through this concern with the self, Li Po was able to liberate himself from some of the most restrictive aspects of the poetic tradition: the passivity of the perceiving subject, the repression of human will, and the tyranny of the external world. Wang Wei may have been the "master craftsman," but Li Po was the first true "genius." Indeed, Li Po's manner came virtually to define genius in poetry.

This alien and superior Li Po was the subject of one of Li's poems included in the *Ho-yüeh ying-ling chi*; Yin Fan's selection of the poem suggests that the self that Li Po created was appreciated in the T'ien-pao.

Dialogue in the Mountains 山中問答

You ask me why I lodge in these emerald hills; 問余何意棲碧山
I laugh, don't answer—my heart is at peace. 笑而不答心自閑
Peach blossoms and flowing waters 桃花流水窅然去
  go off to mysterious dark, 別有天地非人間
And there is another world,
  not of mortal men.
     [08465]

If Li Po was to be separate from the society of other men, then he would have the separateness of the immortals or those who dwell at Peach Blossom Spring. The "dialogue" of the title does not occur; there is no social intercourse, because Li Po is cut off from the mortals of this world. Li Po assumes for himself the role of the unanswering fisherman of Kao Shih's poem (pp. 67–68). Other poets may claim to have encountered such a figure, but Li Po claims to *be* the figure.

A famous Wang Wei poem also employs a blocked dialogue, but the way in which it differs from Li Po's poem above is characteristic of the differences between the two poets.

Parting 送別

I get off my horse, drink wine with you, 下馬飲君酒
Ask you where you are going. 問君何所之

You say you feel dissatisfied,   君言不得意
Will go back to rest by South Mountain's edge.   歸臥南山陲
So go off now—I'll ask no more.   但去莫復問
White clouds for eternity.   白雲無盡時
                    [05811]

Part of a dialogue does occur in Wang Wei's poem, but that part covers the essentials of the situation—the details are unnecessary. Thus, the break in the dialogue concerns a shared humanity and fellow feeling that permits instant understanding. Against this is Li Po's interruption in communication, brought about by a fundamental and unbridgeable gap that separates him from other men.

   Much of Li Po's poetry is devoted to forming and projecting an image of the self, and that self is partially defined as the creative poet. This occurs both in personae and in disjunctive techniques that reveal the creative, manipulating poet behind the poem. All major T'ang poets developed some image of the self, but in Li Po the activity was central. Unlike Wang Wei, Li Po was not greatly interested in how the world was perceived; unlike Wang Ch'ang-ling, he was not primarily interested in mood. Li Po wrote about a grand "me"—how I am, what I am like, what I said and did. The world scarcely matters at all, except as a prop to hang his headband on. His was a poetry of self-creation: while the meditative poet might define the self by introspection, Li Po defined the self by individuating acts, by gestures that separated him from others.

Summer Day in the Mountains   夏日山中

Lazily waving a fan of white feathers,   嬾搖白羽扇
Stripped naked here in the green woods,   躶袒青林中
I take off my headband, hang it on a cliff,   脫巾掛石壁
My bare head splattered by wind through pines.   露頂灑松風
                    [08669]

My Feelings   自遣

Facing my wine, unaware of darkness growing,   對酒不覺暝
Falling flowers cover my robes.   落花盈我衣
Drunk I rise, step on the moon in the creek—   醉起步溪月
Birds are turning back now,   鳥還人亦稀
   men too are growing fewer.
                    [08679]

In Li Po's collection there are more social occasional poems than "private" poems like the two above; however, after the *yüeh-fu*, the "private" poems are the form that readers have most strongly associated with Li Po.

   Even in his social occasional poetry, Li Po often placed himself in the center of the stage, as in the famous couplet from "A Parting Banquet for the Collator Shu-yün at the Hsieh T'iao Lodge in Hsüan-chou" 宣州謝脁樓餞別校書叔雲 (08454):

> I draw my dirk and cut the waters,　　　　　　抽刀斷水水更流
> 　　the waters flow on and on.
> I lift my goblet to melt away sorrow,　　　　　舉杯消愁愁更愁
> 　　but sorrow keeps on sorrowing.

Even drinking farewell to a friend, Li Po is the poem's protagonist whose frenzy at parting dwarfs the mere melancholy of others.

Like Wang Chi in the early seventh century, Li Po found in wine the means to achieve freedom of spirit and spontaneity. Also like Wang Chi, Li Po's poems are not so much about drinking as about the drinker. The most famous of such poems is the first of the series "Drinking Alone by Moonlight" 月下獨酌:

> Here among flowers a single jug of wine,　　　　花間一壺酒
> No close friends here, I pour alone　　　　　　　獨酌無相親
> And lift cup to bright moon, ask it to join me,　舉杯邀明月
> Then face my shadow and we become three.　　　對影成三人
> The moon never has known how to drink,　　　　月既不解飲
> All my shadow does is follow my body,　　　　　影徒隨我身
> But with moon and shadow as companions a while,暫伴月將影
> This joy I find will surely last till spring.　　行樂須及春
> I sing, the moon just lingers on,　　　　　　　　我歌月徘徊
> I dance, and my shadow scatters wildly.　　　　　我舞影零亂
> When still sober we share friendship and pleasure,醒時同交歡
> Then entirely drunk each goes his own way—　　醉後各分散
> Let us join in travels beyond human feelings　　永結無情遊
> And plan to meet far in the river of stars.　　　相期邈雲漢
> 　　　　　　　[08651]

Solitude is neither loneliness nor serene seclusion in this poem or in most of Li Po's other work: it is rather an opportunity for the poet to show his creative self-sufficiency, his ability to populate his surroundings with his own imagination. There is no loneliness as long as there is the poetic act (and an audience for it in the mortal world). If the birds and clouds desert him, Li Po can find a more reliable companion.

Sitting Alone by Ching-t'ing Mountain　　　　　　獨坐敬亭山

> The flocks of birds have flown high and away,　　眾鳥高飛盡
> A solitary cloud goes off calmly alone.　　　　　孤雲獨去閑
> We look at each other and never get bored—　　　相看兩不厭
> Just me and Ching-t'ing Mountain.　　　　　　　只有敬亭山
> 　　　　　　　[08678]

Whimsy is possible for the poetic imagination that can structure and interpret the world as it wills.

The poet exposes his presence and creative power not only in his masks,
but also in description and other aspects of poetic technique. The "strangeness" that contemporary and later critics saw in Li Po's work served the
function of calling attention to the poet behind the poem, his originality
and his uniqueness. Wang Wei used syntactic figuration in description to
create a "strangeness" that referred ultimately to the nature of perception;
Li Po went to greater extremes and, in doing so, emphasized the power of
the poet to shape and transform. Li might use bold inversions of perception; three peaks of a mountain appearing above the horizon became
(08569):

Three Peaks, half fallen beneath blue sky's edge.   三山半落青天外

Hyperbole was another device to make the world "strange," as in the
famous "Autumn Banks Songs XV":

Three thousand yards of white hair—   白髮三千丈
Sorrow's conscqucncc, long as sorrow too.   緣愁似箇長
Here, bright in the mirror, I wonder   不知明鏡裏
From where I got this autumn frost.   何處得秋霜
             [08114]

Li's brashness, his hyperbole, and a wit that verges on playfulness all invite
the reader to maintain an ironic distance from the poem. The poet seeks
neither authenticity nor "an illusion of reality"; its artifice is exposed to
reveal the potent artificer. The poet goes a little too far in his frenzy, a
little too far in his hyperbole—just far enough to undermine a reader's
engagement with the poem and reveal Li Po, the creative genius, in full
control.

The poet who devoted so much of his energy to creating a poetic self
could also remove himself entirely from poems that would normally
demand personal response. This is not as paradoxical as it might seem: the
power to create the self implied the power to negate the self as Wang Wei
never could. Precisely because Li Po lacked the capital poet's yearning for
authenticity, his fictional imagination was liberated from the world at hand
and the personal response that complemented it. For example, Li Po's *huai-
ku* were often far closer to *yüeh-fu* than to conventional *huai-ku*, where the
poet's response intruded strongly upon the scene. Other poets might look
upon ruins and see only ruins and their own melancholy; Li Po would see
a pageant of ancient figures.

Observing the Past at Yüeh   越中覽古

When Kou-chien, king of Yüeh,   越王句踐破吳歸
   returned from smashing Wu,

The royal troops went back to their homes
    all robed in fine brocade,
And palace ladies, lovely as flowers,
    filled the springtime halls,
Where now this day are only
    partridges in flight.
        [08617]

義士還家盡錦衣

宮女如花滿春殿

只今惟有鷓鴣飛

The simple diction, the straightforward message, and the bright presences of the imagination are all characteristic of Li Po's work in one mode.

    Critics and biographers have often discussed Li Po's interest in religious Taoism, particularly in the cult of immortality. Li Po consorted with noted Taoists, acquired a Taoist certification as a low-level initiate, and sometimes showed in his poetry a knowledge of Taoist esoterica that was rare in most poets. The imperial patronage of Taoism under Hsüan-tsung made it a speedy and attractive road to court favor, and it was the road Li Po followed. Li never took the *chin-shih* examination, never showed any interest in it, nor is it likely he could have procured the requisite recommendations. Even if he had taken the examination, it is highly unlikely that he could have passed it, considering the combination of social and educational factors necessary for success through the standard "literary" route to favor. Li Po was even less a religious poet than Wang Wei was: he was deeply concerned neither with the cosmic principles of Taoism nor with the protoscience of Taoist alchemy. To Li Po the immortals were objects of speculative fantasy and a means to liberate the imagination. Their alienness answered his personal sense of alienness: "There is another world, not of mortal men."

    Immortals appeared frequently in the *Ku-feng*, and some of Li's finest *yüeh-fu* and "songs" concerned flights through the Cosmos.

Song of Yüan Tan-ch'iu   元丹邱歌

Yüan Tan-ch'iu   元丹邱
Loved the gods and the immortals: 愛神仙
At dawn he drank from clear currents   朝飲潁川之清流
    of the River Ying,
At dusk he returned to purple mists   暮還嵩岑之紫煙
    upon Mount Sung,
And around its thirty-six peaks he whirled   三十六峯長周旋
    around and around.
Long he whirled round,   長周旋
Pacing a comet's tail,   躡星虹
And his body rode a dragon,   身騎飛龍耳生風
    winds rose at his ears,
Then over the rivers, striding the seas,   橫河跨海與天通
    reaching up to Heaven—

I know that on this journey,
  his heart will never fail.
       [08079]

我知爾遊心無窮

In this poem, as in much of Li Po's poetry, the senses are engaged far more than the intellect: as had once been true in the *fu*, the poet is trying to create an immediate, sensuous experience through words.

Two of Li Po's finest visionary encounters with immortals happen also to be occasional poems: "Visiting T'ien-mu Mountain in a Dream: On Parting" 夢遊天姥吟留別 (08332) and "Song of Lu Mountain: To Censor Lu Hsü-chou" 廬山謠寄盧侍御盧舟 (08303).[12] Both poems describe imaginary spirit journeys in the tradition of the *Ch'u-tz'u*, though in the case of the former, the flight through the heavens is rationalized as a dream. Although Li Po mocked quests for the immortals in some of his *ku-feng*, the bright beings held an irresistible fascination for him.

Li Po bore a strange relation to the poetic tradition: never before had there been a poet who knew earlier poetry so well and felt its greatness so lightly. Li Po unabashedly borrowed famous phrases and whole lines from past poets, but he never felt truly compelled to confront another poet's genius—with the possible exception of Ssu-ma Hsiang-ju. Even in poems that were virtually pastiches of lines from other poets, Li Po never sounded like anyone but himself. This may have been true of Meng Hao-jan, but it was far more true of Li Po. In contrast, Tu Fu saw the literary past not as a vast collection of lines but as a series of powerful voices; as a poet Tu tried to master those voices and assimilate them into his own distinctive voice. Li Po greatly admired Hsieh T'iao; he often mentioned Hsieh and borrowed phrases from his work, but never did Li write a poem that in the least resembled Hsieh's characteristic work.

Pao Chao might seem an exception: a few of Pao Chao's *yüeh-fu* were very close to Li Po's style. However, while Li Po might begin a poem in the Pao Chao mode, he quickly turned off in a direction entirely his own. For example, every T'ang reader would have known the sixth poem of Pao Chao's "Hard Traveling" 行路難.[13]

I face the table, cannot eat,
Pull out my sword, strike the column,
  heave a long sigh—
How long can human life last?
How can I bear to hobble about with folded wings?
So give it all up—I quit my post and left,
Went back to my home and took my ease.
At dawn I went out, took leave of my kin,
Now in evening return to my kinsmen's sides.

對案不能食
拔劍擊柱長嘆息

丈夫生世會幾時
安能蹀躞垂羽翼
棄置罷官去
還家自休息
朝出與親辭
暮還在親側

I play with my child in games by his bed, 弄兒牀前戲
Watch my wife at her loom weaving. 看婦機中織
From time's beginning the good and the wise 自古聖賢盡貧賤
    have all lived in poverty,
Even truer for men of my age, upright and alone. 何況我輩孤且直

Any reader familiar with Li Po might guess that in all the corpus of pre-T'ang poetry the opening of this poem would have irresistably attracted him. Indeed, Li Po's own version of "Hard Traveling" opens with Pao Chao's poem clearly in mind, but Li completely undermined the starkness of Pao Chao's lines: Li Po would refuse only the "choicest" foods and the "finest" wines. And once Li Po draws his sword in frustration, he sets off into a wild world all his own:

A golden goblet and clear wine, 金樽清酒斗十千
    ten thousand for a gallon,
A plate of jade with choicest foods, 玉盤珍羞直萬錢
    feast worth a fortune—
I put down my goblet, drop my chopsticks, 停杯投筯不能食
    cannot eat,
Pull out my sword, look all around, 拔劍四顧心茫然
    mind in a daze.
I want to ford the Yellow River— 欲渡黃河冰塞川
    ice blocks the stream.
I decide to climb the T'ai-hang's, 將登太行雪滿山
    but snow fills the mountains.
Then peace of mind comes—I drop my line 閒來垂釣碧溪上
    down into emerald rivers,
And all of a sudden I'm riding a boat 忽復乘舟夢日邊
    in dream beside the sun.
Hard traveling, 行路難
Traveling hard, 行路難
The byways too many— 多歧路
Where am I now? 今安在
But there shall come a time 長風破浪會有時
    when winds will smash the waves,
I'll just hoist my cloud of a sail 直掛雲帆濟滄海
    to cross the dark, dark sea.
[07936]

From Pao Chao, Li Po has borrowed only the gestures of dissatisfaction. A deeper understanding of Pao Chao's poem would have drawn a poet to Pao's psychological starkness, its nervous energy and uneasy resolution. Li follows the stages of Pao's poem until the closing, but his hyperbolic frenzy is an act of poetic bravura that has nothing to do with Pao's credibly human dissatisfaction. One may contrast the ways in which the capital poets sought to understand and interpret T'ao Ch'ien: though they produced High T'ang versions of T'ao that were very different from the Chin poet, their revisions were generated from a genuine interest in T'ao's poetic identity.

From many aspects Li Po was an outsider to the world of contemporary capital poetry. He ignored the capital poets, and they ignored him. In Li Po's work we hear not a word of Wang Wei, probably Li's most famous contemporary, and Wang Wei ignored Li. This may have been because the two men belonged to different social circles or because each poet's conception of poetry was so remote from the other's that they had no common ground on which to meet. Meng Hao-jan did not requite, as far as we know, Li's ecstatic admiration. Wang Ch'ang-ling may have written one very slight poem to Li: while there were some similarities in the way those two poets handled the quatrain, Wang Ch'ang-ling was a gentler, more controlled poet. Of all the poet's in the capital group, only Li Ch'i may have been touched by Li Po's talent, and this possibility is only tentative. But beside Li Po's best work, Li Ch'i's poetry is reduced to blandness and mere bluster.

Li Po was acquainted with at least two major poets: Kao Shih and Tu Fu. When he met Li, Kao was not yet a nationally famous poet, and Kao does not seem to have felt Li Po's influence greatly. When Tu Fu met Li, Tu was simply an admiring youngster, and apart from a few bland poems, there is little evidence that Li Po repaid Tu Fu's adoration. The legendary friendship between the two poets is a product of Tu Fu's poetry to and about Li Po. Li Po did exert an influence on Tu Fu's poetry, but Li's example went through the transforming filter of Tu Fu's own complex poetic personality. Li Po's poetry did have a degree of popularity and influence during the T'ien-pao: distinct echoes of Li can be heard in Ts'en Shen and several minor poets, as well as in the work of Tu Fu and Li Ch'i. Li Po's "strangeness on top of strangeness" played a role in the formation of T'ien-pao taste in eccentric personae, in exotica, and in the visionary imagination. But the influence of Li Po came from admiration for a man apart; it was not the calm transmission of a style through shared poetic exchange. Though his greatness is unquestionable and though his popularity in later ages was immense, Li Po remained, in a profound way, a solitary and unique figure.

吳筠

WU YÜN

Although Li Po was essentially a solitary poet, different aspects of his varied poetic oeuvre can be traced to several poetic traditions. The model of the drunken eccentric can be seen in earlier figures such as Chang Hsü, Ho Chih-chang, and Wang Han. The poet of the *Ku-feng* stood directly in the tradition of Ch'en Tzu-ang and Chang Chiu-ling. And in his poetry on immortals, Li Po's work was closely related to that of his friend and benefactor, the Taoist Wu Yün.

Wu Yün (d. 778) failed the *chin-shih* examination and turned to the occult mysteries of religious Taoism. Where Confucian learning failed, wizardry succeeded, and Wu found imperial patronage and passed the imperial examination in Taoist classics. Summoned to court in 742, Wu brought Li Po with him, and both poets were given posts in the Han-lin Academy. Both also earned the enmity of the powerful eunuch Kao Li-shih, and it seems possible that Li Po's problems at court may have stemmed from his association with Wu. At some time before the An Lu-shan Rebellion, perhaps as early as 744, Wu Yün withdrew from court and spent the rest of his life as a Taoist recluse in the Southeast.

Wu Yün wrote occasional poems, but these occupy an unusually small part of his surviving corpus. The greater part of his extant poetry is found in four poem series: two are on immortals, the twenty-four "Wandering Immortals" 遊仙 (46738–61) and the ten "Verses on Treading the Void" 步虛詞 (46776–85); one series consists of ethical meditations on history, the fourteen "Observing Antiquity" 覽古 (46762–75); and finally there is a series on exemplary recluses, worthies, wizards, and adepts: the fifty "Songs on Lofty Scholars" 高士詠 (46800–849), with a preface.

There was a long-standing association between ethical *fu-ku* poetry and poetry on immortals and neo-Taoist themes; it had appeared in the work of Wang Chi, Ch'en Tzu-ang, Chang Yüeh, Li Po, and elsewhere. Poets were not unaware of the fundamental differences between the Confucian persuasion, the Taoist persuasion, and Buddhism, but those differences were simply not of primary interest to High T'ang poets. Instead, poets conceived the paramount distinction to be between an occasional poetry motivated by social necessity and a poetry of ideas and values that transcended everyday society. Wu Yün's poems on immortals are much more interesting than his meditations on history, but it is not surprising to find the stern observer of the ethical lessons of the past standing comfortably beside the entranced adept soaring up through the tiers of the Cosmos.

During the Early T'ang the "river of stars" had flowed directly down into Lo-yang and Ch'ang-an; its "streamlets" had branched past the sparkling villas of the Wei clan. The landscapes celebrated in court poetry were infused with a luminous magic. As private poetry and informal occasional poetry grew in importance during the K'ai-yüan, the magic immanence left the landscapes, and they took on symbolic value. A landscape of Wang

Wei or Meng Hao-jan might be a "sign" of transcendent meaning, but the "sign" existed in a secular, phenomenal world that could be walked over, sat upon, and fixed in the eye. To some degree, poetry on the immortals satisfied the need to recapture that lost magic in poetry, its luminous immanence. In poetry on immortals the High T'ang tendency to hidden meaning is absent: as in Li Po's "Yüan Tan-ch'iu," the goal was to present a sensually immediate scene. Like Early T'ang court poetry, it was a poetry of presence and celebration. It may not have been a poetry of ideas and values, but it did transcend the social aspect of everyday society.

Though High T'ang poetry on immortals evolved to serve High T'ang needs, it was essentially a recreation of an older poetic form, like the High T'ang *ku-feng* to which it was closely related. Its source lay in the neo-Taoist tradition of "wandering immortal poems" 遊仙詩, of which the most famous examples were written by the Chin poet Kuo P'u 郭璞. Kuo P'u's "Wandering Immortal Poems" preserved in the *Wen-hsüan* are rather sober works when compared to his poems under the same title preserved elsewhere, and it was to those other "Wandering Immortal Poems" by Kuo P'u that Wu Yün's poems were most closely related. Wu Yün's archaic diction and poetic technique were clearly meant to echo this Chin poetic tradition.

Archaism was less prominent in Li Po's poetry on immortals. For example, a High T'ang interest in dramatic contrasts can be seen in the nineteenth *Ku-feng*, as the poet looked down from his high perspective and saw the turbulence of the human world, "where wolves and jackals all wore officials' caps." Wu Yün also had visions of the tininess and turbulence of the mortal world below, but they were only a stage in the stately ascent to transcendence.

Wandering Immortals   遊仙

Nine dragons, coiling, undulating,	九龍何蜿蜿
Bear my ascent up on a cable of clouds,	載我昇雲網
Whence I peer down in love of my native land—	臨睨懷舊國
There wind and dust meld over vast spaces.	風塵混蒼茫
Now into blurriness, far from man's realm,	依依遠人寰
I go ever farther and draw nigh the god's land.	去去邇帝鄉
High I pass upward, beyond stars' network,	上超星辰紀
And gaze back down on the light of sun and moon—	下視日月光
Suddenly I'm past the T'ai-wei,	倏已過太微
Heaven's dwellings blaze, dazzling my eyes.	天居煥煌煌

[46748]

This is one of the most easily intelligible of Wu Yün's poems on the ascent to immortality; in most cases, the arcana of neo-Taoism defy intelligible

translation.[14] The poem above represents the most common norm of
Wu Yün's immortality poems, a graded ascent through the heavens to an
epiphany of vision. But though it is unique, Wu Yün's poetry combines
the two most powerful currents of T'ien-pao poetry: a taste for the exotic
and a renewed impulse to *fu-ku* poetry.

9

高適

Kao Shih

In the poetry of Kao Shih we often find the language of those powerful, masculine emotions and, with it, energy and sturdiness.

Yin Fan, preface to Kao Shih's poetry in the *Ho-yüeh ying-ling chi*

Contemporary comments on a poet's work rarely constitute in themselves a balanced evaluation, but they often provide certain basic insights that clarify and balance our understanding against the varying interests of later critics. Yin Fan's prefaces to the poets whose works he selected are limited in their scope and concerns, but Yin's contemporary point of view can sometimes serve as a useful corrective to the potent myths that have grown up around the major T'ang poets.

"The language of those powerful, masculine emotions" is a free interpretation of Yin Fan's *hsiung-yi yü* 胸臆語 literally "words from the breast." This refers to emotive language, but the emotions involved are of a different quality from the more sensitive and passive *ch'ing* 情, the "emotions" that are closer to English "feelings." The "words from the breast" constitute an intense, powerful response associated with the masculine persona: they are the language of *pei-chuang* 悲壯, "resolute and manly pathos," a modal term associated with the *ku-feng*. Along with the "words from the breast" comes "energy," *ch'i* 氣, the poet's impelling force of spirit that is embodied in a poem and communicated to a reader. Also there is *ku* 骨, "bone" or "sturdiness": this term, discussed earlier, is an inner strength of form and values with strong *fu-ku* associations. All are vague terms with rich associations, and those associations lead ultimately to the T'ang interpretation of Chien-an and Wei poetry, the *ku-feng*.

Yin Fan's *ku-feng* interpretation of Kao Shih's poetry helps dissociate it from the work of Ts'en Shen. Because the two poets wrote extensively of their experiences on the frontier, their names and reputations have been inextricably bound together. But the union of these two poets is a late

147

phenomenon, occurring first in the Southern Sung. To Yin Fan, Ts'en Shen's poetry belonged to a category of style completely different from Kao Shih's, and in this case, the High T'ang critic's perception is the correct one.

Ts'en Shen was the younger poet who wrote in the new style of the T'ien-pao; his was an essentially descriptive talent that delighted in flamboyance and exotica for their own sake. Ts'en Shen belonged to the second generation of High T'ang poets; he was one of the "later born" whose poetic oeuvre developed in confrontation with the preceding generation's genius. In contrast, Kao Shih was a poet of a particular stance and mood. Ingenuity of description played little role in his poetry: his landscapes were those bleak and barren expanses that stirred *pei-chuang*, the "resolute and manly pathos." Moreover, Kao Shih was essentially a poet of the first High T'ang generation and developed his independent style in relative isolation from contemporary capital poetry. Kao Shih was an intellectual poet who knew and felt the influence of the histories more strongly than he felt the influence of his talented contemporaries. After his growing reputation brought him into closer contact with contemporary poetry, Kao became a smoother, less original poet, but except in the coincidence of theme, his work never resembled the work of Ts'en Shen.

During the High T'ang several implicit concepts of the nature of poetry were in competition; none were mutually exclusive, and none appeared in a pure form in any single poet, but they are the norms of contemporary comment on poetry. To most writers, poetry was a specialized form of social discourse, a means to speak to others: poetry persuaded; it justified certain acts and attitudes; and it gave intelligible form to complex emotions, either those of the speaker or of the person addressed.

A related concept was poetry as pure expression of the poet's inner nature, an extension of self: poetry was the means by which an individual might be known or make himself known. This was a very old theory of poetry, and it differed from the preceding social theory more in emphasis than in substance. The theory of expression was fundamental to the use of poetry as a qualification for service through the examination and as an introduction to potential patrons. It presumed that as an authentic expression of a person's inner nature, the poem might make the unknown person "known." Among the major High T'ang poets the theory of poetry as an extension of self gradually freed itself from these social motives and became an end in itself. The eccentric and the recluse were supposed to be disinterested versions of the self, expressed authentically but for their own sakes. Out of this grew a third version of poetry as a free, creative act. This drew from the theory of art and from earlier literary theory a concept of literary creation as corollary to the larger forces of cosmic Creation. Li Po's work was concerned with projecting or expressing the poet's identity, but the expression was neither authentic nor direct. Instead, the oeuvre was an evidence of mastery and power.

The fourth viewpoint also conceived of poetry as expression and response, but this was an independent tradition where response was measured against the responses of earlier poets and the enduring norms of civilization. This was the *fu-ku* tradition, and its poet was an isolated figure for whom poetry was to be found in texts rather than performance. He might write *to* a contemporary, but he was writing *for* posterity and in the context of the full literary past. He aimed for the universal and general, and he spoke the "old" language that High T'ang readers associated with eternal validity, the language of *ku-feng*. Such a poet was Kao Shih.

Although there are good biographical sources for Kao Shih, the date of his birth remains uncertain: dates ranging from 696 to 707 are given by various sources and scholars, but the latter date is preferable.[1] Kao's family was originally from the far Northeast, but Kao himself seems to have been born elsewhere. Kao's father had been a subprefect in modern Kwangtung; this was an extremely undesirable post and evidence of disfavor by the central government. Kao's family was not an eminent one, and biographical sources even say that as a youth Kao was compelled to beg. He spent much of his childhood in Sung-chou, in modern Honan, a region later devastated during the last campaigns of the An Lu-shan Rebellion. On reaching maturity in the mid-720s, Kao traveled to Ch'ang-an to seek advancement, but lacking any connections, he soon returned to Sung-chou in disappontment. Though there were many new poets in Ch'ang-an in the mid-720s, the only one Kao met for certain was Wang Chih-huan.

After "keeping to literary work for ten years" (suggesting both study and the composition that attended study), Kao set off to the northeastern frontier in 737, probably in search of a military appointment. The failure to gain civil office through the central government often led educated provincials to seek service with the military, where appointment was the prerogative of the commanding general. These offices were usually staff posts involving paperwork rather than combat, and of the scores of T'ang poets who served in the imperial army, it is unlikely that more than a few ever lifted a sword in anger. Alliance with a powerful general greatly enhanced possibilities of future civil service in the capital.

The army in the Northeast was on campaign against the Khitan, and Kao remained with the Chinese forces a year, then made his way back to Sung-chou. But that year was a fertile period for Kao's poetry, and the poetry he wrote in the Northeast showed the strong influence of another poet who had served on a Khitan campaign and visited many of the same sites Kao visited—Ch'en Tzu-ang. More than any other poet, Ch'en Tzu-ang was the model of Kao Shih's early poetry: both were outsiders to capital poetry, and both turned to the *ku-feng* and the language of "those powerful, masculine emotions." Li Po looked to the Ch'en Tzu-ang of the *kan-yü*, but Kao Shih was attracted to the Ch'en Tzu-ang of the campaign poems. The former was the *ku-feng* of the fictional imagination—allegory, *yüeh-fu* themes, the *hsien-jen shih-chih* theme, and immortals; the latter was the *ku-feng* of occasional poetry—the *huai-ku*, meditation, and "moral and resolute pathos."

Kao Shih's five poems entitled "Chi Gate" 薊門 (10238–42) were in the same form and the same style as Ch'en Tzu-ang's famous series "Observing the Past at Chi Heights" 薊丘覽古 (04388–94). Both series used six-line poems: the *ku-feng* defined itself not only positively, as an attempt to recapture an ancient style, but also *against* the regulated forms. The six-line poem was the ideal form for short *ku-feng*, because it avoided the two most common regulated genres, the eight-line *lü-shih* and the *chüeh-chü* quatrain. Ch'en Tzu-ang does not seem to have conceived the six-line poem as an independent form, but Kao Shih clearly did: Kao used the form repeatedly, not only in the two series mentioned above but also in several other series written at or near Sung-chou in the 730s and early 740s. The following is the fifth poem of "Chi Gate":

Dark and brooding beyond the Great Wall,	黯黯長城外
The sun sinks and again dust, again smoke.	日沒更煙塵
Though nomad horsemen press us hard,	胡騎雖憑陵
The troops of Han worry not for their lives.	漢兵不顧身
Ancient trees fill the deserted passes,	古樹滿空塞
And brown clouds destroy men with sorrow.	黃雲愁殺人

[10242]

Kao Shih was fascinated with violent, almost colorless landscapes where: (10253):

Whirlwinds sweep over a million trees,	驚飈蕩萬木
And autumn's breath masses on the high plain.	秋氣屯高原

Like Wei Cheng, Li Pai-yao, Hsüeh Chi, and Ch'en Tzu-ang before him, the poet of the occasional *ku-feng* looks out over a vast and barren landscape, finding in it some moral or social truth. In the poem above the poet perceives the loyal resolution of the Chinese troops in the depressing ambience of the frontier scene, and he responds with the direct, archaic expression of heartfelt misery.

Sometimes Kao might use a more characteristically High T'ang gesture of renunciation:

Written in Chi	薊中作

I whipped on my horse out of the desert,	策馬自沙漠
Galloped afar to climb the barrier walls:	長驅登塞垣

So somber and grim, these border ramparts 邊城何蕭條
Where the bright sun darkened in clouds of brown. 白日黃雲昏
Each time I come to some site of battle, 一到征戰處
I grieve that the nomads may return 每愁胡虜翻

True, we have plans to still the frontiers, 豈無安邊書
But our generals have rested too long in favor. 諸將已承恩
I am depressed at this, Sun Wu's vocation— 惆悵孫吳事
I will go home and alone I will lock my gate. 歸來獨閉門
[10323]

Sun Wu was an ancient military theoretician, and his "vocation" is metonymy for warfare. Presumably the generals of the northwestern frontiers are unwilling to take vigorous action for fear of failing and thereby losing the favor they enjoy.

Although poems like the two above occupy the greater part of Kao Shih's poetry in the northeast, Kao's single most famous poem was written in a different style. This is the "Song of Yen" 燕歌行, a heptasyllabic song that combined the descriptive pyrotechnics characteristic of the song genre with Kao's own starker sensibilities. It was probably through the fame of this and a few other heptasyllabic songs that Kao's work came to be associated with Ts'en Shen's. But Kao Shih was a poet of mood rather than the descriptive imagination, and in the flamboyant context of the heptasyllabic song, the "Song of Yen" was a grim, stark piece of writing.

Preface: In the twenty-sixth year of the K'ai- 開元二十六年，客
yüan Reign (738), there was a man who went with 有從御史張公，出
the Grand Censor Chang Shou-kuei out into the 塞而還者。作燕歌
frontier region; when he returned, he wrote a 行以示適。感征戍
"Song of Yen" and showed it to me. Stirred by 之事，因作和焉。
campaign experiences and military life, I
wrote an accompanying piece.

For the House of Han, war's dust and smoke 漢家煙塵在東北
   lie in the Northeast,
And the Han general leaves his home 漢將辭家破殘賊
   to crush the last of the raiders.
True men by their very nature 男兒本自重橫行
   love the long campaign,
And the Son of Heaven has granted them 天子非常賜顏色
   his special countenance.
Strike the kettledrums, beat the tambours 摐金伐鼓下榆關
   down through Elm Pass,
Banners and pennons in far-winding lines 旌旆逶迤碣石間
   move over Chieh Rock.

Dispatches from the colonels
    fly across the Sea of Sand.
The hunting fires of the Great Khan
    are shining upon Wolf Mountain.
Now gloom settles on mountains and rivers
    all through this borderland,
Nomad horsemen press our ranks hard,
    blending with wind and rain;
Our troops fighting in the vanguard,
    half living and half now dead,
While the loveliest maidens dance and sing
    in the tents of the commander.
On the great desert, autumn's end,
    border plants sicken and die,
A lone fortress in setting sunlight
    where troops doing battle grow fewer—
They have tasted His Majesty's favor
    and think nothing of the foe,
But their strength is worn down at forts in the mountains,
    the encirclement not yet broken.
Men clad in armor in far garrisons,
    their sufferings long endured;
Surely many a lady wept silver tears
    after many a parting.
As south of the city a young wife's heart
    is on the point of breaking,
North of Chi a man marching
    turns to look back in vain.
Whirled back and forth on the borderlands,
    how can they ever cross over?
In this farthest realm's vast reaches
    nothing there is at all.
For three seasons long, winds of destruction
    form into phalanx of cloud;
Sounds in the cold: the whole night through,
    the ringing of watch kettles.
They look on each other: bare blades of silver
    where snow comes drifting down,
Steadfast to death, and never a thought
    of glory or reward.
Haven't you seen on those tracts of sand
    the pain of marching and battle?
But even today there is memory of
    our general, Li Kuang.　[10358]

校尉羽書飛瀚海

單于獵火照狼山

山川蕭條極邊土

胡騎憑陵雜風雨

戰士軍前半死生

美人帳下猶歌舞

大漠窮秋寒草腓

孤城落日鬭兵稀

身當恩遇常輕敵

力盡關山未解圍

鐵衣遠戍辛勤久

玉筋應嘀別離後

少婦城南欲斷腸

征人薊北空回首

邊庭飄飄那可度

絕域蒼茫無所有

殺氣三時作陣雲

寒聲一夜傳刁斗

相看白刃雪紛紛

死節從來豈顧勳

君不見沙場征戰苦

至今猶憶李將軍

The significance of the "memory of our general, Li Kuang," is double-edged. That great Han "Flying General," claimed by the T'ang royal house as its ancestor, was an extremely successful campaigner, and the closing line may suggest a yearning for past competence in face of present incompetence. In the words of Wang Ch'ang-ling (06785):

If only the Flying General of Lu Fort were here,　　但使盧城飛將在
He would never let nomad horses cross Yin Mountain.　不敎胡馬度陰山

On the other hand, Kao's closing may suggest that it is the futile desire to emulate Li Kuang which has led to endless campaigns and which results in so much human suffering. And in the context of the heroic self-sacrifice of the troops, the memory of Li Kuang may may serve yet a third function, a reminder of how poorly the state rewards those who serve it well: the Han general cut his own throat in response to the ingratitude of his superiors. Kao's song was written in response to someone else's "Song of Yen" (see preface), and it is possible that a reference to Li Kuang in the original version, now lost, would have clarified its function here.

Although most elements in Kao's song were commonplaces of frontier poetry, the poem is strikingly original in its overall effect and well deserved the fame it achieved. Like Wang Wei's short "Army Song" (05782), perhaps from the same year, and Li Po's "Fought South of the Wall" (07930), of an undetermined date, Kao's "Song of Yen" forms something resembling a narrative out of a series of short scenes. In contrast to Ts'en Shen's interest in exotic frontier scenery for its own sake, the focus of Kao's poem is on the troops, their courage and their suffering; the scenery is only an instrument of their misery. In his social concerns Kao Shih foreshadowed the songs of Tu Fu, but artistically he was more conservative. The songs of Ts'en Shen and Tu Fu in the late 740s and early 750s were more unified works, the former in description, the latter in narrative; but the "Song of Yen" is in the K'ai-yüan style, an impressionistic pastiche of scene fragments that only hint at narrative sequences.

A large body of of Kao's poetry was written in Sung-chou, but whether before or after his northeastern journey of 737–38, it is impossible to tell. The Sung-chou poems were strongly in the *ku-feng* tradition, and one series, "In Sung" 宋中 (10313–22), was even closer to Ch'en Tzu-ang's "Observing the Past at Chi Heights" than the "Chi Gate" series. The first poem of "In Sung" concerns the ruins of the palace of the fabled Prince of Liang:

When long ago Liang's prince was in his glory,　梁王昔全盛
Among his guests were many men of talent.　　賓客復多才
And now remote, across a thousand years,　　　悠悠一千年

There are only the ruins of his high terrace.　　　　陳跡唯高臺
In utter silence I face the autumn grasses,　　　　寂寞向秋草
And a sad wind comes from a thousand miles.　　　悲風千里來
[10313]

Compare Ch'en Tzu-ang writing on Prince Chao of Yen: no single line of Kao's poem echoes Ch'en's poem, yet in sentiment and style the two poems are identical:

To the south I climbed the lodge of Chieh Rock,　　南登碣石館
And gazed afar on his terrace of gold.　　　　　　遙望黃金臺
The hills are all covered with high trees,　　　　丘陵盡喬木
But Prince Chao of Yen—where is he now?　　　　昭王安在哉
Sad how his plans to be overlord are done,　　　　霸圖恨已矣
I ride my horse back down again　　　　　　　　驅馬復歸來
[04389]

Both the language and the message are simple, yet the modal associations of the style and theme touched contemporary readers deeply, evoking an ancient simplicity of feeling and a sense of vanished nobility.

> Were be they that beforen us weren,
> Houndes laden and havekes beren,
> And haden feld and wode.

To translate the medieval lyric into modern English—"Where are those who lived before us, who led hounds, carried hawks, and possessed fields and woods?"—is like translating the *ku-feng* of Kao Shih and Ch'en Tzu-ang: the considerable literary values of the poems lie in the reader's sense of cultural and literary history, which is touched by an archaism, a turn of phrase, or a simplicity that is romantically projected into the past.

Kao was capable of a more arcane and formal style, but the *ku-feng* continued to appear through his work of the 740s. At times Kao Shih's *fu-ku* impulse went beyond the *ku-feng* and approached the extreme archaism of midcentury poets like Yüan Chieh; for example, the "Three Poems on Lord Fu's Lute Hall" 登子賤琴堂賦詩 (10306–8) included a preface that explicitly summarized the moral purport of each poem. The practice of including ethical commentary with poems was associated with the high moral purpose of "ancient poetry" and came from a variety of sources: Mao's topical interpretations of the *Shih-ching* were set in texts as prefaces to individual *Shih*, and Shu Hsi's 束晳 series "Filling in the Lyrics of Lost Songs" 補亡, included in the *Wen-hsüan*, also used the technique. Kao Shih's "Three Poems on Lord Fu's Lute Hall" are among the earliest T'ang examples and probably antedate Yüan Chieh's version of "Filling in the Lyrics of Lost Songs." Later, when Po Chü-yi wrote the "New *Yüeh-fu*," he enunciated the principle in his preface to the series: "A prefatory sentence at the head of each poem states the topic."[2]

In 744 Kao Shih met Li Po and Tu Fu in his home region of Sung-chou. The few months that the three poets spent together greatly impressed the ever impressionable Tu Fu, but neither Li Po nor Kao seem to have felt the momentousness of the occasion. At this time Kao Shih's reputation as a poet was just beginning, and shortly thereafter Kao was recommended to the capital. During the ministerships of Chang Yüeh and Chang Chiu-ling, provincials had had some hope of advancement, but in the T'ien-pao the great Li Lin-fu came to power, and Li feared an excess of rusticity around His Majesty. Probably more as a matter of course than out of special enmity, Li Lin-fu blocked Kao's chances for a post in the central government much as he tried to block Tu Fu's. Instead, Kao received the lowest of all positions in the official hierarchy appointed by the capital, that of office chief—in Kao's case, of Feng-chou in northern Honan. Understandably, Kao was little pleased with his new post. In 749, as part of his duties, Kao went again to the northeastern frontier, this time as an escort for a a levy of local troops.

Kao Shih's political fortunes changed abruptly in 752, when he attracted the notice of one of Hsüan-tsung's most important generals, Ko-shu Han. Ko-shu Han made Kao his secretary and took him along to his command in Central Asia in 754. Kao had met the young poet Ts'en Shen in the capital in 753, and though both served in Central Asia the following year, they do not seem to have corresponded. At the same time that Ts'en was writing wildly descriptive songs on the wonders of the Central Asian landscape, Kao was smoothing out the roughness of his *fu-ku* style. His recent contacts with some of the most famous poets of the capital had subtly affected his own work, mellowed some of his idiosyncracies, and brought him closer to the various styles popular in the capital in the early 750s. The following poem, a *lü-shih*, differs from Kao's earlier, old-style frontier poetry largely as a function of generic differences; but for a poem on this topic, the very choice of the polished *lü-shih* and the rejection of the *ku-feng* is significant.

The North Tower of Golden Fort	金城北樓
From the North Tower my westward gaze is filled with clear sky,	北樓西望滿晴空
Massed waters and linked mountains lovelier than a painting.	積水連山勝畫中
A swift current over the rapids, its sound like an arrow's,	湍上急流聲若箭
The waning moon over the fort— form of bent bow.	城頭殘月勢如弓
I've bid farewell to P'an Creek's elder, his fishing line still dangling,	垂竿已謝磻溪老
But my mind is still on the old frontiersman	體道猶思塞上翁

who lived within the Way.
Should you ask me of these borderlands,
    what else there is out here—
Ever and now the nomad flutes
    sing bitterness without end.   [10432]

爲問邊庭更何事

至今羌笛怨無窮

P'an Creek's elder was T'ai-kung, who was fishing in the creek when King Wen of Chou met him and raised him to his councillor. The story became a standard metaphor for imperial recognition and quick promotion to high office. Kao Shih's T'ai-kung is still awaiting "discovery," but Kao himself takes his leave, giving up hope of recognition. The consolation for Kao's hopelessness comes in the following line, from a story in the *Huai-nan-tzu*: once there was an old man whose horse wandered into nomad territory; his neighbors all offered their sympathy, but the old man simply said, "How do you know this isn't a piece of good luck?" Later the horse returned leading an entire herd of nomad horses; his neighbors then all congratulated the old man, who replied, "How do you know *this* isn't a misfortune?" Afterwards the old man's son, who was out riding one of the nomad horses, was thrown and broke his thigh; again the neighbors commiserated, and again the old man questioned the nature of his fortune. Finally, during a nomad incursion, all the young men of the region were drafted into the militia and most died on the campaign. Only the old man's son, with his broken thigh, was left at home. Kao finds consolation in this story, and it allows him to question whether his apparent misfortune in failing to achieve office might not finally turn out for the best. The consolation had a prophetic truth.

When the An Lu-shan Rebellion broke out and Lo-yang fell, Ko-shu Han was commanded to hold T'ung Pass, the major stronghold on the road to Ch'ang-an. Under pressure from the central government, Ko-shu Han was forced to quit the fortifications and do battle with An Lu-shan's army in the open. The imperial army was defeated decisively, but Kao Shih managed to escape with his life and to make his way to Hsüan-tsung's refuge in Ch'eng-tu. There Kao made a defense of Ko-shu Han's defeat, and as a result Kao was made a censor. Later the new emperor, Su-tsung, decided to give military commands to the various imperial princes, and as censor, Kao opposed the plan vigorously. When the inept revolt of the prince of Yung broke out (the one that involved Li Po), Kao Shih was credited with great perspicacity and rewarded with a number of high posts, including that of regional commander (*chieh-tu-shih*). In this last function, he took part in the suppression of the prince of Yung.

Like most of the new officials appointed to central government offices during the rebellion and especially those associated with the disgraced minister Fang Kuan, Kao lost his position after the capitals were retaken. Kao was transferred to the post of prefect of P'eng-chou in Szechwan in 760. There Kao again showed his military talents and was instrumental in crushing two rebellions against the central government. After his first success, he was again made a regional commander. Then, in 763 there was a Tibetan invasion of the Kansu region, and Kao Shih responded by leading his troops out of his home region to meet them. This time his military talent failed him, but he was recalled in honor to the capital, enfeoffed, and given several high offices. Shortly thereafter, in 765, Kao died. As the *Old T'ang History* observed, "Though the course of the T'ang, Kao Shih is the only example of a poet who became a true political success."

It is hardly surprising that the demands of political success exacted a price in his poetry: relatively few of Kao Shih's poems can be dated from his last years, after the An Lu-shan Rebellion. This contradicts the most curious piece of biographical data on Kao's life, a notice in the *Old Tang History* that Kao began to pay serious attention to poetry only at the age of fifty, and that over the course of a few years, his style changed completely. This comment is not a commonplace in biographies of literary men and must have had some basis in a contemporary source, perhaps a lost letter or preface. However, no matter how one juggles the date of Kao's birth, the greater part of Kao's extant poetry was done well before he was fifty. Moreover, in his later years Kao did gradually abandon his youthful *ku-feng* style, but there was nothing like a radical change in his work. The most likely explanation involves the traditional association of style and an emperor's moral influence: one can imagine Kao or a preface writer making such a comment as a tribute to the ascension of Su-tsung and the "restoration" of dynastic power in 756.

Writing to Tu Fu in 762, Kao Shih showed something of the mellowness of Tu Fu's later work, but rather than a mark of stylistic change, this signals a general weakening of Kao's poetic identity and a submission to the styles of other groups and poets.

On the Day of Mankind: To Tu Fu	人日寄杜二拾遺
On the day of Mankind I write this poem to send to your thatched hut	人日題詩寄草堂
From afar with love for a dear old friend yearning for native land.	遙憐故人思故鄉
The play of colors in willow branches I cannot bear to see,	柳條弄色不忍見
And plum blossoms filling the boughs break my heart in vain.	梅花滿枝空斷腸
Here I am on the southern borders, nothing to cheer my mind,	身在南蕃無所預

My heart filled with countless griefs,　　　　　　　心懷百憂復千慮
　　innumerable concerns.
This year on the day of Mankind　　　　　　　　　今年人日空相憶
　　we remember each other in vain,
Next year on the day of Mankind　　　　　　　　　明年人日知何處
　　I wonder where we will be.
Once like Hsieh An I lay on East Mountain,　　　　一臥東山三十春
　　resting for thirty years,
Unaware that with book and sword　　　　　　　　豈知書劍老風塵
　　I'd grow old in the wind-blown dust.
Now decrepit with age, they've raised my salary—　龍鍾還忝二千石
　　two thousand pounds of rice,
And I must stand embarrassed, facing you,　　　　愧爾東西南北人
　　who go north, south, east, west.

[10360]

The "day of Mankind" was the seventh day of the first month, the preceding days having been devoted to lesser animals. The poem is famous primarily because of its dedication to Tu Fu, but the half-humorous deprecation of the closure is very effective.

Kao Shih's collection, now comprising almost two hundred and fifty poems, originally made up twenty *chüan*; however, there is no way to know the proportion of poetry to prose in that larger collection. Since the length of a *chüan* and the number of characters per page varied greatly, one cannot say that part of the collection has been lost simply because extant editions have fewer *chüan* than are indicated in the original bibliographical notices. However, the preservation in early anthologies of many poems not included in the main body of Kao's works does suggest that Kao Shih's collection in its present form is far from complete.

With a few exceptions, such as the brilliant "Song of Yen," Kao Shih's poetry is probably more difficult for the modern reader to appreciate than the work of any other major T'ang poet. In the T'ang, especially in the mid-eighth century, Kao's reputation was high: to Tu Fu, who was admittedly prejudiced in favor of Kao, the old poet was one of the heroes of the age (11173):

In this age when we speak of men of talent,　　　當代論才子
How many others are a match for you?　　　　　　如今復幾人

But as Kao's name became increasingly linked to that of Ts'en Shen, he came to be regarded as only a border poet, the author of the "Song of Yen." In this deforming mask, Kao has come to be thought of as a weak second to Ts'en.[3] Modern readers have been understandably attracted to the flamboyance of the T'ien-pao style, and judged against that standard, it is not surprising that Kao seems inferior to Ts'en. But to appreciate the talents for which Kao Shih was admired in the T'ang, his poetry must be read in a context of aesthetic values different from those of the T'ien-pao song writers.

Kao Shih was the least visual of the major T'ang poets and, with the exception of Tu Fu, the most intellectual. Much of Kao's later poetry possesses an allusiveness and rugged formality that defies aesthetically pleasing translation; there he was the great public poet, celebrating the myths of imperial order, the deeds of the great, and the moral values of traditional Chinese civilization. The element of personal response in Kao Shih's poetry was not a signal of individuality, but rather it sought to embody the normative reaction of a sensitive and morally concerned Confucian intellectual. In the "Song of Yen" Kao wrote effectively of the hardships of campaign, but he also celebrated with formality Li Fu's campaign against the Thai state (10309):

Our Sage glowed wrathful in his rage,	聖人赫斯怒
Ordered attack on the southwest tribes;	詔伐西南戎
Sternly, gravely, in halls of council	肅穆廟堂上
They deliberated deeply on the power of command.	深沉節制雄

When Ko-shu Han defeated the Tibetans (10437):

The streams spurt blood of the many tribes,	泉噴諸戎血
Winds drive the souls of dead nomads,	風驅死虜魂
Heads fly as they gather thousands of pikes,	頭飛攢萬戟
Hands tied behind, massed at the general's gate.	面縛聚轅門
Ghosts weep in the brown dust of evening,	鬼哭黃埃暮
And the heavens grieve as the bright sun sinks.	天愁白日昏

This was not Ts'en Shen's fascination with border warfare as part of an exotic, alien world, but rather the treatment of warfare as an adjunct of imperial policy. The violence that was repressed in so many High T'ang poets here can be expressed directly, legitimately as a manifestation of imperial power.

For complicated reasons much of Kao's private poetry is even more inaccessible than his public poetry. Kao Shih was a modal poet, but one of a very different sort than Wang Ch'ang-ling. Wang Ch'ang-ling's poetry retained its popularity because it was sensuous. In contrast, Kao Shih's poetry depended heavily on the affective energy with which T'ang readers invested the *ku-feng*. As the T'ang sense of the *ku-feng* began to fade in the mid-ninth century, interest in the poetry that grew up around it faded too. The following poem, the first of a series entitled "Written on the Tung-p'ing Road" 東平路作 (10342–44) appealed to aesthetic values peculiar to the T'ang.

My plans to go south never reached fruition,   南圖適不就
This rushing eastward is not to my heart.   東走豈吾心
Now moaning, moaning a chill wind rises,   索索涼風動
On and on I go, as autumn floods deepen.   行行秋水深
The cicada sings, leaves fall from the trees,   蟬鳴木葉落
And again this evening, the long rains of fall.   茲夕更秋霖

[10342]

Two allusions require explanation: the "plans to go south" refer to the P'eng, the world-spanning Great Bird that for T'ang readers was a symbol of spiritual and political greatness. According to the *Chuang-tzu*, only when the P'eng was lifted thousands of miles high on a mighty whirlwind could it "plan to go south" to the Southern Sea at the other edge of the universe. Thus, the phrase referred to aspirations of greatness. The "autumn floods" also comes from the *Chuang-tzu*, where the rivers of autumn, swollen but still bounded "Ways," all rush toward the vast undifferentiation of the sea, the ultimate Way. But the melancholy mood of the poem suggests a more ominous vision of the floods, the vision found in *Analects* XVIII.6, where Confucius had "missed the ford" and met the mad Taoists Chang-tsu and Chieh-ni. When Confucius sent his disciple to Chang-tsu and Chieh-ni to ask of the ford," they took the question metaphorically and responded with a vision of the world in flux and flood, a world without a direct "Way" or ford. To Confucius their vision represented not a state of nature but the decay of human civilization.

Kao Shih's poem goes far beyond these two allusions. Almost every line evokes the autumn mode of Chien-an and Wei poetry, a bleak world of ruin in which the poet feels increasingly isolated. The poet rushes along a road with no apparent direction, and the landscape through which he passes is a bleakness without color, without place-names or landmarks, a landscape of wind, bare trees, and rising waters. The poem lacks the usual spatial and geographical orientation of occasional poetry: it is "everywhere." The characteristically High T'ang objective closure sustains the mood and projects it into an unknown future: waters will continue to rise, and turbulent floods will spread everywhere as the world sinks in the Yin darkness of evening and year's end.

Although Kao Shih's later poetry approached more closely the work of his contemporaries, he began, like Li Po, as a solitary poet. He felt the attraction neither of his great contemporaries among the K'ai-yüan capital poets nor of court poetry and its craft. In his early years "poetry" was what Kao had read in Ch'en Tzu-ang and the *Wen-hsüan*; it was not primarily an activity practiced at certain times but a collection of texts. The material of poetry was not an ornamental craft applied to set topics, but rather what Kao had read in the classics, philosophers, and histories, as well as in earlier poets. Kao's work became a model of seriousness, "literature" in its fullest Chinese sense, but only one poet truly responded to the model: that poet responded to all the myriad forms of literary genius and made them his own—Tu Fu.

PART TWO

The "Later-Born": The Second and Third Generations of the High T'ang

A poetic generation is not a historical entity but a relationship, and it cannot be defined purely in chronological terms. The poets who reached artistic maturity in the K'ai-yüan constituted a generation, and their generation was loosely unified by a negative relationship to court poetry and the Early T'ang style. The work of the capital poets may have been more deeply infused with the craft of court poetry than the work of outsiders like Kao Shih and Li Po, but all the poets of the K'ai-yüan generation possessed a freedom of innovation that would have been impossible in the Early T'ang. Renewed interest in the values of reclusion, eccentricity, creative autonomy, and the meritocracy of virtue set the individual and his inner identity above social role.

Genius came easily in those years, partly because there had been no truly great poets for centuries.[1] There was much space for individual talent. On a profound level, there were no "great" court poets because court poetry had been an essentially anonymous venture; "genius" awaited Li Po and a concept of poetry as an expression of individual indentity.

The young poets of the 740s and 750s faced a range of established individual talents unparalleled in earlier Chinese literature. Young Wang Wei may have admired the craftsmanship of a Sung Chih-wen or Shen Ch'üan-ch'i, but mastery of their craft presented no threat to his own developing poetic identity. In the 740s young Ts'en Shen admired Li Po, but mastery of Li Po's art could raise him at best only to a weak echo of Li. Writing in the style of Sung or Shen, Wang Wei would be called "master craftsman"; writing in the style of Wang Wei or Li Po, Ts'en Shen would be called "imitator," for the poetic voice he used carried the name of another. Nor were the first-generation masters dead and gone when many second-generation poets were growing to poetic maturity;

Wang Wei and Li Po were at the heights of their creative powers when Ts'en Shen, Tu Fu, Yüan Chieh, and Ch'ien Ch'i were trying to find their own poetic voices.

Thus, the poets of the second generation became what might be called *hou-sheng* 後生, the "later-born." Their unity as a generation lay in the priority of the first-generation masters and in the very fact that the "later-born" had to respond to that earlier genius in their poetry. In some cases the younger poets were overwhelmed by their predecessors and became true "followers." Such poets were primarily in the tradition of capital poetry, of which Wang Wei came to be considered the undisputed master. Through the second and third generations of capital poets, the shared style of the K'ai-yüan was carried virtually unchanged into the ninth century.

In other cases, younger poets tried to surpass their predecessors, and the passion to surpass manifested itself in a poetry of stylistic, thematic, and modal excess, the flamboyant T'ien-pao song style (as *kuo* 過 links the ideas of "surpassing" and "excess"). Still other younger poets sought to repudiate their talented predecessors, and the polemical, antithetical nature of the *fu-ku* tradition provided a means to assert superiority over all "modern" poetic efforts. Finally, there was the most difficult stance: to assimilate one's predecessors and master the masters. From these possible responses came Ch'ien Ch'i and a host of others, the conservators of the capital poetic tradition; Ts'en Shen, the overreacher and master of the T'ien-pao song style; Yüan Chieh, the *fu-ku* radical; and finally, Tu Fu, the poet who assimilated and transcended all his predecessors.

So much has been written on the cultural trauma caused by the An Lu-shan Rebellion that it would be redundant to discuss it here. Indeed, except in the case of Tu Fu, there was a nearly universal retrenchment in postrebellion poetry. The work of Kao Shih, Ts'en Shen, and Yüan Chieh turned markedly more conservative in the later 750s; even the ebullient Li Po seems less daring in the poetry datable to his last years. Then, one after another, the poets of the midcentury passed away, and amid the decades of military and political troubles that wracked the fragile T'ang state, a rigid conservatism ruled capital poetry. No longer able to respond creatively to past genius, poets of the third High T'ang generation were content to walk competently in the shadow of K'ai-yüan and T'ien-pao greatness.

But during the decades from 760 to 790, the Southeast became a center of poetic activity to rival the capital. There the most talented poet of the later eighth century, Wei Ying-wu, wrote in an idiom appropriate to the age: elegiac reminiscences of past glory—literary, political, and cultural. At the same time, the southeastern monk Chiao-jan learned an important lesson from the poetic diversity of the century, a lesson he may have passed on to several admiring younger poets who were to become major figures in the Mid-T'ang. Poetry was neither a timeless craft nor a single "ancient" style to be advocated above all others, nor even a body of used-up possibilities from which the "new" poet should differ; rather, the literary past became a vast collection of individual voices and period styles, each with its own identity, quality, and associations. These idioms could be used by a poet as he chose; they did not preclude innovation, but they were, in their totality, the material and language of poetry. It was Chiao-jan who first attained a full literary-historical perspective on the poetic tradition, and he embodied his catholic taste in his own work. That ability to move freely between the styles of periods and individual poets was to become one of the most important characteristics of later poetry in China.

10

岑參

Ts'en Shen
The Search for Difference

In his diction Ts'en Shen favored the strange, and his style was massive and daring; his ideas also were ingenious and strange. Couplets like:

> Steady winds blow white rushes,
> Wildfires burn barren mulberries.

mark a lofty, dispassionate talent. And couplets like:

> A mountain wind blows on the empty forest,
> And in its rustling someone seems to be there.

capture the very essence of reclusion.

> Yin Fan, preface to Ts'en Shen's poems in the *Ho-yüeh ying-ling chi* [753]

In phrasing he admired clarity; in ideas he valued those that touched readers immediately and sharply. He was usually at his best in creating a perfect scene.

> Tu Tui 杜碓, preface to the *Chia-chou chi* [ca. 800]

As Kao Shih needed to be saved from a reputation as Ts'en Shen's less gifted twin, so Ts'en Shen needs to be redeemed from his well-deserved fame as the master of frontier poetry. T'ang comments on Ts'en Shen's poetry praised a master craftsman, a stylist who succeeded in creating daring effects. By the twentieth century, this poet whose couplets captured the "essence of reclusion" had become the greatest frontier poet, whose attraction lay not in the realm of craft but in a "realism" that attended writing from direct experience:

Of all the poets of the K'ai-yüan and T'ien-pao, Ts'en Shen had the greatest affection for things foreign. . . . Many T'ang poets wrote of the frontiers, but they were clutching after winds and shadows. Ts'en Shen, on the other hand, wrote every line from personal experience.[1]

169

Such a drastic change in the qualities for which Ts'en Shen's poetry was admired reflects a basic difference between the interests of T'ang and later audiences. Certainly, the major High T'ang poets went beyond concerns of craft, but with the notable exceptions of Li Po and the poets of the *ku-feng*, mastery of craft remained a major concern of both poets and readers. Craft applied primarily, but not exclusively, to the regulated genres. To think of Meng Hao-jan's poetry in terms other than those of craft was to think about Meng Hao-jan the person; to consider Meng Hao-jan's poetry as poetry meant a consideration of craft, of the "perfect lucidity" of a couplet. The High T'ang conception of craft may have differed from that of the Early T'ang, but in this concern High T'ang poets were closer to their six-century and seventh-century predecessors than they were to the poets of the Mid-T'ang. To Yin Fan, the sound of footsteps seeming to emerge through the rustling of the leaves was an aesthetic triumph quite apart from the quality of the poem as a whole. True, a poet might excel in some themes and be weak in others, but poets were less frequently indentified with their themes in the High T'ang; rather, identities of mood and style and the quality of performance were primary.

In contrast, later readers could not help seeing a historical dimension in High T'ang poetry; it was the most accessible evidence of the myth of the High T'ang as the apogee of poetry and medieval civilization. Thus, Ts'en Shen came to be distinguished not by the subtle qualities of his craft, but by a theme that represented one aspect of that civilization: T'ang expansion into Central Asia. The first hint of this shift in interest appeared in the *Ts'ang-lang shih-hua* in the Southern Sung, when Ts'en's work was first linked to Kao Shih's; Yen Yü inappropriately described Ts'en's poetry as *pei-chuang*, the modal quality of *ku-feng* often associated with frontier poetry.

Ts'en Shen's poetry was not widely discussed during the Sung, and the revival of interest in his work seems to have grown out of Ming neoclassicism and its exclusive devotion to High T'ang poetry. In a postface to Ts'en Shen's *Chia-chou Collection* 嘉州集, the neoclassicist Pien Kung 邊貢 went so far as to say that Ts'en was superior to both Li Po and Tu Fu because his work united the essential qualities of both; however, this excess was probably no more than Pien Kung justifying his own poetry, which stood in the shadows of *his* more famous contemporaries. After the Ming, Ts'en Shen's reputation rose steadily, and his frontier poems came gradually to define his work.

But Ts'en Shen was a more versatile poet than his modern critics allow, and the exotica of Central Asia in his work were simply convenient topics to satisfy the T'ien-pao thirst for the strange. Exotic themes were a corollary manifestation of Ts'en's interest, noticed by Yin Fan, in "strange diction" and "ingenious ideas." All these various aspects of Ts'en Shen's prerebellion poetry were dedicated to a newness that could carry the poet beyond the work of his predecessors.

Ts'en Shen was born in about 715 into a declining branch of a great family, the Nan-yang Ts'en's. The Nan-yang Ts'en's had held a succession of high government posts since the Later Liang, and three of its members had been ministers during the T'ang, including Ts'en Shen's great-grand-father, who had been a minister of T'ai-tsung. However, in the decades before Ts'en Shen's birth, another branch of the family had risen to prominence, and Ts'en Shen's father spent his life in a series of provincial posts, rising only as high as prefect. Ts'en Shen's family was a respectable one but no longer great, either in social standing or in power.

We know very little of Ts'en Shen's early life except that his father died while the poet was still very young and that afterwards the family took up residence in the Sung Mountain region south of Lo-yang. Ts'en spoke with conventional modesty of his family holdings in the Lo-yang region, and in his preface, Tu Tui even called Ts'en "poor." But the family was probably moderately well-off.

In about 734, Ts'en Shen journeyed to Ch'ang-an and presented a memorial to the throne in hopes of obtaining office. The choice of this route to public office rather than the more hazardous examination may suggest that Ts'en had such confidence in the family name that he did not feel he needed to take the examination. His petition was not granted, and he returned to the capital later as part of the regional quota of examination candidates.

Ts'en Shen's most characteristic poetry did not begin until the mid-740s, but some earlier poems survive. This early work is highly significant, because it shows the strong influence of Wang Wei, of Meng Hao-jan, and, later, Li Po. Ts'en's relationship to the great poets of the first generation was not social: he seems to have known neither Wang nor Meng, and an acquaintance with Li Po is only a possibility. It was the genius of their poetry that attracted him to their style rather than the social pressure to join their company. In the 730s the poetry of reclusion and the T'ao Ch'ien revival were at their peak, and young Ts'en Shen, in his busy search for office, wrote serenely (09546):

In evening I grow more distant from the crowd	夕與人羣疏
And love still more the valleys and hills.	轉愛丘壑中
Waters and trees match a stillness in the heart,	心澹水木會
Fish and birds comprehend seclusion's joy.	興幽魚鳥通

In the same poem Ts'en played Meng Hao-jan:

Valley clouds pale autumn's countenance	谿雲淡秋容

echoing Meng Hao-jan's already famous:

Faint clouds pale the river of stars.   微雲淡河漢

Another line in the same poem—

I know contentment in its wonders only all alone.   勝愜只自知

is unmistakably close to a famous line from Wang Wei's later poetry: (05968):

I know all about its wonders, without motive and alone.   勝事空自知

Clearly the Ts'en Shen of the late 730s cannot be imitating the Wang Wei of the late 750s, but the diction is so characteristic of Wang Wei that one can only presume Wang had written something similar in an earlier poem now lost. Other early poems by Ts'en Shen show Wang Wei's influence even more strongly (09645):

How can I explain the experience of wondrous scenes?   勝事那能説
My prince has gone off and not yet returned.   王孫去未還

In this couplet young Ts'en succinctly combines the highpoints of the whole tradition of eremitic poetry. There is a hint of the sublime experience of nature that cannot be explained, as in T'ao Ch'ien's famous "Drinking Wine" V; but the seeming ineffability of the experience modulates into an inability to express oneself for want of an appreciative friend, as in the poetry of Hsieh Ling-yün. And that absent friend turns out to be the "prince" of the "Summons to the Recluse" in the *Ch'u-tz'u*, a figure Wang Wei appropriated several times for the closure of his poems (05967, 06107).

    If in the mid-720s Wang Wei felt (06954):

My heart is as calm as the broad stream,   心與大川閒

then Ts'en Shen found the ideal recluse-fisherman had (09631):

A heart as clear as Ts'ang-lang's waters.   心與滄浪清

While Ts'en was still under the spell of Wang Wei's beautifully controlled style, a new poetic luminary appeared in the capital in the early 740s—Li Po. At about the same time the various masks of Li Po also made their appearance in Ts'en Shen's poetry. As Li Po had celebrated carousals in Hsiang-yang in the 730s, so Ts'en Shen, passing the ancient city of Han-tan in 742, celebrated the famous locale in a voice unmistakably echoing Li Po (09633):

Han-tan girls sell wine by night,   邯鄲女兒夜沽酒
  Face the guests,
swing lanterns from poles,   對客挑燈誇數錢

show off the few coins they've gotten;
And I'll be roaring drunk till the sun is high next noon—
A verse of crazy song, then sleeping in the tavern.

酩酊醉時日正午
一曲狂歌爐上眠

Specific borrowings and stylistic echoes of both Wang Wei and Li Po are found throughout Ts'en Shen's poetry. From time to time it seems almost as if Ts'en were engaging in his own private competition with Li: if Li Po had written brilliantly of the waterfall on Lu Mountain (08570–571), then Ts'en Shen would have to describe a cascade even more furious and dazzling (09511). Ts'en Shen's later use of the heptasyllabic song in occasional poetry may have come from the precedent of Li Po. But the most significant attractions of Li Po's work for young Ts'en Shen were Li's imaginative descriptive technique, his image of the wild poet-singer, and his fascination with extremes. It was no accident that Yin Fan characterized the work of both Li Po and Ts'en Shen as "strange" 奇. Yet another great poet of the age, Wang Ch'ang-ling, was known to Ts'en personally, but fewer direct echoes of Wang Ch'ang-ling's poetry appear in Ts'en Shen's work; however, Ts'en owed much to Wang Ch'ang-ling in his quatrain techique.

Like other young poets of the 740s, Ts'en Shen felt the spell of the masters of the first generation, and he often succumbed to the temptation to fall into their style. But Ts'en managed to escape the trap of his admiration by an original synthesis of capital poetic craftsmanship and the new style of the T'ien-pao. This was accomplished in the couplet, and the combination of formal restraint and imaginative metaphor was very effective.

Much stylistic interest was concentrated in what was later to be called the "eye" of the line—the third-position word in the pentasyllabic line. In the 740s Ts'en Shen began to use bold metaphors in this position, as in the following couplet from a poem of 742 (09644):

A lonely lantern sets ablaze the sojourner's dream,
Cold washing mallets pound the sorrow of home.

孤燈然客夢
寒杵搗鄉愁

As the poet awakes from his dream, he sees the flame of the lantern in his eyes, and it seems to set the images of his dreams ablaze. The sound of washing blocks makes the traveler think of home, and thus, synaesthetically the sound seems to "pound" his sorrow.

The use of a metaphorical verb in the third position of the pentasyllabic line had been a characteristic of court poetry, but never before had the metaphors been so bold and difficult. Such couplets appeared often in Ts'en's regulated verses of the 740s (09759):

An herb basin's waters shake the mountain's reflections,
The fishing line, belted by a scar in the water.

藥椀搖山影
魚竿帶水痕

But like the bold simplicity of Li Po's dog barking amid the sounds of water, these metaphorical couplets (moderate by Western standards) unbalanced the regulated verse. In both cases the remainder of poems would surround brilliant couplets with embarrassed flatness. Ts'en Shen was capable of sustaining descriptive ingenuity in his frontier songs, but it was not possible in the aesthetics of the High T'ang regulated verse.

In 744, Ts'en Shen passed the *chin-shih* examination and received an insignificant post in the guard of the crown prince, a sign of his lack of influence. In 749 the great general Kao Hsien-chih came to court, and probably because Ts'en's former post in the guard counted as experience in "military" administration, Kao took Ts'en on his staff and returned with him to his command at An-hsi, Kucha in Central Asia. In 751, Kao Hsien-chih was badly defeated by forces of the Caliphate at the Battle of the Talas River, and he returned to the capital in disgrace.

In 752, Ts'en himself returned to the capital, and there he became friends with Tu Fu and Kao Shih. In 754, Ts'en returned to Central Asia, this time to Beshbalik (Pei-t'ing) and Bugur (Lun-t'ai). There he served on the staff of Regional Commander Feng Ch'ang-ching as a military judge. Ts'en was still in Central Asia when the An Lu-shan Rebellion broke out; in 756 he set off for China and reached the temporary capital at Feng-hsiang in 757.

The period from 749 to 757 was Ts'en's most creative. During his service in the Northwest he composed the frontier songs for which he is now famous, and he also wrote many other fine works during the brief interlude in Ch'ang-an between 752 and 754. As the literary historian Cheng Chen-to pointed out in the passage quoted earlier, Ts'en Shen did have personal experience of those regions in Central Asia that most poets knew only by report and poetic convention. Still, it is important to remember that the Central Asia of poetry was primarily a literary topic: the styles associated with it, the elements that constituted a frontier scene, and the appropriate responses had developed out of a long tradition of poems by men who had never been anywhere near the frontiers. Ts'en Shen knew Central Asian lore more thoroughly than any of his predecessors, and he showed greater familiarity with the place-names and exotic details in which frontier poets delighted. But the greater scope of Ts'en Shen's frontier poetry was built upon a basis of convention: he followed precedent in omitting description of actual battle and in including sections on drinking in camp, descriptions of the desertscape, hyperbole for the cold, and so forth. It was not that Ts'en Shen was *trying* to be conventional; rather, the poetic tradition taught the educated visitor what to look for in a frontier scene.

Though Ts'en Shen's frontier poetry is deservedly famous, he was, in fact, at the end of a tradition, the last of the important High T'ang poets to write extensively on frontier life. Before him were Wang Han's "Songs of Liang-chou," Kao Shih's "Song of Yen," Li Po's "Fought South of the Walls," and Wang Ch'ang-ling's many frontier songs. Kao Shih, Li Po, and others had already adapted the conventions of frontier poetry to the heptasyllabic song. Ts'en Shen was a poet of great talent, but in these, his most famous poems, he was no innovator: to surpass Kao, Li, and Wang Ch'ang-ling he had to outdo them in their own "kind" of poetry. As a results, Ts'en produced some of the finest poetry of that "kind."

Song of the White Snow: Sending Off Judge Wu on His Return to the Capital	白雪歌送武判官歸京
The north winds roll up the earth, white grasses snap.	北風捲地白草折
In the Tartar skies of September the snow is flying.	胡天八月即飛雪
Suddenly it's as though in one entire night the spring wind comes,	忽如一夜春風來
And on thousands of trees, millions of trees, blossoms of pear appear	千樹萬樹梨花開
That come scattering through the beaded curtains, melt soaking lacework drapes,	散入珠簾溼羅幕
And our fox furs give us no warmth, our quilts of brocade are too thin.	狐裘不煖錦衾薄
The general finds that he cannot draw his bow stiffened with horn,	將軍角弓不得控
The armor of the viceroy is nearly too cold to wear.	都護鐵衣冷難著
Far and wide over the Gobi a hundred yard thickness of ice,	瀚海闌干百丈冰
And unmoving mass of somber cloud darkens thousands of miles.	愁雲黲淡萬里凝
In the central divisions we bring out wine to toast a home-bound friend,	中軍置酒飲歸客
Here the Turkoman lute, the round guitar, the flute of nomads,	胡琴琵琶與羌笛
As this blizzard of evening snow descends over the general's gate	紛紛暮雪下轅門
And winds clutch the red banners that freeze, no longer shake.	風掣紅旗凍不翻
At the eastern gate of Bugur we send you on your way,	輪臺東門送君去
And as you go the snow will fill the Heaven Mountain Road.	去時雪滿天山路

As the mountain bends, so the road will turn,
   and we will no longer see you,

山迴路轉不見君

Leaving only the marks in the snow
   to show where your horse has passed.

雪上空留馬行處

[09591]

The theme of the cold on the frontiers was one of the most popular topics for elaboration in frontier poetry: comparison of the snowflakes to pear blossoms, panoramas of ice and snowclouds, the stiffness of a bow, and the drinking of warm wine in camp all belonged to the theme. But the colorful descriptions and dramatic juxtapositions of the T'ien-pao poetic art charged the old images with an energy they had never before possessed. Moreover, the closure here is particularly effective, and it is clever (Yin Fan's "ingenious ideas"); in fact, its cleverness so resembles quatrain technique that it seems almost an independent quatrain appended to a song.

The appeal of "Song of the White Snow" was much the same as the appeal of poems on immortals and swaggering bravos: it was a poetry of "otherness," a poetry that created enchanting illusions about how it might be somewhere else, in some other flesh, in some other time. It is interesting to note that none of the frontier songs were anthologized in the T'ang itself or in the early Sung: the exotic illusions they create had the greatest appeal to later readers, for whom Ts'en's borderlands were even more alien.

Sometimes Ts'en clearly chose his topics for their exotic qualities; for example, a poem on a volcanically heated lake (09592) or a poem on the cinder clouds from a volcano.

Volcano Clouds: Parting

火山雲送別

A volcano stands, thrusting high
   through the Ch'ih-t'ing Gap,

火山突兀赤亭口

And from the volcano in the month of June
   fire clouds rise thick.

火山五月火雲厚

These fire clouds cover the mountains,
   unmoving, unbreaking,

火雲滿山凝未開

And birds in flight for a thousand miles
   dare not come near.

飛鳥千里不敢來

Then all at once in the dawnlight
   they break with the Tartar winds,

平明乍逐胡風斷

And at dusk they turn back once again,
   blown with the rain from the passes,

薄暮渾隨塞雨回

Coiling around they slant down and swallow
   the trees by Iron Gate;

繚繞斜吞鐵關樹

Puffing out, swelling, they half cover over
   the Yarkhoto Garrison.

氛氳半掩交河戍

Far in the distance a road lies,
    east of the volcano,
And on the volcano a single cloud
    now follows your horse away.
           [09596]

迢迢征路火山東

山上孤雲隨馬去

In this and in other songs composed for social occasions, Ts'en would describe some element of the frontier scene with vigor, then tie it in the most tenuous way to the occasion. It has even been suggested that the occasional closings were added to songs already written.[2] In "Song of the White Snow" the descriptive main body and the closing quatrain were integrated successfully and enigmatically, but in "Volcano Clouds" there is a "travelogue" description of the cinder clouds from which the poet incongruously cuts a tiny puff to follow the traveler on his way.

The heptasyllabic songs of Ts'en Shen closely resemble those of his friend Tu Fu. It is not clear who learned from whom. Ts'en's "Song of Regional Commander Wei's Roan" 衛節度赤驃馬歌 (09616) of 758 clearly owes much to Tu Fu's "Grand Marshal Kao's Dapple" 高都護驄馬行 (10505) from earlier in the 750s; both draw from a broader tradition of poetry on horses (e.g., 04301, 04279). On the other hand, Ts'en seems to have preceded Tu Fu in poetry on the dance (09617).

Nowhere is the flamboyance and daring of the T'ien-pao poets clearer than in one of the most interesting encounters between the second-generation poets and their predecessors: in 752 Hsüeh Chü (702?–?), Kao Shih, Ch'u Kuang-hsi, Tu Fu, and Ts'en Shen all climbed the Wild Goose Pagoda of the Temple of Compassionate Mercy in Ch'ang-an.[3] Though only thirteen years separated the eldest of these poets from the youngest, Ts'en Shen, there was a clear distinction between the more formal and ornamented style of the older poets Ch'u and Kao (Hsüeh Chü's poem does not survive) and the more vigorous and imaginative T'ien-pao style of Tu Fu and Ts'en Shen. Ch'u Kuang-hsi's poem began with a mixture of formal ornamentation and the conscious simplicity of the capital poets:

From the golden shrine rises a holy vault,
Straight up to the edge of blue clouds.
The place is still, my heart at peace as well.
I climb it in the season of autumn's clarity.
Green and flourishing, the Yi-ch'un Gardens,
A sheet of emerald, K'un-ming Pool.
Who says that the River of Heaven is high?
The spirit's free wanderings happen right here.
          [from 06560]

金祠起眞宇
直上青雲垂
地靜我亦閒
登之秋清時
蒼蕪宜春苑
片碧昆明池
誰道天漢高
逍遙方在茲

The extent of the differences between the two generations can be seen in the kinetic description, metaphor, and hyperbole of Ts'en Shen's version:

In shaping the pagoda seems to bubble up   塔勢如湧出
High and alone, jutting to Heaven's palaces.   孤高聳天宮
I climb for the view and bypass world's bounds   登臨出世界
On a stairway of stone that winds through the void.   磴道盤虛空
Upthrusting, it weighs down the holy domain,   突兀壓神州
Towering as though of demon's work.   崢嶸如鬼工
Its four corner eaves blot out the bright sun,   四角礙白日
Its seventh story rubs the blue sky's vault.   七層摩蒼穹
I peer down, point to high-flying birds,   下窺指高鳥
Bend my ears, listen to roaring gales: 俯聽聞驚風
A string of mountains like mighty waves   連山若波濤
Rush eastward like rivers to the court of the sea.   奔湊似朝東
Green linden line the royal highway   青槐夾馳道
Where halls and palaces glitter and sparkle.   宮館何玲瓏
Now autumn's countenance comes from the west   秋色從西來
And a rich green fills the capital region,   蒼然滿關中
There Five Barrows on the northern plain,   五陵北原上
For eternity lies in blue haze.   萬古青濛濛
At last I am enlightened to that Pure Truth,   淨理了可悟
Having always honored perfect Cause—   勝因夙所宗
I vow to put off my cap of office,   誓將掛冠去
Aware of the Way, I rely on What is Forever.   覺道資無窮
                                [09534]

Ts'en's inspiration clearly failed him midway through the poem; the last half consists of the worst banalities of temple-visiting and pagoda-climbing poems. In fact, the imaginative vigor in the first part of Ts'en's poem is no less a form of "ornamentation" than Ch'u Kuang-hsi's more traditional rhetoric. As in his frontier poetry, Ts'en Shen was not a radical innovator: he said precisely what he was supposed to say in such a poem, that the temple "approached" Heaven, provided a lofty perspective, and taught him a spiritual truth. But despite the continuities of thematic and structural convention, Ts'en's "ornamental vigor" appealed to new aesthetic values. Tu Fu's poem was somewhat less brash than Ts'en's and followed the same structural conventions, but his was the truly innovative genius that changed the conventions into something deeper.

Some of Ts'en Shen's finest quatrains were also written between 749 and 757. The frontier quatrain was an even more strongly established sub-genre than the long frontier song, and in Ts'en Shen's treatment of the form one cannot miss the vignette technique of Wang Ch'ang-ling.

Song for General Chao 趙將軍歌

November on Heaven Mountain, the wind like a knife, 九月天山風似刀
South of the walls a hunting horse, 城南獵馬縮寒毛
  pelt matted short by the cold.
Our general gambles at chess, wins victory in every game, 將軍縱博場場勝
And has won in the stake the sable-fur greatcoat of the Khan. 賭得單于貂鼠袍
                          [09882]

    As often in Wang Ch'ang-ling's quatrains, the literary values here are modal, and the poem's effectiveness lies in the suggestive juxtaposition of the scenes of the two couplets. Both the army and the horse are in winter quarters, idle and waiting. Chess is the substitute for battle, and the general's victory and his "booty" are good omens in the mood of resolute expectation.
    One of Ts'en's finest quatrains is "Meeting an Envoy on His Way Back to the Capital" 逢入京使:

I gaze eastward to my homeland, 故園東望路漫漫
  the road stretches endlessly,
My two sleeves drenched with tears, tears that never dry. 雙袖龍鍾淚未乾
I meet you now on horseback, no paper here, no brush, 馬上相逢無紙筆
I trust you to take them word—tell them all is well. 憑君傳語報平安
                          [09877]

    Inversion of expectations was a common technique in the closure of quatrains, with long traditions in the epigrammatic wit of sixth- and seventh-century quatrains; but rarely would a first-person persona say exactly the opposite of what was meant; the injunction is serious: the lie is in the message. Like Li Po's "Song of the Roosting Crows," the attention of the readers is drawn painfully to the difference between appearance and reality, but in this case the protagonists of the poem share that knowledge with the reader: the only person to be deceived is the recipient—a friend or relation —and the deception is an act of love.
    In 757, Ts'en Shen joined the temporary court of Su-tsung at Feng-hsiang, and on the recommendation of his friend Tu Fu, Ts'en was made Omissioner of the Right. Ts'en accompanied the court on its return to Ch'ang-an, but in 758 the former minister Fang Kuan was disgraced and his entire faction purged. Ts'en Shen, Tu Fu, Kao Shih, and many other newly appointed officers of the court were demoted to provincial posts. This was also the year when Wang Wei, member of the old ruling families, was pardoned and raised to high office.
    Ts'en Shen was sent to a post in Kuo-chou between Ch'ang-an and

Lo-yang. Ts'en's years in Kuo-chou had some joys, but they also contained a period of genuine depression during which Ts'en wrote a number of brooding meditative poems concerning his removal from the central government and his sense of personal failure in his political career. In contrast to the sensuous and daringly metaphorical earlier poetry, this was a bleak poetry devoid of description.

On the West Tower in Kuo-chou   題虢州西樓

Miscarried, mishandled—a lifetime's affairs,   錯料一生事
Slipping and stumbling and now, white hair.   蹉跎今白頭
My plans and stratagems all fell through;   縱橫皆失計
I feel my shame even before wife and children.   妻子也堪羞
Though my wise prince has cast me from him,   明主雖然棄
Loyalty still ceases not in my heart,   丹心亦未休
But grief comes, and I've nowhere to go—   愁來無去處
I can only climb this, the western tower.   祇上郡西樓
                           [09774]

Of course, the western tower is the tower that faces Ch'ang-an.

    After completing his tour of duty in Kuo-chou, Ts'en was recalled to the capital, where he held a series of middle-level posts until 765. Then he was sent again to the provinces as prefect of Chia-chou in Szechwan. Raids by Uighurs and Tibetans followed by a local rebellion caused Ts'en to delay his departure until the following year. Ts'en found little pleasure in his Chia-chou post, but this time he did not respond with the gloom of his Kuo-chou years, but rather with a whimsicality rare in his poetry. Interestingly, a similar whimsicality appears in the Szechwanese poetry of Kao Shih and Tu Fu written at about the same time.

An Account of a Visit to Chamberlain Yang's Cottage   尋楊七郎中宅即事

Millions of problems, welling up in confusion,   萬事信蒼蒼
But my heart long ago lost ambitious motive.   機心久已忘
For no special reason I was sent here as prefect—   無端來出守
Not at all because I was bored as secretary.   不是厭爲郎
Now rains drip the banana leaves red,   雨滴芭蕉赤
Frost hurries the oranges' deepening yellow.   霜催橘子黃
And I meet you with an open-mouthed smile—   逢君開口笑
What place can we call a strange land?   何處是他鄉
                           [09757]

The gentle irony of the second couplet—secretary was the post Ts'en had held in the capital—is particularly reminiscent of Tu Fu's Szechwanese years. Ts'en's last line is cheerfully pilfered from the closure of a quatrain by Li

Po (08593) and echoes a popular High T'ang theme of consolation: home defined by the presence of friends.

The conservatism of postrebellion poetry is apparent in the two poems above from Kuo-chou and Chia-chou. The vivid juxtaposition, the hyperbolic descriptions, and the bold metaphors virtually disappeared from Ts'en's work, and there remained only hints of his former style. Images of burning recur throughout Ts'en's poetry: lamps metaphorically set dreams ablaze, and a Central Asian volcanic lake sets "nomad clouds on fire" (09592). In the following poem from Chia-chou the fires remain, but here they take the shape of a forest fire that merely burns the clouds. The image is less contrived, and the *lü-shih* regains its proper shape, but one senses also the loss of those qualities that gave Ts'en Shen's work an individual style.

Traveling by River and Spending the Night at Dragon Roar Rapids, I Gazed Out in Longing for the Recluse on Mount O-mei: Sent Also to Various Gentlemen in Camp	江行夜宿龍吼灘 臨眺思峨眉隱 者兼寄幕中諸 公

A government lodge looks down on the river's mouth,	官舍臨江口
And by now I'm accustomed to the rapids' sound.	灘聲人慣聞
Misty waters let through a moon of clear sky,	水煙晴吐月
Night fires in the mountains burn the clouds.	山火夜燒雲
Now I'd like to seek out my friend the wizard—	且欲尋方士
I lack the heart that yearns to be prefect.	無心戀使君
How can I stay on in this strange land?	異鄉何可住
More strongly felt now, long gone from the herd.	況復久離羣
[09646]	

In 768, after just a short time in office, Ts'en renounced his post and took up residence in Ch'eng-tu, where he died in 770.

It is impossible to tell if Ts'en Shen's collected works were put into circulation immediately after his death, but in 800 Tu Tui made an edition in which the poems were arranged topically. The earliest printed edition is from the Ming, but it is clear that this came from a continuous tradition and was not reconstructed from anthologies. Approximately four hundred poems are extant. Yin Fan thought highly of Ts'en's poetry, but it did not appear in the *Kuo-hsiu chi* and was not well represented in the later T'ang anthologies.

Ts'en Shen lacks the stature of the greatest High T'ang poets, but he is perhaps the best representative of the second generation. He was one of dozens of T'ien-pao poets whose works had only modest popularity in the T'ang; but by chance his collection survived and touched the interests of later readers. What they appreciated in his work was only one very limited aspect of the T'ien-pao style. But the vitality they saw was worthy of their admiration, and the general lack of interest in Ts'en's poetry during the T'ang is more a mark of the T'ang tendency to ignore, if not its greatest poets, then its "very good" poets.

II

杜甫

Tu Fu

He attained all the styles of past and present and combined the unique, particular masteries of each other writer.

Yüan Chen, "Tomb Inscription for Tu Fu"

Tu Fu *is* the greatest Chinese poet. His greatness rests on the consensus of more than a millenium of readers and on the rare coincidence of Chinese and Western literary values. Within the Chinese poetic tradition Tu Fu is almost beyond judgment, because, like Shakespeare in our own tradition, his literary accomplishment has itself become a major component in the historical formation of literary values. The peculiar nature of Tu Fu's greatness lies beyond the limited scope of literary history.

By the early ninth century Yüan Chen 元稹 had already discerned the essential characteristic of Tu Fu's genius, its sheer variety and many-sidedness. Tu Fu assimilated all that preceded him and, in doing so, changed his sources irrevocably. The variety of Tu Fu's work became a quarry from which later poets drew isolated aspects and developed them in contradictory directions. Indeed, one of the commonplaces of Tu Fu criticism was to list which famous later poet developed his own style out of which aspect of Tu Fu's work. Each age found in Tu Fu's poetry what they were seeking: an unrivalled mastery of stylistic invention, an authentic personal "history" of a period, the free exercise of the creative imagination, the voice of the moral man exposing social injustice. The impact of Tu Fu's poetic oeuvre was not felt until several decades after his death, but once his preeminence was established, he became the towering figure of Chinese poetry whom no later poet could entirely ignore.

Because he played such a formative role in the future directions of poetry, it is probably inappropriate to say that he was "ahead of his time." Yet Tu Fu possessed a protean talent and personality in an age when poets had just developed the unified and unitary poetic personality against the powerful centrifugal influences of subgeneric traditions. Tu Fu was the master stylist of regulated verse, the poet of social protest, the confessional poet, the playful and casual wit, the panegyricist of the imperial order, the poet of everyday life, the poet of the visionary imagination. He was the poet who used colloquial and informal expressions with greater freedom than any of his contemporaries; he was the poet who experimented most boldly with densely artificial poetic diction; he was the most learned poet in recondite allusion and a sense of the historicity of language. One function of literary history is to account for a poet's identity; Tu Fu's poetry defies such reduction: the only aspect that can be emphasized without distorting his work as a whole is the very fact of its multiplicity.

Multiplicity is manifest not only in the full corpus of his poetry, but also in the individual poems, where rapid stylistic and thematic shifts join to represent a problem or experience in several dimensions. Out of this "shifting style" grew new aesthetic values that eventually supplanted older concerns with unities of mood, scene, time, and experience. On a deeper, textual level, multiplicity appears in an ambiguity of syntax and referent, as well as in an awesome ambivalence in point of view.

In traditional comment on Tu Fu, particularly by T'ang writers, the language of cosmogony and Creation 造化 plays an important role: these associations suggest not only an analogue to the generative forces of nature, they also point to a unifying poetic identity that transcends its particular manifestations. This same awareness of the multiplicity of Tu Fu's work may also in part account for the intense biographical interest in the traditional reading of Tu Fu: the poet that unified such variety could not be identified by any simple, reductive type—a poet of reclusion, a *fu-ku* poet, or a "doleful" poet. Rather, the unifying poet could only be the historical being, the man who wrote the poems.

In its concern with conventions, norms, and their mutations through time, literary history is of only limited usefulness in understanding Tu Fu's poetry. In earlier T'ang poetry, questions of convention were essential because convention silently guided the creating hand. A poem was a more or less individuated version of a shared body of artistic material. The generative power of convention was such that among minor poets a poem virtually "wrote itself." For major poets like Wang Wei, convention was the "language" through which a poet might speak individually: the poet might use convention, avoid it, or transform it into something individual, but poetic convention remained the great norm that gave all variation significance. Even the archindividual, Li Po, attained his separateness by laughing at convention, by a stance of defiance that required something to defy.

Tu Fu's liberation from convention was of a different and more profound variety. One of the clichés of critical comment on Tu Fu was that "every word had its source": this is untrue not only on the surface level, but on the deeper level of Tu Fu's use of the past. Tu Fu's command of earlier literature far exceeded that of any poet before him, but he truly "used" the past, with all the implications of control and mastery that belong to the word *used*. Very rarely did past literature and convention guide his creations. One must look carefully in Tu Fu's poetry to find the familiar structures of T'ang poetry, and when they are found, one realizes how small a role they play in the poem as a whole. For example, the ascent of a mountain as the correlative imitation of the process of attaining enlightenment was a venerable theme that had generated hundreds of poems. Wang Wei created a beautiful and highly personal version of the theme in "Climbing Pien-chüeh Temple" (pp. 42–43). Nevertheless, the structural and thematic convention was the raw material that shaped the poem: like other poems of the kind, "enlightenment" was the true subject of the poem. The same convention can be seen in one of Tu Fu's earliest poems, "Gazing on the Peak"; not only is the conventional pattern hidden, its role is subordinate, and the true artistic and intellectual concerns of the poem lie elsewhere (pp. 187–88). In reading Tu Fu it is essential to recognize how the poet made use of specific earlier texts and styles, but that large and ever-changing body of poetic convention is not sufficient or even primary for the understanding of his poems.

Given the quantity of Tu Fu's poetry (about fifteen hundred poems), the value placed on it, and its close ties to historical occasion, it is natural that centuries of scholars have devoted great energy to tracing the details of Tu Fu's life and to precisely dating his poems. Many difficult questions have been resolved, and other, insoluble questions have been hotly debated. I have no aspirations to add anything new to the historical problems here; rather, I will often back away from many precise, but insecure conclusions achieved by perceptive inference and great erudition.[1] For literary history, biography is only a framework, and it usually does not require exact dating. In reading many individual poems, however, the precise historical background of occasion may be of much greater relevance.

Many of Tu Fu's poems can be read without reference to their biographical or historical contexts, but an equally large body of poetry responds to the momentous events of political history with a far greater engagement than the work of most of his contemporaries. This engagement with political history, particularly with the events surrounding the An Lu-shan Rebellion, has earned for Tu Fu the title of *shih-shih* 詩史, the "poet-historian." Tu Fu's involvement in political and social problems should neither be overestimated nor underestimated. The historical context must be excluded where it is irrelevant or unknowable, but in other poems contemporary political problems play a major role in the surface subjects, in the diectics, and, more important, in the way traditional readers have understood Tu Fu's poetry. The political and biographical context was an enriching dimension to many poems, and they were read as the utterances of a particular individual at a particular moment in history.

Tu Fu came from an old and respectable family of Tu-ling in the capital region, and the family seems to have had links to the Lo-yang region as well. Tu Fu was the first T'ang poet whose clan base was in the capital region, with the partial exception of Wang Ch'ang-ling, who seems to have been from a branch of the T'ai-yüan Wangs who had based themselves in the capital. It is possible that Tu Fu's enduring concern for the empire was colored by his clan ties to the capital region: only there would the sense of empire have entirely overshadowed regional affiliations. The great clans, which produced poets like Wang Wei, had strong ties to the ruling house, but less to the concept of empire itself.

The greatest luminary of the Tu clan during the T'ang had been Tu Fu's grandfather, Tu Shen-yen 杜審言, a court poet of Empress Wu and Chung-tsung. As a clan, however, the Tu's enjoyed neither great social prestige nor great power. Unlike many of the provincials who came to Ch'ang-an to seek their fortunes, Tu Fu had no lack of contacts with members of the great clans, but his relationship to them was highly subordinate.

Tu Fu's birth in 712 coincided with the beginning of Hsüan-tsung's long reign. Of his youth little is known: the poet was later to speak of himself as a youthful prodigy whose precocious talents were acclaimed by older men of letters. He doubtless hoped that this item of biographical convention would be duly noted by his later biographers (as indeed it was). Tu Fu was no less concerned with his self-image than Li Po, but he usually addressed posterity more strongly than his contemporaries, and those future biographers were neccessary contributors to the posthumous fame for which he yearned. Like many other young poets and intellectuals, Tu Fu made a journey through the Southeast in his late teens. Then, in 735 or 736, during the ministership of Chang Chiu-ling, Tu returned to Ch'ang-an and took the examination as a candidate from the capital prefecture. He failed. Again the poet set off on travels, this time through the Northeast, and finally he returned to Lo-yang, where he resided for several years.

By his own account, Tu Fu wrote prolifically during his early years. A few such early poems may have survived, now scattered through his collection under later dates; but the earliest poems to which probable dates can be assigned come from the late 730s, and not until the first half of the 740s, when Tu Fu was already in his thirties, are there poems that can be dated with certainty. In these "earliest" poems Tu Fu appears as a poet without an apprenticeship, a fully mature poet with a sure hand and a strong individual voice. It is possible that Tu Fu's youthful works were lost in the turmoil of the An Lu-shan Rebellion and in the vicissitudes of the poet's later travels, but it is equally possible that Tu Fu excluded from his collection virtually all he wrote before the T'ien-pao as well as the greater part of his prerebellion poetry.

The following poem, "Gazing on the Great Peak" 望嶽, was written either on Tu Fu's first trip to the East in the late 730s or on a later journey in 744. Even this poem, one of the earliest by traditional dating, has the indelible marks of Tu Fu's personal voice:

And what is T'ai Mountain like?	岱宗夫如何
Over Ch'i and Lu a green unceasing.	齊魯青未了
Here Creation concentrated unearthly glory,	造化鍾神秀
Dark north slope, the sunlit south	陰陽割昏曉
divide dusk and dawn.	
Sweeping past breast growing layered cloud,	盪胷生曾雲
Eye pupils split, moving in with homing birds.	決眥入歸鳥
The time will come when I pass up to its very summit,	會當凌絶頂
And see in one encompassing vision	一覽衆山小
how tiny all other mountains are.	
[10498]	

The stylistic brilliance of this poem pales in translation. It is an "old-style" poem that wears the half-mask of a *lü-shih*. Its quick stylistic shifts are characteristic of Tu Fu's art: it moves from discursive, prosaic diction in the opening couplet, through a grand and gnarled density of poetic diction in the middle couplets, to the straightforward expectation of the closure, which echoes Confucius's ascent of T'ai Mountain when he "thought the whole world small" (*Mencius* VII A. 24).

More accessible in translation are intellectual interests, equal to those of Wang Wei but very different in kind. The almost religious reverence accorded the great mountains of China contributes to Tu Fu's massive, symbolic vision of the mountain in a cosmic position between Yin and Yang, Dark and Light. (See line 4: the "dark north slope" is Yin; the sunlit south [slope] is Yang.) The mountain is a mystery to be "known," (line 1), and in the quest for that knowledge, the poet is acutely aware of the difference between knowing the mountain by gazing "at" it and knowing it by gazing "from" it. The answer to the question "What is T'ai Mountain like?" can be found only in the balance between these two kinds of knowledge that are the points that define the ascent of the mountain—the journey's beginning with a gazing "at," the journey's close with a gazing "from." The mountain has no shape in Tu Fu's imaginary ascent; beginning with a broad vision of the whole range that straddles the ancient states of Ch'i and Lu, Tu Fu sees only an endless green that modulates into an interface between Light and Dark. Gradually he ascends the mountain with his eyes, following the birds in flight, until finally he imagines the completion of the ascent when he attains the complementary large vision *from* the summit.

What are the poetic traditions behind this, one of Tu Fu's earliest extant poems? There is nothing of Ts'en Shen's close imitation of the first-generation poets; the poet neither submits to nor avoids the poetic tradition, but rather puts it to his service. The tripartite form survives as a purely formal framework, but thematically the poem breaks into two quatrains. The closing response is not a "conclusion" from the experience but a balancing alternative. Instead of a linear chronological progression, the poem moves from present vision to contemplation of the past, back to present, and finally to the future.

The opening question is the essential problem of the *yung-wu* tradition, yet the poem is like no *yung-wu* before. As the correlative to enlightenment, the ascent of the mountain in the imagination has antecedents in Sun Ch'o's *fu* "Visiting Mount T'ien-t'ai" 遊天台山賦 and probably in Li Po's visionary visits to Lu Mountain (08303) and T'ien-mu Mountain (08332). But in their use, these traditions were not isolated patterns subject to any combination that pleased the poet: they carried certain concomitant elements—in this case, Buddhist enlightenment or Taoist vision. But Tu Fu did use the theme of the mountain ascent as an isolated pattern subject to reinterpretation: instead of Buddhist or Taoist values, he echoes Confucius's ascent of Mount T'ai and the mountain's position in the cosmic order, standing between Yin and Yang. The poet's reinterpretation may seem mild enough—the substitution of one visionary experience for another—but it shows a freedom in handling traditional material that appeared very rarely in the works of his T'ang predecessors.

In 744, near Lo-yang, Tu Fu met Kao Shih and Li Po; Li was then journeying east after his loss of favor at court. Tu Fu traveled in the East with these two poets and visited the aging intellectual Li Yung, whom Tu Fu had known earlier in Ch'ang-an. Much has been written on the friendship of Li Po and Tu Fu, and delineating the contrasts between the two poets has been one of the favorite occupations of Chinese critics, traditional and modern. Li Po and Tu Fu were indeed very different poets, fascinating in juxtaposition, but the contrast between them does not constitute a basic antithesis in the values of Chinese poetry, as some critics have suggested. With some justification, Tu Fu would have seen himself as a poet in the same tradition as Li Po, and the more significant contrast lies between a kind of poetry represented by the work of Li and Tu, and the capital poetic tradition represented by Wang Wei.

Tu Fu was much in awe of Li Po, but awe of other poets was a characteristic of Tu Fu, and it extended to many poets whose stature was consider-

ably beneath that of Li Po. However, Li Po was of special importance to
Tu Fu: in Tu Fu's prerebellion poetry the voice of Li Po can be heard more
clearly than that of any other poet. As suggested earlier, their famous
friendship was onesided; their greatest common ground may have been
a shared admiration for Li himself. Tu Fu addressed poems to Li Po throughout his life, and many have become famous more for the aura of the poets'
mythical friendship than for any intrinsic merit. One of the best of such
poems is an early quatrain, "Given To Li Po" 贈李白, from 744:

Autumn comes—I look on you, still tumbleweed blown by winds,	秋來相顧尚飄蓬
Immortality's pill, not yet compounded— shamed by comparison to Ko Hung.	未就丹砂愧葛洪
Get roaring drunk, sing wild songs, pass your days in vain,	痛飲狂歌空度日
The wild gestures and all the frenzy to show your powers to whom?	飛揚跋扈爲誰雄

[10914]

Ko Hung was the author of the *Pao-p'u-tzu*, a neo-Taoist miscellany that
included much alchemical lore.

An unmistakable melancholy undermines the frenzied intensity
described in the poem, a sense of failure and futility, of wasted energy in
the dying world of autumn. Complications of tone and context change
the values of typological conventions, in this case the popular "type" of
the wild eccentric so often assumed by Li Po. A similar ambivalence recurs
in almost every personality type Tu Fu described, and it led him to complicate the representation of human nature more deeply than any poet
before him.

Leaving Kao Shih and Li Po, Tu Fu returned to the capital in 745,
again determined to seek office. In 747 a perfect opportunity seemed to
present itself when the emperor decreed a special examination for prior
examination failures. However, the minister Li Lin-fu had all the candidates
failed and assured His Majesty that no person of talent had slipped through
the net of earlier examinations. Tu Fu spent virtually the entire decade
between 745 until 755 trying to make the connections necessary to secure
him a position in the government. In 751 the poet resorted to the expedient
of presenting the emperor with three *fu*, and according to Tu himself,
these found special favor with His Majesty. As a result, Tu Fu was given
a special examination, passed, and told to await a position at the Bureau of
Selection.

Qualification for an appointment and actually receiving one were
very different matters: even if an appointment were forthcoming, its

quality would depend greatly on a man's social and political connections. In Tu Fu's case, years passed without assignment. Much has been made of the animosity of Li Lin-fu, first in trying to block Tu Fu's qualification and later in blocking his appointment to office. It is unlikely that Li Lin-fu any special animosity for a person as insignificant as Tu Fu then was: more likely, opposition to Tu Fu was probably a matter of routine for anyone with the social connections Tu Fu did possess—links to real enemies of the minister, men like Li Yung.

When Li Lin-fu died and Yang Kuo-chung became minister, Tu Fu still received no appointment. In 754, at the age of forty-three, the poet attempted to follow the example set by Ts'en Shen and Kao Shih, but his application to Ko-shu Han for a military post was ignored. Then came the torrential rains and resultant famine of 754, and Tu Fu took his family north to Feng-hsien. On his return to the capital, Tu Fu's posting finally came through, the lowest county post appointed by the central government. Tu Fu seems to have refused this highly unattractive position and was given an alternative appointment in the shadow government of the crown prince. Late in 755 he set off to join his family in Feng-hsien, and during his absence, the imperial armies of the northeast rebelled under the leadership of An Lu-shan.

Tu Fu's prerebellion poetry shows more clearly than his later work elements common to other contemporary poetry. Heptasyllabic songs like "Eight Drinking Immortals" 酒中八仙 (10520) grew out of the poetry of drunken eccentricity by Li Po and Li Ch'i. Some heptasyllabic songs like "Lovely Ladies" 麗人行 (10522) were topical transformations of the heptasyllabic song style popular in the early eighth century. Horse poems like "Grand Marshal Kao's Dapple" (10505) were parallel to poems of Ts'en Shen, as were some poems of imaginative fantasy like the "Mei-p'i Lake Song" (10524). Two series of poems on visiting the mountain villa of a General Ho (10936–50) drew on the traditions of occasional capital poetry. Even the famous "Ballad of Army Wagons" 兵車行 (10504) had a pale, contemporary parallel in the "Answer for the Old Man of Pei-chou" 代北洲老翁答 (09450) by Chang Wei 張謂. But these correspondences only serve to illustrate how radically Tu Fu transformed whatever he touched: his shared interests with his contemporaries were only in the broadest stylistic, thematic, and modal categories.

Tu Fu's relation to Ts'en Shen can be taken as a case in point. By the early 750s, Ts'en Shen was already writing the kind of imaginative, descriptive songs seen in the preceding chapter. Accompanying Ts'en Shen and his brother to Lake Mei-p'i near Ch'ang-an, Tu Fu wrote a song echoing the style of Ts'en Shen and his "passion for wonders." As a gesture of friendship and respect, Tu Fu was following the common practice of modeling one's style on that of one's host or companion. But one need only compare the result of Tu Fu's "imitation" with any of Ts'en Shen's songs to see both the superiority and the deep originality of Tu Fu.

A Mei-p'i Lake Song

渼陂行

The brothers Ts'en have a passion for wonders
And took me to visit Mei-p'i far away.

岑參兄弟皆好奇
携我遠來遊渼陂

The earth and sky were ashen and somber—
   their color suddenly changed,

天地黯慘忽異色

Thousands of acres of mighty waves,
   a hoard of amethyst,

波濤萬頃堆琉璃

And into amethyst vistas spread
   our boat set sail.

琉璃漫汗泛舟入

The experience strange, elation crested,
   then grim thoughts came—

事殊興極憂思集

Of behemoth rising and leviathan,
   swallower of ships—these are known no more,

鼉作鯨吞不復知

But, alas who will be by my side
   in cruel winds and white water?

惡風白浪何嗟及

My host's brocaded sails
   unfurled on my behalf,

主人錦帆相爲開

And the boatman's joy is great
   that murky fog is gone,

舟子喜甚無氛埃

Ducks scatter in confusion
   as the rowing song begins,

鳬鷖散亂棹謳發

While murmurings of far music come
   through the formless azure air.

絲管啁啾空翠來

Depths unmeasured
   by plumbline or pole,

沈竿續蔓深莫測

Leaves of water chestnut, blossoms of lotus
   drift as if freshly scrubbed.

菱葉荷花淨如拭

And now in the very midst of the waters,
   clear as some arm of the sea,

宛在中流渤澥清

Sinking infinite beneath us,
   the black form of South Mountain—

下歸無極終南黑

South of midslope all the hill
   lies here submerged,

半陂已南純浸山

A shimmering reflection stirred
   in a plain of vast waters.

動影裊窕冲融間

Upon its darkness our skiff raps
   the cliff temple, Edge of Clouds,

船舷暝戛雲際寺

Till the moon comes out on the face of the waters
   through the pass at Indigo Fields,

水面月出藍田關

Which now is a coal-black dragon puffing
   a pearl from its jaws;

此時驪龍亦吐珠

Then the God of Waters strikes his drum,
    the herds of dragons scurry,　　　　　　　馮夷擊鼓羣龍趨

Singing and dancing the spirits come forth,
    the Han's Maidens, the Ladies of the Hsiang,　湘妃漢女出歌舞

Tassled poles golden, kingfisher banners,
    a radiance hovering in the half-real,　　　　金支翠旗光有無

Right here before me—yet I worry
    at the thunder and rain of the god's coming:　咫尺但愁雷雨至

Then empty spaces infinite and the god's intent,
    not understood.　　　　　　　　　　　蒼茫不曉神靈意

Youth endures not,
    no escape from old age,　　　　　　　　少壯幾時奈老何

Yet still there has ever been
    much sorrow, great joy too.　　　　　　向來哀樂何其多
          [10524]

As the moon emerged from the passes at Indigo Fields and became, in its reflection on the lake, a pearl exhaled from the jaws of a black dragon, Tu Fu's visionary imagination reduced Ts'en Shen's hyperbolic descriptions of desertscapes to blustering timidity. Tu Fu correctly saw that Ts'en Shen's essential trait was his "passion for wonders," a desire to surpass others by novelty; here the surpasser was surpassed.

    Among the many elements that separate this poem from Ts'en Shen's work or the work of any of Tu Fu's contemporaries was the deliberate violation of modal unities, the "shifting style" that marked Tu Fu's poetry throughout his life. Moreover, it was perhaps this very quality that denied Tu Fu the full admiration of his contemporaries and immediate successors. The demand for unity of mood was powerful in the eighth century: Ts'en Shen may not have concerned himself with structural unities when he appended an occasional ending to a frontier song, but he was very careful to observe a unity of mood. One wonders what Tu Fu's contemporaries could have thought of a song like the one above, a song that undergoes as many shifts in mood and style as it describes shifts in weather. Beginning with a straightforward statement of the occasion, "A Mei-p'i Lake Song" soon turns to a terror of storm and imaginary monsters, followed by a cheerful boating song, then to a journey "up" the reflected mountain. As might be expected, the culmination of the ascent is a luminous vision of the gods in revelry, but Tu Fu undermines his epiphany with a timorously human storm-fear at the "thunder and rain" that accompanies the god's coming. The closing lines are consciously archaic, a commonplace from Han Wu-ti's "Song of the Autumn Wind" 秋風歌, and their position suggests the message of the "god's intent" that was not understood by the too mortal poet, apprehensive at the tempest of divine presence. All the while,

Tu Fu was crossing the boundaries of couplets in his topics, then breaking them off midcouplet.

Tu Fu's protean exuberance may have been too much for his contemporaries, but it was precisely this richness in the transformations of experience that drew many later admirers. Weather, mood, and topic changed; playfulness and awe rested comfortably side by side. The poetic tradition was not forgotten: the lake trip might be an ascent to heaven (cf. Chang Yüeh, 04821); a poem might close with an archaic truth, as in some of Wang Wei's poems; the bright vision of the gods traditionally could not be spoken of; but never had a poet missed the "god's intent" out of worry over the perturbations of the weather.

As Tu Fu willfully ignored modal unities, so he felt unhindered by the usual decorum of topic that obtained in poetry. No reader who reads Tu Fu's work in the context of the poetry that preceded him can fail to notice that Tu Fu wrote about things that other poets simply did not mention. If later poets learned from Tu a naturalism in treating the details of everyday life, they rarely showed themselves capable of Tu Fu's freedom in attitude and point of view. This freedom gave Tu Fu's poetry a sense of tolerant humanity apparent even to modern western readers. This freedom might occur on the simplest level, as the ability to say the thing most natural to the occasion: visiting his nephew Chi, Tu Fu tells him not to put himself out on account of his uncle (10517):

I have come on behalf of the clan	所來爲宗族
and not for a plateful of food.	亦不爲盤飱

On a grander level, the freedom can appear in a flicker of humor in a grave situation, a humor that in no way detracts from the gravity. The following is the second poem of a series on the flood rains of 754 秋雨歎三首 (10508–10):

Wind of ruin, lurking rain, autumn flurrying turmoil,	闌風伏雨秋紛紛
Seas and wastelands circling the earth share a single cover of cloud.	四海八荒同一雲
Horses going, oxen coming— can no more tell them apart.	去馬來牛不復辨
The muddy Ching and clear Wei, when again can we distinguish them?	濁涇清渭何當分
Fungus grows on the heads of rice, the wheat turns black.	禾頭生耳黍穗黑
From farmers and from field workers, no news yet,	農夫田父無消息
While here in the city a measure of rice can be had for your bedroll—	城中斗米換衾裯

"Done!" and never a question asked
    if their values are the same.
            [10509]

相許寧論兩相直

The closing vignette on market value previously had been the stuff of chronicles and anecdotal collections rather than poetry. The closest poetic parallel was from the third-century "Unclassified Poem" 雜詩 by Chang Hsieh 張協:

Foot of firewood worth more than a yard of cassia,
Brown grain more valuable than garnets or jade.

尺爐重尋桂
紅粒貴瑤瓊

But Chang Hsieh's couplet, with its hyperbole and ornamental variation for parallel, represents Chin poetics. It belongs to a different world from Tu Fu's market scene, with the language of a bargain struck and struck willingly. More important is the slight touch of whimsy in Tu Fu's scene, a bemused distance from the purchaser—perhaps himself—who so eagerly exchanges his expensive bedding for a "mere" measure of rice. The whimsy in no way undermines the real gravity of the situation, and it points to a real order of values in the priority of rice, as opposed to the false values of the marketplace in ordinary times. Tu Fu was one of the first Chinese poets to discover the energy of tragicomedy, and in the conjunction of its antithetical impulses, there appears yet another aspect of the multiplicity that informs Tu Fu's work. In Tu Fu the inclination is ever to complicate, to draw in opposing dimensions, and to "complete" knowledge of a thing or an experience.

Equally apparent in the poem above is the "shifting style": the poem begins in grand poetic diction with a cosmic vision of all the world under one vast cloud, then proceeds to the ethical and philosophical associations (line 3, from the *Chuang-tzu*; line 4, convention) in the second couplet. The third couplet draws from a farming proverb and leads to the urban vignette of the last couplet. Moreover, the opening belies the idea that "every phrase has its source": not only are there no known antecedents for the phrases "wind of ruin" (?) 闌風 and "lurking rain" (?) 伏雨, no commentator is completely certain what the phrases mean. The phrases are sonorous and ominous, a confusion with menacing, destructive overtones; the confusion and uncertainty with which they begin the poem continues throughout the poem in the inability to tell things apart, the lack of news, and the final confusion in values.

Nowhere did Tu Fu's multiplicity appear more strongly than in the long narratives of personal experience that the poet wrote throughout his life. The first major example came from 755, just before the outbreak of the rebellion; this was "Going from the Capital to Feng-hsien, Singing

my Feelings" 自京赴奉先縣詠懷五百字 (10534). A few years later this was
followed by the more famous and fully developed examples of the form,
the "Song of P'eng-ya" 彭衙行 (10557) and the "Journey North" 北征
(10558). "Going from the Capital" is too long to quote in its entirety, but
some extracts can provide an idea of the variety of the poem. The poem
begins with the curious mixture of self-mockery and assertive pride that
was to become characteristic of Tu Fu's self-image.

In commoner's robes a man of Tu-ling,	杜陵有布衣
As he ages, his ideas fall deeper into naïvete and foolishness,	老大意轉拙
And the goals to which he vows himself— simpleminded—	許身一何愚

In the secret heart comparing himself
    to Hou Chi, Chou's ancestor,
    to Chieh, the Shang's founder.
	竊比稷與契

But he may be deceived and instead become a useless vacancy,	居然成濩落
Hair now white and willing to meet long suffering:	白首甘契闊
When the coffin lid closes, the matter is done.	蓋棺事則已
And yet my goals still and forever long for fulfillment.	此志常覬豁

Discursive self-analysis did have its antecedents in Chinese poetry,
but the complexity of Tu Fu's statement—its combination of mockery,
grandeur, and bitterness—reflect an ambivalence and depth that no earlier
poet could match. The first thirty-two lines of the poem are an extended
monologue in which the poet argues with himself and defends his continuing search for office despite repeated failures. Then, in line 33, the poet shifts
abruptly to the narrative of the journey that is the subject of the poem.

It was year's end; all plants shriveled and fell,	歲暮百草零
The rushing wind split the high hills,	疾風高岡裂
35 The avenues of the capital were dark canyons	天衢陰崢嶸
As the traveler set out at midnight.	客子中夜發
His stiffened belt cracked in the harsh frost,	霜嚴衣帶斷
And fingers, stiff and straight, could not tie back the ends.	指直不得結
Then, by dawn's breaking, I passed the Li Mountain Villa,	凌晨過驪山
40 A royal bed set on towering heights	御榻在嵽嵲
Where battle flags blocked a cold and empty sky,	蚩尤塞寒空
Where slopes and valleys were worn smooth by the tramp of armies.	蹴踏崖谷滑
There from the hot springs, vapors curled upward	瑤池氣鬱律
past the clack and clatter of the Household Guard.	羽林相摩戛

Tu Fu's journey through the chill darkness of early morning is ominous
and mysterious. The palace he passes in the early morning is not the court
poet's compound of groves, pools, halls, and terraces; rather, it is a garrison-
like fortification in which the Household Guard seems more functional
than decorative, as they were in most poetry. Tu Fu continues in speculation
on the world behind the ranks of patrolling guards, a world of feasts and
gifts given to the great. Such feasts would be familiar to the T'ang reader,
but Tu Fu balances them with a description of the poverty and suffering
of the common people, who provided the feasts and gifts.

Next Tu Fu turns to a condemnation of the emperor's relatives by
marriage:

67 Around Vermilion Gates, the reek of meat and wine   朱門酒肉臭
   Over streets where lie the bones of the frozen dead.   路有凍死骨

Quickly the poet shifts back to a narrative of his journey, vividly describing
the desparate crossing of a creaking bridge over a river in flood, the travelers
all joining hands to draw one another across. Finally, Tu Fu reaches Feng-
hsien, where his family is staying.

85 I came through the gate, I heard a crying out,   入門聞號咷
   my youngest child had died of starvation   幼子飢已死
   . . . .
   And this thought obsesses me—as a father,   所懷爲人父
90 Lack of food resulted in infant death;   無食致夭折
   I could not have known that even after harvest   豈知秋禾登
   Through our poverty there would be such distress.   貧窶有倉卒
   All my life I've been exempt from taxes,   生常免租稅
   and my name is not registered for conscription.   名不隸征伐
95 Brooding on what I have lived through, if even I   撫迹猶酸辛
      know such suffering,
   the common man must surely be rattled by the winds;   平人固騷屑
   then thoughts silently turn to those who have lost   默思失業徒
      all livelihood
   and to troops in far garrisons.   因念遠戍卒
   Sorrow's source is as huge as South Mountain,   憂端齊終南
   a formless, whirling chaos that the hand cannot grasp.   澒洞不可掇
                              [10534]

Such experiences played little role in poetry before Tu Fu; where
they occurred (as in the "Lament for a Wife" subgenre 悼亡, or in Lu Chao-
lin's lyrics on his disease), they were usually stylized beyond recognition.
But Tu Fu was not merely being confessional: he wove together private
experience and public experience; private values and public values; per-
suasive argument, narrative, symbolic description, and lyric meditation.

Against the centrifugal impulses of such multiplicity, Tu Fu bound the poem together with new principles of unity: analogical echoes (the emperor's provision for the state and a father's provision for a child), subtle resumptions of themes (the poet's longing to be, like Hou Chi and Chieh, the founder of a great line, and later, the death of his child), and the tradition of hermetic topical symbolism (an excess of the Yin principle in government echoed in images of darkness and the flood scene). There is no sense of artifice in these orderings; rather, Tu Fu seems to have possessed an unconscious sense of the inner pattern of events, and this swallowed up conventions of earlier poetic structure.

The rebellion of the northeastern armies under An Lu-shan was the central event of the mid-eighth century. The High T'ang poets could hardly have been blind to its magnitude, and the fact that the momentous events of the 750s were so rarely treated in poetry was more a function of the general concept of the nature of poetry than an indication of aloof indifference. To Ts'en Shen a Central Asian snowstorm was an appropriate topic for a poem; the Battle of the Talas River was not. The wars were given passing mention in parting poems, in personal narratives, and in poems on visiting the sites of battle; only rarely did poets write about the rebellion itself. That the An Lu-shan Rebellion is now considered one of the great topics of T'ang poetry is due almost entirely to Tu Fu, to his poems on its battles and his personal experiences of it.

Late in 755 the Army of the Northeast descended upon Lo-yang, and while An Lu-shan set himself up as emperor in Lo-yang, the rebel troops smashed the imperial armies to the west and took Ch'ang-an. Hsüan-tsung fled the capital in precipitous haste, and during his flight the imperial guard demanded and received permission to execute the minister Yang Kuo-chung and the emperor's favorite Yang Kuei-fei. In the summer of 756, Hsüan-tsung abdicated in favor of the crown prince, soon Su-tsung, who was organizing the defense at a temporary capital in Feng-hsiang, west of Ch'ang-an.

Tu Fu seems to have been north in Feng-hsien when the rebellion broke out; he quickly moved his family even farther north to a place called Ch'iang Village. A few years later he wrote a narrative of this journey, the "Song of P'eng-ya."

I remember when first we fled the rebellion,	憶昔避賊初
Hurrying north, we passed through hardship and danger.	北走經險艱
The night was deep on the P'eng-ya Road,	夜深彭衙道
And the moon was shining on Whitewater Mountain.	月照白水山
The whole family had been traveling long on foot—	盡室久徒步
Most whom we met seemed to have no shame.	逢人多厚顏
Here and there birds of the valley sang,	參差谷鳥吟

We saw no travelers going the other way. 不見遊子還
My baby girl gnawed at me in her hunger, 痴女飢咬我
And I feared wild beasts would hear her cries: 啼畏虎狼聞
I held her to my chest, covered her mouth, 懷中掩其口
But she twisted and turned crying louder in rage. 反側聲愈嗔
My little son did his best to take care of things, 小兒強解事
With purpose went off and got sour plums to eat. 故索苦李餐
It had thundered and rained half the past week, 一旬半雷雨
We clung together, pulling through mud and mire, 泥濘相牽攀
And having made no provision against the rain, 既無禦雨備
The paths were slippery, our clothes were cold. 徑滑衣又寒
At times we went through great agony 有時經契闊
Making only a few miles in an entire day. 竟日數里間
Fruits of the wilds served as our provisions, 野果充餱糧
Low-hanging branches became our roof. 卑枝成屋椽
Then early in mornings we went through the runoff, 早行石上水
To spend the evening at homestead smoke on horizon. 暮宿天邊煙
We stayed a while in T'ung-chia Swamp 少留同家窪
And were about to go out Lu-tzu Pass, 欲出蘆子關
When an old friend of mine, Sun Tsai by name— 故人有孫宰
His great goodness reached the tiers of cloud— 高義薄曾雲
Welcomed us as night's blackness was falling, 延客已曛黑
Hung out lanterns, opened his many gates, 張燈啟重門
With warm water had us wash our feet, 煖湯濯我足
Cut paper flags to summon our souls, 剪紙招我魂
Then afterward brought in his wife and children, 從此出妻孥
Whose eyes, seeing us, streamed with tears. 相視涕闌干
As if unconscious, my brood was sleeping; 眾雛爛漫睡
He woke them kindly and gave them plates of food. 喚起霑盤飧
And I make this vow to you, 誓將與夫子
That forever I will be your brother, your kin. 永結爲弟昆
Then he emptied the hall where we sat, 遂空所坐堂
I rested peacefully—he offered what gave me joy. 安居奉我歡
Who else would be willing in times of such trouble 誰肯艱難際
To show his good heart so openly? 豁達露心肝
Since we have parted, a year has run its course, 別來歲月周
And still the barbarian weaves his calamities. 胡羯仍構患
When shall I ever have the wings 何當有翅翎
To fly off and alight before your eyes? 飛去墮爾前
[10557]

The great differences between this poem and "Going from the Capital" caution against generalizations about Tu Fu's treatment of any given theme: instead of the "shifting style," the "Song of P'eng-ya" is a simple, moving narrative poem treating an experience more naturalistically than any poet before Tu Fu. Tu Fu called the poem a "song" (or "ballad," *hsing* 行), but it was not recognizable as such according to any eighth-century concept of a "song." It was, in fact, an occasional poem of a specific type: a personal narrative presented to someone, a verse letter. The *yüeh-fu* overtones of the generic title allowed the naturalistic detail and gave the experience a universal dimension.

After removing his family to safety, Tu Fu returned south and was captured by rebel forces. He appeared next in rebel-held Ch'ang-an, lamenting the repeated defeats of the imperial armies and the desolation of the great city. In the spring of 757, Tu Fu escaped through the rebel lines and made his way to the temporary capital at Feng-hsiang. There he received the respectable post of Reminder. After some serious trouble for his support of the inept, but well-meaning minister Fang-Kuan, Tu Fu requested permission to go and visit his family. It was on this journey to Ch'iang Village that the poet wrote his most famous long narrative, "Journey North."

A few months after Tu Fu's arrival in Ch'iang Village, Ch'ang-an was retaken and, following that, Lo-yang; factions of the rebel army still held the East and Northeast. Su-tsung and the retired Hsüan-tsung returned to Ch'ang-an, as did Tu Fu, resuming his post as Reminder. In 758, in the great purge of Fang Kuan's adherents and other new appointees during the rebellion, Tu Fu was demoted to a low provincial post in Hua-chou, between Ch'ang-an and Lo-yang. Like Ts'en Shen in nearby Kuo-chou, Tu Fu was deeply dissatisfied with his demotion: in 759, at the age of forty-eight, Tu Fu resigned his post and set off for Ch'in-chou, far in the Northwest. Out of Tu Fu's fifteen hundred poem, approximately five of every six poems were written after the poet's departure for Ch'in-chou, during the last eleven years of his life.

The poems written by Tu Fu during the rebellion include many of his most famous works, but for the most part they constitute no real change from Tu Fu's earlier poetry. The emotions described are often more intense, and the style is more controlled, but in their immense variety most belong to types of poems Tu Fu had been working with before the rebellion. Thus, the famous "Lament by the Riverside" 哀江頭 (10540) grew in part from the heptasyllabic song style of "Fair Ladies" (10522); the six ballads of social protest, grouped as the "Three Clerks" 三吏 (10578–80) and the "Three Partings" 三別 (10581–83) grew out of the "Song of the Army Wagons" (10504). But from this period also came some of the only geuinely conventional poetry that Tu Fu ever wrote: during his service as Reminder, Tu composed a small group of occasional poems and poems on court service; these are among the best of their kind, but are basically in the same mold as poems by his fellow officers Ts'en Shen, Chia Chih, and even Wang Wei, to whom Tu Fu dedicated one poem.

One area in which significant innovations did appear in this period was in Tu Fu's regulated verse. Wives and family had occupied little place in poetry apart from passing mention in a few topics and subgenres (for instance, in reclusive poems in the T'ao Ch'ien mode): they certainly did not belong in regulated verse. Not only did Tu Fu write extensively of his family in "old-style" poems like "Song of P'eng-ya," he could also write lovingly of his wife in regulated verse, as in the following famous poem from his captivity in Ch'ang-an.

Moonlit Night   月夜

The moon tonight in Fu-chou   今夜鄜州月
She watches alone from her chamber,   閨中只獨看
While faraway I think lovingly on daughters and sons,   遙憐小兒女
Who do not yet know how to remember Ch'ang-an.   未解憶長安
In scented fog, her cloudlike hairdo moist,   香霧雲鬟濕
In its clear beams, her jade-white arms are cold.   清輝玉臂寒
When shall we lean in the empty window,   何時倚虛幌
Moonlit together, its light drying traces of tears.   雙照淚痕乾
[10974]

Remarkable here are not only the supremely human sentiments, but also the transformation of some of the oldest and most artificial poetic tropes. Tu Fu's wife is formed out of the conventional attributes of "fair ladies": she is reduced to jade-white flesh and a coiffure surrounded by scent and moisture. These are the attributes of courtesans, court ladies, and the stylized personae of *yüeh-fu*, but never one's own wife. There is the venerable trope of the moonlight shared by parted friends or lovers, united by the same moon and identical gazing; there is the reflexive longing where the poet thinks on someone far away and imagines that they in turn must be longing for him, as in Wang Wei's famous quatrain to his brothers (06137). And the poem closes with a piece of wit as clever as anything from the age of court poetry—a moonlight that can dry tears because it is shared side by side. Out of this stylized legacy Tu Fu wrought a poem that has been read for centuries as a movingly natural testimony of conjugal love.

As in his earlier poetry, Tu Fu wrote more naturalistically on topics hitherto unmentionable. Poets might legitimately complain of the constraints of office and might long to escape to a freer life, but such poems never admitted a hint of what their authors were compelled to do that was so burdensome. To speak of sitting at one's desk piled with oppressive paperwork had no place in the poetic strife between service and the private life. But Tu Fu spoke of it vividly in a playful topic from Southern Dynasties poetry, "Suffering from the Heat" (also treated by Wang Wei, 05849).

Suffering the Early Autumn Heat,   早秋苦熱堆案相仍
   My Desk Keeps on Being Piled High

The seventh month, the sixth day,
    I suffer the sultry heat.   七月六日苦炎蒸
I face my food, eat a bit,
    then I can take no more,   對食暫飡還不能
And constantly worried when night comes
    of scorpions everywhere;   每愁夜中皆是蠍
Worse now after autumn's begun—
    more and more flies.   況乃秋後轉多蠅
My tight belt drives me mad,
    I want to scream out loud.   束帶發狂欲大叫
More papers, every one "urgent,"
    keep coming in succession.   簿書何急來相仍
Just gaze to the south to the green pines
    that frame a little vale—   南望青松架短壑
Oh, to tread with my feet bare
    the thick, thick ice down there!   安得赤脚踏層冰

[11027]

Wang Wei must have felt much the same way in his own "Suffering from the Heat," but Wang, sensitive to the rules of poetic decorum, treated the theme with gentle hyperbole and kept the excessive heat from touching too closely the drudgery of everyday life.

    More important for Tu Fu's future development was a deepening sense in his poetry of an inner symbolic order in the world. Most T'ang poetry was nonfictional: the poet observed the physical world and found implicit in it a meaningful structure. In the works of most poets the order of the world was relatively simple and intelligible (such as, a mountain structured to lead one "upward" to transcendence); moreover, all parts of a scene need not be significant—the reader could allow elements in a poem to be present simply because they were present in the scene (though they might contribute to mood). In Tu Fu's poetry the possibilities of meaning and order can become complex to the point of contradiction, and they echo through every word in a poem.

Facing the Snow   對雪

Weeping over battle, many new ghosts,   戰哭多新鬼
In sorrow reciting poems, an old man all alone.   愁吟獨老翁
A tumult of clouds sinks downward in sunset,   亂雲低薄暮
Hard-pressed, the snow dances in whirlwinds.   急雪舞迴風
Ladle cast down, no green lees in the cup,   瓢棄樽無綠
The brazier lingers on, fire seems crimson.   爐存火似紅
From several provinces now news has ceased—   數州消息斷
I sit here in sorrow tracing words in air.   愁坐正書空

[10973]

The political conditions described here have led the traditional commentators to date this poem to Tu Fu's period behind rebel lines in Ch'ang-an, after the defeats of the imperial armies at Ch'ing-fan and Ch'en-t'ao.

In the symbolic cycle of the seasons, winter was the nadir that followed the destruction of autumn; it was the season of Yin and Darkness, but it was also the season that promised rebirth. The correspondences between the political world, the cosmic cycles manifest in the seasons, and the scene before his eyes all come together in Tu Fu's vision of the snow scene.

The title, "Facing the Snow," involves a primary opposition between the poet and the winter world outside. Indeed, Tu Fu's treatment of the topic has strong echoes of the formal amplification of seventh-century poetic rhetoric. The first couplet repeats the primary opposition in nominal terms: out there, on the battlefields beyond the horizon, many "new" ghosts, the young dead slain unnaturally before their time; within is the solitary "survivor," the old man for whom death would be appropriate. The city disappears in the poem: there is only the poet who "faces" and the snow world that is "faced," the world of death and winter. This is one of the earliest examples of a characteristic scene in Tu Fu's poetry, the self alone in an uninhabited or haunted world.

In the second couplet the world faced grows closer, first in clouds on the horizon, then in the snow whirling before the window. These are nature's correlatives of disorder and rebellion: *luan* 亂 clouds, "clouds of rebellion," a "tumult of clouds"; *chi* 急 snow, the "snow of war's alarums (*chi*)," "hard-pressed snow." Double meanings mark the secret correspondences between the human world and the uninhabited scene. The poet faces a world of disorder, white in the growing darkness of night, and the predominance of black and white, darkness and light, echo (as elsewhere in Tu Fu's poetry) the interplay of cosmic forces.

As the second couplet treats "what is faced," the third couplet treats the balancing "one who faces"—the poet and the world inside. Each couplet treats one term of the primary opposition, amplifying one line of the first couplet. The antithesis of the winter world is warmth, light, and color—the wine that is gone and the fire that is dying, growing redder as it burns down to the embers.

The poem has been focusing inward, from beyond the horizon ever closer and into the room, to the spot of warmth and color that is the brazier. The "response" of closure demands a corresponding outward movement, but before that can occur, a new term must be introduced into the "facing" relationship: this is blockage, news blocked coming in and messages blocked going out. The poet makes his futile gesture of response upon the interface between the two worlds, words written in air, hopeless signs of communication that cannot cross the barrier into the world of winter and disorder. In form, style, and concerns, "Facing the Snow" is an early example of the "classic" Tu Fu *lü-shih* in which the poet confronts a world of hermetic correspondences. Here the hermetic world can be deciphered; in his later poetry the world can be a configuration of fragments, insistently symbolic, but never falling into such an easily intelligible patttern.

Giving up his post in Hua-chou, Tu Fu traveled northeast to Ch'in-chou in 759; he stayed there less than two months. No longer seeking a career in the central government, Tu Fu seems to have begun to devote himself almost entirely to poetry, though he never entirely abandoned his public values, as did most poets who withdrew to private life. During the last eleven years of Tu Fu's life, political events and the "outer biography" receded in importance, and the "inner biography" of the poet became dominant. Great changes occurred in the poetry of Tu Fu's last eleven years, but the outer biography may be summarized briefly.

In 760, after traveling in the Ch'in-chou region, Tu Fu crossed the mountains to the southwest and came to Ch'eng-tu, the greatest city of the West, where several of his friends had already been posted. Soon after Tu Fu's arrival, Yen Wu, a friend and son of a friend, became military governor. Tu Fu built himself the famous "thatched hut" 草堂 on the outskirts of the city and spent some of the happiest years of his life there. In 762, while Yen Wu was away in the capital, the Ch'eng-tu garrison revolted, and Tu Fu slipped away from the city, probably to avoid being implicated. The rebellion was crushed, Yen Wu resumed his post, and Tu Fu was appointed a military advisor, an appointment that was more likely an act of patronage than an homage to Tu Fu's military genius. In 765 Yen Wu died, and in the same year Tu Fu began a journey down the Yangtze, lodging in various cities along the way. The longest of these stops was in K'uei-chou, White Emperor City, where Tu Fu spent the years from 766 to 768: there the poet wrote almost a quarter of his extant poems, including many of his most famous works. From K'uei-chou the poet went on downstream to Chiang-ling, then to Tung-t'ing and the lakes region, where he died in 770.

When most poets vowed to give up public service and lead the simple life of the "recluse," they possessed sufficient properties and estates to permit graceful enjoyment of their reclusion. Tu Fu clearly had no such means. The decision to abandon a political career and his office in Hua-chou and to set off for the uncertainties of Ch'in-chou was both drastic and dramatic. It was one of those serious life decisions that could not but affect the work of an author who wrote in the context of a concept of poetry as *shih-yen chin* 詩言志, "poetry articulates intention," the expression of individual response to a historical world.

Ch'in-chou was a period of changes in Tu Fu's poetry. Probably the most famous poems of the period are the twenty "Unclassified Poems of

Ch'in-chou" 秦州雜詩 (11036–55). Close contact with the capital poets during his former period of service in the capital can be heard faintly in some of these; for example, the tenth poem of the series resembles the late work of Wang Wei transferred to a frontier setting.

Vapor of clouds touches the K'un-lun Range,   雲氣接崑崙
Then rain from the passes, streaming densely.   渗渗塞雨繁
A nomad boy watches the River Wei,   羌童看渭水
The royal envoy heads to the Yellow River's head.   使客向河源
Smokey fires: the tents of an army camp,   煙火軍中幕
Cattle and sheep: a village on the ridge.   牛羊嶺上村
Where I dwell the autumn grass is still,   所居秋草靜
Just now as I close my wicker gate.   正閉小蓬門
                    [11045]

Of all Chinese poets, Tu Fu was perhaps the least willing to let nature be herself: little seems random or accidental; rarely is something note-worthy simple because it exists, as is true in some of the best poetry of Meng Hao-jan. The physical world is replete with meaning, sometimes in obvious correspondences and sometimes teasingly hidden. But even this observation is subject to exception according to the larger truth of multiplicity in Tu Fu's poetry. In some of the Ch'in-chou poems, particu-larly in the "Unclassified Poems of Ch'in-chou," the symbolic world is absent, and in its place can be found a gray version of the modal poetics of Tu Fu's contemporaries: the objects of the world are not hieroglyphs of a hidden order but indices of a complex state of mind. The following is the seventeenth poem of the series:

On the frontiers fall shadows swiftly turn evening,   邊秋陰易夕
No more can we make out the light of dawn,   不復辨晨光
Rain from eaves streams down curtains in disorder,   簷雨亂淋慢
Clouds from mountains cross low over my wall.   山雲低度牆
A cormorant peers into a shallow well,   鸕鶿窺淺井
Earthworms climb far into the hall.   蚯蚓上深堂
Drearily horses and carriages pass by,   車馬何蕭索
And before my gate all the plants grow tall.   門前百草長
                    [11052]

With its lengthening nights and dark autumn skies, Ch'in-chou becomes the modal emblem of the North—of darkness, wetness, and isolation.

"View of the Wilds" 野望 is traditionally ascribed to the Ch'in-chou period: the grounds for dating it then are weak when based on internal evidence, but credible to centuries of critics who had a sharp sense of the changes in Tu Fu's style. It is one of the more overwhelmingly stark of Tu Fu's poems, combining the modal interests of the Ch'in-chou months with the symbolic mode in the interplay of the cosmic forces of light and dark, as darkness gradually overwhelms the barren immensity of autumn.

Clear autumn—cannot gaze to its limits,	清秋望不極
And in the distance layers of shadow rise.	迢遞起層陰
Far waters pure and level with the skies,	遠水兼天淨
Deep away, a lone fortress shrouded in fog.	孤城隱霧深
Leaves few now—the wind brings more down,	葉稀風更落
Mountains remote as the sun begins to sink.	山迴日初沉
How late the solitary crane returns—	獨鶴歸何晚
The crows of dusk have already filled the woods.	昏鴉已滿林

[11089]

Yin-Yang symbolism played an important role in Tu Fu's poetry, and the terms of cosmology were the most readily available vocabulary in which to speak of universals. The poet who was so often drawn to contradictions would not miss the paradox in the traditional attributes of autumn: its famous clarity that permits the distant vision of the first line, and the ascendancy of darkness and the forces of Yin that closes the poem. Shadow sweeps in over autumn's vistas, opened in part by the interstices between the tree branches stripped of their leaves. But as the darkness encroaches, the fallen leaves are replaced by new specks of darkness, by the black of the ill-omened crows that have come to roost in the blackness of night. In the midst of the darkness is the solitary crane, nature's correlative of the poet, alone and unable to find a resting place.

One of Tu Fu's most characteristic responses to escape from the world of darkness and dissolution was the optative. It appeared early in his poetry as young Tu Fu faced the unclimbed T'ai Mountain; it recurred often in his later poetry, as when in Ch'eng-tu the poet made his imprecation for a great mansion to house all the poor scholars of the world, after his own roof had been blown away by the autumn wind. What is limited by the forms of the physical world finds release in the optative.

Thousand League Pool	萬丈潭

The blue creek fuses dark mystery within,	青溪合冥寞
A holy creature, sometimes appearing, sometimes concealed—	神物有顯晦
A dragon resting in massed waters coiled,	龍依積水蟠
His lair sunken under a thousand leagues.	窟壓萬丈內
Pace each step with care, pass over cliff rim,	蹋步凌垠堮
Bent for balance go down into mist and haze,	側身下煙靄
Look out over a stretch of mighty waves,	前臨洪濤寬
Then stand back on a greatness of gray stone.	却立蒼石大
The mountain is steep, the one path here now ends	山危一徑盡
Where sheer banks form two facing walls:	岸絕兩壁對

Thus were they hewn, rooted in nothingness,　　　　　削成根虛無
Their inverted reflections hung in shaking waters.　　倒影垂澹瀨
The black tells of the vortex's bottom,　　　　　　黑知灣澴底
The clear parts display a shattered sparkling.　　　清見光炯碎
Deep within it a lone cloud comes,　　　　　　　孤雲到來深
And the birds in flight are not outside.　　　　　飛鳥不在外
High-hung vines for its battle tents,　　　　　　高蘿成帷幄
The winter trees rank its legions' standards.　　　寒木疊旌旆
Streams from afar twist their flows to reach here,　遠川曲通流
Caves give subterranean vent to swift scouring.　　嵌竇潛洩瀨
I have come to a place hidden, a realm without men,　造幽無人境
The response it stirs is all our own.　　　　　　發興自我輩
Now, asking my leave, unwillingness hangs strongly on,　告歸遺恨多
As old age approaches, this visit, the finest.　　將老斯游最

Hiding himself away, he sleeps in long scales;　　　閒藏修鱗蟄
The mighty stone blocks his going and his coming—　出入巨石礙
Oh, when shall the blazing skies of summer pass,　　何當炎天過
That his will may exult in the meeting of wind and rain.　快意風雨會

[10632]

The hidden dragon near Ch'in-chou belongs to a different world than the
exuberant epiphany of "A Mei-p'i Lake Song." In Ch'in-chou the gnarled
style of Tu Fu's later years begins to appear, and though the topic shifts,
the style is relatively consistent (especially true of the Ch'in-chou poems
and the poetry of the journey to Szechwan). But the contrast with "A
Mei-p'i Lake Song" is even stronger on the level of the differing relationships between the poet and the world he perceives.

　　The visit to Lake Mei-p'i had been an opportunity for the exercise of
the free imagination, and the fantastic speculations had essentially been
ends in themselves. The "ascent" of reflected mountain was not part of a
unified symbolic vision, but rather a part of the occasion that was "material"
for the imagination. The message of the bright god was not understood;
the poem closed with the "ancient truth" of the variability of mortal pleasures, and as in its Han source, that "truth" referred to the experience of the
outing itself.

　　In "Thousand League Pool" reflection becomes the mirror of the
world, and the mysterious, cliff-ringed tarn casts back an image of the
poet surrounded by stone that is "rooted in nothingness." The reflecting
surface is an interface across which only the dragon can pass, as it stretches
out and upwards from its hibernation and rises to reveal its powers among
the clouds. The full significance of the vision may not be completely intelligible—such is the nature of "mystery"—but the experience is not intended to display the poet's powers of invention; rather, the poet is striving

to represent portentous experience. The imperial theme plays a role in the poem, but no simple allegorical equation can be made between the emperor and the dragon: the dragon embodies a power that is incarnate also in the emperor.

To commemorate his passage over the mountains from the Ch'in-chou region to the Ch'eng-tu plateau, Tu Fu composed a number of grand landscape poems, similar in style to "Thousand League Pool." But once the poet arrived in Ch'eng-tu, he seems to have felt more at ease with himself and the world. The years in Ch'eng-tu were rich ones for Tu Fu, as he continued old poetic interests and developed new ones. Perhaps the most characteristic stance of the Ch'eng-tu poems is a mellow, half-humorous vision of himself as an old man. This self-image clearly grew out of the conventional "type" of the old eccentric, but Tu Fu's version was too complicated to resemble closely its antecedents.

The seven quatrains "Walking Alone by the Riverbank Seeking Flowers" 江畔獨步尋花七絕句 (11218–24) are among the most famous examples of this figure of the self. The following is the second poem of the series.

Dense flowers, a riot of stamens, make the riverbank terrible,	稠花亂蘂畏江濱
But I walk on, precariously tottering, truly afraid of spring,	行步欹危實怕春
And bear still the drivings of wine and of song, I endure,	詩酒尚堪驅使在
Not yet finished off—this white-haired old man	未須料理白頭人

[11219]

The poem may be read with humor or with terror, but the characteristic multiplicity appears in the poet's "in-between" state, young enough to be "driven" by the oppressive lushness of spring, but already too old for it— "tottering precariously." But the primary function of being old is the distance from the other, driven self, the distance that allows him to observe himself with wry horror.

Nowhere is the half-humorous, half-pathetic vision of the self more apparent than in the famous "My Thatched Roof is Ruined by the Autumn Wind" 茅屋爲秋風所破歌:

In the high autumn skies of September the wind cried out in rage,	八月秋高風怒號
Tearing off in whirls from my rooftop three plies of thatch.	卷我屋上三重茅
The thatch flew across the river, was strewn on the floodplain,	茅飛度江灑江郊

The high stalks tangled in tips
    of tall forest trees,

高者掛罥長林梢

The low ones swirled in gusts across ground
    and sank into mud puddles.

下者飄轉沉塘坳

The children from the village to the south
    made a fool of me, impotent with age,

南村羣童欺我老無力

Without compunction plundered what was mine
    before my very eyes,

忍能對面爲盜賊

Brazenly took armfuls of thatch,
    ran off into the bamboo,

公然抱茅入竹去

And I screamed lips dry and throat raw,
    but no use.

脣焦口燥呼不得

Then I made my way home, learning on staff,
    sighing to myself.

歸來倚杖自嘆息

A moment later the wind calmed down,
    clouds turned dark as ink,

俄頃風定雲墨色

The autumn sky rolling and overcast,
    blacker towards sunset,

秋天漠漠向昏黑

And our cotton quilts were years old
    and cold as iron,

布衾多年冷似鐵

My little boy slept poorly,
    kicked rips in them.

嬌兒惡臥踏裏裂

Above the bed the roof leaked,
    no place was dry,

床頭屋漏無乾處

And the raindrops ran down like strings,
    without a break.

雨脚如麻未斷絶

I have lived through upheavals and ruin
    and have seldom slept very well,

自經喪亂少睡眠

But have no idea how I shall pass
    this night of soaking.

長夜沾濕何處徹

Oh, to own a mighty mansion
    of a hundred thousand rooms,

安得廣廈千萬間

A great roof for the poorest gentlemen
    of all this world,
    a place to make them smile,

大庇天下寒士俱歡顏

A building unshaken by wind or rain,
    as solid as a mountain,

風雨不動安如山

嗚呼

Oh, when shall I see before my eyes
    a towering roof such as this?

何時眼前突兀見此屋

Then I'd accept the ruin of my own little hut
    and death by freezing.

吾廬獨破受凍死亦足

          [10686]

Tu Fu moved with ease between the naturalistic world of vignette and the world of symbolic vision: the allegorical mansion differs from the frail cottage of thatch in stability and in size, rather than in the more radical distinction between the real and the metaphorical. The worlds are united by the figure of the poet, at once ridiculous and grandly heroic, pathetic and funny. The personal narrative becomes petition, not to the authority of the state, as in the songs of social protest, but to the higher authorities of the cosmic order. Yet speaking to those unseen powers, the poet uses the device of imperial memorial, expressing the petitioner's willingness to die as evidence of his sincerity.

As Tu Fu's self-image matured and deepened in the Ch'eng-tu years, a new fascination with the nature and role of the poet appeared. In some cases Tu Fu made grand statements of the value of literature: in later years he spoke of literature as (11547):

. . . a deed of eternity,	文章千古事
Whose failure and success is known	得失寸心知
in the mote that is consciousness.	

But beyond these echoes of traditional literary theory, the poetic nature becomes part of Tu Fu's self-image (11167):

As a man my nature's lopsided	爲人性僻躭佳句
and addicted to lovely lines.	
If my lines don't startle others,	語不驚人死不休
in death I'll find no rest.	
And now in old age my poetry	老去詩篇渾謾興
is really getting relaxed.	

The easygoing, colloquial tone of these line was characteristic of Tu Fu's Ch'eng-tu years and mockingly reflected the self-image of the eccentric. The famous second line has a serious side in the playful context: that poetry should "startle" people was based on T'ien-pao values of "strangeness" that appeared so often in Yin Fan. But even more significant is the implicit importance granted to poetry: if it failed to produce the desired effect, the poet would find no rest even in death.

Both Li Po and Tu Fu granted an importance to poetry not found in the works of their contemporaries. For Li Po poetry was the means for the genius to find recognition in this world (the "qualifying" theory of poetry as a means to make oneself known); for Tu Fu poetry was involved in his future reputation, with his place in history. Having failed in the political world, Tu Fu increasingly invested his ambitions in his poetry. Tu Fu was ill at ease with attacks on famous poets, and it is not surprising that in the illusory conflict between *fu-ku* and the poets of the sixth and seventh centuries, Tu Fu was one of the rare open defenders of the poetry of the preceding centuries. Tu Fu did admire both the ancient poets and the *fu-ku* poets, but he set out to redeem the poets that *fu-ku* writers attacked, particularly Yü Hsin and the Four Talents of the Early T'ang. The clearest example of his defense was in an exceptionally difficult series of epigrams, the six "Playful Quatrains" 戲爲六絶句 (11228–33). The following, a defense of Yü Hsin that begins the series, is one of the more intelligible:

The writings of Yü Hsin
    grew more perfect as he grew older,   庾信文章老更成
A mighty brush, overtopping the clouds,
    a mind roaming as it pleased.   凌雲健筆意縱橫
But men today ridicule and criticize
    his *fu* that were handed down,   今人嗤點流傳賦
Unaware that even an ancient sage
    might be in awe of the later-born.   不覺前生畏後生
                        [11228]

In his last line Tu Fu referred to *Analects* IX. 22 to suggest the possibility that the moderns, the "later-born," might surpass the ancients. Despite scriptural validation, this was a heady suggestion in the T'ang, whose poets had hoped at best to recapture and thereby equal antiquity. By freeing Yü Hsin and the Four Talents from the stigma of "modernity," Tu Fu was also clearing space for his own greatness.

    Of Yü Hsin's *fu* that were "handed down," one in particular touched Tu Fu deeply: "The Barren Tree" 枯樹賦, in which the leafless or dying tree became an allegorical figure of greatness and failure. That the same subject was treated several times by Lu Chao-lin and Lo Pin-wang may have been partially responsible for Tu Fu's defense of the Four Talents. In a group of four poems on sick or barren trees, Tu Fu consciously echoed this tradition.

Sick Cypress   病柏

A cypress there was that grew on a lofty hill,   有柏生崇岡
Spreading wide like a coach's canopy.   童童狀車蓋
Aloft it reared its tiger and dragon form,   偃蹙龍虎姿
Stood master in meeting of wind and cloud.   主當風雲會
Since divine power lies with the upright and straight, 神明依正直
Old men often bowed to it with respect.   故老多再拜
Who could have known that its thousand-year roots   豈知千年根
Would lie, beauty broken, midroad.   中路顏色壞
It lacked not good place in its growing,   出非不得地
Became large and tall, coiling and grasping the earth. 蟠據亦高大
The year turned cold, all at once it had nought to depend on, 歲寒忽無憑
Through day and night its boughs and leaves changed.   日夜柯葉改
The cinnabar phoenix, leading its nine chicks,   丹鳳領九雛

Cried out in sorrow, hovered beyond it,
And owls had their way with it,
Raising their young in its bored-out holes.
From what land have you come, sir,
That you stand here so long marveling:
If with clear head you seek to know
  the law of the essence of things—
It is flood, wild and surging, and not to rely on.

哀鳴翔其外
鴟鴞志意滿
養子穿穴內
客從何鄉來
佇立久吁怪
靜求元精理

浩蕩難倚賴

[10676]

Though the barren tree was a "modern" theme, Tu Fu treated it in the allegorical mode associated with *fu-ku*. A topical referent may have been present, but it is no longer accessible. Though *fu-ku* in mode, the poem bears no resemblance to any "ancient" form: the interlocutor of the last quatrain was a High T'ang device, and the closing shift away from the main topic was characteristic of Tu Fu.

Through the Ch'eng-tu years, Tu Fu's work in the *lü-shih* assumed ever greater importance. In addition to the heavy seriousness of *lü-shih* like "Facing the Snow" and "View of the Wilds," Tu Fu also developed a *lü-shih* style that showed all lightness of "old-style" reclusive poetry. In such poems there often appeared the vision of mellow self-satisfaction, of the old eccentric living in simplicity in his little hut, surrounded by the beauty of nature.

A Guest Comes

客至

North of my cottage, south of my cottage,
  spring waters everywhere,
And all that I see are the flocks of gulls
  coming here day after day,
My path through the flowers has never yet
  been swept for a visitor,
But today this wicker gate of mine
  stands open just for you.
The market is far, so for dinner
  there'll be no wide range of tastes,
Our home is poor, and for wine
  we have only an older vintage.
Are you willing to sit here and drink
  with the old man who lives next door?
I'll call to him over the hedge,
  and we'll finish the last of the cups.

舍南舍北皆春水

但見羣鷗日日來

花徑不曾緣客掃

蓬門今始爲君開

盤飧市遠無兼味

樽酒家貧只舊醅

肯與鄰翁相對飲

隔籬呼取盡餘杯

[11139]

The lightness of touch set in formal perfection made this poem a favorite, and there was scarcely a major poet who did not imitate the first couplet.

After the succession of political troubles in Ch'eng-tu, the poet made his way down the Yangtze, coming eventually to K'uei-chou. Tu Fu's years in K'uei-chou were fertile ones when the poet was at the height of his powers. A sobriety and even a somberness often replaced the wryness and half-humorous self-image of the Ch'eng-tu poems. K'uei-chou and the years that followed contained Tu Fu's most radical experiments in style, and the symbolic worlds of the K'uei-chou poems were his most hermetic and the most bewildering in the multiplicity of their possible referents.

After his Ch'eng-tu years, Tu Fu's poetry increasingly concerned himself. He was a poet of fundamental questions, and as in his early years he had asked what the great Mount T'ai was like, so going downriver he turned to the question "What am I like?" Time and again he found answers in the forms and creatures of the great river. (11433):

Tossed about by winds, what is my semblance?	飄飄何所似
Of Heaven and of Earth, a single sand gull.	天地一沙鷗

Tu Fu saw himself in the largest contexts of all, contexts that inevitably reduced him to the dignified but impotent infinitesimal—Heaven and Earth, Ch'ien and K'un, the Darkness and Light of days and seasons, the Elements. He lived at junctures between Earth and Sky, Stone and Water, high in a tower between cliff and river:

A visible darkness grows up mountain paths,	暝色延山徑
I lodge by river gate high in a study,	高齋次水門
Frail cloud on cliff edge passing the night,	薄雲巖際宿
The lonely moon topples amid the waves.	孤月浪中翻
Steady, one after another, a line of cranes in flight;	鸛鶴追飛靜
Howling over the kill, wild dogs and wolves.	豺狼得食喧
No sleep for me. I worry over battles.	不眠憂戰伐
I have no strength to right the universe.	無力正乾坤

[11465]

Many of the themes and questions of Tu Fu's earlier poetry recurred in the K'uei-chou poems, and often the K'uei-chou poems have become so famous that the earlier treatments have been reduced to obscurity. The famous "Song of the Old Cypress" 古柏行 (10768), written on the temple cypress of the Chu-ko Liang shrine in K'uei-chou, grew out of his earlier poems in the barren tree tradition, but the depth and complexity of the later poem made it the classic treatment of the theme. Chu-ko Liang, the minister of the Shu-Han state during the Three Kingdoms period, haunted the poetry of Ch'eng-tu and K'uei-chou: Chu-ko Liang was the man of genius born in the wrong times, the man who had tried in vain to restore the unified empire. This figure of the great failure, honored and remembered, had special meaning for the poet: he had treated Chu-ko Liang during his Ch'eng-tu years in a famous regulated verse, "The Minister of Shu" 蜀相 (11101). In K'uei-chou Tu Fu returned to the theme time and again, most prominently in "The Eight Formations" 八陣圖 (11519) and in several of the five "Singing My Feelings on Traces of the Past" 詠懷古跡 (11556–60), perhaps Tu Fu's most successful and difficult *huai-ku*.

The *lü-shih* of Tu Fu's K'uei-chou years are particularly memorable. The pentasyllabic *lü-shih* constitute the majority, but it was the formal perfection of Tu Fu's heptasyllabic *lü-shih* that made the deepest impression on later crities. The K'uei-chou *lü-shih* include a large number of poems on weather and the parts of the day (sunset, midnight); these were treated as the manifestations of the interplay of cosmic forces and merged with Tu Fu's interest in Yin-Yang symbolism, the Elements, and the great river that was the incarnation of Change. Famous among the K'uei-chou *lü-shih* are "Spending the Night in a Tower by the River" 宿江邊閣 (11465, translated earlier); "Night in the Tower" 閣夜 (11474): "The Highest Tower in White Emperor City" 白帝城最高樓 (11527); and "Sunlight Cast Back" 返照 (11659). "Night in the Tower" will serve as an example:

In the evening of the year Yin and Yang hurry the shortening daylight.	歲暮陰陽催短景
On sky's edge the frost and snow clear in the cold of night.	天涯霜雪霽寒宵
Drums and horns of night's fifth watch, notes both strong and sad,	五更鼓角聲悲壯
In the Three Gorges the river of stars, reflections stirring, shaking.	三峽星河影動搖
Weeping in wilderness, how many families, hear of attack and battle,	野哭幾家聞戰伐
Barbarian songs in several places rise from fishermen, woodcutters.	夷歌數處起漁樵

Sleeping Dragon Chu-ko Liang,
    Leaping Horse Kung-sun Shu,
    heroes turned to brown soil.
	臥龍躍馬終黃土

All word of events in the human world are lost in these vast silent spaces.	人事音書漫寂寥

[11474]

The poetry of Tu Fu's old age often used indefinite syntax to create a world in which relationships were only potential: images of a line do fit together, but absent are the exclusions of other possibilities that makes propositional discourse possible. It is a haunting language in which the world is an insistent omen that can be interpreted in many, often contradictory ways.

In line 5 of the poem above it may be that the "families" are weeping over those dead in battle or that they are hearing weeping from the battlefield, or it may be that the poet is hearing either weeping from the battlefield or the weeping of displaced families. The parallel line, which is supposed to help resolve ambiguous syntax, is no help, because it demands the one syntactic interpretation of the preceding line that is not possible.

The reflected world, seen earlier in "A Mei-p'i Lake Song" and "Thousand League Pool," recurs here briefly in line 4, as the stable, orienting constellations are shaken by the river's waves. It is a world where order is falling apart, where intelligible relationships are distintegrating, and where all sound and sight is dying away in the growing darkness and empty, silent spaces.

The centerpieces of Tu Fu's K'uei-chou poetry are two sequences, the five "Autumn Wilderness" 秋野五首 (11490–94) and the eight "Autumn Meditations" 秋興八首 (11548–55) . In these complex meditations on the autumn world and its significance, the richness of the K'uei-chou poetry was at its height. "Autumn Wilderness" addressed more directly the problem of civilization and its disintegration, wilderness and cultivation, and the poet's reconciliation with old age. The "Autumn Meditations" have a strong claim to be the greatest poems in the Chinese language.[2] In this latter series Tu Fu wove together scenes of K'uei-chou with his memories of court and, in doing so, produced an extended meditation on the relationship of time and memory to the poetic art.

A poem sequence is an integrated unit, and one cannot offer even the sketch of an interpretation of an individual poem apart from the context of the sequence as a whole. However, to suggest a few of the themes of the sequence, we may consider the seventh "Autumn Meditation":

The waters of K'un-ming Pool, deed of the days of Han,	昆明池水漢時功
The banners and pennons of Emperor Wu here before my eyes.	武帝旌旗在眼中
Silk of the loom of the Weaving Girl empty in moon of night,	織女機絲虛月夜
Scales and fins of the whale of stone stir in autumn wind.	石鯨鱗甲動秋風
The waves toss a kumi seed, black in sinking cloud,	波漂菰米沈雲黑
And dew chills the lotus pod, red of falling powder.	露冷蓮房墜粉紅
Barrier passes stretch to the heavens, a road for only the birds;	關塞極天唯鳥道
Lakes and rivers fill the earth, one aging fisherman.	江湖滿地一漁翁

[11554]

The K'un-ming Pool was actually an artificial lake in Han Ch'ang-an. The Weaving Girl was a constellation and denizen of the heavens (appearing frequently in court poetry); her statue, like the statue of the stone whale, belonged to the palaces of Han.

The world of the immortals and the Han past (the standard metaphor for the T'ang court and empire) merge with the past of Hsüan-tsung's court: all are equally lost in their pastness or their remoteness (in Heaven or in Ch'ang-an, beyond the barrier passes of line 7). Yet strangely they become equally accessible through the poetic imagination and memory: the "days of Han" are "here before the eyes." This past of the imagination is ghostly and uninhabited, filled with "deeds" and monuments but not with people. And the abandoned statues seem portentous in their isolation, weaving empty fabric in/of moonlight or swimming with mechanical fins through the autumn wind of destruction. The eyes of the imagination focus on the minutest detail, a tiny seed being tossed about by the waves (which, of course, mirror the clouds of Heaven) and the red powder falling from the autumn lotus. In "Autumn Meditations" the past of the imagination is usually brightly colored, in contrast to the grays and whites that usually describe the present autumn of K'uei-chou. These colors of the imaginary world are echoed in the last poem of the series by the allusion to the "brush of many colors" of Kuo P'u.

Even the infinestimal world of the wave-tossed seed and the red powder is filled with omens—of helplessness, dissolution, endings, and autumn. The seventh line brings the poet back to the present in K'uei-chou, facing the barriers that block him from Ch'ang-an and the past. Finally, the last line draws in one of the most sophisticated uses of the analogical possibilities of parallelism, a technique used throughout "Autumn Meditations"—structural repetition. From a new perspective the form of the seed in the "huge" pool reappears in the vast water world that is inhabited only by the single fisherman, the contemplative poet dreaming and writing of the brightly colored past, of the red that has fallen.

The poetry that Tu Fu wrote after he left K'uei-chou was not significantly different than the poetry of his K'uei-chou years. But some poems possess a bleakness and austerity of which even Wang Wei was not capable.

Yangtze and Han	江漢
At the Yangtze and the Han a voyager longing to go home,	江漢思歸客
Between Ch'ien above and K'un below one broken-down man of learning.	乾坤一腐儒
A wisp of cloud, the sky shares this distance,	片雲天共遠
Endless night, the moon an equal in solitude.	永夜月同孤
In setting sun a heart still young, still strong,	落日心猶壯

Through autumn's wind, my sickness growing better.　　秋風病欲蘇
From ancient times they've sustained old horses　　　古來存老馬
That they need not take to the long-faring road.　　　不必取長途
                              [11627]

Ch'ien and K'un are the two primary cosmic principles of the *Yi-ching*:
Heaven and Earth, Yang and Yin. The reader does not know whether the
cloud or the poet is as far as the sky. It is a strange world of emblems of the
self, culminating in the image of the old horse as the aging official, who
should be cared for and not turned loose to endless travels in his dying years.

> Efter our wrettingis, thesaurer,
> Tak in this gray hors, Auld Dumbar,
> Quhilk in my aucht with service trew
> In lyart changeit is in hew.
> Gar hows him now aganis this Yuill,
> And busk him lyk ane bischopis muill,
> For with my hand I have indost
> To pay quhatevir his trappouris cost.

For Tu Fu's petition, unlike for Dunbar's, there was no *respontio regis*.

　　Except for the brief period of court service after the recapture of the
capital, Tu Fu was never at the center of the poetic world of his own day.
His last and most productive years were spent wandering through the
provinces. Fan Huang's 樊晃 preface to a short edition of his works put out
soon after his death notes that Tu Fu's larger collection was in circulation
in the South. Therefore it is not greatly surprising that his work was largely
ignored for thirty years after his death. What is surprising is that in a very
short time he went from great obscurity to being acknowledged (along
with Li Po) as the greatest poet of the dynasty. In the late eighth century he
was virtually unmentioned, and echoes of his poetry were rarely heard;
in the first decade of the ninth century his name was being used with Li
Po's as the accepted standard of literary greatness.

　　Laudatory comments on Tu Fu in his own day cannot be entirely
trusted; rather than recognitions of genius, they fall largely under the
rubric of social politeness. A small circle of admirers he did have, but there
was no general recognition of his greatness. Even Fan Huang's preface
was unusually restrained in its praises. One exception may be the poem
addressed to Tu Fu by Jen Hua 任華 (13475); this piece praises Tu Fu with
the same blustering hyperbole that Jen Hua also gave to Li Po and the
calligrapher-monk Huai-su.[3]

　　The men responsible for Tu Fu's rehabilitation in the early ninth
century were the dominant literary figures of the Mid-T'ang: Han Yü

(17828, 17922), Yüan Chen (21415, and the preface to the "*Yüeh-fu* with Traditional Titles," and the "Tomb Inscription for Tu Fu"), and Po Chü-yi (22636, and the "Letter to Yüan Chen"). In addition to these relatively direct evaluations of Tu Fu's merit, there were many more casual references to Li Po and Tu Fu by Han Yü, Yüan Chen, and Po Chü-yi as well as by their less famous contemporaries. Such references began to use the catch-phrase "Li and Tu" as the accepted standard of greatness in poetry.

But the real tributes to Tu Fu's pre-eminence were not in the praises and anecdotes (Chang Chi is reputed to have swallowed an infusion made from the ashes of Tu Fu's poems in order to absorb Tu Fu's genius), but rather in the repeated echoes of his poetry in the works of Mid-T'ang writers, particularly in Han Yü, but also in the poetry of Meng Chiao, Chang Chi, Po Chü-yi, and Yüan Chen. Many of the most famous poems of the Mid-T'ang resonate with Tu Fu's voice; the "New *Yüeh-fu*" of Po Chü-yi and Yüan Chen, or Han Yü's famous "Song of the Stone Drums" 石鼓歌 (17913), echoing Tu Fu's "Song for Li Ch'ao's Pa-fen Script" 李潮八分小篆歌 (10824). Reference to and use of Tu Fu continued throughout the ninth century, and by the Northern Sung, Tu Fu held the universally accepted pre-eminence that he holds in classical Chinese poetry to this day.

Individual poems by Tu Fu were echoed by a millenium of later poets, but Tu Fu also made important general contributions to the development of Chinese poetry. Of these, Tu Fu's treatment of subgenre was one of the most important. Prior to Tu Fu, subgenre had probably been the dominant factor in *what* poets wrote about and *how* they wrote about it. Not only did Tu Fu write extensively outside the limits of traditional subgenres; he also expanded the scope of established topics and created hybrid forms by recombining elements from disparate poetic "kinds." Tu Fu's rise to pre-eminence in the Mid-T'ang coincided with a vastly diminished importance of subgenre in poetic composition; in many ways this reflected specifically Mid-T'ang interests, but the range of the major Mid-T'ang poets was also a reflection of the example of Tu Fu.

Tu Fu's treatment of the poetry of indefinite occasion was particularly significant.[4] Throughout the early eighth-century poems of indefinite occasion had been growing in importance, and it was in that form that many of Wang Wei's and Li Po's most famous poems were written. However, such indefinite occasional poems had been generally limited to situations in which there was already an established occasional subgenre; for instance, Wang Wei's "Parting" 送别 or "Villa on Mount Chung-nan," in the tradition of visiting poems. Particularly in his later poetry, Tu Fu's poems of indefinite occasion constitute a large percentage of his works. Tu Fu expanded the form into less common subgenres ("A Guest Comes" 11139) and used it for new occasions ("Siting My House" 卜居, 11102). In many cases, poems of indefinite occasion merged with older, purely rhetorical topics; for example, when Tu Fu wrote a poem entitled "Rain" (as he did many times), it was usually a poem of indefinite occasion rather than a rhetorical exercise in the *yung-wu* tradition; however, it retained some of the generality of referent that was characteristic of *yung-wu*.[5] The poetry of indefinite occasion became one of the most important ways in which the Chinese lyric, with its deep roots in occasion and the nonfictional world at hand, moved towards general significance. And Tu Fu's freedom in writing on new topics—his son's birthday, the destruction of a tree in his yard, an excess of office work—provided a model for the immense range of Mid-T'ang poetry, and particularly for Sung poetry. Poetry was no longer tied to certain formalized events, but was appropriate to a wide range of life's experiences.

The poem sequence was another of Tu Fu's major contributions to the poetic tradition. There had been a tradition of writing frame poems for poem series, but Tu Fu was the first poet to develop fully the poem sequence, in which individual poems made full sense only in the context of the sequence as a whole. The sequence was the perfect solution to a central problem of the Chinese lyric: how to give a topic extended treatment without sacrificing the elliptical density and intensity of the short poem. The initial impulses to the poem sequence appeared in some of Tu Fu's earlier series, like the "Unclassified Poems of Ch'in-chou"; there the poet picked up themes and images from earlier poems in the series to bind the individual works into a rough continuity. By the K'uei-chou years, when Tu Fu wrote "Autumn Meditations," he had combined this binding technique with some older serial techniques, such as repetitions of last and first lines in adjacent poems (as in Ts'ao Chih's, "To the Prince of Pai-ma" 贈白馬王彪). In addition, the first three poems of the sequence were even more closely joined by a chronological progression, from an evening to the following morning. In "Autumn Meditations" these various continuities produced a complex sequential development, in which structural patterns, themes, and images underwent multiple revisions and metamorphoses: the Yangtze of K'uei-chou will be replaced by the Twisting River of Ch'ang-an, then by the "river of stars," or by the Yü-su; images of blocking and penetration recur in numerous shapes; worlds of color alternate with worlds of black and white.

Tu Fu is generally acknowledged to be the master stylist of the poetic language, but his virtuosity does not admit easy characterization. Critics looking for the popular poet point out what seem to be colloquialisms in his poems. (William Hung even suggests that such an inclination toward popular language caused him to fail the examination.) Critics looking for the scholar point out archaisms and echoes of earlier usages. Critics looking for the aesthete point out perfectly chosen words. Critics looking for linguistic experimentation point out passages of unusual syntactic and semantic daring. All these elements exist in Tu Fu's poetry; all go beyond what was conventional in mid-eighth-century poetic diction; but none define Tu Fu the stylist.

Tu Fu worked in plain styles and archaic styles, but his most original stylistic traits involved a linguistic complication that was correlative to his thematic complications. Here multiplicity appears in the aspect of ambiguity, and it can be seen in two stylistic extremes: propositional language and the "imagistic" language of the parallel couplet. In both cases the ambiguity in Tu Fu's work can sometimes approach unintelligibility.

Ambiguity in propositional language is the most disturbing, because the propositional style signals to the reader that the lines can be reduced to stable semantic message. There are no finer examples of Tu Fu's propositional ambiguity than the "Six Playful Quatrains." The following is the fifth poem of the series:

Without belittling the moderns, loving the ancients:	不薄今人愛古人
Clear phrases, lovely lines shall surely be my neighbors.	清詞麗句必爲鄰
Secretly yearn for Ch'ü Yüan, Sung Yü as right to ride side by side,	竊攀屈宋宜方駕
But afraid that with/compared to Ch'i and Liang I'll be the dust behind.	恐與齊梁作後塵

[11232]

The style and the subgenre pretend to epigram here, and in Chinese the poem reads with deceptive smoothness. Earlier in the series Tu Fu had been defending Yü Hsin and the Four Talents of the Early T'ang against their *fu-ku* detractors among Tu Fu's contemporaries. The first line involves the problem of whether the "moderns" are the writers of his own age or (using the conventional ending of the "ancient" period in literature) the poets from his own age back through the times of Yü Hsin and the Four Talents of the Early T'ang. Similarly, we may wonder if the "ancients" are Yü Hsin and the Four Talents or the pre-Ch'in poets like Ch'ü Yüan or Sung Yü. The term *moderns* tends to refer to contemporaries, while the term *ancients* tends to refer to poets before the fifth century; however, the conventional period associations of these terms leaves a gap of three centuries that includes Yü, the Four Talents, and the Ch'i and Liang mentioned in line 4.

These serious problems of referent are only the insecure foundation upon which the real linguistic problems rest. The first line reads equally well:

> I don't belittle the moderns'
>   love of the ancients,
> But clear phrases and lovely lines
>   will surely be *my* neighbors.

"Clear phrase and lovely lines" would be strongly associated with the Ch'i, the Liang, Yü Hsin and the Four Talents. In this version Tu Fu is saying that he can accept his contemporaries love for the pre-fifth-century poets, but his preference is for Yü Hsin and the Four Talents. But the relationship between the first two lines is radically determined by how the reader sees "ancients" and "moderns":

> I don't belittle my contemporaries, but love the poets of
>   long ago [either Yü Hsin et al or the pre-fifth century],
> Their [poets of long ago, either version] clear lines . . . .

or, with magnanimity to all:

> I don't belittle recent poets [Yü et al.] *and* love the ancients,
> But their [recent poets] clear lines . . . .

or perhaps:

> I don't belittle the moderns' love of the ancients.
> They [moderns] should have clear lines and lovely phrases [of
>   the ancients] as their neighbors.

On the other hand, Tu Fu may be trying to dispel what he considers a false opposition between the ancients and more recent poets like Yü Hsin and the Four Talents:

> Their [ancient poets and more recent poets like Yü] clear lines
>   and lovely phrases should be recognized as neighbors [i.e.,
>   the post-fifth century poets and pre-fifth-century poets have
>   more in common than is usually claimed]

If this were not confusing enough, there is a legitimate uncertainty in line 3 as to whether Tu Fu is the subject (in which case he is stating his goals and modestly admitting failure), or whether Tu Fu's contemporaries, the detractors of Yü and the Four Talents, are the subject (in which case he is mocking them). And is it Tu Fu or the detractors who are the "dust behind" even the Ch'i and Liang? Or is it that he and his contemporaries join the Ch'i and Liang as "dust behind" the ancients. The reader who approaches the poem with the expectations of *fu-ku* values (which Tu Fu sometimes espoused) reads one poem; the reader who expects to see Tu Fu's admiration of the poetry of the Southern Dynasties and Early T'ang reads a different poem; the reader who expects a self-assertive Tu Fu and the reader who expects a modest Tu Fu come up with completely different versions. This innocent quatrain presents the illusion of pointed epigram, but the "point" shifts wherever the reader's predilections point.

Uncertainty of referents and indefiniteness of relationships was a more common stylistic feature of *lü-shih*, particularly of the parallel couplet. However, the ambiguity of Tu Fu's *lü-shih*, particularly of his late *lü-shih*, far exceeded anything by his contemporaries. This has appeared earlier in the third couplet of "Night in the Tower" and in the second couplet of "Yangtze and Han." But such ambiguity might also appear in an opening couplet, as in "Winter's Depths" 冬深 (11632):

Flowers, leaves—only at Heaven's will,   花葉惟天意
Yangtze and creek—shared roots of stone.   江溪共石根

Does the first line mean that spring will come only at Heaven's will? Or that the poet will live to see spring only at Heaven's will? Or, as Ch'ou Chao-ao 仇兆鰲 suggests, the "flowers and leaves" are the shapes of clouds whose mutating forms follow Heaven's will? Do the Yangtze and the creeks that flow into it share common sources in the stone of the mountains? Or do the river and streams share roots of stone with the plants that will bear "flowers and leaves" in springtime? Or do the waters share roots of stone with the flower-and-leaf cloud formations (clouds would be the most conventional association of "roots of stone," the origin of the clouds in the mountains)? Or do they share roots of stone with the poet, who like the river has come down from the mountains of the West—the poet who so often compares himself to a drifting cloud? Or is it "*on* Yangtze and creek" that one of the possible elements shares "roots of stone" with another possible element. The couplet that follows this only compounds the complications. Tu Fu managed to create a major poetry that was strangely coherent out of these objects of the world, objects pregnant with symbolic value and set in ill-defined relationships with uncertain referents. In doing so he carried the openness of Chinese poetic diction to limits beyond which it could not go.

The full range of Tu Fu's artistic and intellectual concerns lies far beyond the scope of this chapter, but as an example, we may consider one pattern that recurs in diverse forms through his poetry: this pattern may be broadly defined as the opposition of civilization and barbarism or, in an analogical pair (with interesting parallels in the Western tradition), art versus nature. Arranged in sequence, this antithetical pair appears as the process of decline and disintegration and is sometimes subsumed into the larger processes of Change in Chinese cosmology.

No simple formulation can articulate Tu Fu's "position" on this opposition. At times Tu Fu shows an awe of the natural that is shared by many of his contemporaries, but on the whole, Tu Fu is one of the rare T'ang poets to lean to the side of order, civilization, and its arts. In "Autumn Meditations" art and memory have a tenuous claim to recapture and preserve a civilization that is dying. In "Autumn Wilderness" the response is a futile farming, ordering the wilderness, along with Confucian values to oppose decay and barbarism. But usually the most nobly constructed human artifice is consumed and replaced by the permanent forms of nature.

The opposition has seasonal manifestations, as in the confrontation of antithetical worlds in "Facing the Snow." But it appears most commonly in autumn, the seasonal interface between the vegetative lushness of summer and winter's bleakness. During the day an analogous interface occurs at evening, particularly in the moment of *fan-chao* 返照, "sunlight cast back," the last brilliance of the setting sun before the world turns dark.

Art is essentially a gesture against time, "a deed of eternity" against the mortality of civilization, whose dissolving splendors of order art seeks to conserve or recapture. In K'uei-chou Tu Fu saw Lady Li perform the *chien-ch'i* dance. Lady Li had been the student of the great court dancer Lady Kung-sun, and Tu Fu, who had seen the original court dance as a child, could not help but view the present performance in the context of its past and the loss of K'ai-yüan glory (10818):

In the Music Academy those who followed the arts have vanished like the mists.	梨園弟子散如煙
Here the dancer, remnant beauty, shines in the cold winter sun.	女樂餘姿映寒日
To the south of the Tomb of Golden Grains the boughs of the trees form arches,	金粟堆南木已拱
While on the stone wall of the Chü-t'ang Gorge winds howl through the grasses.	瞿唐石城草蕭瑟

The Tomb of Golden Grains was Hsüan-tsung's, and over its pathway the commemorative trees have already grown large enough to touch branches. The dance in K'uei-chou preserves the past dance, and the art of the poem preserves the present dance. Yet each stage removed from the original work changes the meaning of the conserving art, until that art signifies only the fact of loss.

Against this elegiac entropy of art grew a countervision of art that could become real. This occurred most often in poetry on painting, working through the central theme of that subgenre: the ability of art to create an illusion of reality. In Tu Fu's poetic universe this tired trope was often transformed into a painted subject that strained to break free from the limits of the painting, to intrude into the physical world and become real (e.g., 10705, 10922). But more often the demiurge failed and his artifice was exposed: the hawk that tried to break free of the silk might be "pinched between the fingers" (10922), and the illusory landscape (10671)

I wish I had a razor-sharp knife from Ping-chou,	焉得幷州快剪刀
And I'd cut for myself half the river Sung in Wu.	剪取吳松半江水

Art is mortal; nature, immortal. In contrast to the painting, the original in nature will be free and seemingly immortal. In the closing of a poem on a mural of cranes by the early eighth-century poet and painter Hsüeh Chi, Tu Fu spoke of the paintings as faded but still noble, then commented (10716):

Before this high hall had collapsed,	高堂未傾覆
These always consoled the honored guests,	常得慰嘉賓
But now, left exposed on the rear wall,	曝露牆壁外
I sigh how the wind and rain threaten them.	終嗟風雨頻
The true ones are off in vermilion clouds,	赤霄有眞骨
Ashamed to drink of the turbid pools and fords—	恥飲洿池津
In the dark, dark sky they go where they will.	冥冥任所往
Free and unfettered, none can tame them.	脫略誰能馴

The closing juxtaposition of the real cranes with the painted ones changes radically the significance of the paintings: their nobility is reduced to a pale and mortal reflection of the vital, immortal crane.

Ultimately, all art was a manifestation of human civilization and subject to its entropy and disintegration.[6] As civilization wanes, nature mockingly replaces its artifacts with her own superior forms, as in the beautiful elegy on the ruins of T'ai-tsung's Yü-hua Palace:

The creek gully turns, long winds through pines,	溪回松風長
Gray rats scuttling over ancient tiles,	蒼鼠竄古瓦
I wonder what prince's hall that lies,	不知何王殿
A construct abandoned, beneath sheer cliff wall.	遺構絕壁下
In its shadowed chambers ghost-fires green,	陰房鬼火青
Over shattered avenues a dirge of torrents stream.	壞道哀湍瀉

The million cracks and vents that pipe nature's music—these the true orchestra,	萬籟眞笙竽
Just now as autumn's visage shows serene indifference.	秋色正蕭灑
Its lovely ladies are the brown soil	美人爲黃土
Still more infused with their craft of powder and paints.	況乃粉黛假
Of those that once waited on the coach of gold,	當時待金輿
Now only the tomb-horses of stone.	故物獨石馬

Depression comes, smooth back the grasses, sit,	憂來籍草坐

Sing wildly, let the tears cover your open hands.
Then go ever onward and on the road of your travels,
Meet none who prolong their fated years.

浩歌淚盈把
冉冉征途間
誰是長年者

[10561]

Nature's permanent "art" stands in for the decaying artifice of man: its cliff "wall" looms above the crumbling palace "construct"; its fires inhabit the deserted rooms; its true music (Chuang-tzu's "music of Earth") stands in for the lost palace orchestra. It swallows up the adorning "craft" (假, implying falseness) of the palace ladies and the ladies themselves. It even performs the "dirge" that the absent humans can no longer perform. Of all the works of the summer palace, nature leaves only the stone funerary horses as mocking signals of human mortality.

In face of the absolute impermanence of human endeavor, Tu Fu stood, making the poetic gesture of permanence, order, and civilization In his confidence he might see his work as a "deed of eternity," but he also felt (11433):

In literature my name will not be known,
Sickness, old age demand resignation of post—
Tossed about by winds, what is my semblance?
Of Heaven and of Earth, a single sand gull.

名豈文章著
官應老病休
飄飄何所似
天地一沙鷗

12

元結　篋中集

Fu-ku Revival
Yüan Chieh, the *Ch'ieh-chung chi*,
and the Confucian Intellectuals

There is now the shining example of Yüan Chieh of Tao-chou, to whom the old phrase may apply: "The sage of olden times can stand in awe of the later-born."
Tu Fu, "A Companion Piece to Yüan's 'Ballad of Ch'ung-ling'"

His mind of antiquity, his deeds of antiquity, and antiquity's language.
Yen Chen-ch'ing, "Funerary Inscription for Yüan Chieh"

When I compiled the *Ch'ieh-chung chi* [*The Satchel Anthology*], someone asked how I decided upon the poems I included. I told him: the ancient principles of poetry [*feng-ya*] have lain dormant for almost a thousand years, yet are there not men nowadays capable of such poetry, but lost to the world? There are those whose names and reputations remain obscure, who do not live out their full span of years, who lack friends to understand their worth, who go unpraised and unsung, who simply die and that's an end to it. Can anyone claim there are none such?

　　Most writers of recent times imitate their predecessors ever more closely and are hampered by tonal regulations. Their greatest delight is in similitude, and they follow transient fashion in their diction, unaware that by doing so they bring ruin to what is right and proper. Isn't it true? Such poets write about the flora and fauna of each season, then set their works to the music of stringed instruments and pipes. That may be just fine for the lewd and deluding songs of singing boys and dancing girls in private chambers, but for an upright and educated man, a gentleman of the Great Odes—I don't think it is right that such a man listen to that kind of poetry or chant it himself.
Yüan Chieh, "Preface to the *Ch'ieh-chung chi*"

The High T'ang had successfully domesticated antiquity in the *ku-feng*; the great "decline" of literature had been accurately located in a recent past

that was ever receding, a "bad past" layered between antiquity and the restoration of antiquity's values in the present dynasty (see 07865). But the
radical *fu-ku* sentiment that fathered the T'ang *ku-feng* was by nature
polemical and unsatisfied. Li Po and others might congratulate present
writers on their restoration of literary antiquity, but such complacency
was alien to *fu-ku's* first inclinations—though it would approve of the
gesture of loyalty to the dynasty implicit in the claim that antiquity had
been restored.

The reformist zeal of *fu-ku* could not remain long satisfied by the *ku-
feng*. The second generation of the High T'ang produced a new *fu-ku* radicalism in Yüan Chieh. Yüan took aim not at the long-dead frivolities of
Southern Dynasties poetry, but at the poetry of the High T'ang itself. In
the above section of the preface to *The Satchel Anthology*, Yüan Chieh
insisted that the truly worthy poets were unknown, their virtues hidden
by the eminence of contemporary poets who had become famous for
pernicious poetic practices: themes of nature, tonal regulation, and poetry
written to be sung. One can only wonder who these amoral composers
for courtesans and catamites might have been—Li Po? Wang Ch'ang-ling?
Wang Wei?

Like other second generation poets, Yüan Chieh had to confront an
entire generation of genius and poetic fame; he protected the identity of
his own work and that of his friends by espousing a poetics in which fame
was the mark of inferiority. Nor had the *fu-ku* sentiment lost its force: Yüan
Chieh's opinions and his radical *fu-ku* stance were praised by a whole generation of intellectuals. But unlike his great *fu-ku* predecessor Ch'en Tzu-
ang, Yüan Chieh's poetry and that of the poets he admired was largely
ignored. Yüan had tried to create a new language for poetry to answer the
moral seriousness that *fu-ku* demanded of poetry, but he was successful only
when he moved to compromise with established poetic modes. His goal of a
powerful poetry that embodied Confucian cultural values was to be fulfilled only half a century later in the poetry of Meng Chiao and Han Yü.

Originally *fu-ku* sentiments had shown a strong affinity to men who
were outside the circles of capital poetry. As can be seen in the passage from
the preface above, in Yüan Chieh that affinity had become a cult of unsuccess. True *fu-ku* writing had to emanate from the poet forgotten by the age,
the poet who lived in dire poverty, the unrecognized man of moral value
with talent for both state service and literature. If *fu-ku* was antithetical to
the worldly splendor of capital society, its proponents must likewise be the
antithesis of the eminence that attached itself to the literary figures of the
capital. Conversely, it was equally true that the age was indicted by its failure to recognize such worthy men. *Fu-ku's* disjunction from established
literary and political power led it to social criticism: within strict limits,

it came to speak for the downtrodden, to take the part of the peasants against the government. Yüan Chieh even praised barbarians above civilized Chinese (a possibility raised in the *Analects* IX. 13), though that was an extreme to which few *fu-ku* writers would go.

Yüan Chieh was born in 719 into a clan descended from the Hsien-p'i rulers of the Later Wei.[1] Like the great Wang's of the capital, the Yüan's were originally from T'ai-yüan, but during the T'ang, the clan had been steadily losing its ability to procure the best posts for its members. Yüan Chieh's father had briefly held a very low post in the central government, but had moved to Lu County in Honan, where he lived out his life as a private citizen. As with other poets, we should remember that a central government post did not necessarily reflect a man's wealth or his local power and prestige.

The most important figure in Yüan Chieh's early life was his cousin Yüan Te-hsiu 元德秀. Yüan Te-hsiu was probably the closest T'ang approximation to a Confucian saint. An exemplar of filial piety, a successful local administrator who governed by moral force, and a *fu-ku* poet (whose works are no longer extant), Yüan Te-hsiu became the subject for both prose and poetic hagiography (e.g., 20033–42, 33474). Yüan Chieh spent much of his youth living with Yüan Te-hsiu and probably met the great intellectuals like Hsiao Ying-shih who were acquainted with his cousin. And Yüan Chieh became the *fu-ku* moralist that such an upbringing might have been expected to produce.

Yüan Chieh's first datable poem, "Pity for Dissolution" 閔荒 (12574), came from 746. In that year Li Po was off wandering in the Southeast after his dismissal from the capital; Wang Wei was holding a respectable post in Ch'ang-an and producing graceful poems for court outings along with the serene poetry of reclusion; Ts'en Shen was in the crown prince's guard, trying to build a personal style on the models of Li Po and Wang Wei. Yüan Chieh's "Pity for Dissolution" was technically a *huai-ku*, occasioned by a visit to the old Sui canal built by Yang-ti. But Yüan Chieh's *huai-ku* differed radically from earlier *huai-ku*: its title suggested general rather than occasional significance; explicit moralizing occurred throughout; its diction was idiosyncratically archaic; and the poem showed a deep concern for the proper function of poetry. These were to become important characteristics of Yüan Chieh's prerebellion poetry.

"Pity for Dissolution" was not so much occasioned by Yüan's visit to the canal as by five Sui folk songs that Yüan found, songs that seemed to express the bitterness of the Sui populace against Yang-ti's extravagance. These songs fulfilled one of the canonical functions of poetry set forth in the "Great Preface" to the *Shih-ching*—to be the voice of the people directed upward, informing the ruler and the gods of the evils the people suffer.

Lest some remarkably obtuse reader miss the poem's internal moralizing, Yüan Chieh provided the poem with a preface to underline the ethical dimensions of the situation:

> I obtained the five "Songs of Wrongs Suffered," and when I investigated their purport, I could see that they were expressing grievances against the ruler. So I amplified the idea and selected a song [as Confucius "selected" the poems of the *Shih-ching*] to write my "Pity for Dissolution."

Straightforwardness was one of the qualities most admired by *fu-ku* writers, and the preface afforded an opportunity to reinforce a poem's moral or intellectual point, as well as providing the occasional context. It is therefore not surprising to find that Yüan Chieh's collection has more prefaces to poems than the collection of almost any other T'ang poet.

"Pity for Dissolution" is not an exciting poem either in the original or in translation, but it is an excellent example of the amplification of a moral problem in history. The middle section seems to contain one of the Sui folk songs, which complains about "Heaven's Prisoner" (the ruler) who feels that the mortal confines of the world are "Heaven's Jail"; both terms are also names of stars.

15 Barge and galley, shapes of dragon and cormorants	舸艫狀龍鶂
Sailed along as though bearing his palace towers,	若負宮闕浮
And before his dissolute pleasures were done,	荒娛未央極
He came to the edge of the blue sea.	始到滄海頭
At once he saw the mountain straits to the ocean.	忽見海門山
20 And he thought on erecting a sea-gazing tower,	思作望海樓
Unaware that his capital Hsin-tu then	不知新都城
Had become a hill of attack and battle.	已爲征戰丘
In this age we have the songs of that time	當時有遺歌
Which express great wrong and suffering:	歌曲太寃愁
25 "All this sea-bound world denounces Heaven's Jail,	四海非天獄
And why do we denounce Heaven's Prisoner?—	何爲非天囚
Heaven's Prisoner is a wicked ruthlessness,	天囚正凶忍
Our enemy, ours—the millions of people.	爲我萬姓讎
And men will seize the scythe of Heaven,	人將引天�
30 And men will take Heaven's carving knife—	人將持天鍁
What we want is to fulfill our desires,	所欲充其心
To join and cease this misery."	相與絕悲憂
I found these songs of the Sui,	自得隋人歌
And each was the Sui ruler's shame.	每爲隋君羞
35 If you sang them in bright days of spring,	欲歌當陽春
You could almost feel the world turn autumn;	似覺天下秋
Keep singing them, and before you're done,	更歌曲未終
The aura of their wrongs will float about you.	如有怨氣浮

Surely the king's heart was clouded indeed, 奈何昏王心
40 That he took no heed of their spite and rage: 不覺此怨尤
  If just one man would sing these songs, 遂令一夫唱
  All the world would raise lances joyously. 四海忻提矛
[12574]

Righteous rebellion, the power of poetry and the people's ill-will to influence the seasons, royal responsibility—these were ancient and potent themes, but themes usually suppressed in poetry. A bold poet might speak of the hardships suffered by imperial armies or even, at times, the suffering of the peasantry; but to see those same peasants taking up their great scythes on Heaven's authority to put an end to an unrighteous ruler— that was taboo as a poetic topic, however legitimate it might have been in Confucian political theory.

Like Tu Fu and Kao Shih, in 747 Yüan Chieh presented himself for the special examination set to discover hidden talent that had been overlooked in previous examinations and in the usual channels of recommendation and privilege. Like all the others, Yüan Chieh was failed on Li Lin-fu's orders, and the ensuing disappointment surely contributed to the conviction on the part of Yüan and many other intellectuals that there were indeed numerous unrecognized men of talent. The praise of the virtues of unsuccess that appeared in the preface to *The Satchel Anthology* had roots in contemporary political experience as well as in the *fu-ku* tradition. And in his own unwitting way, the great aristocrat Li Lin-fu contributed to the midcentury *fu-ku* revival.

When in the capital for the special examination, Yüan Chieh presented his ten "Two Kinds of Airs" 二風詩 (12527–36). Written in archaic tetrasyllabic meter, this series consisted of five poems on examples of good government and five poems on misgovernment. Each poem was provided with a short preface that stated explicitly the moral of the poem. And to clarify the obvious, Yüan added a "discussion" (*lun* 論) explaining the plan of the series. The seriousness and self-consciousness with which Yüan invested the series were far more important than the series itself. Court poetry had possessed tacit rules about *how* poetry should be written, but only *fu-ku* possessed articulate principles of what poetry should be. Aesthetically pathetic, Yüan Chieh's early series did represent a planned, internal order, written to fulfill a prior concept of what poetry should be. Literary self-consciousness in the eighth century was still largely technical; *fu-ku* retained the monopoly on the vision of the broad goals and function of poetry.

During the years after 747 Yüan Chieh perfected his attempts to create a new *fu-ku* poetry. The twelve "In the Succession of the *Yüeh-fu*" 系樂府 (12547–58) of 751 were aesthetically far more successful than the "Two Kinds of Airs." The diction became somewhat less archaic and was adopted to the pentasyllabic line, as was appropriate to *yüeh-fu*. The series represented the primitivistic *fu-ku* interpretation of *yüeh-fu* as the poems selected for the Han Music Bureau (*Yüeh-fu*), expressing the sentiments of the populace. Yüan Chieh gave the series a general preface stating the purpose of the poems, but the series lacked the individual prefaces and internal unity of the "Two Kinds of Airs."

The most remarkable of these poems is the first, "Thinking on High Antiquity" 思太古, in which the golden age of the past is found in the primitive tribes of the south:

To the southeast three thousand miles	東南三千里
The Yüan and Hsiang form Grand Lake,	沅湘爲太湖
And by lakeside are deep mountain valleys	湖上山谷深
Where people live, that seem so simple:	有人多似愚
They lodge their children in treetops,	嬰孩寄樹顛
And in the waters catch crowfish, perch.	就水捕鰷鱸
Their joys are shared by birds and beasts,	所歡同鳥獸
And no constraints bind body or mind.	身意復何拘
I have traveled all China's nine regions	吾行遍九州
And nowhere else can such ways be found.	此風皆已無
What has become of our sages' teachings?!	吁嗟聖覽教
Unconsciously I waver here long.	不覺久踟躕
[12547]	

The closure is borrowed from the *ku-feng*, the straightforward act of deep emotional turmoil, but the language of the poem as a whole has an artlessness that differs greatly from the *ku-feng* style. It is the artlessness of "High Antiquity" and its primitive simplicity that still can be found in the southern tribes. If the Chinese "noble savage" was not as potent a myth as his Western counterpart, he at least had a millenium's priority.

From about the same time as "In the Succession of the *Yüeh-fu*" came another series, "Amplifying Thoughts Stirred" 演興 (12570–73), four poems on the gods in the manner of "The Nine Songs" of the *Ch'u-tzu*. As the plainness of the preceding poem was to echo the *yüeh-fu* of Han, these songs employed the rich, expressive vocabulary of the *Ch'u-tzu* tradition. Undatable but probably also from this prerebellion period were two other archaic series by Yüan: "Filling in the Lyrics of Ancient Songs" 補樂歌 (12537–46) and *Yin-chi* 引極 (12576–79), an untranslatable title that Yüan endeavored to explain in the preface as "complete expression of emotions stirred." Like "Amplifying Thoughts Stirred," the *Yin-chi* were in the Ch'u song tradition, but "Filling in the Lyrics of Ancient Songs" was an attempt to write lyrics for song titles preserved in ancient texts. The models for "Filling in the Lyrics" were the *Shih-ching*, other poetry of antiquity preserved in various texts (most of which is now recognized as spurious), and Shu Hsi's series of "Filling in the Lyrics of Ancient Songs" (p. 156).

Yüan Chieh's prerebellion poetry was remarkable in the seriousness with which Yüan sought to create a new *fu-ku* poetry. Equally remarkable was the consistent use of the preface as a theoretical text to justify the poet's experiments. Though Yüan tried many styles, their variety was unified by a conscious avoidance of conventional poetic diction. When simple, Yüan's style was an artless simplicity entirely unlike the artful simplicity of Wang Wei; when difficult, Yüan's style was difficult by rich archaism rather than by syntactic and semantic play. Like Ts'en Shen, Yüan Chieh strove to be different from those contemporary poets who "imitated their predecessors ever more"; Yüan achieved "difference" in his poetry more perfectly than Ts'en Shen did, but that radical difference was no guarantee of aesthetic success. Indeed, his success in being different was directly proportional to his lack of success in the poetic art.

In 754 Yüan Chieh passed the examination and returned to Shang-yü Mountain, where he had been living with his cousin. When the rebellion broke out late in the following year, the family fled south, finally taking up temporary residence at Jang Creek in Kiangsi. Then, in 759 Su Yüan-ming 蘇源明, known in the T'ang as a *ku-wen* master like Yüan himself, recommended Yüan to the central government. As a result, in the early 760s Yüan held a series of military commands to organize regional resistance against the various insurgent groups contending in the countryside.

It was during this period, in 760, that Yüan Chieh put together *The Satchel Anthology*, the *Ch'ieh-chung chi* 篋中集, and began a new period of poetic activity. Perhaps basing himself on the model of the *Ch'ieh-chung* poets, Yüan Chieh moderated his *fu-ku* radicalism and turned to a more discursive, less archaic poetry. Abstract discussion, emblematic allegory, and archaic imitation were all part of the vocabulary of the *fu-ku* poet, but these were so alien to the mainstream of T'ang poetry that it was unlikely that major poetry could emerge from them. A preferable aternative, equally legitimate in the *fu-ku* tradition, was to write of some exemplary situation that incarnated "ancient" values of public morality. To Yüan Chieh, with his new administrative experiences, the peaceful and simple society of the golden age could be glimpsed in this world, and wherever it might be found, it was inimical to and threatened by the political exigencies of the age. Jang Creek in Kiangsi became the incarnation of this harmonious society and the dangers that threatened it.

To my Neighbors at Jang Creek

In 758 I took my family to Jang Creek to preserve them from harm. In this year of 761 I find myself in charge of troops from Ching-nan garrisoning Nine Rivers. Here on military duty I don't get to see my old neighbors from Jang Creek as I once did. But

與瀼溪鄰里

乾元元年，元子將家自全于瀼溪。上元二年，領荊南之兵鎮九江。方在軍旅，與瀼溪鄰里不得如往時相見遊。又知

I know that the people there are finding themselves
in ever-increasing difficulties and poverty. So I wrote
this poem for them.

瀼溪之人，日轉窮困。
故作詩與之。

In recent years, in rebellion's hardships,
My entire clan fled southward:
Each day we went ten or twenty miles,
Then halted from love of your mountain village.
Peak and valley gaped in light shining,
And no house lacked its private spring;
Everywhere tall bamboo lined the road,
And tiny boats were at every gate.
Jang Creek's shores twist in the middle,
On its sunny side are peaceful gardens.
In those days our neighbors gave word to us:
"We accept you and your offspring."
Whenever necessities were wanting,
Our neighbors willingly shared with us;
Whenever we were distressed,
Our neighbors then took care of us.
People like these now grow ever poorer,
Have not missed the injustice of forced labor.
I end with this plea for Jang Creek—
Let the world not speak of it.
                [12582]

昔年苦逆亂
舉族來南奔
日行幾十里
愛君此山村
峯谷呀回映
誰家無泉源
修竹多夾路
扁舟皆到門
瀼溪中曲濱
其陽有閒園
鄰里昔贈我
許之及子孫
我嘗有匱乏
鄰里能相分
我嘗有不安
鄰里能相存
斯人轉貧弱
力役非無寃
終以瀼濱訟
無令天下論

Presumably, if Jang Creek became known, it would suffer even greater
difficulties. The poem stands uneasily between the Confucian impulse to
manifest ethical and social problems in order to rectify them and, on the
other hand, the quietist impulse to the safety of obscurity. The poet also
stands divided between a public posture and the yearning for a perfect polity
in which the unseen, unacting government disappears behind a harmonious
agrarian society.

    Returning to Jang Creek, Yüan experienced an even more disquieting
sense of membership in an unsuccessfully manipulative government from
which the people rightly felt alienated.

The Lesson of a Former Visit to Jang Creek

喻瀼溪鄉舊遊

In years gone by on the shores of the Jang,
The people acted all unselfconsciously.
But now when I visit this land again,
Seeing me people are instantly ill at ease.
My own heart's relation to the people of Jang
Makes no distinction of "grand" and "humble"—
No, the people of Jang have changed *their* hearts,
And surely because of my government robes.
In ancient times wise men hated this

往年在瀼濱
瀼人皆忘情
今來遊瀼鄉
瀼人見我驚
我心與瀼人
豈有辱與榮
瀼人異其心
應爲我冠纓
昔賢惡如此

And therefore refused high office:　　　　　　　　　所以辭公卿
In their native towns they grew old in proverty,　　貧窮老鄉里
Quit, went back to labor at the plow.　　　　　　自休還力耕
They would feel it more strongly still,　　　　　　況曾經逆亂
　　had they, like I, lived through rebellion.
I grow daily more weary of hearing of battle.　　　日厭聞戰爭
And most I love this single creek　　　　　　　　尤愛一溪水
That keeps the name Jang, meaning "Yield."　　　而能存讓名
In the end I will surely come to its shores,　　　終當來其濱
Drinking, munching, live my life to full span.　　飲啄全此生

[12587]

Though the informing values are different, this poem is reminiscent of Meng Hao-jan seeing Lu Mountain and thinking on the recluses there (07631): Meng expressed his desire to be a recluse, but excused himself from immediate withdrawal because of a government mission; then, in compromise, he promised that someday he would return. Wang Wei may exclaim at the pastoral scene "Why not go now?!" (05861), but in poetry the joy deferred is the rule. Yüan Chieh's poem is discursive in the extreme, and one might be tempted to call it "prosaic" were it not that a writer was even less likely be so discursive in prose. In the context of contemporary poetics, the poem was a species of "antipoetry" that aimed for authenticity in its ramblings. It is the secret twin of Wang Wei's great goal, the self-conscious poet using his manipulative powers to defeat self-consciousness, the yoking of art to defeat art.

　　After completing his years of military service, Yüan Chieh spent the remaining years of his life, until his death in 772, alternating between periods of retirement and serving in regional prefectural posts. It was in Tao-chou, located in the southern part of Hunan, that Yüan experienced the worst contradictions of practical politics and social realities: his precarious situation was set forth in the preface to the "Ballad of Ch'ung-ling" 舂陵行 (12576):

In the year 763 the "Easygoing Old Man," as I call myself, was made prefect of Tao-chou. Previously Tao-chou had consisted of over forty thousand households, but since the rebellion not even four thousand are left, and the greater part of these are incapable of paying taxes. It had not even been fifty days since I assumed office when I received over two hundred legitimate demands from government clerks (for taxes and expropriations). Every one of these said that if I failed to meet the quota, my crime would be punishable by dismissal and having my name removed from the registers of official exemptions. What a situation! If I were to fulfill these commands to the minutest detail, the prefecture would revolt, and then how could I escape punishment? On the other hand, if I were not to fulfill the commands, I certainly would be gravely punished. I have taken this office to soothe the people and give them respite, but the office turns out to be no more than a period awaiting punishment. This prefecture was once called Ch'ung-ling, so I wrote a "Ballad of Ch'ung-ling" to bring the sentiments of those below to those above.

The closing phrase, "to bring the sentiments of those below to those above" 以達下情, is one of the canonical Confucian functions of poetry: poetry is the effective/affective use of language that not only states the position of the people, but states it in such a way as to touch and convince those in power. The ballad itself is rather too long to quote here in its entirety, but the following passage illustrates the pathetic picture it paints of the suffering populace:

What they eat at dawn are the roots of plants;	朝飡是草根
What they dine on at dusk is bark of trees.	暮食是木皮
When they speak, their breath seems about to fail,	出言氣欲絕
Swiftly they speak, but their movements are slow.	言速行步遲
I cannot bear to summon them,	追呼尚不忍
Still less, to whip or flog them.	況乃鞭扑之

Several years earlier Tu Fu had written similar narrative poems on the plight of the common people and specific social abuses, and since Tu Fu was later to write a companion piece for the "Ballad of Ch'ung-ling," it may be that Yüan was familiar with Tu Fu's work. But despite this coincidence of their interests, the two poets were profoundly different: perhaps the strongest element in their difference was Yüan Chieh's *fu-ku* self-consciousness: Yüan could not resist closing the "Ballad of Ch'ung-ling" with a statement of the canonical poetic function: to speak on behalf of the people as though he were "selecting" the *Kuo-feng*, that portion of the *Shih-ching* that was supposed to make the sentiments of the common people known to the ruler:

Who is there now to select the "Airs of States"?	何人采國風
Only I, who hereby present these lines.	吾欲獻此辭

Though Yüan Chieh was able to obtain a temporary reprieve for Tao-chou's taxes, the essential conflict between Confucian social values and the coercive realities of contemporary politics remained.[2] While we might conceive of a true social heroism as accepting compromise and helping the people as best one can, the Confucian tradition validated absolute virtue only by absolute success; if absolute success was denied by the conditions of the age, the only recourse for absolute virtue was flight. But when Yüan finally made that gesture of flight, he retained a dimension of public morality in his flight by echoing the peasant speaker of *Shih* 113, fleeing oppression to a "happy land." The poem was Yüan Chieh's famous "After the Raiders Have Gone: To Clerks and Officials" 賊退示官吏:

In 763 raiders from the western plateaus attacked Tao-chou, burning, looting, and murdering. They left only when everything was virtually gone. The following year the raiders struck again, this time at Yung-chou, smashing Shao, but they turned back before they crossed the boundaries of this prefecture. We do not seem to be able to control the enemy by force, and can do no more than endure the wounds we suffer. But how, after all this, can the government envoys increase our hardships with more demands and exactions of taxes? For this purpose I wrote this poem to be shown to the clerks:

癸卯歲，西原賊入道
州。焚燒殺掠，幾盡
而去。明年，賊又攻
永州，破邵。不犯此
州邊鄙而退。豈力能
制敵歟。蓋蒙其傷憐
而已。諸使何爲忍苦
微歛。故作詩一篇，
以示官吏。

In past years I lived in an age of peace,	昔歲逢太平
Twenty years amid mountains and forests.	山林二十年
Springs lay by the door of my yard,	泉源在庭戶
Caves and ravines, right before my gate.	洞壑當門前
Field taxes were taken at regular times;	井稅有常期
At sundown a man could still sleep in peace.	日晏猶得眠
All at once we came into times of trouble,	忽然遭世變
And I served several years under battle flags.	數歲親戎旃
Now, as I govern this commandery,	今來典斯郡
The mountain tribes are running wild.	山夷又紛然
The city, so small the raiders didn't sack it.	城小賊不屠
But its people are poor, their wounds to be pitied.	人貧傷可憐
Thus, when the neighboring regions were plundered,	是以陷鄰境
This prefecture alone remained intact.	此州獨見全
Then come commisioners with royal commands—	使臣將王命
Surely they must be better than the raiders!	豈不如賊焉
But with their exactions and their collections	今彼微歛者
They harry us like a simmering fire—	迫之如火煎
What kind of person would end men's lives	誰能絕人命
To be a great worthy of the age?	以作時世賢
How I long to cast down my symbols of office,	思欲委符節
Take fishing pole, punt my own boat away,	引竿自刺船
Go with my family where there's fish and grain,	將家就魚麥
To live out my life by the Yangtze and sea!	歸老江海邊

[12577]

The poem is framed by the idyllic world seen earlier in the Jang-chou poems and in "Thinking on High Antiquity." Yüan, the public poet, was gradually changing into a private poet: the poem still exists for a social function, "to be shown to clerks and officials," but in the end the self-aware, moral poet yields to the poet who acts for himself. Yüan Chieh's poetic development was consciously tied to his social and political experiences: this was Yüan's chosen myth about the nature of poetry—a literature alive in the political and social world, serving to articulate and change the relationship between moral value and political reality.

Even before his experiences in Tao-chou, Yüan Chieh had taken to calling himself the "Easygoing Old Man" 漫叟, a pseudonymn that affected the private values of the eccentric. Even though he was to accept public office one more time after his second term in Tao-chou, the public poet disappeared forever, and in his place appeared the landscape poet and the eccentric. In many ways this later poetry of Yüan's is more attractive than his *fu-ku* poetry. But even though Yüan brought to such private poetry his wide vocabulary and stylistic range, his later poetry was fundamentally a retreat into poetic conservatism, a retreat that signaled the failure of *fu-ku* poetics in midcentury. One of Yüan's favorite themes in his later poetry was relativity—large things seeming small and small things seeming large (e.g., 12601, 12614). This visual relativity was inextricably linked to the relativity of values in the *Chuang-tzu*, and one cannot help but see in this theme an apology for his abrogation of public responsibility, for which *Chuang-tzu*'s moral relativity might serve as a convenient excuse.

Wine Cup in Stone Hollow   宛樽詩

Tiny mountain of stone, upjutting sheer,	巉巉小山石
Some peaks face my resting place by a hollow:	數峯對宛亭
This hollow in stone can serve as my wine cup,	宛石堪爲樽
Though I can't give a name to what kind it is.	狀類不可名
I wend a circling course round a few square feet	巡回數尺間
And seem to see here the immortals' isles,	如見小蓬瀛
For when the wine first brims this "cup,"	樽中酒初漲
There are isles and peaks appearing.	始有島嶼生
Sure enough, we have here Sungazing Peak	豈無日觀峯
That looks straight down on the dark, dark sea.	直下臨滄溟
I love the place, don't notice I'm drunk,	愛之不覺醉
I lie down drunk, wake up sober again—	醉臥還自醒
To grow drunk then sober by this, my wine cup,	醒醉在樽畔
Has now become my very nature.	始爲吾性情
And as if I've conceded the dispute to Form,	若以形勝論
My sitting nook looks down on the district capital:	坐隅臨郡城
A level lake lies near my stairs,	平湖近階砌
And far mountains are a green upon green.	遠山復青青
There are twenty or so unusual trees	異木幾十株
Whose branches and boughs crown columns, eaves,	枝條冒簷楹
And whose twisting roots fill these rocks,	盤根滿石上
All taking the shapes of serpents and dragons.	皆作龍蛇形
In my wine hall I've stored away vats of brew,	酒堂貯釀器
And the doors and windows, all filled with jugs,	戶牖皆罌餅

So this "wine cup" can be kept full forever—   此樽可常滿
Now who really is T'ao Yüan-ming?   誰是陶淵明
                    [12607]

When Yüan Chieh "concedes the dispute to Form," he is referring to
"Form, Shadow, and Spirit" 形影神, the famous debate poem by T'ao
Ch'ien (T'ao Yüan-ming). There Spirit advocates Taoist passivity; Shadow
advocates social values and personal reputation; but Form represents an
inebriate epicureanism that neither transcends life's concerns nor faces them,
but forgets them in the self-pleasing stupor of wine. "Form" does most
accurately represent the T'ang "type" of the drunken eccentric, but reference to the debate poem undermines the assurance of the role and casts the
discursive poetry of drunkenness in the terms of defense and apology.

Yüan Chieh's last extant poems date from 767, a series of five "Rowing
Songs" 欸乃曲 (12620–24). Yüan had just been in the capital and was returning to his district: the moralist and the intellectual had receded into a
mellow irony that was not unlike some of the late poetry of Tu Fu or of
Han Yü fifty years later:

My name and deeds by chance   偶存名跡在人間
    survive in the world of men.
I follow custom, but in these times   順俗與時未安閑
    find myself ill at ease.
I went to greet the grand masters of state, 來謁大官兼問政
    to ask them how one governs,
And now my boat goes back again   扁舟却入九疑山
    into Nine Doubts Mountain.
                    [12620]

Fame is haphazard; the times are awry; and the poet, once the self-assured
fu-ku moralist, speaks with a wry humor as he reports of asking the great
in Ch'ang-an "how one governs." Now he returns to the real world of
doubts and uncertainties, manifest in nature's great topographical pun, Nine
Doubts Mountain.

Yüan Chieh was more an "important" poet than a great one. He was
an innovator who opened the way for better poets who followed him in
the late eighth century. With a firm conviction of what poetry should be,
he set about to create that kind of poetry; yet he found that such poetry was
no more successful in the aesthetics of the real literary world than its Confucian values were successful in the political world. Confucian values had
to be put into practice in society; if they collapsed into private values, they
tended to merge with the private values of Taoism. The differences between
the Confucian recluse and the Taoist recluse were of tone rather than sub-

stance. Like Yüan Chieh, Tu Fu took part in the midcentury *fu-ku* resurgence, but for Tu Fu art occupied a position at least as important as
his social values. Thus, when those values were threatened by the disinte-
grating fabric of the empire in the 760s, Tu Fu's poetry did not undergo
the dramatic retreat into the conservatism of Yüan Chieh's poetry.

POETS OF THE *CH'IEH-CHUNG CHI*

The poets of the *Ch'ieh-chung chi* represented a style, a mood, and a
theme. The theme was the virtuous man in poverty and difficulty, the "resolute endurance of hardship" (*ku-ch'iung* 固窮) of the *Analects*. That the virtuous man lived in such a condition was an implicit indictment of the age.
The style was the occasional *ku-feng*, whose archaism was intensified by the
frequent use of particles, pronouns, and prose constructions. But all in all,
the style of the *Ch'ieh-chung* poets was less radically archaic than the early
poetry of Yüan Chieh and closer to the *ku-feng* works of their more eminent contemporaries.

The *Ch'ieh-chung chi* is a very small anthology, consisting of twenty-
four pentasyllabic "old-style" poems by seven poets. Yüan Chieh insisted
upon the obscurity of the worthy, and most of the *Ch'ieh-chung* poets fulfilled his conditions admirably: only two of them have significantly more
poems than the handful anthologized in the *Chieh-chung chi*: Wang Chi-yu
王季友, who has thirteen extant poems (of which two are of questionable
authenticity) and Meng Yün-ch'ing 孟雲卿, with seventeen extant poems.
According to Yüan Chieh, the anthology was constituted of poems by
Shen Ch'ien-yün 沈千運 and his followers, though Shen is no more fully
represented than the others.

There is nothing particularly inspiring about Shen Ch'ien-yün's poetry: the theme of the unrecognized man of talent had a powerful resonance
for T'ang intellectuals, but in Shen's extant poems the theme is not handled
with great genius. The poems of Yü T'i 于逖, Chang Piao 張彪, Chao
Cheng-ming 趙微明, and Yüan Chi-ch'uan 元季川 are perhaps superior
to Shen's, but much in the same vein. The *Ch'ieh-chung* style is best represented by the two poets who were most widely known beyond Shen's circle: Wang Chi-yu and Meng Yün-ch'ing.

Among the *Ch'ieh-chung* poets, Wang Chi-yu is unique, for his poetry
was also anthologized in the *Ho-yüeh ying-ling chi*, which provides a less
partisan view of his poetry than Yüan Chieh's. To Yin Fan, Wang Chi-yu
"adored the strange and devoted himself to daring, going far beyond ordinary sentiments. But that he wore poor commoner's garb in white-haired
old age is to be lamented." The typology was similar to Yüan Chieh's

"virtuous man in obscurity," but Yüan placed greater emphasis on moral value than exceptional genius. Wang Chi-yu also had contacts in the larger world of contemporary poetry; pieces were dedicated to him by Ts'en Shen and the later capital poets Ch'ien Ch'i and Lang Shih-yüan.

The two poems of Wang's included in the *Ch'ieh-chung chi* represent that aspect of Wang's talent closest to Shen Ch'ien-yün; but Wang Chi-yu was clearly the stronger poet:

To Wei Tzu-ch'un   寄韋子春

When you left the mountains, fall clouds were bright,	出山秋雲曙
Now the mountain trees have again turned spring.	山木已再春
You ate my herbs of the mountains,	食我山中藥
But do not remember the mountain man.	不憶山中人
Who in these mountains is my intimate?	山中誰余密
This white hair of mine, my only kin.	白髮惟相親
Both day and night, no rats nor wrens—	雀鼠晝夜無
They know my kitchen and pantry are bare.	知我廚廩貧
But the flourishing pine of north cottage	依依北舍松
Wearies not of its neighbor to the south.	不厭吾南隣
All that have feelings are cast from me—	有情盡棄捐
Earth and stone, the same body as I.	土右爲同身

[13411]

Elements of this poem are remarkably close to the severity of Meng Chiao in the 790s. However, this poem was also included in the *Ho-yüeh ying-ling chi*, where it has a different title, a change in the first line, and an incongruously obsequious occasional ending added. There is no way to know which version is "correct" (if, indeed, both are not correct), but an important conflict in sensibility can be seen in the differences between the two versions. To Yin Fan, the *Ch'ieh-chung* version would have been too harsh: the occasional closure softened it:

You, sir, are a thousand-foot tree, fine substance,	夫子質千尋
From Heaven's moisture branch and leaf flourish anew.	天澤枝葉新
While I, with the long life of poor timber,	今以不材壽
And without wisdom, can still avoid the axe.	非智免斧斤

The proud austerity of the recluse, the body that is earth and stone, is politely given a self-deprecating qualification in the *Ho-yüeh ying-ling chi* version. On the other hand, to Yüan Chieh, compiling the *Ch'ieh-chung chi* seven years after the *Ho-yüeh ying-ling chi*, the occasional closure would have entirely destroyed the integrity of the poem and the firm, proud stance of the moral man. Appending an occasional message to a poem was entirely consonant with High T'ang poetic practice, but most modern readers would probably agree that in this case, Yüan Chieh's instincts were correct.

The *Ho-yüeh ying-ling chi* also anthologized heptasyllabic poems by Wang Chi-yu, a form that Yüan Chieh excluded from his anthology. Among these can sometimes be seen the roughness of the *Ch'ieh-chung* poems, but there is also the "strangeness" and "daring" that Yin Fan and many T'ien-pao readers so admired. Yin Fan singled out the following poem for special praise.

Seeing Grand Secretary Yü's Landscape Mural	觀于舍人壁畫山水
A man of the wilds will spend the night in a mountain home but seldom,	野人宿在山家少
When at dawn I saw these mountains, said, "It's morning in the mountains."	朝見此山謂山曉
Still settled over half your wall are clouds upon the peaks,	半壁仍棲嶺上雲
And I opened the curtains to permit escape for the birds upon the lake.	開簾放出湖中鳥
Now who is that fellow sitting alone under a towering pine?	獨坐長松是阿誰
Again and again I wave to him— why's he so slow to rise???	再三招手起來遲
The great Lord Yü gives a hearty laugh, and then he says to me:	于公大笑向予説
"Little brother, can you paint in the red and green a painting such as this?"	小弟丹青能爾爲

[13418]

Wang Chi-yu was playing the role of the naïve rustic for the amusement of Lord Yü, and there is little dignity in his self-mockery. It is not a pose Yüan Chieh would have greatly admired, but it indicates a participation in the more common world of contemporary poetry that made Wang socially one of the best known of the *Ch'ieh-chung* poets.

Meng Yün-ch'ing (b. ca. 712–13) was the most serious *fu-ku* poet of the *Ch'ieh-chung* group and, judging from what survives, also the best. Like Wang Chi-yu, Meng Yün-ch'ing was an acquaintance of Tu Fu's, and he was an especially close friend of his fellow countryman Yüan Chieh, who believed Meng superior in every way to himself (12594 preface). Meng's apparent fame removes him from the *Ch'ieh-chung* model. Wei Ying-wu said of him: "Your lofty writing stirs the falling wave" (09168), alluding to the first of Li Po's *Ku-feng* where Ssu-ma Hsiang-ju and Yang Hsiung halted the general decline of literature by "stirring the falling wave." In the ninth-century *Shih-jen chu-k'o t'u* 詩人主客圖, an elaborate and idiosyncratic classification of poets by exemplary couplets, Chang Wei 張爲 considered Meng Yün-ch'ing to be the foremost representative of a style he called "nobly ancient and loftily abstruse" 高古奧逸. In one edition of the *Chung-hsing hsien-ch'i chi* 中興間氣集, the T'ang critic Kao Chung-wu 高仲武 was more moderate: "His master was Shen Ch'ien-yün, and he hunted and fished in Ch'en Tzu-ang. The import of his verse was of mournful resentment . . . but if you compare him to Shen and Ch'en, you will see he is not quite up to them."[3]

Meng Yün-ch'ing was a less radical *fu-ku* poet than Yüan Chieh at his most archaic; Meng's work falls comfortably into the High T'ang *ku-feng*, of which he is perhaps the most talented representative. But even in the few poems that survive, Meng Yün-ch'ing was a better poet than Yüan Chieh. Kao Chung-wu was correct in tying Meng's work to that of Ch'en Tzu-ang. At times Meng Yün-ch'ing's poetry approached that of Ch'en very closely, as in Meng's two "Grieving over the Times" 傷時 (07570–71). The title indicates topical allegory, and it is particularly tempting to read the second of the pair as an allegory against Yang Kuei-fei (though Su-tsung's empress would be another attractive target):

The Great Void flows the pale moonlight—	太空流素月
How bright it is midmonth!	三五何明明
Its radiant beams invade bright sunlight's realm,	光耀侵白日
Of sage and fool we are led astray in its perfect essence.	賢愚迷至精
But the four seasons change on and on,	四時更變化
Heaven's Way has both waxing and waning.	天道有虧盈
I ever expect it to sink tonight,	常恐今夜沒
But in an instant it appears again.	須臾還復生

[07571]

The poem closely echoes the first of Ch'ien Tzu-ang's *Kan-yü* (04347). The moon stands for the Yin principle, the empress, that infringes on the imperial male Yang and fails to wane as it should.

Seven of Meng Yün-ch'ing's poems are *yüeh-fu* or in the *yüeh-fu* manner, and these belong to the primitivistic interpretation of *yüeh-fu*, seen also in the work of Tu Fu and Yüan Chieh. Primitivism appears clearly in the use of certain devices; for instance, certain forms of repetition and opening binomes, didactic closure, aphorisms, and exclamations. These were picked up forty years later by Meng Chiao. The style had strong associations for T'ang readers, an authenticity in emotional directness and a concomitant moral sense. In addition, Meng tried to approximate the indefiniteness and anonymity of the Han *shih* style: the intricate particularities of place and circumstance were stripped away, leaving the bare frame of an emotional situation.

Sadness   悲哉行

The lone child goes from loving parent,   孤兒去慈親
The far traveler loses his host: 遠客喪主人
Don't sing me the songs of sorrow—   莫吟苦辛曲
Who can bear to hear such songs?   此曲誰忍聞
Hear them you can, but meet you cannot,   可聞不可見
Go off ever farther, no sight, no traces.   去去無形跡
The man walking broods on the journey ahead,   行人念前程
Waits not on Orion's setting, not Antares'.   不待參辰沒
At dawn he always suffers from hunger,   朝亦常苦饑
Evenings too he suffers from hunger,   暮亦常苦饑
Wind-whirled over thousands of miles,   飄飄萬餘里
And poverty, full of inner struggles.   貧賤多是非
May no youth set out on faraway travels,   少年莫遠遊
From faraway travels men seldom return.   遠遊多不歸

                           [07563]

The speaker here is neither the conventional persona of *yüeh-fu* nor the poet himself as in occasional poetry: rather, it is the everyman of the Han poems and the Nineteen Old Poems.

Fu-ku poets tended to be activists: they believed in the incarnation of moral order in the world and considered it their duty to maintain and preserve it. T'ang poems were dominated by the lyric diad of scene and response, world and self; the *fu-ku* version usually required that the poet respond with a moral position. The moral position manifest in such poems may in turn affect the natural order: if the songs of the angry Sui peasants could turn spring into autumn, a sincere statement of the moral order could likewise rectify natural imbalance. This was a cosmic extention of the moral poet's presumed ability to rectify social imbalance, and it appeared commonly in the Mid-T'ang in the poetry of Meng Chiao and Han Yü. In the following poem by Meng Yün-ch'ing, the causal relation between the moral stand and the clearing of the weather is not stated explicitly, but it is implicit in the juxtaposition at the close of the poem.

Blocked by Winds on the Pien River   汴河阻風

In clear dawnlight I went from Liang and Sung,   清晨自梁宋
Hung up my sail to go to Ching and Ch'u,   挂席之楚荊
But once offshore, the wind and the tide grew rough,   出浦風潮惡
And by a rapids my boat began to turn sideways.   傍灘舟欲橫
The great river pours on eastward,   大河復東注
The herds of creatures grow blurred and hazy.   羣動皆窅冥
White fogs: breath of fish and dragon;   白霧魚龍氣
Brown cloud: forms of tigers, of cattle.   黃雲牛虎形
A blur all around me, I lost my bearings,   蒼茫迷所適

All apprehensive, not even a moment's peace:
Put trust in this, that in this world of ours
Nothing is lighter than human life,
But if a grown man has not attained his goal,
His inclination must be to preserve sincerity.
For the journey ahead I put up my boat and go on;
In the southeast there should be an evening clearing.

危懼安暫寧
信此天地內
孰於身命輕
丈夫苟未達
所向須存誠
前路捨舟去
東南應晚晴

[07573]

THE INTELLECTUALS

Ch'en Tzu-ang had been a well-known prose stylist as well as a poet, and Yüan Chieh became even more famous for his prose than his poetry. The *Ch'ieh-chung* poets may have been exceptions, but in general, prose was even more strongly associated with *fu-ku* values than poetry. This is not an indication that *fu-ku* writers felt poetry should be subordinate to prose; rather, because the language of Confucian moral and social values had developed primarily in classical prose, prose rather than poetry seemed the most natural vehicle for them.

The great mid-century intellectuals loosely constituted a group,[4] to which Yüan Chieh was linked through his cousin Yüan Te-hsiu. The two dominant figures of the group were Hsiao Ying-shih 蕭穎士 (717–69) and Li Hua 李華 (d. ca. 766). The hostility towards parallelism, tonal regulation, and similitude Yüan Chieh expressed in his 760 preface to the *Ch'ieh-chung chi* was not unique to Yüan. Similar statements had been made earlier by Hsiao Ying-shih and were to be made again later by Tu-ku Chi 獨孤及.[5] To Hsiao, writing in the late 740s or early 750s (07515 preface):

Literature [*wen*] does not refer to similitude or to drawing comparisons of kind, positioning them in parallel construction and letting them go wild with frivolous conceit. In such cases, what is said will always turn out to be shallow and perverse. Devotion to the revitalization of the lesson of classical restraint and to making manifest what is factually true is, on the whole, unlike the crowd's conception of literature. Alas, they think that I am idiosyncratic.

Ornament, *fu-ku*'s old enemy in court poetry, was still a great foe, but both here and in Yüan Chieh a new evil had become the target—"similitude" and "comparisons of kind." One hesitates to use the term *metaphor* in this case because Western metaphorical operations have significant differences from their Chinese counterparts. It is clear that Hsiao Ying-shih was offended by the "hiddenness of meaning" that had assumed such an important role in eighth-century poetry: the significance of the text could be discovered only by "associations of kind." Instead, Hsiao would have the poem represent what was "factually true." Though they rejected the general metaphoricality of poetry, the Confucian intellectuals would admit one form of true metaphor: allegory, in which the surface text was only a disguise for an indentifiable and controllable "meaning."

On one occasion—probably in the 740s and probably while Yüan Chieh was living with his cousin—Hsiao Ying-shih paid a visit to Yüan Te-hsiu (07519). At the time Hsiao was already considered one of the most brilliant young scholars of the age, and he had already begun to experiment in archaic poetic forms and to make pronouncements like the one quoted above. Hsiao's example may well have been important influence on Yüan Chieh's early archaic experiments.

Just as Yüan Chieh and Yüan Te-hsiu were descendants of the Later Wei ruling house, Hsiao Ying-shih was a scion of the royal house of Liang, one of the great families of the Southern Dynasties. But in contrast to Yüan Chieh, who grew up in obscurity and spent most of his life in relative obscurity, Hsiao Ying-shih was a renowned intellectual, a student in the imperial academy, and an unusually young *chin-shih* in 735. Hsiao began his career in the imperial library but soon became embroiled in the factional disputes of the T'ien-pao. Banished to Kuang-ling by Li Lin-fu, Hsiao wrote a history of the Period of Disunion on the model of the *Ch'un-ch'iu* and was recalled to the Bureau of History. The enmity of Li Lin-fu again drove Hsiao from government, and he was no more popular with Li's successor, Yang Kuo-chung. Hsiao was in such disfavor that when a Japanese envoy asked especially to see the famous intellectual, the government refused, probably knowing that Hsiao would have been less than kind in his comments on the ruling party. Hsiao escaped the forces of An Lu-shan when they swept over the district to which he had been posted, and he spent his last years acting the part of the upright Confucian, trying to give moral and political advice to a government that would not listen.

Hsiao Ying-shih's experiments in archaic poetry were modeled on the *Shih-ching*—on its metrics, its diction, and its stanzaic form. Hsiao Ying-shih's imitations of the *Shih* were generally more accurate in their archaism than the tetrasyllabic poetry of his contemporaries (though in this case "accuracy" refers to fidelity to the canonical interpretations of the *Shih*, particularly in the particles, which Hsiao used generously). Like Yüan Chieh's archaic poems, Hsiao's *Shih* imitations were provided with prefaces, particularly apt in Hsiao's case because of the "lesser prefaces" of the *Shih-ching* model. However, Hsiao's archaic poetry (07511–15) was even less successful than that of Yüan Chieh: the *Shih* model was too restrictive and overinterpreted, while Yüan Chieh's models were more flexible.

Hsiao Ying-shih's pentasyllabic poetry ranges from modifications of *Shih* meter and syntax (e.g., 07521–22) to the more domesticated High

T'ang *ku-feng* (e.g., 07517–18) to the smooth occasional verse of his contemporaries, filled with bewitching similitudes and lovely scenes ranged in parallel construction (e.g., 07530). Hsiao faced the perennial problem of the *fu-ku* poet: the more closely he fulfilled the social and ethical values he espoused, the less compelling his work became artistically. The *ku-feng* was still the most successful compromise between *fu-ku* values and the eighth-century poetic art. Equally effective but less widely practiced was the mid-century resurrection of *yüeh-fu* as an instrument of social protest and to express public values. The possibility of a "new *yüeh-fu*" might be apparent to Yüan Chieh, whose military and civil experiences justified his speaking "for the people," but such a form was less available to Hsiao Ying-shih, who was bound more closely to the intellectual society of the capital.

Li Hua was Hsiao Ying-shih's friend and the second great intellectual and prose stylist of the midcentury. Li Hua passed the *chin-shih* examination in 735, in the same year as Hsiao and Li Ch'i. Like Hsiao Ying-shih, Li Hua became widely known without ever rising to high position in the government. When Hsüan-tsung fled to Szechwan, Li Hua hurried out of Ch'ang-an to rescue his mother, but was captured by the rebels and given unwanted office. After the restoration, Li was punitively exiled to an administrative post in Hang-chou. In 760 when he was again offered a post in the central government, he refused. Late in his life, Li turned to Buddhism, and he died in 766 or a few years thereafter. In his old age Li Hua was one of the most respected men of letters in the empire, the sponsor of many famous intellectuals of the later eighth century, including Tu-ku Chi, Huang-fu Jan, and Han Yü's uncle, Han Yün-ch'ing 韓雲卿.

Li Hua did not experiment with archaic models, but instead worked in the *ku-feng*, writing seven "Unclassified Poems" (07482–87) and eleven poems on history (07488–98). The *fu-ku* poet's passion for symmetrical order appears in the first three "Unclassified Poems": these poems treat the "proper music," the "proper colors," and the "proper tastes," respectively. The fourth "Unclassified Poem," in which "Yin light engulfs the universe," is probably topical allegory directed against an empress. The fifth poem is on the decline of honor paid to Confucian values, while the sixth poem is on the choice of scholars as friends. Though Li Hua avoided the radical archaism of Hsiao Ying-shih, his *ku-feng* were more uncompromisingly didactic than Hsiao's tetrasyllabic poems. Similarly, the poems on history each treat a separate historical incident, never failing to draw the appropriate moral lessons for the reader.

But Li Hua differed from Hsiao Ying-shih in his undeniable descriptive genius, apparent both in his prose and in his more conventional occasional poetry. The few landscape poems in his few surviving works possess a rich vocabulary and imaginative capability equalled by few of his contemporaries (07499–501). Particularly interesting is the survival of Li Hua's examination poem, written to the topic "The Bright Moon Rises over the Sea" (07506) : this work shows a perfect mastery of formal rhetorical amplification and ornamentation, and it is ironic that for the Confucian intellectual to participate in the public world, he had to submit himself to an artistic discipline so alien to his inclinations.

Hsiao Ying-shih and Li Hua were the central figures of a large group of intellectuals and writers, most of whom did not write *fu-ku* poetry. Younger members of the circle, like Tu-ku Chi and the Huang-fu brothers, Jan and Tseng, were linked to capital poetry and followed the bland poetic conservatism of the second half of the century. Famous intellectuals like Han Yün-ch'ing and Liang Su 梁肅 have no extant poems, while Li Shu 李 紓 has only one ceremonial cycle extant.

13

Minor Poets of the K'ai-yüan and T'ien-pao

The rubric of "minor poets" is designed to include those poets, outside the major groupings, whose work survives only in fragments. Their "minorness" is a function only of the limited scope of their extant works and of our inability to judge their work as a whole. On the one hand, the category encompasses poets possessing great talent without originality, poets who wrote in one or more of the shared styles of the age. On the other hand, there are also poets who do seem to have had independent poetic identities, but too few of whose works survive to characterize them adequately.

Wang Chih-huan 王之渙 was a poet who wrote with brilliance in the shared style of the age. He was well known as a poet during the K'ai-yüan, but no collection of his poems seems to have been made.[1] Though only six of his poems survive, all quatrains, almost every one has become a minor classic.

Hooded Crane Tower 登鸛雀樓

The bright sun rests on the mountain, is gone, 白日依山盡
The Yellow River flows into the sea. 黃河入海流
If you want to see a full thousand miles, 欲窮千里目
Climb one more story of this tower. 更上一層樓

[13284]

This famous quatrain represents a distinct type in which the persona makes or proposes some mysteriously significant gesture in the closure. Here the reader is invited to consider the relationship between the sunset, the poet's range of vision, and climbing higher in the building: out of that problematic relationship, the reader realizes that not only does one increase the range of vision by climbing higher in the tower, the sunlight is also briefly regained. (In later poetry this phenomenon was often described as the evening sunlight "rising" on a tower or mountain, instead of the shadow of some intervening mountain rising.)

The following poem is also a deservedly famous anthology piece, even though it is comprised entirely of commonplaces.

Parting   送別

Willows, trees of the eastern gate,   楊柳東門樹
Richly green, lining the royal moat,   青青夾御河
Recently have suffered broken twigs—   近來攀折苦
Surely because partings have been many.   應爲別離多

[13285]

"Willow" (*liu* 柳) was homophonous with the verb "stay on" (*liu* 留), and as a result, willow twigs were snapped off at parting to indicate an unwillingness to let the traveler depart. The poem uses the evidence trope, as the poet reads a hidden message in the forms of the physical world. However, the broken willow branch was probably the most common poetic image of parting, and the truth "discovered" is the expected one. As in Wang Han's second "Liang-chou Song," the straightforward presentation of the expected indicates a conscious naïvete, and the innocence of the speaker's inference conceals an immensity of shared sorrows in the evidence of the broken branches.

Ts'ui Kuo-fu 崔國輔, a friend of Wang Chih-huan, passed the *chin-shih* examination in 726, in the same year as Chi-wu Ch'ien and Ts'ui's fellow southeasterner Ch'u Kuang-hsi. Ts'ui's subsequent appointment to a low provinvial post was a measure of his lack of political connections, but he also formed no strong literary ties among the capital poets. Indeed, Ts'ui may possibly have been linked to the party opposed to Chang Chiu-ling, because he was given a capital post in the early T'ien-pao or last years of the K'ai-yüan. Although a capital appointment at this time suggests a connection to Li Lin-fu, Ts'ui was also involved with Li's opponents: he was probably acquainted with Li Po, and he recommended Tu Fu's *fu* to the throne despite Li Lin-fu's opposition. In 752, when Yang Kuo-chung came to power, Ts'ui was again sent off to a poor provincial post in the Southeast, and nothing more is known of him.

Yin Fan spoke of Ts'ui Kuo-fu's poetry as having a "tenderness with exhilarating clarity" 婉孌清楚, referring particularly to Ts'ui's *yüeh-fu* quatrains. Ts'ui shared with Li Po an interest in *yüeh-fu* quatrains in the tradition of folk songs and popular songs, and most of Ts'ui's quatrains were on southeastern subjects.

Song for South of the Lake   湖南曲

South of the lake they send you on your way,   湖南送君去
North of the lake they come with you homeward,   湖北送君歸
Then the mandarin ducks in the lake   湖裏鴛鴦鳥
Pair by pair fly off on their own.   雙雙他自飛

[05667]

Mid-Current Song 中流曲

I came back when the sun was still high, 歸時日尚早
I'd wanted to go on farther, 更欲向芳洲
    to the isles of sweet scent,
But at the crossing the current was swift— 渡口水流急
My boat was whirled around, out of my control. 迴舟不自由
                    [05668]

These quatrains are modeled on the quatrain folk songs of the Southern Dynasties (or, perhaps, on lost contemporary folk songs of the Southeast): they are simple love poems which make frequent use of puns and erotic metaphors. In "Mid-Current Song" that tradition leads the reader to find the metaphor of woman as flower in the "isles of sweet scent" and to hear a suggestion of unmanageable passion in the description of the driving current. In "Song for South of the Lake" there is also something of the extreme simplicity of Wang Wei's quatrain style. Such quatrains, almost entirely *yüeh-fu*, make up twenty-six of Ts'ui Kuo-fu's forty surviving poems.

    The *Ho-yüeh ying-ling chi* is a rich source for gifted and well-known High T'ang poets with only a handful of extant works. It includes Ho-lan Chin-ming 賀闌進明, a *chin-shih* of 728, whose surviving works consist of two *ku-yi* 古意 (07581–82) and five excellent versions of the *yüeh-fu* "Hard Traveling" 行路難 (07583–87). Also included are T'ao Han 陶翰, a *chin-shih* of 730, and Ts'ui Shu 崔曙, a *chin-shih* of 738, both gifted practitioners of the shared style of the age. The *Ho-yüeh ying-ling chi* also anthologized the works of two friends of Meng Hao-jan, who probably, like Meng, worked largely outside of capital circles: Yen Fang 閻防 and Liu Shen-hsü 劉脊虛. Though Yin Fan praised him generously, Liu Shen-hsü is a less interesting poet than Yen Fang. All five of Yen Fang's extant poems are eremitic landscape pieces with a descriptive genius that would surely have have made Yen an important figure in the period had more of his works survived.

    One of the saddest losses to High T'ang poetry is the collection of Hsüeh Chü 薛據, almost all of whose extant poems survive in the *Ho-yüeh ying-ling chi*. Hsüeh Chü may be remembered as one of the poets who climbed the pagoda of the Temple of Compassionate Mercy with Tu Fu, Ts'en Shen, Kao Shih, and Ch'u Kuang-hsi. Unfortunately, his poem on that occasion has been lost. Hsüeh Chü was a very well known poet during the T'ien-pao and the following decade; he was a poet with wide-ranging friendships that spanned groups and generations—from Wang Wei to Tu Fu and Kao Shih to Liu Ch'ang-ch'ing. Tu Fu, always generous to his poet friends, seems to have particularly admired Hsüeh Chü's work, and it may not be out of place to see something of the older Hsüeh in Tu Fu's own poetry. To Tu Fu, Hsüeh "opened the dark recesses of literature" (11096);

he was "the master who covered the generation, / The force of whose talent grew more godlike as he grew older" (10852). Moreover, from other comments by Tu Fu (11573) and Kao Shih (10264), it is clear that Hsüeh Chü's work was strongly associated with the *ku-feng*. In Yin Fan's characterization: "As a man he was firm, honest, and full of spirit; what he wrote was the same."

The *ku-feng* appears clearly in several of Hsüeh's twelve extant poems. His work possesses that personalizing of moral values that so appealed to T'ang readers. The opening of "Strong Feelings" 懷哉行 is a fine example of Hsüeh's version of the *ku-feng*, and its public seriousness finds a counterpart in Tu Fu's work.

No man is wasted in our brilliant age,　　　　　　　　明時無廢人
For the grand edifice, no timber cast aside.　　　　廣廈無棄材
But the master craftsmen pay me no heed;　　　　良工不我顧
Use I have, but won't chase a lover on my own.　　有用寧自媒
With plans in my breast, I gaze on my Lord's gates,　懷策望君門
And tarry there in vain till the year's end.　　　　歲晏空遲迴
The city of Ch'in is filled with horses and coaches,　秦城多車馬
At day's evening swirls of dust fly.　　　　　　　日夕飛塵埃
Then with rolling drums the palace gates open,　　伐鼓千門啓
Horse-bangles ringing pass paired watchtowers,　　鳴珂雙闕來
And I hear how His thunder and rain are bestowed,　我聞雷雨施
None but are covered by Heaven's enriching grace.　天澤罔不該
                                    [from 13295]

This is not a lush description as one find's in poems on court attendance, but an attempt to represent the moral grandeur of the imperial presence. Modern readers would find Hsüeh's other poems more appealing than his *ku-feng*; these possess something of Tu Fu's rich imagination and vocabulary.

Another poet whose work parallels aspects of Tu Fu's was Chang Wei 張謂, a *chin-shih* of 743 who lived well into the 770s. Chang Wei's later poems fall into the blandness of postrebellion capital poetry, with one unusual feature: they are filled with echoes of the poetry of Li Po (e.g., 09451, 09452, 09476). Chang Wei's *chin-shih* of 743 corresponds to the height of Li Po's popularity in the capital, and this may in part account for his influence on Chang's work. But Chang Wei's most important poem was "Answer for the Old Man of Pei-chou" (09450), a *yüeh-fu* of social protest that used an exemplary lower-class figure to articulate criticism of contemporary social conditions. As Yin Fan singled this poem out for special praise, it must have been well known by 753, and thus it may have exerted some influence on Tu Fu, who was also experimenting with protest *yüeh-fu* at about the same period.

Chia Chih 賈至 (718–73) was a friend of Li Po's and an acquaintance of Tu Fu's. Chia came from a distinguished family: his father had drafted the proclamation for Hsüan-tsung's assumption of the throne, while Chia Chih himself drafted Hsüan-tsung's edict of abdication in favor of Su-tsung. As might be expected of such a figure, Chia was a master of the formal public style, and there are similarities between his work and the poetry of Kao Shih. Also like Kao, Chia Chih wrote a "Song of Yen" (11959), though it a less interesting piece than Kao's.

Chia Chih's best poetry is to be found in his quatrains, several of which are memorable as example of High T'ang vignette technique, with its violent shifts and dramatic juxtapositions.

The White Horse   白馬

A white horse with spots of purple joined   白馬紫連錢
Whinnies before the Cinnabar Gate,   嘶鳴丹闕前
Hears the bridle-pendants and sets off prancing,   聞珂自踥蹀
And you need not strike down with the golden whip. 不要下金鞭
                          [11973]

Out the Passes   出塞曲

Thousands of miles of level sands,
   a single puff of dust: 萬里平沙一聚塵
A winged dispatch flying southward,
   another man coming north—   南飛羽檄北來人
It carries the news that at Wu-yüan
   the beacon fires blaze alarm: 傳道五原烽火急
Last night the Great Khan
   made a raid upon New Ch'in!   單于昨夜寇新秦
      [11975]

Chia Chih's most famous extant poems are three quatrains written on meeting Li Po in the South after the rebellion: the first of these is remarkable for the nominal closing couplet made up of a string of modal images:

On First Arriving at Pa-ling: Sailing on Lake Tung-t'ing   初至巴陵與李十二
   with Li Po and P'ei, the Ninth of His Clan   白裴九同泛洞庭湖

On the river we meet once again,
   all former comrades in travel,   江上相逢皆舊遊
And we constantly gaze at Hsiang River mountains
   with a sorrow that cannot be born: 湘山永望不堪愁
Bright moonlight and autumn's wind,
   waters of Lake Tung-t'ing,   明月秋風洞庭水
A lone goose, the falling leaves,
   a single tiny boat.   孤鴻落葉一扁舟
       [11982]

Though the poets above are "minor," they are in the "mainstream." Scattered through the surviving corpus of High T'ang poetry are indications that there were also individual poets and groups of poets who concentrated their efforts in certain of the less common subgenres. Wu Yün and a fragmentary tradition of neo-Taoist poetry represents one such group. "Palace poetry" and poems in the tradition of the *Yü-t'ai hsin-yung* represent another such subgroup. In the High T'ang, Li K'ang-ch'eng 李康成 compiled a continuation of the *Yü-t'ai hsin-yung*, the *Yü-t'ai hou-chi* 玉臺後集, to carry the Yü-t'ai style from the Ch'en Dynasty through the mid-eighth century. The *Yü-t'ai hou-chi* does not survive, but since some of Li K'ang-ch'eng's poems are in the Yü-t'ai style, they may well have been part of the anthology (09969–72). At about the same time another poet, Liang Huang 梁鍠, also seems to have specialized in poetry on women (09912–26). Except in cases like Li Chiao's collection of *yung-wu* poetry, which survived independently, poets with clear "specializations" have not survived well, probably because the topical arrangement of the great early Sung anthologies permitted only limited representation of a given topic.

14

The Traditions of Capital Poetry
in the Later Eighth Century

The K'ai-yüan and T'ien-pao reigns were decades of innovation and the growth of the individual poetic identity; but beginning in the decade after the rebellion, a tenacious conservatism came to dominate the world of poetry, particularly in the capital. The dominant poets of the later eighth century present a less attractive face than their predecessors in Hsüan-tsung's reign. Whether by chance or the vagaries of taste, there survives a large corpus of poetry by writers active between the late 750s and early 790s. The majority of these poems were not worthy of survival: all too often they represent the bland norm of T'ang occasional poetry—hundreds of parting poems, visiting poems, and banquet poems, most in pentasyllabic verse with hackneyed sentiments, images, and rhymes. Generic and subgeneric distinctions in style remained, but one rarely finds those strong individual voices that characterized the best work of the first two generations of High T'ang poets. A pentasyllabic, regulated parting poem by Liu Ch'ang-ch'ing is largely indistinguishable from one by Li Chia-yu, Huang-fu Jan, Ch'ien Ch'i, Han Hung, or dozens of others.

Innovation and individuation, however, are not the only criteria for literary judgment. The Sung Dynasty saw the formation of a poetic "orthodoxy" that exerted a strong influence on the literary activity of later dynasties. Orthodoxy was the spiritual descendant of the more ill defined *fu-ku* concerns of the T'ang, and it sought universal standards for poetry, standards manifest in particular periods of literary history. To Sung and post-Sung orthodoxy the period that most perfectly embodied the universal values of poetry was the reign of Hsüan-tsung, the High T'ang.

Orthodoxy would agree with an individualist view that later-eighth-century poetry (referred to as Ta-li poetry, after the longest reign in the period 766–79) was inferior to that of Hsüan-tsung's reign, but its reasons were different: "At its best, the poetry of the Ta-li had not lost the High T'ang; at its worst, it slipped into the Late T'ang style." Here the nascent orthodoxy of Yen Yü's 嚴羽 *Ts'ang-lang shih-hua* 滄浪詩話 considers later-eighth-century poetry important precisely because it was conservative. The ossification of High T'ang poetic convention and the disappearance of the individual poetic voice were considered less important than the approximation of the invariable standard set by the first two generations of High T'ang poets.

From poetic orthodoxy and its individualist alternatives developed the complex canons of T'ang poetry which have survived into modern times. But the capital poets of the later eighth century provide a third point of view on their own age; they too formed a canon of their recent poetic past, and their view differs significantly from that of later ages. They did not see themselves as the preservers of an invariable standard of excellence, but as the inheritors of the mainstream of the poetic art.

The continuity of that capital poetic tradition was inseparable from an awesome continuity of social relations among its poets. Wang Wei had served in the court of Li Fan with Yen Chao-yin, a court poet of Empress Wu and Chung-tsung. Ch'ien Ch'i knew and wrote poems with Wang Wei; Lu Lun knew and wrote with Ch'ien Ch'i; Li Yi knew and wrote with Lu Lun. Adding the hundreds of other capital poets, this chain becomes a web of social relations that firmly linked the poetry of the later seventh century to the poetry of the early ninth century. These capital poets wrote primarily social occasional poetry, and they were responsible for the slow evolution of regulated verse. It was from this group that emperors usually chose their favorite poets, allowing the decorous lag of a generation. Thus, Hsüan-tsung especially admired Chung-tsung's courtier-poets Su T'ing and Li Chiao; Tai-tsung greatly admired Wang Wei; Te-tsung and Hsien-tsung showed a partiality for Lu Lun and Li Yi.

Having this strong sense of the mainstream of the poetic art, writers of the later eighth century began to form their canon of T'ang poetry:

After more than a thousand years we came to Shen Ch'üan-ch'i and Sung Chih-wen . . . and by that time the subtle delineation of emotions had been perfected. Even though poetry had gone ever farther from the "Odes" [*Ya*] and though it may have gone to excess in ornamental beauty, still its relation to the poetry of antiquity was like the development of the four-sided court ceremonial drum out of the plain pottery drum or the growth of elaborate seal scripts from their origins in the tracks of birds. After Shen and Sung died, Wang Wei and Ts'ui Hao were the towering figures of the K'ai-yüan and T'ien-pao reigns. And of their followers in our own age, no more than a few can approach them. The Omissioner Huang-fu Jan is such a man [Tu-ku Chi "Preface to the Collected Works of Lord Huang-fu of An-ting, former Omissioner of the Left"].

After Ch'ien Ch'i passed the examination, his official's cap stood high in the forest of verses. The grand old man of letters, Wang Wei, acknowledged the loftiness of his manner. And after Wang's death, Ch'ien became the pre-eminent figure . . . . Men of letters were fond of saying: "Before there were Shen Ch'üan-ch'i and Sung Chih-wen; now we have Ch'ien Ch'i and Lang Shih-yüan" [Kao Chung-wu, note on Ch'ien Ch'i in the *Chung-hsing hsien-ch'i chi*].

It is to be expected that this embryonic canon would have the enthusiastic support of a spokesman for capital poetic taste like Kao Chung-wu. More remarkable is the qualified support of a *fu-ku* writer like Tu-ku Chi. It is not a canon that later readers would recognize: it admits Shen Ch'üan-ch'i and Sung Chih-wen, but excludes Ch'en Tzu-ang; it reasonably includes Wang Wei, but leaves out not only Meng Hao-jan, Li Po, and Tu Fu (the present canon that grew out of the *fu-ku* resurgence of the Mid-T'ang), but also omits poets like Wang Ch'ang-ling and Ch'u Kuang-hsi, who shared with Wang Wei the adulation of the K'ai-yüan and T'ien-pao. Later capital taste was drawn to the formal art of Shen Ch'üan-ch'i and Sung Chih-wen and saw in Wang Wei not the austere intellectual but the master craftsman and honored poet of capital society.

Literary history and the formation of canons of major poets had been the exclusive province of *fu-ku*. Between the 750s and its great resurgence in the 790s, *fu-ku* poetics went through a period of decline. Few poets wrote extensively in the *ku-feng* or in the archaic modes, and the commonplaces of the *fu-ku* history of poetry were less often heard. Kao Chung-wu might say of Ch'ien Ch'i that he "mowed down the frivolity of the Ch'i and Sung, and pared away the sensuality of the Liang and Ch'en," but this is only a pale echo of *fu-ku* values set amid a strong renewal of interest in the poetry of the Southern Dynasties. The recluse-poet Ch'in Hsi 秦系 was closer to contemporary taste when he praised Ch'ien Ch'i as another Ho Hsün, one of the most artificed of Southern Dynasties poets (13449).

The decline of *fu-ku* poetics can be heard clearly in the preface to Huang-fu Jan's collected works: there Tu-ku Chi, pupil of the great Li Hua, was compelled to retreat from many venerable *fu-ku* positions. Instead of condemning regulated verse, Tu-ku Chi praised Huang-fu Jan for having "taken the *pi-hsing* ["metaphor and stimulus," with ethical associations] of antiquity and put them in modern tonal regulation." The poetry of the Chien-an and Wei had been the model of the *ku-feng*, but Tu-ku Chi condemned it as possessing an excess of *chih* 質 ("unadorned substance") and an insufficiency of *wen* 文 ("ornament"/"aesthetic qualities"). He allowed that the Southern Dynasties and Early T'ang may have gone to the other extreme, to an excess of *wen*, but contrary to all *fu-ku* tenets, he saw in this the natural process of high civilization, like the "development of the four-sided ceremonial drum out of the plain pottery drum." Implicit in Tu-ku Chi's comments was that Wang Wei and Huang-fu Jan had achieved the perfect balance between "substance" and "ornament": this was an old Confucian value, and one espoused by Li Hua, but it was a value at odds

with the *fu-ku* impulse to return to the simplicity and blunt honesty of
ancient poetry. The most significant aspect of Tu-ku Chi's preface, however, is the metaphor of the drum and script: these represent the first serious challenge to *fu-ku* poetics on its own terms, insisting that literary sophistication is not inherently inimical to, but rather part of, the natural
process of civilization.

Capital poetry was the rival, sometimes the enemy, of *fu-ku* poetics,
and as *fu-ku* values weakened in the later eighth century, the greatest of the
capital poets became the hero of the age. Wang Wei's influence was everywhere in the poetry of the period, and dozens of writers aspired, with varying degrees of success, to recreate his style. When Kao Chung-wu granted
Ch'ien Ch'i the mantle of Wang Wei, in the passage above, he was implicitly acknowledging Wang's unique supremacy. And when the *Chi-hsüan
chi* 極玄集, an anthology of the early ninth century, surveyed the poetry
of the preceding half decade, it began with the work of Wang Wei.

Wang Wei's poetry was not a "rediscovery" of the later eighth century: the continuity of admiration for his work was unbroken. Wang's
reputation was founded in his youth, but he reached the height of his fame
in the last years of his life, honored by the emperor and surrounded by
admiring younger poets like Ch'ien Ch'i and Huang-fu Jan. Other famous
poets of the K'ai-yüan and T'ien-pao may have been virtually forgotten,
but Wang's reputation and influence continued to grow after his death in
761.

The *Wang Stream Collection* provides an excellent example of Wang
Wei's influence. Many poets tried to reproduce the distinctive simplicity of
Wang's quatrain style, and a number of programatic series were modeled
on the collection, including Ch'ien Ch'i's twenty-two "Miscellaneous
Songs of Lan-t'ien Creek" (12484–505) and Huang-fu Jan's five "Songs in
the Mountains" (13056–60). The style of the *Wang Stream Collection* was
easy to imitate and impossible to imitate well. Compare Wang Wei:

In deserted mountains no one is seen,	空山不見人
Yet heard, the traces of men's voices.	但聞人語響
Sunlight cast back enters deep in the woods	返景入深林
And shines again upon the green moss.	復照青苔上
[06082]	

to Huang-fu Jan:

The mountain lodge is ever silent,	山館長寂寂
Restful clouds come from dawn till dusk.	閒雲朝夕來
What is found in the empty yard?	空庭復何有
The setting sun shining on green moss.	落日照青苔
[13060]	

Huang-fu Jan catches everything in Wang Wei's quatrain style except the animating talent.

Through the course of the eighth century, capital poetry continued independent of the private directions developed in the work of Meng Hao-jan, Li Po, Tu Fu, and even in the work of the master himself, Wang Wei. Capital poetry was still a poetry of "performance" and the mark of culture and status; as Kao Chung-wu wrote of Lang Shih-yüan: "From the minister on down when anyone went out to take a provincial post, if they did not have Ch'ien Ch'i and Lang Shih-yüan at their parting banquet, contemporary opinion would consider them lowborn and unsophisticated." Wang Wei may have been greatly admired and imitated after his death, but only a living poet could truly serve the world of capital poetry and satisfy the insatiable appetite for new compositions.

The homogeneity of style among the capital poets makes grouping them difficult. Later readers identified the poetry of the age with the so-called Ten Talents of the Ta-li 大歷十才子. This convenient term presents numerous problems, not only in the exact composition of the Ten, but also in the usefulness of the grouping. The Ten Talents were first listed in the *Chi-hsüan chi* of the early ninth century. This list probably most closely represents the original sense of who made up the group; however, the grouping may not have been current in the later eighth century, and even if it had been, it might well have been used without a shared consensus of who all ten of the talents were.

The list of the Ten Talents in the *Chi-hsüan chi* includes Li Tuan 李端, Lu Lun 盧綸, Ch'i Chung-fou 吉中孚, Han Hung 韓翃, Ch'ien Ch'i 錢起, Ssu-k'ung Shu 司空曙, Miao Fa 苗發, Ts'ui Tung 崔洞, Keng Wei 耿湋, and Hsia-hou Shen 夏侯審. Of this group, Ch'ien Chi and Han Hung represented an older generation, and the only occasions on which *both* Ch'ien and Han might have been with the younger Ten Talents were the poetry parties given by Princess Sheng-p'ing 昇平, Tai-tsung's daughter. Thus, the grouping of the Ten Talents may have been from these occasions.

The remaining eight of the *Chi-hsüan chi* list were close friends, exchanged poems frequently, and saw themselves as a group. They appear together in the title of a long elegiac poem by Lu Lun (14712), in which the names of neither Ch'ien Ch'i nor Han Hung appear. Lu Lun's elegy was written in response to another, lost elegy by Ch'ang Tang 暢當, a poet who also belonged to this circle despite his omission in the *Chi-hsüan chi* list. These younger poets saw themselves as the successors of Wang Wei and the circle of capital poets, even though many of them resided for long periods in the Southeast and had literary friendships there as well as in the capital.

In this chapter the capital poets of the later eighth century are divided roughly into two groups. The younger group consists of the poets named in Lu Lun's elegy; the older group, many of whom had known Wang Wei and other first-generation poets, includes Ch'ien Ch'i and Han Hung, along with two poets who spent much of their creative lives in the provinces (while retaining close ties to capital society): Liu Ch'ang-ch'ing and Li Chia-yu. Also included in this older group is Lang Shih-yüan 郎士元, whose name was frequently linked with that of Ch'ien Ch'i, as well as the Huang-fu 皇甫 brothers Jan 冉 and Tseng 曾. Around these central figures of capital poetry were a host of lesser figures, such as Yen Wei 嚴維 and Pao Jung's two sons, Pao Chi 包佶 and Pao Ho 包何.

These poets were what they aspired to be, master craftsmen, and they achieved a smoothness and competence that their predecessors in the K'ai-yüan and T'ien-pao could rarely match. They perfected the poetic inheritance they received, and if they were on the whole timid poets, their timidity should not diminish their achievement: in many ways they spoke the poetic language they inherited better than its creators, and in doing so, they produced many poems that were remembered and often anthologized.

The peculiar talents and limitations of these capital poets appear clearly in the work of Liu Ch'ang-ch'ing 劉長卿, whom the prose master Ch'üan Te-yü extravagantly called "the Great Wall of the pentasyllabic line." An undeniably bland poet is hidden beneath the grandeur of that epithet, but Liu's very blandness touched the aesthetic interests of many later readers. Liu's poetry seems to have been quite popular in the later eighth century, but, curiously, Kao Chung-wu had reservations about its quality: "There is nothing novel or arresting [*hsin-ch'i* 新奇] in his style, but it is extremely well crafted. After ten poems or so, you will find that his diction and themes are pretty much the same." The thirteenth-century critic Fang Hui 方回 seems to note much the same qualities, but from a positive viewpoint: "His poetry has a delicate understatement that does not flash out at you. A contemplative reader should taste it slowly." [1] Kao's criticism and Fang's positive revaluation contrast sharply with the strength implicit in "the Great Wall of the pentasyllabic line," but Kao and Fang are closer to the truth.

Liu Ch'ang-ch'ing had been born to the first-generation of High T'ang poets, but his extant poetry comes almost entirely from the last years of his life, in the period after the rebellion. It is impossible to say whether Liu only took up poetry late in life or whether his extant poems represent only part of his work. In either case, Liu's late public appearance as a poet is related to certain anomalies in his life. Liu was a native of Hopei in central China and passed the *chin-shih* examination in 733, but thereafter, instead of seeking public office in the capital, Liu lived a private life in the Southeast. After the rebellion, Liu returned to the capital and held a position in the censorate. From the censorate, Liu passed through a series of respect-

able provincial posts, broken only by an imprisonment and exile to Kwangtung for an unknown offense. He died probably in the mid-780s.

The occasional poetry of Wang Wei and his circle is echoed strongly
in Liu Ch'ang-ch'ing's work, in direct borrowings and even more in a general similarity of imagery and style. Liu Ch'ang-ch'ing's conservatism and
his lack of interest in the more daring poetry of the T'ien-pao can be partially understood through his biography: the decorous restraint of capital
poetry was the style of his youth, and Liu evidently was not in the capital
to witness the new poetry of the T'ien-pao. Probably more important,
Liu's poetry was consonant with the style fashionable in the capital in the
decades immediately after the rebellion. Liu possessed thet requisite mastery of craft, producing hundreds upon hundreds of competent, lovely
poems that never lapsed into awkwardness, but also never dazzled the
imagination.

Liu and the other late capital poets often are most attractive in their
couplets. One touchstone of Wang Wei's genius had been a grand simplicity of couplet construction, basic components in straightforward syntax;
the very simplicity of his couplets pointed the reader to hidden depths of
significance. It was, however, a remarkably easy style to imitate, and in
hundreds of poems Liu did so with abandon. Occasionally Liu used the
style with something of the genius of Wang Wei, as in (06988):

River trees look down on an evening of isles,	江樹臨洲晚
Sand birds face the cold of waters.	沙禽對水寒

or (06998)

Autumn winds scatter a thousand riders,	秋風散千騎
And cold rains moor a solitary boat.	寒雨泊孤舟

or (07019)

The birds scatter, a hawk of autumn drops,	鳥散秋鷹下
Men rest in peace while springtime grasses grow.	人閒春草生

In Liu's poetry can be found all the proven techniques of High T'ang
poetics: the evocative closing image (07007):

Tomorrow at daybreak I'll look on misty trees	明發看煙樹
And only hear the bells from north of the river.	唯聞江北鐘

or the solitary figure set in a vast scene in order to reduce it to loneliness
and insignificance (07339): "Ten thousand miles of green mountains, one
solitary boat" 青山萬里一孤舟. The use of these standard poetic techniques
did not preclude genius, as in Tu Fu's (11433) "Between Heaven and Earth,
a single sand gull" 天地一沙鷗 or (11554) "Lakes and rivers fill the earth,
one aging fisherman" 江湖滿地一漁翁. But more often than not they had
become compositional formulas to produce poems easily and fluently.

Even more than the work of his contemporaries, Liu Ch'ang-ch'ing's poetry was sentimental rather than emotional, picturesque rather than de-criptive of a scene whose order reflected the structure of cognition or the latent order of the world. The innovative and complex concerns of K'ai-yüan and T'ien-pao poetry had become a uniform melancholy of migrat-ing birds, falling rain, setting suns, and the lonely poet in his solitary boat or on his lone horse.

Through repeated use, certain images had become linked to fixed moods, which could be evoked by picturesque scenes built of those images.

Facing the Moon on the River   江中對月

Over deserted isles the evening mists drawn in,   空洲夕煙斂
And I gaze at the moon on the autumn river.   望月秋江裏
Clear in my eyes, a man on the sands   歷歷沙上人
Crosses the water alone in moonlight.   月中孤渡水
                              [06984]

Seeing off His Reverence Ling-ch'e   送靈澈上人

Dark and blue, a temple in groves of bamboo,   蒼蒼竹林寺
From far away, the evening sounds of bells.   杳杳鐘聲晚
Wearing his rainhat, lit by setting sun,   荷笠帶夕陽
To green hills afar he returns alone.   青山獨歸遠
                              [06981]

Compare Liu Tsung-yüan's famous "River Snow" 江雪 from early in the ninth century:

On a thousand mountains flights of birds have ceased,   千山鳥飛絕
On ten thousand paths, men's footsteps sink away.   萬逕人蹤滅
A lone boat, an old man in rainhat and raincoat   孤舟蓑笠翁
Fishes alone in the snow of the cold river.   獨釣寒江雪
                              [18520]

There was a strong continuity of convention in the picturesque quatrain vignette, and virtually the same scene would appeal to and be recreated by generation after generation of T'ang poets. "River Snow" is one of the best known T'ang quatrains; Liu Ch'ang-ch'ing's two quatrains are largely unknown. An argument might be made for the superiority of Liu Tsung-yüan's little poem, but taken in isolation, Liu Ch'ang-ch'ing's two quatrains are probably just as effective.

If the "Great Wall of the pentasyllabic line" had referred to mass rather than strength, it would have been an appropriate epithet for Liu Ch'ang-ch'ing: Liu possessed an extraordinary fertility in the pentasyllabic *lü-shih*. Almost half of Liu's five hundred and twelve poems were in this form, and the majority of these were for social occasions. The pentasyllabic *lü-shih* tended to a certain consistency of style, but the homogeneity of Liu's work is exceptional. Even his programmatic series and *yung-wu* series (07181–90; 07208–15; 07191–98) do not differ markedly from his occasional style.

The long regulated *p'ai-lü* usually demanded more rhetorical figuration than the *lü-shih*, and Liu's *p'ai-lü* are no exception. But even in these Liu was prone to repeat himself; contiguous lines in one poem (07283):

I have clearly seen the appeal of lakes and mountains.	頗見湖山趣
Dawn vapors merge with the clouds of Ch'u	朝氣和楚雲

may appear slightly altered as a couplet in another poem (07286):

I have found clearly the appeal of lakes and mountains,	頗得湖山趣
River vapors merge with the clouds of Ch'u.	江氣和楚雲

Such minor plundering from one's own work or from the work of others was common compositional practice in the T'ang, but the frequency of it in Liu's poetry attracted the attention even of Kao Chung-wu.

Perhaps because of Liu's repetitiousness, Kao was unusually harsh in his evaluation: "His thought is dull and his talent narrow." But in spite of Kao's criticism, Liu's poetry retained its appeal for later readers, and he was one of the most widely discussed poets of the later eighth century. Especially from the point of view of poetic orthodoxy, Liu's poems possessed a balance, clarity, and technical perfection that seemed to maintain the continuity of the High T'ang style.

After the Ch'ing-ming Festival in Early April, Climbing the City Wall and Gazing Afar	清明後登城眺望

The scenery after the Ch'ing-ming:	風景清明後
Clouds and mountains before these battlements.	雲山睥睨前
All the flowers as in days gone by,	百花如舊日
But new smoke rising near thousands of wells.	萬井出新煙
Of grasses' color no place is barren,	草色無空地
The river's flow merges with distant sky.	江流合遠天
But where, oh, where is Ch'ang-an?	長安在何處
I point afar, to beside the setting sun.	遙指夕陽邊

[07067]

Poetic orthodoxy was concerned with universals, and poems such as these located the universal human response in the conventional poetic response. What they lacked was a quality much admired in the later eighth century: as Kao Chung-wu noted, nothing in Liu's poetry was *hsin-ch'i*, "novel and arresting."

The poet whose work *was* "novel and arresting" (in the opinion of Kao Chung-wu and Yao Ho, the compiler of the *Chi-hsüan chi*) was Ch'ien Ch'i. Ch'ien was born in 722 and passed the examination in 751. After the rebellion, Ch'ien made the acquaintance of Wang Wei and gradually became the darling of capital poetry. Kao Chung-wu placed him first in the *Chung-hsing hsien-ch'i chi*, saying, "He stands alone, at great remove from the others, none of whom can consort with him." Ch'ien's official posts were never high, but he was much sought after for his literary talents. Ch'ien's wide range of acquaintances included most of the poets active in the later eighth century. He passed the greater part of his remarkably uneventful life in the capital, loved and admired by all until his death in around 780. His collection consists of over four hundred poems.[2]

By all indications, Ch'ien's personality was anything but reclusive, yet as Wang Wei's successor, he inherited a tradition of eremitic interests in capital poetry.

Sending Off Inquest Judge Yüan on his Return   送元評事歸山居
　　to His Mountain Dwelling

Remembering home, you gaze to a road through clouds,   憶家望雲路
Alone go off eastward, a faint shape in haze.   東去獨依依
For night's lodging on rivers, you follow the fishermen's fires,   水宿隨漁火
Travel through mountains to reach a bamboo gate.   山行到竹扉
The flowers of the cold hurry the wine to readiness,   寒花催酒熟
A mountain dog rejoices in the man's return.   山犬喜人歸
Here from afar, you yearn to be there by library window,   遙羨書窗下
Where a thousand peaks emerge from azure mist.   千峯出翠微
　　　　　　　　　　　　　[12167]

This poem shares many superficial traits with Wang Wei's work, but it lacks the deeper intellectual interests of Wang Wei. Wang would transform the conventions of the parting poem by raising problems of the perceiving consciousness or by discovering the order of human experience immanent in the structure of the landscape. In Ch'ien Ch'i's poem the "return" is a physical trip from one place to another.

Ch'ien begins his poem with a standard opening of parting poetry: two lines, a "here" and a "there," between which the traveler is set in motion. This is the "departure" couplet, followed by a "traveling" couplet an "arrival" couplet, and finally a couplet on how it will be at the traveler's destination. The "traveling" couplet develops the idea that the traveler will spend time (days and nights) moving through a "landscape" (*shanshui*, "mountains and waters"): this becomes a line about night lodging on waters parallel to a line on daytime movement over mountains. Parting poems that treated the parting banquet rather than the journey often built their third couplets out of a line on wine parallel to a line on song. Ch'ien Ch'i cleverly transposes this to his "arrival" couplet: instead of the parting drinks, the judge will enjoy warm wine in the autumn chill of his mountain home; instead of the sad songs of parting, the judge will hear the dog's joyful barking at the return of his master. Finally, Ch'ien uses the suggestive closing scene—not to embody any special significance for the "return," but as a sensual consolation in the pleasure that the judge will feel as he looks through his library window. The poem is a flawless, even gifted rendition of a thoroughly conventional form.

As a master of the couplet, Ch'ien Ch'i was Wang Wei's equal. To Kao Chung-wu, Yao Ho, and many T'ang readers, literary value appeared primarily through the craft of the couplet, which usually meant the middle couplets of regulated verse. Though there were individual and period differences in the treatment of the couplet, it was on the whole an anonymous craft. On these terms Ch'ien Ch'i could compete with, sometimes even excel the major poets of the K'ai-yüan and T'ien-pao. The aesthetic dominance of the parallel couplet was such that the opening and closing couplets often served a function similar to that of the title, signaling the thematic context and the appropriate mood in which to read the middle couplets.

Written on the Cottage Wall of the Old Man of Jade Village	題玉山村叟壁
Mouth of Valley, the recluse, loves stream and stone;	谷口好泉石
Whoever dwells here can sink on dry land.	居人能陸沈
Cattle and sheep are tiny, going down mountains,	牛羊下山小
Smokey fires are far, off beyond the clouds.	煙火隔雲深
A single path enters the creek ravine's color,	一徑入溪色
Several houses are linked to the shade of bamboo.	數家連竹陰
Hidden rainbows take leave of the evening rain,	藏虹辭晚雨
An updarting hawk brings down the last of the birds.	驚隼落餞禽
When I go through some appealing spot, my eyes always rove,	涉趣皆流目
Now about to return, I yearn to be in these forests.	將歸羨在林
I recall my service in yellow ribbons of office	却思黃綬事
How I've run counter to this heart set on immortal herbs.	辛負紫芝心

[12249]

The first couplet sets the theme of reclusion in a lovely landscape, and the closure offers the conventional balance between present service and a desire to lead a private life. But the poem lives by its middle couplets, and it was in his couplet style that Ch'ien Ch'i merited the epithet "novel and arresting." The juxtaposition of the hawk's sudden soaring upward with the descending bend of the rainbow shows that very genius for similitude, structurally analogous patterns, that had been denounced in the preceding decades by Yüan Chieh and Hsiao Ying-shih. At times Ch'ien's similitudes possessed the artificed daring of Lo Pin-wang, Yü Hsin, and the masters of court poetry, as in a snow scene where (12273):

Raging billows heap on stairs of stone,	怒濤堆砌石
A new moon gestates in the curtain hook.	新月孕簾鈎

Ch'ien Ch'i's poems often praised eremitic and Buddhist values, but at heart Ch'ien was a sensual poet, drawn by the bright surfaces of things and not by their intellectual implications. In the poetry of Wang Wei there had been a tension between the sensuality of the physical world and the observer's mask of dispassion; that tension is absent in the poetry of Ch'ien Ch'i. Although Ch'ien echoed Wang throughout his poetry, the effect is always different. Nowhere did Ch'ien Ch'i try harder to emulate Wang Wei than in the twenty-two poems on Lan-t'ien Creek. But instead of the enigmatic understatement of the *Wang Stream Collection*, Ch'ien Ch'i produced a celebratory exultation of the physical world.

Egret Returning in Evening   晚歸鷺

It never wearies of calm in the pool,   池上靜難厭
Only late it's ready to go off among clouds: 雲間欲去晚
Suddenly flies, its back to the setting sun,   忽背夕陽飛
Going with its whim afar in the clear wind.   乘興清風遠
                    [12488]

There is no mysterious hidden significance here: the poem belongs securely in a *yung-wu* tradition and glories in the creature.

Kingfisher with Fish in Beak   銜魚翠鳥

Its mind is on something among lotus leaves—   有意蓮葉間
In the blink of an eye, down from the tall tree.   瞥然下高樹
Splitting the waves it takes the sunken fish,   擘波得潛魚
Then a single dot of azure light departing.   一點翠光去
                    [12500]

However in a few cases, especially when describing scenic spots as in the *Wang Stream Collection*, Ch'ien almost attains the simple dignity and mystery of Wang Wei's style. In the last line of the following poem, the reader does not know why the poet adds his information and how he comes to know it.

Bamboo Isle   竹嶼

Secluded birds on the clear ripples—   幽鳥清漣上
When the mood comes, I can't watch them enough.   興來看不足
New clumps of bamboo press the water low   新篁壓水低
Where last night mandarin ducks had stayed.   昨夜鴛鴦宿
                    [12494]

Ch'ien Ch'i's name was usually paired with that of Lang Shih-yüan 郎士元. In its present state, Lang's collection seems to have been reconstituted from anthology poems and is much smaller than Ch'ien Ch'i's collection—only seventy-three poems, including many of questionable attribution. Despite the admiration of Kao Chung-wu and many of Lang's contemporaries, Lang's extant poems reveal a much weaker poet than Ch'ien Ch'i. Indeed, the comparative devaluation of Lang seems to have begun in the T'ang: the Late T'ang anecdotal collection, the *Yün-hsi yu-yi* 雲溪友議, tells that when Liu Ch'ang-ch'ing heard the catchphrase "Before there were Sung Chih-wen, Shen Ch'üan-ch'i, Wang Wei, and Tu Fu; now we have Ch'ien Ch'i, Lang Shih-yüan, Liu Ch'ang-ch'ing, and Li Chia-yu," Liu Ch'ang-ch'ing objected violently at being placed in the same category as Lang and Li—Ch'ien Ch'i's pre-eminence was undisputed. The story is almost certainly a ninth-century invention, an elaboration of a more common, shorter catchphrase that included only Ch'ien and Lang. (The inclusion of Tu Fu's name is a good indication that the story is late.) But the story does show a clear distinction in the evaluation of Ch'ien and Lang Shih-yüan.

The devaluation of Li Chia-yu 李嘉祐 may be less justified. Li Chia-yu was a *chin-shih* of 748 who, like Liu Ch'ang-ch'ing, was poetically most productive in the postrebellion period. Like Liu, Li Chia-yu served much of his career in provincial posts, but was well known in the capital. Li Chia-yu came from an eminent branch of the Li's that included the calligrapher Li Yang-ping, the intellectual Li Shu, and Li Tuan, one of the younger Ten Talents. To Kao Chung-wu, Li Chia-yu's style seemed entirely different from that of Ch'ien Ch'i or Lang Shih-yüan: Li was "always moving into the style of the Ch'i and Liang—delicate, lush, and ornamented." At times, as in this case, Kao Chung-wu's refined distinctions elude this author. If any differences appear between Li Chia-yu's poetry and that of his contemporaries, it would be that Li was far sterner in his treatment of the civil wars and foreign raids that plagued the later eighth century. While other poets tended to treat scenes of war's desolation with an unremitting melancholy, Li Chia-yu was capable of irony about a world in which "Everywhere Tartars are on campaign, while people are growing fewer" (10120).

Written on the Road While Returning from Ch'ang-chou to Chiang-yin	自常州還江陰途中作
Everywhere desertion and desolation—	處處空離落
The Yangtze villages I cannot bear to see.	江村不忍看
No one around, the flowers' colors are gloomy,	無人花色慘
In continual rains the voices of birds, cold.	多雨鳥聲寒
A Huang Pa, arriving at his first post,	黃霸初臨郡
Or a T'ao Ch'ien, not yet having quit office.	陶潛未罷官
Enjoy the spring, work hard at campaign and attack,	乘春務征伐
None willing to ask of the ruin done.	誰肯問凋殘

[10081]

In the third couplet the poet presents alternative models for the outcome of his present provincial post: either he is destined to become minister as Huang Pa did or to retire to a private life like T'ao Ch'ien. The melancholy opening gives way to a strange irony in the closure.

Only rarely did Li Chia-yu's poetry take on a biting edge: more commonly his poetry possessed a sensual vividness similar to Ch'ien Ch'i's. As with his contemporaries, Li had a particular fondness for objective closure, and at times he carried it beyond the picturesque, as in a poem (10138) that ended:

I imagine that at Hua-chou   想到滑臺桑葉落
   mulberry leaves are falling,
And the Yellow River is pouring eastward   黃河東注荻花秋
   a whole autumn of flowers of reeds.

The following poem by Li is representative of the best pentasyllabic regulated verse for which the later capital poets were known.

Written at the Tung-ch'ing-yang Lodge of Chü-jung   句容縣東清陽館作
County

The thousand peaks of the Chü-ch'ü Mountains darken,   句曲千峯暮
A homebound man heads into faraway mists.   歸人向遠煙
The wind shakes leaves nearing waters,   風搖近水葉
As cloudbanks guard the almost clearing skies.   雲護欲晴天
Evening sunshine lingers on this mountain lodge,   夕陽留山館
And autumn light falls on the grassy fields.   秋光落草田
The road to be traveled lies by setting sun,   征途傍斜日
There a single rider, trotting on alone.   一騎獨翩翩
[10045]

To a later reader this poem would have the unmistakable stamp of the period, but we might consider what elements differentiate it from the K'ai-yüan style on which it is based. Perhaps the most obvious characteristic is the poet's unwillingness to intrude into the poem: such concealment of self derives from the style of Wang Wei and the aesthetic decorum of capital taste, the legacy of court poetry. The suppression of the self that responds to or comments upon the scene can lead, as here, to a failure to distinguish between scene and emotion, *ching* and *ch'ing*. Instead of being confined to one part of the poem, subjectivity and an emotional coloring infuse the whole: the poem is anything but emotionally neutral. Wang Wei had used images with set modal associations, but he tended to use them sparingly. Like Liu Ch'ang-ch'ing, Li Chia-yu builds this poem of images that carry intense and inescapable modal associations, all pointing to the melancholy of a homeward journey on an autumn evening.

The middle couplets are excellent specimens of couplet craft, as in the second couplet's visual parallel between the clear stream flanked by leaves and the open sky flanked by banks of clouds. The closing image of the solitary rider outlined in the setting sun is picturesque, and, indeed, the picturesque may be one of the dominant traits of later eighth-century capital poetry. Out of the variety of the physical universe, the artist creates a conventional "kind" of scene possessing easily apprehended aesthetic values to evoke an expected response. Descriptive convention played an important role in K'ai-yüan and T'ien-pao poetry as well, but in the later eighth century the conventions were more restrictive, the variations more limited, and the modal values more fixed.

Also part of this circle of capital poets were the brothers Huang-fu Jan and Huang-fu Tseng. Tseng was much inferior to his elder brother, Jan, who rivaled Ch'ien Ch'i and Lang Shih-yüan as a favorite of capital society. Jan had been a youthful prodigy, supposedly admired by none other than Chang Chiu-ling (though problems of dating make this unlikely). Jan began a moderately successful career in the mid-760s as secretary to the minister Wang Chin, Wang Wei's brother.

Kao Chung-wu was effusive about Huang-fu Jan's poetry, gracing it with his favorite epithet, "novel and arresting." Jan could

from a superior position gaze upon the P'an brothers and Chang brothers (of the Tsin), and pay the respects of an equal to Shen Yüeh and the Hsieh's (Ling-yün and T'iao). Consider his poem on Wu Mountain—the piece is wondrously beautiful from beginning to end. Since the Tsin, Sung, Ch'i, Liang, Ch'en, and Sui, there have been countless poets, yet only the Omissioner Huang-fu Jan has obtained these perfectly matched pearls. It makes former worthies lose their footing and later generations stand back. How could one attain this except through the aid of Heaven?

Since Kao included Huang-fu Jan's "Wu Mountain High" in the *Chunghsing hsien-ch'i chi*, his lush praise promises a good indication of contemporary taste. Reading the poem itself, however, one can only wonder at the values that informed Kao's taste: if the poem is effective at all, it is effective through the modal associations of Wu Mountain: the king of Ch'u's fleeting sexual encounter with the goddess and the mournful cries of the gibbons that make travelers weep. And the inclusion of the poem in the *Chi-hsüan chi* and the *Yü-lan-shih* suggests that Kao's admiration was not idiosyncratic.

Wu Mountain High 巫山高

East of Pa, the Wu Gorges appear, 巫峽見巴東
Emerging afar, half covering the sky. 迢迢出半空
Clouds conceal the goddess's lodge, 雲藏神女館
But her rain reaches the Ch'u king's palace. 雨到楚王宮
From dawn to dusk stream sounds descend, 朝暮泉聲落
In cold or sun's heat, trees' colors the same. 寒暄樹色同
I cannot listen to the gibbons' clear voices— 清猿不可聽
Especially in the ninth month, autumn's end. 偏在九秋中

[12995]

To readers of later ages it would have been incredible that Kao Chung-wu might prefer this poem to anything by Li Po or Meng Hao-jan, yet this timid piece surely answered the later eighth-century conception of the poetic art more perfectly than any work by those more individual poets of the first generation.

In his youth Huang-fu Jan had close contacts with many capital poets of the first generation, and especially with Wang Wei; and of all Wang Wei's contemporaries, Huang-fu Jan was most strongly under his spell. Ch'ien Ch'i's different sensibility led him to make his own use of Wang Wei's legacy, but Huang-fu Jan often adhered slavishly to the example of the master and, in doing so, usually exposed his own inferiority. One of Wang Wei's most famous quatrains ended (06107):

Next year spring grasses will be green again,   明年春草綠
But will my prince return again or not?   王孫歸不歸

Wang Wei's "prince" was drawn from the closing of the "Summons to the Recluse" in the *Ch'u-tz'u*: it was through Wang Wei's use of the term that the "prince" came to refer to an honored, perhaps aristocratic friend in the poetry of the later eighth century. If this ending had been successful for Wang Wei, Huang-fu Jan must have thought it would be successful for him as well (13030):

Richly green, spring grasses darken,   青青草色綠
At last awaiting only my prince's return.   終是待王孫

or (13024):

Everywhere on the islets are fragrant plants—   處處汀洲有芳草
My prince is not at all willing to think of return.   王孫詎肯念歸期

Earlier in this chapter was given a similar effort of Huang-fu Jan to recreate Wang's famous image of evening sunlight on green moss.

Ninth-century poets used the work of their High T'ang predecessors no less than the later capital poets used Wang Wei, but there were important differences in how they treated the literary past. Ninth-century poets tended to respond to the larger aspects of their predecessors' work: to themes (cf. 17913 and 10824); to complex "types" (cf. 20685 and 07867); and even to the form of specific poems, couplet by couplet (cf. 31900 and 11554). Capital poets like Huang-fu Jan found only lines and images in the work of Wang Wei, fragments that could be "spent" again and again like coins. When they borrowed more than a fragment, they received hollow forms and seemed incapable of understanding how their predecessors had animated the forms. Thus, when Huang-fu Jan wrote a pair of Ch'u songs (13021–22) in imitation of Wang Wei's "Songs for the Worship of the Goddess at Yü Mountain" (05905–6, see p. 37), all that had made Wang Wei's songs memorable disappeared—the mystery of the goddess' advent and departure and the literary historical dimension as exile poems. Huang-fu Jan's songs were exercises in filling a hollow form.

Around these central figures in the world of capital poetry were a host of other poets in no way inferior to the four men discussed above. Such poets have often been remembered for the sake of one or two poems that have appeared often in anthologies. But on the fringes of this capital circle were two poets whose work presents certain anomalies: Han Hung and Tai Shu-lun.

Although the *Chi-hsüan chi* included Han Hung in its list of the Ten Talents, the only other figure of the group with whom Han seems to have had a close relationship was Hsia-hou Shen. But Han Hung also participated in Princess Sheng-p'ing's poetry gatherings with Ch'ien Ch'i and Li Tuan, and he was at least acquainted with Lang Shih-yüan, Li Chia-yu, and perhaps Huang-fu Jan. Kao Chung-wu said of Han that "every piece, every song was prized by the gentlemen of the court," and indeed, Han does seem to have had a large circle of social acquaintances in the central government, many of whom he praised as poets. Almost none of their work survives, however, and on the whole, they represent a different group than that of the capital poets discussed above.

Han Hung won the highest honors in the *chin-shih* examination of 754, but he left office, probably during the rebellion, and reappeared in public life only in the mid-770s. He was in office in the mid-780s and probably died in that decade. Han Hung became one of the better known poets of the later eighth century, but his fame rested largely on his appearance in a prose romance, the "Tale of Miss Liu" 柳氏傳, and in the many later versions of the story.

As a poet Han Hung is less interesting than as the legendary lover of Miss Liu. He was a heavier poet than his contemporaries, and there is something in his work reminiscent of Kao Shih. Kao Chung-wu saw in his poetry a "craftsmanship that approaches the histories," probably referring to his frequent use of historical, cultural, and geographical references. A link to Kao Shih is not impossible: some of Han's early poems are in the T'ien-pao song style popular in his youth, and he had even written a poem to Kao Shih's onetime patron, General Ko-shu Han (12704).

It was probably through his early work in the T'ien-pao song style that Han Hung developed one of his favorite forms, an "old style" poem beginning in pentasyllabic lines and shifting to heptasyllabic lines. But with a few exceptions, these poems lack the imagination and exuberance of the best T'ien-pao songs: instead, Han was content to evoke one of the moods conventionally associated with poetry in the heptasyllabic line.

Though Han Hung's regulated poetry was popular with Princess Sheng-p'ing and Te-tsung, it seems less inspired than that of his contemporaries: he lacked the descriptive talents of Ch'ien Ch'i and the evocative simplicity of Liu Ch'ang-ch'ing. His best lines often involved an apt historical reference. But at times his quatrains possess something of Lu Lun's vivid imagery.

Cold Food Festival   寒食

Not a place in the city of spring
  but the flowers are blossoming,   春城無處不開花
Cold Food Festival: in the east wind
  the royal willows are slanting.   寒食東風御柳斜
At sunset in the palace of Han
  wax torches are passed around,   日暮漢宮傳蠟燭
And light smoke scatters off and away
  into homes of the Five Lords.   輕煙散入五侯家
                    [12817]

Though his social relations with the capital poets were not close, Tai Shu-lun 戴叔倫 (732–89) should be included on the fringes of the capital circle. Tai's occasional poems mention Ch'ien Ch'i, Lang Shih-yüan, Huang-fu Jan, Chu Fang, Ssu-k'ung Shu, and Keng Wei among others, but none with the frequency that would indicate close ties. Though the majority of Tai Shu-lun's poems fall comfortably within the scope of capital poetry, his work also contains some of the most interesting and anomalous pieces of the period. However, problems in his biography and in the present form of his collection suggest that the collection is corrupt and requires caution when discussing his work in a literary-historical context.[3]

Tai Shu-lun had been one of Hsiao Ying-shih's finest disciples, and he served with distinction both in the central and provincial governments, ultimately being enfeoffed as a baron. However, his work shows little trace of Hsiao Ying-shih's *fu-ku* concerns. The exceptions are some mediocre attempts at philosophical poetry (e.g., 14281), topical allegory (e.g., 14285), and some very interesting *yüeh-fu* style narratives of social criticism.

Girls Plowing the Fields   女耕田行

Fledgling swallows enter their nests,
  the sprouts grow to bamboo,   乳燕入巢筍成竹
From what household, those two girls
  planting the new grain there?   誰家二女種新穀
With neither men nor oxen
  they cannot plow: 無人無牛不及犂

Knives in hand, they chop at the earth,
    but the earth turns to mud. 持刀斫地翻作泥
They tell me that their family's poor,
    that their mother is growing old, 自言家貧母年老
That their elder brother is in the army
    and has not married yet. 長兄從軍未娶嫂
Last year, an epidemic,
    and the cattle feedbin is empty, 去年災疫牛圈空
So they cut their plain silks to buy these knives
    in the capital market. 截絹買刀都市中
With their turbans they've covered their faces,
    afraid to be recognized, 頭巾掩面畏人識
Using knives instead of oxen—
    who does the same as they? 以刀代牛誰與同
Two sisters hand in hand,
    hearts bitter as can be, 姊妹相攜心正苦
They see not the men on the road,
    they only see the soil. 不見路人唯見土
They build embankments and ridges throughout
    to keep sprouts from running wild, 疏通畦隴防亂苗
They set in order the furrows and drains
    awaiting the seasonal rain. 整頓溝塍待時雨
When the sun is right above south hill,
    they go back for their meal, 日正南岡下餉歸
Thinking fondly on the pheasants of dawn
    that startle up with commotion. 可憐朝雉擾驚飛
At their eastern neighbor's and the west cottage
    the flowers have all come out— 東鄰西舍花發盡
They both cherish the last of the fragrance,
    and tears fill their robes. 共惜餘芳淚滿衣
        [14298]

The technique here is close to that of the social protest *yüeh-fu* of the Mid-T'ang, especially to the work of Wang Chien and Chang Chi. The poem is, in fact, much closer to the Mid-T'ang than the only other social *yüeh-fu* of the later eighth century, those of Wei Ying-wu. It is therefore particularly unfortunate that the unreliability of Tai's collection forces us to regard his social *yüeh-fu* with some suspicion.

    Much of Tai's regulated poetry is in the restrained, evocative style characteristic of the age. But Kao Chung-wu did not rate him highly and said "his style does not go above the middle rank . . . its 'bone' is soft, and therefore poets have thought little of his work."[4] Tai fell particularly short of the couplet craft of his contemporaries. But he also possessed the ability to write of the self with a playful, casual voice that is rare in later eighth-century poetry.

Feelings at the End of Spring II   暮春感懷二首之二

"Forty years old and unknown"—   四十無聞懶慢身
　　this lazy, lolling body
Whose feelings go free among valley and hill   放情丘壑任天真
　　at the will of my true nature.
An endless stream of past events: 悠悠往事杯中物
　　the "thing in the wine cup,"
The glittering glory of fame in the age   赫赫時名扇外塵
　　is the dust beyond my fan.
With a short staff, I watch the clouds,   短策看雲松寺晚
　　evening at a temple in pines,
Through spaces in curtains I listen to rain—   疏簾聽雨草堂春
　　spring at my thatched hut.
Mountain flowers and birds of the river   山花水鳥皆知己
　　all are my close friends:
We visit each other hundreds of times—   百遍相過不厭貧
　　they're not annoyed at poverty.
　　　　　　　　　[14428]

This is Tai Shu-lun at his best, but it is unfortunately not characteristic of most of his work. Like his contemporaries he plundered K'ai-yüan and T'ien-pao poetry, sometimes creating whole poems of clichés and lines from other poets (e.g., 14305). Wang Wei's voice can be heard everywhere (e.g., 14331.7–8; 14465.4), and like Liu Ch'ang-ch'ing, Tai often borrowed from himself (e.g., 14465 and 14475; 14460 and 14524).

　　Tai Shu-lun is best known for a statement on poetry echoed in Li Shang-yin's famous "Brocade Zither" (29092) and quoted by the critic Ssu-k'ung T'u: "The scene a poet creates is as when the sun is warm on Indigo Fields and the fine jade gives off mist: you can gaze on it, but you cannot fix it in your eyes."[5] Despite their deep differences, both the later eighth century and the Late T'ang were interested in a poetry of mood, and Tai Shu-lun's statement suggested one means to achieve such a poetry —a poetry in which the effect transcended perceptual clarity and rational understanding.

　　Some of Tai Shu-lun's finest poems are to be found among his almost one hundred and twenty quatrains. Interesting innovations appear in these too, but these innovations must remain suspect because of doubts about Tai's collection. For example, the collection contains a set of quatrains amplifying a couplet of a poem sent to him: five quatrains on "The night rain drips on the empty stairs" 夜雨滴空階 (14444–48) and five on "The dawn lantern leaves the darkened chamber" 曉燈離暗室 (14449–53). The following is the first of the series:

Rain falls, it soaks the lonely traveler,
The heart is startled like a roosting bird.
On empty stairs the dripping is dense by night,
A confusion that I'm sure will last till dawn.

雨落溼孤客
心驚比棲鳥
空階夜滴繁
相亂應到曉

[14444]

Each set of five develops the theme of the line into a meditation on Tai's personal experiences.

Though the quatrain above is consistent with the modal poetics of the later capital poets, Tai was usually a less elegant poet than his contemporaries. Thus, when he tried to recreate the enigmatic understatement of Wang Wei's quatrain style, he was often more successful than poets like Ch'ien Ch'i or Huang-fu Jan.

Crane in the Pines

松鶴

Rain-soaked shadows of pines are chill,
And the wind brings down tiny blossoms:
A solitary crane, loving purity, seclusion,
Flies here, does not fly away.

雨溼松陰涼
風落松花細
獨鶴愛清幽
飛來不飛去

[14470]

The point of the poem is more obvious than in Wang Wei's quatrains, but the last line is worthy of the master.

Taken as a whole, however, Tai's collection does not escape the poetics of mood of the later eighth century. Everywhere are found those picturesque and melancholy images, scenes that touch the sentiments but "cannot be fixed in the eyes."

Su Creek Pavilion

蘇溪亭

By Su Creek Pavilion
    the grasses spread everywhere—
Who is it leans to the east wind
    on the twelve railings there?
The swallows do not return,
    the last events of spring:
A whole sandbar of misty rain
    and the pear blossoms cold.

蘇溪亭上草漫漫

誰依東風十二闌

燕子不歸春事晚

一汀煙雨杏花寒

[14510]

The younger Ten Talents knew and wrote poems with older poets such as Ch'ien Ch'i, the Huang-fu brothers, and Li Chia-yu, but they formed a more tightly knit group among themselves. The period of their poetic activity extends from the late 750s until roughly the mid-790s, with the greater concentration of their work falling in the latter part of the period. Their poetic style was largely indistinguishable from that of their elder contemporaries, with a few exceptions to be discussed later. The poetry of no one of them stands high above the poetry of the others; if they considered any of their number the leader, it would have been Ch'i Chung-fou (see 14712, 15151). Ch'i, Miao Fa, and Hsia-hou Shen each have only one or two extant poems. Of Ts'ui Tung's poetry only one *chüan* survives, but he was certainly the least talented poet of the group. The group is best represented by the four poets with the largest collections: Lu Lun, Li Tuan, Ssu-k'ung Shu, and Keng Wei.

The voice of Wang Wei remained strong in the work of the younger Ten Talents: it had become a part of the shared style of capital poetry, but it could be heard even more distinctly in situations that had some direct link to the master, as in the following poem by Ssu-k'ung Shu:

Visiting the Recluse Hu and Seeing Uncollected Writings by Wang Wei	過胡居士觀王右丞遺文
He whom you knew in former days so well is gone,	舊日相知盡
Now dwelling deep away, your one body alone.	深居獨一身
There is snow pointlessly blocking your gate,	閉門空有雪
And you gaze on bamboo, ever without another.	看竹永無人
You always vowed to withdraw to the hills out there,	每許前山隱
And he pitied your poverty in this narrow alley.	曾憐陋巷貧
The poems he wrote are still here today—	題詩今尚在
For my sake you brush off the drifted dust a while.	暫爲拂流塵

[15545]

Wang's poem no longer survives, and Ssu-k'ung Shu's poem is probably referring to passages in it. But in a more general sense, Ssu-k'ung Shu perfectly echoes Wang Wei's austere plainnes.

A visit to Wang Stream led Li Tuan to write in Wang Wei's descriptive style.

Visiting Wang Stream After a Rain	雨後遊輞川
A sudden downpour returns to the mountains, is gone,	驟雨歸山盡
And the falling sunlight enters Wang Stream.	頹陽入輞川
To see rainbows climb high in the evening villa,	看虹登晚墅
And tread stones to cross a springtime creek.	踏石過春泉
Purple creepers hide the immortals' well,	紫葛藏仙井
Yellow flowers come out in the wild fields.	黃花出野田
Knowing myself there's no road to go farther,	自知無路去
I turn back my steps to the smoke of men's dwellings.	迴步就人煙

[15192]

Wang Wei not only taught his successors the poet's craft; he also provided the terms in which to express a variety of human situations. On the Double Ninth young Wang Wei had felt: "Each time I meet this holiday, I long doubly for my kin" (06137). This can provide a response for Lu Lun on

Cold Food Festival: "Even more when I meet Cold Food Festival, I long doubly for my home" (14929). Like the elder Ch'ien Ch'i and Huang-fu Jan, the younger Ten Talents also tried to recreate the *Wang Stream Collection* (15584–93). Wang Wei's influence was pervasive, and it is particularly interesting to note that poems addressed to Ch'ien Ch'i echoed Wang Wei's style very strongly: this suggests that whatever the real differences between the two poets, Ch'ien's work was already clearly associated with that of Wang Wei (e.g., 13965, 15261, 15541).

For most social occasions, the younger Ten Talents produced pentasyllabic regulated verses as voluminously as their predecessors. Some of the poems, such as the following piece by Lu Lun, have been widely anthologized and much appreciated. Yet the choice of such poems from the massive corpus of their occasional poetry seems virtually arbitrary, and one wonders precisely what separates simple dignity and grace from mere facility.

Parting from Li Tuan 送李端

In the ancient pass are dying grasses everywhere, 故關衰草徧
And parting—of course, to be lamented. 離別自堪悲
The road goes out beyond cold clouds, 路出寒雲外
The man returns, at the time of evening snow. 人歸暮雪時
Orphaned young, you early were a wanderer, 少孤爲客早
Then suffered much—I came to know you late. 多難識君遲
We wipe away tears and face each other; 掩淚空相向
In the windblown dust where can we meet again? 風塵何所期
[14881]

The reader may remember Liu Ch'ang-ch'ing's (06984):

Clear in my eyes, a man on the sands 歷歷沙上人
Crosses the water alone in moonlight. 月中孤渡水

or his parting from Ling-ch'e (06981):

Wearing his rainhat, lit by setting sun, 荷笠帶夕陽
To green hills afar he returns alone. 青山獨歸遠

or Ch'ien Ch'i's farewell to Judge Yüan (12167):

Alone go off eastward, a faint shape in haze. 東去獨依依

or Li Chia-yu's (10045):

The road to be traveled lies by setting sun, 征途傍斜日
There a single rider, trotting on alone. 一騎獨翩翩

In the context of these couplets we read Lu Lun's:

The road goes out beyond cold clouds,   路出寒雲外
The man returns, at the time of evening snow.   人歸暮雪時

At partings or on long journeys, this kind of scene had a natural place in the physical or speculative eye. But whether that single, distant figure passed through evening snow, haze, moonlight, or the setting sunlight, the poetically trained eye was directed by convention to frame the scene and take the snapshot. Similar scenes had appeared in parting poems from the Early T'ang on, but contrast the T'ien-pao poet's impulse to distinctive variation: saying farewell to a friend on the frontier, Ts'en Shen closed with a figure of a lone horseman in the distance, but Ts'en's horseman was pursued by a cloud of steam from a volcano (09596):

Far in the distance a road lies, east of the volcano,   迢迢征路火山東
And on the volcano a single cloud now follows your horse 山上孤雲隨馬去
    away.

Ts'en's idiosyncratic treatment of convention ran the danger of grotesqueness—*ch'i* 奇 in the T'ien-pao sense of "strange" rather than in the later eighth-century sense of "arresting." The modal associations of images were fragile and easily disrupted: if a poet sought to embody a mood gracefully and naturally—and later eighth-century poets did seek this—it was necessary to suppress what was saliently individual.

    As the renaissance blazon enumerated the parts of a woman's body, so certain T'ang subgenres had their own blazons. A *huai-ku* on a ruined dwelling or battlefield had its set components to be enumerated: thus, as Keng Wei passed scenes of desolation of civil war in what had been the pre-Ch'in state of Sung:

At sunset brown clouds merge,   日暮黃雲合
As years deepen, the bare unburied bones grow few.   年深白骨稀
Of a former village tall trees endure,   舊村喬木在
In autumn grasses a man returns afar.   秋草遠人歸
Mosses grow thick on the ruined wells,   廢井莓苔厚
Paths grow fainter over fields run wild.   荒田路徑微
All that remains—the color of nearby mountains,   唯餘近山色
Facing me as if filled with longing.   相對似依依
                   [13823]

Keng has produced a beautiful poem entirely out of cliché images, literary formulas of the lyric: he has performed a theme "the continuity of nature and the impermanence of man and his civilization."

    As with the poets of the preceding generation, the art of the couplet played an important role in the poetry of the younger Ten Talents. Already in the work of Ch'ien Ch'i there is the suggestion of movement away from

the relative simplicity of the K'ai-yüan couplet and toward a visual ingenuity like that of the Early T'ang: such descriptive complexity is even
more apparent in the work of the younger Ten Talents.

There was a miniature genius in the art of the couplet: it was not a
genius which in itself pointed to the identity of the poet; rather, it lay
in the perception and representation of related patterns. Though it always
was manifest in the physical world, it was basically an art of abstracted
relationships. This may, in fact, be the best explanation for the extreme
conventionality of imagery in the parallel couplet of the later eighth century: the focus of attention was not on the items of the scene but on their
relationships. When in Ts'en Shen's waking eyes a lamp "set the wanderer's
dream ablaze," the genius was of metaphor and of the fresh perception of
an experience; but it was not truly the art of the parallel couplet, which
lives in the relations between lines. An example of true couplet art might
be a morning scene involving a transition from fog to brightness, a balance
of scattering and gathering, a hazy, scurrying movement of dislocated fragments transforming into a solid, radiant, clearly outlined mass—for instance,
Lu Lun (14915):

Clerks of the way station scurry through cold fog,	亭吏趨寒霧
The mountain city gathers in early morning light.	山城斂曙光

Or there may be a daylong and nightlong assault of water upon precariously upright forms, water from above and below on a massive and tiny
scale—Li Tuan (15277):

Night tides dash against aging trees,	夜潮衝老樹
Morning rains smash the light rushes.	曉雨破輕蘋

In this art-in-miniature so important in Chinese poetics, the younger Ten
Talents often surpassed their great predecessors of the K'ai-yüan and T'ien-
pao, and it is significant that their couplets were often selected in later lists
of exemplary couplets (*chü-t'u* 句圖).

A few significant differences separate the work of the younger Ten
Talents from that of the preceding generation. In a small number of poems
new topics made their appearance, and these topics suggested the breakdown of the old decorum of capital poetry and anticipate the Mid-T'ang
fascination with the "unpoetic." When Ssu-k'ung Shu can write a playfully hyperbolic song on the virtues of noodle soup (15625), it is impossible not to think ahead to the poetry of Han Yü. Heptasyllabic songs appeared more frequently in the work of the younger Ten Talents than in
the poetry of their immediate predecessors, and the song and the quatrain
were the forms most open to accommodating new topics. Thus, Lu Lun
finds a legitimate occasion for a poem when "Meeting a Sick Soldier" 逢
病軍人:

You have walked much and sickness is in you,
  no provisions when you halt,
行多有病住無糧

Thousands of miles returning to home,
  and not back to home yet.
萬里還鄉未到鄉

With tangled locks you groan in sorrow
  beneath an ancient wall,
蓬鬢哀吟古城下

Unable to bear the breath of autumn
  entering metal's scars.   [14716]
不堪秋氣入金瘡

The diction of this poem is so simple that it probably could have been understood by an unlettered soldier. The scars are "metal's" because they were made by weapons, and they have a special affinity with the "metal wind" of autumn, the wind of death and destruction. Another example of an unusual topic appears in the poetry of Ssu-k'ung Shu:

Sick, Sending Away a Concubine
病中遣妓

All life's events wound my heart,
  they are before my eyes,
萬事傷心在目前

My whole body drenched with tears,
  facing our flowered mat.
一身垂淚對花筵

I used up all my bright gold
  to teach you songs and the dance—
黃金用盡教歌舞

Now I leave you to another
  to take pleasure in your youth.   [15601]
留與它人樂少年

Though modern readers might not feel great sympathy for Ssu-k'ung's depression at an investment gone wrong, in the context of the later eighth century such a poem would have been immensely personal precisely because it represented the sort of situation that usually had no place in poetry.

Much of the best and most original work of the younger Ten Talents was done in the quatrain. With its ability to treat new topics and its links to *yüeh-fu*, the quatrain made it easier for a poet to go beyond the bland decorum of capital regulated verse. Lu Lun's six "Frontier Poems: Matching Poems by Governor Chang" from the late 780s contain probably the most famous poems of all the later capital poets. The first poem below refers to a story about the great Han general Li Kuang: one night the general shot an arrow at what he thought was a tiger, and in the morning the arrow was found embedded in a stone:

The forest is dark, grasses startle the wind,
林暗草驚風

The general draws his bow by night.
將軍夜引弓

At dawn they searched for the white feathers—
平明尋白羽

They were sunk deep in a cleft of stone.   沒在石稜中
[14747]

The moon is black, the geese fly high,   月黑雁飛高
The Great Khan is fleeing by night;   單于夜遁逃
About to go after him with our light cavalry,   欲將輕騎逐
A snowstorm covers our bows and blades.   大雪滿弓刀
[14748]

There is little difference between these poems and the frontier vignettes of the K'ai-yüan and T'ien-pao, though they lack the complications found in Wang Ch'ang-ling's quatrains. They are no less concerned with mood than the occasional *lü-shih* of the period, but their energetic mood contrasts with the prevailing melancholy of regulated verse. They are deservedly famous, but there is nothing new or individual about them. Keng Wei's most famous poem was also a quatrain, and also distinguished primarily by its perfect treatment of a received art.

Autumn Day   秋日

Sunlight cast back enters the village lanes,   反照入閭巷
Grief comes—to whom can I tell it.   憂來與誰語
An ancient road, no one walking there: 古道無人行
The autumn wind stirs the stalks of grain.   秋風動禾黍
[13955]

A rich tradition lies behind the imagery of the poem—Wang Wei (05837) and *Shih* 65, in which the grain covers over the ruins of the old Chou capital. But that rich legacy is used for simple purposes of mood, the desolation of autumn and longing to return home.

The younger Ten Talents walked no less in the shadow of the K'ai-yüan and T'ien-pao than Ch'ien Ch'i, Liu Ch'ang-ch'ing, and the other later capital poets; but the younger Ten Talents made use of a far wider range of K'ai-yüan and T'ien-pao poetry. Their heptasyllabic songs (e.g., 14727–36; 15170–79; 15652) possessed something of the imagination and energy of T'ien-pao songs and were far superior to the feeble attempts in the form by Ch'ien Ch'i and Huang-fu Jan. Particularly interesting is Li Tuan's "Ballad of the Lean Horse" (15172), because it seems to echo several poems by Tu Fu. Tu Fu was largely forgotten in the decades immediately following his death, yet in this ballad and in a few other poems by the younger Ten Talents (e.g., 15263, 15330, 15575) there are hints—no more than hints—that they may have been familiar with at least a few of Tu Fu's poems.

The younger Ten Talents had numerous contacts with the poet-monks of the Southeast, and Li Tuan is even supposed to have studied with

Chiao-jan. They shared with the monks an interest in poetic craftsmanship and a sense of poetry as the motive rather than as an adjunct for social gatherings. In the works of the younger Ten Talents there are numerous references to "poetry meetings," "poetry discussions," and to linked verse, which was then being practiced in the Chiao-jan circle.

The "poetry discussions" probably consisted of technical prohibitions and classifications such as we find in the criticism of Chiao-jan and in the texts taken to Japan by Kūkai and included in the *Bunkyō hifuron*. On the other hand, such discussion probably also involved impressionistic descriptions of individual style such as are found in the *Ho-yüeh ying-ling chi* and its successor, the *Chung-hsing hsien-ch'i chi*. In his elegy for the group (14712), Lu Lun characterized the poetry of his friends. Ch'i Chung-fou is:

The Underdirector, Lord of Letters,	侍郎文章宗
Genius risen, divinity of Huai-Ch'u,	傑出淮楚靈
Fu-master, like Earth's music piping,	掌賦若吹籟
Word-ruler, as a jug on roof spilling downward.	司言如建瓴

Ssu-k'ung Shu is:

| An outswelling pine bearing snow, | 鬱鬱松帶雪 |
| Sad cries of geese entering dark, dark skies. | 蕭蕭鴻入冥 |

And Miao Fa:

| A moonlit fragrance drifting over cassia fruit, | 月香飄桂實 |
| A dripping that nurses, falling on jade blossoms. | 乳流滴瓊英 |

Keng Wei seems to possess that "lingering taste" that later critics prized so highly:

| A well-brewed wine, stored longer, ever purer, | 九醞貯彌潔 |
| Thrice-flowering trees, still more fragrant in the cold. | 三花寒轉馨 |

Such was the way in which they saw their own art, and such were also the values they sought to embody in their poetry. The fate of their poetry was linked to the fortunes of such values. In ages when the subtleties of mood and craft were primary concerns, the later eighth-century capital poets were popular. But in ages dominated by strong, individual poets, they were largely ignored. Their poetry truly was, as Su Shih wrongly described the poetry of Meng Hao-jan, the "wine of monks."

15

Literary Activity in the Southeast

Faint in the distance, before the Cha's temples,
Are white rushes filled with clear breezes.
Visited long ago, the poetry parties were full;
Visited now, the poetry parties are gone
· ·
In recollection I recite the theories of those times
When people came there truly without end.
But the Yangtze songs cannot be attained again—
The dust of the capital covers me in vain.

Meng Chiao, "Sending Lu Ch'ang off on His Way Home to Hu-chou: I Trust Him to write This Poem on the Graves of My Old Friends, Chiao-jan and Lu Yü [19958]

In the later eighth century the lower Yangtze region had become a center of poetic activity rivaling the capital. Most of the famous literary men of the day visited, governed, or took refuge in the Southeast; and in the congenial atmosphere of the southeastern literary circles, they discussed the fine points of their art, wrote of the famous landscapes, feasted, toured, and forgot for a while the constant troubles that beset the northern half of the empire. The Mid-T'ang poet Meng Chiao, himself a southeasterner, grew up during this brief period of southeastern literary glory, and as a youth he joined in these gatherings of famous poets. But by 808, when Meng wrote the lines quoted above, the values of poetry had undergone major changes, and few other writers would look back with such fondness on the poetry of the later eighth century. Even Meng Chiao recalled not a flowering of genius, but an ambience of literary parties and discussions of poetry.

In the Southeast, capital poets like Liu Ch'ang-ch'ing, Li Chia-yu, the Huang-fu brothers, Keng Wei, and Li Tuan made the acquaintance of local writers like young Meng Chiao and of the poet-monks, whose monasteries often served as the setting for literary gatherings. At such gatherings the linked verse had its first true flowering since the Southern Dynasties; also the first *ch'ang-ho chi* 唱和集, collections of poems exchanged between two poets, were composed.[1] And it was in this atmosphere of poetry discussions and literary parties that the monk Chiao-jan wrote his critical works.

There are many indications that poets were becoming increasingly reflective about the art of poetry, and that reflectiveness was inseparable from the social context of the literary group. In the southeastern circles the dominant attitude thought of poetry not as self-expression, not as a vehicle for moral values, not as a pure art divorced from occasion, and not even as a craft to be mastered for social advancement: rather, as in the Southern Dynasties, poetry was conceived as a social art that existed for its own sake, a pastime that was in itself an occasion for social intercourse. And at the center of this poetic activity were the poet-monks.

THE POET-MONKS

The best-known poet monks have mostly come from the lower Yangtze region. Ling-yi ("Numinous One 靈一) was the source; Hu-kuo ("Guardian of the State" 護國) carried on; Ch'ing-chiang ("Clear River" 清江) stirred the waves forward; Fa-chen ("Dharma Spreads" 法振) followed the current. But these men were tiny strings with a single tone that passed the ear in a flash; they did not represent the Grand Music [of the ancient tradition]. Only His Reverence Ch'ing-chou (清晝; i.e., Chiao-jan) mastered all the forms; and after him, Ling-ch'e (靈徹) carried on the work.

> Liu Yü-hsi, "Notes on the Collected Works of Ling-ch'e" [2]

In the passage above Liu Yü-hsi describes a tradition of poetry by southeastern monks as the movement of a river. The river was also a common metaphorical model by which to describe the history of literature by secular writers, and in Liu's description these two streams are independent and do not "flow together." The separateness that Liu saw was an illusion fostered by a convention of Chinese historiography, the clear differentiation between secular and religious figures. It is more accurate to see the poet-monks as the stable elements in a larger pattern of literary activity in the Southeast. Secular poets and monks wrote together and wrote in much the same way, but while the great poets of the capital came and went, the monks usually remained.

Poem exchanges reveal how closely the monks were linked to secular writers and to each other. The earliest of the southeastern monks, Ling-yi, was acquainted with Ch'ien Ch'i, Lang Shih-yüan, Liu Ch'ang-ch'ing, Li Chia-yu, the Huang-fu brothers, and Wei Ying-wu, to mention only the most prominent. Ling-ch'e even studied composition under the capital poet Yen Wei. And Chiao-jan, while he had connections with the same group as Ling-yi and Ling-ch'e, was closely associated with the group of secular intellectuals who compiled the rhyming dictionary *Yün-hai ching-yüan* 韻海鏡源, directed by the great calligrapher Yen Chen-ch'ing. Both in their social relations and in their poetic practice, the poet-monks were an integral part of the literary world of the later eighth century. They were in no sense religious poets: with a few exceptions, when Buddhism appeared in their work, it was the lay Buddhism of capital poetry.[3]

Ling-yi's (727–62) forty-two extant poems may have constituted the single *chüan* of his poetry recorded in the Sung. The earliest of the southeastern poet-monks, Ling-yi learned to write in the style of capital poetry even before the massive influx of secular writers into the Southeast in the 760s. Apart from three poems on famous monks (44220–22), the reader can find Ling-yi's Buddhism only incarnate in the natural world of occasional poetry.

A New Spring at Yi-feng	宜豐新泉
Recently the source of a stream gushed forth,	泉源新湧出
And breaking through, reflects the slender clouds.	洞澈映纖雲
The level of lotus pond sinks somewhat lower,	稍落芙蓉沼
As it first covers the streaks of moss.	初掩苔蘇文
At last it cleanses the illusion of bright beauty;	了將空色淨
It has always been distinct from the average stream.	素與衆流分
Whenever the moon's out on a clear night,	每到清宵月
You can hear it trickling in your dreams.	泠泠夢裏聞
[44216]	

It is tempting to find a Buddhist poet in this poem, in terms such as "the illusion of bright beauty" and in conventional Buddhist metaphors, such as the reflecting surface of the pure stream. But the degree and seriousness of Buddhist reference in this poem derive largely from the reader's knowledge that the poet was a monk: exactly the same poem might have been written by a secular poet in praise of the garden of a capital aristocrat. Since at least one technical Buddhist term is used, it is legitimate to find Buddhist values in the poem, but these appear primarily through a "situational frame of reference," reading intellectual implications into natural imagery according to the circumstances of composition, in this case the presumed religious concerns of the author.

The language of most Buddhist texts was less figured and syntactically more direct than the language of secular prose and poetry. The monks' education in such texts might lead one to expect the development of corresponding forms of poetry, and indeed the remains of such a tradition can be seen in the collections of Han-shan and Wang Fan-chih. Though the southeastern poet-monks seemed anxious to prove their sophistication in the secular poetic tradition, a very small number of their works—usually epigrammatic quatrains—do draw from their background of Buddhist learning. The following quatrain by Ling-yi uses the problem of free will playfully and colloquially.

About to Leave Yi-feng Temple: I Leave This Written on a Mountain Chamber	將出宜豐寺留題山房
Lotus flowers in the pool don't blossom of their own will;	池上蓮荷不自開

Flowing waters in the mountains
   likewise come by chance.   山中流水偶然來
Should you claim that meeting and separation
   necessarily arise from the self,   若言聚散定由我
Consider—how can we manage to turn back,
   before it's our time to turn back.   未是回時那得回
                [44249]

At parting, a real or hypothetical interlocutor implies that Ling-yi can come back if he desires. Ling-yi's quatrain is a playful rebuttal, arguing against free will, not by karmic determinism but by a theory of accident: even if one claims free will to return at a given time, how can one know that the "choice" is not fated or accidental? But less important than Ling-yi's argument is that, as in Wang Wei's most abstrusely "doctrinal" poetry, the philosophical problem is subordinate to the motives of occasional poetry.

Although Liu Yü-hsi regarded Ling-ch'e's poetry more highly than that of Ling-yi, fewer of his works have survived, only sixteen poems out of a collection once in ten *chüan*. Ling-ch'e's long life (746–816) spanned the later eighth century and the Mid-T'ang, but so many of his poems are from late in his life that he should probably be considered a Mid-T'ang poet. Yet unlike Meng Chiao, Ling-ch'e was well known as a poet in literary circles of the Southeast: he was a student of Yen Wei, a friend of Ling-yi and Chiao-jan, as well as of Keng Wei and Lu Lun. Indeed, the monk's poetry was so highly regarded that he was recommended to the capital, where his work was said to have enjoyed imperial favor.

Like other southeasterners, such as Ho Chih-chang and Ku K'uang, Ling-ch'e was known for his quick repartee and sharp wit. A mild specimen of his wit survives in his most famous poem, an epigram. The professed yearning of secular officials to retire to the hills was a subject that begged for a satiric gibe, but for obvious reasons the satiric reply was seldom offered. Early in the ninth century, Wei Tan, the commander of Hung-chou, wrote of his desire for the recluse's life (07590), and Ling-ch'e composed this famous answer:

Now old, my heart is at peace,
   and nothing external bothers me.   年老心閒無外事
The robes of hemp and seat of grass—
   enough for my body.   麻衣草座亦容身
Everyone I meet tells me
   how grand it would be to quit office;   相逢盡道休官好
Yet never once here in the woods
   have I seen a single one.   林下何曾見一人
                [44264]

The genius of this epigram lies less in its gentle barb than in its play on a durable convention of reclusive poetry: "seeing no one" in the deserted forest (cf. 06082).

If Liu Yü-hsi considered Ling-ch'e one of the two best poet-monks, it was probably because Ling-ch'e's work was marked by the Mid-T'ang taste for bold, original imagery and propositional language (and also because he had been Liu Yü-hsi's friend). It is impossible to tell if this characterized Ling-ch'e's total oeuvre or only his later poems. The following is one of Ling-ch'e's finest quatrains, written on a visit to a deserted Buddhist temple. "Effigy worship" (line 3) is a kenning for Buddhism.

Spending the Night at East Forest Temple	宿東林寺
The skies are cold; fierce tigers roar through the snow of peaks;	天寒猛虎叫巖雪
Here in the forest, no one— and moonlight shines unseen.	林下無人空有月
A thousand years of effigy worship is heard no more today,	千年像教今不聞
And the burning of incense is pleasing only to the ghosts.	焚香獨爲鬼神說

[44261]

The quatrain is a brilliant *huai-ku* rooted in a secular poetic tradition. The "tiger's roar" was a potent image of Ch'an thought, but the tigers of Ch'an are only remote echoes in this quatrain; rather, these are the real tigers of the wilderness that creeps over the decaying sites of human habitation, the tigers of a *huai-ku* (e.g., 02641).

Like Ling-ch'e, Ch'ing-chiang survives only in a handful of poems: twenty-one pieces, of which several are also attributed to other peoets. But judging from his extant work, Ch'ing-chiang possessed a poetic gift that should have raised him above Liu Yü-hsi's derogatory "tiny string with a single tone." 'Chiao-jan may have been a more important poet with a broader range, but Ch'ing-chiang's best poems have an intensity and grandeur that Chiao-jan never achieved. There is in his poetry an ability to speak with dignity on the larger element of the universe and a public seriousness that are reminiscent of Tu Fu. (Fan Huang's early preface to Tu Fu's collection states that it was in circulation primarily in the South.) The following poem was addressed to the capital poet Yen Wei.

Setting Out Early from Hsia-chou: On the road, Sent to Yen of the Imperial Library	早發陝州途中贈嚴秘書
Though this body of mine has no earthly ties,	此身雖不繫
Concern for the Way still troubles my life.	憂道亦勞生
A million miles—a dream of rivers and lakes;	萬里江湖夢

A thousand mountains, walking through rain and snow.　千山雨雪行
Men's dwellings rest against former battlements,　　人家依舊壘
Barrier roads shut out Layered Wall.　　　　　　關路閉層城
The Chiao-ho nomads are not yet gone,　　　　　未盡交河虜
And Thinwillow Garrison still encamps troops.　　猶屯細柳兵
In hardship I sigh for these hard travels;　　　艱難嗟遠客
Sojourning, rely on the warmth of men's hearts.　棲託賴深情
Sickness and poverty will be my lot:　　　　　貧病吾將有
To perfect my spirit, I take leave of Shao-ch'ing.　精修謝少卿
                                              [44311]

Layered Wall was the highest spot in the K'un-lun Mountains, and there
the mythical Queen Mother of the West was said to dwell. In this poem
the K'un-lun of myth merges with the geographical K'un-lun of Central
Asia, as the barrier passes simultaneously block the traveler from immortal
worlds as well as holding back the Tibetans and steppe peoples. In this
context, Shao-ch'ing refers to Jen An, to whom Ssu-ma Ch'ien wrote his
famous letter in defense of his decision to accept the imperial punishment of
castration so that he could finish the *Shih-chi*. It would appear that Ch'ing-
chiang is assuming the role of Ssu-ma Ch'ien to offer Yen a defense of some
decision (perhaps to remain a cleric) which would be clearer if the full
biographical context were known.

　　Most reminiscent of Tu Fu are the grand, general statements concerning
self and universe, as in the third couplet of the following poem.

Early Spring, Writing my Feelings: To Magistrate　早春書情寄河南崔少府
　　Ts'ui of Honan

With days of spring the east wind comes,　　　春日春風至
But its gentle warmth seems unevenly shared:　陽和似不均
My sick body pointlessly grows older,　　　　病身空益老
My sad locks show no knowledge of spring.　　愁鬢不知春
In this universe I've become a thing left behind;　宇宙成遺物
Light and dark speed an illusion-body on.　　　光陰促幼身
Still wandering, feel pain at the end of the road,　客遊傷末路
All the heart's concerns directed to travelers.　心事向行人
Weak in the Way, still loving comfort,　　　道薄猶懷土
The times hards, I weary of poverty.　　　　時難欲厭貧
If my modest talents had a place to lodge,　　微才如可寄
I'd find home and kin on imperial soil.　　　赤縣有鄉親
                                      [44312]

As the great official inevitably yearns for the pure, unfettered life of the
recluse or monk, so here the monk longs for the secular life, on "imperial
soil" rather than in the wilderness where "no man is seen." Ch'ing-chiang
showed a particular fondness for quoting the *Analects*, a fondness not shared

by his secular contemporaries. In this poem, "loving comfort" is from *Analects* IV.11, where "The good man loves virtue; the lesser man loves comfort."

Ch'ing-chiang was as adept as any of his contemporaries in composing couplets, but as can be seen in the poems above, he possessed a special gift for self-analysis, "speaking his intention" 言志 according to the canonical function of poetry. Paradoxically, it is his self-doubt about his own religious conviction that makes him perhaps the most religiously serious of the southeastern poet-monks. In place of the serene description of reflecting streams and vacant thoughts, we sometimes find in Ch'ing-chiang's poems the cry of an unconvinced soul (44323):

Unable to comprehend the Dharma-nature, 未能通法性
How can I avoid the ruin, the dissolution? 詎可免支離

皎然
CHIAO—JAN

His poet friends at Shan-yin
    were rowdy when they met—
The lovely lines flew back and forth
    without destroying Ch'an.

The couplet above appears at the end of a poem by Chiao-jan on the Southern Dynasties monk Chih-tun (44840), but Chiao-jan could just as easily have been speaking for himself. Even more than the other poet-monks, Chiao-jan was entirely caught up in a secular social world and a secular poetic world, so much so that he could not avoid some sense of conflict with his religious vocation. Though he did write a few genuinely religious poems, these form only a tiny part of his corpus of nearly five hundred poems in seven *chüan* (with another *chüan* of linked verse). If Chiao-jan was not the best poet of the later eighth century, he was certainly the most interesting poet of the period—a critic, writer of linked verses, and a master stylist who experimented with a wide variety of period styles. Though a monk, he was, more than any other writer of the age, a man of poetry.

Chiao-jan was a native southeasterner, a Hsieh and tenth-generation descendant of Hsieh Ling-yün. Born around 734, he took his monastic vows in the early 750s and led a relatively uneventful life among the scenic beauties and social pleasures of the lower Yangtze region. Though he defended Chih-tun's poetic activity, Chiao-jan himself was said to have renounced poetry in the late 780s. Whether the report of that renunciation is true or not, he did write poems after that date, perhaps giving way to the social pressures brought upon him by his considerable poetic fame. He was still alive in 791 and surely dead by 809, but the exact date of his death is uncertain. In 792 a copy of his works was presented to the Imperial Library, and this may indicate that he was no longer alive.

Chiao-jan's poetry exhibits a range of styles greater than any other poet of the later eighth century. But most significant is the integrity of the period styles he used: this is a Mid-T'ang trait and contrasts with the High T'ang tendency to stylistic variation according to subgeneric proprieties. For example, a parting poem by Chiao-jan might be in the conventional pentasyllabic regulated verse of the capital tradition (44750–65); it might be an archaized *yüeh-fu* (44819); it might be a heptasyllabic song in the T'ien-pao style (44874, 44876, 44880, etc.) Earlier in the eighth century there had been some freedom of generic choice in treating an occasion, but Chiao-jan's work shows not only a greater range of choice, it also usually shows a careful consistency in the use of a style characteristic of a certain period or author. Generic differences in style remained, and the formality of an occasion still exerted an influence on the choice of genre and style, but there is a *historical* variety in Chiao-jan's style that is hard to find earlier.

This new sense of the literary past had been developing for several decades and was probably connected to the waning of strict *fu-ku* values. In many ways this literary historical sense foreshadowed the entire future development of poetry in traditional China. No longer was the poet confronted with the choice between contemporary style and a single "archaic" alternative: that simple choice was rooted in the *fu-ku* opposition of "ancient" and "modern," and the opposition deemphasized the true variety of both "ancient" and "modern." *Fu-ku* literary history was predicated on a single standard that was being effaced through time: it did not admit variety and multiple standards. As in the history of Western literary criticism, a sense of literary history as change rather than decline meant a relativity of values. And as we shall see, in his criticism, Chiao-jan made just such an argument for literary-historical change.

As he catalogued stylistic variety in his critical work, so he demonstrated it in his poetry. Chiao-jan's range was like that of Tu Fu, but there was an important difference: Tu Fu assimilated the literary past and generated a poetic variety that was all inimitably Tu Fu: Chiao-jan preserved the integrity of past styles and "used" them. Chiao-jan could be the early *yüeh-fu* poet (44818); he could be the Chien-an poet (44565, 44644); he could write with the rich formality of fifth-century poetry (44560 and passim); he could perform a *yung-wu* theme with all the grace of a court poet (44835); he could be Ch'en Tzu-ang (44847–52) or Chang Chiu-ling (44835); he was a master of the T'ien-pao song (44869–902); and he could write in the highly archaic style of Yüan Chieh (44862).

Several factors contributed to Chiao-jan's catholicity of taste and literary-historical variety. Foremost among these was the literary self-consciousness that accompanied his criticism and the poetry discussions that flourished in southeastern literary circles. Another factor was the contemporary revaluation of the poetry of the Southern Dynasties and Early T'ang, which weakened the simple *fu-ku* opposition between ancient and modern. Finally, there was Chiao-jan's deep interest in his ancestor Hsieh Ling-yün, whose very individual style Chiao-jan tried to reproduce in many poems.

The following poem, a composition to a set topic, shows Chiao-jan's skill in handling a delicate later Southern Dynasties and Early T'ang style.

On the Topic "Stone Bridge Stream": Sending Off Ts'ui K'uei	賦得石梁泉送崔逵

A frame of stone reaches cliff of rose cloud,	架石通霞壁
The sheer slope scatters emerald sands.	懸崖散碧沙
When the sky is clear, shadow of rainbow crosses,	天晴虹影渡
When the wind is faint, silky streaks slant.	風細練文斜
Striding upward, meeting in a hidden place blocked,	攀陟幽期阻
Up and downstream, the traveler's thoughts go far	沿洄客意賒
This is not the road of the Yellow River bridge,	河梁非此路
But there too parting's bitterness is limitless.	別恨亦無涯

[44799]

The Yellow River Bridge had been the site of the famous parting of Li Ling and Su Wu. Court poetry's rules of rhetoric are followed carefully here: each line in the first two couplets matches a line on the bridge with a line on the stream; the third couplet repeats the antithesis and introduces the theme of parting, to which the last couplet offers a response through a comparison to a famous precedent.

Chiao-jan could equal any of his contemporaries in the evocative quatrain with its suggestive closing image, as in the following poem on the immortal Red Pine:

Along the bank through dense foliage, then out to see the sky:	綠岸蒙籠出見天
Sunlit sands sparkling clear, and the water rushing on.	晴沙瀝瀝水濺濺
I wonder where that winged being is ever washing his herbs,	何處羽人長洗藥
Whose ruined flowers in countless numbers follow the flowing stream.	殘花無數逐流泉

[44842]

The closing scene is the physical evidence of some hidden truth, on which the third line speculates.

Almost the entire final *chüan* of Chiao-jan's collection is devoted to the heptasyllabic song. The genre's position in the collection corresponds to its position in Wei Ying-wu's works and in some of the collections of the younger Ten Talents. This probably reflects the late-eighth-century sense of generic hierarchy: the heptasyllabic song is placed last because it seemed the "newest" and most unorthodox of the poetic genres. There was a strong element of generic evaluation in the arrangement of poem collections, and the values accorded to genres in different periods was independent of their true history.

A perfect rendition of the T'ien-pao song style can be seen in the following piece. It is a parting poem, and as in many of Ts'en Shen's occasional songs, the occasional message is loosely attached to the end.

Song of the Soaring Hawk: To His Excellency Wang 翔隼歌送王端公
 on Parting

The ancients esteemed the godlike and glorious, 古人賞神駿
And what can compare to the hawk on the kill? 何如秋隼擊
It hovers alone at the highest point, 獨立高標整霜翮
 straightens frost-white feathers;
I'm sure in its eyes Heaven's canopy 應看天宇如咫尺
 seems but a foot away.
Then circling low it brushes the earth, 低迴拂地凌風翔
 and soars up over the winds:
The fledgling phoenix dares to alight, 鵬雛敢下雁斷行
 and the wild geese break formation.
You look all around in the sunlit sky, 晴空四顧忽不見
 it's suddenly not to be seen,
Then for a moment emerges alone 有時獨出青霞傍
 by the edge of blue clouds.
Dark winter's end, and the chill sun 窮陰萬里落寒日
 sets over a million miles,
When the air is of death and the grasses dry, 氣殺草枯增奮逸
 it exults ever more on high.
Through cloudy passes it flies on a slant, 雪塞斜飛攬葉迷
 lost in a flurry of wisps,
Then straight up it goes into snowy skies, 雪天直上穿花疾
 piercing through snowflakes swift.

In this I see your own soaring heart 見君高情有何屬
 finds friendship in like kind,
And as parting gift I sing you this song 贈別因歌翔隼曲
 of the wild hawk's soaring.
The pavilion of parting grows somber and still 離亭慘慘客散時
 as the guests are scattering:
The song is done, your road is long, 歌盡路長意不足
 and my meaning not well enough said.
     [44874]

Comparison to the tame songs of contemporary capital poets reveals Chiao-jan's mastery and freedom in using the T'ien-pao song style.

Like the other poet-monks, in his occasional poems Chiao-jan used monastic settings and the lay Buddhism of capital poetry. But Chiao-jan also composed some Buddhist poems in the more colloquial, casual style of Wang Fan-chih and Han-shan. A reference in his criticism indicates that Chiao-jan was at least partially familiar with the Wang Fan-chih corpus, but it is impossible to know if he was aware of the Han-shan corpus. A poem entitled "Cold Mountain" ("*Han-shan*" 寒山 44814) from the "Miscellaneous Songs of My Southern Pool" 南池雜詠 (44811–15) suggests the symbolic value of the "cold mountain" that is so prominent in the Han-shan corpus, but the image is probably too commonplace to indicate a true link.

Encroaching on the emptiness, riot of color,	侵空撩亂色
I love this uniquely, my own middle peak.	獨愛我中峯
No cares at all, I lean on light staff,	無事負輕策
I walk on calmly, following hidden tracks.	閒行躡幽蹤
On all the mountains falling of leaves is over,	衆山搖落盡
And cold, azure mists form, layer upon layer.	寒翠更重重

[44814]

The style is casual, but somewhat more literary than most of the Han-shan poems. However, there are other poems that are even more "unpoetic," and closer to the style of Wang Chi, Han-shan, and Wang Fan-chih.

Playful Poem	戲題
Yammering, squabbling—all of it in a world bound by "true" and "false";	喧喧共在是非間
Who understands the peace of mind I feel the whole day long?	終日誰知我自閒
A chance visitor sings wildly— and why does he do what he does?	偶客狂歌何所爲
He wants only to force himself to care about human affairs.	欲於人事強相關

[44845]

Like many of the Han-shan poems, this piece belongs thematically to the tradition of the eccentric recluse, but there are other poems more directly concerned with Ch'an.

Spontaneous Poem I	偶然五首之一
Joy in Ch'an, my heart seems swept along,	樂禪心似蕩
And my Way is never hindered.	吾道不相防
Alone and enlightened I sing and laugh—	獨悟歌還笑
Who says I get crazier in old age?	誰言老更狂

[44853]

The last phrase, "crazier in old age," appears verbatim at the end of Tu Fu's "Crazy Man" (11107), written when Tu Fu was in Ch'eng-tu. In a few other cases Chiao-jan seems to echo Tu Fu's poetry, and a citation in his criticism confirms that Chiao-jan had some knowledge of Tu Fu's work.

Wang Wei and Ch'u Kuang-hsi had both composed series of "Spontaneous Poems," but the short poems of Chiao-jan's series (44853–57) make the earlier poets seem decorously controlled in style and theme. It is tempting to read the following poem as a defense of Chiao-jan's secular entanglements, a defense based on the Ch'an impulse to invert conventional religious values:

I hide my heart and not my deeds,	隱心不隱跡
And I even desire to dwell in men's world.	却欲住人寰
If I lack trees, I transplant one in spring;	欠樹移春樹
If I miss the mountains, I look at a painting.	無山看畫山
I reside in noise, and I haven't gone wrong—	居喧我未錯
Truth is here.	眞意在其間

[44855]

The cultivated tree supplants the natural tree; the painting replaces the landscape. Though the poet begins with the conventional assertion that he hides his heart, most of the poem involves a true inversion of eremitic values and not the older Taoist tradition of the recluse in the city. Rather than finding the surroundings unimportant, as when T'ao Ch'ien looks past his town to the hills beyond, Chiao-jan finds truth in the "noise" of the human world. The poem speaks to the Mahayana commandment to dwell in the secular world, but it does so through the Ch'an pleasure in surprise and thwarted expectations. The following poem treats the Ch'an delight in inversion directly and humorously:

I don't like foreign languages; I won't study them;	虜語嫌不學
And I've never translated barbarian words.	胡音從不翻
Tell you of Ch'an? It's what's topsy-turvy,	説禪顚倒是
What makes the Prince of the West die of laughter.	樂殺金王孫

[44856]

The "Prince of the West" is the Buddha. While Chiao-jan's attitude does not misrepresent Ch'an, it should also be remembered how comfortable such a position was for Chiao-jan or any monk: it allowed one to reside in secular society and be spared the more intellectually demanding tasks of Buddhism, such as translating sutras.

Early bibliographies list three critical works on poetry by Chiao-jan: the *Shih-shih* 詩式, the *Shih-p'ing* 詩評, and the *Shih-yi* 詩議. Of these, the *Shih-p'ing* may have been part of the longer version of the *Shih-shih*.[4] Unless the *Shih-p'ing* formed part of the *Shih-shih*, both it and the *Shih-yi* survive only in fragments. But the *Shih-shih* was clearly the work to which Chiao-jan and his contemporaries accorded the most importance. The *Shih-shih* survives in several one-*chüan* versions and in a much longer five-*chüan* version.[5]

Here we are concerned less with the *Shih-shih*'s important place in the history of T'ang criticism than its relation to Chiao-jan's poetry and the literary values of the later eighth century. Chiao-jan inherited the terms of literary-historical discourse from his *fu-ku* predecessors of the seventh and eighth centuries. *Fu-ku* turns of phrase occur almost unconsciously, especially in evaluative comments; for example, to praise the work of his ancestor Hsieh Ling-yün, Chiao-jan says that he "passed on high to the Feng [*Kuo-feng* of the *Shih-ching*] and Sao [*Li-sao* of the *Ch'u-tz'u*], well above the works of the Chien-an, Wei, and Tsin" (*Shih-shih* 1.4b). But from other references in the *Shih-shih* it is clear that Chiao-jan did not believe Hsieh Ling-yün was so much superior to Chien-an and Wei poets as different from them, nor did he believe that the "Feng and Sao" were the absolute standards of judgment. Though Chiao-jan was struggling with the *fu-ku* terms of discourse and their presumptions, *fu-ku* offered the strongest model of literary-historical evaluation.

In many cases Chiao-jan tried to oppose or modify the commonplaces of *fu-ku* literary theory. In his preface to Ch'en Tzu-ang's collection, Lu Ts'ang-yung claimed that Ch'en had restored ancient greatness to poetry after five hundred years of decline; Chiao-jan scoffed at such conventional *fu-ku* hyperbole, and in rebuttal listed his favorite poets of the five hundred years of "decline." Then Chiao-jan filiated Ch'en's poetry to that of Juan Chi, which falls within the "decline" period, and asserted the superiority of the Wei poet (*Shih-shih* 3.1a–1b). Elsewhere, Chiao-jan went beyond the mere defense of poets and undermined the very basis of *fu-ku*, while appearing only to modify its principles. Chiao-jan maintained that in literary history there must be both "change" (*pien* 變) and "return" *fu* 復); Ch'en Tzu-ang was then cited as an example of a poet who "returned too much and changed too little" (*Shih-shih* 5.1b). The admission of the necessity of "change" makes explicit what was implicit in Tu-ku Chi's metaphors of the ceremonial drum and script (pp. 254–56). The legitimacy of "change," even balanced by "return," struck at the heart of *fu-ku*'s presumption of universal and unchanging standards for poetry.

The revaluation of the poetry of the Southern Dynasties and his argument for the necessity of literary change came together in a spirited defense of the poetry of the Ch'i and Liang dynasties. Here the opposition to *fu-ku* values was most radical: Chiao-jan objected that literary-historical evaluation had been too closely tied to the moral judgments of political history, and went on to defend the period by saying, "It can be maintained that the style of poetry changed, but not that the Way [of poetry] had declined" (*Shih-shih* 4.1a–1b).

Directly following this is a peculiar passage in which Chiao-jan attacked the poetry of the capital poets of his day.

During the Ta-li Reign the majority of poets have lived in the Southeast: Huang-fu Jan, Yen Wei, Chang Chi, Liu Ch'ang-ch'ing, Li Chia-yu, and Chu Fang. These men have usurped the green mountains, the white clouds, the spring wind, and the fragrant grasses as though they belonged to them and them along. I acknowledge that the "decline of poetry" belongs right here—why find fault with the Ch'i and Liang? The rolling wave of their influence has grown stronger and stronger until the present, and the younger generation has imitated so much that many have been swallowed up by this style. But at the end of the Ta-li, these gentlemen changed course—I suppose because they realized how wrong they had been.

The charge Chiao-jan raises against the capital poets is one of "usurpation." It is possible that the former owners of the stolen poetic landscape were the local poets of the Southeast, in which case Chiao-jan would be referring simply to the influence and cultural arrogance of the capital poets. But the passage occurs in the context of Chiao-jan's defense of the Ch'i and Liang, those who had owned and written of the southeastern landscape long before. Thus, it seems likely that Chiao-jan is referring to the capital poets' ignorance and rejection of the former "local poets," those of the Ch'i and Liang whose literary landscape the capital poets have arrogantly usurped. Chiao-jan was essentially correct: one of the strongest traits of late-eighth-century capital poetry was a lack of literary-historical awareness and depth, precisely the qualities that enrich Chiao-jan's own work. Their "reform" at the end of the Ta-li would be an abandonment of the *fu-ku* disapproval of Southern Dynasties poetry and the acceptance of the more tolerant and catholic views of Chiao-jan. Besides their literary-historical naïveté, Chiao-jan would have disapproved of the bland simplicity of capital poetry: Chiao-jan often praised complexity and difficulty (*Shih-shih* 1.1a; 1.5b), and in his own work he avoided the ease of capital poetry, even if the results were often awkward and mannered.

Chiao-jan's criticism was closely related to his poetry, which was not always the case among Chinese poet-critics. His stylistic catholicity found a counterpart in his critical catholicity of taste. His assertion of the value of literary change freed him from both the decorum of capital poetry and its *fu-ku* antithesis in the poetry of high antiquity. Though many Mid-T'ang poets reasserted the *fu-ku* model, the self-consciousness and catholicity of Chiao-jan became one of the dominant traits of Mid-T'ang poetry. And it was in the Chiao-jan circle that the oldest of the important Mid-T'ang poets, Meng Chiao, served his poetic apprenticeship.

It is impossible to say to what extent Chiao-jan's literary historical opinions were shared by the circle around him, but there is one fascinating linked verse, "Lecture on Ancient Writing" 講古文聯句 (43241), which puts forward an account of the history of poetry very different than the conventional *fu-ku* history. This linked verse was composed between Chiao-jan and several of the less famous figures of his circle: P'an Shu 潘述, P'ei Chi 裴濟, and T'ang Heng 湯衡. The view of literary history offered is most eccentric and can perhaps be understood only in the context of the strong southern bias suggested in the passage translated above: the poets write favorably of earlier poetry up to the Ch'en Dynasty and seem to condemn everything written after, evidently including the T'ang! But T'ang Heng was presenting something similar to Chiao-jan's balance of "change" and "return" in his lines on the "imitations" of the Liang poet Chiang Yen:

Chiang Yen's "Poems in Various Styles"—	江淹雜體
There one can see power of talent;	方見才力
His imitations were truly well done,	擬之信工
Resembling without crowding [the originals].	似而不逼

Chiang Yen's imitations of his own major poetic predecessors can be seen as the model for Chiao-jan's catholic use of earlier styles. It also offered an alternative to *fu-ku* in the means to creatively use the literary past.

THE LINKED VERSES

If Chiao-jan was ambivalent about his associations with the capital poets, there was another group of secular intellectuals with whom his relations were quite warm: this was the group around Yen Chen-ch'ing 顏眞卿. In the titles of Chiao-jan's poetry there is evidence of extensive poetic activity in this group, but apart from the collection of Chiao-jan, almost nothing of it has survived. Yen Chen-ch'ing's collected works now consists primarily of prose writings, with only a handful of poems, none of which are commensurate with his genius as a calligrapher. Of Li Shu's works only a cycle of ritual survives, while Lu Yü 陸羽, the author of the *Tea Classic*, is represented by a few songs and scattered couplets. Less well known writers such as P'an Shu and Li O 李萼 survive only in the linked verses. Of the luminaries of capital poetry only Keng Wei was closely associated with this group.

The great anomaly in the poetry of the Yen Chen-ch'ing circle is that while their conventional poetic oeuvre survives only in fragments, they are represented by a sizable number of linked verses, *lien-chü* 聯句 —over fifty in all. These are preserved at the ends of the collected works of Yen

Chen-ch'ing and Chiao-jan. Since linked verse was not considered serious poetry, it is particularly surprising to find these poems extant when more respectable poetry was lost. One possible explanation is that a separate collection of linked verses survived and was later divided and appended to the Chiao-jan and Yen Chen-ch'ing collections.[6]

Linked verses and their near relations, Po-liang verses, appeared earlier in the T'ang only infrequently. The linked verse was a form associated with the Southern Dynasties, and it is likely that the later-eighth-century revaluation of Southern Dynasties poetry played a role in the resurgence of the linked verse.[7]

The linked verses of the group around Yen Chen-ch'ing and Chiao-jan are mild in comparison to the rambunctious linked verses between Han Yü and Meng Chiao, but they represent an even greater variety of forms and topics. They were, of course, written to set topics, often *yung-wu* topics, and usually involved a group of more than two participants, thus diminishing the possibility for the quick repartee found in many of the linked verses between Han Yü and Meng Chiao. Of great formal variety, they include verses in trisyllabic lines (43153) and hexasyllabic lines (43254), as well as two tetrasyllabic, archaic "lecture" linked verses (43240–41), one on virtue and one on the literary tradition. The unit of alternation was either the quatrain, the couplet, or the single line.

One of the most amusing groups of these linked verses is a series on playful topics (43155–60), between Yen Chen-ch'ing, Chiao-jan, Li O, and Chang Chien. With one exception, these are quatrains in which each participant gives an example of the subject.

Big Talk   七言大言聯句

Chiao-jan:
   I sing loud on Lang-feng,
      step over to Ying-chou;   高歌閬風步瀛洲
Yen Chen-ch'ing:
   I broil me a roc, fry up leviathan,
      and my dinner's still not done.   焯鵬燴鯤餐未休
Li O:
   I go up and down at the ends of the earth
      where nothing lies beyond;   四方上下無外頭
Chang Chien:
   I take a sip and instantly dry
      the streams of the dark blue sea.   一啜頓涸滄溟流
                       [43155]

Lang-feng was a peak of K'un-lun, the mountain of the immortals in the far west; Ying-chou, reached in a step, was the isle of immortals far in the Eastern Ocean.

Happy Talk [is]: 七言樂語聯句

Li O:
  When the River of Suffering's crossed, 苦河既濟真僧喜
    and the true monk rejoices,
Yen Chen-ch'ing:
  Or when new friends fill your table, 新知滿座笑相視
    with laughing looks exchanged,
Chiao-jan:
  Or when an old campaigner comes home, 戍客歸來見妻子
    and sees his wife and children,
Chang Chien:
  Or when a student on vacation 學生放假偷向市
    steals off to the marketplace.
                [43157]

Gluttonous Talk 七言饞語聯句

Li O:
  Plucking a dumpling, he licks his fingers, 拈餤舐指不知休
    he cannot stop himself;
Yen Chen-ch'ing:
  He stands expectant at the barbeque, 欲炙侍立涎交流
    the drool oozing down;
Chao-jan:
  Passing the butcher's shop, he chews grandly— 過屠大嚼肯知羞
    does he feel no shame?
Chang Chien:
  Sure—he can force himself to hold back a moment 食店門外強淹留
    at restaurant door.
                [43158]

In all these cases Chang Chien is the man with the "punch line." Though such verses hardly represent the glory of T'ang poetry, this kind of poetic play was surely more widely practiced than is evidenced in extant poetry. Wei Ying-wu, for example, does have a pair of similar poems: "Hard Talk" (09421) and "Easy Talk" (09422). But poems of this sort were often excluded from a poet's formal collection and preserved only in anecdotal sources.

Linked verse was not limited to playful topics and *yung-wu*: a group of poets might turn to a more "serious" topic, as in the following *huai-ku* linked verse, written at the temple of Hsiang Yü, the general who competed with the Han founder to destroy the Ch'in Dynasty.

The Ancient Temple of Hsiang Yü 項王古祠聯句

P'an Shu:
  Windblown dust gathers in the abandoned temple, 遺廟風塵積
  Years and months eat away at the grass-grown path. 荒途歲月侵

Chiao-jan:
　The bright soul now is grown silent,　　　　　英靈今寂寞
　His guardian figures still brood darkly.　　　　容衛尚森沈
T'ang Heng:
　Where now, his ambition for Ch'u's hegemony?　霸楚志何在
　Still his deeds were so great in bringing down Ch'in.　平秦功亦深
P'an Shu:
　The feudal lords submitted, then deserted him;　諸侯歸復背
　Through the histories, past lasts on to the present.　青史古將今
Chiao-jan:
　The stars were arrayed, his fate was settled,　　星聚分己定
　Heaven destroyed him—what avail was his might?　天亡力豈任
T'ang Heng:
　If we may offer him white artemisia gathered,　采繁如可薦
　We'll lift wine in libation and sprinkle it　　舉酒灑空林
　　in the deserted forest.
　　　　　　[43242]

According to the traditional interpretation of *Shih* 13, the "white artemisia" was a proper ritual offering. In this verse the poets were not competing in cleverness but working together to produce a poem as unified as that by any single poet.

顧況

KU K'UANG

The mood and form of Wu's mountains and streams possess a clear beauteousness and marvelous allure: the strange stones of Great Lake, the crimson fruits of Lake Tung-t'ing, the clear cry of the crane at Hua-t'ing, and all the Buddhist temples at Tiger Hill and Indian Mountain winding in succession, a splendor unrivaled. From all this Ku K'uang emerged, uniting its etherial clarity in his nature, binding its cold purity/waves in his substance, hatching forth its fresh appearance in his lines. Especially in his aloof songs and long poems he burst forth boldly and with extreme vigor, everywhere piercing the very heart of Heaven and passing up beside the moon. Not commonly attained were those unexpected phrases that so startled readers—these are most pleasing. Li Po and Tu Fu are dead—who but you could be their peer?
　　　　　　　　　Huang-fu Shih, "Preface to the Poems of Ku K'uang" [8]

　　In the mannered rhetoric of the Mid-T'ang, Huang-fu Shih excessively praises a poet of an earlier generation for that poet's own excess. The literary values of the Han Yü circle can be heard clearly here, particularly the values of Huang-fu Shih. Prefaces can rarely be trusted for balanced evaluations of a poet's work, particularly in a case like this, when Ku K'uang's filial son,

Ku Fei-hsiung 顧非熊, had requested the preface in tears from Huang-fu Shih, who had known Ku K'uang in his youth. But if the preface errs in enthusiasm, it also reveals a Mid-T'ang writer looking back over the later eighth century, ignoring the monks and capital poets, and finding there a writer whose interests paralleled those of his own age. The survival of poets like Wei Ying-wu and Ku K'uang, relatively minor figures in their own age, was probably due in part to the admiration of Mid-T'ang writers. Wei Ying-wu's talent was more multifaceted, and his work survived the eccentricities of Mid-T'ang taste. But while Ku K'uang's poems might have had special appeal to the Mid-T'ang, interest in them waned as Mid-T'ang values waned.

Huang-fu Shih saw in Ku K'uang the tutelary spirit of the south-eastern landscape, an embodiment of the recent literary past when the Southeast was an important center of poetry. In fact, Ku K'uang was one of the most anomalous figures of the later eighth century. Ku was from Su-chou and passed the *chin-shih* in 757; he lived to a ripe old age and died probably sometime in the late 790s (13721). Though in the Southeast Ku K'uang developed a passing acquaintance with Chu Fang and Wei Ying-wu, he seems to have had no association at all with most of the capital poets. Both in the capital and in the Southeast, Ku was closely associated with Confucian intellectuals Li Mi 李泌, Liu Hun 柳渾, and Liu Tai-chen 劉太眞; the last two were linked to the great midcentury intellectuals like Hsiao Ying-shih and Yüan Te-hsiu.

Ku K'uang was known both as a poet and as an artist, but he seems to have been most famous for his quick wit and sharp tongue. His drollery is usually mentioned without supporting examples, and many of the examples that do survive are suspect. The patronage of Li Mi and Liu Hun obtained for Ku several minor posts in the central government, but after the death of Li Mi, Ku was demoted to a low provincial post in Kiangsu, supposedly on account of an offense occasioned by his sarcasm. In fact, one version of the story of his demotion suggests that the cause was an unkind comment on the death of his patron. After giving up his provincial post, Ku K'uang lived the rest of his life in the Southeast, in the same general area where Chiao-jan and Wei Ying-wu were active.

Even if we cannot entirely trust its authenticity, the following anecdote probably reveals the kind of jest that earned Ku enemies. A certain provincial graduate had composed the line (47716–17):

I halted my horse and climbed the mountain's fold, 　　　　駐馬上山阿

and was trying unsuccessfully to produce a proper capping line. Ku capped it for him:

Breezes came, the fragrance of shit wafting everywhere. 　　　　風來屎氣多

Ku may have been referring to the literary qualities of the graduate's line (a common metaphorical mode in linked verses and poem exchanges), but he may have simply been intruding some playful scatology into a high "poetic" style.

Another story, cited in the preface to Ku's *Hua-yang chi* 華陽集 (*Ssu-k'u ch'üan-shu chen-pen*, ed.), provides a more decorous example of Ku's wit. Young Po Chü-yi had sent Ku a poem as an introduction, and Ku is said to have punned on Po's given name Chü-yi (居易, "reside-easy," actually from the *Chung-yung* in the *Li-chi*): "Chü-yi—in Ch'ang-an everything is so expensive that 'residing' there long will not be 'easy' at all." But when Ku read Po Chü-yi's famous early poem "Grass on the Ancient Plain" (22409):

Wildfires do not burn it all away,   野火燒不盡
And the spring wind blows it to life again.   春風吹又生

Ku said, "On the other hand, with lines like these residing there may not be so hard. I teased him before, but now I'll sing his praises."

Ku K'uang's collection was once in twenty *chüan*, of which over two hundred and thirty poems are extant, along with some interesting prose pieces. Among the prose pieces are prefaces to the collections of several earlier poets. Ku's *fu-ku* associations can be clearly seen in a series of eleven archaic poems in the tradition of "filling in the lyrics of lost ancient songs" (13572–83). These are provided with short prefaces stating the ethical significance of the poems, and though they are of only minimal literary interest, they constitute a link between the archaic experiments of Yüan Chieh and Hsiao Ying-shih and the culmination of T'ang archaic poetry in Han Yü's "Lute Songs" (17780–87).

Ku K'uang was singularly ungifted as an occasional poet in regulated verse. In his quatrains he often aimed for the lovely simplicity of Wang Wei, as in the programmatic series "Fourteen Poems on the Lin-p'ing Bank" 臨平塢雜詞 (13706–19), but Ku was even less successful in the Wang Wei style than the contemporary capital poets. Ku's true talent lay in *yüeh-fu* and the heptasyllabic song. In these can be heard echoes of first- and second-generation poets, particularly of Li Po. Ku's pentasyllabic *yüeh-fu* "Song of the Abandoned Wife" (13583) was even erroneously included in Li Po's collection.

Ku K'uang was intensely aware of the poetry of the K'ai-yüan and T'ien-pao. The impulse to recreate and outdo his predecessors is strong in his poetry and particularly in his songs. His "Song on Attendant Li's Performance on the Harp" (13650) is a tour de force in musical description and can be read with Wang Ch'ang-ling's fine harp song in the background (06739). Ku's "Song of Yellow Crane Tower: Sending Off Tu-ku Chu"

(13658) should be read with Ts'ui Hao's famous poem (06244) and Li Po's imitation of it (08569). Ku's "The Cascade of Lu Mountain: Sending Off Li Ku" (13659) should be read with Li Po's famous poems on the cascade (08750–51) in the background.

If the reader of the mid-eighth century saw in Li Po's work "a strangeness on top of strangeness," Ku K'uang sought an even more extreme strangeness: the boldness of his imagery anticipated the work of Meng Chiao, Han Yü, and Li Ho. It was certainly this descriptive boldness that attracted Huang-fu Shih to Ku's work. Ku usually used traditional song themes, but his treatment often possesses an almost hallucinatory aura.

Song of the Young Nobles	公子行
A gallant and a rake,	輕薄兒
His face white as jade,	面如玉
In the purple lanes the breeze of spring enwraps his horse's feet.	紫陌春風纏馬足
On the hanging gold of his paired stirrups thread peregrines fly,	雙鐙懸金縷鶻飛
His long gown, pierced by snow, strapping in living rhinos.	長衫刺雪生犀束
Green ash trees line the road, their shade is just become full,	綠槐夾道陰初成
How many joints of coral, the match of shooting stars?	珊瑚幾節敵流星
Rosy flesh, fluttered by wind, and wine rays feral,	紅肌拂拂酒光獰
And on the avenues at the back he pushes the ranks of the *chin-wu* guard.	當街背拉金吾行
At dawn he strolls to the thundering roll as the sound of the drums begins;	朝遊鼕鼕鼓聲發
In evening strolls to the thundering roll as the sound of the drums is ending.	暮遊鼕鼕鼓聲絕
Once in his gates he's unwilling to alone ascend to the hall,	入門不肯自升堂
A lovely lady supports his steps in the moonlight of golden stairs.	美人扶踏金階月
[13621]	

Behind this poem lay a long tradition of sensual description of the life of young noblemen in the capital, but in Ku's poem the rapid shifting of unusual descriptive details lends the theme a distorted perspective that it never before had. In seventh-century and early-eighth-century treatments the theme usually closed with some lament for the transience of human pleasures, but Ku K'uang turns to the evocative closing image of late-eighth-century poetry, here transformed into an eerie scene of drunkenness.

The *yüeh-fu* "Hard Traveling" 行路難 often produced poems in which the mood was one of near hysteria; in Ku K'uang's version the distress at some unnamed malaise reaches the point of raving:

Have you not seen them	君不見
Bearing snow to block up a well,	擔雪塞井空用力
spending their strength in vain,	
Or steaming pebbles to be their rice—	炊砂作飯豈堪食
how shall they ever eat it?	
For a lifetime a faithful heart	一生肝膽向人盡
has been exhausted for others,	
And those who recognized it were worse	相識不如不相識
than those who recognized it not.	
From the winter green of trees there hangs	冬青樹上挂凌霄
the transempyrean vine,	
At the year's close its flowers wither,	歲晏花凋樹不凋
but the tree does not.	
Each of every living thing	凡物各自有根本
has its own root, its nature;	
The planted grain will never grow	種禾終不生豆苗
the sprouts of beans.	
Hard traveling, traveling hard,	行路難
Where are there level roads?	何處是平道
Whoever's heart is untroubled	中心無事當富貴
must be noble and rich,	
As now I look on you,	今日看君顏色好
the well-being in your face.	

[13627]

Ku K'uang's wildness is closer to the bluster of Mid-T'ang poets like Ma Yi and Lu T'ung than to the genius of Han Yü, Meng Chiao, and Li Ho. But Ku's impulse to extreme positions was the symptom of a deeper dissatisfaction with the limits of conventional poetry. And it was out of that dissatisfaction that the Mid-T'ang grew.

16

韋應物

Wei Ying-wu
An Elegy for the High T'ang

Since the Sung Dynasty Wei Ying-wu has been considered primarily as a great landscape poet—with Wang Wei, Meng Hao-jan, and Liu Tsung-yüan, one of the four T'ang masters of natural description and the reclusive mode. This view had its roots in the ninth century and became commonplace in the Sung. In Wei's poetry, Sung critics saw a gift for the limpid, serene style to which many Sung writers themselves aspired. According to Chu Hsi 朱喜, Wei Ying-wu was superior even to Meng Hao-jan and Wang Wei by his "absence of sound, visual appearance, smell, and taste."[1] Wei's poetry was seen to possess a plainness that did not draw the reader by sensual attraction, a natural language in which "not a single word was consciously 'fashioned.'"[2] As was often the case in the Sung, the "mirror" of the T'ang was polished so brightly that the Sung reader saw in it primarily the reflection of his own face.

T'ang views of Wei Ying-wu were more varied: Wei was a multi-faceted poet in whom a reader easily found what he came to seek, and T'ang readers brought to his work a wide range of concerns. Consonant with the southeastern defense of the poetry of the Southern Dynasties, Liu T'ai-chen wrote to Wei:

Ku K'uang came and showed me your "Banquet in the Prefectural Library" [08907]. I was amazed that the expression of sentiments could unite such richness and such nobility. During the Liu-Sung and Ch'i dynasties, Shen Yüeh, Hsieh Ling-yün, Hsieh T'iao, Wu Yün, and Ho Hsün first reached the essence of the natural principles of things and their significance. Thus, in their accurate delineation of emotion and in their use of natural phenomena as subjects, they fulfilled the precepts of the Poets [of the *Shih-ching*]. Later writers lost the source, but you have controlled their tendency to break from the channel in the wrong direction. "Music Master Chih assuming office; The First *Shih*'s Coda" [*Analects* VII.15]— these I see in your writing.[3]

Later-eighth-century writers were remarkably free in their variations on the supposedly invariable principles of *fu-ku*: Like a *fu-ku* poet, Wei Ying-wu is seen to "restore" a lost poetic glory; but as in Chiao-jan's criticism, the lost height of poetry is located not in antiquity but in the Liu-Sung and Ch'i. To a *fu-ku* writer like Ch'en Tzu-ang or Yüan Chieh, a more unorthodox position can scarcely be imagined.

Po Chü-yi saw a very different Wei Ying-wu. While still in his teens, Po had met Wei, and he greatly admired the older poet. In later years, Po was to see in Wei's heptasyllabic songs the antecedents of his own "New Yüeh-fu," and in Wei's occasional poems, he found the gracious ease that characterized his own occasional poetry. It was this latter view of Wei's occasional poetry which Sung critics amplified.

In recent years the songs of Wei Ying-wu have gone beyond mere dazzling description to closely approach the principles of *hsing* and *feng* [from the "Great Preface" of the *Shih*: *hsing* is an affective image to elicit moral response, while *feng* was traditionally interpreted as covert social criticism]. Moreover, his pentasyllabic poetry is characterized by a lofty grace and calm limpidity. He constitutes a style in his own right. Who of those who grasp the writing brush these days are up to his work? And while he was alive no one honored him greatly.[4]

In Wei Ying-wu, Po Chü-yi heard a *yüeh-fu* voice criticizing specific social abuses; Meng Chiao, with his radical *fu-ku* concerns, saw the exemplar of an ancient literary severity that possessed almost canonical authority through the *fu-ku* principles that informed it. As in Liu T'ai-chen's letter, the model of Hsieh Ling-yün is important, but Meng Chiao's Hsieh/Wei is altogether different from Liu's:

To Governor Wei of Su-chou (19855)   贈蘇州韋郎中使君

Master Hsieh chants a single note,	謝客吟一聲
Frost falls, the ears of the crowd hear more clearly.	霜落羣聽清
His writing bears the suppleness of Primal Essence,	文含元氣柔
And he drums all things easily into movement.	鼓動萬物輕
A fine tree, planted in accord to its nature,	嘉木依性植
Will never grow any warped boughs.	曲枝亦不生
Dust specks—the lines of Yü Hsin, Hsü Ling;	塵埃徐庾詞
Gold and jade—the fame of the Ts'ao's, of Liu Chen.	金玉曹劉名
His works are wrought with grace and uprightness,	章句作雅正
So our mountains and rivers grow more luminous.	江山益鮮明

Here the terms of the Confucian moral order and the praise of Chien-an poets signal a resurgence of the strict interpretation of *fu-ku* and an opposition to the contemporary tolerance for the poetry of the later Southern Dynasties. Consonant with Meng Chiao's version of Wei, the Late T'ang critic Chang Wei places Wei Ying-wu second only to Meng Yün-ch'ing as the master of "noble ancientness and lofty abstruseness" 高古奧逸.[5]

Each of the preceding views can be justified in Wei Ying-wu's poetry, nor are they entirely contradictory. Like Tu Fu and Chiao-jan, Wei Ying-wu wrote in a wide variety of styles; however, he lacked Tu Fu's strong unifying identity or Chiao-jan's literary-historical sense of the integrity of period styles. But despite his failure to develop a fully coherent poetic identity, he was the most talented poet writing between the death of Tu Fu and the rise of Meng Chiao and Han Yü in the 790s. His variety foreshadowed many Mid-T'ang interests, but "foreshadowed" may be the wrong word: Wei's poetry was admired by and certainly influenced the important poets of the Mid-T'ang: Han Yü, Meng Chiao, and Po Chü-yi.

Wei Ying-wu was born probably in 736 or 737; his clan had been one of the most powerful capital families during the seventh and early eighth centuries.[6] As a youth Wei served in the Imperial Guard, and after the rebellion he entered the Imperial Academy. But probably because of the Wei clan's declining fortunes, the poet never rose high in office, as had his forebearers. Some of his earliest poetry dates from 763, when Wei was assistant subprefect in Lo-yang. These early poems contain a new kind of *fu-ku* voice that was to be adopted by young Meng Chiao several decades later. Characteristic of this style are opening evaluative metaphors used almost like aphorisms, a straightforward prosaic diction, certain kinds of repetition, and explicit statement of principles (e.g., 09359, 09407). In the following poem from 765, Wei requested to be relieved of his post:

The square bore will not admit the circular,	方鑿不受圓
Straight wood will not form a wheel:	直木不爲輪
Capabilities measured, each has his own use,	揆材各有用
To belie one's nature is to cause suffering.	反性生苦辛
The waist-snapping bow is not my vocation,	折腰非吾事
Drinking ice water, not my kind of poverty.	飲冰非吾貧
I submit my resignation, lie in the empty lodge,	休告臥空館
Nurse my illness, now free from the raucous dust.	養病絕囂塵
The free-wandering fish form into schools,	遊魚自成族
Birds of the wilds too have their flocks.	野鳥亦有羣

[09316]

Though echoes of this unmistakable style appear throughout Wei's poetic career, most datable poems entirely in the style came from the 760s. The style is neither the domesticated High T'ang *ku-feng* nor the radically archaic poetry of writers like Yüan Chieh; its closest analogue is in the poetry of Meng Yün-ch'ing, whom Wei met once and admired greatly (09165).

The events of the decade that followed Wei's resignation are obscure, but in 775 Wei burst into activity again with a series of nineteen elegies on the death of his wife (09203–21): these were written in a more conventional *ku-feng* style, though the metaphors of his earlier *fu-ku* poems still appeared. Couplets like the following were to have numerous echoes in the poetry of Meng Chiao (09203):

The white, dyed, is turned utterly black;　　　　染白一爲黑
The wood, burned, is become wholly ash.　　　　焚木盡成灰

T'ang readers found a moving eloquence in such direct metaphors, a primitive simplicity that was the *fu-ku* counterpart of the authenticity sought by more "artful" poets.

　　　Like Yüan Chieh, Wei Ying-wu eventually turned to a more conservative grace in his later reclusive landscape poetry, but during the 760s and 770s (which, except for his brief service in Lo-yang, Wei probably spent in or around Ch'ang-an), his work was at great variance with contemporary capital poetry. It was not an age for originality, and Wei's poetry seems scarcely to have been noticed by the famous poets of the day. The role of the outsider had strong links to *fu-ku* poetics, and it was a role that attracted Wei—though it is difficult to imagine any member of the Wei clan as an outsider in capital society. True worth is overlooked in a world that honors the ostentatious and superficially attractive: this theme had a long tradition and many guises in the T'ang, but Wei Ying-wu gave it a novel and amusing expression in a song about a fashionable tavern in Ch'ang-an.

Song of the Wineshop　　　　　　　　　　　酒肆行

Where men of power buy their wine　　　　　豪家沽酒長安陌
　　on the lanes of Ch'ang-an,
One morning a great building rose　　　　　　一旦起樓高百尺
　　a hundred feet high.
With sparkling emerald latticework　　　　　碧疏玲瓏合春風
　　filled with winds of spring,
Its name in silver, bright-colored pennons　　銀題彩幟邀上客
　　to invite the honored guest.
Behind, you look out on the Rose Phoenix Towers,　迴瞻丹鳳闕
Ahead, you can see Lo-yu Park—　　　　　　直視樂遊苑
Its praises are sung everywhere,　　　　　　四方稱賞名已高
　　its fame has become great,
Horse and coach from Five Mounds suburb　　五陵車馬無近遠
　　come regardless of distance.
The sunlit scene spreads far and wide　　　　晴景悠揚三月天
　　through the skies of May,
Peach blossoms flutter across the trays,　　　桃花飄俎柳垂筵
　　willows hang over the mats—
A flurry of strings, the shrill pipes　　　　　繁絲急管一時合
　　play together in concert,

And other taverns, neighboring inns—
    how silent they have become!
The innkeeper is insatiable,
    wants the profits all to himself,
And the price of a hundred bushels of grain
    is spent on a single cup.
First comes strong wine, then the thin,
    thus the clients are robbed,
But the drinkers know much of fame,
    and little they know of taste.

Deep behind another gate, an unknown brew
    to which clients rarely come:
All the year through, the finest strong wine
    whose quality doesn't change.
But the drinkers of Ch'ang-an
    go jostling on in vain
And pass it by on the roadside—
    How can its worth be known?
              [09387]

他壚鄰肆何寂然
主人無厭且專利
百斛須臾一杯費
初釀後薄爲大偷
飲者知名不知味

深門潛醞客來稀
終歲醇釀味不移
長安酒徒空擾擾
路傍過去那得知

During the late 770s, Wei Ying-wu held office in the district administration of the Ch'ang-an region, but with the fall of his patron, the prefect Li Kan, Wei retired to a small estate west of the capital. In 781 the poet returned to the government to serve a brief period in the central administration. The poems from these years begin to show the "lofty grace and calm limpidity" for which Wei was best known in later ages. It may be significant that also during this period there are indications of casual relationships with the capital poets Ch'i Chung-fou and Hsia-hou Shen.

Though his use of *fu-ku* styles and themes diminished, Wei never truly wrote in the capital poetic style. Wei was more comfortable writing *ku-shih*—not the *ku-shih* of *fu-ku* poetry, but a *ku-shih* that blended descriptive elements of regulated poetry, echoes of Tsin and early Southern Dynasties poetry, and discursive *ku-shih* modes.

The Meditation Hut at Shan-fu Temple: For Various
    Gentlemen

善福精舍示諸生

Murky and heavy, the shadows of fine trees,
Clear dew in the night scene's gloom.
Somberly now, all things grow still,
And the high tower seems a shadowy peak.
Here in this silent, mysterious place
How can worldly fame, past experience intrude?
In Dharma's marvels we think not of return,
Alone here, embrace a pure, unanxious mood.

湛湛嘉樹陰
清露夜景沈
悄然羣物寂
高閣似陰岑
方以玄默處
豈爲名跡侵
法妙不知歸
獨此抱沖襟

In the fasting hut there is nothing more   齋舍無餘物
Than earthen vessels and single sheets: 陶器與單衾
Often these gentlemen sit here in a row,   諸生時列坐
Their shared passion—how wind fills the forest.   共愛風滿林

[08960]

    After losing his post in the capital in 782, Wei served three term in provincial posts in the lower Yangtze region: in Ch'u-chou, Chiang-chou, and Su-chou. It was during his final term in Su-chou that Wei seems to have developed the acquaintance of southeasterners like Meng Chiao and Chiao-jan. Wei probably died in 791, shortly after his Su-chou term expired. By those last years, he had probably achieved a modest poetic reputation. The laudatory comments by Liu T'ai-chen, Meng Chiao, and Chiao-jan (44439) indicate sincere appreciation, but it was a local fame, and there is no evidence that his work received the more prestigious admiration of capital circles. Kao Chung-wu did not include Wei in the *Chung-hsing hsien-ch'i chi*, and Po Chü-yi specifically stated that Wei's reputation was not established until after his death.

    The poems Wei wrote in the Southeast after 782 contain his most famous works, among which are the kind of poems that Chu Hsi would have praised as having "not a single word consciously 'fashioned.'" Wei's small corpus of quatrains has been particularly admired. In contrast to his longer discursive poems in the *Wen-hsüan* style, Wei's quatrains have the controlled simplicity typical of the eighth century. The following is from Wei's tenure in Ch'u-chou:

Spending the Night in Yung-yang: To the Taoist   宿永陽寄璨律師
   Rule-Master Ts'an

I know that tonight far away   遙知郡齋夜
   by the prefectural library
The freezing snow is encasing pine and bamboo.   凍雪封松竹
At one moment a monk from the mountains comes,   時有山僧來
Hangs up his lantern, spends the night there alone.   懸燈獨自宿

[09012]

Such speculation on a faraway scene appeared often in Wei's later poetry, as in the famous:

Autumn Night: To Ch'iu Tan   秋夜寄丘二十二員外

My thoughts of you belong to this autumn night   懷君屬秋夜
As I stroll and chant to the cold sky.   散步詠涼天
The mountains are empty, a pine cone falls—   山空松子落
I'm sure the recluse is not asleep either.   幽人應未眠

[09027]

However, in the same period Wei Ying-wu wrote lush banquet poems like the piece so admired by Ku K'uang and Liu T'ai-chen:

At the Prefectural Library in the Rain: Banqueting   郡齋雨中與諸文士燕集
  with Various Literary Men

The guards, a dark mass of painted pikes,	兵衛森畫戟
As we feast reclining, a clear scent hangs in air.	宴寢凝清香
Then from over the sea, the wind and rain arrive,	海上風雨至
And we stroll through the cool of pond and tower.	逍遙池閣涼
A troublesome malady recently melted away,	煩疴近消散
And fine guests once again fill my hall.	嘉賓復滿堂
I'm ashamed that I dwell so loftily	自慙居處崇
That I cannot observe my people's welfare,	未覩斯民康
When principle is grasped, dilemmas are put aside;	理會是非遣
When one's nature is fulfilled, act and form are forgotten.	性達形跡忘
Though fresh meat is forbidden by season,	鮮肥屬時禁
Fruits and vegetables fortunately can be enjoyed.	蔬果幸見嘗
One moment I drink a cup of wine,	俯飲一杯酒
The next moment hear compositions, gold and jade.	仰聆金玉章
The spirit rejoices, the body feels light,	神歡體自輕
The imagination ready to soar over winds.	意欲凌風翔
Wu is rich in history and culture,	吳中盛文史
Its many talents now pour out literary wealth.	羣彥今汪洋
Now I realize that the land of Great Marches	方知大藩地
Should not be thought of as the frontier,	豈曰財賦疆
good for tax and tribute.	

[08907]

Poems like this suffer greatly in translation: the rich formality of the Liu-Sung and Ch'i style, so admired by Liu T'ai-chen, has no effective counterpart in English. But surely one important reason for Ku K'uang's admiration was Wei's bow to regional loyalties in the closing praise of the Southeast.

Wei Ying-wu's ten-*chüan* corpus of over 530 poems is arranged primarily by subgenre, beginning with *ku-feng* poems and ending with heptasyllabic songs. The first *chüan* contains two *ku-feng* series: twelve "Imitations of the Old Poems" (08869–80) and five "Unclassified Poems" (08881–85). Though some elements of Wei's *ku-feng* poems are characteristically T'ang, on the whole Wei was more faithful in his recreation of the second-century style than his T'ang predecessors. He captured the autumn mode of Chien-an and Wei poetry as well as the indefinite persona of the Nineteen Old Poems and the tradition of "unclassified poems" (*tsa-shih*). The sixth of Wei's "Imitations of the Old Poems" 擬古詩 is a fine recreation of the Han and Wei *shih*:

The moon is full, the autumn nights grow longer,   月滿秋夜長
In the north forests startled crows cry out.   驚烏號北林
Still high overhead, the star river stretches,   天河橫未落
The Dipper's handle set to southwest.   斗柄當西南
The cold cricket grieves deep in the chambers,   寒蛩悲洞房
Of the notes of sweet birds, none remain.   好鳥無遺音
Then one evening gusts of autumn come,   商飆一夕至
One who sleeps alone thinks fondly on thick quilts.   獨宿懷重衾
Past loves are a thousand miles farther each day,   舊交日千里
Blocked from my drifting and my sinking.   隔我浮與沈
Man's life is not as the grass and trees;   人生豈草木
Still the season's changes can stir the heart.   寒暑移此心
                            [08874]

The relation between literary history and the arrangement of a collection can be seen in the poems immediately following the two *ku-feng* series; in accord with the history of poetry, there are two imitations of T'ao Ch'ien (08886, 08889) and two quatrains imitating Ho Hsün (08887–88). Critics have often emphasized Wei's relationship to T'ao Ch'ien, and echoes of T'ao do occur throughout Wei's collection. But in contrast to K'ai-yüan poets like Wang Wei and Ch'u Kuang-hsi, Wei Ying-wu did not treat T'ao as the dominant figure of past poetry: like his contemporaries, Wei had a wider appreciation of the poetic past than his K'ai-yüan predecessors, and Hsieh Ling-yün, Wang Wei, and other poets can be heard as often in Wei's poetry as T'ao Ch'ien.

The greater part of Wei Ying-wu's collection consists of occasional poems arranged by subgenre. The eighth *chüan* contains poems on miscellaneous topics, poems of indefinite occasion, and *yung-wu*. Songs and *yüeh-fu* comprise the last two *chüan* of Wei's collection, and it was here that Po Chü-yi saw the antecedents of his own "New *Yüeh-fu*." Wei, Chiao-jan, and Ku K'uang were the only poets of the period who wrote extensively in the song genre; however, the three poets used the form very differently. Like Li Po, Ku K'uang drew on the set modal associations of the heptasyllabic song to project a manner of spontaneity and wild eccentricity; with his literary historical interests, Chiao-jan sought to recreate the variety of the T'ien-pao song, but was particularly fond of the occasional use of the song, as found in Ts'en Shen's work. In some cases, Wei Ying-wu also treated traditional *yüeh-fu* themes in the Kai-yüan and T'ien-pao manner, but many of his *yüeh-fu* and songs were innovative—historical songs, songs of personal reminiscences, and songs on contemporary subjects, such as "Song of the Wineshop."

Topical criticism appears clearly in a few of Wei's songs (e.g., 09420), but Po Chü-yi's comments indicate that he saw this as the general characteristic of the whole corpus.[7] To arrive at topical interpretations, the majority of Wei's songs must be treated allegorically (as is not the case in the majority of Po's "New *Yüeh-fu*"). In certain cases, a topical allegorical interpretation is probably justified, as in the songs on birds (09389–91), but their precise referents are uncertain. Many other songs consist simply of the poet looking back fondly on his youth during Hsüan-tsung's reign; and if there are hints of disapproval of the great emperor, these are inseparable from a private wistfulness that is quite distinct from the censorious stance of the social balladeer. Another group of songs involve immortals and Han themes: these might be taken to refer to Hsüan-tsung's excesses, but when these themes are used in topical criticism, their target is so broad that it is impossible to know which of many inept reigns Wei might have been criticizing. In the following poem, the third of the "Miscellaneous Songs of Han Wu-ti" 漢武帝雜歌, a hyperbole that potentially might criticize martial excess is indistinguishable from a hyperbole praising martial prowess:

The Han Son of Heaven	漢天子
Observed the custom, went from his southern fiefs:	觀風自南國
His boat sailed the great river, stood mountain-fast, would not advance—	浮舟大江屹不前
A great dragon sought combat, the wind and waves turned black.	蛟龍索鬪風波黑
His Majesty was in the prime of years, gifted with warlike powers.	春秋方壯雄武才
He bent his bow, shouted at waves, and their hill-like ridges opened wide.	彎弧叱浪連山開
The onlookers shuddered with alarm, a crowd of a million,	愕然觀者千萬衆
Then, raising their pennons, they shouted together as his first shot struck home:	擧麾齊呼一矢中
The dead dragon floated up, divinity no longer,	死蛟浮出不復靈
For the thousand-mile line of sterns and prows the river's waters cleared.	舳艫千里江水清
The echoes of their mighty drums lasted several days,	鼓鼙餘響數日在
The sea god sank deep under, fish and turtles leapt in fear.	天吳深入魚鼈驚
To his left, a tz'u-fei huntmaster to bring down the frost-white wings,	左有伙飛落霜翮
To his right was the "orphan" to pierce the armor of rhino hide.	右有孤兒貫犀革
So why was it He stood over the depths and shot the dragon himself?	何爲臨深親射蛟

To show forth his might and thereby awe
   the spirits of feudal lords.

示威以奪諸侯魄

His might was to be feared,

威可畏

His nobility to be reverenced,

皇可尊

Of his stockade hunts in level fields
   writings still tell,

平田校獵書猶陳

But of this day why did his attendants not speak?

此日從臣何不言

The renown of his might was singular,
   spreading through all time—

獨有威聲振千古

Don't you see why his successor honored him,
   posthumously, called him Wu-ti, Martial Emperor.

君不見後嗣尊爲武

          [09412]

Poems on immortals and on imperial history might take on topical reference to contemporary politics or they might treat their subjects for their own sake. But Wei did show a great interest in historical themes in their own right. His song for the famous suicide of "Green Pearl" is unusual in that it treats the events in a larger historical context (09394). Another example of Wei's historical interests is his song on "The Stone Drums" (09402), ancient monoliths inscribed with poems. Wei Ying-wu's version was the inspiration for Han Yü's more famous and more richly developed poem on the same subject (17913).

   Like Chiao-jan's interest in literary history, Wei Ying-wu's songs on historical subjects are a manifestation of a backward gaze that dominated the later eighth century. Wei often wrote of the days of Hsüan-tsung as a splendor irrevocably past: even more than Tu Fu, Wei spoke with an elegiac voice, a voice of memories. The theme of man's impermanence amid the continuity of nature leaves the ruins of the *huai-ku* and appears in a temple revisited.

Climbing to the Heights of Pao-yi Temple: Re-
   visiting a Place of Former Travels

登寶意寺上方舊遊

Azure ridges, incense terraces
   emerge midsky,

翠嶺香臺出半天

Misty trees of a million homes
   fill the sunlit stream.

萬家煙樹滿晴川

The monks live nearby.
   I do not recognize them.

諸僧近住不相識

I sit and listen to the faint bell
   recording the years gone by.

坐聽微鐘記往年

          [09236]

The quatrain opens with a High T'ang vision of a landscape, everywhere echoing poems from earlier in the century. But Wei sees this landscape among strangers, among monks different from those he had known in his younger years. Poetically and personally it is a landscape of memories, and the temple bell, which reminded so many of his predecessors of the vacuity of existence, becomes for Wei the occasion for retrospect.

Wei Ying-wu's sense of distance from the recent poetic past often led to an ironic breakdown in the values of High T'ang poetry. "Planting melons" became the vocation of the Ch'in marquis of Tung-ling after losing his fief with the fall of the Ch'in. In the poetry of the K'ai-yüan and T'ien-pao, he was the exemplar of the contented recluse who lived at peace with his changed status. In Wei Ying-wu's poetry we find the failed melon planter, the man who embodies those honored traits of spontaneity and unconcern, but whose very perfection of the ideal causes him to fail in farming. The poet laughs at himself in the poem, but it is an ironic laugh of failed values, a laugh that the High T'ang farmer-recluse cannot be realized in experience. It is not the gentle humor of Tu Fu, juxtaposing grand values with personal failure; it laughs at the failure of the values themselves. The poem strongly foreshadows the Mid-T'ang and has parallels throughout the work of Han Yü, Meng Chiao, and Po Chü-yi.

Planting Melons 種瓜

When I act as my nature dictates, I'm careless;	率性方鹵莽
I'm too easygoing to keep my life in order.	理生尤自疏
This year I tried planting melons,	今年學種瓜
In a garden overrun with weeds.	園圃多荒蕪
All kinds of plants shared the rain and dew,	眾草同雨露
And the new sprouts alone were shaded over.	新苗獨翳如
And just when spring work was most pressing,	直以春窘迫
The time passed—I had no chance to hoe.	過時不得鋤
Farmhands laughed at this foolish waste,	田家笑枉費
As day by day the plot grew more bare.	日夕轉空虛
This really isn't work for a person like me—	信非吾儕事
So I'll just read the books of the ancients.	且讀古人書

[09360]

The humorous, casual tone of T'ao Ch'ien survives in a poem where farmer and reader are no longer the same person, as they were in T'ao Ch'ien. The Taoist principle of nonintervention can ruin a garden.

High T'ang poems often closed with an epiphany of the landscape, a scene that seemed to embody the theme, mood, or resolution of the main body of the poem. Wei Ying-wu also experienced such epiphanies, but often they are located "elsewhere," in some other place or some other time, absolutely separated from the poet. The vision becomes a desire, a mark of something lacking.

Climbing the Tower   登樓

Daily I climb this tower and gaze,   茲樓日登眺
The drifting years slip secretly away.   流歲暗蹉跎
Just now I'm sick of governing Huai-nan,   坐厭淮南守
Now when in autumn hills the red trees are so many.   秋山紅樹多
                          [09241]

The vision of the landscape can also be placed in a larger context of a moment
lost or to be lost. The High T'ang poet sought the recluse, and when the
recluse was not at home, the poet could assimilate the essence of reclusion
simply by being in the recluse's natural surroundings (e.g., 08680, 06200).
In the following poem by Wei, the landscape vision is a "weekend" experience, the one day off in ten; the poet returns from the world of the
recluse not satisfied but "marveling"; and what Wei "marvels" at is not
a life-changing experience of nature but the subject of a poem.

On a Day Off Going to Meet Censor Wang and   休暇日訪王侍御不遇
    Not Finding Him In

Nine days of hustle and bustle,   九日驅馳一日閒
    one day of peace;
I sought you, didn't find you,   尋君不遇又空還
    and returned home in vain.
But I marveled how poetic reverie   怪來詩思清人骨
    clears a man to the bones,
Where your gate faces the cold stream   門對寒流雪滿山
    and snow fills the mountains.
                          [09172]

The hermit's melons do not grow, and the landscape makes you want to
"change your life" only on your day off. The Mid-T'ang too felt the
diminished power of the landscape and natural order; again and again
they framed the epiphany of nature in the quotidian. Thus, Han Yü found
it difficult to climb "South Mountains" and wanted to reach the summit
because (17790):

When I reckon up the days and months tied to my post,   拘官計日月
I want to go on for I won't be able to come here again.   欲進不可又

    Anomalies had begun to fracture the integrated and harmonious worlds
of High T'ang poetry. Throughout Wei's poetry can be found faint marks
of alienation from the old values of poetry. In his imagination Wang Wei
could participate in the life of farmers; the modern reader may see the
difference between the sophisticated aristocrat and the fieldhands that
worked for him, but to Wang's cool eye all were part of a harmoniously

functioning whole. Echoing Wang Wei's agrarian poems, Wei Ying-wu too looked to the fundamental values of agrarian society, but Wei was equally conscious of his own distance from that world.

Watching the Fieldhands 觀田家

In the light rains all plants spring anew, 微雨眾卉新
With a thunderclap waking from hibernation starts. 一雷驚蟄始
How many days can the fieldhands take their ease? 田家幾日閑
Plowing and planting begin from this time. 耕種從此起
All the strong men are out in the wilds, 丁壯俱在野
The gardens too they go to prepare. 場圃亦就理
When they go home, the sun is always sinking, 歸來景常晏
As they water their calves at the western stream. 飲犢西澗水
Toil from hunger brings them no suffering, 飢劬不自苦
Rich moisture in ground brings them joy. 膏澤且為喜
But there's no great store in government granaries, 倉廩無宿儲
And public labor is still required. 徭役猶未已
Now I feel shame at men who do not plow— 方慚不耕者
Our salary, our food, comes from those villages. 祿食出閭里
[09263]

Wei's poem looks back to the agrarian poetry of Wang Wei and Ch'u Kuang-hsi, but it is even closer to the Mid-T'ang, to the famous poem by Po Chü-yi which it inspired, "Watching the Reapers" (21748).

Traditional critics have been attracted primarily by Wei's fluency and stylistic control, by the serene mood with its "absence of sound, visual appearance, smell, or taste." Critics could have found these qualities in many poets of the later eighth century. The true attraction of Wei Ying-wu's poetry may have been in something more disturbing, in his sense of loss combined with a clear vision of what had been lost, as in the following famous poem:

To a Taoist on Ch'üan-chiao Mountain 寄全椒山中道士

This morning the district library is chill, 今朝郡齋冷
I suddenly think on one who sojourns in the hills: 忽念山中客
In the bed of a stream he bundles kindling, 澗底束荊薪
And goes back to boil white stones. 歸來煮白石
I would take this single gourdful of wine 欲持一瓢酒
To comfort him afar on an evening of wind and rain. 遠慰風雨夕
But fallen leaves fill the deserted mountains— 落葉滿空山
Where can I find the traces of his passage? 何處尋行跡
[09003]

In the poetry of this later-born Wei, the deities of the upper heavens no longer stroll about the shimmering earth as they had at Wei Ssu-li's villa in the first decades of the century. The ideal recluse still does exist, but he can be seen only in vision; in the physical world he cannot be tracked down.

Nowhere is the sense of absence and loss stronger than in the most famous of Wei Ying-wu's poems: the poem is often interpreted allegorically, but allegory is brought to the poem only to resolve the disturbing enigma offered the reader at the close of the poem.

West Stream at Ch'u-chou	滁州西澗
Alone I cherish the hidden plants that grow beside the stream,	獨憐幽草澗邊生
Above which the yellow oriole sings deep within the trees.	上有黃鸝深樹鳴
Spring's high water, bearing rain, comes swiftly with evening:	春潮帶雨晚來急
A ferry in the wilds, no one there— the boat crosses by itself.	野渡無人舟自橫

[09369]

The poem develops like a typical High T'ang quatrain, building to a serene, visual epiphany of the natural world. But the natural world the reader sees is all too natural—or perhaps too unnatural—as the unsteered boat cuts across the current. One may explained the image allegorically; one may speculate on the positions of the banks to resolve the enigma. But in the poem the unsteered boat occupies the place of the evocative closing scene of nature, and it is an eerie, animate nature that takes over the functions of absent humanity. That very absence is the focus of interest in the poem.

Wei Ying-wu was not a Mid-T'ang poet: he was still deeply tied to High T'ang styles and themes. But many of his best poems are High T'ang poems with cracks in them, whose beauty lies in their complicating imperfections. In those places where the old values of poetry were beginning to fail, Wei Ying-wu foreshadowed and influenced the great Mid-T'ang poets. If he was the poet whom "no one honored greatly" when he was alive, he spoke precisely to the poetic interests of the succeeding generation.

List of Abbreviations

Ccc	*Ch'ieh-chung chi* 篋中集. See *TjhTs*.
CCh'ens	*Ch'üan Ch'en shih* 全陳詩. See Ting.
CCs	*Ch'üan Ch'i shih* 全齊詩. See Ting.
Chao	Chao Tien-ch'eng 趙殿成, *Wang Mo-chieh ch'üan-chi chien-chu* 王摩詰全集箋注. Kwong chi reprint. Hong Kong, n.d.
Chc	*Chi-hsüan chi* 極玄集. See *TjhTs*.
Chhcc	*Chung-hsing hsien-ch'i chi* 中興閒氣集. See *TjhTs*.
Chiu-chia	*A Concordance to the Poems of Tu Fu.* (containing the Chiu-chia edition) Harvard-Yenching Institute Sinological Index Series, Supplement No. 14, vol. 2. Taipei, 1966.
Ch'ou	Ch'ou Chao-ao 仇兆鰲. *Tu Shao-ling chi hsiang-chu* 杜少陵集詳註. Hong Kong, 1966.
CHs	*Ch'üan Han shih* 全漢詩. See Ting.
Cjc	*Chiao-jan chi* 皎然集. SPTK.
CKhsc	*Ch'u Kuang-hsi shih-chi* 儲光羲詩集. *Ssu-k'u ch'üan-shu chen-pen.*
CKkc	*Ch'ien K'ao-kung chi* 錢考功集. SPTK.
CLs	*Ch'üan Liang shih* 全梁詩. See Ting.
CLw	*Ch'üan Liang wen* 全梁文. Reprint of 1894 edition. Taipei, 1969.
CPCs	*Ch'üan Pei-Chou shih* 全北周詩. See Ting.
CSks	*Ch'üan San-kuo shih* 全三國詩. See Ting.
CSs	*Ch'üan Sung shih* 全宋詩. See Ting.
CTs	*Ch'üan T'ang shih* 全唐詩. Peking, 1960.
CTsins	*Ch'üan Tsin shih* 全晉詩. See Ting.
Hanabusa	Hanabusa Hideki 花房英樹. *A Concordance to the Poems of Li Po.* Kyoto, 1957.
HfJsc	*Huang-fu Jan shih-chi* 皇甫冉詩集. SPTK III.
HHs	*Hou-Han shu* 後漢書. Chung-hua standard histories.
HJAS	*Harvard Journal of Asiatic Studies.*
Hs	*Han shu* 漢書. Chung-hua standard histories.
Hsiao	Hsiao Chi-tsung 蕭繼宗. *Meng Hao-jan shih-shuo* 孟浩然詩説. Taipei, 1961.
HTs	*Hsin T'ang shu* 新唐書. Chung-hua standard histories.

Hyylc	*Ho-yüeh ying-ling chi* 河嶽英靈集. See *TjhTs*.
Juan	Juan T'ing-yü 阮廷瑜. *Kao Ch'ang-shih shih chiao-chu* 高尚侍詩校注. Taipei, 1965.
KCsc	*Kao Ch'ang-shih shih chi* 高常侍詩集. *SPTK*.
Khc	*Kuo-hsiu chi* 國秀集. See *TjhTs*.
KHyc	*Ku Hua-yang chi* 顧華陽集. *Ssu-k'u ch'üan-shu chen-pen*.
Li	Li Kuo-sheng 李國勝. *Wang Ch'ang-ling shih chiao-chu* 王昌齡詩校注. Taipei, 1973.
LScsc	*Liu Sui-chou shih-chi* 劉隨州詩集. *SPTK*.
Ltsh	*Li-tai shih-hua* 歷代詩話. Taipei, 1956.
MC	Middle Chinese.
MHjc	*Meng Hao-jan chi* 孟浩然集. *SPTK*.
Sc	*Shih chi* 史記. Chung-hua standard histories.
SPPY	*Ssu-pu pei-yao* 四部備要.
SPTK	*Ssu-pu ts'ung-k'an* 四部叢刊.
Stcyths	*Shih tz'u ch'ü yü-tz'u hui-shih* 詩詞曲語詞滙釋. Shanghai, 1962.
Syhc	*Sou-yü hsiao-chi* 搜玉小集. See *TjhTs*.
TCcs	*Ts'en Chia-chou shih* 岑嘉州詩. *SPTK*.
Ting	Ting Fu-pao 丁福保, ed. *Ch'üan Han San-kuo Tsin Nan-pei ch'ao shih* 全漢三國晉南北朝詩. Yi-wen reprint of 1916 ed. Taipei, n.d.
TjhTs	*T'ang-jen hsüan T'ang-shih* 唐人選唐詩. Hong Kong, 1958.
Tscs	*T'ang-shih chi-shih* 唐詩紀事. Taipei, 1960.
Tsh	*T'ang shih hsüan (Tōshi sen)* 唐詩選. Japanese notes and translation. *Kanshi taikei*, vols. 7–8.
Tshhc	*T'ang-seng hung-hsiu chi* 唐僧弘秀集. *Ssu-k'u ch'üan-shu chen-pen* 四庫全書珍本 ed.
Tsin	*Tsin shu* 晉書. Chung-hua standard histories.
TSscy	*T'ang Sung shih chü-yao* 唐宋詩舉要. Taipei, 1960.
Ttc	*Ts'ai-tiao chi* 才調集. See *TjhTs*.
Twt	*T'ang wen ts'ui* 唐文粹. *SPTK*.
Wang	Wang Ch'i 王琦. *Li T'ai-po ch'üan-chi chiao-chu* 李太白全集校注. Kwong chi reprint. Hong Kong, n.d.
WCcc	*Wei Chiang-chou chi* 韋江州集. *SPTK*.
Wh	*Wen hsüan* 文選. *SPTK*.
Whtl	*Wen-hsin tiao-lung hsin-shu* 文心雕龍新書. Peking, 1951.
WsTjcc	*Wan-shou T'ang-jen chüeh-chü* 萬首唐人絕句. Reprint Peking, 1955.
Wycc	*Wang yu-ch'eng chi* 王右丞集. *SPTK*.
Wyyh	*Wen-yüan ying-hua* 文苑英華. Reprint of Wan-li ed. Taipei, 1965.
Yfsc	*Yüeh-fu shih-chi* 樂府詩集. *SPTK*.

Yhc   *Yu-hsüan chi* 又玄集. See *TjhTs.*
Yls   *Yü-lan shih* 御覽詩. See *TjhTs.*
YTsc   *Yüan Tz'u-shan chi* 元次山集. Shanghai, 1960.
YTswc   *Yüan Tz'u-shan wen-chi* 元次山文集. *SPTK.*
Yu   Yu Hsin-li 游信利. *Meng Hao-jan chi chien-chu* 孟浩然集箋注.
                  Taipei, 1968.
Ywlc   *Yi-wen lei-chü* 藝文類聚. Taipei, 1974.

Notes to the Text

INTRODUCTION

1 Most traditional literary historians would have the Mid-T'ang begin after the death of Tu Fu or earlier, directly after the An Lu-shan Rebellion. Although this effectively severs the great High T'ang poets from their less vital successors and although it does correspond to certain political changes, the poets of the later eighth century remained largely within the stylistic and thematic bounds of their predecessors. "High T'ang" is used in this book as a convenient term for the period style; it is not an evaluative designation encompassing only the "height" of that period style.

CHAPTER 1

1 Stephen Owen, *Poetry of the Early T'ang* (New Haven, 1977), pp. 14–22, 153–223, 301–2. Hereafter referred to as Owen.
2 Owen, pp. 303–24.
3 Wang Ting-pao 王定保, *T'ang chih-yen* 唐摭言 (Taipei, 1967), p. 9.
4 For the series of court poems on sending off Chang Yüeh, see *Wyyh* 177. 3a–9a.
5 Owen, pp. 271–73.

CHAPTER 2

1 For examples and a further discussion of Kuo Chen's poetry, see Owen, pp. 291–93, 299, 316–17.
2 Quoted in *Tscs*, p. 81.
3 Owen, pp. 311–14.
4 Hu Chen-heng, *T'ang-yin kuei-chien* 唐音癸籤 (Taipei, 1964), p. 39.
5 For a more extensive discussion of Chang Yüeh's poetry, see Owen, pp. 387–412.
6 For a discussion of the first poem of this pair (07557), see Owen, pp. 419–20.
7 E.g., 02739; see Owen, pp. 96–97.
8 Though "Reaching the Foot of Pei-ku Mountain" is preserved in a slightly later source than "Mood of the Southland," other indications of the priority of the "Reaching the Foot of Pei-ku Mountain" version reinforce the sense of stylistic progression. When poems became popular and were widely circulated, general titles would often be substituted for occasional titles. It is unlikely that an occasional title ("Reaching the Foot of Pei-ku Mountain") would be substituted for a general title ("Mood of the Southland").
9 *Chiu T'ang-shu* 190B.
10 Ibid.
11 *Tscs*, p. 616.
12 See Cheng Chi-hsien, *Analyse formelle de l'oeuvre d'un auteur des T'ang: Zhang Ruo-xu* (Paris, 1970).
13 Because the capital was the ultimate arbiter of poetic taste and determined the survival of collections, very little is known of truly regional poetry in the T'ang. There are, however, many hints of lively poetic activity in the Southeast during the first half of the eighth century. Yin Fan, the compiler of the *Ho-yüeh ying-ling chi*, also compiled the lost *Tan-yang chi* 丹陽集, an

anthology of poets from the region around modern Chiang-ning in Kiangsu. Local poets who achieved fame in the capital (Pao Jung, Ch'u Kuang-hsi) were represented, but there were also many poets who seem never to have left the region.

Another interesting hint is found in a passage by Meng Chiao, himself a southeasterner (19966):

> K'ai-yüan monks in the dialect of Wu,
> With tones and rhymes, lofty and smooth.

Provided that Meng Chiao is not referring to monks from the many "K'ai-yüan Temples," this suggests poetic activity in the southeastern monasteries even before their prominence in the later eighth century. If there was a true dialect poetry at this time, I have been able to find no examples of it. Of course, dialect pronouns and particles were common in the southeastern literary mode, but Meng's reference to "tones and rhymes" suggests something more. A true dialectical poetry would have appeared most clearly in the rhymes, but it is possible that poems could have been composed and chanted in Wu pronounciation with allowances made to keep the rhyme categories of the poetic koine.

14 From the various sources, it appears that Liu Hsi-yi lived from 651 to 679; flourished in the 750s; and still managed to be Sung Chih-wen's nephew, which in the normal succession of generations, would place his short life in the last decades of the seventh and first decades of the eighth century. The dates 651–79 have been reconstructed around a single *chin-shih* date in the late and unreliable *T'ang ts'ai-tzu chuan*. The floruit of the early 750s is given in the *Ming-huang tsa-lu*, cited in the *T'ang-shih chi-shih* (*SPTK*) 25.7b. That date can be disregarded, because Liu is listed as flourishing with several other poets, clearly deceased by 750.

A date in the late seventh to early eighth century is suggested by the following evidence. Three of Liu's poems appear in the *Kuo-hsiu chi*, which contains the work of no other poet who wrote exclusively in the seventh century. Also, both the *Kuo-hsiu chi* and the *Wen-yüan ying-hua* (in its subsections) arrange poets in roughly chronological order and in both cases, the positioning of Liu's poems suggests a late-seventh or early-eighth-century date. Furthermore, the recipient of at least one of Liu's poems (04337) can be identified with some probability: Yin Yao, whose death was lamented by Wang Wei. (See *T'ang-jen hang-ti-lu*, p. 94.) If, as is commonly supposed, Yin Yao died in the late 740s, an eighth-century date for Liu Hsi-yi's poem is strongly suggested. Finally, Liu's presumed relationship to Sung Chih-wen would make the late seventh and early eighth centuries likely.

Other factors are more convincing to the literary historian than to the historical biographer. Liu Hsi-yi's poetry is filled with themes, structural devices, and turns of phrase that do not appear elsewhere until the eighth century; for instance, his poem on hearing music from an unseen source (04315). Taken singly, none of these pieces of evidence would warrant revision of the traditionally accepted dates, but together they make a strong case that Liu's period of poetic activity was in the first decades of the eighth century.

15 Hsin Wen-fang 辛文房, *T'ang ts'ai-tzu chuan* 唐才子傳 (Taipei, 1964), p. 10.

16 Owen, pp. 115–18.

CHAPTER 3

1 Compare 04010 for Chung-tsung and 03989 for Hsüan-tsung, both by Su T'ing.

2 See Owen, pp. 256–73.

3 *Tscs*, p. 231.

4 *Ssu-k'ung Piao-sheng wen-chi* (*SPTK*) 2.4a.

CHAPTER 4

1 There was a roughly contemporary programmatic series in Ch'u song meter by a single poet, Lu Hung-yi 盧鴻一 (05740–49).

2 The *Wang Stream Collection* is presumed to bear some relation to a painting of the estate by Wang. The painting survives only in copies. For a study of the relationship between the poems and the

painting, see Kobayashi Taichirō, *Ōi no seigai to geijutsu* (Osaka, 1944), pp. 202–79.

3 *CLs* 8.1a.

4 Owen, pp. 364–66.

5 There is another, radically different way in which this kind of closing image may be read. The issue is whether the last line signifies more than itself. Using "Rapids by the Luan Trees" as an example, this alternative reading would see in the egret an epiphany of the natural world, a presence that is important purely for its own sake and without meaning beyond its self-contained existence. Such a mode of reading has roots in Sung poetics, with its fascination with the "accidental." This theory is presented—not as a mode of reading but as a universal principle of Chinese poetry—by Wai-lim Yip in his *Hiding the Universe: Poems by Wang Wei* (New York: Grossman, 1972) and later expanded in *Chinese Poetry: Major Modes and Genres* (Berkeley: University of California Press, 1976).

The mode of reading suggested in our chapter would have the image of the egret as an enigma, as an indecipherable omen whose actions seem to incarnate some larger pattern of the natural order: the image cannot be reduced to a single meaning, but it points beyond itself to some larger significance. Though the Yip reading of such images as "pure phenomenon" cannot be excluded entirely, the strong tradition of pointed closure in the quatrain (often making some clever, metaphorical point through some object or scene) suggests that a T'ang reader would have looked for some larger significance. Once the issue of "other significance" is raised in the reader's mind, the image can no longer stand as "pure phenomenon"; it can only be indecipherable, an omen and an enigma.

6 For example, the antithesis of "love" is "hate," but its negation is "neutrality."

7 Owen, pp. 104–15.

8 A serious use of past poetry must be distinguished from the natural intertextuality of the Chinese poetic language. The language used by Chinese poets was largely a language constituted of usages in other poems. All T'ang poets drew lines, images, and themes from past poetry; some of these echoes are conscious, but the majority were probably either unconscious or half-remembered. A large proportion of the "citations" that catch the learned commentator's eye are either commonplaces that were associated strongly with no single earlier text, or the poet's reading, thoroughly digested and reappearing in the process of composition.

The myth of the infallible memory of all Chinese writers begs challenge; contrast with the modern Westerner's modest capabilities of memory blurs the distinction between a good, trained memory and superhuman eidetic recall. The Chinese literary language was grounded in texts and particular usages rather than in open paradigms, and the fact that its phrases usually have earlier textual sources developed naturally out of an educational process based on memorization (not on the "grammar" of the Western pedagogic tradition—the open paradigm). It is precisely this *general* textuality of the literary language which forces us to recognize that not every use of a phrase with an earlier source involves "reference" to that source.

Knowing when the literary past *is* being consciously called to the reader's attention is a much more complicated problem. In different periods certain subgenres, certain phrases, and certain kinds of phrase are "coded" with pastness and may call to mind an author, modal associations of an age, or the full context of an earlier source. I do not believe any general rule can be deduced for their operation; rather, they can only be learned on a case-by-case basis from wide reading.

To use a phrase Ts'ao Chih used probably would not call to mind the Chien-an, but to begin a poem with the location formula X *yu* Y, "at X there is Y," does call to mind the Chien-an and Wei. One learns this association from repeated use of the formula in *ku-feng* poems and poems with other Chien-an and Wei associations. To speak of "homing birds" will not necessarily call to mind T'ao Ch'ien (though in certain contexts, as in a poem on T'ao Ch'ien, it could); but to speak of "chrysanthemums by the hedge" will almost inevitable call T'ao Ch'ien to mind. There is a wide gradation between phrases that always refer to a source and phrases that never, in themselves, refer to their source. To judge the value of such usages, the source text must be known, but the source text in itself is far less important than a sensitivity to parallel usages in works contemporary with the referring text. Contemporary context is the "dominant": a phrase that in Tu Fu is an echo of the Southern Dynasties style is, in the twelfth century, more likely an echo of Tu Fu. See also James Hightower, "Allusion in the Poetry of T'ao Ch'ien," in Cyril Birch, ed., *Studies in Chinese Literary Genres* (Berkeley, 1974), pp. 108–32.

9 Suzuki Shūji, *Tōdai shijin ron* (Tokyo, 1973), 1: 110–25.

CHAPTER 5

1 Many modern anthologists and literary historians (e.g., Hsü Wen-yü 許文雨, *T'ang-shih chi-chieh* 唐詩集解 [Taipei, 1954], 2: 1) speak of a "Wang Wei group," referring to those of Wang's contemporaries and "spiritual relations" who were interested in the theme of reclusion and in landscape description. The grouping of capital poets here is a larger and looser entity which tries to reflect literary-historical realities more accurately.

2 象雅而不素, 有大體, 得國士之風. This text follows *Tscs* (*SPTK* version) 26.2a. The present edition of the *Hyylc* reads 象雅而平, 素有大體: "Hsiang is decorous and level, always in the grand style." Not only is X 而不 Y a common descriptive pattern, the *su-t'i* 素體, "flat style," was a commonly recognized, though usually positive, mode.

3 See *Wen fu* 文賦, 11.91–93.

4 *Liu Meng-te wen-chi* (*SPTK*) 23.10b–11b.

5 *Tscs*, p. 284.

6 For an example of how such a quatrain structure sounded to later readers, see Chou Pi's discussion of "Second Couplet Parallel" 後對 in the *San-t'i shih* 三體詩; Murakami Tetsumi, *Santai shi* (Tokyo, 1966), p. 204.

7 *Tscs*, p. 311.

8 The note that Ch'u was from Shantung is clearly erroneous or, at best, respresents his clan's original home.

9 See 06471–75. The tone of these poems suggests failed political ambitions.

10 This preference may have been because of several factors: provincials' lack of ease in a regulated poetry which was primarily a phenomenon of the capital upper class (perhaps related to a difficulty of developing an "ear" for tonal balance in the capital dialect—compositional occasions demanding strict adherence to tonal regulation would have been most common in the capital, and a poet who grew up in the Southeast would have less opportunity to practice regulated forms and have them judged.) or the association of southeastern themes and the whole southeastern mode with nonregulated forms.

11 Of course, to speak of T'ao Ch'ien's poetry as "old style" verse is an anachronism, though it is an anachronism true to the way T'ang readers would have heard T'ao's poetry.

12 A good contrast can be found in comparison with the rustic vignettes of the Sung poet Fan Ch'eng-ta, in which naturalistic details of rural life are celebrated for their own sake.

CHAPTER 6

1 For instance, 07764 for line 1; 07767 for line 4; 07752 for line 8.

2 For the main outlines of Meng Hao-jan's life, I have followed the reconstruction of Meng's biography by Daniel Bryant in *The High T'ang Poet Meng Hao-jan: Studies in Biography and Textual History* (Diss., University of British Columbia, 1978), supplemented by Ch'en Yi-hsin's *Meng Hao-jan shih-chi k'ao-pien, Wen-shih* 4 (1965): 41–74. I have, however, preferred to leave in uncertainty certain conclusions that they admit seen probable rather than certain.

3 *P'i-tzu wen-sou* (*SPTK*) 7.11a.

4 *Hou-shan shih-hua* 後山詩話, 9a, in *Li-tai shih-hua* (Taipei, 1956).

5 Bryant, *The High T'ang Poet Meng Hao-jan* contains an excellent discussion of the text and editions of Meng Hao-jan's poetry.

　　Very little is known about the compilation and circulation of poem collections in the eighth century. Poems on social occasions were given to the addressee or sometimes written on walls, but the poet himself usually seems to have kept a copy. Editions of a poet's works were usually put together late in his life or posthumously, and the circulation of poems during a poet's lifetime was based on copies of the originals, on copies of copies, or, I suspect, a poem was often written down from memory, after hearing it recited. (The last conjecture would help explain the large number of homophonic variants.) The texts of poems preserved in anthologies and anecdotal collections suggest how vulnerable poems were to textual variation through this method of circulation. Whether poets kept a *complete* set of their poems or not is uncertain, but some poets (Li Po, for example) did compile a collection that they wanted "published." When Wang Chin noted that Wang Wei's prerebellion poetry was largely lost, he was probably referring to such a master set of poems. To reconstitute his brother's collection, Wang Chin would have had to use the prerebellion poems of Wang Wei that he himself possessed, as well as gathering other poems from their original recipients, from walls, and from copies in circulation.

It is possible that poets willfully excluded some poems from their collected works, but given the tendency of Chinese editors to include everything, especially when editing a posthumous collection such aesthetic exclusions are unlikely. Most K'ai-yüan and T'ien-pao poets are known to have been present at many occasions from which poems do not survive. In addition, incomplete poem exchanges indicate missing poems. Therefore, we know that the editions of most K'ai-yüan and T'ien-pao, poets are incomplete, but whether that incompleteness is due to aesthetic exclusions, to the loss of master copies in the An Lu-shan Rebellion, or to the failure to keep complete master copies is, in most cases, uncertain.

The master copy, whether complete or incomplete, would be entrusted to an "editor," usually a relative or close friend, to copy out with a preface. The degree of textual care involved in such "editing" is uncertain. In many cases, a filial descendant would prepare the collection from a set of poems handed down in the family; in such cases, the descendant would usually request a preface from some well-known contemporary writer. Then editions would often be presented to the Imperial Library, where presumably they would serve as the stable texts from which copies could be made. Individual poems, however, might still be circulated and memorized quite apart from the standard text, and such very popular poems are often characterized by numerous variants and sometimes by problems of attribution. Anthologies compiled during a poet's lifetime often have texts quite different from the standard editions, and one may presume this was because anthologies were compiled from circulating manuscripts.

The facts presented in occasional titles are often crucial to the understanding of a poem; however, there seems to have been very little sense of the *textual* integrity of titles. In their own sets, poets probably kept titles as notes on the occasion of a poem, but it seems likely that when someone took a poem from a wall, he would include that fact as part of the title (*t'i* 題 "written on the wall of . . ."). Poems with wide circulation would often develop nonoccasional titles, and one should be suspicious of such titles given to clearly occasional poems. Furthermore, it seems probable that when poems were gathered up for collections, individuals might claim that they or some relative was the addressee. In short, in occasional poems what we call the "title" is more properly "information on the circumstances of composition." This probably accounts for much of the variation in poem titles and may also affect many poems whose titles do not have variants.

There are also problems of forgery and mistaken attribution when gathering poems for a collection or anthology. The anthology fragment from Tun-huang contains some glaring misattributions and suggests a laxness in many "popular" anthologies. Poets like Li Po, who possessed what seemed an easily identifiable manner, inevitably attracted the attribution of certain kinds of poems.

Excessive caution is unnecessary when a collection has a secure early manuscript history (e.g., Wang Wei's collection). In the case of Meng Hao-jan, it is possible that Meng Hsi-jan's collection of his brother's poems found its way into later editions (though only the Wang Shih-yüan and Wei T'ao prefaces survive). We know that later in the eighth century, a poet's family members felt a responsibility to preserve and disseminate their relative's work, and even if they were not able to keep a complete collection, they could be expected to have good texts. But if our present editions are based entirely on Wang Shih-yüan's edition—put together from scattered sources by a stranger—there were probably numerous errors in text and attribution even before the problems of printed editions. In such cases, the use of titles as biographical evidence presents clear dangers.

6 For a more extensive discussion of this poem, see Hans Frankel, *The Flowering Plum and the Palace Lady* (New Haven, 1976), pp. 111–13.

CHAPTER 7

1 Wen I-to, *Wen I-to ch'üan-chi* (Hong Kong, 1968), 4: 198. Wen presumably arrived at this date from a poem in which Wang Wei referred to Wang Ch'ang-ling as "elder brother": from this we may infer only that Wang Ch'ang-ling was born before Wang Wei, the date of whose birth is also in dispute.

2 T'an Yu-hsüeh, *Wang Ch'ang-ling hsing-nien k'ao*, reprinted in *T'ang-shih yen-chiu lun-wen chi* (Hong Kong, 1970), vol. 3.

3 Owen, pp. 406–8.

4 Owen, pp. 320–21.

CHAPTER 8

1 The earlier Szechwanese poet is Ch'en Tzu-ang: see 04417. 5; 04452. 5; and Owen, pp. 158–62.

2 Kuo Yün-p'eng 郭雲鵬 ed., *Fen-lei p'ien-tz'u Li T'ai-po wen* 分類編次李太白文 (Taipei, 1969), 26.17a–17b.

3 For an excellent summary of the long and heated controversy over Li Po's background, see Suzuki Shūji, *Tōdai shijin ron* (Tokyo, 1973), 1: 253–61.

4 For an extensive discussion of the tradition and values of the bravo, see James Liu, *The Chinese Knight-Errant* (Chicago, 1967).

5 *Hsi-ching tsa-chi* (*SPTK*) 2.4a.

6 Ibid., 3.5a.

7 Kuo Yün-p'eng, op. cit., 26.16a.

8 *Ting-an wen-chi pu-p'ien* (*SPTK*), 2.19a–19b.

9 For a discussion of spurious attributions, see Chan Ying, *Li Po shih lun-ts'ung* (Peking, 1957), pp. 45–63.

10 No reader after 755 could miss the parallel to Hsüan-tsung and Yang Kuei-fei in "Song of the Roosting Crows." Ho Chih-chang's comment may well have been preserved because readers presumed that he was referring to the analogy to the contemporary political situation. "Song of the Roosting Crows," however, certainly antedates the An Lu-shan Rebellion, probably by at least a decade and a half; there is no evidence, apart from Li Po's later claim to prophetic foresight, that the song had any topical intent. Moreover, the quality of Ho Chih-chang's comments have other analogues in the T'ien-pao.

11 *Pen-shih shih* 本事詩, 7b, in *Hsü Li-tai shih-hua* (Taipei: Yi-wen, n.d.).

12 For a translation and discussion of these two poems, see Elling O. Eide, "On Li Po," in Arthur Wright and Denis Twitchett, ed., *Perspectives on the T'ang* (New Haven, 1973), pp. 367–87.

13 *Pao-shih chi* (*SPTK*) 8.3a–3b.

14 For a brief discussion of Wu Yün, see Edward Schafer, *Pacing the Void* (Berkeley, 1977), pp. 244–46.

CHAPTER 9

1 Here and elsewhere in Kao's biography, I follow Juan T'ing-yü, *Kao Shih nien-p'u*, in Juan's *Kao Ch'ang-shih shih chiao-chu* (Taipei, 1965), pp. 9–38.

2 *Po-shih Ch'ang-ch'ing chi* (*SPTK*) 3.1a.

3 Lu K'an-ju 陸侃如 and Feng Yüan-chün 馮沅君, *Chung-kuo shih-shih* 中國詩史 (Hong Kong, 1968), pp. 440–41.

PART TWO: INTRODUCTION

1 Most modern literary historians would consider Yü Hsin a major talent, but the kind of reverence accorded to Yü by Tu Fu and later readers was not at all in evidence in the K'ai-yüan.

CHAPTER 10

1 Cheng Chen-to, [*Ch'a-t'u-pen*] *Chung-kuo wen-hsüeh shih* (Hong Kong, n.d.), pp. 324–25.

2 Suzuki Shūji, op. cit., 1: 423.

3 For a detailed discussion of this event, see Maeno Naoaki, *Tōdai no shijintachi* (Tokyo, 1971), pp. 88–149.

CHAPTER 11

1 In the biographical sections I have usually followed only those points on which there is consensus and good evidence. A more detailed biography can be found in William Hung, *Tu Fu: China's Greatest Poet* (Cambridge, 1952).
2 An excellent study of the sequence is Kao Yu-kung's and Mei Tsu-lin's "Tu Fu's 'Autumn Meditations': An Exercise in Linguistic Criticism," *HJAS* 28 (1968): 44–80.
3 The Jen Hua poems appear first in the *Yu-hsüan chi* (preface 900), and if they are genuine, they are unique pieces of poetry for the mid-eighth century. In style and sentiment they seem to me more typical of the early ninth century.
4 A poem of "indefinite occasion" is one that purports to represent a specific moment, an occasion, but the definition of the occasion in the title and the treatment of the occasion in the poem are general. Thus, the poem is both about the specific moment and the general case; for instance, "Recent Clearing" and "Autumn Night." The term is mine and not a Chinese distinction.
5 This mode probably grew out of the use of *yung-wu* topics in occasional heptasyllabic songs, an increasingly common practice during the T'ien-pao.
6 There was no T'ang concept of "fine arts" that linked dance, painting, and poetry, but they were unified by their associations as manifestations of refinement and civilization.

CHAPTER 12

1 For Yüan Chieh's biography I follow Sun Wang, *Yüan Tz'u-shan nien-p'u* in *Yüan Tz'u-shan chi* (Peking, 1957).
2 We must read such heart-rending descriptions of gouging government demands with a degree of skepticism. We must consider the possibility that from the government's point of view, local officials might exaggerate the gravity of the local situation in order to maintain their popularity in a district (and perhaps to protect their own financial interests), thus denying the central government the resources it so desperately needed during its struggle for survival in the 750s and 760s.
3 *TjhTs*, p. 314.
4 For an extensive discussion of this group, see David McMullen, "Historical and Literary Theory in the Mid-Eighth Century," in Arthur Wright and Denis Twitchett ed., *Perspectives on the T'ang* (New Haven, 1973), pp. 307–42.
5 *P'i-ling chi* (*SPTK*) 13.1b–2a.

CHAPTER 13

1 No collection of Wang Chih-huan is included in the *HTs* bibliography, and thus it was probably not in the Imperial Library.

CHAPTER 14

1 *Ying-k'uei lü-sui*, cited in Shen Ping-hsün, *Hsü T'ang shih-hua* (Taipei, 1974), 10.1a.
2 One hundred "Untitled Poems Traveling by River" (12373–472) are sometimes attributed to Ch'ien Ch'i and are included in the *SPTK* edition of his poetry. The evidence that these poems are not by Ch'ien Ch'i but rather by the Late T'ang poet Ch'ien Hu is presented in the *T'ang-yin t'ung-chien* and cited by the compilers of the *Ch'üan T'ang shih*. To their evidence I might add the nineteenth poem of the series (12931), in which the poet speaks of chanting the poetry of Tu Fu, a most unlikely activity for Ch'ien Ch'i.
3 According to the strong authority of Ch'üan Te-yü's funerary inscription, Tai Shu-lun's death occurred in 789. However, several sources give the date of his *chin-shih* as 800. See Nunome Chofu and Nakamura Takahashi, *A Study of the Tang-cai-zi-chuan* (Kyoto, 1972), p. 302. Fur-

thermore, Tai's collection contains poems addressed to the Early T'ang poet Ts'ui Jung (14320) and to Mid-T'ang poets (14325, 14420, 14421, 14460). If we disregard the poem to Ts'ui Jung, it would be possible to resolve these and other anomalies by presuming there were two Tai Shu-lun's: the later Tai would have been a Mid-T'ang poet whose works were mixed in with the earlier, more famous Tai. This, however, would not resolve some strange improprieties in the problem poems; for instance, addressing a heptasyllabic regulated verse to Meng Chiao. It is possible that the poems to Meng Chiao and Liu Yü-hsi were written in those poets' youths, but there are no poems to Tai in Meng's or Liu's collection; had they met the famous Tai Shu-lun, they would surely have written and preserved a poem on the occasion. Furthermore, Tai's poems to them and the other Mid-T'ang poet are suspiciously without toponymn or clan rank. Unfortunately, the most likely explanation is that Tai's collection was put together carelessly at a late date and may contain much unreliable material.

4 This passage is not in all editions of the *Chhcc*; see *TjhTs*, p. 306. The passage is also cited in *Tscs*, p. 456.
5 *Ssu-k'ung Piao-sheng wen-chi* (*SPTK*) 3.3a. It is uncertain whether the last part of the statement was supposed to be by Tai or an explanation of the metaphor by Ssu-k'ung T'u.

CHAPTER 15

1 *Ch'üan Tsai-chih wen-chi* (*SPTK*) appendix, pp. 330–31. Occasional exchange collections like the *Wang Stream Collection* can be seen as the ancestors of the *ch'ang-ho chi*.
2· *Liu Meng-te wen-chi* (*SPTK*) 23.17a–17b.
3 See 23180, cited also in Ichihara Kōkichi, "*Chūtō shoki ni okeru kōsa no shisō ni tsuite*," *Tōhō gakuhō* 28 (1958), p. 222.
4 Kuo Shao-yü, *Chung-kuo wen-hsüeh p'i-p'ing shih* (Taipei, 1969), 1: 207–9.
5 Though there are doubts as to the authenticity of the five-*chüan* edition of the *Shih-shih*, I accept is as Chiao-jan's work. Many sections not in the shorter editions of the *Shih-shih* raise issues of singular interest to poets of the later eighth century. References are to the *Pai-pu ts'ung-shu chi-ch'eng* reprint of the *Shih-wan-chüan-lou ts'ung-shu* edition.
6 This may have been the work listed in the *HTs* bibliography (p. 1624) as *Ta-li-nien Che-tung lien-ch'ang chi* 大歴年浙東聯唱集.
7 For evidence of other linked verses in the period, see *Ch'üan Tsai-chih wen-chi* (*SPTK*) 39.1b–2a and *P'i-ling chi* (*SPTK*) 14.7b–8b. For an extensive discussion of the origin and development of the Chinese linked verse, see David Pollack, *The Chinese Linked Verse* (Diss., Berkeley, 1976).
8 *Huang-fu T'e-cheng wen-chi* (*SPTK*) 2.7b.

CHAPTER 16

1 *Chu-tzu ch'üan-shu* (Imperial preface, 1714), 65.16b.
2 Ibid.
3 *Tscs*, p. 400.
4 *Po-shih Ch'ang-ch'ing chi* (*SPTK*) 27.7b.
5 *Shih-jen chu-k'o t'u* 詩人主客圖, 5b, in *Hsü Li-tai shih-hua* (Taipei: Yi-wen, n.d.).
6 For Wei Ying-wu's biography I have generally followed Thomas Nielson, "Wei Ting-wu: His Life and Career," in Nielson, *A Concordance to the Poetry of Wei Ying-wu* (San Francisco, 1976).
7 For a topical reading of Wei Ying-wu's songs, see Fukazawa Kazayuki, "*I Ōbutsu no kakō*," *Chūgoku Bungaku hō* 24 (1974), pp. 48–74.

Notes to the Poems

INTRODUCTION

In response to the encouragement of some and the insistence of others, I am including my notes to the poems in this volume. These notes are directed both to the intermediate student and to the scholar. The notes treat not only factual identifications, but also discuss matters of text, style, interpretation, semantics, and parallels to other poems. Problems treated in the main body of the volume are not discussed again in these notes; furthermore, with a few exceptions, no notes are given for the numerous couplets and short passages quoted. The format and conventions of the notes are as follows:

1. The Kyoto index number will be given first to identify the poem. Since the notes are given in the sequence of the poem's appearance in the text, a finding list will follow the notes.

2. Following the Kyoto index number are the source texts: these will include the page number in the *Ch'üan T'ang shih* (Peking, 1960), the critical editions used (where applicable), the *SPTK* edition, and sources in early anthologies. For Li Po's poems, the poem number in the Hanabusa index is given for cross-referencing with other editions. The Harvard-Yenching index to Tu Fu's poems provides similar cross-references, correlated to the Chiu-chia edition. I have used the typeset critical editions of the *Tjh Ts* anthologies and *Tscs*. See the list of abbreviations.

3. For texts of the poems, I have followed critical editions when available, and when I deviate from those editions, the fact is mentioned in the notes. Where critical editions have been available, I have made comments on variants only when they were of particular interest. For poems without critical editions, I have given the early textual variants, though omitting obvious errors in poor texts.

4. The rhymes of the poem are given with the line number and the Middle Chinese reconstructions from Hugh Stimson's *T'ang Poetic Vocabulary* (New Haven, 1976). Where *t'ung-yün* are used, I have made a note; otherwise, all the rhymes are *p'ing-shui yün*.

5. After the rhymes, I have in many cases made comments on the tone patterns. Rather than observing a strict division between regulated and "old style" verse, I have treated regulation as couplet based, and note regulated passages in unregulated poems. No note usually indicates an unregulated poem. If a poem is entirely regulated, I simply note "regulated." The term "A" form couplet refers to *p'ing-ch'i* 平起 couplets; "B" form refers to *tse-ch'i* 仄起 couplets.

6. In the section "Title" I will sometimes note secondary discussions of the poem; this is solely for the reader's convenience and is in no way meant to be exhaustive. My main concern in this volume has been to cover the essential primary materials; the voluminous secondary material on some of the better-known poets has been unavoidably slighted.

7. I have tried to use Middle Chinese reconstructions wherever possible in discussing words and phrases. Stimson's reconstructions have been used, and when words do not appear in *T'ang Poetic Vocabulary* I have converted the reconstructions of the *Kuang-yün sheng-hsi* 廣韻聲系 to Stimson's system. Despite the uncertainties of Middle Chinese reconstructions, they reflect the sounds of T'ang poetry more accurately than Mandarin, and their use is a forceful reminder that T'ang poets did not chant their works in a perfect Peking dialect. However, for the sake of the reader's patience and convenience, I have retained the more familiar Wade-Giles for proper names.

8. When making cross-references to other T'ang poems, I have used the Kyoto index number, sometimes with the line number following a decimal point.

9. When a commentator raises a point that is not obvious or when he cites a source that

328

is not common knowledge, I cite him, either in parentheses or in the text of the note. However, such citation is not given for obvious information, such as place-names and biographical information from the standard histories.

10. To avoid redundancy, when a problematic word, phrase, or allusion recurs, I will usually refer the reader to a previous note.

11. I have followed Legge's numbers for references to the *Analects* and *Shu* (though I have followed the commentaries that would have been available in the T'ang). *Shih-ching* poem are identified by their number. Passages from the *Chuang-tzu* are identified by the page, chapter, and line(s) from the text given in the Harvard-Yenching concordance to the *Chuang-tzu*. Passages from the standard histories are identified by their page number in the punctuated Chung-hua editions. *Wen hsüan* texts are cited by their location in that anthology, but all other Han to Sui poems are identified by their location in Ting Fu-pao; I have used a reprint of the early edition rather than the punctuated edition because it is to the early edition that the Harvard-Yenching index of names is correlated.

Notes to the Poems

CHAPTER 2

04771: *CTs*, p. 977; *Chang Yüeh-chih wen-chi (SPTK)*, 5.8a (title only); *Tscs*, p. 199.
Rhymes: 2 *zhiə*, 4 *shiə*. Unregulated.

    1. For 樂無極 *CTs* gives variants 方知樂 (*Tscs*) and 樂無窮. All have approximately the same meaning, and the variation may be due to imperfect reconstruction through oral circulation. *Tzuì-hoù* 醉後 clearly refers to drunkenness itself rather than to the end of drunkenness; cf. 08651.12.
    2. *CTs* gives 全 as variant for 彌. *Miɛ* 彌 may mean "increasingly (better than ...)," but I take it as "fully," describing the state rather than the process.
    3. *Iong* 容 is the poet's "manner" or "bearing." For the use of *zhiɛ* 是, cf. 10539.6. The spontaneity of the poet's dancing and poetry playfully echoes the origin of poetry as described in the "Great Preface" of the *Shih-ching*: "Emotions are stirred within and take form in speech. When speech is inadequate, we speak them in sighs; when sighs are inadequate, we sing them; and when song is inadequate, unconsciously our hands and feet dance and tap them out."

07558: *CTs*, p. 1605; *Khc* in *TjhTs*, p. 139.
Rhymes: 1 *lɑn*, 2 *hɑn*, 4 *qɑn*. Regulated.
Title: Liang-chou was an important military prefecture northwest of Ch'ang-an in modern Kansu
    Province. The melody of the Liang-chou Song (涼州詞 or 涼州歌) was supposedly first brought
    to Ch'ang-an in the K'ai-yüan; see *Yfsc* 79.10b. However, Wang Han's two quatrains are not
    included in the *Yfsc* versions of the song.

    1. Ch'in is the standard poetic term for the capital region. *Xua-děu* 花鳥 indicate spring. The use of *qiəng* 應 is important, because it signals an indirect assumption, letting the reader know that the persona is elsewhere, thinking of Ch'ang-an.
    2. The *ga* 笳 was a small flute or pipe, originally imported from Central Asia and associated with the region. The song *Jiet iɑng-liǒu* 折楊柳 made its first appearance in the Liang Dynasty, supposedly an importation from the North; see *Yfsc* 22.5b. The song was originally classed as a "Nomad Piping Song," and the earliest recorded version goes:

I got on my horse, wouldn't take the whip,	上馬不捉鞭
Instead I broke off a branch of willow.	反拗楊柳枝
I got off my horse, played the horizontal flute,	下馬吹橫笛
Causing terrible grief to the traveler.	愁殺行客兒

Though the music may have been of Central Asian origin, the governing metaphor of the song, its association with parting, depended on a purely Chinese pun between *liou* 留 "stay" and *liǒu* 柳 "willow."
    4. *CTs* reads 意氣 for 氣盡. Though most modern texts of the song follow *CTs*, here I have followed the older *Khc* version. The closure is probably an echo of 02758.

05527: *CTs*, p. 1170; *Hyylc* in *TjhTs*, pp. 108–9; *Khc* in *TjhTs*, p. 186; *Tscs*, p. 220 (*Hyylc* version).
Rhymes: 2 *dzhen*, 4 *huen*, 6 *nen*, 8 *ben*. Regulated.
Title: Pei-ku Mountain 北固 is on the Yangtze close to its mouth, in modern Kiangsu Province.

The *Hyylc* version, entitled 江南春, reads: 南國多新意，東行伺早天，潮平兩岸失，風正一帆懸 (third couplet identical). 從來觀氣象，惟向此中偏. The *Hyylc* version maintains regulation.

    3. The *Hyylc* reading of 失 for 闊 implies that the river is so wide the shores can no longer be seen.

    4. The *jièng* 正 of the wind means that it is blowing in the same direction as the poet's course.

    7–8. The point of the last couplet is that on his travels it will be difficult for letters from home to reach him; however, his own letters can be sent with the migrating geese, bearers of messages, north to Lo-yang.

04335: *CTs*, pp. 885–86; *Syhc* in *TjhTs*, pp. 705–6; *Wyyh* 207.2b–3a; *Tscs*, p. 184; *Yfsc* 41.3a–3b. A somewhat different version of the song appears under the title "Longing for Someone" 有所思, attributed to Sung Chih-wen in *Twt* 18.12b–13a and in the Sung Chih-wen collection (*SPTK* 2nd series) 1.21b–22a. Furthermore, ten of the first twelve lines appear as "Longing for Someone," attributed to Chia Tseng 賈曾, 03860, *Ttc* in *TjhTs*, pp. 590–91. For a discussion of the poem, see Suzuki Shūji 鈴木修次, *Tōdai shijin ron* 唐代詩人論 (Tokyo, 1973), 1: 23–29. The *Tscs* notes the theory that Sung Chih-wen stole the song from Liu, but no early evidence exists to prove the attribution of the poem to either poet. Sung's attack on Liu is mentioned in the *Ta-T'ang hsin-yü* 大唐新語 (Li Mu t'ang ed. of *Pai-hai* 稗海) 8.13b–14a; the *Ta-T'ang hsin-yü* accepts Liu's authorship of the poem under the title *Bhaek-dhou ngyim* 白頭吟 and claims that Sun Yi 孫翌 considered it the best work in his anthology, the *Cheng-sheng chi* 正聲集 (now lost). In his *T'ang-shih pieh-ts'ai chi* 唐詩別裁集 (1973 rpt. of 1763 ed.) 5.4a, Shen Te-ch'ien 沈德潛 disputes the attribution to Liu on the grounds that Sung Chih-wen was the better poet and that the *Ta-T'ang hsin-yü* is an unreliable source. In apparent support of Ch'ien's position, Suzuki (p. 28) notes that Chia Tseng's abbreviated version has the same title as the full version by Sung Chih-wen, and that Chia Tseng had at least one one occasion matched poems with Sung (03852). If, however, Sung and Liu were roughly contemporary and acquainted with one another, Chia could just as easily have known Liu. The most disturbing aspect of the Chia Tseng version is how Wei Hu 韋縠, the compiler of the *Ttc*, could have included such a well-known poem in his anthology under Chia Tseng's name. However, in the *T'ang-shih chi-chieh* 唐詩集解 (Taipei, 1970), Hsü Wen-yü 許文雨 notes (p. 77), that Kuo Mao-ch'ien not only accepts the Liu attribution in the *Yfsc*, he also includes the song under the title *Bhaek-dhou ngyim*, one of the two titles under which the song is attributed to Liu. Given the usual astuteness of Kuo in *yüeh-fu* categories, it seems likely that Kuo discounted the Sung version. In the final analysis, the attribution of the song remains uncertain, though most readers have accepted it as Liu Hsi-yi's, and his seems the better case.

Rhymes: 1 *xua*, 2 *ga*; 3 *shriək*, 4 *siək*; 5 *gǐ*, 6 *dzhǒi*, 8 *xǐ*; 9 *dung*, 10 *biung*, 11 *ziǐ*, 12 *dhung*, 13 *tziǐ*, 14 *qung* (note interlocking rhymes); 15 *len*, 16 *nen*, 18 *dzhen*, 20 *sièn*, 22 *ben*; 23 *zhiə*, 24 *siə*, [25 *dhì*], 26 *byi*. The sixth, ninth, tenth, and twelfth couplets are regulated.

Title: Here I accept the title given in *Syhc*, *Wyyh*, and *Yfsc*; *Tscs* and *CTs* read 代悲白頭翁. *Twt* and the Sung Chih-wen collection have 有所思.

    1. *Tsh* commentaries note that the opening echoes the beginning of the 董嬌饒詩 by 宋子侯: "On the road east of Lo-yang's walls / Peach and plum grow by the roadside" 洛陽城東路，桃李生路旁 (*CHs* 2.15b–16a). Through that echo, and particularly in the mention of Lo-yang, Saitō Shō (*Tsh*) suggests that the opening suggests the Eastern Han. Indeed, a Han setting was common in heptasyllabic songs of the period, and Han Lo-yang is also the setting for 04940 and 05881. By the T'ang, "peach and plum" had become emblems of an ephemeral beauty strongly associated with young women. The association of the flowers with female beauty appears early, in *Shih* 6 and 24. In the biography of Li Kuang, Ssu-ma Ch'ien cites the proverb "Peach and plum do not speak; paths form to them all by themselves" 桃李不言自成蹊; the application is to a moral beauty that attracts people effortlessly (*Sc*, p. 2878). The sensual associations of the image ultimately vanquished its moral dimensions, as in 02762.40: "Together we will spend the night at the courtesans' home, on the path of peach and plum" 共宿娼家桃李蹊; cf. also 03443.37–38, 04148.47.

    3. For 洛陽 the Sung Chih-wen and Chia Tseng versions have the more ornamental 幽閨. For 惜, *CTs* reads 好; the Chia Tseng version reads 愛.

    4. 行逢 is the *Syhc*, *Wyyh*, and *Yfsc* reading; other versions have 坐見. Note that in this

case textual variation takes the form of a categorical pair, especially in the exchange of *haeng* 行 and *dzhuǎ* 坐.

5. For the last four characters of this line, the Chia Tseng version reads 聞君不侍, but as the Chia Tseng version omits the following couplet, the use of *zhià* 侍 leaves this couplet rhymeless. Again we may wonder how Wei Hu could have included the song in this form.

7–8. The Chia Tseng version omits this couplet, probably because its allusiveness shifts attention away from the scene at hand. *Tsh* commentaries note the echo of a couplet from the fourteenth of the "Nineteen Old Poems:"

Ancient tombs are plowed into fields,	古墓犂爲田
Their pines and cypress broken into kindling.	松柏摧爲薪

An interesting possibility in compositional method is that the *Ku-shih* echo led the poet to think of *dhen* 田 in the second line of the couplet. In the *Ku-shih* couplet, the destruction of the *ziong-baek* 松柏 suggests the desecration of the tombs where they were planted; here they are used in their most common function in T'ang poetry as long-lived evergreens in contrast to the ephemeral beauty of peach and plum. Oceans changing places with mulberry fields, an interchange that takes place over vast eons, was a literary commonplace suggesting the impermanence of even the most durable topographical features.

9. For 無復 the Chia Tseng version reads 不共.

10. For 人還 the Chia Tseng version reads 來空. The poet is developing a contrast between the mortality of the individual and permanence through cyclical recurrence. Thus, the ladies sigh facing the flowers, recognizing in them emblems of their own mortality; yet the situation and its general components, ladies and flowers, are recurrent, therefore permanent. What differentiates the recurrent people from the recurrent flowers in the next couplet is, of course, an awareness of their identity, and of that identity's impermanence.

11–12. This couplet ends the Chia Tseng version. The Sung Chih-wen version reads 年季 in both lines for 年年; the Sung version destroys the tonal balance of the couplet. This is supposedly the couplet that Sung Chih-wen coveted. The phrase *nen-nen siuèi-siuèi* 年年歲歲 echoes the closing of Lu Chao-lin's "*Ch'ang-an: ku-yi*" 長安古意 (02762), where every year the cinnamon blossoms fall around Yang Hsiung's secluded dwelling.

13. For another example of "sending the burden" in a heptasyllabic song, see 02761.33. *Hung-ngan* 紅顔 as "ruddy faces" is traced by *Tsh* commentaries to Juan Chi's *Yung-huai* IV 詠懷; there, as in the T'ang, it was an epithet for youth; e.g., 04148.83.

14. For 須 *Tscs* and *CTs* read 應. For 死 one edition of *Tscs* reads 謝, interesting as an example of euphemistic substitution in textual variation.

17. *Gung-tziǎ* 公子 and *hiuɑng-suən* 王孫 appear commonly in songs and *yüeh-fu* as the reckless, aristocratic youth of the capital.

19. *Tscs* and *CTs* read 開 for 文. The Chamberlain 光祿大夫 referred to is Wang Ken 王根, the extravagance of whose estates was said to have infuriated Han Ch'eng-ti; see *Hs* pp. 4023–25. Parks and richly ornamented buildings were often described in terms of brocade.

20. The reference here is to the mansion of the powerful Liang Yi 梁冀, whose walls bore murals of the gods; see *HHs*, pp. 1181–82. Both this and the allusion in the preceding line describe a glory tinged with dangerous excess and portending fall.

21. *Syhc* reads 知己 for 相識. The "sickness" 病 probably refers to the feebleness of old age, which comes on so swiftly it seems to occur in a "single morning," *qit-djiɐu* 一朝. The isolation of the old man may be owing to the deaths of his former companions, but it is more likely the result of the desertion of his admirers after a fall from power, as in Lu Chao-lin 02761.19: "In one morning fallen, no one asks after you" 一朝零落無人問. The situation finds a more sententious expression in Lo Pin-wang 04148.82: "Once ennobled, once humbled—there friendship's feelings are revealed" 一貴一賤交情見; this in turn comes from *Sc*, p. 3114.

22. *Sɑm-chuin* 三春 may refer to the third month, but here it probably refers to the three months of spring. Note the use of *ben* 邊 as a general location marker, as in 05527.8, perhaps for the sake of rhyme.

23. *Qiuɑěn-djiuěn* 宛轉 describes something "bending" or "winding around," and perhaps through the popularity of this song, it became a conventional epithet for "moth (beautiful) eye-

brows." Its most famous occurrence is in Po Chü-yi's *Djhiang-hàn ga* 長恨歌, 22335.38: "The gracefully curving moth eyebrows died before the horses" 宛轉蛾眉馬前死.

24. *Sio-io* 須臾, as in line 21, is to emphasize the swiftness of change. *Hak-biaet* 鶴髮, "crane-hair," is hair that has become white with old age. Though the crane's longevity and whiteness make it a natural association for the white hair of old age, the phrase seems to be a transformation of *hok-biaet* 鵠髮; see *HHs*, p. 950. For an early usage of "crane-hair," see *CLs* 7.17b.

25. *Syhc*, *Wyyh*, and the Sung Chih-wen version read 古 for 舊. The closing *memento mori* is strongly reminiscent of the closing of Wang Po's 03443:

Look where high terraces were in olden days— 君看舊日高臺處
Brown dust rises where there was Po-liang and Copperbird. 柏梁銅雀生黃塵

The phrase *ga-miǒ dhì* 歌舞地 is the source for the use of the phrase in Tu Fu's 11553.7.

26. For 悲 *Wyyh* and the Sung Chih-wen version read 飛. As the cries of evening birds were a standard mark of closure in banquet poetry, so the melancholy cries of birds at a deserted site became one way to close a *huai-ku*; cf. 02781.7.

CHAPTER 3

02949: *CTs*, pp. 567–68; *Wyyh* 312.2a–2b; *Ch'ü-chiang hsien-sheng wen-chi (SPTK)* 3.4a; *Ch'ü-chiang chi (SPPY)* 2.14b.

Rhymes: 2 *tziɛng*, 4 *dzhiɛng*, 6 *shraɛng*, 8 *zhiɛng*, 10 *qiɛng*, 12 *jiɛng*, 14 *iuɛng*, 16 *miaɛng*, 18 *bhiaɛng*. Allowing for a violation in the fourth position of the fifth line, the first four couplets are regulated; the seventh couplet is also regulated.

Title: Shih-hsing 始興 was the commandery (in modern Kwangtung) in which Chang's native Ch'ü-chiang 曲江 was located. The river in the poem is probably the Chen 湞, known also in the area as the Greater Shih-hsing River 大始興江. Thus, from the geography and sentiments expressed, the poem probably comes from the very end of Chang Chiu-ling's life.

1. *Shra-ièn* 沙衍 are sandflats in the middle of rivers: the line seems to describe the sinking of the high waters of autumn.

2. *Tziɛng* 晶, "crystalline," had become a favorite term for the autumn atmosphere in the later seventh and early eighth centuries; e.g., Sung Chih-wen 03221.1: "Chill wind in the eighth month, the atmosphere crystalline" 八月涼風天氣晶; Shen Ch'üan-ch'i 04970.5: "Autumn's crystalline clears the bending ravines" 秋晶澄回壑; Chieh Yen-jung 42599.16: "At the *tziɛ-miəi* the lovely air is crystalline" 紫微佳氣晶. *Ten-hiǒ* 天宇 can refer to the whole "world" or, as here, specifically to the "sky"; see the Wu-ch'en exegesis of *Wh* 26.29a–29b: 天宇謂天之覆地如屋宇. Whatever the original cosmic significance of the phrase, here it is a poeticism like the English "sky's vault." The Wu-ch'en exegesis of *ten-hiǒ* was for its use in an autumn poem by T'ao Ch'ien, a poem similar in subject and tone to Chang's poem and using the same rhyme.

3. The phrase *bhiuk-hăm* 伏檻 is from the *Chao-hun* 招魂: "Sit in the hall hunched at the railing, looking down into the winding river" 坐堂伏檻臨曲江些. Note that "winding river" is Ch'ü-chiang, where Chang is at the time.

4. The line reads literally "Path and ford: many distant emotions"; i.e., on seeing the paths and river crossings, all leading back to the capital, the poet thinks on those faraway places, and his emotions are stirred. Thus, in the next couplet, longing comes from beyond the range of the poet's vision, which is blocked by clouds and mist. From the time of Wang Ts'an's *Teng-lou fu* 登樓賦 on, this situation was common in poetry: a longing gaze from a high vantage point blocked by clouds, mists, and mountain ranges.

7. As so often in T'ang poetry, the physical features of the landscape, once named, take on significance in a broader intellectual context. *Tau-tau* 滔滔 describes a river in flood, but in addition to the river before the poet's eyes, its use here clearly echoes *Analects* XVIII.6, where Confucius sends the disciple Tzu-lu to "ask of the ford" (問津, cf. l.4), and one of the eccentric plowmen answers "A rolling flood—thus is the entire world" 滔滔者天下皆是也. The plowman was referring to the chaotic state of the world in which there is no ford/Way/Tao. *Biət dzhì bhyěn* 不自辨 echoes the "Autumn Flood" 秋水 chapter of the *Chuang-tzu*, in which autumn floods so swell the river that from one side to the other "one cannot distinguish an ox from a horse" 不辨牛馬 (*Chuang-tzu*

42/17/1). Such a loss of distinction is, of course, the threat of the "rolling flood" in the *Analects* passage.

8. Perhaps picking up the echo of the *Chuang-tzu* in the preceding line, this line paraphrases a passage from the "Equalizing Things" 齊物論 chapter of the *Chuang-tzu*: "To toil constantly through one's life and see no accomplishment" 終身役役而不見其成功 (4/2/19).

9. The use of *sop* 颯 as "windblown," thus tangled, echoes Hsieh T'iao's "How could I feel pained that my dishevelled tresses are wind-shaken?" 寧傷蓬鬢颯 (*CCs* 3.18a).

10. Chang is being sardonic here. The phrase *piɛu hua-qiɛng* 飄華纓 is taken from a *Yung-shih shih* 詠史詩 by Pao Chao, where it is an attribute of "one in state service" 仕子 (*Wh* 21.23b).

11. The "stabled horse" was a common emblem of being tied down, lacking freedom, as in Ts'ao P'i's "An old steed stabled, but its intense thoughts are to go a thousand *liɔ̌*" 老驥伏櫪, 志在千里 (*CSks* 1.2a).

12. As "the stabled horse" in the preceding line, the "caged bird" was an emblem of captivity. Chang is "caged" by his exile, but the more common "cage" is that of state service.

13. For 向 *Wyyh* reads 生. *Siuɛi-qim* 歲陰 is technically a series of positions of the planet Jupiter, the "year star," but in poetry it usually refers simply to the "end of the year." *Qiuǎn-miaɛ̌n* 晼晚 is a binomial expression indicating evening or sunset, but it is commonly extended to the "evening of the year" or the "evening of one's life."

14. For 夕 *Wyyh* reads 久.

15. *Dɔk-siɛng* 得性, "fulfilling one's nature," was often spoken of in terms of animal, fish, or insect analogies, where such creatures were able to "fulfill their natures" only in certain media or places. At this point the argument of the poem begins to reverse itself, claiming that separation from the capital might actually be a liberation and that his earlier sense of captivity was only a state of mind.

16. This refers to Chang's former high position in the central government.

17. For *nuɔ̀i-gò* 內顧 see *Analects* X.17; presumably the poet is "looking back" on the previous course of his life. The situation and phrasing of the line unmistakably echo T'ao Ch'ien's "Return" 歸去來辭:

Truly I have not gone far on the wrong path,	實迷途其未遠
I realize now I am right and then I was wrong.	覺今是而昨非

18. Though the poet attempts to resolve his sorrow by insisting that his separation from the capital was "right," the poem ends with an admission of failure in the consolation, as the poet still feels sorrow at what is past.

CHAPTER 4

06137: *CTs*, p. 1306; Chao, p. 203; *Wyc* 3.9b; *Tscs*, p. 236.
Rhymes: 2 *tsin*, 4 *njin*. Regulated.

4. The *zhio-io* 茱萸, "dogwood," was part of the ceremonies of the Double Ninth festival. At that time the berries were ripe, and these were either put in a "dogwood bag," used in wine (cf. 06084.4), or worn at the waist—all to protect and prolong life and to ward off misfortune; see *Ywlc*, p. 1541. The verb *chraep* 插 implies that the dogwood sprigs are being "stuck in" something, and the verb is used with putting things in a bag. But even though *bi n* 徧 might suggest "everyone" was putting berries in the bag, it seems more likely that the brothers are putting them in their clothing.

06057: *CTs*, p. 1295; Chao, p. 137; *Wycc* 2.7a; *Wyyh* 179.13a; *Yhc* in *TjhTs*, p. 356.
Rhymes: 2 *giung*, 4 *djiung*, 6 *lung*, 8 *kung*. Regulated.
Title: *Tjiɔk* 勅 are the "imperial orders" by which the prince of Ch'i is granted permission to use the summer palace. The Chiu-ch'eng palace at Feng-hsiang was originally built by Sui Wen-ti, then restored and renamed Chiu-ch'eng by T'ang T'ai-tsung as a retreat for his father (Chao). Passing the site in 757, Tu Fu wrote a well-known poem on the dilapidated structure (10562). *Qiɔng-gau* 應教 is the technical term for a poem written to the command of an imperial prince.

1. *Dèi-tziǎ* 帝子 refers specifically to an imperial prince, the child of an emperor (cf. 03444.7), but the phrase carries with it a divine and legendary aura from its use in the *Hsiang-fu-jen* 湘夫人 in the "Nine Songs" 九歌. There it refers to a "princess-goddess," the divine daughter of the sage-emperor Yao. The "Rose Phoenix Gates" 丹鳳闕 was the south-central gate of the Ta-ming Palace in Ch'ang-an (Chao).

2. Wang here follows one of the more common opening forms for a travel poem, in which the first two lines match starting point with destination, while at the same time giving the occasion for the journey. In later poetry the use of *hiuaěn* 遠 and *iɛu* 遙 in the same couplet of a regulated poem might have been considered a fault, especially, as here, in the same position in their respective lines. *Ten-shiu* 天書, literally "Heaven's writings," was a T'ang term for imperial commands. *Tsuì-miəi* 翠微 may refer to a mountain slope, but here (as it usually does in T'ang poetry) it refers to the blue mountain mists (Chao).

3. That clouds are generated in this spot suggests its otherworldliness. The opposition between such a place and the mortal world appears even more clearly in a poem from the *Wang Stream Collection* (06080.3–4):

I had no idea that the clouds in the beams   不知棟裏雲
Would go off and be rain in the mortal world.   去作人間雨

Both passages by Wang echo the dwelling of the Taoist in the second of Kuo P'u's "Wandering Immortals" 遊仙詩 (*Wh* 21.29a):

Clouds grow in the beams and rafters,   雲生梁陳間
Winds come out the windows and door.   風出窗戶裏

4. For another example of a landscape "entering" 入 something in Wang's early poetry (in this case a decorated, perhaps reflecting screen), see 06111.

8. *Syhc* and some other texts read 簫 for 笙. In that case the line would refer to the story of Hsiao-shih 簫史 and Nung-yü 弄玉, who rode off to heaven together on a phoenix. In the usage of court poetry, this allusion would be proper if the prince were accompanied by his wife.

05848: *CTs*, p. 1250–51; Chao, p. 53; *Wycc* 6.3b.
Rhymes: 2 *nga*, 4 *ga*, 6 *ma*, 8 *ha*. Unregulated.
Title: Ch'ing-ho Commandery lay in modern Hopei.

1. *Piaèm jiou* 汎舟 echoes *Shih* 26, "Drifting, that cypress boat" 汎彼柏舟. The Mao-Cheng gloss for *piaèm* is "floating manner" 流貌, with the implication that in drifting, the boat may not make it across the stream: 亦汎汎其流不以濟渡也. The Little Preface to *Shih* 26 suggests the propriety of the echo for an exile poem: "'Cypress Boat' tells of a good [officer of state] who did not find favor [with his ruler]" 柏舟言仁而不過也. The exegesis of *Shih* 26 makes it clear that the concern in the traditional reading of the poem is whether the boat will "get across" or not; in other words, whether the officer will be successfully employed. Thus, the flood that Wang Wei first sees marks the danger of not being able to "get across," to be of use; cf. *Analects* XVIII.6. The "Great River" is the Yellow River.

2. *Tziɛk-shuǐ* 積水 usually refers either to a deep pool or to the depths of the ocean; in this case, because of Ch'ing-ho's proximity to the sea, the association is probably the latter.

5. *Zhiɛng-zhiǎ* 城市 is the walled-in market area.

6. *Qiuaěn-njiɛn* 宛然 usually means "right here/there," "clearly." Kobayashi Taiichirō (*Ō I*. Tokyo, 1964) offers the attractive suggestion that here the phrase is used in another of its meanings as "swelling" or "full," applied to the mulberry and hemp (p. 130). Though I have followed this interpretation in an earlier treatment of the poem, I am no longer convinced this reading can be justified, and here take the phrase simply as "clearly."

8. *Miěu-mɑn* 淼漫 describes a vast expanse of water, either the sea or a very wide river.

06087: *CTs*, p. 1300–1301; Chao, p. 192; *Wycc* 4.4a; *Tscs*, p. 241.
Rhymes: 2 *tziɔk*, 4 *shiɔk*. Unregulated.
Title: Chao gives a brief discussion of *djhaek* 垞. According to the *Chi-yün*, 垞 (alternately written 隯) is the name of a hill; others take it as an old form of 宅, a miswriting of the proper form 疣.

Here I have followed the latter interpretation. Harada Kenyū (*Ō I*. Tokyo, 1964, p. 321) notes that present copies of the Wang Stream paintings have for this a small hill with a cottage.

1. For examples of why this must mean 'go off to" rather than "go off from," see 08241.5; 08367.1; 08394.1; and 08462.5.

3. The English "shore" refers to anything reasonably close to the water; the Chinese *pǒ* 浦 is narrower. Thus, *gɛk-pǒ* 隔浦 means "on the other side of the (far) shore."

4. Here is an excellent example of a case where *siang* 相 must mark a direct object and not mean "mutually": the poet is gazing at the homes, but there is no hint that the homes are gazing back at him.

05984: *CTs*, p. 1279; Chao, p. 121; *Wycc* 6.3b; *Wyyh* 296.8b.
Rhymes: 1 *bən*, 2 *iɛn*, 4 *tən*, 6 *hyɛn*, 8 *njiɛn*.

1–2. For the opening couplet *Wyyh* gives:

With royal mandate I withdrew from Heaven's gates,   銜命辭天闕
In a single coach I visit the frontiers.   單車欲問邊

Harada Kenyū (*Ō I*. Tokyo, 1964, pp. 238–39) gives a long argument defending the *Wyyh* version on the grounds of geographical accuracy and also on grounds of the tone pattern. In fact, the *Wyyh* opening may be a good example of the kinds of modifications that occurred in earlier poems after regulated verse was codified. In the form given in the text, the poem begins with two "A" form couplets, very common in Early T'ang regulated verse, but later considered a violation; see Stephen Owen, *Poetry of the Early T'ang*. (New Haven, 1977) pp. 429–31. In the *Wyyh* a new, filler line has been added, the second line has been shifted to the first position, and a line has been removed to make the opening conform to standard regulated pattern. *Zhiɛn-giu* 單車 is a "single carriage," indicating the poet's solitude lacking an entourage. Its use here, however, strongly echoes Li Ling's "Letter to Su Wu" 答蘇武書: "Long ago, an envoy in a single coach, you went to the barbarian ruler" 且足下昔以單車之使適萬乘之虜 (*Wh* 41.7b). *Jiok-guǝk* 屬國 refers to the non-Chinese kingdoms that acknowledged Han suzerainty. In T'ang literary texts the term might apply to actual client states, but it was also a literary fiction. Chü-yen 居延 refers to both a river and a client state, but the term is used here less for geographical accuracy than to echo the exploits of the great Han general Huo Ch'ü-ping 霍去病 who passed Chü-yen when he achieved a great victory (*Sc*, pp. 2930–31; *Hs*, p. 2480). Notes to both these versions take Chü-yen as the river, and thus in this context Wang's poem might be saying that he will "cross the Chü-yen." But Chao cites another version in the *Hs* where the notes take Chü-yen as a place and not the river. Though the first line suggests that the second line may be a speculation on the future, it is not clear whether Wang is going to pass the region or the river. In either case, just as the phrasing of the first line casts him in the role of Su Wu, so here the poet thinks of retracing the steps of the great Han general.

3. The *bhung* 蓬 is a plant that dries up in autumn and whose top breaks loose in the wind and blows away; "tumbleweed" is a botanically inaccurate translation of convenience, though the tumble weed does have a similar life cycle. However, in poetry the *bhung* became a set metaphor for the traveler, torn from his "roots" and carried here and there by the vagaries of chance. Chao notes this particular phrase, 'voyaging *bhung*" 征蓬, as having a source in a poem by Wu Yün (*CLs* 8.13a), but the phrase is simply one variation among a number of similar descriptive epithets applied to the *bhung*. The metaphor, of course, applies to Wang himself and shifts the tone from the heroic to the pathetic. "Leaving the Passes" 出塞 was a common *yüeh-fu* title.

4. The "homebound goose" 歸雁 is going north into the frontier region, marking the season as spring. Regionalizing Heaven as "Tartar skies" 胡天 is much more striking in Chinese than in English, and thus Chao feels the necessity to cite a precedent in Liang Chien-wen-ti's "Blocked in Return" 阻歸賦: "The trees of Lung are full of the wind, / The Tartar skies lack color" 隴樹饒風, 胡天少色 (*CLw* 8.3a). In any case, the parallel position word in Wang's poem, *Xǎn* 漢, begged a corresponding *Ho* 胡.

5. For the "one column of smoke standing straight," Chao cites a line by Yü Hsin: "Fortress in wilderness: one column of smoke stands straight' 野戍孤煙直 (*CPCs* 2.8a). Chao then cites the *P'i-ya* 埤雅 of Lu Tien 陸佃 for the comment that signal fires were made of dung to cause a straight,

dense column of smoke, or that the dust devils of the desert caused the smoke to stay together. Chao then praises the excellence of Wang's firsthand observation. Without denying that the scene is appropriate, I might add that it was also a staple poetic image and not confined to border scenes (e.g., 02832.6).

7. Hsiao ramparts 蕭闊 was one of the fortified passes to the frontiers, somewhat less than three hundred kilometers northwest of Ch'ang-an. *Hòu-ghyè* 候騎 echoes a couplet by Ho Hsün (*CLs* 9.12a):

A mounted patrol emerges from Hsiao ramparts,   候騎出蕭闊
The pursuit troops go off to Horseburg.   追兵赴馬邑

One can only marvel at Wang Wei's propensity to see in real frontier scenes the imaginary frontier scenes of Southern Dynasties poet .

8. If the grand marshal were indeed at Mount Yen-jan and if Wang were indeed seeking him, then the poet would have a long way to go in a somewhat different direction. Mount Yen-jan was where the Han general Tou Hsien 竇憲 made a commemorative inscription for his victory over the Hsiung-nu (*HHs*, p. 814). Thus, the patrol's news marks a Chinese victory and the deep penetration of enemy territory. However, Harada Kenyū (op. cit., p. 399) cites the closing line (?) of a poem by Wu Yün which shows that even this stirring, surprising news has its poetic past: "The general is at Jade Gate Pass" 將軍在玉門 (*CLs* 8.1a); though there the surprise seems to be that the general is too far out to meet an incursion).

05968: *CTs*, p. 1273; Chao, p. 28; *Wycc* 3.11b; *Wyyh* 250.5a, and 318.1b (title only); *Hyylc* in *TjhTs*, p. 59; *Khc* in *TjhTs*, p. 159; *Twt* 16B.3b.
Rhymes: 2 *zhiuε*, 4 *djiε*, 6 *zhiə*, 8 *ghiə*. The third couplet is regulated.
Title: The villa is the Wang Stream Estate. *Hyylc* and one instance in the *Wyyh* give the title as "Entering the Mountains: Sent to a Friend in the City" 入山寄城中故人. This variation accounts for the poem's double classification in *Wyyh*. The *Khc* title is "First Reaching the Mountains" 初至山中. The frequent anthologizing of this poem and the numerous echoes of its third couplet attest its popularity.

1. To "love the Way" 好道 was no modest interest but a passion that might carry a person away from home and into the mountains; cf. *Lun-heng* (*SPTK*) 7.3b, and the "Tale of Liu Yi" 柳毅, where the dragon-princess is born into a human family in which the father "late in life grew to love the Way, went wandering alone among clouds and streams, so that no one knows where he is" 晚歲好道獨遊雲泉今不知所在矣 (*T'ang-jen hsiao-shuo*, p. 67). Indeed, the phrase can have an almost pejorative sense, a religious motivation that contrasts to more dispassionate forms of freedom from society, as in *Wh* 22.30b:

It wasn't because his heart was in love with the Way,   寧爲心好道
It was only because his mood was endless.   直由意無窮

Of course, the "Way" to which Wang refers is Buddhist, and the poem does not confess a secret penchant for Taoism. *DKW* cites the *Yün-chi ch'i-chien* 雲笈七籤 to the effect that there are three categories of Taoist devotees, and that those of "middle years" (in this case 中年 rather than 中歲) are in their forties and fifties.

2. *Miaěn* 晚 is clearly used in contrast to the "middle age" of the first line and suggests a gap between the stirring of his desire and the time when he was able to fulfill it. "South Mountain" is the Chung-nan formation, just southwest of Ch'ang-an.

3. *Xiəng* 興 is an "excitement" or "elation," but I have translated it as "mood" to retain the sense of following one's whim. Wang's emphasis on going sightseeing alone should be understood in the context of the usual T'ang practice of group outings.

4. This is a notoriously difficult line. *Shiəng-jrhiə* 勝事 is literally a "wondrous occurrence" or "excellent experience," though the quality of "wondrousness" was commonly associated with beautiful landscapes. This may have been a phrase commonly used at the time to describe sightseeing in the region, as in the line by Ts'en Shen from the mid-740s (and thus before the date of this poem): "I've heard tell that at Wang Stream there are many experiences of wonders" 聞道輞川多勝事 (09817). The use of *djiε* 知 may have been suggested by rhyme, but it was a felicitous

suggestion, because it calls to mind the compound *djiɛ-jrhiə* 知事, an eminently practical "knowledge of how things go," which becomes wry in this context. To take *kung* 空 as "emptiness," the object of "know," would be highly unnatural. But *kung* does describe the mode of knowing: "emptily," suggesting lack of purpose, motive, or attachment. *Dzhì* 自 likewise suggests solitude and that the "knowing" occurred quite in its own course. The emphasis on spontaneity here may be to counter the implications of motivation in "loving the Way," from the *Wh* usage cited earlier.

    5. The line means that the poet followed the streams to their sources, an act of emblematic significance.

    6. The antithesis in this couplet is a transformation from activity (*haeng* 行) to rest (*dzhuǎ* 坐). This is the only tonally regulated couplet in the poem and is an excellent example of categorical parallelism producing problems for English translator while presenting no difficulties for the Chinese reader; one can "walk to a place," but it is difficult to "watch times." However, the categorical matching in the couplet is perfect. Clouds are generated from the heights of mountains.

    7. The poet may go off alone with no prearranged plan, but human companionship can be recovered if it is "by chance" 偶然.

05906: *CTs*, pp. 1263–64; Chao, p. 6; *Wycc* 1.5b; *Hyylc* in *TjhTs*, p. 61; *Twt* 17A.4b; *Yfsc* 47.9b. Rhymes: 1 *dzhen*, 2 *iɛn*, 3 *djhiuɛn*, 4 *shrɛn*, 6 *hɛn*, 7 *ziuɛn*, 9 *hyuɛn*.
Title: The *Hyylc* includes the name of the goddess, misnaming her Ch'iung-chih 瓊智; her proper name is Chih-ch'iung 智瓊. Though the story of Chih-ch'iung exists elsewhere, Chao cites a version in the *Shu-cheng chi* 述征記 in which she appears to a certain Hsien Chao 絃超 in the mid-third century, is denounced as an evil spirit and cast out, then reappears to Hsien five years later on Yü Mountain (in modern Shantung).

    1. *Piən* 紛 often appeared as the first word in *Ch'u-tz'u* lines, glossed by Wang Yi variously as "abundant" 盛貌 or "disorderly" 亂貌. Presumably this refers to the temple dancers. *Yfsc* gives 舞 as a variant for 拜 (to clasp hands and bow slightly as an act of respect).

    2. *Gyuèn-gyuèn* 眷眷 occurs twice in Han *Ch'u-tz'u*, once in Liu Hsiang's "Nine Sighs" 九歎, where it refers to the soul's melancholy gaze, and once in Wang Yi's own "Nine Longings" 九思. However, Kobayashi Taiichirō (op. cit., p. 136) is probably correct in referring to a Li Shan gloss for *gyuèn-liuèn* 眷戀 as "longing" (*Wh* 19.21b). The "mats like jade" 瓊筵 are a conventional synecdoche for a fine feast, here the offering. Though there are no verbal echoes, the situation of the song is very reminiscent of the "Lord of the East" 東君 in the "Nine Songs."

    4. That the goddess "is the evening rain," *tzɑk mò hiǒ* 作暮雨, is a clear reference to the goddess of Wu Mountain and her sexual liason with the king of Ch'u; see *Wh* 19.1a–1b.

    5–6. This is in fact one line with the *hei* 兮 omitted. The *hei* is included in the *Yfsc* version. I have taken the "grieving" and "longing" as attributes of the music, but if one follows the model of the "Lord of the East," with the goddess reluctant to depart, the lines could just as easily read: "She grieves for the shrill pipes and longs for the flurried strings."

    7. The "carriage of the goddess" 靈之駕 appears commonly in prose and poetry in the form *leng-gà* 靈駕 and in numerous alternate forms such as *jhin-gà* 神駕, *siɛn-gà* 仙駕, or *leng-chia* 靈車.

    9. The *jrhɛn-hyuɛn* 潺湲 of the waters after the goddess's departure echoes its use in the *Hsiang-chün* 湘君 and the *Hsiang-fu-jen* 湘夫人 of the "Nine Songs"; in the case of the *Hsiang-fu-jen*, it is what one sees when gazing for the absent goddess. Poems on immortals often closed with marks of absence or lingering reminders of their visit; for instance, the closing of Pao Chao's "Song of Hsiao-shih" 蕭史曲 (*CSs* 4.7a) and 03224.8–10.

05902: *CTs*, p. 1262; Chao, p. 4; *Wycc* 1.4a–4b.
Rhymes: 1 *miəi*, 2 *hiuəi*, 4 *giuəi*.
Title: Because of the mention of the Secretariat and the use of Chung-nan, Kobayashi Taiichirō suggests that this poem is from Wang Wei's last years; see Harada Kenyū, op. cit., pp. 344–45. If the subject of the poem were Wang himself ("One evening I came out . . ."), such dating might be warranted by Wang's tenure in the Secretariat. But more suggestive evidence occurs in the use of the term *Tziɛ̌-miəi* 紫微 for the Secretariat, its official title between 714 and 717. This in itself does not constitute evidence for an earlier dating, because the terms was sometimes poetically

applied to the Secretariat after 717. It seems likely, however, that this poem was dedicated to Hsü Ch'u-pi 徐楚璧 (better known by his later name, Hsü An-chen 安貞), who was grand secretary 中書令人 in the K'ai-yüan: in fact, grand secretary is given first in a list of offices Hsü held in the K'ai-yüan (*HTs*, p. 5690). This would make the poem a very early one by Wang, either from the time that the Secretariat was called the *Tziĕ-miəi* or shortly thereafter. At that time Sung Chih-wen's experiments in the Ch'u song style would have been very recent memory; see Owen, op. cit., pp. 364–66. Moreover, association with men such as Hsü Ch'u-pi, later of the Li Lin-fu party, would help to explain why Wang had so few difficulties when Li Lin-fu came to power.

    1. Hsü is evidently leaving work late, exasperated by the demands of "worldly affairs" 塵事.

    2. *Shrang-zhiò* 雙樹 is probably a reference to the "two-trunked *sāla* tree" 娑羅雙樹 under which Sakyamuni achieved enlightenment. The tree seems to have an inspirational effect on Hsü as well.

    4. It is uncertain whether *giuəi* 歸 refers to "going back" to the Secretariat, "going off" to the mountains, or actually "going home."

06090: *CTs*, p. 1301; Chao, p. 193; *Wycc* 4.4b; *Tscs*, p. 242.
Rhymes: 2 *siă*, 4 *hă*. Unregulated.
Title: *Luæn* is a name applied to several kinds of trees; I am uncertain which is meant here.

    1. *Sop-sop* 颼颼 is a descriptive binome, perhaps onomatopoetic, describing the wind.

    2. *Tsiĕn-tsiĕn* 淺淺 is a descriptive binome for the swift flowing of water. Wang's line is in fact a reworking of a line in the *Hsiang-fu-jen* of the "Nine Songs": 石溜兮淺淺. Similarly, the first line echoes the *Shan-kuei* 山鬼 in the "Nine Songs."

06108: *CTs*, p. 1303; Chao, p. 196; *Wycc* 5.12a.
Rhymes: 2 *ghiək*, 4 *siək*. Unregulated.
Title: Chao notes that *Ws Tjcc* does not have *Lim gæu-dhəi* 臨高臺, and indeed *Yfsc* does not include this quatrain under its versions of the song: *Yfsc* 18.2a–4a. Moreover, none of the songs quoted under the title in the *Yfsc* are quatrains. On the other hand, almost all versions of the *yüeh-fu* have the poet seeing birds in flight and flowing water as he looks down from the terrace. Though Wang keeps the spirit of the *yüeh-fu*, the *Lim gæu-dhəi* part of the title may have been added from the text. Note that though *lim* 臨 is usually followed by what is "looked down on," it is clear from the context of this *yüeh-fu* tradition that in this case *lim* means "look down from." Reminder Li is probably Li Hsin 黎昕; see Tsuru Haruo. *ŌI* (Tokyo, 1958), p. 29.

    3. The situation and phrasing echo T'ao Ch'ien's famous "Drinking Wine" V 飲酒:

| The mountain air is fine in the sunset, | 山氣日夕佳 |
| Birds in flight join and return. | 飛鳥相與還 |

05861: *CTs*, pp. 1253–54; Chao, pp. 56–57; *Wycc* 6.5b–6a.
Rhymes: 2 *kiù*, 4 *gò*, 6 *tsiò*, 8 *sò*, 10 *gò*, 12 *chiù*, 14 *lò*, 16 *gò*, 18 *mò*. This poem uses *t'ung-yün*.
Title: *Ngŏu-njiɛn* 偶然 indicates that the poem was supposed to have been composed without any premeditation or purpose (especially social purpose). Though this is one of the earliest works using this title, which was later to become a common subgenre, interest in this compositional mode can be traced back to the preface of T'ao Ch'ien's "Drinking Wine" series.

    1. The T'ai-hang Range runs between Honan and Hopei. The poem is probably from Wang's Chi-chou exile.

    2. *Djhim-ngyim* 沈吟, "fall into brooding," means literally "going 'hmmmm' deep down," with the implication of confusion or uncertainty. The phrase may also mean "to chant a poem broodingly," and it is possible that that meaning is applicable here.

    3. The enallage in the unmarked introduction of an interlocutor is typical of poetic narrative: literally, "I ask you why that is so."

    4. *Miăng* 網 is a "net," which as *ten-miăng* 天網, "Heaven's net," catches up all things and ensnares malefactors, and as *djhin-miăng* 塵網, "the dusty net," or as *shiĕi-miăng* 世網, "the net of the world," entangles all who are involved in human society. The final *gò* 故, "because," is prosaic.

5–6. The mention of family and family concerns was a feature of reclusive poetry from T'ao Ch'ien to Wang Chi.

7–8. Indeed, Wang's salary in Chi-chou would not have been great, but it is unlikely he was in any real poverty, as is implicit in the mention of the family stores in the eighth line.

11. Sun Teng 孫登 (*Tsin*, p. 2426) was a Tsin recluse encountered by Juan Chi 阮籍 on Su-men Mountain. When Juan tried to discuss occult questions, Sun refused to answer, and Juan final departed with a long *sèu* 嘯, "whistle" (or "yodel"). Soon after Juan heard the hills and valleys resounding with a sound like that of a phoenix, and this sound turned out to be Sun Teng's whistling (*Tsin*, p. 1362). Chao notes that there actually was a "Long Whistling Terrace" in the region.

14. Just who the "old friend" or "old friends" might be is uncertain.

15. This couplet echoes the second of T'ao Ch'ien's "Returning to Dwell in my Fields and Garden" 歸園田居:

The mulberry and hemp daily grow taller,   桑麻日已長
My land daily grows broader.   我土日已廣

Qèi-njiĕm 愛染, "stained with desire," is a Buddhist term for one of the carnal passions.

16. *Zhiɛn-dzhek* 禪寂, "meditation's stillness," is a Buddhist term for the condition of *dhyana*, *ch'an*.

17–18. Wang's exhortation for himself to go off is clearly reminiscent of T'ao Ch'ien's exhortations to himself in the *Kuei-ch'ü-lai tz'u* 歸去來辭. Wang's "Why wait" 寧俟 picks up T'ao's "Why tarry on here" 胡為遑遑 (*Wh* 45.29a). In addition, the lines echo Ch'ü Yüan's resolve to escape an unappreciative world by flight into the wilderness or world of immortals. "I resolve to go" or "I'm about to go" 吾將行 occurs three times in the *Ch'u-tz'u*, twice preceded by "suddenly" 忽乎. In the *Li Sao* Ch'ü Yüan "selects a lucky day and is about to go" 歷吉日乎吾將行: Wang Wei will not wait that long. And at the close of *She-Chiang* 涉江 in the *Chiu-chang* 九章, the Ch'ü Yüan persona gives a final complaint that his worth is not appreciated and "suddenly resolves to go" 忽乎吾將行兮 (Chao). The same line recurs in the *Yüan-yu*. The passionate seriousness of these echos belies the casual discursiveness of an "offhand composition" and adds depth to the poetic voice. The last line may simply mean "why wait until the year's end," rather than "wait until late in life."

05969: *CTs*, pp. 1276–77; Chao, p. 96; *Wycc* 4.7a; *Wyyh* 160.3b–4a.

Rhymes: 2 *hɛn*, 4 *huan*, 6 *shrɛn*, 8 *guan*. Loosely regulated; permitted violation in the fourth position of the first line, and unacceptable violation in the fourth position of the third line.

Title: Sung Mountain lies east-southeast of Lo-yang, and when Wang might have been "returning" there is a puzzle. As the journey from Chi-chou back to Ch'ang-an would probably have taken Wang "beneath the heights of Mount Sung," one would like to take the title as "Returning Past Mount Sung" and read the last lines as: "Far, far from beneath the heights of Mount Sung / I will return . . ." However, *giuəi* 歸 most naturally takes the destination of the return as its object, and even if Wang meant only to pass Mount Sung, generations of readers have probably had him returning *to* it.

1. Chao cites two passages from the poetry of Lu Chi, the first of which reproduces this line exactly (*Wh* 28.8a). The Wu-ch'en gloss for *bhɑk* 薄 is "plants growing in clusters" 草木叢生. *Djhiɑng* 長 most likely refers to their continuous growth all along the banks of the stream.

2. *Hɛn-hɛn* 閑閑 is a binome describing the swaying movement of carriages, from its use in *Shih* 26. Note that the postposition of the adverbial binome is a poetic usage. The relation between the first and second lines of this poem is problematic: the terms in which the scene of the first line is described create barriers for the movement in the second line. The reader may interpolate a bridge, ford, or movement parallel to the stream in the mind's eye, but the juxtaposition forces us to call into question the physical relationship of the elements.

3. "To have purpose" 有意 suggests that the stream, in knowing to "return," possesses the semblance of conscious intention.

4. Echo of T'ao Ch'ien's "Drinking Wine" V; see *CTsins* 6.15a.

8. Though "closing one's gate" has a broader significance in Wang Wei's poetry, the terms in which it is expressed here, *bèi-guan* 閉關, are particularly resonant. As Harada Kenyū points

out (op. cit., pp. 181–82), the phrase is used in the *hsiang* 象 of the hexagram *Fu* 復, "Return": "On the first day of winter, the former kings closed the gates and merchants did not travel" 先王以至日閉關，使商旅不行. But more than its seasonal and ritual significance, the link with the hexagram *Fu* is significant, adding a dimension of universal pattern behind the private act.

05961: *CTs*, p. 1275; Chao, p. 117; *Wycc* 5.19b–20a; *Wyyh* 234.2a–2b.
Rhymes: 2 *zhiɛng*, 4 *bhiaeng*, 6 *shiɛng*, 8 *shraeng*. Regulated.
Title: The precise location of Pien-chüeh Temple is uncertain. Harada Kenyū (op. cit., pp. 258–61) notes that Ch'u Kuang-hsi has a poem on the same temple (06523) and cites some parallel poems that strongly suggest the temple is on Mount Hua, which also has a "Lotus Peak" (mentioned in line 2). The only problem with having the temple on Mount Hua is that it makes the geography of line 3 outrageously hyperbolic.

    1. The use of *dzhiong* 從 in this line is somewhat troublesome. In some cases it can mean "to come from," usually with a direction following it. In this usage the line reads: "A bamboo path leads one out from the First Stage." But with "path" in the same line, the most natural way to take *dzhiong* is "follow," as of a path: however, this creates a poetic hyperbaton: "The bamboo path is followed in the First Stage." I prefer the second interpretation because I generally give probabilities of compound-determination precedence over probabilities of syntactic determination: the semantic value of a given usage is more likely to be determined by a set compound relation to a near-by word than by syntactic position. *Chriu-dhì* 初地, "First Stage" or "First Land," appears in various sutras as the first of the "Ten Stages" 十地 in the progress toward enlightenment. The "First Stage" is that of "sensual delight" 歡喜地. The final stage appears in line 8 as "Clouds of Law" 法雲.

    2. The "City of Illusion" 化城 is from a parable in the *Lotus Sutra* in which an expedition, on its way across a desert, becomes discouraged and wants to turn back. Thereupon the leader uses magic to create a great city, in which the travelers refresh themselves and regain heart. When the expedition sets out again with renewed purpose, the city disappears. The reference is, of course, to expedient means to draw the soul towards enlightenment, and in this poem the natural beauty of Pien-chüeh Temple represents just such expedient means. The use of the verb *chuit* 出, here "to make come out," (what mountains do to clouds), intensifies this sense of magical production.

    3. "All Ch'u," *sɑm-Chriǔ* 三楚, is literally "the three regions of Ch'u"—east, south, and west (Chao). The regions covered are well to the south of Mount Hua, and as suggested earlier, either the poet's gaze has been extended by hyperbole, or Pien-chüeh Temple is located somewhere in the Ch'u region.

    4. "Nine Rivers," *Giǒu-gang* 九江, refers to several areas, all in the lower Yangtze region. The geographical problem is the same as in the third line. How certain positions in a landscape invert the usual order of perception was a favorite in landscape description; for instance, Hsieh Ling-yün's "Gazing back down on the tops of tall trees" 倪視喬木杪 (*CSs* 3.11b) or Tu Fu's (10558):

I had already gone to the water's edge,	我行已水濱
But my servant is still in the treetops.	我僕猶木末

    5. *Pio-dzhuǎ* 趺坐 is a technical Buddhist term for a yoga posture. The line is adapted from a passage in the *Hua-yen Sutra*: "Where the grasses are soft and pliant on the earth, sit cross-legged in meditation" 地草弱輭結跏趺坐; see Harada Kenyū. op. cit., p. 263. Harada is certain that the line refers to a story in the *Kuo-ch'ü hsien-tsai yin-kuo Sutra* in which Sakyamuni receives "pliant grasses" from Indra in mortal guise, sits on them in the *pio-dzhuǎ* posture, and achieves enlightenment; see Harada, op. cit., pp. 263–64. The allusion is a convincing one and creates a problem with *zhiǝng* 承: either the grasses "receive" the person sitting, or Sakyamuni is "receiving" the grasses from Indra. The second interpretation of *zhiǝng* would demand that the line be translated "The pliant grasses are received by one who would sit in the *pio-dzhuǎ* posture." Though in itself *zhiǝng* favors the second interpretation, it seems to me to distort the line excessively.

    6. *Bhiaèm-shiɛng* 梵聲 may be the celestial "sounds of Brahmā" rather than the more secular "sounds of sutra chanting."

    7. For the "Clouds of the Law," see note to line 1.

    8. *Mio-shraeng* 無生 is used in its technical Buddhist sense, borrowed and modified from

Taoism, of "not living and not perishing," *mio-shraeng mio-niɛt* 無生無滅; i.e., transcending the world of birth and rebirth.

05845: *CTs*, p. 1250; Chao, p. 49; *Wycc* 5.18b.
Rhymes: 2 gǒu, (3 dhou), 4 kǒu, 6 hǒu, 8 mǒu.
Metrics: Chao includes this poem among Wang's "old style" verse, while Tsuru (op. cit., pp. 124–25) treats it as regulated: neither category applies. The poem begins with two "A" form couplets in a *tse* rhyme. The fifth line begins with a proper "B" form regulated couplet, but violates the pattern by *shrɛn* 山 in the sixth line (though it is a matter of debate how strong the violation is). The fourth couplet, if taken as regulated, not only contains violations, it also is another "B" form couplet, and though "B" form couplets occasionally follow one another in *tse*-rhyme poems, "B" form sequences are uncommon. Metrically, the poem "falls out of regulation," and that process parallels the regression described in the text.
Title: For the more original *Miaĕn-miɑng* 晚望, Chao cites the variant *Iǎ-miɑng* 野望, an established subgeneric title. Though we might expect *tzèi* 霽 rather than *dzhiɛng* 晴 for skies clearing after a rain, earlier usage supports this interpretation, as in P'an Yüeh: "After light rain, newly cleared skies" 微雨新晴 (*Wh* 16.8b). Moreover, the usage appears often in Tu Fu; e.g., 11655.

2. *Piən-gǒu* 氛垢 is probably a variation for the sake of rhyme on *piən-qəi* 氛埃, used with the associations of "the world's filth"; cf. *Yüan-yu*, "To get past the drifting dirt and exceed in goodness" 絕氣埃而淑尤. *Ghiək-miuk* 極目 is an established compound meaning "to gaze as far as the eye can see," as in the coda of the *Chao-hun*: "The eyes stretch a thousand *liǎ*, wounding a spring heart" 目極千里兮傷春心.
3. This is a favorite Wang Wei scene; cf. 05969.5.
5. *Bhaek-shuǐ* 白水 probably refers to the silvery clarity of the water rather than to the "white water" of rapids; cf. its metaphorical use in *Tso*, Hsi 24. This interpretation is reinforced by Chao's citation of Liu Chen's: "The square pool holds white water within" 方塘含白水 (*CSks* 3.8b). Note how Wang's descriptions all take the form of spatial relationships.
7. *Nong-ngiuaet* 農月 are the months of summer when farm work is busiest. Meng Chiao may have been ironically echoing this line when he wrote (19920.1–2):

They have ground green mountains into dust,	青山輾爲塵
Under the bright sun no one takes his ease.	白日無閒人

The reader, expecting a description of farm labor, may be surprised to find that these hard-laboring folk are men greedy for wealth and power, hurrying through the mountains to Ch'ang-an.
8. *Kiuɛng-ga* 傾家 is an interesting phrase; it can mean "the entire family" (cf. 08726.15), but it also means to "ruin the family," a compound on the model *kiuɛng-guɛk* 傾國 and *kiuɛng-zhiɛng* 傾城. However, the *kiuɛng-ga*, "family ruiner," is more often a wastrel than a lovely lady. The use of *jrhiǝ* 事 as "work on" is formal and archaic. In addition to the *Shih* passage cited in the text, *nom-mǒu* 南畝 occurs elsewhere in the *Shih* and other early texts as the fixed epithet for "the fields."

05914: *CTs*, p. 1266; Chao, p. 95; *Wycc* 3.4b.
Rhymes: 2 hyɛn, 4 zhiɛn, 6 gen, 8 dzhen. Regulated.
Title: *Hɛn-giu* 閒居 is a set poetic topic, from P'an Yüeh's "Dwelling in Ease" 閒居賦 (*Wh* 16.1a–10a), also about life on a private estate outside the capital.

1. This line is clearly a reworking of Hsieh T'iao's (*CCs* 3.10a):

In azure blue I gaze on chill mountains.	蒼翠望寒山
Towering high, they peer down on level land.	崢嶸瞰平陸

Hsieh is describing winter mountains; Wang, autumn ones. In his poem Hsieh mentions the evergreen bamboo, which perhaps explains the "azure" of winter hills, but the context of Wang's poem suggests that the azure is a mist after the rain. The only other way in which autumn mountains could grow "ever more azure" is by the presence of evergreens, which might seem to get brighter in contrast to the rest of the scene.
4. *Lim-biung* 臨風 is to "face into the wind."

5–6. This very common poetic construction may be called, for want for a better term, a "Fred" (The arbitrariness of a personal name may redeem the construction from the questionable application of Western grammatical terms). One may debate in English whether a Fred is an inversion, a transitive (sometimes causative) verb, a modifying construction, or an impersonal verb. Since none of these distinctions do or can appear on the level of Chinese poetic word order, we may dispense with them as syntactic categories. If analogous distinctions occur on the level of "meaning," we should perhaps look for those distinctions in determinations from context and from the history of specific usage of lexical items. Usually a Fred occurs when an antepenultimate verb is followed by what the reader would assume is the subject of the verb. A Fred *is* distinguished from normal word order and does have its own value, though that value is not a determination of transitivity, inversion, modifying construction, or impersonal verb. It is rather a much broader category within which the determinations above can occur. Essentially, a Fred weakens the syntactic space of the caesura and implies some necessary rather than accidental relation between the two parts of a line. The use of *iu* 餘 in line 5 is particularly striking and implies some special relation between the spot and the lingering of the last sunlight. Such a relation would be missing (and the tone pattern ruined) if the line were *dhò-dhou lɐk-njit iu*. On the other hand, *iu*'s "having the sunlight linger there" is different from a topographical feature that "catches and keeps" the last of the sun, for which the proper poetic term is *liou* 留 (tonally just as acceptable as *iu* in the third position). Except in the special cases of causatives, which usually fall within the domain of Freds, the Fred-construction is essentially untranslatable. Line 6 echoes T'ao Ch'ien's first "Returning to Dwell in my Fields and Garden" 歸園田居: "Faint in the distance, smoke over a village" 依依墟里煙 (Chao). The T'ao Ch'ien echo seems to lead the way into the last couplet.

    7–8. See text.

06072: *CTs*, p. 1298; Chao, p. 146; *Wycc* 4.11b–12a; *Wyyh* 319.8a.
Rhymes: 1 *djhi*, 2 *jriə*, 4 *liɛ*, 6 *ghui*, 8 *ngiə*. Regulated.
Title: *Tziɛk-hiǒ* 積雨, literally "massed rain," probably suggests a pervasive sogginess and appears to be a new construction on the model of *tziɛk-shuǐ* 積水 and *tziɛk-siuɛt* 積雪.

    1. *Djhi* 遲 describes either the "slow" rising of the smoke or the "slow" burning of the damp wood.

    2. *Lei* 藜 is a goosefoot whose sprouts can be steamed. A soup of *lei* was supposed to have been eaten by Confucius when he was in dire straits; see *Chuang-tzu* 79/28/59–60. That it continued to be thought of as a food for the poor can be seen in Han Yü (17826):

From now on you will be rich in furs and horses,	從茲富裘馬
Surely no longer will you eat goosefoot and bracken.	寧復茹藜蕨

Shiǎng 餉 refers to sending food to field laborers. *Jriə* 菑 are fields just recently put into use; it may also refer to fallow fields, but that does not seem to be the case here.

    3–4. Chao cites a famous dispute about this couplet: according to the *Kuo-shih pu* 國史補 Wang Wei is supposed to have pilfered and modified this couplet from Li Chia-yu's 水田飛白鷺, 夏木囀黃鸝. Yeh Meng-te 葉夢得 (1077–1143) in his *Shih-lin shih-hua* 石林詩話 (*Ltsh* ed. I.11a–11b) responded that the real genius of Wang's couplet lay in the first two characters of each line, and that Wang had taken a dull couplet and transformed it into a great couplet. However, the couplet does not survive in the present version of Li Chia-yu's collection, and while it is possible Li Chia-yu did write the couplet before Wang's version, Li's poetic activity generally postdates Wang's. Furthermore, it is unlikely that Li Chao 李肇, the compiler of the *Kuo-shih pu*, could have had any greater authority for his claim than very old gossip. *Mɐk-mɐk* 漠漠 probably came to Wang's mind from the mention of the "eastern acreage" in line 2: a Hsieh T'iao poem entitled "Wandering in the *Eastern Fields*" 遊東田 (emphasis mine) contains the line: "Rising mists spread out in disorder" 生煙紛漠漠 (*Wh* 22.25b), with the Wu-ch'en gloss for *mɐk-mɐk* as "spreading out" 布散也. The context of the Hsieh T'iao usage makes it likely that in Wang's line it is "mists" that are *mɐk-mɐk*, and not the birds themselves.

    5. Chao cites two Liang poems as earlier examples of *zip-dzhiěng* 習靜: 苦熱 *CLs* 9.9a; 對雨 *CLs* 13.5a. The phrase does occur earlier and clearly possesses some religious value, but it is equally clear from the Liang poems that "practicing stillness" is an escape from the heat of summer,

equally appropriate in this poem. The *giǒn* 槿 is a kind of hibiscus whose blooms last only a single day; it thus serves as a meditative emblem for the impermanence of things.

6. The "fasting" here is obviously not complete abstinence but rather eating only pure foods such as mallows. The poet literally "snaps off the dewy mallows," the seventh-month food of *Shih* 154. Wang's calmness, coolness, and gathering wild plants as food contrasts strongly with the farm labor in the first half of the poem.

7–8. See text.

05829: *CTs*, p. 1246; Chao, pp. 50–51 *Wycc* 5.21b–22b.
Rhyme.: 2 *miuk*, 4 *liuk*, 6 *guk*, 8 *miuk*, 10 *djhiuk*, 12 *luk*. Unregulated.

1. Though "going out the eastern gate," *chuit dung-mən* 出東門, is a poetic act with a long history (e.g., *Shih* 93), the primary association of the line would be with *yüeh-fu* and the Nineteen Old Poems; e.g., for 步出 ... 門, see *Yfsc* 37.3b; for 出東門, see *Yfsc* 37.7b–8a; see also *Ku-shih* XVI 驅車上東門. The line that follows "going out east gate" is usually some form of gazing. That Wang has indeed gone out of the capital's eastern gate is obvious from lines 5 and 6. It may be objected that if Wang did indeed go out the capital's eastern gate when he wrote the poem, the line would be stating fact rather than echoing past poetry. But it seems more likely that the poetic past was the stimulus for the historical experience and its transformation into a poem; Wang probably did not go out the eastern gate *because* it occurred so often in past poetry; rather, past poetry lent a special significance to his happening to go out the eastern gate.

2. The "thousand-*liǒ* eye" 千里目 is an eye that can see a thousand *liǒ*; see note to 05845, line 2. *Tjiěng* 騁, "gallop," "let free," forms a compound with various eye and sight words, as *tjiěng-miuk* 騁目 or *tjiěng-miɑng* 騁望, and describes a sweeping gaze, unobstructed by anything near at hand.

4. *Chiɛk* 赤 is the color of the south and high Yang (as well as of reddish soil, in which shade the translation "crimson" would be singularly inappropriate). Chao cites a line by Ho Hsün: "The crimson sun descends over the city round" 赤日下城圓 (*CLs* 9.8a). Wang's fondness for similar images may be recalled from 05984.6. *Wycc* notes the excellence of Wang's use of *dhuɑn* 圍, presumably because Wang avoids its more common synonymn *hyuɛn* 圓.

5–6. These lines describe the historical geography of Wang's gaze. Han-tan was the capital of the ancient state of Chao, in Hopei, and here Wang's gaze is surveying the roads north of the Wei and Yellow River to the east-northeast. Han-ku Pass lay directly east on the road to Lo-yang and was one of the famous passes that created the distinction between East-of-the-Passes and Within-the-Passes.

7. This refers to Ch'ang-an's symbolic position as the center of the empire and of the world.

8. *Miuk* 牧, literally "pastor," was the archaic term given to the governors of the Nine Regions. Here the term is a poetic anachronism for the T'ang provincial governors and probably suggests the embassies sent by provincial governors to court every New Year.

9–10. Hsien-yang, the old Ch'in capital whose ruins lay just outside T'ang Ch'ang-an, is here used for Ch'ang-an itself. The line probably refers to the traffic of officials—"caps and (carriage) awnings"—on their way to dawn court.

11–12. Such visits between the nobility and upper officialdom were an established part of the capital theme; cf. 02762.

13–14. Having achieved great fame and favor as a court poet, Ssu-ma Hsiang-ju grew sick and retired to the Mao-ling suburb. When the emperor sent an emissary to gather up his writings, he found that Ssu-ma Hsiang-ju had already died, leaving only his famous "Treatise on the Feng and Shan Sacrifices"; see *Sc*, p. 3063.

29160: *CTs*, p. 6156; *Li Yi-shan wen-chi* 李義山文集 (*SPTK*) 6.8b; *Yü-hsi-sheng shih chien-chu* 王溪生詩箋注 (*SPPY*) 2.30b; *Li Yi-shan shih-chi* 李義山詩集 (Chu Hao-ling commentary rpt. Taipei, 1967) 1.27a–27b (pp. 157–58).
Rhymes: 1 *giu*, 2 *shiu*, 4 *njiu*. Regulated.
Title: The addressee is Ling-hu T'ao 令孤綯, son of Ling-hu Ch'u 楚. For Li's relationship to Ling-hu T'ao, see James Liu, *The Poetry of Li Shang-yin* (Chicago, 1969), pp. 18–19, 23–24. Feng Hao (*Yü-hsi-sheng shih chien-chu*) dates the poem 843–44.

1. *Li Yi-shan wen-chi* reads 高 for 嵩: 嵩 is necessary for the internal parallelism. Feng notes that this refers to Li's previous activities in the two capitals. Ch'in stands for Ch'ang-an; Mount Sung, for Lo-yang. At the time of composition, Li was away from the capitals; see Liu, pp. 20–22.

2. As both Feng and Chu note, the carp-form letter-case, literally the "paired carp" 雙鯉, is a reference to the *yüeh-fu* "Watering My Horse at a Watering Hole by the Great Wall" 飲馬長城 窟行 (*Wh* 27.20b). The letter in the poem is probably from Ling-hu T'ao to Li asking the kind of question Li forbids in the third line; but it is possible that it refers to the message Li is sending to Ling-hu T'ao.

3. Before Ssu-ma Hsiang-ju became a poet in the court of Han Wu-ti, he served in the court of Prince Hsiao of Liang (*Sc*, p. 2999). The prince, known as a kind and generous patron, gathered about him many of the famous literary men of the day, and in this poem Li uses the allusion to refer to idyllic earlier times, probably when he was still enjoying the patronage of Ling-hu T'ao's father, Ling-hu Ch'u.

4. See note to 05829, lines 13–14.

05797: *CTs*, p. 1239; Chao, p. 22; *Wycc* 3.8b.
Rhymes: 2 *shia*, 4 *ia*, 6 *liɛ*, 8 *ziə*, 10 *byɛ*, 12 *jiɛ*, 14 *zhiə*. Only second couplet regulated.

1. *Biung-giaĕng* 風景, "scenery" or "atmosphere," had become a fairly common term in the T'ang, but occurred only occasionally earlier; it does not, for example, appear in the *Wen hsüan*. In one way the term "scenery" is an appropriate translation, because *biung-giaĕng* was a term for a scene and ambience linked to an appreciating subject. It differs from "scenery," however, in that it is a quality of "good viewing" which one particular place can possess or lack depending on the weather, season, and so forth. The quality of the term can be seen in the following early use from the biography of the famous Tsin magistrate Yang Hu 羊祜: "He took joy in the mountains and waters, and whenever there was a 'scenery,' (每風景) he would go off to Mount Hsien, set out wine and chant poetry, never tiring the whole day through" (*Tsin*, p. 1020). Here *biung-giaĕng* is almost synonymous with "good weather," and it does not entirely lose that dimension in T'ang usages. For *njit-ziɛk gɛi* 日夕佳, see text.

3. *Dhàm-njiɛn* 澹然 refers primarily to the mood of persons, though it could conceivably refer to the skies as well.

4. The *njiu-qiə* 如意, "as-you-please," was a kind of rough staff used to scratch oneself with (Chao).

7. *Qài-qài* 曖曖 is a "haziness," probably referring to the sun shining through the steamy summer sky. *Guei* 閨 is usually the women's chambers and tends specifically to implicate women. It is not a place where Wang would be entertaining P'ei Ti, and Wang's inferential description of its sultriness seems stragely out of place.

8. *Dhen-ga* 田家 can either refer to someone of a farm family or to the home itself. The former is slightly more common in poetry, and the translation reflects this interpretation. If, however, the second meaning applies, the line becomes: "To the farm home they bring word." The lines that follow may be the news of spring that is brought.

9. *Xiən-xiən* 欣欣 usually refers simply to joyousness, but the usage here strongly echoes its special application in T'ao Ch'ien's *Kuei-ch'ü-lai tz'u*: "The trees are joyous and almost in full burgeoning" 木欣欣以向榮 (*Wh* 45.28b). From this *xiən-xiən* becomes a descriptive metaphor for vegetative growth.

10. For *dhàm-dhàm* 澹澹 Chao cites Li Shan gloss "full and level," applied to its use in the *Kao-t'ang fu* 高唐賦 (*Wh* 19.3a). In fact, the gloss cited by Chao is to *dhàm-dhàm* 淡淡, a descriptive binome closely related to *dhàm-dhàm*. Soon after the use of *dhàm-dhàm* in the *Kao-t'ang fu*, *dhàm-dhàm* occurs (*Wh* 19.3b), where it is glossed as "the manner of water shaking" on the authority of the *Shuo-wen*. The contradictory meanings of "still" and "agitated" appear in early glosses of the character *dhàm* alone, and both meanings appear in literary uses. I have decided to keep agitation ("churning") on the authority of the *Shuo-wen* gloss. The use of *shraeng* 生 is interesting, because it may suggest that the waters first "appear" (i.e., rise) against the banks or embankments meant to contain them.

12. The use of the pronoun *ghiə* 其, "their," is a strong mark of the *ku-shih* style in general and the style of T'ao Ch'ien in particular.

13. Chao feels constrained to note that *chrɛk* 策 refers to P'ei's walking stick rather than to "plans"; the line could easily, but perhaps incorrectly, be read "make ready plans to return."

14. *Gàm-gàu* 敢告 means literally "to be so bold as to inform you." The "boldness," *gàm*, was conventionally used with conveying opinions and information to the court or superiors. Its use here is surely playful, a mock trepidation in telling P'ei he should go home because Wang, the "farmer," has to attend to his seasonal duties. P'ei, indeed, has a special obligation to leave Wang alone because *nong-zhiə* 農時, "time for farming," is something one should not interfere with, a time "not to be missed": 不遺農時 (*Mencius* IA.3).

CHAPTER 5

05732: *CTs*, p. 1221; *Wycc* 4.13b; *Tscs*, p. 243.
Rhymes: 1 *lo*, 2 *djio*, 4 *njio*. Regulated.
Title: Ts'ui of the title is Ts'ui Hsing-tsung 崔興宗, onetime Omissioner of the Right and at this time living as a private citizen. Lu's quatrain is one of a series written during a visit by Lu, Wang Wei (06144), Wang Chin (06159), and Pei Ti (06191). There is also a quatrain in the series by Ts'ui himself (06197); see *Tscs*, p. 243.

1. *Qiaèng* 映 means "to cast light on" something, "to have light cast on" something, "to reflect," or to have two colors or forms "offset" one another. Probably from the meaning of having one object showing up through another, it can mean "screen" or "conceal." However, in specific poetic usages, it is often very difficult to tell which of these relationships is implied. In many cases it seems to refer to something "half-hidden" (e.g., 07101.6; 18031.2), but it is often very difficult to tell which of the objects is in the foreground; e.g., in 10064.6 映竹五湖村, we do not know if the villages appear "against a background of bamboo" or if they are "half-hidden in the bamboo." As *qiaèng* suggests, the juxtaposition of colors and forms is seen as "casting light." In the case of this line, because the visitors must rely on the evidence of their ears, *qiaèng*, usually a visual word, must mean either "hiding," or it must be something like "sunlit." From other uses of *qiaèng-djiuk* 映竹, the former interpretation seems more likely.

2. The point of this couplet is that while approaching Ts'ui's dwelling, the visitors heard evidence of human presence, but when they came closer, the house seemed to be deserted. Peering in the windows and seeing no one there was part of the theme of "seeking the recluse and not finding him in" (cf. 06200.4); this is somewhat out of place in this situation.

3. *Gau-nguà* 高臥, "to rest on high," is what a recluse does; *gau* combines the physical "height" of mountains with the moral "height" of noble values and an "aloofness" of disposition which keeps its distance from the common world. The connection between "resting on high" and sickness can be seen in the title and first lines of *Wh* 26.8b–9a.

4. *Huan-dǒ* 環堵, the "circling wall," has canonical echoes as the humble dwelling of a man of learning; see the *Ju-hsing* 儒行 chapter of the *Li-chi*: "A man of learning possesses an estate of one *mǒu* [ca. 1.82 acres], a dwelling with a low circling wall" 儒有一畝之宮環堵之室 (*SPTK* ed., c. 19, section 41, p. 180). The implication is that a scholar should live in humble circumstances, and indeed, the "low circling wall" characterizes the dwelling of the anonymous recluse of T'ao Ch'ien's *Wu-liu hsien-sheng chuan* 五柳先生傳. *Mung-lung* 蒙籠 suggests not only a dense tangle of vegetative growth, but also involves concealment, as is appropriate for the recluse. The implication is clearly that the low wall is overgrown. This juxtaposition in the last line is striking, and it would not be inappropriate to hear it behind Tu Fu's famous "*Ghyɛn* and *Kuən*—one worn out man of learning" 乾坤一腐儒 (11627).

06270: *CTs*, p. 1334; *Hyylc* in *TjhTs*, p. 110; *Khc* in *TjhTs*, p. 188; *Chc* in *TjhTs*, p. 324; *Yhc* in *TjhTs*, p. 376; *Wyyh* 318.2b–3a; *Tscs*, p. 285.
Rhymes: 2 *sim*, 4 *lim*, 6 *qim*, 8 *ghyim*. Regulated.
Title: *Hyylc* adds 遊 before the title; for 氏 *Khc* reads 門. The frequent early anthologizing of this poem attests to its popularity, due largely, I suspect, to its third couplet.

1. For 居 *Hyylc* reads 本 and *Khc* reads 在; note that *Khc* again unimaginatively reads 在 for 映 in line 4.

2. *Qiǎn-sim* 隱心 is a new compound, probably a variation for the sake of rhyme on the common *qiǎn-dzhiɛng* 隱情. *Shraeng qiǎn-sim* 生隱心 literally means "it gives rise to a reclusive mind/heart."

4. The Feng runs into the Wei just upstream from Ch'ang-an, and its course lies between the capital and the Chung-nan Mountains. For the problems of *qiaèng* 映, see note to 05732, line 1: either the Feng "reflects the gardens and groves," or it reflects light back upon them.

5–6. This famous couplet is an excellent example of poetic diction: literally "Roof covers pass-through-winter snow; courtyard darkens not-yet-evening shadows." It is clear that the snow is what is doing the covering and the shadows are doing the darkening. We have a Fred that resolves nicely into a passive, with the *qiu* 於 marking agency implied after the verb (see 05914n, ll. 5–6).

7. The descriptive binome *leu-leu* 家家 implies vastness and tranquillity; its primary semantic element is "emptiness." The *njin-giaěng* 人境, which the Su villa lies beyond, echoes the "realm of men" within which T'ao Ch'ien built his reclusive dwelling in "Drinking Wine" V.

06291: *CTs*, p. 1337; *Hyylc* in *TjhTs*, pp. 110–11; *Twt* 16A.11a; *Wyyh* 155.2b; *Tscs*, p. 284.
Rhymes: 2 *duan*, 4 *han*.
Metrics: Note the violation on *tzèi* 霽 in the third line: it is interesting in connection with Tsu Yung's assertion of the poem's completeness, that this violation would be acceptable as the seventh-line, fourth-position violation that often occurs in an eight-line regulated poem.

3. Under the pressure of composition to a set topic, a poet can always raid the *Wh*, as Tsu Yung has done here and in the second line. What comes to Tsu's mind is a couplet of Hsieh T'iao (*Wh* 27.7b):

At the edge of the clouds, Ch'u's mountains appear,   雲端楚山見
Beyond the woods, Wu's peaks are tiny.   林表吳岫微

Though the use of *biěu* 表 would not have puzzled anyone with much education, its formality is evident in the fact that Li Shan felt it necessary to gloss it as "beyond" 外也. The more common *nguài* 外 would have served Tsu Yung just as well in the tone pattern, but it lacked the formal elegance of *biěu*.

06417: *CTs*, p. 1368; *Hyylc* in *TjhTs*, p. 89; *Yhc* in *TjhTs*, p. 380; *Wyyh* 166.6a–6b; *Tscs*, p. 288.
Rhymes: 2 *ngóu*, 4 *kóu*, 6 *dóu*, 8 *hóu*, 10 *sóu*.
Metrics: Note that this is one of those "old style" poems that willfully avoids any couplet that might seem regulated. Occasional "old style" verse tended to slip into regulation in one or more couplets during the seventh and eighth centuries, but during the eighth century there were more and more poems like this which avoided regulation even beyond the probabilities of random tone distribution. Nor is it any accident that the poet is a southeasterner writing of a southeastern location on a theme that stands opposed to the public demands of capital poetry.
Title: Jo-yeh Creek runs beneath Jo-yeh Mountain in Shao-hsing County of modern Chekiang, and from there into Mirror Lake. This is the famous "Washing Gauze Creek" 浣紗溪 where the ancient beauty Hsi Shih was discovered.

3. For 晚 *Wyyh* reads 好.
4. For 花路 *Wyyh* reads 落花. The trail of flowers coming out of the creek's mouth indicates that blossoming trees lie upstream, and the poet, on entering the creek, will be going up toward the source. The association with Peach Blossom Spring is particularly strong here.
5. The phrase *tzièi-ià* 際夜, "to meet night," "at night's edge," is very unusual for this use of *tzièi* as "reach"; it usually occurs only with "reaching" physical things.
6. For 南 *Yhc* reads 北, presumably to have the poet gazing wistfully back toward the capital—an incongruous suggestion.
7. *Iong-iong* 溶溶 was a binome from the *Ch'u-tz'u*, not then in common use in *shih*. *Iong-iong* describes the rolling of waves; see Wang Yi's gloss 波貌. Underlying the use here is the common compound "mists and waves" or "misty waves," *qen-hɑ* 煙波.
8. For 月 *Hyylc* incomprehensibly reads 風.
9. Here I follow the interpretation of *tsiǎ* 且 as 正, "just now at their most," suggested by

Chang Hsiang in *Stcyths*, p. 86. In T'ang poetic language the real values of some poetic particles are perhaps the most difficult elements to recover. The general practice of those studying poetic particles is to list the classical glosses, then see which make the most sense in a given line. Chang Hsiang, in contrast, often extrapolates from contexts, sometimes successfully and sometimes not. But particles add a subtle quality of tone or mood to a line, and we should not feel secure with either system of resolving their meaning. There is a great difference between the true and the plausible. Equally plausible resolutions for *tsiǎ* here are glosses like 尚, "still a rolling flood" or 己, "have become a rolling flood."

    10. Literally "I want to be a fishing-pole-holding old man."

06171: *CTs*, p. 1313; *Wycc* 4.2a; *Tscs*, p. 241.
Rhymes: 2 *liò*, 4 *gò*. Unregulated.
Title: *Miən-haěng* is an apricot wood with straight grains, poetically associated with the beams of a fine dwelling; e.g., *Wh* 16.12b. As in most of the poems of the *Wang Stream Collection*, nothing in P'ei's poem could be construed as a response to Wang's poem on the same topic.

06229: *CTs*, p. 1326; The poem occurs in the *T'ang-yin t'ung-chien* (which was probably the source for the *CTs* version), and the *Tytc* had a source for a number of Ts'ui Hao's poems which is either no longer extant or which I have not been able to locate.
Rhymes: 2 *siɛn*, 4 *jhiuɛn*; 5 *gěn*, 6 *ghiǎn*, 8 *dzhin*. The second rhyme group in this poem is *t'ung-yün*.

    2. This suggests she is going to meet a lover.
    5. *Gěn* 緊 implies a special keenness or sharpness to the wind; cf. 08027.15 for a similar usage.
    6. Heng-t'ang 橫塘 could be the Heng-t'ang near Hsiang-yang, thus evoking the ambience of the *yüeh-fu* "Songs of the West" 西曲; cf. 20662.1, where Heng-t'ang is obviously near Hsiang-yang. But here it is most likely the Heng-t'ang embankment near Chin-ling, as in Ts'ui's 06251.
    7. A river's being *liok* 綠, "dark green," suggests a southern or southeastern river and evokes the ambience of Wu; cf. 05539.3; 06650.1.
    8. *Sim-ziǔ* 心緒 with related compounds like *dzhiəng-ziǔ* 情緒, *qiə-ziǔ* 意緒, and *siə-ziǔ* 思緒, are a group of terms describing emotions. Members of the compound group first appear in the Southern Dynasties, and the group becomes common in the T'ang. *Ziǔ* is used twice by Lu Chi in connection with emotions, in *Wh* 16.19b and 24.25b. These terms do not so much describe general emotions as refer to emotions about something or stirred by something.

06244: *CTs*, p. 1329; *Khc* in *TjhTs*, pp. 155–56; *Yhc* in *TjhTs*, p. 365; *Ttc* in *TjhTs*, p. 615; *Twt* 16A.9b; *Wyyh* 312.6a; *Tscs*, p. 311.
Rhymes: 2 *lou*; 4 *iou*, 6 *jiou*, 8 *jrhiou*. Second half regulated.

    1. *CTs* notes 黃鶴 as a variant for 白雲, but no early text supports it.
    2. For 此 *Khc* and *Wyyh* read 茲. For 餘 *Ttc* reads 作 and *Wyyh* reads 遺.
    4. For 載 *Khc* reads 里. The image is of the skies in which the crane never returns.
    5. Han-yang is near where the Han River empties into the Yangtze.
    6. Parrot Isle lies in the Yangtze near this spot. It is supposed to have received its name because Mi Heng, author of the "Parrot Fu," was killed there.

06522: *CTs*, p. 1387; *CKhsc* 2.9a.
Rhymes: 2 *mǒu*, 4 *hiǒu*, 6 *tziǒu*, 8 *tzǒu*, 10 *liǒu*, 12 *iǒu*, 14 *dǒu*, 16 *biǒu*. Unregulated.

    2. The T'ang *mǒu* was about 5.8 acres, so Ch'u's farm is approximately 174 acres.
    3. In other words, silk from mulberry-eating silkworms and millet for food.
    7. As in the Cheng interpretation of *Shih* 82. *CTs* gives 善 as a variant for 喜.
    10. As in line 11 of T'ao Ch'ien's first *Kuei-yüan-t'ien chü* 歸園田居 (*CTsins* 6.5a).
    11. The use of *jhiəng* 乘 here is somewhat strange. One can *jhiəng-ngiuaet* 乘月, *jhiəng-shiə* 乘時, or do something *jhiəng-njit* 乘日, but in these cases *jhiəng* does not really mean "during." One parallel usage occurs in an "Unclassified Poem" of Ho Shao (*Wh* 29.31a), where a chill wind rises *jhiəng-ziɛk* 乘夕, but the usage is sufficiently unusual for Li Shan to gloss *jhiəng* as 陵 or 侵.

Jhiəng means to "carry" or "ride," and thus to "go along with." In Ch'u's poem it must mean that the friends return "with the coming of night."

12. Literally, the winds blow through "door and windows." Note that the "chill winds" are what *jhiəng-ziɛk* in the *Wh* passage alluded to above. This is a good indication that Ch'u had Ho Shao's poem in mind when he invented *jhiəng-ià* 乘夜.

13. *Tsiɛ̆n* 淺 applies to water and is appropriate here because the Milky Way is a "river." Ch'u's compositional technique was strongly associative, and his associations here move among the "unclassified poems" and related Old Poems in *chüan* 29 of the *Wh*. Here Ch'u is unmistakably echoing "Old Poem" X: "The river of stars is clear and shallow" (*Wh* 29.6b).

14. Again we have a line that is a transformation of a line from an "Unclassified Poem" in *Wh* 29. Fu Hsüan's "The Dipper swiftly rises and sinks" 北斗忽低昂 (*Wh* 29.26b). The intrusion of the solitary and pensive mode of Chien-an and Wei poetry into a georgic vignette is characteristic of T'ao Ch'ien's poetry.

16. This is reminiscent of the closing invitation of T'ao Ch'ien's "Drinking Wine" IX or of Wang Chi 02606. The closing invitation to have a drink becomes common in T'ang poetry, the most famous examples being 11139 and 22761, the latter being particularly close to Ch'u's ending here.

06503: *CTs*, p. 1385; *CKhsc* 2.3b–4a; *Hyylc* in *TjhTs*, p. 97; *Wyyh* 319.11b; *Tscs*, p. 323.
Title: *Hyylc* omits 即; *Wyyh* reads 書情 for 即事.
Rhymes: 2 *tziə*, 4 *zhiə*, 6 *jriə*, 8 *biəi*, 10 *giəi*, 12 *byi*, 14 *giuəi*, 16 *iɛ*. *T'ung-yün*. The fifth and seventh couplets are unregulated. The first line has compensatory violations in the fourth and fifth positions, and the second and third couplets are two "A" form couplets.

1–2. This is an echo of T'ao Ch'ien's *Kuei yüan-t'ien chü* 歸園田居 II (*CTsins* 6.5a). *Bho-iɛp* 蒲葉 are the leaves of a kind of cattail or calamus (*chiəng-bho* 昌蒲). Lines 3 and 4 suggest these serve primarily as seasonal markers, but the white parts of the roots are also edible. For 杏 *Wyyh* give 荇 as a variant and notes that this is the reading in Ch'u's collected works. Though this is not the reading in the present version of Ch'u's collection, there is no reason to suppose that the collection as possessed by the *Wyyh* editors was superior.

4. Injunctions not to miss the proper time for farming occur often in early texts; see note to 05797.14.

5. Though *DKW* glosses *ngiaeng-jhin* 迎晨 as "toward dawn," *ngiaeng* has an almost ritual significance, as when the emperor "greets" the seasons, the new year, or the sun.

6. The *dung-jriə* 東菑 are referred to elsewhere in Ch'u's poetry (06512) and may be remembered as the scene of farm labor and repose in Wang Wei 06072; see note 06072.

8. Here and in line 13 *Wyyh* reads 鳥 for 烏.

9. There is a question whether the *hop* 合 refers to the "joining together" of the crows' voices or their actual "coming together" to form a flock. The former seems more likely. *Duk-sàu* 啄嗛 is an original compound combining "pecking for food" and *sàu*, the raucous sound of many birds.

10. Though *ngɑu-ngɑu* 嗷嗷 originally had the association of the sad cries of geese from *Shih* 181, it came to be associated with any sad cries, especially from groups. It is impossible to tell if 道飢 is *dhàu-giəi*, "telling of their hunger," or *dhàu-giəi*, "hungry on their ways." One does find some remote parallels for the second, but I suspect *dhàu-giəi* is the more likely here.

11. The discussion of *chriək-qiən jiə sim* 惻隱之心 can be found in *Mencius* IIA.6. It is the "origin of humaneness" 仁之端也, which makes a person respond to a child about to fall into a well, regardless of knowing the parents or hoping for personal advantage. We may doubt, however, that Mencius would have approved of the application of it Ch'u Kuang-hsi has made here.

12. The referent of *liǎng* 兩, "both," is uncertain, but I take it as the poet's sympathy for both the starving crows and for the earthworms that are about to be eaten.

13. *Wyyh* reads 發食餉田鳥. The use of *bɑt* 撥 here is difficult. Since the poet has been plowing, it must be seeding time; otherwise it would be tempting to take *bɑt* in its common sense of "pull up" (cf. 撥鑷), the poet taking out growing grain and giving it to the crows. The same meaning of *bɑt* could conceivably be applied to the poet "taking out" seed grain and giving it to

the crows. I prefer to take it in the sense of *biaet* 發, as "distribute," to cast the seed grain out for the birds to eat.

15. For 誚 *Hyylc* reads the equally plausible 笑.

16. *Iɛ-sim* 移心 is a variation on the more common *iɛ-dzhiɛng* 移情.

06446: *CTs*, p. 1374; *Ckhsc* 1.2a–2b.
Rhymes: 2 *liou*, 4 *gou*, 6 *jiou*, 8 *bhiou*, 10 *iou*, 12 *jiou*, 14 *xiou*. Unregulated, except for second couplet.

1–2. In other words, each loves to be closer to the source.

4. *Zhiuɛ-gou* 垂鈎, literally "to let the hook hang down," is a conventional kenning for fishing. The question of the line lies in *dzhiɛm* 潛, "hide," whether the hook is hidden from the sight of the fisherman (as it obviously is), hidden from the sight of the fish (as the bait is not), or the fisherman's position is hidden from the sight of the fish or of other people; see line 6.

7. *Dzhiĕng-ngiaen* 靜言 is probably simply "calmly" or "silently," with the *ngiaen* interpreted as a particle, as in *Shih* 26: "Silently brood on it" 靜言思之. *Shih* 26 begins with the image of the "drifting cypress boat," which is comparable to the fisherman's situation here; furthermore, *Shih* 26's 靜言思 is clearly parallel to Ch'u's 靜言念, though the misery implicit in the *Shih* line is inapplicable. In Ch'u's poem the parallel with *qɑn-dzhu* 安坐 might suggest that the *ngiaen* is actually "speaking," but it is interesting to note that a Lu Chi use of *dzhiĕng-ngiaen* in parallel to "long whistle" 長嘯 has *Shih* 26 given as its source by Li Shan (*Wh* 28.1b). What this suggests is that a sophisticated T'ang commentator like Li Shan saw parallelism simply as a matching of characters, whether those characters formed a semantic pair or not; i.e., *ngiaen* used as a particle in its *Shih* sense can be set in parallel position to a verb of the same kind like *dzhuǎ* and still not be forced into the meaning "speak." This is all the more remarkable here since *dzhiĕng* and *qɑn* form such a perfect match. *Jiung-shǐ* 終始 is literally "ending and beginning," commonly used from early texts on to mean "from beginning to end," "continuity" of an event.

8. *Djhim-bhiou* 沈浮 is a common antithetical compound for "quiescence and activity," "hiding oneself away and coming forth." Precisely what object in the scene serves as the contemplative emblem of *djhim-bhiou* is uncertain.

10. Literally, "His mind, faraway, wanders with the clouds." In literary Chinese, if one's mind is "on something," the mind is "out there with it." Cf. Lu Chi, *Wen-fu* 文賦: "Intention goes far, far, and looks down on the clouds" 志眇眇而臨雲, or in the *Shen-ssu* 神思 chapter of the *Wen-hsin tiao-lung*: "Thus, when the principle of thought is at its most essential, the spirit wanders with things" 故思理爲妙神與物遊 (p. 80).

11. *Ngiaek-làng* 逆浪 is used to describe waves that cause difficulty for boats, presumably "waves which run against" the boat. It may also be taken as a verb-object compound, "to go against the waves." This is one of those English grammatical discriminations which is not made in the physical scene or in poetic Chinese.

12. Ts'ang-chou lies in modern Hopei, not too far from the Yellow Sea.

13. Echoing T'ao Ch'ien's *Kuei-ch'ü-lai tz'u*: "I have made my own mind the servant of my physical form" 既自以心爲形役 (*Wh* 45.27a).

14. I have taken here what is perhaps the less likely interpretation of *haeng-xiou* 行休 as "moving and halting," because it more perfectly fits the context. However, *haeng-xiou* is used in the *Kuei-ch'ü-lai tz'u*, and especially considering the allusion to the *Kuei-ch'ü-lai tz'u* in the preceding line, it should be perhaps taken in the sense it is used there, as "about to die": "I am stirred that my life will soon be over" 感吾生之行休 (*Wh* 45.29a). In this case, Ch'u's line would read "His joy is in being about to die." Note that this is very different from saying that he awaits death with equanimity; rather it means that his joy resides in death's proximity—an extreme sentiment to say the least.

10384: *CTs*, p. 2224; Juan, pp. 119–20; *KCsc* 5.3a–3b.
Rhymes: 1 *sǒu*, 2 *shiǒu*, 4 *kǒu*; 5 *qiǝi*, 6 *giǝi*, 8 *giuǝi*. Unregulated.

2. *Djiò-ngĕn* 駐眼 is not the usual way to say "fix one's gaze" (but cf. 10793.5), and the construction seems to be an expansion of the paradigm of compounds like *tjiĕng-miuk* 騁目. Note that following the verb-less first line, there are three verbs of motion in this line.

3. Literally, "he wants to get to know his family name and given name." The wordiness of this line is appropriate for the heptasyllabic song style.

4. The use of *ta* 他 as a third-person-pronoun direct object is strongly colloquial at this period; its use contrasts to old style and prosaic *jiə* 之, and to the tendency of poetic diction to omit the direct-object pronoun altogether or use *siang* 相. See also the use of *lip-tziə* 笠子 in line 5, and *lèu-dək* 料得, instead of the more poetic *qiəng* 應.

7. For *miɔ dhèng-jiə* 無定止, see 08070. 14, where it describes the "never-resting" changes of fortune.

06469: *Cts*, p. 1377; *CKhsc* 1.7a–7b.
Rhymes: 2 *ghiək*, 4 *shriək*, 6 *siək*, 8 *jriək*, 10 *djhiək*. Unregulated except for the third couplet.
Title: Mao Mountain 茅山 was, of course, the center of one of the most important Taoist covens. The references to the "peak of immortals" and to "pines and cypresses" in the end may suggest the coven, but on the whole, the poem is a straightforward landscape poem.

1–2. Note how much closer Ch'u stays to the Hsieh Ling-yün model than Meng Hao-jan.

3. *Chriu-qiaĕng* 初景 refers to the "new light" of spring, or to the "new scene," *chriu-giaĕng*, from its use in a landscape poem by Hsieh Ling-yün (*Wh* 22.12a).

4. This use of *hom* 含 as a vegetative scene "holding in" some color or quality like "moisture" is common in poetry.

5. The initial *njiə* 而 is decidedly prosaic.

6. Besides indicating wish or fulfillment of wish, as I take it here, *leu* 聊 may mean "for a while."

06648: *CTs*, p. 1418; *CKhsc* 5.11b.
Rhymes: 2 *miən*, 4 *ngiaen*. Regulated.

1. In common poetic usage, *guà* 過 may mean "stop by" as well as "pass."

2. *Huèn-bhiuk* 袨服 are robes of black and yellow (the primal colors of Heaven and Earth), and were associated with wealth and glory.

4. *Hom-dzhiɛng* 含情 usually does not mean simply to "have feelings" about something, but to "keep one's emotions hidden"; see Li Shan gloss, *Wh* 22.26b. *Pèn-ngiaen* 片言 is an incomplete statement, the full meaning of which must be inferred.

06649: *CTs*, p. 1418; *CKhsc* 5.11b.
Rhymes: 2 *jiò*, 4 *lò*. Regulated, *tse* rhyme, sequence of two "A" form couplets, with compensation in the first line.

4. This is a striking use of the evidence trope, perhaps serving as the model of Tu Mu's famous (28142):

Who would have known on the West of Bamboo Road　　　　　　誰知竹西路
That Yang-chou is there, where the songs and piping are.　　　歌吹是揚州

06660: *CTs*, p. 1419; *CKhsc* 5.13a; *Wyyh* 204.9a; *Yfsc* 29.6b.
Rhymes: 1 *biəi*, 2 *qiəi*, 4 *giuəi*. Regulated.

2. *Lɑ-qiəi* 羅衣 are the mark of a fair lady, but singularly inappropriate for the far north.

3. For 殿 *Yfsc* reads 帳. *Ghiăng-ləi* 强求 does not means that her attendants drag her out, but rather that they urge her or insist. She may, in fact, be compelling herself to go out.

CHAPTER 6

05951: *CTs*, p. 1273; Chao, p. 209; *Wyyh* 268.6a.
Rhymes: 2 *shriu*, 4 *liu*, 6 *shiu*, 8 *xiu*. Regulated.

Attribution: This poem is attributed to Wang in the *Wyyh*, and Meng Hao-jan's collection is given as the source. It should surprise us neither that such a poem does not appear in the early edition of Wang Wei's collection nor that it does not appear in the *SPTK* edition of Meng's poems. Occasional poems like this were often excluded from collections, and it may even be that Meng retained the only copy; furthermore, Wang's collection was compiled from what could be gathered together of his works after the An Lu-shan Rebellion. The *Ying-k'uei lü-sui* attributes the poem to Chang Tzu-jung; however, the *Wyyh*, for all its faults, had access to better and earlier sources, and in this case is precise about its source.

1. For 欲 *Wyyh* notes that the "collection" (presumably Meng Hao-jan's) reads 復. *Bhioù* 復 is clearly the easier reading.

2. *Shièi-dzhiɛng* 世情 are feelings like desire for advancement, fame, and profit.

3. The structure is unusual here: the prosaic exhortation in this line is explicitly a comment on the topic of the first two lines. Though Wang uses *djhiɑng-chrɛk* 長策 elsewhere (05922), the phrase has a history of political usage, like "policy." The quality of the statement here is "Do not think to make public policies—the only policy you should form is to return home."

5. *Dhen-shià* 田舍 was a hut built in the fields during the the season of fieldwork.

7. This line is strongly colloquial.

8. *Xiaèn* 獻 is literally to "present [the "Master Emptiness" *fu* to the throne]." In the context of parting poetry, this piece by Wang to Meng Hao-jan is singularly cool. The expected statement of personal loss at departure is totally absent. Even the praise of the private life is directed specifically to Meng's case, and there is no general statement in favor of the private over the public: "This is best for *you*." Indeed, it may not be overreading the poems to see a distinct indifference in Wang Wei's poem and a petulance in Meng Hao-jan's (see 07698).

07623: *CTs*, p. 1623; Yu, pp. 1–3; Hsiao, pp. 1–2; *MHjc* 1.1a; *Wyyh* 219.4b.
Rhymes: 2 *tsuì*, 4 *jì*, 6 *kiɔì*, 8 *ghyè* (*t'ung-yün*), 10 *suì*, 12 *mì*, 14 *iɔ̀*, 16 *ziɔ̀*, 18 *qiɔ̀*, 20 *kì*.
Title: Yu notes three different Fragrance Mountains, two in Honan and one in Kiangsu. Though, as Yu notes, it is uncertain which is meant here, the landscape described best suits the lower Yangtze region. Furthermore, in another poem to the monk Chan (07609), Meng speaks of his "late (in life?) path" 晚途, which if referring to his life, would more likely be from the time of one of his visits to the lower Yangtze region than to the time he was in Lo-yang (Honan).

1–2. This couplet is modeled on the opening of Hsieh Ling-yün's 登臨海嶠初發彊中作與 從弟惠連可見羊何共和之 (*Wh* 25.35a–35b). As Yu notes, *kung-tsuì* 空翠 appears in Hsieh Ling-yün's 過白岸亭 (*CSs* 3.11b–12a), but not only does the usage there suggest the phrase was already in use, it had gained even greater poetic currency during the T'ang. *Kung-tsuì* is literally "empty (formless or of the sky) azure," and the *tsuì* refers either to mists or vegetation. Though Meng's own "Empty azure lets fall (sinks to) the yard's shadow" 空翠落庭陰 (07755) tends somewhat to the side of vegetation's azure, Wang Wei's "Empty azure soaks a person's robes" 空翠濕人衣 (06123) almost surely refers to mist (because with *kung* vegetation would require a distant perspective, which is not the case here). Also suggesting the predominance of the sense of mist is P'ei Ti's "Mountain azure brushes a person's robes" 山翠拂人衣 (06170); clouds and mists are more often said to "brush" and "sweep" than vegetation. One could say that the mountain was "in" the azure vegetation, but it seems more plausible to have it in azure mists. This then would be picked up in the *piɔn-qiuɔn* 氣氳 of the following line.

6. The "incense in air," *xiɑng-kiɔ̀* 香氣, by which the poet recognizes the presence of the temple, is also the "fragrance," *xiɑng* 香, of Fragrance Mountain.

9. *Zhiɛk-mɔn* 石門 were standard elements of a secluded mountain dwelling. The use of *zhio* 殊 here is peculiar and is without close analogue in the *Wh* or contemporary poetry. It could relate the two elements that surround, having the gate "hard by" the ravine, but it seems better to take it as modifying *xɑk* 壑, a "sheer ravine" or a "strange ravine."

10. *Djiuɛ̌n* 轉 is the standard way to mark continuous change of state in poetry.

11. *Biaɛp-liǔ* 法侶, as noted by Yu, is a kenning for a monk; see *CLw* 6.16b. It is only one of several such kennings appearing in the Southern Dynasties; e.g., 法徒 (*CLw* 13.13b).

12. *Tsiɛng-dhɑm* 清談, translated freely as "speculative discussion," is the form of clever philosophical chat which flourished in the third and fourth centuries. *Xɛ̌u biɔt mì* 曉不寐 is literally "(even) at dawn we do not sleep." Note that the poem begins at dawn and comes here to dawn again, at which point the poet begins his meditation.

13. *Mò* 慕 also carries the sense of "admire." Thus, the line could easily read: "I have admired the true recluse." The genuineness of true reclusion is no hollow attribute; the alternative "false recluse," who pretends to lead a hermit's life while actually awaiting an invitation to serve, was satirized in the *Pei-shan yi-wen* 北山移文 (*Wh* 43.35b–40b).

14. *Leng-iə* 靈異 initially referred to specifically supernatural phenomena, but like many such words, it was steadily diminished until it came to refer only to what was "extraordinary," great men and fine landscapes. In the translation I have kept something of the otherworldly quality, even though Meng is not hoping to find feys. Rather, the bucolic scenes of the next couplet are a spiritual *leng-iə*.

18. *Gǒ-qiə* 古意 is difficult: it is usually either a significance embodied in the past or derived from thinking on the past. *Dhəi-bək* 苔壁 might be taken as "mossy cliffs," but these would seem to provide eternal verities; *gǒ-qiə* would more likely come from reminders of mortal impermanence on moss-covered walls. The use of *njiɛu* 饒 is particularly striking, and the line as a whole has an element of catachresis which is rare in Chinese poetry.

19. *Ngiuaèn-ngiaen* 願言 is a *Shih* phrase interpreted as "constantly," which was occasionally borrowed in later poetry. (*ngiaen* serves as a particle, as is common in the *Shih*). *Dhou* 投, however, usually refers to only temporary lodging, and thus runs at cross purposes to *ngiuaèn-ngiaen*. I have decided to keep the more orthodox interpretation of *ngiuaèn-ngiaen*, but it is possible that Meng is using the phrase in the sense of a Wu-ch'en gloss as "longing" 相思 (an interpretation based on its context in the *Shih*); see gloss to use in a letter by Ts'ao P'i to Wu Chin, *Wh* 42.10b. In that case the line would read, "I yearn to lodge on this mountain."

20. As Yu notes, the last line here is identical to the last line of Pao Chao's *Yung-shih shih* 詠史詩 (*Wh* 21.23b). The *Chuang-tzu* passage cited by Yu (deriving from Li Shan's note to Pao Chao's line) is not directly relevant.

07644: *CTs*, p. 1627; Yu, pp. 79–80; Hsiao, pp. 55–56; *MHjc* 1.15b.

Rhymes: 2 *dhep*; 4 *tziɛp*; 5 *xiəi*, 6 *qiəi*, 8 *giuəi*. Rhyme shifts are rare in poems as short as this. Often when rhyme shifts in a long heptasyllabic song, a rhyming couplet will mark the shift; this occurs here, but the effect is strange in a short pentasyllabic poem. The tone pattern is equally unusual: the first two couplets avoid any hint of tonal balance, then when the poem shifts from a *tse* to a *p'ing* rhyme, a regulated rhyming couplet appears (appropriate only at the beginning of poems). Then the seventh line breaks that pattern up violently with a series of four level tones in a row.

Title: Yu quotes a poem by Shen Yüeh and a tetrasyllabic poem of P'an Yüeh, cited by Li Shan, associating the phrase *tsəi-dzhiɛu* 採樵 with P'an Yüeh. This, however, seems unnecessary; "gathering firewood" is simply a bucolic activity.

2. The *djhiong-dhep* 重疊, "layering," of the streams occurs because the poet encounters stream after stream as he goes up and down the hills. The term is more commonly applied to the mountains themselves. The linking device whereby *shim-shrɛn* 深山 is inverted and repeated has been seen earlier in 07623 and is a strong mark of "old style" poetry.

3. *Bəng* 崩, marking the collapse of mountains, states, city walls, and the deaths of emperors, is a powerful word in this context, and it indicates that the bridge seems to have fallen in one catastrophic crash, rather than a gradual crumbling. *Nguà-jrha* 臥查, a "recumbent log," is an unusual phrase; as *jrha* usually refers to a log in the water, Meng is using the log to get across the stream.

5. The *bhǎn* 伴 may suggest that Meng went gathering firewood with others, but more likely the "companions" are figurative, other people encountered by chance in the mountains. The emptying out of the mountain landscape with the coming of evening was one of the events commonly noted in reclusive poetry.

6. *Bhèi-qiəi* 薜衣 are not really "burlap robes" but robes woven out of a kind of creeping vine; these form the mantle of a true recluse.

7. "Long songs" are a specific *yüeh-fu* category on the brevity of human life, but here, as often in T'ang poetry, the poet is simply singing a long time.

07646: *CTs*, p. 1628; Yu, pp. 40–41; Hsiao, pp. 32–33; *MHjc* 1.8a–8b; *Wyyh* 291.6b.

Rhymes: 2 *guɑt*, 4 *bɑt*, 6 *kuɑt*, 8 *mɑt*, 10 *tɑt*, 12 *xuɑt*. Meng Hao-jan tends to intrude one or two regulated couplets into his longer "old style" poems; here the fourth couplet is loosely regulated (*kiš* 起 being a moderate violation in line 7), and the fifth couplet is perfectly regulated.

Title: As Yu notes, Yü-p'u recalls one of Hsieh Ling-yün's finest and most famous landscape poems, "Fu-ch'un Isle" 富春渚 (*Wh* 26.33a–34a). It is hard to imagine that Meng could have written on this landscape without Hsieh's poem in mind. Both poems derive a spiritual liberation from the experience of the landscape, but in contrast to Hsieh's strenuous description of the landscape's physical form and complex meditation on its significance, Meng Hao-jan's poem is almost willfully rambling.

4. *Bat* 撥 is a problem: in this context it should mean to "punt" the boat. If *shiɛng* 槳 is the subject of *bat*, then it must mean something like "issue forth," but if the boatmen are the implied subjects, as I take it, then it is used for "handle (the oars)." Thus, the line is literally, "Oars' sound— in darkness they mutually ply them."

5. *Kiǝi-ziàng* 氣象 is a term suggesting both "atmosphere," in the sense of ambience, and "weather," specifically the signs of the weather.

10. As Yu notes, "otters offering fish" alludes to two passages in the *Li-chi*: one, in the *Yüeh-ling* 月令, associates the event with the first month of spring; the other, in the *Wang-chih* 王制, explains that otters take carp, display them in all directions, then offer them and do not eat them.

07734: *CTs*, p. 1645; Yu, pp. 158–59; Hsiao, pp. 79–80; *MHjc* 3.3a.
Rhymes: 2 *dhan*, 4 *guan*, 6 *kuan*, 8 *han*. Regulated.
Title: Ch'ien-t'ang County was in the area of Hang-chou (modern Chekiang). As Hsiao notes, Yen, otherwise unknown, must be the county magistrate. *Iǔ* 與 may indicate simply "accompanying" a poem of the same title by Yen.

1. As Yu notes, the first line involves an elaborate play on *bhaek-liš* 百里 as the domain of a county magistrate, a common reference. This is complicated by a double reference to the Judgement under hexagram 51, *Jin* 震, "Shock":

The Shock comes terrifyingly,	震求虩虩
Then laughter, ho-ho:	笑言啞啞
The Shock startles a hundred miles,	震驚百里
Does not make one lose ladle and fragrant wine.	不喪匕鬯

Through this text the thunder shock is always thought to have a range of a "hundred miles," *bhaek-liš*, and as Yu notes, when Mei Sheng describes the metaphorical thunder of the Ch'ien-t'ang bore, its sound can be heard a "hundred miles." Yu cites the *Po-K'ung liu-t'ieh* 白孔六帖, showing how the area of a magistracy and a thunder shock are combined in the kenning *Luǝi-biong* 雷封, a "Thunder fief," for a county magistracy. Thus, if we were to try to incorporate these associations in the translation, the first line would read, "Across your domain of a 'hundred miles,' the thunderous sound of the tidal bore rolls, in its accustomed range."

2. As Yu notes, this alludes to the common story of Fu Pu-ch'i 宓不齊, a disciple of Confucius, who when he governed Tan-fu spent his time playing his *ch'in*, and still Tan-fu was well governed. This is, of course, a compliment to Yen, and likewise a justification of the entertainment that seems to be in progress when the tidal bore comes.

4. If syntactic parallelism is maintained, the second hemistich of this line will read, "gaze out, awaiting the tide."

5. The *tsiou-hiuǝn* 秋雲 may refer to the spume of the tide rather than to real clouds.

6. The Po Sea usually refers to the sea off the northern coast; here it is simply a metaphor for the sealike breadth of the tidal bore.

7. Snow or snow-capped mountains were common metaphors for whitecaps and large billows.

8. *Qit-dzhuǎ* 一坐 refers to "everyone present in a group." The closing evocation of chill is strongly reminiscent of Tsu Yung's 06291.4.

07770: *CTs*, p. 1652; Yu, pp. 164–65; Hsiao, pp. 83–84; *MHjc* 3.4a.
Rhymes: 2 *iɛu*, 4 *djhiɛu*, 6 *ghyɛu*, 8 *biɛu*. Regulated.

1. *Miɑng* 望, the "view" of the title, unites "gazing," direction, and "hope" or desire. Here *miɑng* is not only the poet's southeastern "gaze," but the southeastern "heading" of the set sails. *Ziɛk* 席 are specifically "mat-sails," and *guèi* 挂 is the proper verb for "setting" them (Yu, citing Li Shan).

2. *Shuĭ-guɑk* 水國 was a common poetic term for the lower Yangtze region.

3. Yu cites the advice of the *Yi*: "It is advantageous to cross the great stream" 利涉大川. This is, at best, an ironic echo. The second hemistich divides more naturally *jrɛng-lì zhiɛp* 爭利涉, "to cross, struggling for advantage."

4. *Njim* 任, translated as "at the will of," is actually a more personal "trusting themselves to."

5. The intrusion of an imaginary interlocutor in the middle of a poem was common, but more common in "old style" poetry than in regulated verse; here it strongly violates parallelism.

6. T'ien-t'ai Mountain 天台山, with its famous stone bridge, was one of the most famous scenic spots in the Southeast. The perilous ascent of the mountain had long been associated with the quest for immortality, most notably in the imaginary ascent described by Sun Ch'o in the *Yu T'ien-t'ai-shan fu* 遊天台山賦.

7. I have preferred to take *dzhuɑ* 坐 in its basic meaning "to sit"; however, several of the colloquial poetic usages given by Chang Hsiang in the *Shih-tz'u-ch'ü yü-tz'u hui-shih* would be applicable here, especially "and so . . ." or "at this moment. . . ."

8. As Yu notes, this line echoes *Yu T'ien-t'ai-shan fu*: "One Redwall Mountain rose clouds rise, setting up a marker" 赤城霞起而建標 (*Wh* 11.4a). Li Shan cites the *T'ien-t'ai-shan t'u* 天台山圖 to the effect that Redwall Mountain was the "south gate" on the journey to T'ien-t'ai. Li also glosses *biɛu* 標 as "something (set up) by which a thing can be recognized." Seeing rose clouds from his boat, the poet is reminded of the rose clouds that Sun Ch'o wrote of rising from Redwall Mountain, a stage on the journey to T'ien-t'ai. *Ngiɑ-zhiĕ* 疑是 could be taken as a slightly more dubious "I wonder if they are," but the quality of the phrase is closest to "they seem to be. . . ."

07729: *CTs*, p. 1644; Yu, pp. 168–69; Hsiao, pp. 85–86; *MHjc* 3.4b–5a.
Rhymes: 2 *zhiɛng*, 4 *miaeng*, 6 *haeng*, 8 *huaeng*. Regulated.

1. On the advice of Daniel Bryant, I have decided here to follow Yu's suggested reading of 愛 for 友. The "Master of Ultimate One" 太一子 refers to a Taoist adept, also mentioned in 07640 and probably the adept meant in 07683.

2. See note to 07770, line 8. *Tsɑn-ha* 飡霞, "feeding on rose clouds," or more properly "gulping rose clouds," was a form of Yang-ingestion commonly used in poetry to refer to an immortal or to someone aspiring to be an immortal.

3. The Peak of Flowers was the highest ridge of T'ien-t'ai. The subject of the line could possibly be the Master of Ultimate One, but since the verb *zim* 尋, "seek," is the same as the "visit" of the title, it most likely refers to the poet's search for the adept.

4. As Yu and Hsiao note, Evil Creek was indeed the name of a prodigy-infested creek near T'ien-t'ai, but as Hsiao suggests, the line also refers to a common story found in various versions that Confucius or Tseng-tzu would not drink from Robbers' Spring and/or stop at a village called Conquering Mother because they "hated the name" 惡其名; see *Wh* 28.1a–1b with commentary.

5. *Bhiɑng* 憑 is an elegant variation on the poetic location-marker *qiɑi* 依, as "among."

6. The use of *dzhet* 截, "to cut straight through," for a water journey is rather unusual, but not without some precedent.

07727: *CTs*, p. 1644; Yu, p. 147–48; Hsiao, pp. 65–66; *MHjc* 3.1a.
Rhymes: 2 *gyim*, 4 *lim*, 6 *shim*, 8 *gyim*. Regulated.

1. *Dhɑi-ziɑ* 代謝 is a compound describing one thing taking the place of another; in the translation I have decided to keep both components, the "loss," *ziɑ*, of one thing and its "replacement," *dhɑi*, by another. It is possible to take *njin-jrhiɑ* 人事 simply as "human life," as does Frankel, but here I have taken it as "human affairs" to emphasize the events and experiences in life. The line strongly recalls T'ao Ch'ien's: "(In the relation) of winter's cold and summer's heat there is succession, loss" 寒暑有代謝 (CTsins 6.12b).

2. *Hiuǎng-ləi* 往來 may refer to the restless physical movement of people as well as, by extension, to the "coming and going" of their lives, the change of generations. It is precisely this process which "forms past and present."

3. Frankel takes *shiəng-tziɛk* 勝迹 as referring to the beauty of the landscape which is "kept" alone; Yu takes *shiəng-tziɛk* as the "traces of glorious men." *Tziɛk* 迹 is usually an artifact or identifiable natural thing or scene that reminds a viewer of someone that has been there before. Though my translation straddles several possibilities, I think *shiəng-tziɛk* refers to the "traces of men past in the glorious scene."

4. *Ngǎ-bài* 我輩 is simply "we," "our group," but the group is clearly defined in distinction from those who have been to the place in the past, hence the translation.

5. As Yu notes, Fishweir Islet lies in the Mien River (part of the Han River) and was the dwelling of P'ang Te-kung 龐德公, a famous recluse of Hsiang-yang to whom Meng refers often in his poetry. Fishweir is thus a *tziɛk*, a "site" that reminds the viewer of someone past.

6. Yün-meng Marsh would be associated not only with the ancient kings of Ch'u but also with Ch'ü Yüan.

7. Like Yu and Frankel, I must here quote the relevant passages in the *Tsin History*:

Yang Hu delighted in the mountains and rivers. Whenever the atmosphere was particularly fine, he would always go off to Mount Hsien, and there would drink and recite poetry, never tiring the whole day through. But once, overcome by emotion and sighing, he said to Tsou Chan and others, "As long as the universe has been, so long has this mountain been. Many have been the worthies and great men who, just like I and you now, have climbed here to gaze afar. They have all perished and are heard of no more—this is what gives me sorrow. If after my lifetime I still have any consciousness, then surely my soul will still climb to this spot." And Tsou Chan said, "Your virtue crowns the whole world; your way continues that of the wise men of the past. Such noble reputation and admiration will surely continue on with this mountain. But for people like myself, it will be just as you have said." . . . [After Yang Hu's death], the people of Hsiang-yang erected a stele and built a temple at the spot where Yang Hu used to take his ease on Mount Hsien, and every year they would make sacrifices to him. And not a single person who looked on the stele could help shedding tears, so that Tu Yü gave it the name "the stele of tears" (*Tsin*, pp. 1020, 1022).

07767: *CTs*, pp. 1651–52; Yu, pp. 151–52; Hsiao, pp. 69–72; *MHjc* 3.1b; *Hyylc* in *TjhTs*, p. 92; *Yhc* in *TjhTs*, p. 381 (incomprehensibly ascribed to Meng Chiao!); *Wyyh* 160.4a; *Tscs*, p. 348. Rhymes: 1 *shiu*, 2 *liu*, 4 *shriu*, 6 *djhiu*, 8 *xiu*. Regulated.
Title: *Nom-shrɛn* 南山 here clearly refers to the mountains of Hsiang-yang rather than to Chung-nan, as is often the case. It seems, however, that readers unfamiliar with the specifics of Meng Hao-jan's biography might easily have taken *nom-shrɛn* as Chung-nan.

1. "Palace gates," *bək-kiuaet* 北闕, are literally the "northern palace gates," the place to which, as Yu notes, letters seeking employment and interviews were sent; see *Hs*, p. 64. *Zhiǎng-shiu* 上書 was a standard Han term for a memorial in the Han, though its primary sense is a "letter sent to a superior"; in the T'ang, *zhiǎng-shiu* were usually addressed to high officials, often requesting favor or advancement.

2. *Bhièi* 弊, translated as "poor," is usually taken as a term of humility referring to one's own dwelling. While this is undeniably true, it is not so common in poetry that the semantic element of "poor" disappears altogether. Note that the first couplet is not only a rhyming couplet, it is also perfectly parallel.

3. Though one might expect *mio-dzhəi* 無才 (*mio* does occur in expanded forms; *mio* . . . *dzhəi*), *biət-dzhəi* 不才 is the frozen archaic form for "untalented." The precise value of *miaeng* 明 in the bound form *miaeng-jiǒ* 明主 has been a question of debate; it seems to refer primarily to discernment, and it is clearly this quality which is called to mind here.

4. *Shriu* 疏 may be taken as translated, "fewer," though it may just as easily refer to "estrangement," the fact that his old friends "keep their distance" from him.

5. *Tsuəi* 催 occurs often in poetry when the mark of something is treated as a cause that "hurries on" the state it marks.

6. *Tseng-iɑng* 青陽, translated as "spring's green force," is literally "green-Yang," a kenning for spring with the authority of the *Erh-ya*, where it is the explanation of spring. *Biək* 逼 is a forceful proximity which is best translated as "pressing": what is suggested here is that evidence of the "green-Yang" of spring marks and moves one forcibly closer to New Year's Day, *siuèi-djhiu* 歲除.

7. Though I have translated *hiuaĕng-huaei* 永懷 as the characters are given, "constantly with som thing on one's mind," I suspect that the proper interpretation here is *hiuaèng-huaei*, taking 永 in the sense of 咏, "to sing of what is on one's mind."

8. The relations between the string of images in the last line are willfully indeterminate. The window suggests either the poet is gazing out or that light and shadows are being cast in. The "emptiness" of the window indicates that it is unblocked, but it also suggests the insubstantiality of moonlight and shadows as well as the "lack of purpose" in the poet's life.

07855: *CTs*, p. 1668; Yu, p. 279; Hsiao, p. 205; *MHjc* 4.12a–12b; *Wyyh* 291.6b; *Tscs*, p. 348. Rhymes: 2 sin; 4 njin. Regulated.
Title: The Chien-te is the name given to the Che River above Chien-te County in Chekiang. For a discussion of this poem and 07848, which follows, see Paul Kroll, "The Quatrains of Meng Hao-jan." *MS* 31 (1974–75): 344–74.

1. *Iɛ-jiou* 移舟 implies volition.
4. The proximity of the moon's reflection is probably what is meant here.

07848: *CTs*, p. 1667; Yu, pp. 279–80; Hsiao, p. 205; *MHjc* 4.1b; *Wyyh* 157.5b. Rhymes: 1 xĕu, 2 dĕu, 4 shiĕu. Regulated, with two "A" form couplets in succession.

1. *Gak* 覺 combines the notion that the poet was "unaware" of dawn and that he did not "wake up" with dawn. To qualify *men* 眠 with *chuin* 春 is rather unusual, just as "sleeping in spring" is in English: the interesting circumstance of the poet's sleeping is not that it is daytime, night, or darkness, but that it is in spring.
2. This is the moment, the first perception, and perhaps the cause of waking.
3. *Ià-ləi* 夜來 is a bound form, usually meaning "last night."

07630: *CTs*, p. 1624; Yu, pp. 11–12; Hsiao, pp. 10–11; *MHjc* 1.2b–3a. Rhymes: 2 *jiŭ*, 4 *iŭ*, 6 *niŭ*, 8 *ngiŭ*. The first two couplets are loosely regulated, *tse* rhyme: the second two couplets are unregulated, with the final line, a quotation from the Nineteen Old Poems, made up entirely of deflected tones.
Title: For Jo-yeh Creek, see note on title, 06417.

4. *Lim-piaèm* 臨泛 might conceivably be taken as "about to set out floating," but *lim* is so often used with looking down into the water, that it probably here means "looking down into the drifting current." *Iong-iŭ* 客與 describes a contented carefree wandering, which, as Yu notes, hearkens back to the *itineraria* of the *Ch'u-tz'u*.
6. The "girl washing gauze" is to be a beauty like Hsi Shih, discovered washing gauze in Jo-yeh Creek.
7. I have here followed Yu's suggestion to read 似 instead of 未.

07698: *CTs*, p. 1639; Yu, pp. 153–54; Hsiao, pp. 73–74; *MHjc* 3.2a; *Wyyh* 286.9b. Rhymes: 2 *giuəi*, 4 *hiuəi*, 6 *xiəi*, 8 *biəi*. Regulated.

1. I have chosen to read 寂寞 here with Yu, rather than the 寂寂 of *MHjc* and some other texts. The repetition of this compound in line 7 violated later prohibitions against redundancy, and the variation is the sort of "improvement" on a text that we should regard with extreme caution. *Dzhek-mɑk* implies silence, isolation, and a somberness that belongs both to the scene and to the person in the scene. The *giaèng hə zhiə* 竟何時 is a variation on a *yüeh-fu* tag.
2. Though it is tempting to make Meng's "return" one of those spiritual returns that occur so often in Wang Wei's poetry, it may be that every morning Meng returns from a futile search for employment. The line is supremely vague.
3. As both Hsiao and Yu suggest, this line suggests Ch'ü Yüan's going off to pick fragrant plants, without involving any specific textual allusion. Picking fragrant plants is an emblem of cultivating one's goodness.
5. *Dang-lò* 當路 means to "hold power in government," from *Mencius* II A.1.1 (Yu).
6. As Yu notes, this echoes the fifth of the Nineteen Old Poems (*Wh* 29.4a):

One pities not the singer's suffering itself,   不惜歌者苦
But feels pain that those who understand are few.   但傷知音稀

"Those who understand (the tone)," *djiɛ-qyim* 知音, are the "true friends" of the translation. Meng's line is taken verbatim from a Lu Yün poem, *Wh* 25.5b.

7. This line seems to respond directly to Wang Wei's injunction to Meng in 05951.

8. The gesture of returning home and closing one's gate occurs very often in Wang Wei's poetry.

06891: *CTs*, p. 1461; *Hyylc* in *TjhTs*, p. 51; *Yhc* in *TjhTs*, p. 357; *Twt* 17A.2b–3a; *Wyyh* 234.9b; *Tscs*, p. 486.
Rhymes: 2 *lim*, 4 *shim*, 6 *sim*, 8 *qyim*. Regulated. (Note that the poem was nevertheless included in *Twt*.)
Title: This was probably the Hsing Fu Temple 興福寺 on Broken Mountain 破山 in Kiangsu. The poem was so popular in later centuries that it was carved on a stele and set up in the temple.

1. It is ambiguous as to whether the poet is "entering" the temple or the dawnlight is "entering." *Njip* 入 would more likely refer to the human, but there are cases where light and scenes enter places.

2. For 照 *Twt* reads 明 and *Wyyh* reads 曜.

4. In later poetry it became a commonplace to contrast the austerity of Buddhist meditation to the sensual distractions of a spring garden.

6. The reflecting surface of a pool is the Buddhist emblem of the illusory nature of the sensuous world: its forms are *kung* 空, "empty," "insubstantial." Thus, the mind that meditates on such illusion becomes itself *kung*, "void."

7. The *miaèn-lài* 萬籟, translated as "nature's sounds," are literally the "ten thousand pipes" of Heaven and Earth, described in the *Ch'i-wu lun* 齊物論 chapter of the *Chuang-tzu*.

8. *Jiong-kèng* 鐘磬 are literally "bells and chimes," a pre-Buddhist musical category here used for the temple bell, whose insubstantial tones remind the listener of the vacuity of existence.

06878: *CTs*. p. 1459.
Rhymes: 2 *kuət*, 4 *mət*, 6 *kiuaet*.
Title: "Drifting at White Dragonhole: Sent to One Studying the Way on T'ien-t'ai" 白龍窟汎 舟寄天台學道者. The first six of twenty lines are quoted.

5. This image is based on the common poetic assertion that the color of waters joins that of the sky.

6. Ch'ang Chien's use of *hiuən-kiuaet* 雲闕 is unusual in that the phrase usually refers to "palace gate-towers like clouds," rather than to "clouds like palace gate-towers."

06875: *CTs*: p. 1458.
Rhymes: 2 *shi*, 4 *chi*, 6 *jiə*, 8 *shiɛ*.
Title: "Ancient Stirring" 古興. The first eight of twenty-four lines are quoted.

CHAPTER 7

06725: *CTs*, p. 1433; Li, pp. 37–39; *Hyylc* in *TjhTs*, p. 100; *Wyyh* 212.12a–12b.
Rhymes: 2 *zim*, 4 *shim*, 6 *sim*, 8 *qyim*, 10 *gyim*, 12 *ngyim*, 14 *qim*. The first four couplets are regulated, with strong violations in the fourth position of the third line and the fifth position of the seventh line. As the poem breaks into the *yüeh-fu* mode in line 9, regulation disappears, but reasserts itself in the last couplet.

1. The *huaeng-dhek* 橫笛 was a seven-hole flute blown from the side like a Western flute; it was often associated with frontier music. *Qiuaèn* 怨, here translated as "speaks complaint," is a difficult emotion to translate, involving "grief at" something, often with an element of anger or resentment. It is possible that the river moon is the object of the flute's "complaint," in which case the moon would be the reminder of mortality or the player's separation from the Northland.

2. The translation given is the most likely in the context of the expectations of this subgenre. The "small boat," however, could be the object of the poet's search.

3. The "long-drawn-outness," *djhiang* 長, of the notes becomes the "far distance" they travel, going from the southern river scene out beyond "Ch'u's mountains."

4. Passing beyond Ch'u's mountains, the melody reaches its destination in the Tartar passes: this journey is the enactment of the figurative "distance" between the frontier mode of the music and the place in which it is being played.

6. As the music goes out, so the thoughts of the player go afar to the Tartar passes.

7. The shores' chill may be the due to the affective influence of the music and its northern theme. Li's note that *pǒ-ziŭ* 浦溆 refers exclusively to a sea or lake shore is in error.

9. The phrase *zhui ga-tziš* 誰家子 and the situation belong to the world of *yüeh-fu*; cf. Ch'en Tzu-ang 04380.

10. The most common association of Han-tan, the capital of the ancient state of Chao, is with beautiful women, but it often can evoke a conviviality that includes knights-errant, see note 06741. Furthermore, it is a northern city whose northerliness stands opposed to the southern boating scene.

11. *Qiŏng* 擁 involves either "squeezing" (often used with crowds) or "taking something in one's arms," "hugging": the point here is that the people on the boat clasp their oars and forget to row, so entranced are they with the music.

12. The northern music affects both spirits and weather. *Gyim* 襟 unites the emotional and the sartorial.

13. This seems to be a scene or thought evoked by the music, echoing the first of the Nineteen Old Poems, where "The Tartar horse leans into the north wind" 胡馬依北風.

14. Following the order of the couplet from the first of the "Nineteen Old Poems," a mention of Yüeh is appropriate here. The theme of "longing for the north" is briefly abandoned for the more general point that each thing longs for its home. The line alludes to a story told by Ch'en Chen to King Hui of Ch'in:

Chuang Hsi, a native of Yüeh, served the state of Ch'u as a minister. After a while, he grew sick, and the King of Ch'u said, "Hsi was formerly a commoner in Yüeh, yet now he serves as a minister in Ch'u. He has become rich and noble, but I wonder if he still longs for Yüeh." An attendant said, "The average person thinks of his past circumstances when sick. If he's thinking of Yüeh, you will hear the sounds of Yüeh; if he's thinking of Ch'u, you will hear the sounds of Ch'u." The king sent someone to listen to him, and Chuang Hsi was making the sounds of Yüeh" (*Sc*, p. 2301).

Ch'en Chen's story was probably speaking of dialectical differences, but Wang Ch'ang-ling is using the allusion, based on the paradigm of many similar stories, to refer to the music. The "exiles," *tsiɛn-njin* 遷人, apply neither to the case of Ch'en Chen nor to Chuang Hsi, and here probably serves only to intensify the mood of displacement.

15. This refers to the famous white grasses of Central Asia, mentioned in *Hs*, p. 3876.

16. Lung was located almost directly west of Ch'ang-an, in modern Kansu. The position of the troops on the "north side," *qim* 陰, of the city walls suggests preparation for a campaign into the frontier region.

06726: *CTs*, p. 1433; Li, p. 22.
Rhymes: 2 *miəi*, 4 *guiəi*, 6 *biəi*.

4. This line could also be interpreted "the soul dreams of return."

06694: *CTs*, pp. 1425–26; Li, pp. 23–28; *Tscs*, p. 364.
Rhymes: 2 *han*, 4 *xuan*, 6 *kuan*, 8 *dhan*, 10 *njiɛn*, 12 *nan*.
Title: *Dhəi* 代 here is not the marker of a *yüeh-fu*, but rather a poem written "on behalf of" someone else: the poet invents what they say; cf. 04150–51. The discourse attributed to the host begins at line 13. The first twelve of thirty-eight lines are translated.

1. The "breath of killing," or "interficient pneuma," *shraèi-kiəi* 殺氣, is the quality of atmosphere associated with the second month of autumn in the "Ordinances of the Months" in

the *Li-chi*. From the autumn air's destruction of the vegetation, the *shraèi-kiəi* is further associated with warfare and the hunt.

3. Literally, "Drifting dust rises on all four sides." On the one hand, *sì-ben* 四邊 means simply "all around" and the line is purely descriptive of the visual scene; on the other hand, *sì-ben* is more commonly the "frontiers that surround China," and the drifting dust is an emblem of frontier warfare. The second association remains only an ominous overtone behind the predominantly visual scene.

5. *Qiəi-njien* 依然 means "as always" or "as I used to": the implication is either that Wang Ch'ang-ling has been there before or that he lodges there while traveling in the region. The second possibility seems the more likely. Fu-feng was located about 100 kilometers west-northwest of Ch'ang-an; its strongest literary association was the *Fu-feng ko* 扶風歌 of Liu K'un (*Wh.* 28.38a–39a).

6. *Dzhì-kuɑn* 自寬, translated as "ease my spirit," describes a relaxed mental state, an "expansiveness" that contrasts with terms of "crampedness," "pent-up emotions," anxiety.

7. The compound embedded in this line is *liə̌-sim* 理心, to "regulate the mind" or "control the heart." The epithet *tsuə̀n* 寸, "square-inch (of the mind)," is used to emphasize the apparent tininess of the uncontrollable font of emotion.

8. The line is literally "Who can rap the long sword hilt?" The line alludes to the famous story of how Feng Huan became a retainer of Meng Shang-chün: lodged in a guest house Feng beat out time with his sword hilt (or sword) and sang of what he lacked in his poverty; in each case Meng Shang-chün provided the thing missing; see *Chan-kuo ts'e, Ch'i ts'e,* and *Sc,* p. 2359. The implication is that Wang's relation to his host is different from that of Feng Huan to Meng Shang-chün. It is difficult not to hear a melancholy irony here, an awareness that the heroism of ancient days has vanished in this world.

9. For a similar use of *dzhiòu* 就 as "to go to join (someone in a drink)," see 08046.4.

12. "Hardships of Travel" 行路難 is a *yüeh-fu* title strongly associated with Pao Chao: here it concerns the difficulties of past experiences, particularly the host's sufferings on campaign.

06741: *CTs,* p. 1437; Li, pp. 108–10; *Hyylc* in *TjhTs,* p. 102.
Rhymes: 1 *dheu,* 2 *gyɛu,* 3 *siɛu,* 4 *deu,* 6 *shrau* (t'ung). If one were to speculate on the effect of this strange rhyme scheme, there seems to be a strong dissonance in the closing *t'ung-yün* following such a strongly established pattern of *p'ing-shui* rhymes. Unregulated.

4. "Levelplain County," Yüan-p'ing, is in T'ai-yüan Commandery, north of Ch'ang-an. *Chiɛt* 挈, translated as "held on his arm," also implies "kept under restraint." As Li notes, the *giəp-deu* 皂鵰 is a large black eagle or hawk.

06781: *CTs,* p. 1444; Li, pp. 192–94; *Khc* in *TjhTs,* p. 177; *Yfsc* 33.4a.
Rhymes: 1 *shrɛn,* 2 *guan,* 4 *huan.* Regulated.

1. The geography of this couplet covers vast areas, and a single point of view cannot be determined. Kokonor, Ch'ing-hai 青海, lies about 800 kilometers northwest of Ch'ang-an, just south of the Kansu corridor. The Mountain of Snows 雪山 lies about 450 kilometers south-southeast of Kokonor, in the northwestern tip of Szechwan. Jade Gate Barrier 玉門關 lies far northwest of Kokonor, at the very tip of the Kansu Corridor in Central Asia.

4. Kroraina, Lo-lan 樓蘭, was a Central Asian state of Han times; Li suggests it stands for Nop-bhiɑk-bɑ 納縛波 of the T'ang. Li takes the last line as stating the soldiers' hopeless desire to return home, but he also cites Shen Te-ch'ien's comment that it can be either a lament or a heroic vow (though Shen too prefers lament).

06764: *CTs.* p. 1442; Li, pp. 127–28; *Twt* 13.7b.
Rhymes: 2 *chuin,* 4 *njin.* Regulated.

1. *Jriək* 昃 is usually used for the time when the sun is in the western part of the sky.
2. This is a good example of poetic diction: *chuin* 春 applies to both the flowers and the "floweriness" of the door.
3. Though *ngiok-dhei* 玉臺 is a poetic term for the imperial dwelling, the significant compound

here is *giàeng-dhei* 鏡臺, a mirror stand. That it is a "jade stand" suggests a wealthy dwelling, but it does not have any specifically imperial association. Similarly, the *bhan-liong* 盤龍 is a decoration on the mirror and not the imperial dragon.

06794: *CTs*, p. 1445; Li, pp. 136–37; *Wyyh* 204.4a; *Yfsc* 43.4b; *Tscs*, p. 362.
Rhymes: 1 *huang*, 2 *shriang*, 4 *djhiang*. Regulated.
Title: The Ch'ang-hsin Palace was where Pan Chieh-yü was sequestered after Han Ch'eng-ti made the Chao sisters his favorites. Pan Chieh-yü became perhaps the most famous example of the "abandoned consort" and a favorite figure in *yüeh-fu*. *Yfsc* 43.1a–5a is devoted to songs about Pan Chieh-yü, and here Wang Ch'ang-ling's quatrain is listed under the *yüeh-fu* title "Resentment in Ch'ang-hsin Palace" 長信怨. Another group of such songs appears in *Wyyh* 204.4a–5a. In *Wyyh* this quatrain is listed without author after a quatrain by Ts'ui Kuo-fu; this should mean that *Whhy* attributes this quatrain to Ts'ui, but the quatrain was so famous, it seems probable that this is simply an error on the part of the *Wyyh* editors.

    1. *Gyim-tzieng* 金井, the "golden well," is an ornamental term often indicating a palace. Li suggests the yellowness of the pawlonia leaves is a marker of late autumn.

    2. Though *jio-liem* 珠簾 refers to a "beaded" curtain rather than to a curtain of "pearls," the opulent association of pearls is not altogether missing. The line suggests that because the frost first came the night before, this night Pan Chieh-yü will not roll up the curtains.

    3. As Li notes, the *xiuan-liong* 熏籠 is a small bamboo censer used to keep clothes and bedding fragrant: in this case, bedding is probably indicated.

    4. The last line translates literally, "She lies, listens to the clear dripping from south palace stretch long (into the night)." Contrary to Li's suggestion, *nom-giung* 南宮 is probably not the South Palace of Lo-yang, but rather the palace buildings to the south of Ch'ang-hsin within the imperial city.

06393: *CTs*, p. 1363; *Wyyh* 235.3b.
Rhymes: 2 *dzhiuen*, 4 *qen*, 6 *ben*, 8 *ten*, 10 *chiuen*, 12 *ziuen*. Regulated, with acceptable fourth-position violation in line 11, and less acceptable fourth-position violation in line 9.
Title: There were Fragrance Mountains 香山 in various parts of China; it is impossible to tell which is referred to here.

    1. This is a case when *tsuì-miəi* 翠微 probably refers to the verdure of a mountain slope rather than to mists; see note to 06137, line 2.

    3. *Dài* 帶 is a term of which the precise value in poetry is often difficult to determine: its root meaning is a "sash" or "to sash"; from this it is extended to mean "surround" or "wear at waist." In its most extended sense, it simply means to "carry." Here it is used primarily in the sense of "carry," not as a willful "bearing," but rather almost as an adornment.

    5. Reading 殿壯 with *Wyyh*, rather than 衣拂 of *CTs*.

    6. The proximity of a mountain or mountain temple to Heaven was a commonplace in poetry, a commonplace animated in Taoist speculation by corridors through which intercourse between earthly and heavenly realms was possible.

    7. *Dei* 低 could possible mean that coming in through the windows, the peaks and ridges seem to "sink" to the poet's resting place; however, the interpretation in the translation is supported by the topos of the inversion of high and low in mountain poetry; cf. 05961, line 4 note.

    8. *Shièi-gaèi* 世界 was a Buddhist term that was quickly extended in poetry to refer to the sensible world, without the antitheses that formed the older terms of Chinese cosmology.

    11–12. Birds filling the groves and the sorrow at returning home were standard marks of closure in banquet poetry. Here they are transferred to the poet's departure with dawn. *Ngiaenziuen* 言旋 is a *Shih* tag (see *Shih* 187), in which *ngiaen* is interpreted as the first person pronoun.

10544: *CTs*, p. 2269; Chiu-chia 2.19A, p. 42; Ch'ou, c. 4, p. 43.
Rhymes: 2 *xiang*, 4 *dang*, 6 *piang*, 8 *ziang*, 10 *jrhiang*, 12 *huang*. Unregulated.
Title: The "Temple of Great Clouds" 大雲寺 referred to here was the one in Ch'ang-an. This poem is usually dated to the time Tu Fu was trapped behind rebel lines in Ch'ang-an in 757.

1. The metonymy of *mio-zhiuè* 無睡 is striking; the situation of watching the lamplight in sleeplessness was common in poetry, but here it is as though Tu Fu is perceiving the situation from outside himself.

2. Chiu-chia and Ch'ou cite the *Vimalakirti Sutra* concerning a land of many scents. However, olfactory delights were common in many Buddhist stories and were a real part of Buddhist temple life, so no allusion need be present. The use of *djiɛ* 知 is significant, involving recognition rather than simply smelling.

3. The night's *shim* 深 unites the visual qualities of the dark scene with the lateness of the night: both make the scene "deep." *Tuət-nguət* 突兀 is used to describe the whale-leviathan in Mu Hua's "Sea *fu*" (*Wh* 12.9a), but the compound became common in the mid-eighth century to describe buildings and monuments.

4. The *lang-dang* 琅璫 was a metal bell or chime hung at the corner of a building and rung by the wind.

5. It is impossible to tell whether the blackness of the night figuratively "closes up" the garden or whether this is simply a statement that the garden is "closed up."

7. The Chain of Jades, *ngiok-jhiəng* 玉繩, is a pair of small stars near the Northern Dipper. The "chain" is literally a "rope." The "breaking" of the chain/rope probably means that one of the stars disappears behind the building.

8. The "soaring" of the iron phoenix probably describes the movement of a kind of weather vane.

9. Here I follow the interpretation given in the Chiu-chia commentary.

11. *Qok-iǎ* 沃野, the "fertile plain," is given in the *Shih-chi* as the characteristic of the capital region, Kuan-chung, where there was "never a year of famine" (*Sc*, p. 1408).

12. The dust raised from the moist earth of Kuan-chung is the mark of warhorses.

06366: *CTs*, p. 1357; *Hyylc* in *TjhTs*, p. 75; *Twt* 12.16b; *Wyyh* 334.4b–5a; *Tscs*, p. 286.
Rhymes: 2 *paek*, 4 *kaek*, 6 *bhaek*, 8 *shrɛk*; 10 *miaeng*, 11 *tziɛng*, 13 *dzhiɛng*, 15 *dzhiɛng*, 17 *shiɛng*, 19 *miaeng*, 21 *shraeng*; 22 *shrǎ*, 23 *nguǎ*, 25 *hǎ*; 26 *hiuaen*, 27 *mən*; 28 *lì*, 29 *jì*.
Title: The text of the title is the form in which it appears in *Hyylc*, *Twt*, and *Tscs*. It is admittedly a most peculiar construction, especially in the use of *ngiǔ* 語. Probably because of the *ngiǔ* and because *gem* 兼 usually indicates an additional occasional purpose, the *CTs* editors and the modern editors of *Tscs* have changed the phrase to *gem gyè-ngiǔlùng* 兼寄語弄, a more common construction, meaning "also sending these words playfully to. . . ." I feel more comfortable with the revised version of the title, but have retained and tried to make sense of the older form: the fact that *Hyylc*, *Twt*, and *Tscs* all have the form as given suggests that it did not present as many problems to early editors as it did to later ones. *Wyyh*, with its customary laxness about titles, reads 聽董庭蘭彈琴寄房給事 "Listening to Tung T'ing-lan Play the Ch'in: To Grand Secretary Fang." Fang Kuan became grand secretary in 753, and the poem is either from that year or shortly thereafter.

1. Ts'ai Yen 蔡琰 (fl. later second century) was the granddaughter of Ts'ai Yung; she was captured by the Hsiung-nu and, on her release, composed an eighteen-stanza suite for the ch'in called "Nomad Pipe Songs."

2. The *paek* 拍 is usually the "beat" or rhythm" of a song; here it clearly refers to a division or measure, which I have translated as "stanza" (which in Chinese music is properly a *dhep* 疊). The different *paek* may have involved fundamental shifts in rhythm, remarkable in their juxtaposition because they are played "in sequence," "at one sitting," *qit-dhan* 一彈.

3. *Hyylc*, *Twt*, *Wyyh*, and *Tscs* all support the reading 向 over *CTs* 沾. Thus, the "nomad" or "Tartar" weeps, reminded of the frontier region by the song.

4. This refers to the parting of Li Ling and Su Wu.

5. The interpretation of this line can vary greatly depending on how one takes *tsɑng-tsɑng* 蒼蒼. If *tsɑng-tsɑng* is the lush growth of vegetation, then the fortress is abandonned and the beacon fires are literally "cold." If *tsɑng-tsɑng* is the blue of the heavens, then the fortress is outlined against the sky, and the beacon fires give no warmth to the frontier guards. *Tsɑng-tsɑng* also describes the gray color of moonlight, but without the specific mention of the moon, such an interpretation would be forced.

6. Though I have overspecified *dhài-xuɑng* 大荒 as the "steppelands," it is in fact the general term for the "wilderness" that surrounds the cultivated land of China. *Qim-djhim* 陰沈, translated as "sunk in gloom," is one of those descriptive binomes that unites interior mood and exterior description of atmosphere.

7. *Piǝt* 拂 is a particular way of striking a *ch'in* string: it is not a general term for "pluck." *Shang* (*shiɑng* 商), *chüeh* (*gak* 角), and *yü* (*hiǒ* 羽) are the second, third, and fourth positions respectively in a pentatonic series, as well as the second, third, and fourth strings on a *ch'in*. Their relative intervals are determined, but their pitch depends on the mode, *luit* 律, in which they are played.

8. The *sì-gau* 四郊 are the outlands immediately around the capital. *Shrɛk-shrɛk* 摵摵 is glossed in *Wh* 30.1b as the "sound of falling leaves" by the Wu-ch'en commentary, and it is in this sense of sound that it is most often used. However, Li Shan glossed *shrɛk* alone as "withered, shriveled appearance."

9–10. A shift to direct address in trisyllabic lines often occurs in the middle of heptasyllabic songs; cf. 07931. *Jhin-miaeng* 神明 is "divinity," not in the sense of an anthropomorphic god, but a transcendent quality of divinity that lies beyond this world and within the self. Tung T'ing-lan's ability to *tung* 通 that divinity refers to both his ability to "comprehend" it and to make his art "penetrate" to the divine realm. Unfortunately, the examples of the divine realm to which his art penetrates are merely supernatural, the goblins to line 11. An element of the *lùng* 弄, the "playfulness" of the song, may reside in this quick transition from grand mystery to mere spookiness.

11. *Qyɛu-tziɛng* 妖精, translated as "sprites and goblins," is a collective term for minor supernatural beings.

12. The function of *ngiaen* 言 here is problematic: parallelism and context make it seem as though it is used as a particle, but it would be a particle of archaic flavor in an extremely unarchaic context. Furthermore, as an initial particle it would tend to be understood as a first-person pronoun, which is clearly not the case. Moreover, I have been able to find no other usages of *ngiaen* in T'ang texts quite like this, and none as a particle paired with *gaeng* 更. Ch'in music can *ngiaen*, "express" something, but without an object here, such an interpretation of *ngiaen* would be forced. *Gaei qiɑng shiǒu* 皆應手 is literally "in every case answering (the movement of) his hand."

13. As in 06725, not only does music evoke visual images, its movement in time is often spatialized, a "going" and a "returning" that mark an indecisive hesitation that suggests unexpressed emotion. For 旋 *Wyyh* reads 還.

15. For this line *Wyyh* reads 萬里孤雲閑且清. For 晴 *Tscs* reads 明. Both *tsiɛng* 清 and *miaeng* 明 escape the homophonic rhyme of *dzhiɛng* 晴 (and 情, line 13). Here, as often in musical descriptions, the alternation between antithetical qualities is stressed.

16. For 嘶 *Wyyh* reads 悽. *Sei* 嘶 here is the long-drawn-out cry of a bird, with the implication of sadness. *Jrhio* 雛, the "chick" of various bird species, may precede the name of the species, as here, or it may follow it.

17. This line clearly refers to the passage in Ts'ai Yen's *Pei-fen shih* 悲憤詩 (*CHs* 3.3b–4a) in which Ts'ai, on being allowed to return to her home, has to give up the child she bore in captivity:

The child came forward and hugged my neck,   兒前抱我頸
Asking "Mother, where will you go?"   問母欲何之
People say my mother must go,   人言母當去
Nor will she ever return."   豈復有還時

Dhuǎn-dzhiuɛt 斷絕 probably refers to the affect of this musical image.

18–19. Various elements of the natural scene grow silent and still, stirred by the music and in order to listen to it: this appears often in poems describing musical performances.

20. I have here retained the *Hyylc*, *Twt*, and *Wyyh* reading of 烏珠 instead of 烏孫 of *CTs* and later texts. In its modern Mandarin reading, *wu-chu* 烏珠 is the Mongolian word for "head," and there was a Mongol clan, the Uchumuch'in 烏珠穆沁, which appeared in the Ming. There may well have been a tribe of Qo-jio 烏珠 Mongols (?) in the T'ang, but I have been able to find no other mention of them. Clearly, some later editor thought it would simplify matters if this referred to the Qo-suɑn 烏孫 Turks. As in 06725, the playing of frontier music in China suggests the idea of "distance."

21. Lhasa was the capital of Tibet in the T'ang, but the Tibetans were then a warlike people who fought with and often raided China.

22. 幽陰 is the *Hyylc* reading; *Wyyh* reads 幽音; *Twt* and *Tscs* read 出音. *Piɐu-shră* 飄灑 is a kind of brisk windiness, blowing droplets of rain, spray, or snow.

23. *Djhuì* 墮 is a verb that applies to the "falling" of tiles but not of rain. However, it is uncertain whether the "tiles sent crashing" are real tiles or figurative tiles, describing the "crashing" rain of the storm.

25. The deer, sent scurrying past the hall, cry out; that "crying out" is a fixed echo of *Shih* 161, whose orthodox interpretation involved seeking companions for a feast. This image links the description of the music to the occasional closing.

27. The "blue-chain-(patterned) gate" was a gate in the Han palace, which eventually became a poetic term for palace gates in general. For the model of this line, see the first couplet of Fan Yün's 古意贈王中書 (*CLs* 6.1a).

28. *Tuɑt-liɑk* 脫略 describes a free, unrestrained personality and often, as here, takes an object: a "freedom from renown and profit."

06300: *CTs*, p. 1340; Twt 16A.8a.

Rhymes: 2 *iuɐng*, 4 *tziɐng*, 6 *shiɐng*, 8 *seng*, 10 *dheng*, 12 *bheng*, 14 *geng*, 16 *seng*, 18 *zhiɐng*, 20 *gaeng*, 22 *huɐng*, 24 *shraeng*. Unregulated.

Title: Here is the brief opening description of Chang Hsü in *Hsin Ts* (p. 5764): "Hsü, a native of Su-chou in Wu, had a craving for wine, and whenever he would get really drunk, he would give a loud bellow and run wildly, then use his brush, or sometimes even write by dipping his hair in ink. When he sobered up, he would look at what he had done, and see divinity in it; but then he couldn't write as well."

2. *Xuɑt-dhɑt* 豁達 is an "openness" that can describe either a scene or the expansiveness of a person's nature. *Mio shriŭ iuɐng* 無所營 is literally "there is nothing with which he gets himself busy."

4. Great Lake 太湖 is just south of Su-chou. "Genius" is used here in the classical sense, a a spirit that is the "essence" of a thing or place.

5. Chang's "bare headedness" indicates that he does not hold office; the implication is that he is so free-spirited that he doesn't want office. The ho-jrhiɑng 胡牀 was a large folding chair with a backrest.

9. Hǎ 下, in front of a kind of dwelling, is often a term of humility or deprecation; I take it as such here.

10. *Hǒ-dheng* 戶庭, literally "gate and courtyard," is the yard area within the walls of a dwelling compound.

11. This perhaps echoes the emperor's query to the famous recluse T'ao Hung-ching: "What is there in the mountains?" 山中何所有 (*CLs* 11.12b).

13. This echoes a comment by the Chin eccentric Pi Cho to the effect that all he needed in life was a crab claw in one hand and a cup of wine in the other (*Shih-shuo hsin-yü. SPTK*, c. 3A, section 23, 19).

14. *Dɑn-geng* 丹經, translated freely as "alchemical tracts," is literally the *Cinnabar Classic*. It was supposedly an immortal's book, received by Liu An, the Han prince of Huai-nan (*Wh* 22.26a, Li Shan note, citing *Shen-hsien chuan*). *Dɑn-geng* then became part of the title of several alchemical and occult treatises.

16. It is possible that Chang himself does not know "whether he's drunk or sober."

17. This probably describes the occasion on which this poem was composed and "presented to Chang Hsü."

18. A play on Chang Hsü's given name may be involved here: "at dawn" 旭 the guests are "at Hsü's" 旭.

20. *Gaeng* 秔 (*Twt* writes the variant 粳) is nonglutinous rice. The use of *djiŭ* 貯 is noteworthy: *djiŭ* usually applies to the accumulation of grain in private or public granaries, and its use here to describe the rice in the bowls suggests a hyperbolic bounty that verges on the comic. This, incidentally, is the only description of a breakfast party I have seen in T'ang poetry.

21. *Piət-set* 不屑 is something petty, humiliating, beneath contempt—in this case, concern for the personal gain involved in struggle for office.

22. The *bat-huɛng* 八紘 are the eight points that bound the universe.

24. An-ch'i was an immortal who met Ch'in Shih-huang.

CHAPTER 8

08680: *CTs*, p. 1858; Hanabusa 825; Wang, pp. 523–24; *Wyyh* 228.1b.

Rhymes: [1 *djiung*, acceptable in level tone only if rhymes, and as rhyme, the only *t'ung-yün*], 2 *niong*, 4 *jiong*, 6 *piong*, 8 *ziong*. Regulated.

Title: "Going to Visit the Taoist on Mount Tai-t'ien and Not Meeting Him" 訪戴天山道士不遇
According to the Wang Ch'i note, an early gazetteer says that Li Po studied on Mount Tai-t'ien, which was located near Mien-chou, north-northeast of Ch'eng-tu in modern Szechwan.

1. Note that *bhiaèi* 吠 does not occur once in the *shih* of the *Wh*; the word *kuɛn* 犬 occurs only once. Though the *Wh*'s selection of *shih* is far broader than the narrow decorum of court poetry, the absence of these two words gives some indication of the prohibition against certain "low" things.

2. Reading 露 instead of 雨. *Niong* 濃 is a dark, rich color, here probably enhanced by the raindrops. *Niong* also describes a plenitude of dewdrops (or raindrops), and the line may suggest that the blossoms are "laden" with rain or dew.

7. The diction here is particularly prosaic.

08019: *CTs*, p. 1703; Hanabusa 156; Wang, pp. 149–50; *Yfsc* 80.10a–10b; *Tscs*, p. 268.

Rhymes: 1 *iong*, 2 *niong*, 4 *bhiong*. Regulated.

Title: The story of the performance of this song in the inner court occurs in various sources, none of which are very reliable: Wang cites the T'ai-chen wai-chuan 太真外傳; *Yfsc* cites the *Sung-ch'uang-lu* 松窗錄; *Tscs* gives its own version, incorporating the anecdote of Li Po being forced to perform when drunk. The strongest defense one can make for the probability of the occasional frame is that there is no more circumstantial evidence to prove the anecdote unlikely than there is to prove its historical veracity. In any case, it is a firm part of the Li Po legend.

1. There was a tradition of texts reading 葉 instead of 雲. Wang Ch'i attributes this to a slip of the brush and not, as he says, "to a magic touch that turns gold into iron." From the *Ch'u-tz'u* on, cloud-robes have been part of the paraphernalia of goddesses and immortals.

2. For *niong* 濃, see note to line 2, 08680.

3. "Hoard of Jade Mountain" 羣玉山 was the legendary dwelling place of the goddess Hsi-wang-mu.

4. The "Terrace of Jasper" 瑤臺 appears in the *Li Sao*, but it appears often as a dwelling of immortals.

08147: *CTs*, p. 1728; Hanabusa 282; Wang, p. 221.

Rhymes: 1a *biəi*, 1 *ièi*, 2a *dzhuəi*, 2 *tzèi*, 3a *gek*, 3 *shièi*, 4a *sɑng*, 4 *mièi*, 5a *dək*, 6a *miɑng*, 6 *tèi*. The small "a" after line number indicates a rhyme at the hemistich.

Title: Given in the collection as "Song: About to Set Out" 臨路歌; I agree with Wang's suggestion that this is the "Deathbed Song" 臨終歌 mentioned in Li Hua's *mu-chih-ming* (Wang, p. 714).

1. The *bat-ièi* 八裔, like the *bat-huɛng* (see 06300, line 22 note), are the eight points that mark the bounds of the universe.

2. Compare the following line from the *Ai shih-ming* 哀時命 in the *Ch'u-tz'u*: "Cut off mid-road and cannot get through" 路中斷而不通.

3. The line is literally, "His lingering wind will stir things for myriad ages." The *biung* 風 is a combination of "energy" and "manner," which together generate an "influence."

4. This line is a reworking of a line in the *Ai shih-ming*: "My left sleeve caught on Fu-sang" 左袪挂於抙桑. The Wang Yi interpretation here is crucial: "As his robes are all tightly bound up [the preceding line] and cannot be extended, so his virtue is capable of greatness, but he cannot put

it to use. When he travels east, his left sleeve catches on the Fu-sang tree, and there is nothing that it cannot cover." Both here and in Li Po's song, the ancient theme of unrecognized greatness is the central concern.

6. Wang Ch'i takes this as a reference to Confucius's tears when a unicorn was captured and no one recognized it. Now that Confucius is gone, there is not even one person who can recognize true greatness, not even one person to pity the fact that the majority of people don't recognize greatness.

07929: *CTs*, p. 1682; Hanabusa 65; Wang, p. 88; *Hyylc* in *TjhTs*, p. 58; Tun-huang manuscript anthology in *TjhTs*, p. 17; *Twt* 13.11a; *Wyyh* 203.3a; *Yfsc* 48.2b; Tscs, p. 266.
Rhymes: 1 *zhiə*, 2 *shiɛ*; 3 *bit*, 4 *njit*; 5 *dɑ*, 6 *bɑ*, 7 *hɑ*.
Title: Earlier examples of this song by Liang Chien-wen-ti, Liang Yüan-ti, Hsiao Tzu-hsien, and Hsü Ling are all straightforward songs in the southern manner. However, reading these songs from the T'ang, they would inevitably be linked to the image of the Southern Dynasties courts, a menaced hedonism that would seem like a repetition of the historical situation Li Po describes in his song.

1. Ku-su Terrace was supposed to have been built by the voluptuary Fu-ch'a, king of Wu, and it was there that Fu-ch'a was supposed to have spent his days amusing himself with Hsi Shih. It may be that the antithesis between the roosting of the crows and Fu-ch'a's orgies is to suggest the untimeliness and unnaturalness of the latter, in contrast to the rhythms of activity and rest in the natural world.

3. *Xuɑn* 歡 suggests sensual pleasure in this context.

6. *Djhuì* 墮 is particularly strong for the sinking of the moon.

05851: *CTs*, p. 1251; Chao, p. 62; *Wycc* 6.7a; *Hyylc* in *TjhTs*, p. 58; *Twt* 17B.8b; Tscs, p. 238.
Rhymes: 2 *miəi*, 4 *piəi*, 6 *xiəi*. The first six of fourteen lines are quoted.

07950: *CTs*, pp. 1687–88; Hanabusa 86; Wang pp. 104–5; *Wyyh* 193.12a–12b; *Yfsc* 28.14a–14b.
Rhymes: 1 *quəi*, 2 *ləi*, 4 *tzei*, 6 *huəi*; 8 *ten*, 10 *njiɛn*; 11 *huɑ*, 12 *bɑ*, 14 *guɑ*, 16 *dɑ*, 18 *kuɑ*.
Title: *Yfsc* classifies this under "The Sun Comes Out from Its Nook in the Southeast" 日出東南隅行, a fairly common *yüeh-fu*, earlier examples of which bear no resemblance to Li Po's song, though Li's first line does echo the title.

1. *Quəi* 隈, "cove," is a variation on the *ngio* 隅, "corner," of the common *yüeh-fu* title; the variation is probably for the sake of rhyme.

2. *Tsiong . . . ləi* 從 . . . 來 is more colloquial than the more conventionally poetic *dzhì . . . ləi* 自 . . . 來.

4. The "six dragons" are the team that carries the sun chariot. *Qɑn dzhǒi tzəi* 安在哉 is a *ku-feng* tag, usually marking the *ubi sunt* theme. The line translates literally, "Where the six dragons (can) stop—where is it?"

5. The prosaic *ghiə shiǒ iǔ jiung* 其始與終 is a necessary construction to avoid *shiǒ-jiung*, "from beginning to end."

6. In the context of the poem, the translation given is what the line should mean. However, human beings are constituted of a devolved form of the *ngiuaen-kièi* 元氣, and *biəi* 非 constructions like this often are conditional: in this case, the line would be "Were man not made of Primal Stuff, how could he linger with it so long." This would involve an assertion of universal human durability, outlandish even for Li Po.

7. The interpretation of *ziὰ* 謝 offers some problems: a parallel passage cited by Wang Ch'i and the corresponding *qiuaèn* 怨 in the next line suggest the interpretation given in the translation. However, the more common use of *ziὰ* in poetry is "to decline," which would give the plausible "Plants don't refuse to blossom in the spring wind." The translation in the text suggests the emotional indifference of nature to life and death, in contrast to human distress. The second interpretation emphasizes not the lack of feeling, but the acquiescence to natural cycles itself.

9. In the context of the poem up to this point, this line is a rhetorical question, with the answer "no one" confirmed by the following line. However, it raises the possibility of someone

who might wield a whip and drive the seasons along: Hsi-ho, the charioteer of the sun, who appears in line 11.

12. *Xuɑng-qyim* 荒淫 is the dissolute condition of drunkenness, here (as in some earlier texts cited by Wang) combined with the traditional metaphor of morality as a body of water, either with a proper course or promiscuously mingled in flood; see note to line 7, 02949. In Li Po's usage, the ethical dimension is played down, and *xuɑng-qyim* describes a drunken recklessness in Hsi-ho's behavior which is transferred to the waves into which he nightly casts himself.

13–14. The story of how the Lord of Lu-yang, when fighting with Han Kou, turned the evening sun back appeared originally in the Lan-ming chapter 覽冥 of the *Huai-nan-tzu*, but the phrasing of Li Po's lines indicates that he is echoing the allusion to the story in the fourth of Kuo P'u's *Yu-hsien shih* (*Wh* 21.30b). *Djiò-qiaĕng* 駐景 is literally "halted the (moving) light."

15–16. It is impossible to tell whether the perversion of Heaven's will is a condemnation of Lu-yang's act or whether it is grounds to disbelieve that such an act occurred. Line 16 suggests the latter.

17. The *Dhài-kuài* 大塊, the "Big Clod" or "Mighty Mudball," was a common Taoist kenning for the world. To *nɑng-kuɑt* 囊括, "wrap up in a bag," was what Chia Yi described Ch'in Shih-huang as wanting to do to the empire (*Wh* 51.1a).

18. *Mĕng-hĕng* 溟涬 was one of the many binomes the *Chuang-tzu* used to describe the primordial Chaos out of which the world was generated. For *dhung-kuɑ* 同科 see *Analects* III.16.

07931: *CTs*, pp. 1682–83; Hanabusa 67; Wang, pp. 89–90; *Hyylɛ* in *TjhTs*, pp. 57–58; *Twt* 13.7b;
  Wyyh 195.9a–9b and 336.2b (title only, different title identified as *Chiang chin chiu*); Yfsc 17.4b.
Rhymes: 1 *lɔi*, 2 *huɔi*; 3 *hiɑet*, 4 *siuɛt*, 6 *ngiuɑet*; 8 *lɔi*, 10 *bɔi*; 12 *shrɑeng*, 14 *dheng*, 16 *teng*, 18 *seng*, 20 *miɑeng*; 2i *lɑk*, 22 *xiɑk*, 24 *jiɑk*; 26 *ghiou*, 28 *jrhiou*.
Title: *Chiang chin chiu* was one of the eighteen "Han Cymbal Songs" 漢鐃歌, one of the oldest and most important groups of *yüeh-fu*. The theme was, however, little used in literary *yüeh-fu*, and the only literary example in *Yfsc* before Li Po's version is a gentle, festive quatrain by Liang Chao-ming t'ai-tzu.

1. *Giuɔn biɔt gèn* 君不見, literally "do you not see," "have you not seen," is a common and characteristic *yüeh-fu* interjection, establishing an intensity of direct address which is inappropriate in *shih*. The flow of the great rivers to the sea and the whitening of hair were two of the most durable and conventional emblems of impermanence and mortality.

7. *Dzhɔi* 材 is literally "material" or "timber," but its use had been so often mixed with the homophonous 才, "talent," that the two were virtually interchangeable.

9. *Paeng iɑng tzĭ ngiou* 烹羊宰牛 comes from a somewhat less frenzied drinking song, "Harp Song," by Ts'ao Chih (*Wh* 27.26b).

10. Literally, "You must finish three hundred cups in one drinking session." For *huài sio* 會須 see Chang Hsiang, *Shih tz'u ch'ü yü-tz'u hui-shih*, p. 126. *Huài* often indicates a future occasion, and its mood may be imperative, optative, or an assertion of probability. Wang cites the *Shih-shuo hsin-yü* commentary for the famous story of Cheng Hsüan, the great classical scholar of the end of the Han, who drank three hundred cups of wine at one sitting.

11. Exactly who Master Ts'en is remains uncertain, though it is possible that it is Ts'en Shen.

12. Tan-ch'iu is Yüan Tan-ch'iu 元丹邱, a friend referred to several times in Li Po's works.

15. The fact that this line appears almost verbatim in Pao Chao's *yüeh-fu* (*CSs* 4.5b) is less significant as a verbal allusion than as an attempt to recreate the manner of Pao's *yüeh-fu*.

16. *Kiuɛng-njiă* 傾耳 is to "turn the ear (to a sound)" and pay attention.

17. *Jrhiuɛn-ngiok* 饌玉 is literally "morsel-jades": *ngiok* is commonly used as a metaphor for anything that is beautiful or good. *Biɔt tziok giuài* 不足貴 is literally "not worth prizing."

19. *Dzhek-mɑk* 寂寞 is the "silence" of death, but it is also "silence" in that they are not spoken of, in contrast to the drinkers, whose names are remembered. Not only is this statement strictly untrue, it furthermore violates conventional wisdom; its presence here is clearly for its shock value.

21. The prince of Ch'en is Ts'ao Chih, and the mention of P'ing-lo Lodge with line 22 echoes a couplet from Ts'ao Chih's "Famous Capital" 名都篇 (*Wh* 27.28a):

Return and feast at P'ing-lo Lodge,   歸來宴平樂
The fine wine costs ten thousand a gallon.   美酒斗一千

The Wu-ch'en commentary takes the "ten thousand" as the cost of a *dŏu* (in Ts'ao Chih's time a little over two liters, in Li Po's time almost six liters). In Ts'ao Chih's time, the construction could possibly have been a poetic archaism, enumerating the number of *dŏu* of wine at the feast, but the Wu-ch'en commentary's instinctive reading of the number as a predicate (and hence a price) is good indication that Li Po would have used it that way. *Xuan-xiɑk* 歡謔 is the "pleasure and playfulness" that is often said to accompany a feast.

    25. The *ngŏ-xua mǎ* 五花馬 is literally "a horse with flower (patterns) of five (colors)," i.e., a horse with dappled spots. Wang cites another theory that the "five flowers" were a special way of tying the horse's mane into tufts.

07939: *CTs*, pp. 1684–85; Hanabusa 75; Wang, p. 96; *Wyyh* 202.2b; *Yfsc* 69.6b–7a.
Rhymes: 2 *qɑn*, 3 *lɑn*, 4 *hɑn*, 6 *tɑn*, 7 *duan*, 9 *lɑn*, 11 *nɑn*, 13 *gɑn*.
Title: *Djhiɑng siɑng siə* 長相思 originally was a formulaic phrase in the *yüeh-fu* and *ku-shih* tradition; in the Southern Dynasties it became a *yüeh-fu* title in its own right. As a *yüeh-fu*, it belonged to a minority group in which there were some formal restrictions: most *yüeh-fu* with this title begin with two trisyllabic lines, the first of which is *djhiɑng siɑng siə*, followed by a heptasyllabic line. After that, the form was free, and Li Po's trisyllabic closure is highly unusual. *Yfsc* treats this poem as the first of a series of three, the other two of which appear later in Li Po's collection. (08068–69).

    3. *Lɑk-hiuəi* 絡緯 ("reeling woof-threads"?) was an early kenning for the cricket. For *gyim-tziĕng* 金井 see 06794, note for line 1; here the term probably does not refer to a palace.
    4. *Shriək* 色 is the visual surface quality of a thing, exclusive of its form. Since "color" is included in this, we are doomed to it as the closest approximation. The bedmat "looks cold": its whiteness suggest chill, but more than that, a tactile intuition is transferred to a visual impression.
    5. This suggests that the person longing has stayed awake until the lamp has burned down: now he or she is so sleepy the longing is about to cease, but on rising and looking out the window, the emotion is kindled anew.
    7. *Hiuən-duɑn* 雲端 is the "edge of (a mass of) cloud," which blocks vision.

08006: *CTs*, p. 1701; Hanabusa 143; Wang pp. 144–45; *Yfsc* 85.12a.
Rhymes: 2 *dei*, 4 *mei*. Regulated, two "A" form couplets.
Title: 襄陽曲.

    1. *Haeng-lɑk* 行樂 suggests an activity, like English 'have fun."
    2. "Shining Hooves of Bronze" 白銅蹄 (evolved here into the inexplicable "Shining Buskins of Bronze" 白銅鞮) began as a prophetic children's song, but eventually seems to have become something of a local song with variable lyrics. *Bhaek* 白, literally "white," translated as "shining," is the "silvery" or "metallic" appearance of the bronze.

08009: *CTs*, p. 1701; Hanabusa 146; Wang, p. 145; *Yfsc* 85.12a.
Rhymes: 1 *djhiɛ*, 2 *byɛ*, 4 *njiɛ*. Regulated.
    1. Wang cites the *Hsiang-yang chi* 襄陽記, quoted in the *Shih-shuo hsin-yü* commentary, to the effect that Hsi Yü of Hsiang-yang built a pool toward the south side of Mount Hsien, and it became a favorite site for parties. The famous governor Shan Chien had a special fondness for the spot and would always return from the place roaring drunk. The inebriate magistrate soon became the subject of children's songs. It should be pointed out that when Li Po makes reference to such a story, it is highly unlikely that he is alluding to the *Hsiang-yang chi*; rather the *Hsiang-yang chi* simply recorded a bit of local lore that an educated visitor to Hsiang-yang would have heard rather than read.
    2. For the "monument of tears," see note 07727, line 7.
    4. *Shraèi* 殺 here is an intensifier; it is a happy coincidence that "die" serves the same function in "die of laughter." *Sièu-shraèi* 笑殺 is transitive in this line: "makes the children die of laughter."

08045: *CTs*, p. 1709; Hanabusa 183; Wang p. 166; *Wyyh* 194.6a; *Yfsc* 66.4b.
Rhymes: 1 *dung*, 2 *biung*, 4 *djiung*. Second couplet regulated.
Title: Though Li's are the first *Shiĕu-nen haeng* in the *Yfsc*, they are members of a large family of *shiĕu-nen yüeh-fu*.

1. Five Barrows 五陵 was a fashionable pleasure area near Ch'ang-an; the Golden Market 金市 was located in Lo-yang.

2. The use of *dhò* 度 merits some note: *dhò* more commonly applies to the wind's passage than to a horseman's passage, while the syntax favors the horse as the subject. These contrary impulses leave the function of *dhò* strangely indeterminate.

4. *Ho* 胡 (a general appellation for Central Asians, Turks, Tartars, etc.) were often associated with tavern keeping (e.g., 02628), but Li Po's line specifically echoes lines from Hsin Yen-nien's "Officer of the Guard" 羽林郎 (*CHs* 2.15b):

Relying on our general's power,	依倚將軍勢
We tease the Turk of the tavern.	調笑酒家胡
The Turkish wench is just fifteen,	胡姬年十五
On a spring day she stands alone at the bar.	春日獨當壚

08827: *CTs*, p. 1885; Hanabusa 982; Wang, p. 582.
Rhymes: 2 *huəi*, 4 *ləi*. (extemely trite rhymes). Regulated.

1. For Jo-yeh Creek, see note to title, 06417.

08087: *CTs*, p. 1720; Hanabusa 227; Wang, p. 195; *Wyyh* 162.8a–8b.
Rhymes: 2 *qɑk*, 4 *gɑk*.
Title: Heng-chiang was on the north bank of the Yangtze, upstream from the Chien-yeh/Nanking area.

1. *Nong* 儂 is used as the first-person pronoun of the Wu dialect. Its appearance indicates the persona of a southeasterner: poets who happened to be from the Southeast did not write *nong* whenever they wrote the first-person pronoun, only when they wanted to emphasize their "southeasterness."

3. *Qit-biung* 一風 is "one wind" in that it does not stop blowing for three days.

4. Wa-kuan Tower (互棺, "Title Sarcophagus," later written 互官), was located in Shang-yüan County in modern Kiangsu. Li has a poem on climbing the tower (08567)

08091: *CTs*, p. 1885; Hanabusa 986; Wang, pp. 196–97.
Rhymes: 1 *ngiaeng*, 2 *shraeng*, 4 *haeng*. Regulated with strong violation in second position of first line.

1. The *tzin-liə* 津吏 was a minor public employee charged with taking care of ferries and bridges: see Robert des Rotours, *Traité des fonctionnaires et Traité de l'armée* (San Francisco, 1974) pp. 498, 746.

08092: *CTs*, p. 1885; Hanabusa 987; Wang, p. 197; *Wyyh* 162.8b.
Rhymes: 1 *kəi*, 2 *huəi*, 4 *ləi*. Regulated with strong violation in second position of first line; for line 4, see below.

1. For a halo around the moon as an omen of wind, see 07631.1–2.

2. As Wang notes, the description of the *ghiaeng* 鯨 here (to be translated as "whale" or "leviathan" depending on whether its attributes answer our modern sense of the natural or supernatural) derives from the description in Mu Hua's *Hai fu* (*Wh* 12. 9a), where the *ghiaeng's* puffing makes "rivers run back in their courses." *Tzuit* 憂 is a "pressing on" something or "squeezing together."

3. Three Mountains 三山 is a formation overlooking the Yangtze in Chiang-ning.

4. The *mio* 無 in *Gung mio dhò hɑ* 公無渡河 is in the wrong tone, and indeed it would be impossible to integrate the *yüeh-fu* title into a regulated poem without breaking it across the caesura.

The variant *mɑk* 莫 in the *Wyyh* text is clearly to regularize the tone pattern, as *Wyyh* deviations from standard texts often are.

07912: CTs, p. 1678; Hanabusa 48; Wang, p. 72.
Rhymes: 2 *jhin*, 4 *tzin*, 6 *njin*, 8 *chuin*, 10 *sin*. Unregulated.

    1. *Qàn-giuaèn* 按劍 is to "pat" or 'place one's hand on" one's sword, without actually raising it; it is clearly a gesture of menace.
    2. *Xaek* 赫 is essentially to "redden," but it becomes a set epithet of fury, "to turn red with rage." This line is taken almost verbatim from the first of Wang Ts'an's "Army Poems" 從軍詩: "Crimson in rage, he lets his heavenly might thunder" 赫怒震天威 (*Wh* 27.12b).
    3–4. As Wang notes, this story is told in the *San-ch'i-lüeh chi* 三齊略記 cited in *Ywlc* (c. 6, p. 108): "The King of Ch'in was making a stone bridge in order to cross the sea to look on the place where the sun rose. There was a divine person who was able to drive rocks into the sea. When the rocks didn't go quickly enough, he immediately whipped them and they all ran with blood. Even today they are all red—all the rocks of Yang-ch'eng Mountain stand up, towering and leaning eastward, as though moving in file." *Zuin* 巡' is the proper word for an imperial or princely journey. *Xǐ-hiòu* 海右 is literally "the right side of the sea," its western side assuming the proper southerly orientation. As Wang notes, much of the language of these opening lines appears in the first part of Chiang Yen's *Hen fu* 恨賦 (*Wh* 16. 31b–32a).
    5. *Giǒu-njiǒ* 九寓, literally the "Nine Lodgings," is an ornamental variation on *giǒu-jiou* 九州, the "Nine Provinces," all China.
    6. Literally, "He sought only the herbs (for the elixir of immortality) of the island of P'eng-lai."
    7. *Hǒ* 扈 is the same as 扈, used in the sense of 户. Wang cites 04449 and 03222, where the phrase *nong hǒ chuin* 農扈春 is used, in both cases to praise rulers who have given up idle pastimes to "observe the spring (labor) of farm families."
    9. *Zhiɘm* 贍 is often the "adequacy" of provision or strength.

07883: *CTs*, p. 1673: Hanabusa 17 (Hanabusa's division of the *Ku-feng* is different than Wang's and most texts); Wang, p. 56.
Rhymes: 2 *seng*, 4 *tsiɛng*, 6 *haeng*, 8 *xiɑng*, 10 *meng*, 12 *biaeng*, 14 *qiɛng*. (*T'ung-yün*).

    1. Lotus Blossom Peak 蓮華峯 was one of the peaks of Hua-shan.
    2. The *miaeng-seng* 明星 is usually the morning star or Venus, known in Chinese as T'ai-po 太白, which was also Li Po's given name. Wang takes the *miaeng-seng* as the Jade Girl of the Bright Star 明星玉女, an immortal who dwells on Hua-shan; see *HHs*, pp. 1930–31. See also Edward Schafer, *Pacing the Void* (Berkeley, 1977), pp. 132–36.
    4. For an extended discussion of the tradition of *bhò-xiu* 步虛, "stepping in emptiness," see Schafer, op. cit., pp. 234–69. *Tɑ̀i-tsiɛng* 太清 is often used simply as a kenning for Heaven, but here it is probably being used in its technical Taoist sense as one of the levels of Heaven, in which the *kiɘ̀i* 氣 is firm.
    5. As Wang notes, the "rainbow robes" 霓裳 appear in the *Tung-chün* 東君 of the "Nine Songs," describing the coming of the spirits. *Ngei-zhiɑng* 霓裳 was also the name of a famous piece of "new music" of Hsüan-tsung's reign, music to which Yang Kuei-fei danced.
    7. Cloud Terrace 雲臺 was the name of a twin peak in the northeastern section of Hua-shan.
    8. For the immortal Wei Shu-ch'ing, see Schafer, op. cit., p. 225.
    10. *Gà-hung* 駕鴻 is literally "hitching wild geese (to their carriage)." *Tziɛ̆-meng* 紫冥 is a nontechnical kenning for the heavens. The line is a variation on a line in the third of Kuo P'u's *Yu-hsien shih* (*Wh* 21.30a), and clearly the variation to *meng* is for the sake of rhyme. Kuo P'u's line had read *jhiɑng tziɛ̆-qen* 乘紫煙, "riding purple mist," and when *qen* was changed to *meng* for the sake of rhyme, the *jhiɑng* also had to be changed, since the *tziɛ̆-meng* was not something that could be "ridden."
    11–12. Wang takes this as referring to the troops of An Lu-shan, though he cites another opinion that it refers to the T'ang's Uighur allies.
    14. Literally, "*Jrhaei* (a kind of wild dog) and wolves: all caps and cap ribbons." *Jrhaei-lɑng*

射狼 was a set metaphor for the rapacious and cruel. *Guan-qiεng* 冠纓 was a standard synecdoche for officials. The line probably suggests that all the worst people have been made officials, but the emphasis might possibly have been somewhat different, suggesting all the officials are the worst people. A possible further implication is that the *jrhaei* and wolves are decked out in caps and ribbons because they themselves have killed the real officials.

08465: *CTs*, p. 1813; Hanabusa 605; Wang, p. 424; *Hyylε* in *TjhTs*, p. 57.
Rhymes: 1 *shrεn*, 2 *hεn*, 4 *gεn*. Unregulated.
Title: *Hyylε* has "Answering the Question of an Uncouth Person" 答俗人問. There are different
  versions of the title, all combining these various elements in different ways. The poem is consciously
  in the tradition of T'ao Hung-ching's famous epigram (*CLs* 11.12b).

  1. *Sei* 棲, literally "roosting," is a rootless, impermanent mode of lodging, appropriate to
a free spirit with no ties to the world.
  3. *Qĕu-njiεn* 窅然 is one of the many compounds suggesting a quality that is "deep, mysterious,
and far away."

05811: *CTs*, p. 1242; Chao, p. 38; *Wyu* 5.7b.
Rhymes: 2 *jiə*, 4 *zhiuε*, 6 *zhiə*. The first four lines are regulated; the fifth line violently breaks the
  pattern with five deflected tones. The last line ends with proper tonal balance.

  1. 飲 is probably *qyìm* here, "to give someone something to drink."
  5. I perfer to take this as the poet's statement, and the imperative *mak* 莫 as self-exhortation.
However, it is possible to take this as the (distinctly impolite) words of the person asked.

08669: *CTs*, p. 1856; Hanabusa 814; Wang, p. 521.
Rhymes: 2 *djiung*, 4 *biung*. Regulated, two "A" form couplets in sequence.

  2. *Luǎ-dhàn* 裸袒 need not mean completely stripped to the buff, since the characterization
is applied to barbarians who wear breechclouts; however, it is bare enough to offend traditional
nudity taboos.
  4. There is no exact equivalent of *shrǎ* 灑: it usually applies to spray or rain "splattering,"
but here it must refer to the intermittent gusts of the breeze.

08679: *CTs*, p. 1858; Hanabusa 824; Wang, p. 523.
Rhymes: 2 *qiəi*, 4 *xiəi*. Unregulated.
Title: *Kiĕn* 遣, "to drive out," "expel," is often used for the "expression" of emotions, with the
  added implication that once they are "driven out," the person is free of them. *Dzhì-kiĕn* 自遣 thus
  becomes something like "unburdening myself."

  1. Note the similarity between this opening situation and that of 07848.
  4. This is a conventional scene of evening return, redeemed from triteness by the understatement of *xiəi* 稀 (in contrast to the more common isolation of the poet), and by *iεk* 亦. The use of
iεk is particularly fine: it presents the poet as just now noticing a relation between the return of the
birds and the return of people; as those two "returns" were strongly linked in the poetic tradition,
to "notice" that they occur together marks an innocence and freshness of vision, almost a surprise
on the part of the drunken poet. Of course, with this drunken poet, covered in flowers, splashing
around in the moonlight on the creek, it is hardly surprising that nearby birds have taken flight, and
people too might hesitate to linger in the neighborhood.

08651: *CTs*, p. 1853; Hanabusa 796; Wang, p. 515; *Wyyh* 152.7a (title only), 195.6a–6b.
Rhymes: 2 *tsin*, 4 *njin*, 6 *shin*, 8 *chuin*; 10 *luàn*, 12 *sàn*, 14 *xàn*. Old Style.
Title: This is the first in a series of four poems. For a brief discussion of this poem see Frankel,
  op. cit., p. 22.

  2. It was customary when drinking to have someone else pour wine for a person. Of course,
there was enough solitary drinking in T'ang poetry to make this a requisite custom only in convivial
situations, but Li Po's phrasing serves to emphasize the absence of someone to pour for him.

4. The use of *njin* 人 here is remarkable.

7. *Tziang* 將 is used here as a conjunction.

8. *Ghyip-chuin* 及春, literally to "reach spring," suggests either that the poet will achieve a springtime state of mind or, more likely, that his delight will not dissipate until it is spring.

11. *Seng* 醒 usually means to "become sober," specifically after being drunk; however, here it is clearly a more general "sobriety," from which state one becomes drunk. *Gau-xuan* 交歡, translated as "friendship and pleasure," might seem to suggest an almost sexual intimacy from its components; but the compound is used for a more general intimacy.

13. *Mio-dzhieng* 無情, literally "without feelings," is usually a pejorative term; here, however, it is clearly revalued to a positive "freedom from passion," even though that contradicts the "shared friendship and pleasure" of the eleventh line. Yet there is something sly in the use of the term: a Taoist or Buddhist dispassion is usually hard-won, yet the moon and shadow are quite literally "without feelings," and since they are not really *njin* 人, Li Po has "no feelings" toward them.

08678: *CTs*, p. 1858; Hanabusa 823; Wang, p. 523; *Wyyh* 159.5a.
Rhymes: 2 *hen*, 4 *shren*. Regulated
Title: Ching-t'ing Mountain is located in Anhwei, just north of the Yangtze. See Frankel, op. cit., pp. 30–31.

4. Literally, "There is only Ching-t'ing Mountain (to form the 'pair' of mutual gazers)."

08114: *CTs*, p. 1724; Hanabusa 249; Wang p. 206.
Rhymes: [1 *djhiǎng*], 2 *djhiang*, 4 *shriang*. Regulated.
Title: Autumn Banks 秋浦 was south of the Yangtze in modern Anhwei, just east of Ching-t'ing Mountain.

1. A *djhiǎng* 丈 was in fact somewhat over three meters long, so Li Po is actually speaking of 9,330 meters of white hair. Wang Ch'i's comment here is interesting: "The first line is quite strange, but it is resolved in the rest of the poem. Every word forms a subtle meaning. Only an old master can do this: no model follower or line-plucker could say this."

2. *Iuen-jrhiou* 緣愁, translated as "sorrow's consequence," is an unusual, formal way to express cause. For the use of *gà* 箇, see Chang Hsiang, *Shih tz'u ch'ü yü-tz'u hui-shih*, p. 346. Li Po's use of *gà* is unique, even in Chang Hsiang's thorough survey of T'ang particles, and since it lacks poetic or classical parallels, we may presume it is either colloquial or a strange construction of Li Po's devising. It is used as a pronoun, perhaps as a demonstrative pronoun, and its referent is *jrhiou*. *Djhiang* 長 is zeugma.

08617: *CTs*, p. 1846; Hanabusa 758; Wang, p. 500; *Wyyh* 309.6a.
Rhymes: 1 *giuəi*, 2 *qiəi*, 4 *biəi*. Regulated.
Title: After dispatching the beauty Hsi Shih to Wu, King Kou-chien of Yüeh waited until Fu-ch'a of Wu had completely neglected his kingdom in his infatuation with Hsi Shih; see note to line 1, 07929. Then Kou-chien led his army in and defeated Wu.

2. *Ngyè-jrhiǎ* 義士, literally "righteous troops," was the term applied to the imperial army. Using it for the troops of Yüeh asks the reader to adopt the point of view of the king of Yüeh and his people. This is one small but potent mark of Li Po's "negative capability," which separates this poem from the conventional *huai-ku*. The brocade robes of the troops are probably rewards given them for their merit, but they may simply be plunder.

08079: *CTs*, p. 1717; Hanabusa 216; Wang, p. 187; *Wyyh* 332.7a.
Rhymes: 1 *kiou*, 2 *siɛn*, 3 *liou*, 4 *qen*, 5 *ziuɛn*, 6 *ziuɛn*; 7 *hung*, 8 *biung*, 9 *tung*, 10 *ghiung*.

3. Mount Sung, with its thirty-six peaks, was located near Lo-yang and was the source of the Ying River. For the associations of *tziĕ-qen* 紫煙, see note 07883, line 10.

7. A *seng-hung* 星虹, "star-rainbow," is a comet or shooting star with a tail; see Li Shan explanation, *Wh* 54.22b. Wang Ch'i maintains that Li Po is referring to a star positioned in a real rainbow; though this may be less difficult to imagine someone pacing, it is, as far as I can tell, unsupported.

10. Literally, "I know on your wandering the heart will not be exhausted."

07936: *CTs*, p. 1684; Hanabusa 72; Wang, pp. 93–94; *Wyyh* 200.6a; *Twt* 12.10a; *Yfsc* 71.1a.
Rhymes: 1 *tsen*, 2 *dzhiɛn*, 4 *njiɛn*, 5 *chiuɛn*, 6 *shrɛn*, 8 *ben* (*t'ung-yün*); 12 *dzhɔi*, 14 *xɔi*.

1. For *dǒu zhip-tsen* 斗十千, see note 07931, line 21.
4. *Mɑng-njiɛn* 茫然 is one of the many binomes suggesting confusion and indistinctness.
6. The T'ai-hang Mountains were proverbial for their dangers.
11. The multiplicity of byways or crossroads echoes the famous allegory of the division of the Way told in the *Lieh-tzu*, when Yang Chu marveled at the number of people it took to search for one lost sheep because the crossroads were so many.
13. As Wang Ch'i notes, this line echoes the words of Tsung Ch'üeh when asked by his uncle Tsung Ping what his ambition was.
14. *Djhiɔk* 直 here probably means "straightaway" or "all I need do is. . . ."

46748: *CTs*, p. 9642; *Twt* 17B.10a. For a translation of the last part of the poem, see Schafer, op. cit., p. 245.
Rhymes: 2 *gɑng*, 4 *mɑng*, 6 *xiɑng*, 8 *guɑng*, 10 *huɑng*.

1. *Qiuaen-qiuaen* 蜿蜿 is a binome properly reserved for the undulating movement of a dragon.
3. This backward gaze, down to one's native land, occurs at the close of the *Li Sao* and in poems in that tradition.
5. Note the reworking of a couplet from the first of T'ao Ch'ien's *Kuei yüan-t'ien chü* (CTsins 6.5a).
6. *Dèi-xiɑng* 帝鄉 often refers to the "imperial demesne," close around the capital, but here it refers to the dwelling of the Emperor of Heaven.
7. For a discussion of the *giɔ* 紀, translated as "network," the interstellar "strands" of the sky, see Schafer, op. cit., p. 241.
9. The *Tài-miɔi* 太微 (*T'ai-wei*) was an imperial constellation, roughly coordinate with the constellation Virgo; see Schafer, op. cit., pp. 52, 208.

CHAPTER 9

10242: *CTs*, p. 2190; Juan, pp. 94–95; *KCsc* 4.7a; *Yfsc* 61.9b.
Rhymes: 2 *djhin*, 4 *shin*, 6 *njin*.
Title: Chi Gate was very close to modern Peking, though in the T'ang the area was a frontier.

1. *Qaĕm-qaĕm* 黯黯 basically means "dark," but like many descriptives of darkness, it implies a somberness.
2. *Gaèng* 更, meaning "again," usually precedes only verbs, but in some cases, as here, it can precede nouns; cf. 08337.23.
3. *Bhiɔng-liɔng* 憑陵 is a descriptive compound of primarily military associations involving "pressing hard" on people who are holding a position. I have here taken it in an active sense, but some usages would allow it in a passive sense: "Though the nomad horsemen are hard-pressed. . . ."
4. This is, of course, not a historical ballad, and "Han" here refers to the T'ang armies. That the soldiers *biɔt gò shin* 不顧身, literally, "do not look to their bodies," is the standard way to say that the soldiers are willing to die for the empire.
6. *Shraèi* 殺 here is an intensifier.

10323: *CTs*, p. 2211; Juan, p. 6; *KCsc* 1.7a–7b; *Wyyh* 299.5a.
Rhymes: 2 *hiuaen*, 4 *xuɔn*, 6 *piaen*, 8 *qɔn*, 10 *mɔn*.
Title: *Wyyh* has the variant "Written When Returning after Accompanying the Recruits" 送兵還作. For a translation and brief discussion of this poem, see Marie Chan, *Kao Shih* (Boston, 1978), pp. 99–100.

2. *Sɔi-xuɔn* 塞垣 is an elegant variation for the complex of border fortifications known as the Great Wall; see Wu-ch'en commentary, *Wh* 28.22a.
3. *Seu-dheu* 蕭條 is a descriptive binome for a desolation that evokes a mood of gloom.

7. The "plans to still the frontiers" are in the form of written documents 書, probably suggesting memorials to the throne.

10358: *CTs*, p. 2217–18; Juan, pp. 113–16; *KCsc* 5.1a–1b; *Hyylc* in *TjhTs*, pp. 97–98; *Yhc* in *TjhTs*, p. 361; *Ttc* in *TjhTs*, p. 521; *Wyyh* 196.6b–7a; *Twt* 12.14a; *Tscs* p. 342; *Yfsc* 32.6a–6b.
Rhymes: 1 *bɔk*, 2 *dzhɔk*, 4 *shriɔk*; 6 *gɛn*, 8 *shrɛn*; 9 *tǒ*, 10 *hiǒ*, 12 *miǒ*; 13 *bhiɔi*, 14 *xiɔi*, 16 *hiuɔi*; 17 *giǒu*, 18 *hǒu*, 20 *shiǒu*, 22 *hiǒu*, 24 *dǒu*; 25 *piɔn*, 26 *xiuɔn*, 28 *giuɔn*.
Title: The "Song of Yen" 燕歌行 was a *yüeh-fu* title, the first extant version of which was by Ts'ao P'i, and the heptasyllabic meter set by Ts'ao P'i was retained in most subsequent versions. For an extensive discussion of Kao's song, see Marie Chan, op. cit., pp. 101–12.
Preface: Reading 從御史張公 with *Hyylc* instead of Juan's 從元戎.

1. Again, the "House of Han" does not indicate a historical ballad, but rather refers directly to the T'ang; in contrast, many earlier heptasyllabic songs tried to maintain some consistency of historical reference. *Qen-djhin* 煙塵, "dust and smoke," has here lost its visual dimension and has become a true substitution trope, synecdoche for warfare.

2. As Marie Chan notes, this involves an unusual personalizing of the expedition in the *ga* 家, "home." The mention of leaving one's home is common in frontier *yüeh-fu*, where the soldier or adventurer is of low social status, but it usually does not appear when applied to an imperial general. *Dzhɑn-dzhɔk* 殘賊, "last of the raiders," implies that many of the nomads have already been killed, probably by the garrison troops. *Dzhɑn* is used for the troops that "survive" after a battle; *dzhɔk* is a pejorative term, translated as "bandit" or "rebel," applied to anyone who contests imperial authority.

3. *Huaeng-haeng* 橫行 is a term applied to far expeditions into the frontier regions.

4. To "grant special countenance" is to look upon the expedition with great favor.

5. *Chrang gyim* 摐金 seems to be a contracted form of *chrang gyim-gǒ* 摐金鼓, "to beat the kettledrums," used in the *Tzu-hsü fu* 子虛賦 of Ssu-ma Hsiang-ju (Juan). "tambours" for *gǒ*, "plain drums" is translator's license. As Marie Chan notes, the sequence from Elm Pass to Chieh Rock to Wolf Mountain details the progress of the expedition out into the northeastern frontier.

6. *Qyuɛ-i* 逶迤 is a descriptive binome with many applications, the most common, as here, describing something winding off into the distance, in this case the column of troops.

7. The *gàu-qiuǎi* 校尉 was the Han title for the class of officers immediately below the generals; in the T'ang the term was used unofficially. The term *Hàn-xǎi* 瀚海 presents real problems: it can be used for the sea off the North China coast, geographically appropriate here, but it is most commonly applied to the Gobi Desert, geographically inappropriate. It is perhaps best to take it as applying generally to the wastelands of the Northeast.

10. For *bhiɔng-liɔng* 憑陵, see note 10242, line 3.

11–12. These are substantially the same charges later raised against Ko-shu Han.

13. As Juan notes, the use of *bhiɔi* 腓 here for the "sickening" of the autumn plants is an echo of *Shih* 204, traditionally interpreted as a lament for the sufferings caused by misgovernment.

15. As Juan notes, this line may be an echo of *Lao-tzu* 69: "No calamity is greater than thinking little of the enemy." But the allusion must be understood in the context of the conventions of T'ang military poems in which the soldiers often swear to accomplish great deeds to requite the emperor's favor; e.g., 06782–83. In this case the failure of the troops or of their commanders is in "not knowing the measure of their capacities."

17. The emphasis here seems to be that what began as a quick campaign to defeat the nomads has become endless garrison duty.

18. The line begins literally, "They must be weeping jade sinews." *Ngiok-giɔn* 玉筋, a courtly kenning for the strands of tears, is most unusual in this context. Mention of the women weeping at home was a necessity in campaign songs, but Kao Shih has wisely reserved it for a place where their lament has particular force.

20. The turning of the head marks the soldier's thoughts of home.

21. This is another alternative to the swift campaign—a constant movement, "whirled back and forth," never achieving one's goals.

23. As Juan notes, the *sɑm-zhiɔ* 三時, "three seasons," are spring, summer, and autumn.

The *shrat-kiði* 殺氣, "wind of destruction," is a characteristic of autumn, and its presence throughout the year marks the unnaturalness of the frontier world.

24. The *deu-dŏu* 勺斗 were kettles used to sound the watches of the night.

25. I have followed the collection reading of 雪, "snow," instead of the reading 血, "blood," which is supported by virtually all the early anthologies. This is one of the few cases where I have chosen the textually less likely reading: "snow" makes it a great line; "blood" is a melodramatic abomination. The "silveriness" of the blades is literally "white," so with the reading "snow," we have the haunting image of blurred, virtually anonymous forms confronting each other with white blades in the swirling white snow.

26. *Xiuən* 勳 is some kind of acknowledgment of merit, often a reward.

10313: *CTs*, p. 2210; Juan, p. 1; *KCsc* 1.6a.
Rhymes: 2 *dzhəi*, 4 *dhəi*, 6 *ləi*.
Title: Sung-chou, later Sui-yang, was east of Lo-yang and the center of the ancient region of Liang. This poem is translated in Marie Chan, op. cit., p. 74.

1. Prince Hsiao of Liang was a famous patron of letters; he received some of the most famous writers of the Western Han, men like Tsou Yang, Ssu-ma Hsiang-ju, and Mei Sheng. As Juan notes, the phrase *siek dzhiuən zhièng* 昔全盛 ominously recalls its use in Pao Chao's "Fu on the Weed-Covered City" 蕪城賦 (*Wh* 11.13b), where the memory of past splendor is contrasted with the city's present desolation.

6. In connection with the "high terrace" of line 4, the "sad wind" here echoes the opening of the first of Ts'ao Chih's "Unclassified Poems" (*Wh* 29.21b), one of the most famous of Chien-an poems, on which the T'ang *ku-feng* were founded.

04389: *CTs*, p. 896; *Ch'en Tzu-ang chi*, p. 22.
Rhymes: 2 *dhəi*, 4 *tzəi*, 6 *ləi*.
Title: "Observing the Past on Chi Hill: Presented to the Recluse Lu Tsang-yung" 薊丘覧古贈盧居士藏用. The poem quoted is the second of a series of seven and is entitled "Prince Chao of Yen"; see Stephen Owen, *Poetry of the Early T'ang.* (New Haven, 1977), pp. 176–78.

1. Later scholars may have worried about the actual location of the legendary Chieh Rock, but Ch'en Tzu-ang felt secure that it was there, by Chi Hill. The Lodge of Chieh Rock had supposedly been built by King Chao of Yen for his advisor Tsou Yen 鄒衍. The "Terrace of Gold" was built by King Chao for his retainers.

3. *Kiou-liəng* 丘陵 are basically low "hills," but in the context of this scene, they are potentially the sites of Prince Chao's capital and perhaps even the tomb mounds of the state of Yen.

10432: *CTs*, pp. 2233–34; Juan, pp. 197–98; *KCsc* 8.1a.
Rhymes: 1 *kung*, 2 *djiung*, 4 *giung*, 6 *qung*, 8 *ghiung*. Regulated.
Title: Golden Fort 金城 was about 500 kilometers west-northwest of Ch'ang-an, in modern Kansu; it was on the edge of the frontier region, but not deep in Central Asia. A *lou* 樓 is a multistoried building, usually wider than it is tall: *lou* were built on city walls for observation and defense. In this context, to translate *lou* as "tower" is unavoidable, but it gives an unfortunate impression of verticality.

1. *Măn* 滿 is often used for a scene "filling" the eyes or the vision.

2. Literally, "superior to those in a painting." The competition of nature and painting is no less evident in T'ang writing than in the West, though in the T'ang the competition usually takes a somewhat different form.

4. *Shièi* 勢, translated as "form," is a "kinetic form," either a quality of movement or a static form with movement implied. In this case, *shièi* is the particular tension implicit in the form of the bent bow.

6. *Tĕi-dhău* 體道, literally "to take the Way as one's form," means something like "to live consonant with the Way."

7. *Hɑ-jrhiè* 何事 usually means simply "why," but here it clearly means "what is done," "what occurrence is there."

8. For *qiuaèn* 怨, see note 06725, line 2. Presumably the "bitterness" is that of the troops who must serve in the army there.

10360: *CTs*, p. 2218; Juan, pp. 140–41; *KCsc* 5.12b–13a; *Wyyh* 157.8b.
Rhymes: 1 *dhang*, 2 *xiang*, 4 *djhiang*; 5 *iù*, 6 *liù*, 8 *chiù*; 9 *chuin*, 10 *djhin*, 12 *njin*. Note that this poem takes the form of three heptasyllabic quatrains, the third of which is regulated; it is quite possible that a quatrain series has here been conflated into one heptasyllabic "old style" poem.

1. The "thatched hut" was the way Tu Fu referred to his dwelling in Ch'eng-tu; in later dynasties the phrase became inextricably associated with Tu Fu.
2. It is unclear here whether Kao Shih or Tu Fu is the person "yearning for native land." *Len* 憐, translated as "love," also can involve emotions of "concern" and "pity": thus, ". . . with thoughts of concern on how my old friend yearns for his native land." *Gò-xiang* 故鄉 is more locally a "home region."
3–4. The subject here may be Tu Fu rather than Kao Shih. In seventh-and eighth-century poetry, the renewal of nature in the spring usually brings thoughts of return home.
5. *Nom-biaen* 南蕃, translated as "southern borders," is the southern frontier region, to which Ch'eng-tu belonged by its position relative to Ch'ang-an.
6. In its antithesis to *liù* 慮, *iù* 預 here takes on its meaning of "relaxed" or "joyous."
7–8. This couplet is clearly an echo of 04335.5–6.
9. The reference here is to Hsieh An 謝安 (320–85) of the Tsin, who stayed at his villa on East Mountain refusing repeated summons to serve. These refusals won him a great reputation and the general opinion that his service would be the salvation of the empire's troubles; see *Shih-shuo hsin-yü* (*SPTK*) 3B, section 25. 24. *Chuin* 春, "springs," is synecdoche for "years." The "thirty years" refers to Kao Shih's life rather than Hsieh An's.
10. The study of "books" (or "writing") and the "sword" echoes the education of Hsiang Yü.
11. *Liong-jiong* 龍鍾 is a binome often used in poetry to describe the appearance of old age. A *zhiɛk* 石 was a large measure, here used for the rice (or rice-equivalent) that Kao Shih received as a salary. *Tĕm* 添 is often used for a promotion, especially for receiving an additional official position. Two thousand *zhiɛk* was the compensation for the governor of a commandery.
12. As Juan notes, this echoes a famous passage in the first part of the T'an-kung chapter of the *Li-chi*, where Confucius describes himself as a "person of north, south, east, and west." The traditional interpretation of this is that Confucius is a wanderer, with no fixed abode. When Kao Shih applies the epithet to Tu Fu, it is both praise in the implicit analogy to Confucius, and sympathy for Tu Fu's lack of a "position" such as Kao Shih has. Tu Fu is thus one whose position is not commensurate with his greatness, and thus Kao Shih is "ashamed" at his own undeserved office.

10342: *CTs*, p. 2214; Juan, p. 53; *KCsc* 3.2a.
Rhymes: 2 *sim*, 4 *shim*, 6 *lim*.
Title: Tung-p'ing was directly northeast of Pien-chou, in modern Shantung.

3. *Sak-sak* 索索 is a descriptive binome applied to the sound of wind, trees, and crickets; from another meaning, it has the association of restlessness.

CHAPTER 10

09591: *CTs*, p. 2050; *CTcs* 2.2a–2b; *Tscs* p. 353.
Rhymes: 1 *jiɛt*, 2 *siuɛt*; 3 *ləi*, 4 *kəi*; 5 *mak*, 6 *bhak*, 8 *djiak*; 9 *biəng*, 10 *ngiəng*; 11 *kaek*, 12 *dhɛk*; 13 *mən*, 14 *piaen*; 15 *kiù*, 16 *lò*, 18 *chiù*. Some rhymes are *t'ung-yùn*.

1. For the "white grasses," see note 06725, line 15. The imagery of this line is violently hyperbolic: clouds are "rolled up," the wind may "roll up" snow, but nothing "rolls up" the earth. "Snapping," *jiɛt* 折, is what happens when someone picks a plant: it involves separation of one part from another.
2. The function of *tziək* 即 is something like "right then": thus, "In the Tartar skies as soon as it is the eighth month, immediately the snow goes flying."

3. The comparison of snow to pear or plum blossoms was a commonplace, but Ts'en Shen extends the comparison into a full conceit.

5. "Beaded curtains" and "lacework drapes" belong to a boudoir scene and are singularly inappropriate here; Ts'en is writing a poem on falling spring blossoms and applying it to a snow scene; then, in the next line, shifting back to the cold.

6. Literally, "The fox furs are not warm": Ts'en Shen deliberately phrases the line to run counter to the reader's expectations. The reader knows that fox furs are indeed warm, and must infer the extremity of cold that will make them "not warm."

8. The *Do-hò* 都護, "viceroy" or "protector general," was the civil officer in charge of large frontier regions. In the sense of "wear," 著 is pronounced *djiak*, necessary here for rhyme.

9. For *Hàn-xǎi* 瀚海, see note to 10358, line 7. There is some textual indecision as to the extent of the hyperbole here, whether the ice is *baek-chiɛk* 百尺, *tsen-chiɛk* 千尺, or *baek-djhiǎng* 百丈. In any case, the hyperbole must apply to the depth of the ice rather than its breadth; if it were breadth, the ice would be a rather small area on the expanse of the Gobi.

10. *Tsǒm-dhǒm* 黲淡 is a descriptive binome combining often a visual darkness with a sense of gloom. *Ngiəng* 凝, literally "congeal," is an immobility in the clouds, in contrast to their usual fluid changes.

11. An imperial army was divided into three division (*sam-giuən* 三軍), of which the "central division" (*djiung-giuən* 中軍) belonged to the commander-in-chief.

12. All of these are nomad instruments; such nominal enumerations are very rare in *shih* before the T'ien-pao.

13. The *hiuaen-mən* 轅門, literally "Wagon-tongue Gate," was the compound of the commander when an army was on campaign.

14. The use of *chiɛt* 掣 here is strong and unusual: it could mean to "draw out," but I prefer to take it in the more active sense of "clutch and restrain," as in *chiɛt-djiǒu* 掣肘. *Piaen* 翩, not often applied to flags, means to "flutter" or "move with the wind" in this sense.

15. Bugur, or Lun-t'ai 輪臺, was a city far in Central Asia, about 100 kilometers east-southeast of Kucha. The eastern gate of Bugur should mark a journey back toward China, but the Heaven Mountain Range, mentioned in line 16, lies directly north of Bugur.

09596: *CTs*, p. 2052; *TCcs* 2.5b.
Rhymes: 1 *kǒu*, 2 *hǒu*; 3 *kəi*, 4 *ləi*, 6 *huəi*; 7 *zhiò*, 8 *shiò*, 10 *kiù*. (last group *t'ung-yün*).

1. Ch'ih-t'ing was a mountain and stream near Lung-hsi, in modern Kansu.

5–6. In his description, Ts'en Shen draws heavily on traditions of describing ordinary clouds.

6. The use of *huən* 渾 here, in parallel with *jrhà* 乍, is probably "once again," as described in Chang Hsiang, *Shih tz'u ch'ü yü-tz'u hui-shih*, pp. 231–32.

7. "Iron Gate" was probably at Iron Mountain 鐵山, in modern Kansu.

8. Yarkhoto, *Chiao-ho* 交河, was located far to the northwest of the probable site of this poem.

06560: *CTs*, p. 1398; *CKCsc* 3.10b–11a.
Rhymes: 2 *zhiuɛ*, 4 *zhiə*, 6 *djhiɛ*, 8 *tziə*. Old style. The first eight lines of twenty-two are quoted.

1. A *ziə* 祠 is usually a non-Buddhist shrine, though here it is clearly applied to a Buddhist temple; note that the compound *ziə-hiǒ* 祠宇, "shrine-vault," "shrine," has been split up in this line. *Gyim* 金, "golden" or "metallic," is an epithet often applied to splendid buildings, which were often, in fact, gilded. *Jin-hiǒ* 真宇 is glossed as a "dwelling of immortals" in the Wu-ch'en commentary to Tso Ssu's "Fu on the Wu Capital" (*Wh* 5.8b–9a) and here is used in the courtly tradition of describing fine buildings in terms of celestial architecture. The line is a highly ornamental description of the pagoda rising out of the temple complex.

2. *Tseng-hiuən* 青雲 were associated with Heaven and the court, so that an ascent to the blue clouds involved becoming an immortal or rising to high position.

3–4. This couplet shifts diction to the casual, simple style of capital poetry: the theme of stillness, the use of particles like *iɛk* 亦, the use of pronouns like *ngǎ* 我 and *jiə* 之.

5. *Tsang-mio* 蒼蕪, literally "verdant-weedy," is a new compound suggesting the denseness of the early autumn vegetation. The Yi-ch'un Gardens were constructed by the second Ch'in

emperor and were a favorite place for outings in the Han; here the reference is probably to the Ch'ü-chiang Park, southeast of Ch'ang-an.

6. *Pèn* 片 is an untranslatable measure for flat surfaces, as the surface of a lake. K'un-ming Pool was an artificial lake created in the Han.

7. The rhetorical question "Who says?" implicitly denying a statement everyone knows to be true, was a favorite device of court poetry.

8. *Sisu-isu* 逍遙 combines the relaxed strolling of an outing with spiritual freedom, the latter from its use in the *Chuang-tzu*.

09534: *CTs*, p. 2037; *TCcs* 1.19b–20a.
Rhymes: 2 *giung*, 4 *kung*, 6 *gung*, 8 *kiung*, 10 *biung*, 12 *dung*, 14 *lung*, 16 *djiung*, 18 *mung*, 20 *tzong*, 22 *ghiung*. Old style.
Title: "With Kao Shih and Hsüeh Chü, Climbing the Stupa in the Temple of Compassionate Mercy" 與高適薛據同登慈恩寺浮圖.

1. For *shièi* 勢, see note 10432, line 4. *TSscy* (1.39a) notes a passage in the *Miao-fa lien-hua ching* on seven precious pagodas that "bubble up" out of the earth before the Buddha. The description "bubbling" is particularly appropriate for the form of early Indian stupas, but for the Chinese pagoda it is strange indeed.

2. *Ten-giung* 天宮 is the Chinese term for the palaces in Heaven, but it was also the translation of *devapura*, the Buddhist heavenly dwellings.

3. For *shièi-gàèi* 世界, see note 06393, line 8.

5. *Jhin-jiou* 神州 was an old kenning for China proper, the "holly domain." *Qap* 壓 is a term often applied to high mountains, which in their sheerness and height "hang over" and seem to weigh down on what is below.

6. *Giuǎi-gung* 鬼工 emphasizes that the accomplishment seems beyond the capability of humans.

8. *Mɑ* 摩, "rubs," is often said of high things like birds or mountains "touching" the sky. *Tsɑng-kiung* 蒼穹, literally the "blue and vaulted," was a kenning for Heaven. *Kiung* is usually taken as a contraction of *kiung-liung* 穹隆, "domed" or "vaulted," the shape of Heaven: this appears in the K'ung Ying-ta exegesis of *Shih* 257, where *tsɑng-kiung* appears as *kiung-tsɑng*. The "seventh story," *tsit-dzhɑng* 七層, may also be together the "seven stories" of the pagoda.

9–10. These are standard poetic hyperboles of height.

11. Though great waves were frequently compared to mountains, mountains were less often compared to waves. Ts'en Shen's active topography looks forward to the lively landscapes of Han Yü.

12. *Bɑn-tsòu* 奔湊 means literally to "rush together," and the place where the streams come together is the sea. An old set of metaphors compared the movement of rivers toward the sea to the people's gathering to a legitimate ruler. Thus, the rivers were said to *djhiɛu* 朝, "go to the court" of the sea.

13. The *djhiɛ-dhǎu* 馳道 was the highway reserved for the emperor and high nobility.

14. *Leng-lung* 玲瓏 was originally a sound binome, describing the sound of jade; here it is used for the "bright glitter" of the architecture.

17. For "Five Barrows," see note 08045, line 1.

18. *Mung-mung* 濛濛 is a binome describing the haziness of rain or fog. I have translated the text as given, but I suspect *mung-mung* 蒙蒙 is the compound intended, also meaning "indistinct," but more strongly associated with dense vegetation than with fog and haze.

19. *Dzhièng-liǎ* 淨理 is a poetic rather than technical term for the Truth of "principle" of Buddhism.

20. Though *shièng-qin* 勝因, "Perfect Cause," does appear in the *Fo shuo wu-ch'ang ching* (*TSscy*), where it is the "way of producing virtue," Ts'en Shen does not seem to be using the term with any technical precision.

21–22. The closing vow to give up office now that one is aware of the truth of Buddhism or the value of reclusion was one of the most enduring conventions of temple-visiting poems and poems on visiting recluses.

09882: *CTs*, p. 2106; *TCcs* 7.3b; *WsTjcc* 7.3b.
Rhymes: 1 *dɑu*, 2 *mɑu*, 4 *bhɑu*. Regulated.

1. The "wind like a knife" appears in a famous *yüeh-fu* of Wang Ch'ang-ling, 06671. The Heaven Mountain Range was far inside Central Asia, running north of Kucha and Bugur.

2. *Zhiɐng-nom* 城南 usually refers to the area south of Ch'ang-an, though here it must refer to some frontier fortification or city. *Shriuk hɑn mɑu* 縮寒毛 means literally "contracts its cold fur."

3. *Bɑk* 博 is probably *bɑk-iɛk* 博弈, a board game like *go* associated with gambling and, thence, a general name for gambling; see *Ywlc* c. 74, pp. 1276–78. Since *tziòng* 縱 is not the verb generally applied to playing *bɑk*, it must mean something like the general "lets himself go" in playing the game, indulges himself. A *djhiɑng* 場 is probably not an entire game, but rather a series of moves constituting one "battle" within the game.

09877: *CTs*, p. 2106; *TCcs* 7.2b; *Ttc* in *TjhTs*, p. 590.
Rhymes: 1 *mɑn*, 2 *gɑn*, 4 *qɑn*.

2. *Liong-jiong* 龍鍾, besides describing the appearance of old age, also describes something "soaked," as with tears.

09774: *CTs*, p. 2089; *TCcs* 3.31b.
Rhymes: 2 *dhou*, 4 *siou*, 6 *xiou*, 8 *lou*. Regulated.

1. The significant compound in this line is *lèu-jrhiɔ* 料事, "to take care of matters," "to handle things." *Tsɑk* 錯 is an adverb. Thus, there is less of a break at the caesura than the translation would suggest.

2. "Slipping and stumbling," *tsɑ-dhɑ* 蹉跎, refers to all manners of failures: failing to "meet one's proper time," getting into political trouble.

3. Literally, "In my horizontal and vertical alliance stratagems, in all cases my plans did not work."

4. This may mean that "even his wife and children feel shame for him."

5. Probably an echo of 07767.3.

09757: *CTs*, p. 2086; *TCcs* 3.29a.
Rhymes: 1 *tsɑng*, 2 *miɑng*, 4 *lɑng*, 6 *huɑng*, 8 *xiɑng*. Regulated.

1. *Tsɑng-tsɑng* 蒼蒼 is primarily a color description, a gray or green; applied to vegetation it suggests luxuriance, and from that came to suggest a general abundance, here applied to "myriad matters," *miaèn-jrhiɔ* 萬事.

2. *Giɔi-sim* 機心 occurs in the *Chuung-tzu* (31/12/56), where Tzu-kung tries to convince an old gardener to use a well-sweep, and the gardener denounces "contrivances," which he says lead to "problems of contrivance," which further lead to a "contriving mind," *giɔi-sim*. A *giɔi-sim* is thus a mind concerned with achieving certain goals, but primarily concerned with devising means to attain them: thus, all acts have a motive. that determines them. Ts'en Shen's line reads literally, "A contriving mind was long ago forgotten." I have retained "heart" rather than "mind" for *sim* 心 to emphasize the element of inclination, that the poet no longer "has any heart to" deal with the "millions of problems." This lack of personal motive is picked up in the *mio-duɑn* 無端, "for no purpose," of line 3.

3. *Chuit* 出 is the verb used for "go out (from the capital) to serve as. . . ."

4. Note the difference between *biɔt qièm* 不厭, "not bored (being secretary)," and *biɔt zhiɛ qièm* 不是厭, "it (the reason that I came out here as prefect) is not that I was bored (being secretary)."

5–6. This fairly common poetic construction has two verbs: the object of the first verb is the subject of the second verb.

7. An "open-mouthed smile" or "laugh" is a mark of great merriment.

09646: *CTs*, p. 2065; *TCcs* 3.26a–26b; *Wyyh* 253.3a.
Rhymes: 2 *miɔn*, 4 *hiuɔn*, 6 *giuɔn*, 8 *ghiuɔn*. Regulated.
Title: *Wyyh* omits 行. The location of Dragon Roar Rapids is unknown, though from the mention of Mount O-mei and "camp," the poem is certainly from his years of service in Szechwan.

2. For 人 *Wyyh* reads 己.

3. Literally, "Mist on the waters: where clear, it emits moonlight."

5. A *biɑng-jrhiə* 方士 is one who has knowledge of alchemical matters or possesses supernatural skills of some sort.

6. *Liuən* 戀, translated as "yearn," is a particularly intense kind of desire. A *shriə-giuən* 使君, basically an "imperial emissary," became an alternative name for a prefect

7. For this line *Wyyh* reads the very weak 思鄉那可住.

8. *Liɛ-ghiuən* 離羣, "gone from the herd," was a set term for separation from one's kin and companions: here the reference is to the "various gentlemen in camp." Note that the poem takes care of both occasional functions mentioned in the title.

CHAPTER 11

10498: *CTs*, p. 2253; Chiu-chia 1.5, pp. 5–6; Ch'ou c. 1, pp. 2–3.

Rhymes: 2 *lěu*, 4 *xěu*, 6 *děu*, 8 *sièu*. Though in length and the use of parallel couplets in the middle this poem resembles an eight-line regulated verse, the poem avoids tonal balance. The last couplet is close to regulation, though the fifth position in the seventh line is a violation.

Title: The "Peak" is T'ai-shan 泰山.

1. *Tai-tsung, Dhài-tzong* 岱宗, was an honorific kenning for T'ai-shan, used in the *Shu*, II.i.iii.8. Chiu-chia cites the *Feng-su t'ung*, explaining *Dhài* as "primal," and *tzong* as "elder." There is great distance between the archaic elevation of *Dhài-tzong* and the discursive comment *bhio njiu-hɑ* 夫如何.

2. T'ai-shan lay on the boundary of the ancient states of Ch'i and Lu. *Miəi-lěu* 未了 is a particularly active way to speak of the "continuous green" of the mountain.

3. *Jhin-siòu* 神秀 is a "divine excellence," though *siòu* also carries the appropriate seme of "height." As Chiu-chia notes, *jhin-siòu* is the quality that Sun Ch'o says is supreme in T'ien-t'ai Mountain (*Wh* 11.4b), and Li Shan there glosses *siòu* as 異, "wonder," "strangeness." As T'ien-t'ai's supremacy in *jhin-siòu* is the first statement of Sun Ch'o's famous *fu*, it is perhaps appropriate to read Tu Fu's line as a counterstatement: "It is *here* Creation concentrated *jhin-siòu*."

4. *Qim-iɑng* 陰陽 here are the north and south slopes of the mountain, shadow and sunlight in the visual description, and in the context of *Dzhɑu-xuà* 造化, the forces of Yin and Yang. The description here is, of course, of the height of the mountain, which leaves a strong distinction between the sunlit side and the shadowy side.

5. As Chiu-chia and all subsequent commentaries have noted, the strange phrase *dhǎng-xiong* 盪胸 has a precedent in the *Nan-tu fu* of Chang Heng, where the waters of the Yü "sweep (past) the breast" (*Wh* 4.1b). The ever-pedestrian Wu-ch'en commentary notes "i.e., in front of one." Though the visual image of the clouds sweeping like a river before the poet should be retained, the element of "cleansing," "sweeping over" should not be discounted altogether; it survives as a sympathetic exhilaration in watching the cloud scene. *Shraeng* 生, "growing" or "giving birth to," is what a mountain does to clouds, and T'ai-shan was particularly famous for its nubilous world-covering.

6. *Guet-dzhiɛ̌* 決眥 is literally, as translated, "split the eye-pupils," what good archers did to birds in the *Tzu-hsü fu*. Chiu-chia explains the phrase as destroying one's visual abilities in gazing far, and rejects the association of archery. I would agree with the Chiu-chia interpretation and would suggest that the term is transferred from the destruction of eyes to the squinting involved in watching the tiny specks of birds disappear into the mountain. However, the fact that birds are involved both here and in the well-known *Tzu-hsü fu* leads one to suspect that there is some relation between the two. It is possible that Tu Fu is suggesting a close attention to the birds like an archer's taking aim; in this case, the line would be "Watching, as though to shoot and split their eye-pupils, my gaze follows the homing birds into the mountain." *Njip* 入, "enter," clearly refers both to the movement of the birds "into" the mountain and to the poet's vision that follows them "in."

7. *Huɑi-dɑng* 會當 is something like "there will surely be an occasion when. . . ." The phrase may also be taken as an optative. The *huɑi* promises a particular moment so that it alone can carry the future assurance; see Chang Hsiang, *Shih tz'u ch'ü yü-tz'u hui-shih*, p. 126.

8. The primary function of *jiùng* 衆 is as a poetic marker of plurality, but it often, as here, carries the implication of ordinariness.

10914: *CTs*, p. 2392; Chiu-chia 17.17, pp. 272–73; Ch'ou c. 1, pp. 24–25.
Rhymes: 1 *bhung*, 2 *hung*, 4 *hiung*. Regulated.

1. For the *piɛu-bhung* 飄蓬, see note 05984, line 3. The references in this poem are not at all clear: it is impossible to tell whether Tu Fu is speaking of himself, of Li Po, or of them both. *Siang-gò* 相顧 could, for example, be "we look on each other," in which case both are "tumble-weeds." I have chosen to keep the referent exclusively Li Po because Tu Fu was so fascinated with Li's personality; even if the poem refers to Tu Fu alone, it still describes the personality that everyone, Tu Fu included, associated with Li Po.

2. *Dan-shra* 丹砂 is the nugget of refined cinnabar used in elixirs of immortality. *Dzhiòu* 就 is probably used in the sense of "complete" here.

3. *Tùng* 痛 in this sense is an intensifier; *tùng-qyǐm* 痛飲, "drinking terribly much," is used specifically for wines.

4. *Biəi-iang bhat-hǒ* 飛揚跋扈 is a four-character phrase, used in the *Pei shih* to describe Hou Ching. *Biəi-iang* 飛揚 is "taking flight" like a bird, but it also suggests lack of decorum and will-fulness, as in the restlessness of a bird of prey. *Bhat-hǒ* 跋扈 is explained as "leaping over a bamboo fish weir" and is used to describe an unrestrained willfulness and arrogance.

10524: *CTs*, p. 2261; Chiu-chia 2.6, pp. 27–28; Ch'ou, c. 3, pp. 99–101.
Rhymes: 1 *ghyɛ*, 2 *byɛ*, 4 *liɛ*, 5 *njip*, 6 *dzhip*, 7 *djiɛ*, 8 *ghyip*; 9 *kəi*, 10 *qəi*, 12 *ləi*; 13 *chriək*, 14 *shiək*, 16 *xək*; 17 *shrɛn*, 18 *gɛn*, 20 *guan*; 21 *jio*, 22 *tsio*, 24 *mio*; 25 *jì*, 26 *qiɔ̀*; 27 *hɑ*, 28 *dɑ*.
Title: Mei-p'i (Myǐ-byɛ) was located just southwest of Ch'ang-an, at the foot of Chung-nan Moun-tain; as Chiu-chia notes after line 2, the "far away" is poetic exaggeration.

1. Literally, "Ts'en Shen, elder brother and younger": we know Ts'en Shen was on this trip, and this peculiar construction appears because there is no graceful way to say "Ts'en Shen and his brother(s)."

2. *Huei* 攜 is literally "take by the hand," suggesting a companiable spirit in their invitation.

3. *Qǒm-tsǒm* 黯惨 (also written 黯慘) is a binome that, if not of Tu Fu's devising, seems not to have been in common use. Later in the *Yu-yang tsa-tsu* (*SPTK* 20.4b) it is used to describe something dark but not black. Both elements of the binome are used in compounds for dark, gloomy skies, and that somber atmosphere is clearly the primary implication here. The *iə̀* 異, "become different," of *iə̀-shriək* 異色, "changed color," is closely related to the *ghyɛ* 奇, "wonders," for which the Ts'ens have a passion.

4. A *kiuěng* 頃, translated as "acre," is in fact about seventeen acres. *Liou-lyɛ* 琉璃 is usually glass, which in medieval China was treated as a precious stone. But as the Chiu-chia notes, the blue variety was particularly rare and believed to be a natural stone. Hence, I have translated it here as "amethyst," which is poetically effective if mineralogically uncertain. As Chiu-chia and Ch'ou note, the comparison of a body of water to *liou-lyɛ* occurs in the poetry of Liang Chien-wen-ti (*CLs* 2.11b), and the metaphor has a courtly quality.

5. *Hàn-màn* 汗漫 is a binome describing the unbounded vastness of a body of water, such as the ocean, and often extended to the Cosmos and the Way. The *liou-lyɛ* metaphor of Liang Chien-wen-ti's poem applied to a pool, and such gem metaphors were usually applied to miniature objects and landscapes. The application of *liou-lyɛ* to a *hàn-màn* body of water is a peculiar kind of hyperbole involving the mixing of two very different kinds of images.

6. Emotions are often described as processes; thus, when elation "reaches its height," *ghiək* 極, it transforms into its antithesis, sorrow or worry; cf. end of 10818. The line echoes Han Wu-ti's "Song of the Autumn Wind"; see note for lines 27–28.

7. The *dhɑ* 鼉 was a kind of crocodile or alligator, supposed to be over nine feet long (though it is sometimes pictured as an overgrown turtle). *Dhɑ tzɑk* 鼉作 is literally "the *dhɑ* acts," and the actions to which Tu Fu is clearly referring are the *dhɑ*'s drumlike bellows which "emit clouds and bring rain" (*Pen-ts'ao. SPTK* 21.21a). Thus, the *dhɑ* is a storm beast. "Behemoth rising" is too apocalyptic for the "*dhɑ* acts," but a storm-stirring crocodile has no support in the Western tradition.

For the *ghiaeng* 鯨, see note 08092, line 2; here as a "swallower (of ships)," *tən* 吞, it is clearly appearing in its "leviathan" avatar. The point of the line is that this is not a case of a storm beast's tempest or sea monster, so he need not worry about encountering calamity.

8. *Qɑk-biung* 惡風 is an "ill wind." In contrast to *bhaek-shuĭ* 白水 (see note 05845, line 5), *bhaek-lɑng* 白浪, literally "white waves," is the near equivalent of English "white water." *Hɑ tzia ghyip* 何嗟及 is a phrase occurring in *Shih* 69, where it is taken to mean "Alas, with whom will she join?" The phrase, expressing isolation, came to be one of the many *Shih* tags taken over and used in later poetry. In 11829.7, Tu Fu uses the phrase again, but rearranges it to fit T'ang word order: *tzia hɑ ghyip*.

9. As Chiu-chia notes, *gyĭm-bhiaem* 錦帆 occurs in the poetry of Yin Keng (*CCh'ens* 1.12b) and has an ornamental quality. For a parallel use of *siɑng-hyuè* 相爲, see *Wh* 7.20a. *Siɑng-hyuè* is archaic and prosaic: it occurs nowhere else in the poetry of Tu Fu, Li Po, Wei Ying-wu, or Tu Mu.

10. *Piən-qɑi* 氛埃, translated as "murky fog," is a kind of miasmal filth associated with the moral pollution of the world: it occurs twice in the *Yüan-yu* of the *Ch'u-tz'u*.

12. *Siə-guǎn* 絲管 is one of the several variable compounds that are metonymy for the music of stringed instruments and woodwind instruments. *Tjiou-tsiòu* 啁啾 is a binome applied to both the sounds of music and small birds: this suggests a faintness of sound, here probably because of the distance. For *kung-tsuì* 空翠, see note 07623, lines 1–2: here some sort of mist is suggested.

13. Literally, "Allowing the pole to sink and requiring addition to the rope, its depths are unmeasured." *Mɑn* 縵 is a plain rope, here obviously being used as a plumbline. The *gɑn* 竿 is specifically a pole used in punting a boat.

15. *Qiuɑén-dzhɔ̆i djiung-liou* 宛在中流, "right there in midcurrent," is an echo of *Shih* 129. *Bhɔt-gĕi* 渤澥 is actually the name of a part of the Eastern Ocean.

16. This line is very difficult: literally, it translates, "Downward return infinite, Chung-nan black." In the Chiu-chia commentary Chao takes it as horizontal distance: the "return," *giuɑi* 歸, is thus the "flowing away" of a body of water in its return to the sea; the "infinite," *mio-ghiɑk* 無極, is figurative for the distance into which the water flows; and the "descent," *hɑ̀* 下, refers to the waters coming down from Chung-nan. Thus, the line would become "Flowing down and off into the infinite, from South Mountain, blackness." Chao explicitly interprets the "black" as referring to the waters seen in the distance. Ch'ou interprets the "black" as the reflection of the mountain, and I believe this is preferable. *Mio-ghiɑk* thus refers primarily to the depths. The only difficulty here is the interpretation of *giuɑi*: I doubt that it is a specific "return"; e.g., the "infinite" height of the returning to "infinite" depth in reflection. But it probably is the appropriate verb for approaching the seemingly infinite. Thus, in this interpretation the line becomes, "Receding down to infinity—the black (reflection) of South Mountain."

17. *Zhuin* 純, "pure," is the word used for a "pure color," especially "pure black." It also means "entirely" or "completely." Since Mei-p'i lies to the north of the Chung-nan formation, *zhuin* must refer to the lake rather than the mountain. Thus, the line reads literally, "(In the reflection) south of midslope, (the lake is) entirely a steeping of mountain"; i.e., the shadow of the mountain covers a whole section of the lake.

18. *Nĕu-dhĕu* 裊窕 is a new binome, which seems to be closely related to the *nĕu-nĕu* 裊裊 or 嫋嫋 usages, generally applied to things that "bend and wave." Thus, Ch'ou glosses *nĕu-dhĕu* as "the manner of mountain reflections shaking." *Djiung-iung* 沖融 was a binome used in Mu Hua's *Hai-fu*, where Li Shan glosses it as "the appearance of breadth and depth" (*Wh* 12.12b). The line translates literally, "It stirs reflections on the shimmering-quivering broad-and-deep."

19. "Edge of Clouds," *Hiuən-tzièi* 雲際, was a mountain in the Chung-nan Range. Precisely what is occurring in this line is a subject of some disagreement. First, *mèng* 暝 may describe either the "darkness" of the mountain's shadow or of the coming night. In the narrative of the boating excursion, it clearly serves as a pivot between those two topics. *Jhiuɛn-hen* 船舷 is literally the "boat's edge," and poets often wrote of "rapping the boat's edge" (usually using the verb *kŏu* 扣) and singing. Probably from this *topos*, the Chiu-chia interprets this as their "rapping" being heard in the darkness at the temple. Suzuki Toraō (*To Ho* I, p. 169) takes "rapping," *gat* 戛, as the sound of the oars. I think rather that the line is best understood in the context of the old metaphor set in which a journey by boat is treated as a journey through the heavens. This combines with visual play on reflection, common in sixth- and seventh-century poetry. The boat sails over the reflec-

tion of the temple on these heaven-waters and thus seems to rap against it (as it would if the boat were actually in the sky). Clearly, the line is playing on the antithesis between high and low— the physical boat meeting a high mountain temple on a mountain named "Edge of Clouds," a kenning for height. This interpretation of *gat* in which the actual striking is more significant than the sound is supported by a use of *gat-hiuən* 戛雲, "striking the clouds," used by Po Chü-yi to describe the high boughs of a tree (*Po-shih Ch'ang-ch'ing chi. SPTK* 26.3a). Not only was the theme of reflection dominant in the preceding line, it is emphatically retained in the following line by *shuǐ-miȅn* 水面, "on the face of the waters" (lest the eye look up and see the moon in the sky).

20. Lan-t'ien Pass 藍田關, "Indigo Fields," was well to the south. Tu Fu is clearly playing on the color here.

21. The tale of the pearl by the Black Dragon's jaw appears in the Lieh Yü-k'ou chapter of the *Chuang-tzu* (*Chuang-tzu* 90/22/42–45). Though the story is not directly relevant to Tu Fu's use of the image here, it does clarify that the Black Dragon belongs to a deep abyss, and thus the image continues the play on the real heavens and the heavens reflected in the deep lake. Ch'ou suggests that the "pearl" is an image for lanterns on the shore, but Suzuki is clearly correct in taking it as a metaphor for the reflected moon.

22. P'ing-yi 馮夷, the God of Waters, appears often in *fu* and poems on waters: the previous usage closest to Tu Fu's is in Ts'ao Chih's *Lo-shen fu* 洛神賦, where "P'ing-yi makes the drum sound" (*Wh* 19.19b).

23. The "Han's maidens" were the two spirits that Cheng Chiao-fu met by the Han River, and on Cheng's request, they undid their girdle sashes for him. In medieval poetry they suggest an erotic encounter, though in this case, they are simply a seductive vision. The "Ladies of the Hsiang" were the two wives of the sage-emperor Shun, who drowned themselves on hearing of Shun's death and became river goddesses.

24. In keeping with the convivial spirit of the poem, this line echoes the first of the famous *Fang-chung Songs* 房中歌, supposedly written by the Lady of T'ang-shan 唐山夫人 for Han Kao-tsu; in it are mentioned the "tassled golden poles" and "kingfisher flags" (*CHs* 3.1a). The second half of the line is literally, "their light, present and absent." *Hiǒu-mio* 有無 describes something so tenuous that it scarcely seems to exist.

25. *Jiȅ-chiȅk* 咫尺 conventionally is used to describe something very close. "Thunder and rain" were commonly associated with the descent of a divinity. The point of the line is that the poet is delighted at his vision of the spirits, but he is troubled by the storm that is supposed to accompany their visitations. *Jiȅ-chiȅk* could apply to either the spirits or the portended storm.

26. *Tsɑng-mɑng* 蒼茫 is a binome describing indistinctness; here it applies equally to the vision of the gods and the "purport," *qiə* 意, of their visitation, which is "not understood."

27–28. The closing echoes the most famous boating song in Chinese poetry, Han Wu-ti's "Song of the Autumn Wind" 秋風辭, supposedly written when Wu-ti was boating on the River Fen (*Wh* 45.26b). The song closes:

Joy and pleasure crest, 歡樂極兮哀情多
    then mournful feelings are many,
How long does youth last, 少壯幾時兮奈老何
    what can be done about old age?

Line 27 is a direct quotation of this. The last line is literally, "How much joy and sorrow has there been in the past!"

10509: *CTs*, p. 2256; Chiu-chia, 1.16B, pp. 13–14; Ch'ou, c. 3, p. 119; *Wyyh* 331.2a.
Rhymes: 1 *piən*, 2 *hiuən*, 4 *biən*; 5 *xək*, 6 *siək*, 8 *djhiək*. Though this poem is included in the "old style" section, the first half is perfectly regulated; the fifth line, beginning the *ju-sheng* rhyme, is a pivot: as a *p'ing-ch'i* line with a violation in the sixth position, the line continues the tone pattern from earlier in the poem; as a *tse-ch'i* line with violations in the second and fourth positions, it begins the tone pattern of the second half of the poem. There is also a violation in the sixth position of the last line.

1. As noted in the text, *lɑn-biung* 闌風 and *bhiuk-hiǒ* 伏雨 are the subject of controversy, and there are several variants that resolve the problems with suspicious simplicity. For example,

lǝn is taken as "unending" or, with the grass radical, meaning "orchid." *Bhiuk* may be interpreted as "high summer." If a problem of interpretation does not resolve itself naturally at a certain point, one should allow the possibility that a suggestive haziness of reference was permitted by the poet and appreciated by contemporary readers. Such resolutions are dangerous, because they encourage us "later-born" readers to a complacent murkiness of understanding when a T'ang reader might have understood precisely. But despite the danger, there surely were elements of T'ang poetry that were genuinely murky. *Piǝn-piǝn* 紛紛 suggests a large quantity of something in confusion; see note to 05906, line 1.

    2. Echoing *Shih* 210:

Heaven above shares a cover of cloud,   上天同雲
The snow falls in flurrying turmoil.   雨雪雰雰

Note that 雰雰 is essentially the same as 紛紛. *Sì-xǎi bat-xuɑng* 四海八荒 is literally "(All that is within) the four seas and wildernesses lying in the eight directions."

    3. The inability to distinguish horses from oxen clearly echoes the *Ch'iu-shui* chapter of the *Chuang-tzu* in which the Yellow River is so swollen with autumn floods that from one side to another, one cannot tell a horse from an ox (*Chuang-tzu* 42/18/1).

    4. The "muddy Ching and clear Wei," which flow together for three hundred *liǎ* without mixing together, were proverbial and often used as metaphors for moral discrimination. The Chiu-chia commentary suggests that the rain has caused the two to be mixed so that the clear and turbid will not separate themselves. I had previously followed this interpretation, but am now convinced that *biǝn* 分 here means to "distinguish," implying a viewer, as in the preceding line.

    5. The proverb, cited by Chiu-chia and later commentators, is that when there is rain on the first day of autumn, "ears" (fungus) grow on the heads of grain. The "blackness" of the grain is, of course, a mark of its rotting.

    6. The distinction between *nong-bhio* 農夫 and *dhen-bhiǒ* 田父 is not entirely clear, perhaps one of age. The two terms are used together in P'an Yüeh's *Ch'iu-hsing fu* 秋興賦 (*Wh* 13.5a), where the poet, boasting his rusticity, says that these are the only kinds of people he chats with.

    7. *Kyim* 衾 and *djhiou* 裯 appear in *Shih* 21: they are two terms for bed coverings, the second supposedly being lighter than the first. Chiu-chia cites the *Chiu T'ang shu* to the effect that in the K'ai-yüan a *dǒu* of rice cost a few cash.

    8. *Siɑng-xiǔ* 相許 is to "reach an agreement." Yoshikawa (*To Ho* I, p. 49) suggests that this is colloquial, what is said when a bargain is struck. The last character 直 should be pronounced *djhiǝ* when used in the sense of "be worth," as it is here; However, rhyme demands that it be read *djhiǝk*. The only explanation I can suggest is that *djhiǝk*, the primary reading of the character, gradually absorbed the other reading.

10534: *CTs*, pp. 2265–66; Chiu-chia, 2.16, pp. 37–39; Ch'ou, c. 4, pp. 7–12.
Rhymes: 2 *jiuɛt*, 4 *ket*, 6 *kuɑt*, 8 *xuɑt* . . . 34 *liɛt*, 36 *biaet*, 38 *get*, 40 *nget*, 42 *huɑt*, 44 *gɑt* . . . 68 *guɑt* . . . 86 *tzuit* . . . 90 *jiɛt*, 92 *tsuɑt*, 94 *bhiaet*, 96 *set*, 98 *tzuɑt*, 100 *duɑt* (*T'ung-yün*). Note repetition of 卒 in three different pronunciations in lines 86, 92, and 98.

    1. Tu-ling was Tu Fu's ancestral region; it was located about twenty-eight kilometers south of Ch'ang-an. Government officials wore distinctive gowns, so the term *bǒ-qiǝi* 布衣, a plain cotton gown, was one of the most common synecdoches for a commoner.

    2. *Jiuɛt* 拙, translated as "naïvete and foolishness," along with *ngio* 愚, "simple-minded," are difficult and related terms. Both have genuinely pejorative sides and are used when one wants to suggest real stupidity, but at the same time they suggest the clumsiness that marks sincerity and honesty, the antithesis of the English "slick."

    3. *Xiǔ* 許 is the word used when one "promises oneself" to a prince; Tu Fu's "promising himself," *xiǔ-shin* 許身, may be to state service and the dynasty, but it may also be to become like the ancients mentioned in the next line.

    4. Tu Fu's "secret comparison," *tset-bǐ* 竊比, of himself to "Chi and Chieh" is the same thing Confucius does in *Analects* VII.1: "I transmit; I do not invent. I trust in and love the ancients. I secretly compare myself to old P'eng." One interesting topic in the study of Tu Fu would be to

observe how often he assumes the voice of the Sage. Both Hou Chi and Chieh served the sage emperors Yao and Shun, and certainly an important part of Tu Fu's emulation is to become a worthy servant of a sage ruler: this is one side of his *xiŭ-shin*, "promising himself" to the emperor. But among Yao's and Shun's many great servitors, Chieh and Hou Chi happened to be the ancestors of the Shang and Chou dynasties respectively.

5. *Giu-njiɛn* 居然 means basically to "remain in a given state"; from that basic meaning, the compound is used in several rather different ways. One of those usages applies here: an "expectation that will be deceived," something that occurs "contrary to expectations." *Zhiɛng* 成 means not just "become," but to "become utterly." *Huɑk-lɑk* 濩落 (also written 瓠落) is a binome meaning "empty" or "hollow." The commentaries cite its use in the *Chuang-tzu* (2/1/37; 3/1/42), but the term had a fairly wide currency and is probably not a textual allusion here. Its primary extended meaning is "hollow and useless," which is its use here.

6. *Ket-kuɑt* 契闊 is a binome describing a state of suffering, used and glossed in *Shih* 31.

7. *Gài-guɑn* 蓋棺, "covered in one's coffin," was a phrase used often in early texts to indicate the finality of death, after which some problem or desire would cease. Commentaries cite the *Han-Shih wai-chuan*, where Confucius states that he will stop studying only when "covered in his coffin," but Tu Fu's line is a rephrasing of an almost proverbial expression used often in medieval texts.

8. *Gyì-xuɑt* 覬豁 is a compound originating in Tu Fu. *Gyì* means to "look forward to" or "hope for." *Xuɑt* is an "openness" that suggests freedom of spirit or action.

33. The death of all the plants toward the close of the year, when expressed with such simplicity, has numerous echoes in the *Shih* and *Ch'u-tz'u*.

34. *Gɑu-gɑng* 高岡, "high hill," is used in *Shih* 3, 241, and 252. The significance of noting this is not for its own sake but to suggest the quality of the phrase. Since the literary language was built out of a body of more or less memorized texts, phrases often acquired a historical depth impossible to reproduce in English. *Gɑu-gɑng*, for example, has an archaic simplicity; it does not occur once in the *shih* of the *Wen hsüan*. On the other hand, to use *jhriung* 崇, "lofty," as an attribute of a hill has a distinctly "literary" flavor and suggests the Han to Sui period. Though it is used earlier, *liəng* 陵 would be the more modern, T'ang term for *gɑng*. This *Shih* version of archaic simplicity is superimposed on another version, that of Chien-an and Wei *shih*, and the line of Juan Chi noted by the commentators: "A cold wind shakes the mountains and hills" 寒風振山岡 (*Wh* 23.7a). However, this archaic simplicity carries with it overtones of concealed censure: hence the Wu-ch'en commentary to Juan Chi's line indicated that the image is an allegory for the Ssuma's usurping the authority of the Wei, a situation that might suggest analogies to the Yangs' behavior towards the royal house of the T'ang. However, even the most besotted allegorist might hesitate to discover hidden satire in Tu Fu's line here. Rather, the topical dimensions of the image are probably best understood as a submerged part of the general mood of menace which is carried in the style and imagery of the line; that mood, and particularly the topical dimensions of that mood, is historically determined. The use of *liɛt* 裂 is also interesting: Chiu-chia cites the Li Ling letter to Su Wu (*Wh* 41.2a) where it says that the borderland is *tsŏm-liɛt* 慘裂: though Li Shan gives a divided gloss for the compound as "poisonous" and "splitting," the reader knows that this is actually 慘列, a binome describing the "biting" cold. This considerably mutes the violence of Tu Fu's usage, as commentators are wont to do. In fact, Tu Fu's line means precisely what it says: it is a hyperbolic version of the cracking of the earth that occurs in the cold; cf. *Yen-t'ieh lun* (*SPTK*) 3.5a.

35. "The avenues of the capital," *ten-ghio* 天衢, is literally "Heaven's avenues." The commentators note *ten-ghio*'s use in Chang Heng's *Hsi-ching fu*, but it could also mean the paths of the real Heaven, as in Wang Yi's *Chiu-ssu* in the *Ch'u-tz'u*. *Jrhaeng-hiuaeng* 崢嶸 is a binome usually describing the height of mountains and tall buildings: here it describes the avenues as "towered over" by tall buildings on either side. As Yoshikawa Kojirō notes (op. cit., p. 136), the use of *jrhaeng-hiuaeng* to describe a deep-set road has a precedent in the *Wu-ch'eng fu* of Pao Chao (*Wh* 11.16b).

37. *Ngiaem* 嚴 is a conventional attribute of frost. The compound *qiəi-dài* 衣帶 for "sash" occurs in the first of the Nineteen Old Poems; here and throughout this section are compounds and usages from the literature of the Han and Wei.

39. *Liəng-jhin* 凌晨, as Yoshikawa notes, is a literary term for "dawn," originating in the Southern Dynasties. Li Mountain was east of Ch'ang-an, on the south side of the road to Lo-yang. The entrance to the palace there was on the north side of the mountain, so Tu Fu would have seen it in passing.

40. *Ngiù* 御 is the respectful modifier for something belonging to the emperor. The choice of a "bed," *təp* 榻, to designate the imperial presence may suggest that article of furniture of which Hsüan-tsung was making best use in those, his salad days. *Dhet-nget* 嶻嶭 has a *Chi-yün* gloss as "the manner of a mountain's height," but Tu Fu's is the earliest usage of the phrase.

41. *Chiə Hiou* 蚩尤 was the rebel defeated by the Yellow Emperor. It is possible that its use here is as an asterism portending rebellion; however, it was also the name of a military banner, and I have taken it in that sense here. *Sək* 塞, "block up," could more easily be done by banners, portending warfare; but it is just possible that a very bright asterism could be said to *sək* the sky.

42. *Tziuk-top* 蹴踏, "trample over," is used in Chang Heng's *Nan-tu fu* to describe the armies' victorious "trampling over Hsien-yang" (*Wh* 4.13b); here also it suggests the tread of victorious imperial armies. Ch'ou takes the "slipperiness" or smoothness," *huat* 滑, to be the result of the slick frost, thus suggesting hardships for the marching troops. I agree with Chiu-chia that *tziuk-top* suggests the quantity of marching troops, and thus take *huat* as the result of the many armies that have passed over the spot.

43. *Iɛu-djhiɛ* 瑤池, "Jasper Pool," was the place on K'un-lun Mountain where Hsi-wang-mu received King Mu of Chou; here it suggests the pleasure spots where Hsüan-tsung dallies with Yang Kuei-fei, namely, the famous "Warm Springs" of Li Mountain. *Qiuət-luit* 鬱律 is a binome describing the density of vapor, fog, mist, etc.

44. The *Hiŏ-lim* 羽林 was the name of the imperial guard. *Mɑ-gat* 摩戛 is a compound verb first used by Tu Fu, literally "rub and rap."

67. *Jio-mən* 朱門 was a standard synecdoche for the dwellings of the wealthy and noble. *Chiòu* 臭 was originally simply a "scent," but it gradually came to have the sense of "stench," particularly of meat. Meat eating was strongly associated with the extravagance of wealth. The couplet clearly derives from Mencius's criticism of King Hui of Liang: "There are fat meats in your kitchen, fat horses in your stables, the look of starvation in your people, corpses, dead from hunger, in your wilderness' (*Mencius* IA.4).

85. *Hɑu-dhɑu* 號咷 is a phrase from the hexagram *T'ung-jen* 同人, "Fellow Human": "People first cry out; only later can they laugh."

86. *Qiòu* 幼 refers to a child under ten. This line must be read in conjunction with lines 67–68.

90. *Jiɛt* 折 is a somewhat archaic term for "untimely death," literally "to be broken off." By itself, *qyɛu* 夭 implies infant death. This couplet is extremely prosaic, and therein lies part of its power and moral authenticity.

91. Reading 禾, instead of 末 in the Chiu-chia text. This couplet is enjambed: literally, "How could I have known that (even) after the autumn grain was harvested, in our poverty and insufficiency there would be such distress?" *Dəng* 登 here refers to the harvest.

92. The use of *ghiŏ-bhyin* 窶貧, "poverty," is significant: it appears in the first stanza of *Shih* 40, in which a servitor of the state of Wei complains of his poverty, attributes the cause to Heaven, and is reproached by his family when he returns from far travels: the analogies are obvious. *Tsɑng-tsuət* 倉卒 describes a distressed confusion, often associated with the response to death; thus, Ch'ou cites the sixth in Ts'ao Chih's series of poems "Presented to Piao, Prince of Pai-ma" (*Wh* 24.8a).

93. Exemption from taxes was a privilege of even the lower orders of official families; also, exemption from conscription.

94. Literally, "My name is not included in the class of those (destined) for warfare."

95. *Piŏ* 撫, literally "fondle," is often used to describe a pensive consideration of some subject. *Tziɛk* 跡, literally "footprints," is used to describe past experience, always linked to exterior acts: "What I have done"; "Where I have been"; "what I have been through." *Iou* 猶, "still," can refer to the continuity of unhappiness on which the poet thinks, or it can be in relation to the greater suffering of the common people in the following line. The variant 獨 resolves the difficulty in the peculiar use of *iou*.

96. As Ch'ou notes, *sɑu-set* 騷屑 is a binome used in Liu Hsiang's *Chiu-t'an* in the *Ch'u-tz'u* to describe the sound of the wind blowing through autumn trees. To transfer such a description

to the sufferings of the common people is very bold, though it is probably done on the model of various other binomes describing autumn which early took on the general sense of "desolation."

97. Reading 徙 instead of Chiu-chia 迻. *Ngiaep* 業 is essentially something one accumulates (possessions, learning, good deeds) and often that which is passed on. The commoners who lose their *ngiaep* probably have lost their family farms or whatever they had accumulated to live on.

98. Literally, "And thereupon think intently on. . . . "

99. *Qiou-duan* 憂端, "sorrow's source," are those external matters that give rise to the poet's grief: these are the private and public concerns mentioned above. Their being "equal to South Mountain," *dzhei Jiung-nom* 齊終南, expresses their magnitude.

100. *Hŭng-dhŭng* 溷洞 is one of the binomes used to describe the state prior to Creation in the cosmogony of the *Huai-nan-tzu*. Its primary semantic value is "undifferentiation," and it suggests that all the personal and public troubles are inseparably fused so that none can be taken separately and "handled." As with *piŏ* in line 95, *duɑt* 摭, "grasp," belongs to the language of manipulation transferred to mental acts.

10557: *CTs*, pp. 2274–75; Chiu-chia 3.19, p. 58; Ch'ou c. 5, pp. 81–83.

Rhymes: 2 *gɛn*, 4 *shrɛn*, 6 *ngan*, 8 *huən*, 10 *miən*, 12 *chin*, 14 *tsɑn*, 16 *pən*, 18 *hən*, 20 *gɛn*, 22 *djhiuɛn*, 24 *qen*, 26 *guan*, 28 *hiuən*, 30 *mən*, 32 *huən*, 34 *gɑn*, 36 *suən*, 38 *guən*, 40 *xuən*, 42 *gɑn*, 44 *huen* (Ch'ou notes this is the old rhyming pronunciation), 46 *dzhen*. (*T'ung-yün*). In several cases, Ch'ou cites alternative readings for rhyme words in order to make them more regular.

Title: P'eng-ya was located to the north of the capital.

1. *Qiək-siɛk* 憶昔 was a formulaic opening for poems of reminiscence. *Bhiɛ dzhək chriu* 避賊初, instead of the more common word order of *chriu bhiɛ dzhək*, probably places the emphasis on the "beginning," on the event itself rather than on the fact that they fled.

3. The use of *shim* 深 here shows the master's touch: it is both a spatial word and a time word, the "depths" of night. By placing *shim* between "night" and the "P'eng-ya Road," Tu Fu holds its significance indeterminate between the temporal and the spatial: it is "deep" in the night, and that gives a quality of depth to the recesses of the landscape around the road.

6. *Hŏu-ngan* 厚顏, literally "thick countenanced," suggests shameless behavior. There are two ways to understand this line, both equally credible. The first, as I have taken it in the translation, has the *hŏu-ngan* refer to those met; their behavior (staring, begging, accosting the family with questions?) is a shamelessness created by the desperateness of the times and not a mark of immorality. However, *hŏu-ngan* may also refer to Tu Fu's family and their behavior, in which case the mention of their shamelessness is itself a mark of a sense of shame.

7. Ch'ou suggests that the fact that the birds are singing indicates that no one is around, but the singing of birds at night in Chinese poetry often indicates some kind of disturbance, perhaps the presence of animals or other people here. The "uneven distribution," *chrim-chriɛ* 參差, of their cries may suggest potential menace from unseen places.

8. Literally "We did not see travelers returning." Presumably the travelers would be "returning" to Ch'ang-an. The line may also be taken "We did not see any travelers turning back"; i.e., there were others on the road (see line 6), but the menace of the night journey was less than that in a return to the capital.

9. *Tjiə* 癡, "innocent" (or pejoratively "silly," "foolish"), was conventional attribute for young children. *Qău* 咬 is properly "to gnaw a bone," and seems the perfect choice of words to describe "chewing at," without "biting into" or "chewing up."

10. *Xŏ-lɑng* 虎狼 is literally "tigers and wolves"; Chiu-chia takes this as a metaphor for rebels.

13. *Gĕi-jrhiə* 解事 is a general ability to "take care of practical matters": we might translate it as "savvy" were it not used in several official titles. *Ghiăng* 强 means often to "force oneself" to do something, to "try very hard," with the accompanying implication that the object of the *ghiăng* does not come naturally. The little boy wants to take care of his sister's complaint.

14. In poetic usage, *gò* 故 is more emphatic than simple consequence; in this case, the "therefore" becomes a real attribution of purpose to the boy's actions. The boy's true lack of *gĕi-jrhiə* is revealed in his picking "sour plums." Ch'ou cites the counterexample of *gĕi-jrhiə*, an example Tu Fu probably had in mind here: "Wang Jung was once playing with a group of other children by the roadside when they saw a plum tree full of fruit. Everyone but Wang Jung rushed off to

it, and when someone asked him why, he said, 'Whenever there's a tree by the roadside with much fruit, it must be sour plums.' When they took the plums, they found out he was right" (*Tsin*, p. 1231).

15. The "week" is literally a *zuin* 旬, ten days.

18. The poet notes the slipperiness of the paths because of the want of proper footgear, part of the "provision against the rain."

19. For *ket-kuɑt* 契闊, see note 10534, line 6.

21. *Hou-liɑng* 餱糧 are "dried food and grain," the kind of food one takes on a journey.

22. *Quk-djhiuɛn* 屋椽 are literally the "round rafters of the roof," the exact analogue of the branches. There is often in Chinese poetry a particular sensuous precision in metaphors and substitutions: the branches are the analogues of the rafters, not the roof, and they are the analogues of round rafters. Of course, "round rafters," *djhiuɛn* 椽, also rhyme, while "square rafters," *gak* 桷, do not.

23. Literally, "Early we went through water on stone."

24–25. T'ung-chia Swamp and Lu-tzu Pass lie on a journey north from Ch'ang-an through Whitewater County (line 4). Tu Fu ultimately did not go up through Lu-tzu Pass, but instead left his family in Fu-chou.

27. Since *tzɔ̌i* 宰 means to "govern," there is some doubt as to whether Tsai (Tzɔ̌i) is Sun's given name or marks some office. Since *tzɔ̌i* is neither a formal nor a poetic title of office, it is best to take it as a name.

28. To speak of someone's goodness "reaching the clouds," is a conventional and elegantly poetic form of praise; both Chiu-chia and Ch'ou give earlier examples.

29. Literally, "When he received in the guests (us), it was already blackening dusk." *Iɔ̌* 已, "already," may suggest particular generosity in welcoming unexpected visitors so late, especially in such troubled times.

32. "Summons to the soul" were usually reserved for the dead or dying, but the act was applicable to any state of near or total unconsciousness; the Tus are probably in a daze. Ch'ou cites the *Tu-shih Miu-p'ing* 杜詩課評 of Ts'ai Meng-pi 蔡夢弼 to the effect that the ritual of soul summoning here is only figurative, standing for the many kindnesses Sun Tsai did for them. To take it as entirely figurative would be very unusual, but to mention the real ceremony would be almost equally unusual.

33. Ch'ou would have Tu Fu bringing out his wife and children to meet Sun Tsai, perhaps implying that the previous kindnesses had been extended only to Tu Fu himself. Unless a formal introduction is implied (which I do not believe), this would imply a very strange staging of the gate scene. I think rather that Sun Tsai is bringing in his family once the Tus have had the opportunity to rest and refresh themselves. Note that this is the sort of information which the poet and original recipient of the poem could have taken for granted; to later readers this information can be recovered only by inference.

34. It may be that both familes "looked on each other," and everybody wept. *Lɑn-gɑn* 闌干 has a wide range of usages, among which is a description of copious tears. Chao in the Chiu-chia commentary attempts to unify the diverse uses of *lɑn-gɑn* by their application to things that are "continuous."

35. "Brood," *jiùng-jrhio* 衆雛, is literally "brood of baby birds," and in Mi Heng's "Parrot Fu" there is worry that "the brood of chicks lack knowledge (to fend for themselves)" (*Wh* 13.28b). The commentators take *làn-màn* 爛漫 as describing the "depth" of the children's sleep; this is clearly correct, but it derives from the basic meaning of the binome, which is "scattered." As in colloquial English "to be out cold," deep sleep is like unconsciousness, when the soul has "melted away" (*làn-màn*) from the body.

36. *Djiɛm* 霑, translated as "kindly give," is literally "to soak," commonly used for showing generosity and favor.

37–38. There is a difference of opinion among the commentators whether these are the words of Tu Fu or Sun Tsai. Ch'ou cites the *Tu Yi* 杜臆, which emphatically argues that for the continuity of the poem, the lines must be spoken by Sun Tsai. Again we have a problem of referent, which would have been immediately known to Tu Fu and Sun Tsai. *Get* 結, literally to "tie," is to "form a bond (of brotherhood or friendship)."

39. The transitive use of *kùng* 空, "empty," is striking in this line, especially in conjunction with the prosaic modifying construction *shriǔ-dzhuǎ* 所坐.

40. *Bhiǒng* 奉 here means to "present" to someone. *Ngǎ* 我 can be singular, referring to Tu Fu alone, or it can be plural, encompassing Tu Fu's family.

41–42. This couplet in enjambed. In this context, the rhetorical question *zhui kǐng* 誰肯, "who is willing," has its usual function of implying "no one," and simultaneously emphasizes the uniqueness of Sun Tsai because he was, in fact, "willing." *Tzièi* 際 here is an "occasion," a "time when...." *Xuat-dhat* 豁達 is a binome describing an openness or expansiveness of spirit or scene: here it is transferred to a liberality or generosity of disposition.

44. *Ho-giaet* 胡羯 is an imprecise collective term for the nomads of the North, here referring to the rebel armies.

10974: *CTs*, p. 2403; Chiu-chia 19.6, p. 295; Ch'ou, c. 4. p. 29.
Rhymes: 2 *kan*, 4 *qan*, 6 *han*, 8 *gan*. Regulated.

1–2. The first line is the "topic" on which the second line is the "comment." To begin an occasional lyric with a scene which is imagined, a scene specifically located elsewhere, was unusual in poetry. Such speculation was usually reserved for the close of a poem (cf. 06137). Furthermore, the reader would understand that the "moon tonight in Fu-chou" was, in fact, the moon Tu Fu was watching that very night in Ch'ang-an; see Ch'ou's comment that the poet is "facing the moon and thinking of his wife" or the *Tu Yi*, cited in Ch'ou, that Tu Fu is "really longing for his family, but instead imagines his family longing for him." Fu-chou was where Tu Fu had left his wife and children to keep them safe from the rebellion. *Guei-djiung* 閨中 usually refers to women's chambers. The imaginary opening and the fact that the woman looking is unspecified suggests *yüeh-fu*, a female persona longing for a husband far away. The historical occasion is the only thing that specifies the woman as Tu Fu's wife.

3. *Iɛu-len* 遙憐, "far away think lovingly on," locates the speaker of the poem somewhere else, thinking on the family in Fu-chou.

4. "Remembering Ch'ang-an" is precisely what Tu Fu's wife is doing as she gazes at the moon and imagines that Tu Fu is gazing on it too, in Ch'ang-an. That the children are too young to do so protects them from the sorrow of leaving the capital and separation, but it also removes them from the bond that binds Tu Fu to his wife. "Remembering Ch'ang-an" includes thoughts on Tu Fu, but it is more: it encompasses their previous life in the capital and the sorrow over the fall of the great city.

5. Ch'ou cites a controversy among commentators as to how the fog became scented: Ch'ou himself concludes that the scent comes from the *huan* 鬟, the "hair bun." What is interesting here is the reader's desire to discover an empirically coherent scene in what Tu Fu admits is a fantasy, a sensual fantasy of scent, moisture, and hair, and, in the next line, of gleaming flesh. *Hiuən* 雲, "cloudlike," is a fixed attribute of coiffures, but here it is given new vitality as it fuses with the surrounding fog.

6. *Ngiok* 玉, "jade-white," is a fixed attribute of flesh, suggesting beauty and purity. The shining quality of jade bears approximately the same relation to the moonlight that the "cloudlike" hair bears to the fog. The "cold" suggests her isolation and, in the physical scene, that she is standing, gazingly longingly at the moon in the chill of the night, rather than being under the blankets as she would be if Tu Fu were there.

7. *Huǎng* 幌 was a curtain used to cover a window opening. That the curtains are *xiu* 虛, "empty," suggests either that they have been rolled up entirely or, more likely, that there is an open space in them where the poet and his wife can lean. *Qyǐ* 倚 can suggest proximity as well as actual physical "leaning"; the pair can be leaning on the casement or a railing, but they cannot lean on the open space in the curtains.

8. Literally, "Doubly shone upon, tracks of tears dry." When "doubleness" is used in relation to tears, it usually refers the two tracks of tears from the pair of eyes. In that case, it would be the wife's tears which will dry when Tu Fu makes his way to her. On the other hand, in this situation, it is difficult not to take *shrang* 雙 as the "pair" of husband and wife.

11027: *CTs*, p. 2415; Chiu-chia 4.19, p. 73; Ch'ou, c. 6, pp. 121–22; *Wyyh* 210.7b.
Rhymes: 1 *jiəng*, 2 *nəng*, 4 *iəng*, 6 *njiəng*, 8 *biəng*. Only the third couplet is regulated.
Title: The title was originally accompanied by a note, perhaps from the hand of the poet, that

at the time he was in the "Department of Awards" (*ssu-kung* 司功) in Hua-chou. *Duəi-qàn siɑng-njiəng* 堆案相仍 is literally "piled up desks continue in succession."

1. As Ch'ou notes, *hyɛm-jiəng* 炎蒸 occurs in a poem of Yü Hsin (*CPCs* 2.16a), but while Yü Hsin suffered the "blazing steaminess" in the fifth month, midsummer, Tu Fu must endure it even in the "sixth day of the seventh month," when the cooling winds of autumn should be coming.

2. The commentators cite one of Ts'ai Yen's "Nomad Flute Songs" here, but I believe the line is an ironic echo of the inability to eat out of political frustration and unfulfilled ambitions, as in Pao Chao's famous (*CSs* 4.9b):

I face the table, cannot eat,   對案不能食
Pull out my sword, strike the column, heave a long sigh.   拔劍擊柱長歎息

There is more than a little humor in Tu Fu's self-description, especially in the prosaic and anticimactic *huan biət nəng* 還不能.

3. Here I have taken Ch'ou's reading of 皆是 instead of the Chiu-chia 自足. In context and parallel construction *dzhì tziok xyɛt* 自足蠍 should mean "naturally there are ample scorpions"; unfortunately, *dzhì-tziok* is a set phrase that makes it seem that the poet is worried about "self-satisfied scorpions." It may be that *gaei zhiɛ̀* 皆是 was a textual "improvement" generated to redeem this infelicity.

4. *Xiuɑ̀ng* 況 intensifies a previous state (here "worry," *jrhiou* 愁) with a new condition. When *hòu* 後 follows some condition that has duration, it often marks the condition itself, "after the beginning of . . .": thus, *tsiou-hòu* 秋後 here is "after the coming of autumn," not "after autumn"; cf. *tzùi-hòu* 醉後, "while drunk," "after getting drunk."

5. *Shiok-dài* 束帶 is together the "sash" or "belt" (see *Analects* V. 7.4), but the glosses on *shiok* carry the sense of "tightness" and "constriction."

6. *Bhǒ-shiu* 簿書 is here a general term for official documents. This line is literally, "How swiftly and urgently the official documents come in succession!"

7. As Chiu-chia explains, *gà* 架 refers to the branches "framing over" some spot: see Li Shan note to Chiang Yen's imitation of Hsieh Chuang (*Wh* 31.39a); the Wu-ch'en commentary explains *gà* as the pines "growing out horizontally over the sheer slope."

8. Because the slope is shaded by pines, the spot retains its chill even in hot weather.

10973: *CTs*, p. 2403; Chiu-chia 19.5, p. 295; Ch'ou c. 4, p. 34; *Wyyh* 154.9a.
Rhymes: 2 *qung*, 4 *biung*, 6 *hung*, 8 *kung*. Regulated.

1. When the dead in battle are unburied, they linger on as weeping ghosts.

3. *Dei* 低 may be static, the clouds "hanging low" over the horizon where the sun is setting.

4. "Whirlwind," in the modern sense, may be too titanic for *huəi-biung* 迴風, which is a "swirling gust."

5. *Liok* 綠 is a dark green or blue-black, and as an attribute of wine, it indicates the strong and thick brew. In a later form 醁 it is glossed simply as "good wine"; however, the sense of color is present when 綠 is used to describe wine, as can be seen from the parallel here and elsewhere. *Liok* probably does not describe the wine liquid at all, but rather the lees, known as "dark green ants," *liok-ngyě* 綠蟻; see *Wh* 26.9a, with Li Shan explanation. (Note that Ch'ou cites a line using "cup of dark green," *liok-tzuən* 綠樽, from a Shen Yüeh poem written in response to the poem cited above; the Shen Yüeh line appears in *Wh* 30.26b.)

6. I have translated this line following a syntactic parallel with the simplest reading of line 5; however, the structure of the couplet is a far more complicated or indeterminate. What the reader would expect to "linger on," *dzhuən* 存, would be the fire and not the brazier; furthermore, *dzhuən* has a propensity to transitivity. Thus, the most natural way to read the first three characters would be "The brazier keeps the fire," which would be a normal poetic way to say "The fire lasts on in the brazier." However, "fire," *xuǎ* 火, looks like the subject of "seems crimson" or "appears crimson," *ziǎ hung* 似紅. This is reinforced by the relationships of the preceding line, in which *liok* goes with *tzuən*, as in the Shen Yüeh poem. The situation is further complicated by the fact that "crimson," *hung* 紅 (actually a pinkish red), describes glowing braziers but not fires. Thus, following conventional associations of words, the line would be syntactically almost impossible:

"The brazier, keeping its fire, appears crimson." I would suggest that the effect of this conflict between relationships suggested by syntactic position and relationships favored by the history of the association of the words is an indeterminacy of relationship.

8. *Jièng* 正 here means something like "at this very moment."

11045: *CTs*, p. 2418; Chiu-chia 20.1J, p. 320; Ch'ou, c. 7, p. 30.
Rhymes: 1 *luən*, 2 *bhiaen*, 4 *ngiuaen*, 6 *tsuən*, 8 *mən*. Regulated.

1. The K'un-lun Range lay north of Tibet, far to the west-northwest of Ch'ang-an and well outside Tu Fu's range of vision from Ch'in-chou. Tu Fu is observing a cloud covering coming in from the west, and in its immensity, he imagines it stretching to (perhaps originating in) the K'un-lun Range.

2. *Jrhim-jrhim* 淰淰 is a binome describing heavy rain: likewise, *bhiaen* 繁 is the "density" of heavy rain.

3. The Wei flows down to Ch'ang-an, and the enigmatic figure of the nomad boy, standing in the rain and watching the river, leads Chao in the Chiu-chia commentary to suggest that this marks Tibetan warriors watching for an opportunity to attack. Thus, the "royal envoy" in the next line has been dispatched to avert trouble.

4. The "royal envoy" who was sent to find the source of the Yellow River was Chang Chien 張騫 in the Han. However, Tu Fu is probably not describing an expedition of discovery here; rather, he is noting a Chinese official traveling in the rain off into the immensity of the frontier region, and by treating that journey in terms of Chang Chien's expedition, he lends it associations of hardship, distance, and unknown perils.

5-6. The form of these lines is strongly in the tradition of capital poetry: the first hemistich offers precise sensory evidence that leads to the more general scene or conclusion in the second hemistich.

8. *Bhung-mən* 蓬門 is a gate woven out of *bhung* (see note 05984, line 3), and it marks rusticity.

11052: *CTs*, p. 2419; Chiu-chia 20.1Q, p. 321; Ch'ou, c. 7, pp. 32–33.
Rhymes: 2 *guang*, 4 *dzhiang*, 6 *dhang*, 8 *djhiang*. Regulated.

1. Literally, "Border autumn: shadow easily turns evening." The point of the line is that the short, cloudy autumn days are so dark that the transition to evening is swift and imperceptible.

2. Again, it is because of the continuous clouds and rain that the poet cannot distinguish dawn's light.

3. *Lim* 淋 describes rainwater "running off" something, but it may also mean "soak."

5. Commentaries suggest that the cormorant is seeking food here, and the fact that it is looking in a well indicates an avian desperation. Why the well should be shallow after such rain is uncertain.

6. As the commentators suggest, the earthworms are trying to escape the moisture in the ground.

7. *Seu-sak* 蕭索 is a modal binome suggesting autumnnal gloom and desolation.

11089: *CTs*, p. 2425; Chiu-chia 20.34, pp. 330–31; Ch'ou, c. 8, pp. 49–50.
Rhymes: 2 *qim*, 4 *shim*, 6 *djhim*, 8 *lim*. Regulated.

1. Chiu-chia and Ch'ou agree here that the inability to "gaze to the limits" of autumn is because of the shadows of line 2. As usual, the commentator's explanation marks a problem: "cannot gaze to its limits," *miàng biət ghiək* 望不極, can easily be taken as an expression of "limitless vision," especially in the "clarity" of autumn. And if the layered shadows of line 2 make one "unable to gaze to the limit," the waters merging with the horizon in line 3 suggest "unlimited gazing." I would not suggest that there was conscious ambiguity in Tu Fu's use of *miàng biət ghiək*, but the two meanings of the phrase echo the dominant antithesis throughout the poem, opening up and closing off.

2. The initial "and" of the translation is to prevent easy resolution of the problem in the first line: absence of a conjunction would suggest that the statement of line 2 is definitely the

reason one cannot "gaze to the limits." A conjunction like "then" would make *miǎng biət ghiək* refer to limitless vision. A line of Lu Ch'ung, somewhat misquoted by Ch'ou, gives a clear sense of the meaning of "layered shadows," *dzhəng-qim* 層陰: the line is "Folds of ridges have layered shadows" 重巒有層陰 (*CTsins* 7.5a–6b); i.e., degrees of darkness are visible in the overlapping shadows. As in English, "rise," *kiǒ* 起, is used figuratively for "appear."

3. Literally, "Far waters, together with the sky, pure." *Gem-ten* 兼天 can mean both "level with the sky" and "as well as the sky." The former interpretation is somewhat favored by parallelism and the convention that distant waters are said to merge with the sky.

7–8. There has been some debate among commentators as to whether a topical intent is involved here in the antithesis between the noble crane and the raucous crows. I agree with Ch'ou and Chao in the Chiu-chia that such an interpretation is unnecessary; however, the general opposition in the couplet between light (crane) and dark, between one (cranes were usually thought of as solitary) and many, between positive value and negative value is significant.

10632: *CTs*, p. 2294; Chiu-chia 6.2, pp. 88–89; Ch'ou c. 4, pp. 91–92.
Rhymes: 2 *xuə̀i*, 4 *nuə̀i*, 6 *qài*, 8 *dhài*, 10 *duə̀i*, 12 *dhuə̀i* (?), 14 *suə̀i*, 16 *nguài*, 18 *bhài*, 20 *lài*, 22 *bə̀i*, 24 *tzuài*, 26 *ngə̀i*, 28 *huài*. Unregulated, with the exception of lines 23–24.
Title: Thousand League Pool was in T'ung-ku 同谷 County, just south of Ch'in-chou. It is literally "ten thousand *djhiǎng*."

1. A *kei* 溪 is the valley of a stream as well as the stream itself. *Tseng-kei* 青溪, "blue creek," would call to mind the second of Kuo P'u's *Yu-hsien shih*, which opens with a "blue creek one thousand *djhiǎng* down, within which there is a Taoist master" 青溪一千丈中有一道士 (*Wh* 21.29a). *Hop mèng-mɑk* 合冥寞 is strange: *mèng-mɑk* is a descriptive binome primarily meaning "dark," but implying "vague," distant," "mysterious"; it should not be the object of *hop*. Chao's paraphrase in the Chiu-chia commentary irons out the difficulty: "The blue creek is the means by which there is fusing, and then *mèng-mɑk* 青溪所以合而冥寞. Ch'ou's reading of *hom* 含, "holds concealed (mysterious darkness)," is attractive, but it lacks the textual authority of the Chiu-chia.

2. "Sometimes appearing, sometimes concealed," *hiǒu xěn-xuə̀i* 有顯晦, describes the alternation of activity and quiescence that usually characterizes a dragon.

4. Literally, "His cave, pressed down under ten thousand *djhiǎng*."

5. *Ghiok-biò* 蹋步, a "bent pace," describes a cautious, balancing, perhaps crouching walk, here necessary because of the precipitousness of the rock formation. *Ngyin-ngiɑk* 垠堮 is a general term for "boundary," which the commentators note is used negatively when describing formlessness. Tu Fu's peculiar use of the compound to describe the rim of a cliff almost certainly derives from Hsü Shen's gloss to 垠鍔 in Chang Heng's *Hsi-ching fu* as 端岸 (*Wh* 2.22a–22b). However, Tu Fu is also surely retaining something of the compound's cosmological associations, "passing beyond the rim of things."

11. Great Yü's creation of China's waterways is often described in poetry as "hewing" mountains, and the term is then applied to steep, angular rock formations. "Rooted in nothingness" describes either the great depth of the chasm or the fact that the water beneath reflects the emptiness of the sky.

12. As Ch'ou notes, the character 瀨 does not occur in the *Yü-p'ien*, the *Kuang-yün*, or the *Tseng-yün*, so neither the pronunciation nor the meaning are known. *Dhàm-dhuə̀i* (?) 澹瀨 probably refers either to the stillness of the water or to its rippling. Ch'ou offers various alternative characters and explanations, none of which can be accepted without reservations.

13. Reading 知 with Ch'ou rather than 如 as in the Chiu-chia: 知 is a proper match for 見 in the following line. *Quan-huan* 灣澴 is a new compound whose components and contexts suggests waters whirling together in a circle, hence "vortex." For a close parallel to this couplet, see 11648.3–4.

14. *Huěng-guɑng* 炯光 is another new compound suggesting sparkles of light; *huěng-guɑng suə̀i* 炯光碎 is something like "fragments of sparkling."

15. Literally, "A lone cloud, arriving, is deep."

17. As noted in the commentaries, the *topos* that trees and vines can build a "house of nature" occurs earlier in Lu Chi's *Chao-yin shih* (*Wh* 23.3a); cf. also 10557, lines 21–22. *Hyui-qak* 帷幄 are literally "draperies and curtains," but the compound is often used for the commander's tent pavilion, the place where military strategy is made. The compound is less often also applied to the

place where imperial advisors formulate policy. *Tziɛng-ghiə* 旌旗, "pennons and banners," are most commonly used in military contexts, and parallelism suggests the military sense of *hyui-qak* is implied. In the translation I have chosen to clarify and thus emphasize the military associations of both images.

18. Literally, "Cold trees make layers of pennons and banners." Both Chiu-chia and Ch'ou read 壘 here; the variant 疊 (probably an emendation) makes far better sense. *Luĭ* 壘 does have a meaning "to amass" or "put in layers," and Ch'ou cites a couplet that supports such a usage (a couplet I have not been able to locate, and without finding the source, I must doubt its textual integrity). However, *luĭ* in simply not used that way in most poetry: it is the "rampart" of a military fort. Though it would create an attractive image in its boldness, *luĭ* used in this common sense would makes the line a mixed metaphor of the sort that is exceedingly rare in T'ang poetry: "Cold trees make ramparts of pennons and banners." Parallelism also suggests that the line should read either *dhep* 疊 or *luĭ* in its rare sense: in such a case, *dhep* and *luĭ* both would mean something like "to have something in layers."

19. Literally, "Far streams twistingly cause their flow to get through."

20. Literally, "Caves and holes hiddenly let leak through swift water washing over stone."

21. *Tsɑ̀u* 造 here means to "reach": the usage is somewhat formal and archaic. As the commentaries note, the phrase *mio njin giæng* 無人境 is used to describe T'ien-t'ai in Sun Ch'o's *fu* (*Wh* 11.5a).

22. In the Chiu-chia commentary Chao notes that *ngǎ-bə̀i* 我輩 is often used in the Tsin; it is usually an emphatic first-person plural that asserts an "us" as opposed to someone else; cf. note 07727, line 4. Tu Fu took no close companions on his journey to Ch'eng-tu, when the poem was written; he did take his family, though it is unlikely that he would refer to himself and them as *ngǎ-bə̀i*. Moreover, it would be strange to suddenly bring companions into the poem, unmentioned in the title or previously in the poem. In this case, we should perhaps not overlook the necessity of *bə̀i* for rhyme and might take it as a figurative "us": "those of our times." The only "other" to whom *ngǎ-bə̀i* can be opposed would be Sun Ch'o, who also found a "realm without men" in his imaginary visit to T'ien-t'ai. Here Chao's note about the Tsin quality of *ngǎ-bə̀i* becomes significant: they too loved remote and beautiful landscapes, but our elation is no mere repetition of theirs; it is "all our own."

23. The use of *gɑ̀u-giuə̀i* 告歸 is interesting: it is a very formal term used when an official requests leave to return home from the emperor: one of the most common reasons for such a request is old age, as in line 24. It adopts a tone of reverence for the holy creature of the pool, and reemphasizes the link between dragon and emperor already made in lines 17–18. Much, however, depends on the flexibility of *gɑ̀u-giuə̀i*: if it can only be used in the political context, the line means something quite different: "Having requested leave from the emperor (and having been given permission to quit office), there is much remaining bitterness (which is to some degree consoled by this visit)."

24. The use of the demonstrative *siɛ* 斯 is archaic. *Tzuɑ̀i* 最 used in this way is a general superlative, taking to the extreme whatever condition is implicit in the context.

25. In the *T'ien-wen* chapter of the *Huai-nan-tzu* (as Ch'ou notes) and in other early texts, *bèi-dzhɑng* 閉藏, "hiding away," is a condition with set associations of the winter months, when creatures like dragons "sleep" or hibernate," *djhip* 蟄. In the Chiu-chia commentary, Chao suggests this is a criticism of the emperor's inaction and untimely quiessence; however, the poem is a winter poem and speaks strongly of the propriety of such a state.

27. The "blazing skies," *hyɛm-ten* 炎天, are conventionally associated with summer. The poet is looking forward to the autumn rains of the coming year. If the poet were looking forward to imperial benevolence, he would probably be looking forward to spring; autumn rains often have destructive associations, and the most likely association of a dragon in autumn would be the punishment of evildoers.

28. *Kuɑ̀i-qiə̀* 快意 is a kind of joyful satisfaction, while *qiə̀* carries the implication of an "idea" or "intention" that was satisfied. Dragons were often thought of as stormbeasts, drawing clouds after them.

11219: *CTs*, p. 2452; Chiu-chia 23.3B, p. 369; Ch'ou c. 10, p. 11.
Rhymes: 1 *bin*, 2 *chuin*, 4 *njin*. Regulated.

1. Reading 畏, instead of 裹 with Chiu-chia and Ch'ou. *Qiuǎi* 畏 was an old variant, and probably rejected because of redundancy rather than because it "made no sense," as Chao protests in the Chiu-chia commentary. The reading *guǎ* 裹 manages to be insipid and a bizarre usage at the same time: Chao tries to explain the flowers "wrapping" the shore by saying there are flowers on both banks. *Qiuǎi* suggests an awed terror at spring's profuseness, a state of mind reiterated in line 2.

2. *Gyɛ-ngyuɛ* 敧危 is a new compound (imitating a descriptive binome) that combines "tilting" and "precariousness." Ch'ou doesn't like what Tu Fu is clearly saying here, and cites passages to suggest that what Tu Fu means is that he "hates spring" because he is sad and out of tune with the season. Were one to seek one of Michael Riffaterre's "hypograms" for this poem, it would surely be the *Analects* (IX. 22) "One can stand in awed terror of the later-born" 後生可畏.

3. *Kio-shriǎ* 驅使 is to be "sent off under orders." This gives a degree of personification to the "wine and song (poetry)." The syntax of this line is remarkable: the first six characters modify either the implied first-person subject or *dzhǎi* 在, to "endure," to "still be here." *Shiǝ-tziǒu* 詩酒, "poetry and wine," is a topic, on which the next four characters are the comment. "As for poetry and wine, I am still able to endure being sent off under its commands—in such a way I still endure."

4. *Lèu-liǎ* 料理 generally means to "take care of" some matter, to "manage" something. Suzuki Toraō (4:76) insists that the emphasis is on conclusion, hence "to finish up" or "dispose of" some matter. He further argues that what is to be "disposed of" is Tu Fu. Though the Chinese commentators cite other uses of *lèu-liǎ*, I agree with Suzuki here. It is unclear, however, whether "poetry and wine" are the subjects of *lèu-liǎ* ("They need not yet finish off . . .") or whether *lèu-liǎ* is putative ("He's surely not yet finished off—this . . ."). The translation tries to maintain a middle ground between the two.

10686: *CTs*, pp. 2309–10; Chiu-chia 10. 3, p. 137; Ch'ou, c. 10, pp. 19–20.
Rhymes: 1 *hɑu*, 2 *mau*, 3 *gau*, 4 *shrau*, 5 *qau*; 6 *liǝk*, 7 *dzhǝk*, 9 *dǝk*, 10 *siǝk*, 11 *shriǝk*, 12 *xǝk*; 13 *tet*, 14 *liɛt*, 16 *dzhiuɛt*, 18 *tjiɛt*; 19 *gɛn*, 20 *ngan*, 21 *shrɛn*; 22 *quk*, 23 *tziok*. *T'ung-yün*.

1. "Cry out in rage," *nǒ-hɑu* 怒號, is what the winds do in the cavities of the earth in the *Ch'i-wu lun* chapter of the *Chuang-tzu* (3/2/4). The "height," *gau* 高 (note internal rhyme), of autumn's skies was proverbial.

2. *Gyuĕn* 卷 is literally "roll up" the three layers of thatch; cf. note 09591, line 1.

3. *Shrǎ* 灑 is literally "sprinkle down." The *gau* 郊 is the plain outside a city, here probably Ch'eng-tu.

5. As Ch'ou suggests by citing the passage, the *qau-dhɑng* 坳堂, "water-filled depressions," in the famous first chapter of the *Chuang-tzu* (1/1/6) probably lie behind Tu Fu's phrase *dhɑng-qau* 塘坳. Coordinate compounds and binomes were often inverted for the sake of rhyme. The "lowness" of the image in this line and its resonance with Chuang-tzu's discussion of the relativity of values help create some ironic distance from Tu Fu's involvement in the situation. No one can deny the strong element of genuine pathos in this poem, but to read it without some touch of irony and self-mockery in the poet's voice is to do the poem an injustice.

6. *Kiǝ* 欺 means basically to "deceive," but it has a wide range of pejorative uses, including this one, something like the English "make a fool of."

7. *Njin* 忍 means to "bear" to do something and sometimes, as here, carries the implication of performing a morally wrong act. The line translates literally, "Without compunction, they were able, right before my eyes, to act as bandits."

8. *Gung-njiɛn* 公然, translated as "brazenly," is literally "publically."

9. Literally, "Lips scorched, mouth parched, I couldn't get to call them." I have taken *ho biǝt dǝk* 呼不得 as "unable to summon them back"; it would be possible, though less likely, to take it as "unable to call out."

12. For *mɑk-mɑk* 漠漠, see note 06072, lines 3–4. *Xiɑng xuǝn-xǝk* 向昏黑, translated as "blacker towards sunset," is literally "approaching the darkness (of evening)."

14. *Gyɛu* 嬌 is here an epithet of affection applied to one's own children, "dear." I follow Ch'ou in interpreting 惡臥 as *qɑk-nguà*, "sleep poorly," rather than *qò-nguà*, "not want to go to bed." *Liǎ* 裏 here is probably the inner lining of the bedclothes: thus, *top liǎ liɛt* 踏裏裂 is "tamp on the lining and rip it."

15. *Jrhiɑng-dhou* 床頭 is specifically the "head of the bed."

16. Heavy rain was often compared to strands of hemp.

17. *Geng* 經 here is to physically "pass through" areas of *sàng-luàn*, "death and rebellion," as well as to "live through" such experiences.

18. Literally, "The long night's soaking—how can I get through (to dawn)." As Ch'ou notes, *tjiɛt* 徹, "get through," is used in the sense of *tjiɛt-xĕu* 徹曉, "getting through to dawn," i.e., daybreak.

20. *Hɑn-jrhiš* 寒士, literally "cold scholars," is the normal way to refer to "poor scholars," but in the context of Tu Fu's imaginary shelter, the "cold" aspect regains its root force.

11228: *CTs*, p. 2452; Chiu-chia 22.19A, p. 360; Ch'ou c. 11, pp. 53–54.
Rhymes: 1 *zhiɛng*, 2 *huaeng*, 4 *shraeng*. Regulated.
Title: As often in T'ang poetry, the modern reader may wonder what is "playful," or "jesting" about poems that have such terms in the title. It is perhaps best to take such titles as indications to the reader to read the poems with a certain lightness, rather than as descriptions of the contents of the poems. There are a number of articles on the six "Playful Quatrains"; for a translation of all the quatrains and a list of those articles, see John Timothy Wixted, *The Literary Criticism of Yüan Hao-wen* (Diss., Oxford, 1976), pp. 492–93.

2. *Liɑng-hiuɑn* 凌雲, "passing beyond the clouds," is a phrase associated with apotheosis; treating literary greatness as apotheosis became common in the eighth century and appears with particular frequency in Li Po's work. As the commentators note, the term "mighty brush," *ghiaèn-byit* 健筆, is supposed to come from a preface by Yü Hsin, but that preface does not survive in modern editions of his collected works. *Ghiaèn-byit* describes a forcefulness of style. *Tziòng-huaeng* 縱橫 in this context means to "act as one wills." It is interesting to note that Yü Hsin's own discussions of literature also honor the kind of unrestrained power that Tu Fu is praising here; e.g., *Yü Tzu-shan chi (SPTK)* 9.1a–2b; 11.2a–2b.

10676: *CTs*, p. 2306; Chiu-chia 7.18, pp. 112–13; Ch'ou, c. 10, pp. 29–30.
Rhymes: 2 *gɑ̀i*, 4 *huɑ̀i*, 6 *baèi*, 8 *huaèi*, 10 *dhɑ̀i*, 12 *gɑ̀i* (should be *gši*; tone must be changed for rhyme), 14 *nguɑ̀i*, 16 *nuɑ̀i*, 18 *guaèi*, 20 *lɑ̀i*.

1. For *jhriung-gɑng* 崇岡 see note 10534, line 34; the period associations of *jhriung* are reinforced by the use of the compound *jhriung-gɑng* in the opening of Hsi K'ang's *Ch'in fu* as the place where the pawlonia suitable for ch'in-making grows (*Wh* 18.17a). The opening is a variation on one of the most common opening formulae in Chien-an and Wei poetry, a location using *hiŏu* 有, and marks the *ku-feng*.

2. As Chiu-chia and Ch'ou imply by the citation of the passage, this line unmistakably recalls the opening of the biography of Liu Pei in the *San-kuo chih*:

Liu Pei lost his father when he was still young. . . . Over the hedge in the southeastern corner of his house there was a mulberry tree over thirty-five feet tall; seen from afar, it spread wide like the canopy of a small coach. Everyone who passed by it marveled that it was something extraordinary, and some even said that it would surely bring forth some noble person. When Liu Pei was young, he was playing with other children of his clan under the tree and said playfully, "Someday I will surely ride under this feathered screen and canopied coach" (*San-kuo chih*, p. 871).

Liu Pei was one of Tu Fu's heroes, and this omen of his greatness survives in a problematic, even ironic form in the sick cypress.

3. *Qiaĕn-tziuk* 偃蹙, given in the Chiu-chia text, would be a credible new compound meaning "lying prostrate and gnarled," but the tree is clearly still standing tall at this point. Ch'ou's reading of the binome *qiaĕn-kiaĕn* 偃蹇 meaning "rise up high" or "soar aloft," is preferable.

4. The use of *jiŏ* 主 here is difficult, and the variant *jièng* 正 ("right in the conjunction of . . .") is probably an emendation to resolve the problem. But since Liu Pei and dragons are *jiŏ*, it is difficult to dismiss the reading, however unusual the syntax. Moreover, *jièng* is used again in the following line, and while such repetition is not very uncommon, it adds a little weight to retaining the *jiŏ*. *Huɑ̀i* 會, "meeting" or "occasion," is important in Tu Fu's poetry: it is a "conjunction" of circumstances when something should be done. Here the association of the tree is clearly the dragon

(which draws clouds after it) and tiger (which summons the wind), and in that double avatar, it is the "dominant" (*jiǒ*) form in the conjunction of wind and cloud.

5. *Jhin-miaeng* 神明, like English "divinity," is both the quality and the entity possessing the quality.

7–8. This couplet is enjambed. Line 8 is literally, "Midroad its countenance is ruined."

9. *Chuit* 出, translated as "growing," is literally "coming forth" and is also used for choosing an active life of public service.

11. *Siuèi-han* 歲寒 clearly refers to "one winter" and not to the first time it encountered winter. One of the conventions of poems on evergreen and bamboo is that their endurance can be known only in the winter; the cypress should have been able to pass through the winter, but one winter it finds itself failing. The language in which its destruction is described, *mio-bhiang* 無憑, "nothing to rely on," reinforces the link to the human correlative.

13–14. The "cinnabar phoenix" is here primarily the allegorically virtuous bird, but it was also a wooden statue used to carry imperial edicts for promulgation. Without making any direct correlation, we may still say that the "cinnabar phoenix's" appearance here points the reader to a human political context. The auspicious "nine" is the conventional number in a phoenix brood. Phoenixes do not usually roost on cypresses, but the "hovering beyond" it suggests that it will be an unreliable perch.

5. The ill-omened owl is also a prominent species in bird allegory. *Jiò-qiò mǎn* 志意滿 is literally "their intentions were satisfied."

17. This line is a variation on a *yüeh-fu* formula; e.g., *Wh* 27.20b. The use of the interrogative prevents a too easy identification with the poet, though this *kaek* 客 is drawing Tu Fu's own conclusions from the emblem.

18. *Xio* 吁 is an exclamation, here of amazement; *xio-guaèi* 吁怪 is "oooh'ing and marvelling."

19. *Dzhiěng* 靜, "calmly," marks a necessary change to reflectiveness from the observer's initial agitation. *Ngiuaen-tzieng* 元精, "Primal Essence," in a cosmological term for the substance or energy that is part of all things of the world.

20. *Hǎu-dhǎng* 浩蕩 is a binome describing chaotic immensity and a willful freedom of action which from the outside would seem to be a menacing license. Tu Fu's point is that the "principle" behind things is "want of principle," a formless chaos. Its dominant characteristic is that it "cannot be relied on," just as the tree suddenly found it had nothing to rely on in line 11.

11139: *CTs*, p. 2438; Chiu-chia 21.46, p. 355; Ch'ou, c. 9, pp. 139–140.
Rhymes: 2 *lài*, 4 *kài*, 6 *pài*, 8 *bài*. Regulated.

1–2. The function of the *dhàn* 但 in line 2 is to raise the possibility that he might have seen something else, but did not; the "something else" is of course the "guest."

3. *Xua-gèng* 花徑 is a path under flowering trees, and thus a path on which flowers fall. "Sweeping one's path" is a conventional poetic mark of the expectation of guests.

5. Reading 殽 with Ch'ou, rather than 飧 in the Ch'iu-chia. *Bhǎn-suan* 盤殽, literally "a plate of dinner," was one of the standard ways to refer to dinner; its parallel is *tzuən-tziǒu* 樽酒, a "goblet of wine." *Gem-miǒi* 兼味, literally "compound flavors," is a distinctly elegant locution and is strangely out of place in this militantly casual poem. The syntax of this line and line 6 involves two distinct topics and a comment, leaving the reader to supply the relations: "As for dinner, the market is far: (thus) there will be no compound flavors." The tonal requirements of the poem force a rearrangement of more straightforward syntax, which would be 市遠盤殽無兼味.

7. *Kěng* 肯, "be willing," often marks an interrogative or a conditional sentence. The line could also be taken, "If you are willing. . . ." The line is a challenge: presumably the guest is gentry, and it is likely that the man next door is not. Social decorum would insist that guests of such different ranks not be mixed, but Tu Fu's invitation here, like much of the rest of the poem, asks the guest to put aside upper-class ceremony and taste.

8. *Xo-tsiǒ* 呼取 is literally "call to him and (thus) fetch him." This is another highly unceremonious suggestion. Wang Wei may have praised simple rustic values, but he did not shout, "Come on over!" to his neighbors.

11465: *CTs*, p. 2495; Chiu-chia 31.4, p. 487; Ch'ou, c. 17, p. 55.
Rhymes: 2 *mən*, 4 *piaen*, 6 *xiuaen*, 8 *kuən*. Regulated.
Title: "Spending the Night in a Tower by the River" 宿江邊閣.

1. *Mèng-shriək* 暝色 is more than simply "darkness": literally "the surface appearance of darkness," it describes an area of blackness and not a general obscurity. Thus, in the Hsieh Ling-yün usage cited in the commentaries, it is a bounded area of darkness which can be "gathered in" to the valleys as the sun sets (*Wh* 22.15a). In this line Tu Fu is describing the next stage of sunset, as the light rises to the mountain tops: but instead of describing the light "rising," he describes the border of the dark area "extending." I have translated *iɛn* 延 as "grows" rather than "extends" in order to preserve the sense of movement.

2. Ch'ou's note that "High Study," *Gɑu-jraei* 高齋, was in fact the name of the study in which Crown Prince Chao-ming composed the *Wen hsüan* is most intriguing: if Tu Fu knew this, it would add a special depth to the line, but it is quite possible that Tu Fu was ignorant of this bit of Hsiang-yang lore. *Tsì* 次 in this sense means "take up lodgings at." The "river-gate," *shuí-mən* 水門, is the city gate directly on or closest to the river.

4. This refers to the moonlight or moon's reflection being tossed about by the waves. Note how the seeming precariousness of the cloud's situation is picked up by the "falling over" in this line—something very high falling very low.

5. A *hɑk* 鶴 is a crane proper; a *guàn* 觀 is another bird like a crane of ashen gray appearance.

6. *Jrhaei-lɑng* 豺狼 were commonly associated with violent, destructive people—rebels and bandits. The line translates literally, "Wild dogs and wolves, obtaining food, howl."

11474: *CTs*, pp. 2496–97; Chiu-chia 31.43, p. 498; Ch'ou, c. 18, pp. 106–7.
Rhymes: 2 *siɛu*, 4 *iɛu*, 6 *dzhiɛu*, 8 *leu*. Regulated.

1. Ch'ou would have 景 interpreted as *qiaĕng*, which, in the context of evening, must refer to "sunlight" rather than "shadows" (which are growing longer rather than shorter). From similar compounds and from the fact that the four cases in which Tu Fu uses the phrase all seem to be autumn or winter poems, we may presume that *duăn-qiaĕng* 短景 refers to the "shortening daylight" as the year moves towards winter solstice and the individual days move swiftly to their close. The use of Yin and Yang in this line suggests the presence of cosmic forces in the physical relations of day and night.

2. *Ten-ngɛi* 天涯, translated literally as the "sky's edge," is the word used for "horizon," but as one can locate oneself at *ten-ngɛi*, "sky's edge" implies the proper sense of being "out of the way." However, the phrase preserves a central perspective: one's position is seen from a place somewhere else.

3. The night was divided into five watches, and the fifth watch was the period just before dawn. The "drums and horns," *gŏ-gak* 鼓角, indicate a military presence and thus remind the poet of warfare. *Byi-jriàng* 悲壯 is an important and essentially untranslatable category of mood: "strong and sad" are the two essential components, but the phrase is often associated with frontier duty. *Jriàng* often suggests the "prime of life" and a sense of firm resolution that, when brought to restrained sorrow, suggests the concealed intensity of the emotion.

4. The Three Gorges are the Wu Gorges, just downstream from K'uei-chou. Chiu-chia cites a scornful passage from the *Hsi-ch'ing shih-hua* on how most readers miss the allusion to the *Han-shu* in the line, on how "shaking stars" are an omen of suffering masses and coming wars. In fact, it is doubtful that the passage is an allusion: shaking stars as an omen of war were fairly common; moreover, when stars are reflected in the river, they always shake. It is possible, however, that *qiaĕng* 影 refers to the "starlight" rather than to their reflections: "Over the Three Gorges the light from the river of stars stirs and shakes." Whether *qiaĕng* is "light" or "reflections," the image remains an ominous one, though somewhat more subtle and muted in the case of "reflections." What is interesting about the *shih-hua* passage is an indication that most readers were missing the wealth of historical, cultural, and literary background which commentators presumed was present in poems: commentary, especially commentary directed to educated adults rather than children, marks a sense on the part of the scholar that the person with average education will not know the

material provided in the commentary. This obvious fact should be kept in mind when modern readers make presumptions about the vast learning of traditional readers of poetry. In many cases we cannot know with any certainty whether Tu Fu intended and the average reader understood: a specific textual allusion, no textual allusion, or an association derived from one or more texts but in which memory of the texts themselves was not present. In the case of this line, the third possibility seems most likely: the starlight shivering in the water is ominous without being specifically a portent.

5. *Iǎ-kuk* 野哭 is weeping for the dead but not in the proper ritual setting: it is mentioned in the *Li-chi* (*T'ang-kung* I) and in the *K'ung-tzu chia-yü* as something Confucius hated. In this context, *iǎ-kuk* suggests a spontaneous and overwhelming grief. For the ambiguities in the line, see the text.

6. This suggests that the civilized music of the heartland is withdrawing and barbarism is making incursions into the border areas of the empire.

7. Chu-ko Liang, called the "Sleeping Dragon" or "Reclining Dragon," * Nguà-liong* 臥龍 (suggesting poetential power not yet displayed), was the minister of Liu Pei, the founder of the Shu-Han Kingdom. The name "Leaping Horse" for Kung-sun Shu (a rebel during the Wang Mang interregnum in the Han who proclaimed himself emperor in Szechwan) recalls the end of Tso Ssu's *Shu-tu fu*, where "Kung-sun made his horse leap and proclaimed himself emperor" (*Wh* 4.34a).

8. *Qyim* 音 is oral news; *shiu* 書 is written word. The precise sense of *màn* 漫 here is difficult: Chang Hsiang explains it as meaning "moreover"; see *Shih tz'u ch'ü yü-tz'u hui-shih*, p. 228. I think this is too weak and prefer to take it as an adverbial "diffusely," "confusedly," or "uncertainly." The primary semantic values in the binome *dzhek-leu* 寂寞 are "silence" and "emptiness"; see *Lao-tzu* XXV, with commentary of so-called Ho-shang Kung. (Wang Pi glosses *dzhek-leu* as "without fixed form," but that is only the "empty" aspect.) The translation given is an attempt to work around Tu Fu's untranslatable line; literally, "Of human affairs word is confusedly silent-void." The line evokes a sense of vast emptiness and silence through which no news of the outer world comes clearly.

11554: *CTs*, p. 2510; Chiu-chia 30.32G, p. 469; Ch'ou, c. 17, pp. 69–71.
Rhymes: 1 *gung*, 2 *djiung*, 4 *biung*, 6 *hung*, 8 *qung*. Regulated.
Title: The indispensable work for the study of "Autumn Meditations" is Yeh Chia-ying's 葉嘉瑩 *Tu Fu Ch'iu-hsing pa-shou chi-shuo* 杜甫秋興八首集說 (Taipei, 1966): all the major traditional interpretations of the poems are gathered together here, supplemented by Professor Yeh's own discussions of both the commentaries and the poems. The most important work on the poems in English is Mei Tsu-lin's and Kao Yu-kung's "Tu Fu's Autumn Meditations: an Exercise in Linguistic Criticism," *HJAS* 28 (1968): 44–80.

1. Han Wu-ti used K'ung ming Pool to practice naval maneuvers, probably suggested in the banners and pennons of line 2. As Yeh notes, this very clearly specifies the Han and is not using the Han to refer to the T'ang. What this fantasy of the Han means in relation to the contemporary situation in Ch'ang-an is the subject of much speculation on the part of the commentators.

2. The assertion of physically seeing an imaginary scene is strong; cf. 11616.

3. Statues of the Herdboy and Weaving Girl were placed on either side of K'un-ming Pool to correspond to the lovelorn stars separated by the "river of stars." For the history of interpretations of *xiu miaeng-ngiuaet* 虛明月, see Yeh Chia-ying, pp. 369–80.

4. The statue of the whale was supposed to have made sounds when a storm was coming, and its fins were supposed to have moved in the wind. It is possible to take *dhǔng tsiou-biung* 動秋風 as "stir the autumn wind," an illusory inversion of cause and effect; however, a passive reading is equally likely.

5. There is a general agreement among the commentators that a "cloud" of black kumi seeds is meant here. Mine is a somewhat unorthodox interpretation, based on idea that a storm is portended by the movement of the stone whales fins and thus that real storm clouds are present, reflected in the pool. I would further have the image of the kumi seed built on the model of the "celery seed" in *Chuang-tzu* 1/1/6. For the history of interpretations of this couplet, see Yeh Chia-ying, pp. 380–91.

11627: *CTs* p. 2523; Chiu-chia 30.16, p. 463; Ch'ou, c. 23, pp. 60–61.
Rhymes: 2 *njio*, 4 *go*, 6 *so*, 8 *dho*. Regulated.

1. The Han River enters the Yangtze in modern Hupei by Wu-ch'ang. That this poem was classed among the K'uei-chou poems in early editions shows a geographical confusion rare in Chinese editors.

2. Ch'ien and K'un are Heaven and Earth, respectively, in their *Yi-ching* aspects as cosmological principles. "Broken-down man of learning" is perhaps a weak approximation of *bhiǒ-njio* 腐儒: the "learning" is classical and historical Confucian learning, the kind of knowledge that should make one useful to the state, but *bhiǒ* 腐, literally "rotten," imples age and uselessness. As Ch'ou perceptively notes, Tu Fu is both mocking himself and expressing pride in himself.

3–4. As so often in Tu Fu's later poetry, the referents of this couplet are uncertain. Three things are "far": the cloud, the sky, and the poet; three things are "solitary": the night, the moon, and the poet.

11232: *CTs*, p. 2453; Chiu-chia 22.19E, p. 361; Ch'ou, c. 11, p. 55.
Rhymes: 1 *njin*, 2 *lin*, 4 *djhin*. Regulated.

This poem is adequately discussed in the text.

10561: *CTs*, pp. 2276–77; Chiu-chia 3.6, p. 51; Ch'ou, c. 5, pp. 69–70; *Twt* 14B.9b–10a; *Wyyh* 311.6a.
Rhymes: 2 *nguǎ*, 4 *hǎ*, 6 *siǎ*, 8 *shrǎ*, 10 *gǎ*, 12 *mǎ*, 14 *bǎ*, 16 *jiǎ*. Only the third couplet is regulated.
Title: Yü-hua Palace was established in 646 as a summer retreat from the heat of Ch'ang-an; in 751 it was turned into a Buddhist temple. By the time Tu Fu visited it, it was obviously long abandoned.

1. *Djhiang* 長, "long," is used to describe steady winds that seem to come from far away. It is remotely possible that *djhiang* means "tall," referring to wind in the tips of the pines, but *gau-biung* 高風 is the proper term for such wind.

2. *Tsuàn* 竄, translated as "scuttling," is literally "going to hide away," an indication of the poet's entrance onto the scene. It would seem likely that these are fallen tiles, indicating the dilapidation of the structure.

3. As he knows the name of the palace, it is very unlikely that Tu Fu did not actually know that it had been T'ai-tsung's. The point of the line is to suggest the essential anonymity of the ruins, yet the occasional precision of the title and the efforts of Tu Fu's commentators play ironic counterpoint to the poet's feigned ignorance. The problem can be resolved by taking *hiuang* 王 as an "imperial prince," to whom one of the halls belonged, but the commentaries suggest that *hiuang* was read as referring to T'ai-tsung. In a fit of Kung-yang style interpretation, Chao in the Chiu-chia commentary suggests that Tu Fu avoids T'ai-tsung's name as an indirect criticism of the labor wasted on the frivolity of a summer palace.

4. *Ui* 遺 means "left behind," remaining": though the buildings are clearly abandoned, *ui* in itself does not necessarily imply abandonment. *Gòu* 構 is a "building" in its aspect of being something "constructed."

5. *Giuǒi-xuǎ* 鬼火 were natural phosphorescences, believed to have been produced from human blood. That these are "green" (translated as such rather than "blue" to preserve their living, vegetative aspect) is striking and suggests something uncanny.

6. The undermining action of streamlets is the enemy of roads the world over. *Qɔi tuɑn siǎ* 哀湍瀉 is literally "lamenting torrents stream."

7. I have taken some liberties with this line, which translates literally, "Ten thousand pipes: the true *shraeng* and *hio*." The "pipes," *lài* 籟, are the "pipes of Earth" described in the beginning of the second chapter of the *Chuang-tzu*, the vents and fissures in the earth through which the *ch'i* passes, producing sounds (*Chuang-tzu* 3/2/3–8). *Shraeng* and *hio* are two kinds of ocarinas, used especially in court music. The point of the line is that Earth's piping is the "true" music, implying that the piping of the vanished court orchestras was somehow "false; cf. line 10.

8. *Seu-shrǎ* 蕭瀟 is a binome usually applied to people rather than seasons: it suggests a cool, dispassionate, untrammeled manner.

10. Literally, "(If the ladies have turned to earth), it is even more true of their artifice of powder and mascara." *Gǎ* 假, "artifice," "something false," is very strong and negatively echoes the "true" of line 7.

11. The "coach of gold" is, of course, that of the emperor.

15. *Njiĕm-njiĕm* 冉冉 is a binome describing "gradual movement," either of time or, less often, of travel; in this case, the two are combined.

16. Literally, "Who is one with long years"; i.e., a span longer than normal.

CHAPTER 12

12574: *CTs*, p. 2703; *YTsc*, pp. 17–18; *YTswc* 3.1a–1b.
Rhymes: 16 *bhiou*, 18 *dhou*, 20 *lou*, 22 *kiou*, 24 *jrhiou*, 26 *zhiou*, 28 *zhiou*, 30 *sou*, 32 *qiou*, 34 *siou*, 36 *tsiou*, 38 *bhiou*, 40 *hiou*, 42 *miou*. Unregulated. The poem has, in all, forty-eight lines.
Title: *Myĭn-huɑng* 閔荒 is a resonant, archaic-sounding verb-object construction, which seems to have been created by Yüan. *Myĭn* as a term for "grief," "distress," or "pity" has decided archaic qualities. *Huɑng* suggests "dissolute" behavior and portends the "dissolution" of the social body.

15. *Xiang* 舡 is a general term for "boat," sometimes associated with southeastern craft. The variant *jhiuɛn* 船 appears probably because 舡 was sometimes used to represent that word. A *leng* 舲 is a pleasure barge. The emperor's barge was called a "dragon boat," *liong-jhiuɛn* 龍船. Cormorants were common prow decorations.

16. Clearly this describes large galleys and pleasure barges.

17. *Qiang-ghiǝk* 央極 is redundant. *Miǝi-qiang* 未央 by itself means "not yet complete," but *ghiǝk* 極 is the word to describe attaining the limit of pleasure. What is remarkable about Yüan Chieh's *fu-ku* poetry is that in aspiring to ancient authority his language is often highly original (though its construction often appear archaic); compounds and phrases used by poets whom he castigated as "new" far more often have early precedents.

19. This area east of Yang-chou took on the formal place-name 'Straits to the Sea,' *Xǎi-mǝn* 海門, several centuries later.

21. Hsin-tu 新都, literally the New Capital, was the name of the Sui capital built near the site of Han Ch'ang-an, the city that was to become T'ang Ch'ang-an.

22. It is obvious that the use of *kiou* 丘 here, without precedent or special significance, is purely for the sake of rhyme.

23. *Dɑng-zhiǝ* 當時 here can mean either "in this time" or "from that time."

24. In *tǎi qiuɑen jrhiou* 太寬愁 we have yet another peculiar and awkward construction. The line translates literally, "As for those songs, (they are characterized by) extreme resentment-sorrow." *Qiuɑen* combines resentment and sorrow against a wrong done to one or a punishment unjustly inflicted.

25–26. I do not feel certain about the interpretation of these lines. "Heaven's Jail," *Ten-ngiok* 天獄, and "Heaven's Prisoner," *Ten-zhiou* 天囚, were both asterisms portending war and destruction. *Biǝi* 非 more commonly means "is not," and while the meaning "consider wrong" seems best here, the lines could be interpreted, "This sea-bound world is not Heaven's prison, and why are we not Heaven's prisoners?"

27. Again, there is uncertainty about this line. If "Heaven's Prisoner" refers to the asterism (which is itself uncertain), *jièng xiong-njĭn* 正凶忍 may mean "at this moment is wicked and ruthless" (i.e., portends destruction) or "will rectify wicked ruthlessness" (i.e., the war will depose an unjust ruler).

28. The "enemy" is the asterism in the first case above, and the wicked ruler in the second case. *Miaèn-sièng* 萬姓, translated as "the millions of people," is literally the "ten thousand surnames," a hyperbolic variation on the usual term for the peasantry, the "hundred surnames."

29. A *shraèm* 釤 is a very large scythe, a farming implement. It is "Heaven's" insofar as it carries out the will of Heaven in deposing an evil ruler.

30. *Sou* 鏤 is usually just "carving," but in this case it is clearly a "carver." After this line there is an early, perhaps original note in the text that says, "What is investigated from above is

sought by those below" 上所監下所求; the judgments of Heaven are manifest in the actions of the people.

34. *Hyuɛ Ziuə-giuən siou* 為隋君羞 is literally "(ought to) make the Sui ruler feel ashamed."

36. Autumn was the season of war and destruction and the punishment of wrongdoers: the songs generate an unseasonal autumn atmosphere if sung in spring.

37. Literally, "How could it be otherwise than that there was a beclouding of the king's heart."

40. *Qiuaèn-hiou* 怨尤 is "spite and rage" directed against someone who has done a wrong.

12547: *CTs*, p. 2696; *YTsc*, p. 18; *YTswc* 3.2a.
Rhymes: 2 *ho*, 4 *ngio*, 6 *lo*, 8 *gio*, 10 *mio*, 12 *djhio*.
Title: This poem is probably discussed in William Nienhauser, "'Twelve Poems Propagating the Music Bureau Ballad': Yüan Chi'eh's (719–722) *Hsi yüeh-fu shih-erh shou*," in *Critical Essays on Chinese Literature* (Hong Kong, 1976). I have not had the chance to see this essay.

6. The *qio* 鮹 is the piscine metamorphosis of a crow in the ninth month, according to the *Chi-yün*. A *lo* 鱸, loosely translated as "perch," was a fish native to the Southeast, whose fillets were considered such a treat that several southeasterners were reputed to have given up their posts to go back home and eat *lo*.

17. More properly, "What they find pleasure in is the same as that which birds and beasts find pleasure in."

12. *Djhiɛ-djhio* 踟蹰 is one of the several binomes meaning "waver," "pace about with distress or uncertainty."

12582: *CTs*, pp. 2706–7; *YTsc*, pp. 24–25; *YTswc* 3.6a–6b.
Rhymes: 2 *bən*, 4 *tsuan*, 6 *ngiuaen*, 8 *mən*, 10 *hiuaen*, 12 *suən*, 14 *biən*, 16 *dzhuən*, 18 *qiuaen*, 20 *luən*.
T'ung-yün. The first couplet is regulated; no other couplet in the poem is.
Title and preface: Yüan Chich's flight to Jang-hsi may have actually occurred in early 759, with the renewed activity of Shih Ssu-ming. Note that the poet refers to himself as Yüan-tzu 元子, "Master Yüan": this suggests that he saw himself as a thinker more than as a prose stylist or poet.

4. Though *qəi-giuən* 愛君 means to "love one's lord," this construction with a pronoun object followed by a demonstrative pronoun means "this ... of yours"; for a parallel example, see 10501.9.

5. *Nga* 呀, "gape," is often applied to valleys and open features in the landscape. *Huəi-qiaèng* 回映 describes light shining off some feature and seeming cast on other features.

8. This may instead suggest that every gate could be reached by boat, though the qualifying *pi n* 扁 suggests an actual case rather than a general case.

9. I have taken 中曲濱 as *djiung-kiok bin*, making the line nominal, a topic for the following line. The alternative is *djiùng kiok-bin*, "lies between twisting shores": not only is it insipid, it demands an odd, archaic interpretation of *djiùng*. Moreover, *djiung-kiok* is a compound with precedents, while *kiok-bin* is not, and as the second element of a compound, *bin* is used almost exclusively only after river and stream names.

11–12. The absence of an explicit object of *dzhəng* 贈 creates difficulty in the interpretation of this couplet. Uses of *dzhəng* in poetry are about equally divided between offering things and offering words: the form here seems to suggest that the neighbors are "offering" the sentiment expressed in the following line; cf. 17871.24 and the following passage from the second part of the *T'an-kung* chapter in the *Li-chi*:" 子路去魯。謂顏淵曰：何以贈我。曰 ..." *Xiù* suggests an openness and acceptance, but it is unclear why *jiə* 之 is used rather than a first- or second-person pronoun. Pronoun shifts are, however, common in poetic narrative. *Ghyip* 及 is "and" but has some sense of special dispensation—"even including."

13. *Ghyuè-bhiaep* 匱乏 means "hardship" or "want of life's necessities": it has nothing to do with "cabinets."

16. For this use of *dzhuən* 存, cf. 11627.7.

17. The use of *siɛ-njin* 斯人 recalls Confucius's affirmation of fellowship with the two rustic plowmen in *Analects* XVIII.6: "If I am not the fellow of people like these, then of whom?" 吾非斯人之徒與而誰與。

18. *Qiuaen* 寃 is literally the "feeling of being wronged by."

12587: *CTs*, p. 2708; *YTsc*, p. 25; *YTswc* 3.6b–7a.
Rhymes: 2 *dzhiɛng*, 4 *giaeng*, 6 *hiuaeng*, 8 *qiuɛng*, 10 *kiaeng*, 12 *gɛng*, 14 *jrɛng*, 16 *miaeng*, 18 *shraeng*.
Title: *Iò* 喻 in this sense in to draw or offer a lesson from an exemplary case, to "treat as parable."

1. Note that *bin* 濱 is used after the name of the creek; cf. note 12582, line 9.
2. *Miàng-dzhiɛng* 忘情 originally referred to a state of emotional neutrality, beyond any passions; here it has come to describe unself-consciousness and lack of ulterior motive, contrasted to the *giaeng* 驚, "startled behavior," "ill at ease," when Yüan returns to the village.
5–6. Literally, "As for my heart being with the people of Jang, how could there be shame (from humbleness) or grandeur?" This and the two couplets that follow are extremely prosaic.
12. *Xiou* 休 here probably means "give up office."
13. Literally, "How much more (would they have wanted to retire) having passed through rebellion."
16. One of the most common meanings of *njiàng* 讓 (Jang) is to "yield," as in "yielding one's office," "yielding to one of greater virtue," "defer."
18. *Dzhiuɛn-shraeng* 全生 means "to keep one's life whole," to live out one's allotted span of years.

12577: *CTs*, pp. 2704–5; *YTsc*, pp. 35–36; *YTswc* 4.2a–2b; *Tscs*, pp. 328–29.
Rhymes: 2 *nen*, 4 *dzhen*, 6 *men*, 8 *jiɛn*, 10 *njiɛn*, 12 *len*, 14 *dzhiuɛn*, 16 *qyɛn*, 18 *tziɛn*, 20 *hen*, 22 *jhiuɛn*, 24 *ben*.

1. Literally, "encountered an age of peace."
7. *Shièi-byɛn* 世變 is literally a "change in the age," *byɛn* usually implying a change for the worse.
8. *Tsin njiung-jiɛn* 親戎旃 is literally "was kin to battle flags": *tsin* 親 is used poetically to suggest an adherence to something.
9. *Děn* 典 is a slightly archaic word, used in the Han for governing a commandery. Contrast the kind of language used by Ts'en Shen in 09646, line 6. The archaic, prosaic *siɛ* 斯 also lends seriousness to Yüan's sense of his position.
11. *Dho* 屠 is the word use for taking a city and killing its inhabitants.
12. This may imply that even the mountain tribes took pity on the poverty of Yüan's prefecture, hence the tax officials, who do not spare the prefecture, are worse than the raiders (line 16).
16. Literally, "How could they not be as good as the raiders?" *kiǎi-biat* 豈不, "how could they not," is a rhetorical question meaning "surely they are." *Njiu* 如, "be like," in its negative form, *biat-njiu* 不如, almost always means "not be as good as." Thus, the rhetorical transformation of the line is "Surely they must be better than the raiders."
17–18. Literally, "Now those ones who exact and collect (tax) press on them (the people) like a fire's simmering."
23. It is difficult not to hear here the spirit of *Shih* 113, "Big Rat," on the people's flight from oppressive government.

12607: *CTs*, p. 2714; *YTsc*, p. 41; *YTswc* 4.6b–7a.
Rhymes: 2 *dheng*, 4 *miaeng*, 6 *iɛng*, 8 *shraeng*, 10 *meng*, 12 *seng*, 14 *dzhiɛng*, 16 *zhiɛng*, 18 *tseng*, 20 *iɛng*, 22 *heng*, 24 *bheng*, 26 *miaeng*. *T'ung-yün*. Lines 13–14 and last three couplets regulated (with acceptable variation in fourth position of penultimate line).
Title: A *quà-tzuən* 窊樽 was a depression in a rock which could serve as a wine cup.

1. *Jrham-jrham* 嶃嶃 is a descriptive binome properly applied to a towering peak: the kind of oxymoron embedded in this line is not common in T'ang poetry.
3. This is an excellent example of *kom* 堪 being weakened to mean simply "can."
4. *Jrhiàng-luì* 狀類 is literally "form and category": there were different names for different shapes of cup.
5. *Zuin-huəi* 巡回, translated as "wend a circling course," may be comically grand for the act described.

6. Literally, "It is as if I see a little P'eng(-lai) and Ying(-chou)." P'eng-lai and Ying-chou were two of the three isles of the immortals in the Eastern Ocean.

8. This must refer to irregularities in the depression, which protrude above the wine when it is poured in.

9. *Njit-guɑn* 日觀, "Sungazing," was the name of the eastern ridge of T'ai-shan, from which the sun could be observed rising over the sea.

11. The two hemistiches may be more closely related: "As I lovingly appreciate it, I don't notice that I'm getting drunk."

15. Literally, "It's as if Form won in the discussion."

25. A closing question like this implies the answer "I am."

12620: *CTs*, p. 2717; *YTsc*, p. 46; *YTswc* 4.9b; *Yfsc* 82.10a.
Rhymes: 1 *gɛn*, 2 *hɛn*, 4 *shrɛn*. Regulated, but with strong violation in sixth position of second line.
Title: *Qǎi-nǎi* 欸乃 seems to have been a southern binome describing the sound of rowing: after Yüan Chieh's series it became a term for a "rowing song."

1. *Miaeng-tziɛk* 名跡 is literally "name" or "fame" and "traces" of deeds or journeys.

2. *Jhuìn-ziok* 順俗, "to follow custom" (what the average person does), recalls the advice of Jo to the God of the Yellow River: "Whoever follows the custom of his time is a righteous man" (*Chuang-tzu* 43/17/40). The *Chuang-tzu* is, of course, being ironic, speaking of survival and the popular reputation of righteousness. The advice does not work for Yüan Chieh, and he does not feel the comfort he should feel in *jhuìn-ziok*.

3. This passage is unmistakably ironic: "asking how one governs," *miən-jiɛ̀ng* 問政, adopts the attitude of a disciple asking Confucius about a principle; cf. *Analects* XII. 7.1; XIII.1.1.

4. *Giǒu-ngiə* 九疑, "Nine Doubts," is probably a simple writing of the homophonous 九嶷, "Nine Summits." *Giǒu-ngiə* is a mountain with nine peaks, located in modern Hunan.

13411: *CTs*, p. 2889; *Ccc* in *TjhTs*, p. 29; *Hyylc* in *TjhTs*, p. 68; *Wyyh* 252.2b; *Tscs*, p. 392.
Rhymes: 2 *chuin*, 4 *njin*, 6 *tsin*, 8 *bhyin*, 10 *lin*, 12 *shin*, (14 *sin*, 16 *giən*). The *t'ung-yün* of line 16 in a poem entirely in *p'ing-shui* rhymes should raise some questions about the final section in the *Hyylc* and *Wyyh* versions.
Text: The text given is that of the *Ccc*; this is the text given in *Tscs*, with variations in some editions. *Hyylc* and *Wyyh* differ significantly, both from the *Ccc* text and from each other; however, the *Wyyh* text does seem to be loosely based on the *Hyylc* version (in the order of couplets 5 and 6 and in the inclusion of lines 14–16).
Title: The *Hyylc* title is most peculiar: "In the Mountains, Presented to the Fourteenth Member of His Clan, of the Imperial Library, My Elder Brother of the Mountains" 山中贈十四秘書山兄. The *Wyyh* cleans this up: "Presented to my Elder Brother of the Mountains, Wei of the Imperial Library 贈山兄韋秘書.

1. *Hyylc* and *Wyyh* read 秘芸署 for 秋雲曙. The phrase *bhyì hiuən-zhiǔ* 秘芸署 is odd: *bhyì* is an attributive for the Imperial Library, and *hiuən-zhiǔ*, the "Office of Rue," is an ornamental term for the same: but the combinination of the three characters is odd. *Chuit-shrɛn* 出山, "going out from the mountains," suggests giving up a life of reclusion to serve in the government. Thus, the *Hyylc* and *Wyyh* versions translate roughly, "Leaving the mountains (for) the Imperial Library." Of the ways in which variants occur, the most common are synonymn substitutions, homonymn substitutions, and similarity in character form: however, usually only one of these principles is in operation when there is a serial variation of several characters. Here, the variation of 秋 and 秘 is clearly a shape variation, 雲 and 芸 are homonymn variations, and 曙 (*zhiù*) and 署 (*zhiǔ*) are a combination of shape and sound. This suggests strongly that the variation is not accidental.

2. The "mountain tree" is an allegorical figure from the *Chuang-tzu* (51/20/1–6) which preserves itself from woodcutters by being useless: the analogy is to the one who remains in the mountains (Wang Chi-yu), as opposed to the one who goes forth to serve the state. For 木 *Hyylc* reads 色 and *Wyyh* reads 水. The *Ccc* version is by far the most coherent opening couplet, using the change of the seasons to mark the duration of Wei's absence, as is common in T'ang poetry. This suggests that the poem is indeed "sent to" (*gyɛ̀* 寄) Wei rather than "presented to" (*dzhàng* 贈) him in person.

3–4. The use of *ngǎ* 我 suggests that Wei rather than Wang is the subject of the verb. Line 3 could refer either to the past, when Wei ate Wang Chi-yu's herbs, or to the present, to some present Wang sent Wei.

5. For the proper 余密 *Wyyh* reads the inelegant 密余. *Mit* 密, literally "secret," implies a particular personal intimacy, though it does not suggest a sexual relationship.

6. For 惟相 *Hyylc* reads 日相 and *Wyyh* reads 日見. Isolation often leads to unlikely "kin"; cf. 05846 and 07795.

7. "Rats and wrens" were examples of unlovable animals, which stole from a person's foodstocks; cf. also *Shih* 17.

9–10. *Hyylc* and *Wyyh* have these lines as 11 and 12; For 北舍 *Hyylc* reads 舍北. For the line, *Wyyh* reads 依舍北松下: it seems the second 依 has dropped out of this line, and the 不 of the following line has been converted to 下 to produce a line of poetry, albeit a remarkably ugly one. Line 10 may be taken to refer to a real neighbor to the south whom Wang does not weary of: this would admit a simpler explanation of the "my," *ngo* 吾. But it seems far more likely than Wang Chi-yu is the pine's "southern neighbor," and that the *ngo* is either enallage or defining the "southern neighbor" as "myself." Another point of interest in the variation between *Ccc* 北舍 and *Hyylc* 舍北 is that *Hyylc* maintains the positional parallelism of 北 and 南, while *Ccc* keeps the phrases 北舍 and 南鄰 parallel, though in different positions in the line. The latter is consonant with parallelism in *ku-feng* and the style of the poem as a whole; the impulse to positional parallelism is characteristic of "new style" verse. *Qiəi-qiəi* 依依 describes the dense foliage of a tree, though a willow is the tree with which it is usually linked.

11–12. In the *Hyylc* and *Wyyh* versions, this couplet occupies lines 9 and 10. Line 11 could be interpreted, "All that have feelings have cast me off" (encompassing Wei and the sentient rats and wrens, but excluding the pine).

13. Literally, "You, sir, your substance is a thousand *zim* (high)."

14. "Heaven's moisture," *Ten-djhaek* 天澤, was a dead metaphor for imperial favor; but but the use of the conventional tree metaphor returns something of *Ten-djhaek*'s original force.

15. For 以 *Wyyh* reads 也. For *biət-dzhəi* 不材, see note 07767, line 3. The pun between "timber" 材 and "talent" 才 appears here.

16. This is the virtue of the useless "mountain tree" mentioned in line 2.

13418: *CTs*, pp. 2890–91; *Hyylc* in *TjhTs*, p. 67; *Twt* 17A.6a; *Tscs*, p. 392.
Rhymes: 1 *shiĕu*, 2 *xĕu*, 4 *dĕu*, 5 *zhui*, 6 *dzhi*, 8 *hyuɛ*. Regulated with permissible violation for *tse* rhyme in the sixth position of the second line. The second and third couplets are both "B" form couplets, acceptable across a rhyme change.

1. For 山 *Twt* and *Tscs* read 人 ("another man's home"). A "home in the mountains" with a landscape mural would emphasize the poet's mock confusion between the real scene and the painted scene.

2. Light comes in the dwelling and illuminates the landscape mural just as it illuminates the real landscape. *Hiuəi shrɛn shiĕu* 謂山曉 is actually indirect discourse: "claimed morning had come to the mountains."

5. Like the clouds and birds, the figure is painted. *Qà* 阿 is an affectionate and decidedly informal modifier, marking the relationship between the speaker and the person spoken of; it carries no semantic value.

6. Literally, "his rising is so slow."

7. Though it is perhaps extreme to translate *kung* 公 as "lord," it is an appellation of respect. It is sometimes applied on a more modest level, but since Yü is a grand secretary (fifth rank), respect is appropriate.

8. *Siĕu-dhĕi* 小弟, "little brother," is an affectionate term of address to one's juniors and inferiors which rarely finds its way into poetry. *Dɐn-tseng* 丹青, the "red and the green," was the common term for polychrome painting. *Nəng njiĕ hyuɛ* 能爾爲 is literally "can you do it?"

07571: *CTs*, p. 1608; *Chhcc* in *TjhTs*, p. 299; *Twt* 18.10b; *Tscs*, pp. 383–84.
Rhymes: 2 *miaeng*, 4 *tziɛng*, 6 *iɛng*, 8 *shraeng*. First couplet and third couplet regulated.

1. For 空 *Twt*, *Tscs*, and one edition of *Chhcc* read 虛. *Liou* 流 more commonly describes the movement of light than the moon itself.

2. *Sɑm-ngǒ* 三五 is the fifteenth of a lunar month, the time when the moon is full. For the first 明 *Twt* and *Tscs* read 皎.

3. In other words, it appears in daylight.

4. This line closely follows the ending of Ch'en Tzu-ang's first *Kan-yü*: here as there I am uncertain about the interpretation. The agent that "leads one stray" often follows *mei* 迷; cf. *mei-xua* 迷花. That one may well err in regard to who is a sage and who a fool is evidenced in Tu Fu's 11797.50. And in the *Kan-yü* usage, "perfect essence" clearly referred to the moon. Thus, we have one "led astray in regard to who is sage and who fool by its perfect essence."

5. An echo of the third line of Li Po's famous eighth *Ku-feng* (07872).

7. For 夜 *Twt* and *Tscs* read 已.

8. For 還復 *Twt* and *Tscs* read 復更.

07563: *CTs*, p. 1606; *Ccc* in *TjhTs*, p. 31; *Wyyh* 211.5b; *Yfsc* 62.3b–4a; *Tscs*, p. 385.
Rhymes: 1 *tsin*, 2 *njin*, 4 *miɑn* (*t'ung-yün*); 6 *tziɛk*, 8 *mɑt* (pseudoarchaic rhyme); 9, 10 *giɑi*, 12 *biɑi*, 14 *giuɑi* (*p'ing-shui*). I have followed the *Ccc* text here because it uses the kind of approximate, pseudoarchaic rhyme that is also found in Tu Fu. The variants in the later anthologies bring the rhymes in the second rhyme group into greater agreement with conventional practice (5 *shiuɛt*, 6 *bhyɛt*).
Title: *Byi-tzɑi haeng* 悲哉行 is literally, "Ballad: Is It Not Sad!" The *Yüeh-fu chieh-t'i* (cited in *Yfsc*) explains the general theme as "the sadness stirred in a traveler as he encounters things."

2. For 遠 *Tscs* reads 孤. *Sàng* 喪 in this case does not necessarily mean "lose" by reason of death, but rather to "lose" or "leave behind" with no hope of returning; for an analogous use, see Cheng notes to Little Preface of *Shih* 124.

4. For this line *Yfsc* reads 誰忍聞可聞, clearly a textual confusion.

5. For 見 *Wyyh*, *Yfsc*, and *Tscs* read 說. One can "hear" the songs and "hear of" one's loved ones in the songs, but one cannot "see," *gèn* 見, them.

6. For 形迹 *Wyyh*, *Yfsc*, and *Tscs* read 期別. *Heng-tziɛk* 形迹 is literally "form and traces," with "form" referring to sight of the person.

8. *Shrim-zhin* 參辰 refers to the constellations *shrim* 參 and *shiɑng* 商, whose positions were such that they never appeared in the heavens at the same time. Thus, they became a set metaphor for those long parted, who had no chance to meet. It is uncertain why the wanderer might wait on their setting.

9–10. In both lines, for 常 *Wyyh* reads 恒.

12. *Zhiě-biɑi* 是非, translated loosely as "inner struggles," is literally "is so and is not so": *zhi -biɑi* refers to problems of value, propriety, and truth, to situations in which such questions arise. The opposite is not a dangerous amorality, but a freedom of spirit that transcends such concerns.

13–14. In both lines, for 遊 *Tscs* reads 行.

07573: *CTs*, p. 1609; *Chhcc* (variant text) in *TjhTs*, pp. 314–15; *Wyyh* 156.5a–5b.
Rhymes: 2 *giaeng*, 4 *huaeng*, 6 *meng*, 8 *heng*, 10 *neng*, 12 *kiɛng*, 14 *zhiɛng*, 16 *dzhiɛng*. *T'ung-yün*. The fourth and last two couplets are regulated.
Text: The text of this poem is in very poor shape. I have followed the variant *Chhcc* text quoted in the collation in *TjhTs*, but in two cases have taken a *Wyyh* reading over it. Not only is the *Wyyh* text substantially different from the *Chhcc*, the *Wyyh* notes variants from the *Chhcc* which are different from the extant *Chhcc* text.

1–2. The Pien River flows down into the Huai and was the standard river route to follow when going from Lo-yang and Ho-nan to the south. Sung-chou and the ancient region of Liang were on the south side of the Yellow River east of Lo-yang and Pien-chou. The river travelers would reach the Yangtze through the Huai, then travel upstream to reach the ancient region of Ch'u. Ching-chou was a definite location in the south-central region, but Ching was a poetic term for the Ch'u region in general. For 荊 *Wyyh* reads 城. The use of *dzhì* 自 and *jiɑ* 之 as verbs here is somewhat archaic.

3. For 潮 *Wyyh* reads 漸.

5. Using the *Chhcc* version of the line given in Wyyh. The *TjhTs* version of Chhcc reads 大河海東注; *Wyyh* reads 大河噴東注; as another variant *Wyyh* offers 大河東注海.

6. For 眢 *Wyyh* gives 昏 as the *Chhcc* reading. *Ghiuən-dhŭng* 羣動 means "multitudes of animals and birds"; see use in line 8 of Li Po's *Ku-feng* XXV (07889), where "The multitude of creatures compete in flying and fleeing" 羣動爭飛奔: such "flight" and "running" pairs often themselves become ornamental terms for "birds and animals."

8. For 黃 *Wyyh* reads 黑; for 虎 *Wyyh* reads 馬. In the former variant, note that *Wyyh* cleans up the parallelism; in the latter variant, *Wyyh* provides a more common compound, echoing the *Ch'iu-shui* chapter of the *Chuang-tzu*.

9. Here adopting the *Wyyh* reading of 適, instead of the *Chhcc* (*TjhTs*) reading 失.

10. For 危 *Wyyh* reads 色. This is a rhetorical question: "How could I be at peace (even) for a moment?"

11–12. As often, the uncertain archaism of a T'ang poet can lead to problems in interpretation; that the problems are not those of a modern reader alone is indicated by the variants. *Wyyh* reads 爲 for 於, which must have been a somewhat awkward way of saying "Who holds human life lightly?" Another variant given by *Wyyh* for the first two characters in line 12 is 後將. Finally, *Wyyh* offers the incomprehensible 熟於 as the *Chhcc* reading ("I am well familiar with the lightness of human life"??). I have followed the *Chhcc* reading given in *TjhTs*, taking *zhiuk-qiu* 孰於 something like *zhiuk-njiɑk* 孰若: "How can it compare to?"

14. For 存誠 *Wyyh* has the incongruously pragmatic 有成.

16. For 應 *Wyyh* has 仍.

CHAPTER 13

13284: *CTs*, p. 2849; [*Khc* in *TjhTs*, pp. 178–79]; *Wyyh* 312.7a; *Tscs*, p. 394.
Rhymes: 2 *liou*, 4 *lou*. Regulated.
Attribution: In *Khc*, the earliest source for the poem, this quatrain is attributed to the otherwise unknown Chu Pin 朱斌 (09955). Famous quatrains like this one often appear with a variety of authors, and their authenticity is virtually impossible to determine.
Title: The *Khc* version simply has 登樓. *Wyyh* has 鸛鵲樓 (miswritten 觀雀); *Tscs* has 觀鵲樓. This tower supposedly overlooked the Yellow River at P'u-chou, in modern Shansi.

13285: *CTs*, p. 2849; *Tscs*, p. 394.
Rhymes: 2 *hɑ*, 4 *dɑ*. Regulated.

3. Literally, "Recently the suffering of being snapped off...."

05667: *CTs*, p. 1203; *Hyylc* in *TjhTs*, p. 94; *Wyyh* 205.5b; *Tscs*, p. 233.
Rhymes: 2 *giuəi*, 4 *biəi*. Technically regulated, with permissible violation in the fourth position of the first line; however, the repetition in the first couplet goes against the spirit of regulation.
Text: Repetition was permitted in songlike quatrains such as this, but the quatrain has far too much repetition, especially for a regulated poem. The textual variants in the *Wyyh* version try to tone down this excess, and to do away with the painful redundancy in line 3. Thus, the first 送 is changed to 與; the second 送 is changed to 憶. And in the third line, 鳥 is changed to 起.
Title: *Wyyh* gives 古意 as the title.

1–2. I have taken the subject of this couplet to be the mandarin ducks to resolve the problem of *sùng* 送 in the two lines and to explain the *tɑ* 他 in line 4. It would be possible to take the subject as the poet, but in that case we would have an unusual use of *sùng* for meeting the one returning and coming back with him. The use of the mandarin ducks may imply a female *yüeh-fu* persona as the subject, but the difficulty of *sùng* would remain. However, *sùng* would be appropriate if the person in the boat were accompanied by mandarin ducks. (A female *yüeh-fu* persona may still be the implicit point of view.) The *Wyyh* version definitely implies that the poet is the speaker.

4. *Tɑ* 他 implies "elsewhere" (as opposed to "here") or "on their own" (as opposed to "on your behalf" accompanying).

05668: *CTs*, p. 1203; *Ttc* in *TjhTs*, p. 464; *Wyyh* 205.5b; *Tscs*, p. 232.
Rhymes: 2 *jiou*, 4 *iou*. Regulated.
Text: I have followed here the *Ttc* text.
Title: *Wyyh* and *Tscs* give 古意 as the title.

1. For 時 *Wyyh* and *Tscs* read 來.
2. For 更 *Wyyh* and *Tscs* read 却. *Piɑng-jiou* 芳洲, literally "fragrant low, sandy isles," are isles upon which flowering plants and trees grow.

13295: *CTs*, p. 2852; *Hyylc* in *TjhTs*, p. 88; *Wyyh* 211.6a.
Rhymes: 2 *dzhəi*, 4 *məi*, 6 *huəi*, 8 *gəi*, 10 *ləi*, 12 *gəi*.
Title: Literally, "Ballad: Is There Not Something About Which I Feel Strongly?" The first twelve of twenty-four lines are quoted.

4. *Wyyh* reads 因 for 用. Since the traditional metaphor for the relation between ruler and minister is one of lovers, the person who recommends an aspiring official is a "go-between." This line is literally, "I have use, but how could I act as my own go-between?"
11. For 雷 *Wyyh* reads 雲.
12. For 澤 *Wyyh* reads 下.

11973: *CTs*, pp. 2596–97; *Wyyh* 209.8a.
Rhymes: 1 *dzhiɛn*, 2 *dzhen*, 4 *biɛn*. Regulated.

1. For 鑲 *Wyyh* reads 乾: *liɛn-dzhiɛn* 連錢 and *liɛn-ghyɛn* 連乾 both refer to patterns of spots on a horse's pelt.
3. Clearly one function of the *kɑ* 珂, pendants hung on the bridle, was to signal the horse when to go.

11975: *CTs*, p. 2597; *Tjwscc* 3.14a.
Rhymes: 1 *djhin*, 2 *njin*, 4 *dzhin*. Regulated.

3. Wu-yüan was a Han commandery located beyond the Great Wall in modern Suiyüan, almost directly north of Ch'ang-an.
4. New Ch'in was a T'ang county, located in the northern tip of modern Shenhsi, about 300 kilometers southeast of Wu-yüan. The two place-names suggest the swiftness of the khan's movements.

11982: *CTs*, p. 2598; *Tjwscc* 3.14b.
Rhymes: 1 *iou*, 2 *jrhiou*, 4 *jiou*. Regulated, with permitted violation in the sixth position of the third line.
Title: Pa-ling is at the northeast edge of Lake Tung-t'ing. This poem is the first in a series of three.

1. *Ghiòu-iou* 舊遊, translated as "former comrades in travel," is a way of referring to old friends, those one "went around with."

CHAPTER 14

06082: *CTs*, p. 1300; Chao, p. 190; *Wycc* 4.2b; *Tscs*, p. 241.
Rhymes: 2 *xiǎng*, 4 *zhiǎng*. Unregulated.
Title: "Deer Enclosure" 鹿柴.

1–2. This couplet is based on one of the most common kinds of antithesis in a couplet, sight and sound, the two primary senses. *Xiǎng* 響 is not a direct sound, but rather a sound from far away, a sound from someplace unseen, a sound not directed at the hearer.
3. *Biaěn-qiaěng* 反景, like *biaěn-jièu* 反照, refers to the sunlight just before sunset: as the sun moves into the west, its last light is "cast back" eastward, in the direction opposite of the sun's movement. In a grove or a forest on a slope, such light will avoid the blocking foliage and illuminate the interior of the forest.

4. There is some question about the force of *bhiuk* 復 here: it may be no more than a coordinating "and" that joins the two lines; or *bhiuk* might be a strong "again," referring to a previous occasion when the sunlight fell upon the moss. A more serious problem is raised by *zhiăng* 上: in this tone the word should mean "rise," leading some commentators to take the line as "shines upon the green moss and goes up." On the other hand, such an unusual and artificial construction runs entirely counter to the style of the poem and the natural way of reading the line, which begs a dissonant *zhiàng*: "shines upon the green moss." I believe the latter reading is correct and is based on an unconscious misinterpretation of a poem by Hsieh T'iao in which *xiăng* and *zhiăng* are rhymed (*Wh* 30.17a–17b): Hsieh's very artful line reads 蒼苔依砌上, properly translated; "The green moss, along the steps, rises"; however, remembered without its parallel line, the line would read simply, "Green moss lies upon the steps." In its proper interpretation, Hsieh T'iao's is an artful construction, but not an ungainly one; however, to take Wang's line as "shines upon the green moss and rises" would demand an almost grotesque construction of the parts of the line. The legitimacy of Wang's usage may be confirmed by the ability to rhyme rising and falling tones, a practice that was to become common in later centuries.

13060: *CTs*, p. 2806; *HfJsc* 6.48b.
Rhymes: 2 *ləi*, 4 *dhəi*. Unregulated.
Title: "Mountain Lodge" 山館.

1. In addition to silence and stillness, *dzhek-dzhek* 寂寂 implies loneliness and isolation.

06984: *CTs*, p. 1482; *LScsc* 1.4b–5a.
Rhymes: 2 *liə̆*, 4 *shuĭ*. A peculiar kind of regulation, appearing in deflected rhyme poems, where a violation is permitted in the fourth position of the first line of the couplet.

06981: *CTs*, p. 1482; *LScsc* 1.4a–4b.
Rhymes: 2 *miaĕn*, 4 *hiuaĕn*. Unregulated.

1. *Tsɑng-tsɑng* 蒼蒼 can describe either the color of the bamboo vegetation or the color of sky in which the temple is set.
2. *Qĕu-qĕu* 杳杳 implies indistinctness as well as distance; in this case, the indistinctness is of the sounds of the bells.

18520: *CTs*, p. 3948; *TLhsc* 43.10a; *Tscs*, p. 662.
Rhymes: 1 *dzhiuɛt*, 2 *miɛt*, 4 *siuɛt*. Regulated with permissible violation in fourth position of first line: sequence of two "A" form couplets.

07067: *CTs*, p. 1497; *LScsc* 2.8a.
Rhymes: 2 *dzhen*, 4 *qen*, 6 *ten*, 8 *ben*. Regulated with permissible violation in fourth position of seventh line.
Title: The Ch'ing-ming Festival, literally "Clear and Bright," took place at the beginning of the third month.

2. *Pèi-ngèi* 睥睨 initially described a far, sweeping gaze, but it came to be applied to the crenellations in wallworks, which permitted the far, sweeping gaze.
4. The "new smoke" is from the fires rekindled after the three days of Cold Food Festival, ending two days before the Ch'ing-ming.
7. The variant here for 在何處 is 何處是, probably generated to make the tone pattern perfect.

12167: *CTs*, pp. 2635–36; *CKkc* 5.2a.
Rhymes: 2 *qiəi*, 4 *biəi*, 6 *giuəi*, 8 *miəi*. Regulated with permissible violation in the fourth position of the first line.

2. In addition to blurriness because of distance, *qiəi-qiəi* 依依 can suggest yearning. Usually the yearning is of someone not wishing to part from someone else, but in this case it might refer to Yüan's desire to reach his home.

5. The flowers do not actually "hasten the wine to readiness," but as markers of the approaching end of the year, they show the wine is reaching its term.

7. I have taken *iɛu* 遙, "from afar," as referring to Yüan's present position at the parting, yearning to be back home in the mountains; however, it is possible that the "afar" refers to the distance between his windows and the mountains he will see.

12249: *CTs*, p. 2652; *CKkc* 6.4b; *Wyyh* 319.1a; *Tscs*, p. 472.
Rhymes: 2 *djhim*, 4 *shim*, 6 *qim*, 8 *ghyim*, 10 *lim*, 12 *sim*. Regulated, with strong violation in fourth position of third line.
Title: *Wyyh* adds 屋 before 壁.

1. It is possible to take this line as purely descriptive: "At the mouth of the valley, fine streams and stones." However, *guk-kŏu* 谷口 probably refers to the Han recluse Cheng Tzu-chen, who commonly appears as an exemplary hermit in T'ang poetry under the kenning Mouth of Valley, *Guk-kŏu*, the place where Cheng practiced self-cultivation.

2. *Luk-djhim* 陸沈, "sinking on dry land," is a vivid term for reclusion.

3. For 下 *Wyyh* and *Tscs* read 上. *Wyyh* further notes that for 小 Ch'ien's collection reads 去.

4. For 火 *Wyyh* reads 雨; for 雲 *Wyyh* reads 林. The fires are literally "deep beyond the clouds": as the barrier *gɛk* 隔 refers to the edge of the clouds, the fires are simply "deep within the clouds."

5. The "color," *shriɔk* 色, probably refers to the entire creek valley and not just the water: there the path probably "sinks into" the vegetation.

7. Presumably the rainbows become "hidden," *dzhɑng* 藏, because they seem to disappear at the end, perhaps concealed by mist.

8. *Giaeng* 驚 usually suggests a "startled" movement, but here it is applied to the hawk's swift movement upward.

9. For 流 *Wyyh* reads 傷. *Zhiɛp-tsiɔ* 涉趣 is a problematic phrase, whose difficulty is increased because the following line is not parallel; it probably means to "fare through (someplace which has) appeal."

10. *Ziɛn lim* 羨林 would be "you yearn for these forests (from somewhere else)"; *ziɛn dzhəi lim* 羨在林 implies that he yearns to remain there.

11. A *huɑng-zhiŏu* 黃綬, a "yellow seal ribbon," was the mark of a lower official. *Siə* 思 here does not imply desire, as it often does; *kiɑk-siə* 卻思 is to "think back upon with brooding."

12. *Tziĕ-jiə sim* 紫芝心 is literally "purple *jiə* heart": the "purple *jiə*" was probably a kind of mushroom and was associated with the elixir of immortality.

12488: *CTs*, p. 2685; *CKkc* 10.3a.
Rhymes: 2 *miaĕn*, 4 *hiuaĕn*. First couplet regulated, though with violation in fifth position of first line.

1. Literally, "On the pool, so calm it never wearies (of being there)."

4. *Jhiəng-xiəng* 乘興 is literally to "ride one's impulse." The phrase is strongly associated with the famous story of Wang Hui-chih's impulsive journey to visit Tai K'uei, announcing that he had come *jhiəng-xiəng*, and now that the impulse was gone, he had no need to see Tai (*Shih-shuo hsin-yü* 3A, section 21.23)

12500: *CTs*, p. 2686; *CKkc* 10.5a.
Rhymes: 2 *zhiò*, 4 *kiù*. Unregulated
1. *Hiŏu-qiə* 有意 suggests intent.

12494: *CTs*, p. 2685; *CKkc* 10.4a.
Rhymes: 2 *tziok*, 4 *siuk*. Regulated with violation in the fifth position of the first line.

10081: *CTs*, p. 2155; *Wyyh* 292.10a.
Rhymes: 2 *kɑn*, 4 *hɑn*, 6 *guɑn*, 8 *dzhɑn*. Regulated.
Title: Ch'ang-chou just south of the Yangtze near its mouth, in modern Kiangsu.

5. Huang Pa began his career not as a member of the gentry but as a literate clerk; after the usual vicissitudes of official life he became minister (*Sc*, p. 2688). The analogy would have us consider Li's lowly post as an early stage in a glorious career.

6. For 罷 *Wyyh* reads 去.

7. *Zhiəng-chuin* 乘興 is literally "take advantage of the spring": it can suggest either spring pleasures or spring farm labor. *Miò* 務, to "work hard at one's duty," is the wrong word to apply to warfare and leads to a clear irony.

10045: *CTs*, p. 2148.
Rhymes: 2 *qen*, 4 *ten*, 6 *dhen*, 8 *piɛn*. Regulated, with permissible violation in fourth position of seventh line.
Title: Chü-jung was a county, whose location was just east-southeast of modern Nanking, in Kiangsu.

1. Chü-ch'ü was a pair of mountains in Chü-jung; one of the mountains was Mao-shan, famous for its Taoist coven. *Mò* 暮 is literally "darken with evening."

4. The use of *hò* 護, "guard" or "protect," is noteworthy here, and suggests ranks of clouds seeming to "protect" an open space in the sky.

8. *Piɛn-piɛn* 翩翩 is a binome describing a lightness of movement, often suggesting a kind of jauntiness.

12995: *CTs*, p. 2794; *Chhcc* in *TjhTs*, p. 276; *Yls* in *TjhTs*, p. 203; *Chc* in *TjhTs*, p. 338; *Wyyh* 201.3b; *Yfsc* 17.3a; *Tscs*, pp. 416, 782 (in the latter citation, the poem is misattributed); *HfJsc* 3.12b.
Rhymes: 1 *dung*, 2 *kung*, 4 *giung*, 6 *dhung*, 8 *djiung*. Regulated
Title: *Wu-shan Kao* 巫山高 was an early *yüeh-fu* title; *Chhcc* notes that the original Huang-fu Jan collection had 巫山峽 as the title. All anthology texts read *Wu-shan Kao*; indeed, the stability of the text of this poem through so many anthologies is most unusual.

1. "East of Pa," *Ba-dung* 巴東, was the name of a commandery. It is impossible to know whether 見 should be read as *hèn* here ("The Wu Gorges appear from Pa-tung") or as *gèn* ("The Wu Gorges can be seen from Pa-tung"). In either case, the thing that is seen or appears is the Wu Gorges and not Pa-tung: the more normal (and more pedestrian) order of such a line would be 巴東見巫峽.

3–4. This refers to the legend of the king of Ch'u's meeting with the goddess of Wu Mountain: in her parting song, the goddess claimed to be the "clouds" and "rain," which later became a standard metaphor for sexual encounters and appears here in parallel positions in the couplet. The "lodge" may refer to the goddess's dwelling or to the temple the king of Ch'u built for her (*Wh* 19.1b–2a).

8. For 秋 *Chhcc* reads 宵.

12817: *CTs*, p. 2757; *Han Hung shih-chi chiao-chu* 韓翃詩集校注, ed. Ch'en Wang-ho 陳王和 (preface 1973), pp. 404–9; *Ttc* in *TjhTs*, p. 648; *Wyyh* 157.10b; *Tscs*, pp. 468–69 (with anecdote).
Rhymes: 1 *xua*, 2 *zia*, 4 *ga*. Regulated.
Text: I have followed the *Ttc* text.
Title: *Wyyh* reads 寒食日即事.

1. For 開 *Wyyh* and *Han Hung shih-chi chiao-chu* read 飛.

2. These are the willows on the royal moat.

3. For 日暮 *Wyyh* reads 一夜. On Cold Food Festival, all fires were to be extinguished; this describes the relighting of the fires after the third day; cf. note 07067, line 4.

4. For 輕 *Wyyh* reads 青. There were several sets of "Five Lords" in the Han; Han Hung is here using the term to refer to the nobility in general.

14298: *CTs*, p. 3070.
Rhymes: 1 *djiuk*, 2 *guk*; 3 *lei*, 4 *nei*; 5 *lău*, 6 *său*; 7 *kung*, 8 *djiung*, 10 *dhung*; 11 *kŏ*, 12 *tŏ*, 14 *hiŏ*; 15 *giuəi*, 16 *biəi*, 18 *qiəi*.

1. This line sets the time as the spring planting season and functions somewhat like the *hsing* of the *Shih*.

2. The question "from what household," "of what family," *zhui-ga* 誰家, was common in *yüeh-fu*.

3. Lines with *mio . . . biət . . .* 無不 usually mean "no . . . but . . . "; however, here context makes it clear that it means "because they lack . . . they cannot. . . . "

4. *Piaen tzak nei* 翻作泥 is literally "turns over and becomes mud."

7. A *dhǒn* 囷 is a place for storing grain, here probably the grain for cattle feed However, it is possible that *ngiou-dhǒn* 牛囷 means "cattle and stored grain," in which case these are "gone," *kung* 空, because of "natural disasters and epidemics," *tzəi-iuaek* 災疫.

12. *Lò-njin* 路人 may be the "person on the road," the poet himself. The implication here is that they do not have time to chat, but must constantly pay attention to their work.

13. *Shriu-tung* 疏通, "to divide up thoroughly," is more commonly used for intellectual discriminations. *Huei-liǒng* 哇隴 refers to the ridges and embankments that separate one field from another.

14. *Jiěng-duàn* 整頓 is to "marshal" or "put in good order," often applied to military formations.

17–18. The effect of the flowers on the girls is because they are aware of the old metaphor of women as flowers.

14428: *CTs*, p. 3095.
Rhymes: 1 *shin*, 2 *jin*, 4 *djhin*, 6 *chuin*, 8 *bhyin*. Regulated

1. The first four characters are taken from *Analects* IX. 22: "If at forty or fifty a person is not heard of, then such a person is not worthy of awe" 四十五十而無聞焉，斯亦不是畏也已.

2. *Njim ten-jin* 任天真 was what T'ao Ch'ien was supposed to have done in Wang Wei's fourth "Offhand Composition" (05862).

3. *Bəi-djiung miət* 杯中物, the "thing in the cup," was a kenning for wine; it occurs in the poetry of T'ao Ch'ien but has currency later as well.

4. *Xaek-xaek* 赫赫 primarily describes shining light, but very early it came to be applied to the quality of "illustrious" fame and power.

5. A *duǎn-chrɛk* 短策 was originally a short riding crop, but here it is clearly a "walking stick"; *chrɛk* is often used in this sense in T'ang poetry. However, one often finds a play on the meaning of "plan" for *chrɛk*, and in this sense, *duǎn-chrɛk* would be "poor plans" (for self-advancement and service to the state); cf. notes 05797, line 13, and 05951, line 3.

6. If the reader heard a pun in line 5, he might well expect one in a parallel position in this line: *shriu-liɛm* 疏簾, the "blinds with open spaces," easily becomes 疏廉, "remiss in self-restraint."

14444: *CTs*, p. 3098.
Rhymes: 2 *děu*, 4 *xěu*. Unregulated.

4. *Siɑng-luɑn* 相亂 can refer to the external "disorder" of the rain scene, or it can be "throwing me (my heart) into confusion," referring to the effect of the rain in the poet.

14470: *CTs*, p. 3100.
Rhymes: 2 *sèi*, 4 *kiù*. Something seems wrong here: *sèi* and *kiù* are not adjacent *p'ing-shui* categories, and such bold *t'ung-yün* seems improper for this kind of poem. A textual problem may be involved. Unregulated.

1–2. This is a fairly common syntactic form in which some element in the third or fourth position of a pentasyllabic line is the object of what preceded and the subject of what follows: hence, "shadow" is the object of "soaks" and the subject of "chill"; "flowers" is the object of "brings down" and the subject of "tiny." We are speaking here of expected logical subjects and objects rather than bound grammatical functions; indeed, lines like these would admit a great variety of constructions in translation.

14510: *CTs*, p. 3105.
Rhymes: 1 *man*, 2 *lan*, 4 *han*. Regulated.

15545: *CTs*, p. 3314; *Wyyh* 307.4a.
Rhymes: 2 *shin*, 4 *njin*, 6 *bhyin*, 8 *djhin*. Regulated. These rhymes are extremely commonplace; cf. rhymes of 14428.
Title: For 胡居士觀 *Wyyh* reads 湖上觀. The *CTs* reading more accurately reflects the situation of the poem: Ssu-k'ung Shu is clearly speaking to someone here. The interpretation of this poem is highly contingent on the knowledge shared and presumed by Ssu-k'ung Shu and Hu; for example, the person who vows reclusion in line 5 might be either Hu, Wang Wei, or possibly even the poet himself. On the other hand, the *dzhəng* 曾 of line 7, in indicating the past, suggests the poem and its author.

    1. Plausible alternatives for the referents here might be "He whom we knew . . ." "Those whom you knew. . . ." *djiɛ-giə̌* 知己 is a friend who understands one's true nature.
    3. The reason the snow's blockage is "pointless" is because no one ever comes to visit the recluse.
    5–6. These lines probably are making reference to the contents of the poem.
    8. For 流 *Wyyh* reads 留.

15192: *CTs*, p. 3244; Wyyh 318.7b–8a.
Rhymes: 2 *chiuɛn*, 4 *dzhiuɛn*, 6 *dhen*, 8 *qen*. Regulated
Title: *Wyyh* omits 遊.

    2. *Dhuəi-iɑng* 頹陽, "tumbling Yang," is an elegant, courtly phrase for the setting sun.
    5. Perhaps a reference to the spot of 06091.
    7. For 路去 *Wyyh* reads 去路.

14881: *CTs*, p. 3179; *Chc* in *TjhTs*, p. 328; *Yhc* in *TjhTs*, pp. 361–62; *Wyyh* 273.4a; *Tscs*, p. 467.
    Also attributed to Yen Wei, 13534, but with little authority.
Rhymes: 2 *byi*, 4 *zhiə*, 6 *djhi*, 8 *ghiə*. Regulated
Text: The text used is the *Chc* text.

    1. For 衰 *Wyyh* reads 秋.
    3. For 出 *Yhc* reads 入.
    5. For 早 *Tscs* reads 慣.
    7. For 向 *Yhc* reads 見. and *Wyyh* reads 問.
    8. For 所 *Yhc* reads 處.

13823: *CTs*, p. 2976.
Rhymes: 2 *xiəi*, 4 *giuəi*, 6 *miəi*, 8 *qiəi*. Regulated, with permissible violation in fourth position of seventh line.
Title: "In Sung" 宋中.

    2. Literally, "As the years deepen, white bones are (have become) few."
    8. The *ziə̌* 似, "as if," suggests that in this case *qiəi-qiəi* 依依 means "full of longing" rather than "blurry and unclear." The untruth implicit in *ziə̌* would be more appropriate for a transference of human feelings to the mountains.

14716: *CTs*, p. 3147.
Rhymes: 1 *liɑng*, 2 *xiɑng*, 4 *chriɑng*. Regulated with permissible violation in sixth position of third line.
    1. *Haeng-dɑ* 行多 is a particularly unpoetic way to refer to the soldier's long journey.
    3. *Bhung* 蓬 in its various compounds *bhung-dhou* 蓬頭, *bhung-biaet* 蓬髮, and *bhung-bìn* 蓬鬢 refers to messy hair.
    4. *Gyim-chriɑng* 金瘡, "metal scars," are scars from weapons.

15601: *CTs*, p. 3324; *Ttc* in *TjhTs*, p. 544. As 13490, attributed to Han Huang, a version of the poem appears in *Wyyh* 213.2a and Tscs, p. 368.
Rhymes: 1 *dzhen*, 2 *iɛn*, 4 *nen*. Regulated.
Text: I follow the *Ttc* text here; the Han Huang version has a different title and a substantially different first couplet.
Title: The Han Huang version bears the title "Listening to Music: In Depression I Tell of Myself" 聽樂悵然自述. Han Huang's first couplet reads:

All life's events wound my heart, I face the pipes and strings,	萬事傷心對管絃
My whole body holding back tears, I look into springtime mist.	一身含淚向春煙

The title and first couplet make the Han Huang version a very different poem and far less internally consistent than the Ssu-k'ung Shu version.

    1. Literally, "Ten thousand problems wound my heart. . . . "
    2. *Xua-iɛn* 花筵 is a mat woven with flower designs, but *xua* is strongly associated with women, an association that would be called to the foreground in this context, and *iɛn* is a standard synecdoche for a party, here probably a dance performance by the concubine.
    4. *Lɑk siɛu-nen* 樂小年 may be "to give pleasure to his youth" or even "to give pleasure to your youth."

14747: *CTs*, p. 3153; *Yls* in *TjhTs*, p. 216.
Rhymes: 1 *biung*, 2 *giung*, 4 *djiung*. Regulated.
Title: 和張僕射塞下曲.

14748: *CTs*, p. 3153; *Yls* in *Tscs*, p. 216. In *Tscs*, p. 473, this poem is misattributed to Ch'ien Ch'i.
Rhymes: 1 *gɑu*, 2 *dhɑu*, 4 *dɑu*. Regulated.
    1. To say of a moonless night that the "moon is black" was very bold.

13955: *CTs*, p. 3002; *Chc* in *TjhTs*, p. 326; *Yhc* in *TjhTs*, p. 376 (attributed to Li Tuan); *Ttc* in *TjhTs*, p. 476; *Twt* 18.18b; *Wyyh* 151.2b–3a (attributed to Wang Ch'ang-ling!); *Tscs*, p. 465.
Rhymes: 2 *ngiŭ*, 4 *shiŭ*. Unregulated.

    2. It is interesting that only *Chc* gives the classically proper (and tonally preferable) 與誰 here; all other texts read the more colloquial 誰與.
    4. *Huɑ-shiŭ* 禾黍 is literally "rice and millet": in the Little Preface to *Shih* 65, *huɑ-shiŭ* was what was supposed to have been growing over the ruins of the Chou capital; moreover, *huɑ-shiŭ* is mentioned in the song of the Shang prince Chi-tzu, grieving over the ruins of the old Shang capital (*Sc*, p. 1621).

CHAPTER 15

44216: *CTs*, p. 9124; *Wyyh* 163.10b; *Tscs*, pp. 1064–65 (followed by matching poem by Liu Ch'ang-ch'ing).
Rhymes: 2 *hiuən*, 4 *miən*, 6 *biən*, 8 *miən*. Regulated, but with a strong, impermissible violation in the fourth position of the fourth line.
Title: *Tscs* omits 宜豐. Yi-feng was a county in southern Kiangsu.

    2. *Dhùng-tjiet* 洞徹, translated as "breaking through," describes the movement of the new stream downhill, around obstacles.
    3. A *jiɛu* 沼 is a winding, and here probably natural, pond: the "lowering" of the water level of the pond indicates that it is one of the sources of the "new spring."
    5. *CTs* reads here 素將空意合. *Kung-shriək* 空色 is a Buddhist term for the vacuity of all percepts; besides indicating the color or visual qualities of a thing exclusive of form, *shriək* implies a sensuous attractiveness, which can ensnare the unenlightened. The stream "cleans" or "purifies,"

dzhièng 淨, the "bright beauty" (*shriək*) probably by flowing over things and either muting the colors of making them seem illusory.

   6. For 素 *CTs* reads 淨. The *CTs* reading eliminates the ambiguity of *sò* here: the substitution in the *CTs* text suggests that *sò* was taken as "colorless" or "pure"; in that case, the line would be translated, "Its purity is distinct from that of the average stream." However, parallel construction indicates that the *sò* should be interpreted as "always." Here the double function of *sò* should be interpreted as "always." Here the double function of *sò* is so obvious that the word play is probably intentional.

   7. For 每到 *Tscs* reads 若對. *Wyyh* reads 霄 for 宵, but this would seem to be an unintentional error.

44249: *CTs*, p. 9130; *Wyyh* 236.9a.
Rhymes: 1 *kəi*, 2 *ləi*, 4 *huəi*. Regulated.

   3. *Ngǎ* 我, "I," is the technical term for the "self."

44264: *CTs*, p. 9133; *Yün-hsi yu-yi* (Taipei: Kuang-ming, 1970), p. 5; *Tscs*, pp. 685–86, 1064; *Tshhc* 2.2a–2b.
Rhymes: 2 *shin*, 4 *njin*. Regulated.

   2. *Iong-shin* 容身, literally, "admits the body," is commonly associated with adequacy and comfort with little.
   3. *Yün-hsi yu-yi* and the first *Tscs* occurrence read 去 for 好, which appears in the second *Tscs* occurrence and *CTs*. Literally, "When I meet someone, they always say. . . ."

44261: *CTs*, p. 9132; *Tshhc* 2.2a.
Rhymes: 1 *siuɛt*, 2 *ngiuaet*, 4 *iuɛt*. The poem would be regulated if we read *tzǎi* 載 instead on *nen* 年 in the second position of line 3.
Title: An alternative title is 雲門雪夜. From Ling-ch'e's other poems, it is apparent that East Forest Temple was by no means deserted.

   1. For 雪 *Tshhc* reads 穴.
   3. *Tshhc* notes this refers to Master Lung-shu 龍樹大師.
   4. The interpretation of the last line here is uncertain; for a similar use of 說 in connection with "ghosts and gods," see *Kuo-yü*, Ch'u-yü II (*SPTK*) 18.10b.

44311: *CTs*, p. 9144; *Wyyh* 256.10a.
Rhymes: 2 *shraeng*, 4 *haeng*, 6 *zhiɛng*, 8 *biaeng*, 10 *dzhiɛng*, 12 *kiaeng*. Regulated.
Title: Hsia-chou was on the Yangtze, upstream from Chiang-ling and Tung-t'ing.

   2. *Qiou-dhǎu* 憂道 is a phrase from *Analects* XV.31: "The good man is concerned for the Way and not concerned about poverty." It would be easy to transfer "Way" to the Buddhist "way," but the *sui* 雖 of the first line indicates that the Confucian Way of public concern is meant here. Since the monk is on a journey, *qiou-dhǎu* may also have an element of "concern for my journey." It is further possible that *qiou-dhǎu* is coordinate with *lɑu-shraeng* 勞生: "I am concerned for the Way and bring trouble to my life." The meaning is approximately the same in either case.
   7. Chiao-ho 交河 was the Central Asian area around Turfan; except in occasional poetry written on journeys through the frontier regions, poets were often imprecise in their identification of Central Asian tribes and regions. The reference here is uncertain: it may indicate Tibetan incursions, and it may refer to the nomad troops loosely allied to the imperial army.
   8. Thinwillow Camp 細柳營 had been located on the Thinwillow Plain, southwest of Ch'ang-an. An important Han military camp had been located there, and T'ang poets used it commonly to refer to places where the imperial army was mustered.
   12. Reading variant 謝 instead of 許.

44312: *CTs*, p. 9144; *Wyyh* 256.10b.
Rhymes: 2 *guin*, 4 *chuin*, 6 *shin*, 8 *njin*, 10 *bhyin*, 12 *tsin*. Regulated.

6. *Guang-qim* 光陰, "light and dark," commonly are metonymy for the passage of time. *Huàn-shin* 幻身, "illusion-body," is a Buddhist term.

7. *Mɐt-lò* 末路, "end of the road," was a conventional metaphor for the end of life.

8. *Xiàng (haeng) njin* 向 (行) 人 is probably short for *xiàng njin shiuɐt* 向人說, "tell to someone."

10. *Iok qièm bhyin* 欲厭貧, translated as "I weary of poverty," is literally "almost (utterly) weary of poverty."

12. *Chiɛk-huèn* 赤縣, literally the "red county," originally was a kenning for imperial territory, but in the T'ang it was used especially for the capital region. *Xiɑng-tsin* are specifically those of one's native region (who might be presumed, on the model of a village society, to be "kin").

44799: *CTs*, p. 9243; *Cjc* 6.4a; *Wyyh* 285.5b
Rhymes: 2 *shra*, 4 *zia*, 6 *shia*, 8 *nga*. Regulated.
Title: *Biò-dək* 賦得 indicates composition to a set topic.

1. *Già-zhiɛk* 架石 is literally "made a framework of stone"; however, this does not necessarily indicate that the bridge is man-made: the subject could be impersonal. *Ha* 霞, "rose cloud," is a not uncommon attributive for high sandstone cliffs. There was a Rose-Cloud Cliff Mountain in the T'ien-t'ai group and a famous stone bridge on T'ien-t'ai; however, if these famous places were meant, the subject would probably have required more specific allusion to the area.

2. For 壁 *Wyyh* reads 流. *Liou* 流 is the easier reading: not only does it explain the second hemistich, it forms the more common compound *huen-liou* 懸流, "cascade." However, *Wyyh* has a habit of "cleaning up" its texts and providing more obvious readings.

3. The "shadow" or "reflection" is of course the bridge reflected in the stream below.

4. *Sèi* 細, "tiny," first appears as an attribute of wind in the eighth century.

44842: *CTs*, p. 9251; *Cjc* 6.11b.
Rhymes: 1 *ten*, 2 *tzien*, 4 *dzhiuɐn*. Regulated, two "B" form couplets.

1. For *mung-lung* 蒙籠, see note 05732, line 4.

2. *Lek-lek* 瀝瀝 should describe the sound of water, but here, as an attributive of sunlit sands, the binome is probably the homophonous 歷歷, describing clarity or brightness. *Tzien-tzien* 濺濺 describes the swift flowing of water and is closely related to *tsièn-tsièn* 淺淺; see 06090, note to line 2.

3. *Hiò-njin* 羽人, "winged being," was a common kenning for an immortal, here referring to Red Pine.

4. Though the supposed origin of these flowers is different, the image here echoes numerous earlier poems on Peach Blossom Spring.

44874: *CTs*, p. 9257; *Cjc* 7.3b–4a.
Rhymes: 2 *gek*, 3 *hɛk*, 4 *chiɛk* (*t'ung-yün*); 5 *ziɑng*, 6 *haeng*, 8 *bhɑng* (*t'ung-yün*); 9 *njit*, 10 *it*, 12 *dzhit*; 13 *zhiok*, 14 *kiok*, 16 *tziok*.
Title: *Duɑn-gung* 端公 was an alternative title for a Censor of the Court of General Affairs 侍御史. With their duty to exercise moral judgment, censors were often associated with things of autumn, such as frost or, as here, hawks. The comparison of the poem suggests the image of Tu Fu's 10857.12, and near echoes of Tu Fu's poetry occur throughout; e.g., for line 3, cf. 10814.4, 10864.4.

1. *Jhin-tzuìn* 神駿 is properly the "godlike and glorious steed," and it would be just as possible to take the line, "The ancients appreciated godlike and glorious steeds, but how can they compare to . . . ?" But *zhuìn* 駿, written also with the man radical 俊, came to be applied to all forms of excellence, and it is in that general sense I have taken it here: thus, the hawk is the highest example within the larger category *jhin-tzuìn*.

2. *Gek* 擊, translated as "on the kill," is the "striking" of the bird of prey.

4. However one conceived its material composition, "Heaven" was thought of as a plane above the "empty" sky, and thus very high things were said to be "near" it. *Jiɛ̆-chiɛk* 咫尺, "an inch or foot," was commonly used to express close proximity.

6. These birds act out of fear of the hawk's power.

8. *Tseng-ha* 青霞 "blue clouds," like *tseng-hiuɐn* 青雲, suggest spiritual and social "loftiness,"

proximity to heaven and the court. *Ha* 霞 alone usually suggests "rose clouds," but *ha* basically refers to shape, texture, and some color.

10. *Biờn-it* 奮逸 suggests the rapid shaking of wings and soaring up.

11. It is unclear whether *hiuən-sòi* 雲塞, "cloud-passes," refers to actual passes with clouds in them or to formations of cloud that resemble passes. *Gǎu-iɛp mei* 攬葉迷 is literally "disturbs the leaves and is lost." The "leaves" here are probably *hiuən-iɛp* 雲葉, "cloud-leaves," wisps of cloud.

12. *Xua* 花, "flowers" and "snowflakes," is the parallel for leaves in the preceding line.

13. *Zhiok* 屬, to "attach," is often used with letting one's thoughts or feelings consider, hope for, or be stirred by something in the external world. Literally, Wang's "lofty feelings have something to which to attach themselves." The reason Wang's feelings settle on the hawk is affinity, hence the translation "find fellowship of kind."

16. One function of poetry is to "exhaust" intent or emotions; however, the emotions may be so great they "cannot be exhausted." *Qiờ biờt-tziok* 意不足 suggests that the poet has some surplus of emotion or that the connection between Wang and the bird is deeper than he has expressed in the poem.

44814: *CTs*, p. 9246; *Cjc* 6.6a–6b; *Wyyh* 159.5b.
Rhymes: 2 *piong*, 4 *tziong*, 6 *djhiong*. Regulated with strong violation in fourth position of fourth line.

1. *Lěu-luờn* 撩亂 describes confusion and intermingling, here of the colors of the mountain. For 色 *Wyyh* reads 山.

2. To use the first-person pronoun here is strong and merits the playful "my own middle peak."

3. The first hemistich may be conditional: "When there are no problems. . . ."

4. *Niɛp qiởu-tziong* 躡幽蹤 is literally "to tread in secluded traces," i.e., to follow in the footsteps of other recluses who have gone off into seclusion.

6. Literally, "Cold azure, even more layer upon layer." *Djiong-djiong* 重重 refers to the "layers" of mountains.

44845: *CTs*, p. 9251; *Cjc* 6.12a.
Rhymes: 1 *gɛn*, 2 *hɛn*, 4 *guan*. Regulated.

1. Literally, "Raucous, contentious noises, together between 'is so' and 'is not so.'" The people making such noises are caught up in the distinction between "true" and "false."

44853: *CTs*, p. 9252; *Cjc* 6.13a.
Rhymes: 1 *dhɑng*, 2 *bhiɑng*, 4 *ghiuɑng*. Regulated.

1. *Dhɑng* 蕩, "sweep over" or "sweep away," carries implications of freedom from restraint and of cleansing in compounds like this.

44855: *CTs*, p. 9252; *Cjc* 6.13a.
Rhymes: 2 *huan*, 4 *shrɛn*, 6 *gɛn*. Regulated.

1. *Qiǒn-tziɛk* 隱跡 is literally "hide my traces"; i.e., hide the evidence and memory of what I do.

2. *Kiɑk* 卻, translated as "even," indicates a reversal of expectations.

3. *Kiuaèm* 欠, "lack," is highly unliterary in this use in the T'ang.

6. Literally, "Truth is in its midst." *Jin-qiờ* 真意, "true concept," is as close as literary Chinese comes to the abstraction Truth.

44856; *CTs*, p. 9252; *Cjc* 6.13a.
Rhymes: 2 *piaen*, 4 *suən*. Regulated with permissible violation in the fourth position of the first line.

1. *Biət-hak* 不學 may suggest not that he won't try to learn the language but that he won't even try to form the sounds.

2. *Tsiong* 從 here is short for *tsiong-ləi* 從來.

4. *Lɑk-shraèi* 樂殺 is literally "please utterly."

43155: *CTs*, p. 8885; *Cjc* 10.8b.
Rhymes: 1 *jiou*, 2 *xiou*, 3 *dhou*, 4 *liou*. Unregulated.
Title: A "Big Talk" *fu* was attributed to Sung Yü (*Ywlc*, p. 346), and a command series of "Big Talk" and "Little Talk" *shih* from the Liang can be found in *Ywlc*, pp. 345–46. These pieces are exactly the same kind of amusing hyperbole found here.

2. The "roc," *bhəng* 鵬, and "leviathan," *guən* 鯤, are the two fabulous creatures of immense proportions found in the first chapter of the *Chuang-tzu*. That one metamorphoses into the other is of no significance here.

3. Li O's line is the weakest of the three.

43157: *CTs*, p. 8885; *Cjc* 10.8b–9a.
Rhymes: 1 *xiə̌*, 2 *zhǐ*, 3 *tziə̌*, 4 *zhiə̌*. Unregulated.

1. The "River of Suffering," *kǒ-hɑ* 苦河, was a conventional Buddhist emblem of the suffering of the process of life.

4. *Biàng-gǎ* 放假 occurs much later as "to be on vacation": clearly the same meaning existed in the T'ang as well.

43158: *CTs*, p. 8886; *Cjc* 10.9a.
Rhymes: 1 *xiou*, 2 *liou*, 3 *siou*, 4 *liou*. The homophones in close proximity here would not be permitted as rhymes in more formal poetry.

1. *Duəi* 鎚 are Szechwanese steamed dumplings.

2. Literally, "When something is about to be roasted, he stands and waits, the drool flowing criss-cross."

3. *Dzhiɑk* 嚼 is to "grind one's teeth together," here to make gnawing motions. *Kə̌ng* 肯, as often, here indicates a question.

4. I take this line as a mock example of the glutton showing shame.

43242: *CTs*, p. 8933; *Cjc* 10.2b.
Rhymes: 2 *tsim*, 4 *djhim*, 6 *shim*, 8 *gyim*, 10 *njim*, 12 *lim*. Regulated, though there is a violation in the fourth position of the first line of Chiao-jan's second couplet.

1. For *ui* 遺, see note to 11232, line 4. *Biung-djhin* 風塵 often suggests warfare, but here the physical image would be associated with the vicissitudes of history.

2. Note here how that which actually does the "eating away," *tsim* 侵, is transferred to an attribute of the path.

3. Note that *qiaeng-leng* 英靈, translated freely as "bright soul," does not necessarily imply one dead; it can also refer to a superior and living spirit, as in the *Ho-yüeh ying-ling chi* title. In addition to silence, *dzhek-mɑk* 寂寞 implies loneliness and desolation.

4. *Iong-hiuèi* 容衛 are guards, often—but not exclusively—applying to the guardians of a tomb; cf. 06008. *Iong* probably means "adorned" here. For an extensive discussion of this compound, see Chao, p. 128.

5. Hsiang Yü began his struggle for the empire as warlord from the former region of Greater Ch'u.

7. In other words, when they submitted to Han Kao-tsu.

8. The *tseng-shriə̌* 青史 are literally the "green histories," so called because they were written on dried slips of bamboo. In the T'ang the phrase had come to mean simply "histories," and especially "ancient histories."

9. The "arraying of the stars," *seng-dzhiò* 星聚, can be an omen of the appearance of an emperor, in this case Han Kao-tsu.

10. That "Heaven destroyed" him was the complaint of Hsiang Yü before his death (*Sc*, p. 334).

13621: *CTs*, p. 2940; *KHyc* 2.11a.
Rhymes: 2 *ngiok*, 3 *tziok*, 5 *shiok*; 6 *zhiɛng*, (7 *seng*,) 8 *nɛng*, 9 *haeng*; 10 *biaet*, 11 *dzhiuɛt*, 13 *ngiuaet*.

1. *Kiɛng-bhɑk* 輕薄 implies frivolity and lack of depth or seriousness; it is applied particularly to the way a man treats women, but its application is broader.
2. "Jade" color is a mark of beauty.
3. The "purple lanes," *tziɛ̌-maek* 紫陌, were the streets of the capital.
5. *Tsiɛk* 刺, "pierce," describes embroidery on the gown. What the "snow" might be is uncertain unless it is rhino horn (rather than rhino designs). *Shraeng sei shiok* 生犀束 is difficult: *shiok* in this context probably refers to some kind of strapping or belting. If the line is taken in parallel to the preceding line, it becomes "living rhinos are strapped (in)," probably referring to a design on the gown which is crossed by straps. It could, however, be some sort of strap made out of rhino hide.
7. I have no idea what this line refers to, unless it is a metaphor for the trees.
8. "Rosy flesh," *hung-gyi* 紅肌, might possibly describe the young man's wine-flushed skin or the youthful complexion of a young lady, but most likely it is "red meat," as in *Wh* 35.18b. In *KHyc* 凝 is given as a variant for 撑. (The same variant for *nɛng* appears in 20685.) *Piət-piət* 拂拂 should describe the movement of something in the wind, and unless another binome is meant, its application here is uncertain. This line and the preceding line are most unusual; such obscurity, when it is not simply a stylistic posture (as it may well be here), often marks a taboo subject, and the taboo subject most appropriate in this case would be a sexual encounter.

13627: *CTs*, p. 2941; *KHyc* 2.2b; *Ttc* in *TjhTs*, pp. 495–96; *Wyyh* 200.9b (here and in *KHyc* the series is treated as one long poem, with this as the second stanza); *Yfsc* 71.2a.
Rhymes: 2 *liək*, 3 *jhiək*, 5 *shiək*; 6 *siɛu*, 7 *deu*, 8 *myɛu*; 11 *dhǎu*, 13 *xǎu*.

2. For 空 *KHyc*, *Wyyh*, and *Yfsc* read 徒.
3. For 食 *KHyc*, *Wyyh*, and *Yfsc* read 喫.
4. This is the case to which the first two metaphors of futility apply.
5. This could be taken, "Those who recognized me were worse than those who did not."
6. The *liəng-siɛu* 凌霄, "trumpetflower," was a climbing vine that blossomed from summer into autumn. The relation of climbing vines to trees was commonly a metaphor for one's being "elevated" and "given support" by the powerful. A topical application of this and the following lines would be that someone, perhaps the poet, has depended on a powerful person to elevate him to a high position, but has met with a serious reversal that did not touch the one supported him; furthermore, his need for support and inability to stand on his own is from his own nature. For a possible application to Ku's life, see text, p. 299.
10. *KHyc*, *Wyyh*, and *Yfsc* include a repetition of 行路難.
11. *KHyc* reads 不知 at the beginning of this line.
13. For 看 *KHyc*, *Wyyh*, and *Yfsc* read 覺.

CHAPTER 16

09316: *CTs*, p. 1986; *WCcc* 8.1b–2a.
Rhymes: 2 *luin*, 4 *sin*, 6 *bhyin*, 8 *djhin*, 10 *ghiuən* . . . (*T'ung-yün*). The first ten of eighteen lines are quoted.
Title: "In the Post of Assistant in Lo-yang: Asking to Be Relieved" 任洛陽丞請告.

1. A *dzhɑk* 鑿 is a hole or bore, usually man-made.
5. *Jiɛt-qiɛu* 折腰, "breaking the waist," is a kenning for a respectful bow, which from its earlier uses suggests running counter to one's nature.
6. Emending 水 to 冰. In the *Jen-chien shih* chapter of the *Chuang-tzu* (10/4/38) one "drinks ice water," *qyǐm-biəng* 飲冰, in order to cool the "feverish" anxieties brought on by court commands. *Biəng* 冰 and *shuǐ* 水 are often confused in textual transmission.

7. *Xiou-gáu* 休告 is to resign from office.

9–10. These are common emblems of a creature fulfilling its own nature with others of its kind.

09387: *CTs*, p. 1999; *WCcc* 9.2a–2b; *Wyyh* 336.8a.
Rhymes: 1 *maek*, 2 *chiɛk*, 4 *kaek*; 6 *qiuaĕn*, 8 *hiuaĕn*; 9 *ten*, 10 *iɛn*, 12 *njiɛn*; (13 *lì*), 14 *piɔ̀i*, 16 *miɔ̀i*; (17 *xiɔ̀i*), 18 *iɛ*, 20 *djiɛ*.

3. *Shriu* 疏 suggests openwork, here referring to the windows or screens. *Leng-lung* 玲瓏 originally described the sound of jade, but early it was transferred to sparkling and intricate patterns of light, here shining through the *shriu*. *Hom* 含, originally meaning to "hold in the mouth," may retain some of its original force here as the open spaces in the latticework seem to "contain" the spring wind.

4. For "Rose Phoenix Gates," see note to 06057, line 1.

6. Lo-yu Park, founded in the Han, was one of the favorite places for outings from Ch'ang-an.

8. For 無 *Wyyh* reads 於, probably a printing error.

9. *Iou-iang* 悠揚 describes an expanse of sunlit scenery.

12. For 鄰 *Wyyh* reads 酒.

13. In poetry *mio-qiɛ̀m* 無厭 usually means simply "never get tired of"; however, in this case it is clearly used in its older, moral sense of "insatiable." *Jiuɛn-lì* 專利 is literally to "monopolize profits"; like *mio-qiɛ̀m* it is a pre-Ch'in phrase which carries strong moral condemnation.

14. For this line, *Wyyh* reads 百斛一醸斯須美. The *WCcc* text is literally, "A hundred measures in an instant, a single cup's expenditure."

15. Literally, "First the thick, afterwards the thin is a great theft."

20. For 去 *Wyyh* reads 者.

08960: *CTs*, p. 1912; *WCcc* 2.10b.
Rhymes: 1 *qim*, 2 *djhim*, 4 *jrhim*, 6 *tsim*, 8 *gyim*, 10 *kyim*, 12 *lim*. First two couplets regulated, two "A" form couplets.

1. *Dom-dom* 湛湛 is a binome describing the thickness and density of water, vegetation, etc.

2. This and the preceding line echo T'ao Ch'ien's 夕景湛盧明 (*CTsins* 6.10b). *Djhim* 沈, literally "sunken," is both a mood and a visual quality of endfolding darkness.

5. *Huen-mɔk* 玄黙 is the "dark silence" of the sage, a stillness and inaction.

8. *Djhiung-gyim* 沖襟, literally "hollow lapels," refers to a placid, unagitated mood. *Gyim* is commonly used for one's "state of mind."

09012: *CTs*, p. 1922; *WCcc* 3.7b.
Rhymes: 2 *djiuk*, 4 *siuk*. Regulated with compensatory violation in fourth position of first line.
Title: *Luit-shri* 律師 was a title for a class of both Taoist and Buddhist monks, though in this case, Ts'an is clearly a Buddhist.

12. The snow on pine and bamboo is an emblem of the resolute endurance of hardship.

09027: *CTs*, p. 1924; *WCcc* 3.9b; *Wyyh* 255.4a; *Tscs*, p. 714 (with answering poem by Ch'iu Tan).
Rhymes: 2 *ten*, 4 *men*. Unregulated.
Title: Literally, "To Auxiliary Secretary Ch'iu, Twenty-second of his Clan."

1. The use of *jiok* 屬 here is poetic, as in 03503.3.

2. *Sàn-bhò* 散步, literally "scattered pacing," is a random strolling, walking about without going anywhere in particular; the usage becomes current only in the late eigth and ninth centuries, though it occurs earlier. *Hiuaèng liang ten* 詠涼天 can be "chant of the cool sky," as well as chant under it. As in *hiuaèng-miɔt* 詠物, *hiuaèng* often takes the topic of a poem as its object.

08907: *CTs*, p. 1901; *WCcc* 1.8b; *Twt* 15A.7a–7b; *Wyyh* 215.7a–7b; *Tscs*, p. 400.
Rhymes: 2 *xiang*, 4 *liang*, 6 *dhang*, 8 *kang*, 10 *miang*, 12 *zhiang*, 14 *jiang*, 16 *ziang*, 18 *iang*, 20 *ghiang*.
Only the seventh couplet is regulated.

Text: In his *Sheng-yen shih-hua* 升菴詩話 (*Hsü li-tai shih-hua* ed. 8.1b–2a), Yang Shen 楊慎 expresses the opinion that the last lines are a later interpolation by an enthusiast of the Southeast; however, such complimentary occasional closings were entirely consonant with T'ang poetic practice, and an earlier closure at line 16 would be most unusual for a poem of this sort.

2. *Qèn* 宴 is the same as 燕 in the title (though the use of 讌, the character used in the *Wh* category, may have an air of formality). *Qèn-tsǐm* 宴寢 suggests a horizontal feast, like those the Romans held.

5. *Qɑ* 疴 suggests a genuine sickness, rather than simply poor spirits. For 近 *Wyyh* reads 正.

8. In the use of *dǒ* 覩, in the archaic *siɛ-min* 斯民, and in the sentiment expressed, this line is graciously formal.

9–10. These lines represent a version of the principle of government by inaction.

11. *Siɛn-bhiɑi* 鮮肥 is literally "the fresh and fat"; i.e., meat. The line is literally, "The fresh and fat belong to a seasonal prohibition."

13–14. *Biǒ* 俯 and *ngiɑ̌ng* 仰 joined as a compound mean "in a brief time"; the placement of two characters in parallel position usually indicates their significance in compound form; this "in one moment . . . in the next. . . ." However, their basic meanings, "looking down" and "looking up," are physically appropriate to the actions described, and these semes are also present in the line. "Gold" and "jade" are common compliments for literary excellence.

17. *Miən* 文, translated broadly as "culture," is also more specifically "literature."

18. *Ngyèn* 彥 is a person rich in talent and virtue. *Quɑng-iɑng* 汪洋 is a binome describing the boundlessness of the ocean, and like many such water descriptives, it is transferred to the richness of talent in literary composition.

19. The *bhiɑen* 藩 are the "marches," the border feudatories. The *dhɑ̀i-bhiɑen* 大藩 are the important border feudatories, though the application of this language of imperial feudalism to Wu is singularly inappropriate.

20. *Dzhəi-biò* 財賦, literally "property and taxables," is a phrase from the *Shu* (III.II pt.ii. chap. 3.15): these are the factors given consideration in the capital's adjudication of each region's taxes.

08874: *CTs*, p. 1895; *WCcc* 1.3a.

Rhymes: 2 *lim*, 4 *nom*, 6 *qyim*, 8 *gyim*, 10 *djhim*, 12 *sim* (*T'ung-yün*: despite the apparent difference of *nom*, it belongs to an adjacent category).

3. Literally, "Not yet set, Heaven's River stretches athwart (the sky)."

4. This signals the onset of autumn.

7. Literally, the "*shang* gusts," *shang* being the note associated with autumn.

11. An odd, elliptical construction, literally, "Human life—how can it be grasses or trees?" A negative answer to the rhetorical question is implied.

12. *Hɑn-shiǔ* 寒暑, freely translated as "the season's changes," is literally "(winter's) cold and (summer's) heat," a common metonymy for the seasons.

09412: *CTs*, p. 2006; *WCcc* 10.4a; *Wyyh* 332.5b–6a.

Rhymes: 2 *guək*, 4 *xək*; 5 *dzhəi*, 6 *kəi*; 7 *jiùng*, 8 *djiùng*; (9 *leng*), 10 *tsiɛng*, 12 *giaeng*; 13 *hɛk*, 14 *gɛk*, 16 *paek*; 18 *tzuən*, (19 *djhin*), 20 *ngiaen*; 21 *gǒ*, 22 *miǒ*.

2. The events described in the poem are expanded from a brief note on Wu-ti's shooting of a dragon during his journey down the Yangtze in 106 B.C. in *Han shu*, p. 196. In the context of another mention of the journey in *Sc*, pp. 400–401, "southern fiefs," *nom-guək* 南國, may be a proper name Nom. *Guɑn-ziok* 觀俗 echoes the canonical exegesis of *guɑn* in *Analects* XVII.9: "By the *Shih* one can observe" 詩可以觀. *Guɑn* is interpreted as "observe the fruition and decline of customs" 觀風俗之盛衰. This echo reinforces the general theme of Wu-ti's activeness: as he personally shoots the dragon, so he personally goes out to observe customs.

3. *Ngiɑt* 屹 describes the massive solidity of a mountain, here transferred to the immobility of the emperor's boat.

6. *Liɛn-shrɛn* 連山, "linked mountains," is a variation on the standard metaphor of waves as mountains. *Chit* 叱 is to "shout at" someone or something, rebuking or insulting.

7. *Ngiɑk-njiɛn* 愕然 describes the kind of fear that occurs when encountering something unexpected—"startle up in terror."

10. *Djhiuk-lo* 舳艫, "sterns and prows," was a common synecdoche for boats. *Djhiuk-lo tsen-lið* 舳艫千里 is taken verbatim from the *Han shu* passage, immediately following the statement that Wu-ti himself shot a dragon. The commentators explain the phrase as a hyperbolic description of an unbroken line of boats (*Hs*, pp. 196–97).

12. The "sea god" is T'ien-wu (*Ten-ngo* 天吳), described in the *Shan-hai ching* as having a beast's body, eight human heads, eight tails, and eight legs.

13. Tz'u Fei (Tsì Biəi 佽非) was a swordsman of Warring States Ch'u who, when his boat was stopped by a pair of dragons, leapt into the waves and killed them. Written 佽飛, the name became the official title of a Han huntmaster, in charge of shooting with stringed arrows.

14. The referent of "orphan," *go-njiɛ* 孤兒, is uncertain, though it may simply be an expansion of *go* as a conventional deprecatory term for imperial princes and nobility. "Shooting through hide (armor)," *guǎn-gɛk* 貫革, describes the graceless but powerful archery of a warrior interested not in the fine points of the art but in the ability to penetrate a thickness of armor.

15. In other words, given that these others were present to kill the dragon for him, why did Wu-ti kill it himself? The *tsin* 親, "himself," is also used in the *Han shu* source passage.

16. *Dhuɑt-paek* 奪魄 is to cause someone to lose spirit, in this case to "overawe" the feudal lords.

19. The hunts of the emperor are celebrated in the great *fu* on his hunting park by Ssu-ma Hsiang-ju.

20. This line could also be taken as a rhetorical question: "Of this day how could his attendants not speak?" implying that they did. But this seems to promise far more than the brief notice in the *Han shu*, and it is probably best to have the poet wondering why they did not write more of the feat. It would be very easy to read topical criticism into this line.

09236: *CTs*, p. 1970; *WCcc* 7.1b.
Rhymes: 1 *ten*, 2 *chiuɛn*, 4 *nen*. Regulated.
Title: A note, probably the author's, is attached to the title: "The temple is at Wu-kung [about 90 kilometers west of Ch'ang-an]; I once stayed in the temple" 寺在武功，曾居此寺. 方 is probably a mistake for 訪.

1. *Xiɑng-dhəi* 香臺, "incense-terrace," is a kenning for the main image hall of a temple.
2. In other words, in reflection.
3. *Jiu* 諸 is a formal marker of a collective. *Biət siɑng shiək* 不相識 is, in this case, clearly "we do not recognize each other."
4. Rather than its full verbal meaning "sit," *dzhuɑ̀* 坐 here might be one of the particle usages listed in Chang Hsiang, *Shih tz'u ch'ü yü-tz'u hui-shih*, pp. 405–14; however, the parallel word does not give any clue to the function of *dzhuɑ̀* here. *Giə̀-nen* 記年 is to "chronicle," but *giə̀* here might simply mean to "recall." "Recording" in the translation is a weak attempt to preserve the openness of Wei's line, encompassing a metaphorical marking of the years by the bells and the poet's memory of bygone years.

09360: *CTs*. p. 1994; *WCcc* 8.8b.
Rhymes: 2 *shriu*, 4 *mio* (*t'ung-yün*), 6 *njiu*, 8 *jrhiu*, 10 *xiu*, 12 *shiu*. The fifth couplet is regulated; however, the poem as a whole gives the impression of studied carelessness: in contrast to old-style" avoidance of tone pattern, this poem in many of the couplets misses regulation only by one character.
Title: "Planting Melons" recalls the Ch'in marquis of Tung-ling, who after the fall of the Ch'in, became a melon planter outside the Blue Gate of Han Ch'ang-an. In the ninth of Li Po's *Ku-feng*, the marquis's changed status is used as an example of the wheel of fortune.

1. *Lǒ-mǎng* 鹵莽 is a compound used in the *Chuang-tzu* (71/25/38–39) describing "carelessness" in government, transferred from carelessness of farming: commentators explain it as "plowing shallow sowing thinly." *Shruit-sièng* 率性 is to following one's inborn nature. *Biɑng* 方 here marks the apodosis of a conditional construction.

2. *Liă-shraeng* 理生 has the sense of "putting one's life in good order," following the straight and narrow (as in *liă-sièng* 理性). *Shriu* 疏 is to be "remiss" or "lax."

7. The "spring work" is, of course, weeding.

11. *Ngo-jrhaei* 吾儕 is literally "my kind," though Wei is probably referring as much to his ineptness as to his literacy, the mark of his social class.

09241: *CTs*, p. 1971; *WCcc* 7.2b; *Yls* in *TjhTs*, p. 225.
Rhymes: 2 *dhɑ*, 4 *dɑ*. Regulated.

2. *Tsɑ-dhɑ* 蹉跎 primarily meant to "stumble"; it was early extended to mean "miss an opportunity" or to "fail." With a time word such as "years" or "days" as the subject, *tsɑ-dhɑ* means that time "slips away" from one. *Qòm* 暗 means that the poet was "unaware" of the passage of time.

3. For this use of *dzhuà* 坐, see Chang Hsiang, *Shih tz'u ch'ü yü-tz'u hui-shih*, p. 407.

09172: *CTs*, p. 1956; *WCcc* 5.15a; *Yls* in *TjhTs*, pp. 297–98.
Rhymes: 1 *hɛn*, 2 *huan*, 4 *shrɛn*. Regulated.
Title: *Yls* reads 訪李廓不遇.

1. Officials regularly got one day off in ten. *Kio-djhiɛ* 驅馳 is literally to "gallop" a horse; it was sometimes transferred to public service (as were many horse words), implying a person must "rush around" at the behest of others.

3. *Shiə-siə* 詩思 is the process of thinking which leads to a poem.

09263: *CTs*, pp. 1975–76; *WCcc* 7.6a–6b; *Wyyh* 319.12a.
Rhymes: 2 *shiă*, 4 *kiă*, 6 *liă*, 8 *shuĭ*, 10 *xiă*, 12 *iă*, 14 *liă*. Unregulated.

9. *Gyi-ghio* 飢劬 is to be forced to hard labor out of hunger.

11. *Tsɑng-lǐm* 倉廩 are simply "granaries," but the compound is usually used for those granaries kept by the government. *Siuk-djhiu* 宿儲 is literally "accumulation left over from earlier."

09003: *CTs*, p. 1921; *WCcc* 3.6b; *Twt* 17B.11a–11b; *Wyyh* 228.5b–6a; *Tscs*, p. 400.
Rhymes: 2 *kaek*, 4 *zhiɛk*; 6 *ziɛk*, 8 *tziɛk*. Unregulated, except for the second couplet.
Title: Ch'üan-chiao Mountain was near Wei's post in Ch'u-chou (in modern Anhwei).

1. The "chill," first noticed this morning, marks the advance of autumn and oncoming winter.

4. This recalls the recluse "Master White Stone" 白石先生, who boiled white stones as his food.

6. For 慰 *Wyyh* and *Tscs* read 寄.

7. For 滿 *Twt*, *Wyyh*, and *Tscs* read 遍.

09369: *CTs*, p. 1995; *WCcc* 8.9b; *Yls* in *TjhTs*, p. 225; *Yhc* in *TjhTs*, p. 398; *Ttc* in *TjhTs*, p. 467; *Wyyh* 164.7b–8a.
Rhymes: 1 *shraeng*, 2 *miaeng*, 4 *huaeng*. Regulated, two "A" form couplets in sequence.
Title: *Yhc* and *Ttc* read simply 西澗.

2. For 深 *Ttc* reads 遠.

Finding List

Poem Number	Page in Text	Page in Notes
09003	315	422
09012	308	419
09027	308	419
09172	314	422
09236	312	421
09241	314	422
09263	315	422
09316	305	418–19
09360	313	421–22
09369	316	422
09387	306–07	419
09412	311–12	420–21
09534	178	378
09591	175–76	376–77
09596	176–77	377
09646	181	379–80
09757	180	379
09774	180	379
09877	179	379
09882	179	379
10045	266	410
10081	265	409–10
10242	150	373
10313	153–54	375
10323	150–51	373
10342	160	376
10358	151–52	374–75
10360	157–58	376
10384	67	350–51
10432	155–56	375–76
10498	187	380–81
10509	193	383–84
10524	191–92	381–83
10534	195–96	384–87
10544	104	361–62
10557	197–98	387–89
10561	223–24	399–400
10632	205–06	392–93
10676	210–11	395–96
10686	207–08	394–95
10914	189	381
10973	201	390–91
10974	200	389
11027	201	389–90
11045	204	391
11052	204	391
11089	205	391–92
11139	211	396
11219	207	393–94
11228	210	395
11232	219	399
11465	212	397
11474	213	397–98
11554	214	398
11627	216	399
11973	251	407
11975	251	407
11982	251	407

An Introductory Bibliography

EARLY ANTHOLOGIES AND SOURCES FOR TEXTS

A serious student of T'ang poetry must be concerned with texts and their sources. The circulation of poems in manuscript, the probably reconstitution of poems from memory, the upheavals of the late ninth and early tenth centuries, and a cavalier attitude towards textual integrity on the part of many anthologists have resulted in a rich range of variant texts for many of the best-known T'ang poems. An equally disturbing probability is that variants once existed for many poems preserved in a single early text: their textual integrity may be a function only of the loss of other texts. Even when we can trace the history of printed editions, we know almost nothing of the history of a work between its formation and the appearance of Sung printed editions—if we are fortunate enough to have Sung editions. Though a degree of textual uncertainty is present when we treat any T'ang text, knowledge of the source of a poem is of crucial importance in evaluating the credibility of a text and its attribution.

Most of the poets discussed at length in this book have collections that have survived independently. Two exemplary studies of the history of printed editions are recommended:

Hung, William. Preface to *A Concordance to the Poems of Tu Fu*. Harvard-Yenching Institute Sinological Index Series, Supplement 14. Reprint. Taipei, 1966.

Bryant, Daniel. *The High T'ang Poet Meng Hao-jan: Studies in Biography and Textual History*. Diss., University of British Columbia, 1978.

Early anthologies are also important, not only as sources of texts and variants, but also as sources for the history of taste. Hiraoka Takeo 平岡武夫, Ichihara Kōkichi 市原亨吉 and Imai Kiyoshi's 今井清, *Tōdai no shihen* 唐代の詩篇, T'ang Civilization Reference Series 11–12: Institute for Humanistic Studies (Kyoto, 1964–65) provides a poem's source not only in one or more editions of the poet's collection, but also in the early anthologies.

In addition to individual collections and early anthologies, T'ang poems have been preserved in a variety of other sources which include *shih-hua*, anecdotal collections, encyclopedias, stories, gazetteers, and the Japanese sources that went to make up the *Ch'üan T'ang shih yi* 全唐詩逸.

T'ang Anthologies

Sou-yü hsiao-chi 搜玉小集: 1 *chüan*, compiler unknown, but probably put together in the second quarter of the eighth century. The *Syhc* contains primarily poets of the late seventh and early eighth centuries. There is a study by Itō Masafumi 伊藤正文, *Sogyoku shōshū ni tsuite* 搜玉小集について, in *Chūgoku bungaku hō* 15 (1961).

Ho-yüeh ying-ling chi 河嶽英靈集: 3 *chüan*, compiled by Yin Fan 殷璠 and completed in 753. This is the best known of the T'ang anthologies and contains an important general preface and prefaces for the individual poets included; the latter are important sources for contemporary evaluation of High T'ang poets. There is a study by Nakazawa Mareo 中澤希男, *Kagaku eireishū kō* 河嶽英靈集攷, in *Gumma Daigaku kiyō* 1 (1951); and a study of the preface by Wang Yün-hsi 王運熙, *Shih Ho-yüeh ying-ling chi hsü lun Sheng-T'ang shih-ko* 釋河嶽英靈集序論盛唐詩歌, in *T'ang-shih yen-chiu lun-wen-chi* (Peking, 1957).

Kuo-hsiu chi 國秀集: 3 *chüan*, compiled by Jui T'ing-chang 芮挺章 in the late 750s or early 760s. The emphasis in this anthology is on regulated forms and on euphony. There is a study of the text and dating by Nakazawa Mareo 中澤希男, *Kokushūshū kō* 国秀集攷, in *Nihon Chūgokugakkai hō* 3 (1951).

Ch'ieh-chung chi 篋中集: 1 *chüan*, compiled by Yüan Chieh 元結, with a preface dated 760. This is a tiny collection of *fu-ku* poets, many of whom are otherwise unknown; see discussion in chapter 12.

Chung-hsing hsien-ch'i chi 中興閒氣集: 2 *chüan*, compiled by Kao Chung-wu 高中武 in the late 780s with a general preface (missing in some editions) and prefaces to the individual poets. The *Chhcc* is an anthology of poets famous in the 760s and 770s. Modeled on the *Hyylc*, this anthology is an important source for capital taste in the later eighth century.

Chi-hsüan chi 極玄集: 2 *chüan*, compiled in the early ninth century by Yao Ho 姚合. The *Chc* provides short biographical notes on the poets and begins with Wang Wei to cover the poets of the later eighth century.

Yü-lan shih 御覽詩: 1 *chüan*, compiled by Ling-hu Ch'u 令狐楚 by imperial command in the Yüan-ho reign (806–20). The *Yls* is made up primarily of poets popular in the later eighth century.

Yu-hsüan chi 又玄集: 2 *chüan*, compiled by Wei Chuang 韋莊, with a preface dated 900. The *Yhc* contains a wide representation of poets from the eighth and ninth centuries and includes poems by monks and women.

Ts'ai-tiao chi 才調集: 10 *chüan*, compiled by Wei Hu 韋縠 in the Five Dynasties. This is a large anthology with almost a thousand poems (and not one by Tu Fu). The following numbers give some indication of early-tenth-century taste: Wei Chuang, 63 poems; Wen T'ing-yün, 61 poems; Wang Wei, 2 poems; Meng Hao-jan, 2 poems; Kao Shih, 1 poem.

The nine anthologies above have been published together with a fragment of another anthology recovered from Tun-huang as *T'ang-jen hsüan T'ang-shih* 唐人選唐詩 (Hong Kong, 1958). A larger collection of T'ang poems recovered from Tun-huang materials has been made by Wang Chung-min 王重民, *Pu Ch'üan T'ang shih* 補全唐詩, reprinted in *T'ang-shih yen-chiu lun-wen chi*, ed. Chou K'ang-hsieh 周康燮 (Hong Kong, 1971).

Sung Anthologies Important as Sources for T'ang Poetry

Wen-yüan ying-hua 文苑英華: 1000 *chüan*, completed in 987 by Li Fang 李昉 and the other compilers of the T'ai-p'ing encyclopedias. The *Wyyh* is a textual nightmare with errors, "corrections," misattributions, and duplications (often under different titles), but it remains perhaps the single most important source for T'ang writing. The *Wyyh* was based on the model of the *Wen hsüan* and begins in the end of the Liang, where the

Wen hsüan left off. The *Wyyh* includes *fu* and prose, as well as poetry. Later editions include corrections of some errors, and there is a *Wen-yüan ying-hua pien-cheng* 文苑英華辨證 by the Sung scholar P'eng Shu-hsia 彭叔夏.

T'ang wen ts'ui 唐文粹: 100 *chüan*, compiled by Yao Hsüan 姚鉉 (968–1020). The *Twt* was also modeled on the *Wen hsüan* and contains *fu* and prose, but it was compiled with a strong *fu-ku* bias and contains much material not in the *Wyyh*.

T'ang pai-chia shih-hsüan 唐百家詩選: 20 *chüan*, compilation dubiously attributed to Wang An-shih 王安石.

Wan-shou T'ang-jen chüeh-chü 萬首唐人絕句: 101 *chüan* (though there are very different editions), compiled in 1192 by Hung Mai 洪邁.

Yüeh-fu shih-chi 樂府詩集: 100 *chüan*, compiled by Kuo Mao-ch'ien 郭茂倩 in the Sung. The *Yfsc* contains most of the *yüeh-fu* through the T'ang as well as some earlier material on *yüeh-fu*.

T'ang-shih chi-shih 唐詩紀事: 81 *chüan*, compiled by Chi Yu-kung 計有功, earliest published edition from 1224. There is a typeset, collated edition put out by Taiwan Chung-hua (Taipei, 1970). Though much of its material comes from extant earlier sources, the *Tscs* also contains important anecdotes and biographical material.

OTHER IMPORTANT LATER COLLECTIONS AND ANTHOLOGIES:

San-t'i shih 三體詩: compiled by Chou Pi 周弼 in 1250. Though this is a Sung work, its texts are poor and it is more interesting and important as an anthology than as a primary source. The *san-t'i* are the heptasyllabic and pentasyllabic *lü-shih* and the pentasyllabic *chüeh-chü*. Within these three large divisions, poems are further subdivided according to Chou Pi's theories of regulated poetry. Most of the poems are from the later eighth century and from the ninth century. There is a Japanese translation and study by Murakami Tetsumi 村上哲見, *Santaishi* 三休詩, *Chūgoku koten sen* 16–17 (Tokyo, 1969).

T'ang-shih p'in-hui 唐詩品彙: 100 *chüan*, compiled by Kao Ping 高棟 in 1393.

T'ang shih hsüan 唐詩選: 7 *chüan*, published in 1570 after the death of its reputed compiler, Li P'an-lung 李攀龍. This has been the most important anthology of T'ang poetry in Japan. The selection is idiosyncratic and reflects Ming archaist taste: it concentrates heavily on the High T'ang, with some Early T'ang poems, less Mid-T'ang, and no Late T'ang. There are numerous Japanese translations and studies, including Maeno Naoaki 前野直彬, *Tōshisen* 唐詩選 (Tokyo, 1970) and Saitō Shō 齋藤晌, *Tōshisen* 唐詩選, *Kanshi taikei* 6–7 (Tokyo, 1970).

T'ang-yin t'ung-chien 唐音統籤: 1033 *chüan*, compiled by Hu Chen-heng 胡震亨 in the seventeenth century. This massive compendium was one of the primary bases for the *Ch'üan T'ang shih*. The last section, the *T'ang-yin k'uei-chien* 唐音癸籤, is a large compendium of traditional comments on T'ang poetry, random philological notes, and comments on anthologies and editions.

Ch'üan T'ang shih 全唐詩: 900 *chüan*, compiled by ten Ch'ing scholars in response to an edict of 1705, and completed in 1706, then published in 1707. It was reissued in 1887, and Chung-hua published a typeset, punctuated edition in 1960. The typeset edition has corrected some misprints.

Ch'üan T'ang shih yi (*Zen Tōshi itsu*) 全唐詩逸: 3 *chüan*, compiled by Ichikawa Seinei 市河世寧. This work contains T'ang poems that were preserved in Japan and left out of the *CTs*. This is included in modern editions of *CTs*.

GENERAL STUDIES:

Chao Wen-tsao 趙文藻. *T'ang-shih chiang-yi* 唐詩講義. Taipei, 1956.

Cheng-chung Book Company. *T'ang-tai shih-hsüeh* 唐代詩學. Taipei, 1967.

Fang Yü 方瑜. *T'ang-shih hsing-ch'eng te yen-chiu* 唐詩形成的研究. Taipei, 1975. On development of genres.

Hsi Han-ching 席涵靜. *T'ang-jen ch'i-yen chin-t'i-shih ko-lü te yen-chiu* 唐人七言近體詩格律的研究. Taipei, 1976.

Hsia Ching-kuan 夏敬觀. *T'ang shih shuo* 唐詩説. Taipei, 1975.

Hu Yün-yi 胡雲翼. *T'ang-shih yen-chiu* 唐詩研究. Hong Kong, 1959.

Huang Sheng-hsiung 黃盛雄. *T'ang-jen chüeh-chü te yen-chiu* 唐人絕句的研究. M.A. thesis. Taiwan Shih-fan ta-hsüeh, 1972.

Itō Masafumi 伊藤正文. *Sei Tō shijin to zendai no shijin* 盛唐詩人と前代の詩人. *Chūgoku bungaku hō* 8 (1958) and 10 (1959).

Lin Keng 林庚. *Sheng T'ang ch'i-hsiang* 盛唐氣象. *Pei-ching ta-hsüeh hsüeh-pao* 2 (1958).

Liu K'ai-yang 劉開揚. *T'ang-shih lun-wen chi* 唐詩論文集. Shanghai, 1961.

Liu Ta-mei 劉達梅. *T'ang-tai shih-jen fen-che chi yen-chiu* 唐代詩人分析及研究. Taipei, 1976.

Maeno Naoaki 前野直彬. *Tōdai no shijintachi* 唐代の詩人達. Tokyo, 1971.

Ogawa Tamaki 小川環樹. *Tōshi gaisetsu* 唐詩概説. Chūgoku shijin senshū. Tokyo. 1958.

Ogawa Tamaki. *Tōdai no shijin—sono tenki* 唐代の詩人—その傳記. Tokyo, 1975.

Su Hsüeh-lin 蘇雪林. *T'ang-shih kai-shuo* 唐詩概説. Reprint. Taipei, 1967.

Suzuki Shūji 鈴木修次. *Tōdai shijin ron* 唐代詩人論. 2 vols. Tokyo, 1973.

Tu Sung-po 杜松柏. *Ch'an-hsüeh yü T'ang-Sung shih-hsüeh* 禪學與唐宋詩學. Taipei, 1976.

Wang Shih-ching 王士菁. *T'ang-tai shih-ko* 唐代詩歌. Peking, 1959.

INDIVIDUAL POETS

Ch'en Yi-hsin 陳貽焮. *Lun Wang Wei te shih* 論王維的詩. *Wen-hsüeh yi-ch'an* 3 (1956).

—— *Wang Wei sheng-p'ing shih-chi ch'u-t'an* 王維生平事蹟初探. *Wen-hsüeh yi-ch'an* 6 (1958).

—— *Wang Wei te shan-shui shih* 王維的山水詩. *Wen-hsüeh p'ing-lun* (1960.5).

Chuang Shen 莊申. *Wang Wei hsing-lü k'ao* 王維行旅考. *Hsin-ya hsüeh-pao* 1969.9.1.

—— *Wang Wei Tao-chia ssu-hsiang yü sheng-huo* 王維道家思想與生活. *Ta-lu tsa-chih* 33–8 (1966).

—— *Wang Wei yen-chiu* 王維研究. Hong Kong, 1971.

Harada Kenyū 原田憲雄 and Kobayashi Taiichirō 小林太市郎. *Ōi* 王維. *Kanshi taikei* vol. 10. Tokyo, 1964.

Hsü Hsien-te 徐賢德. *Wang Wei shih yen-chiu* 王維詩研究. Taipei, 1973.

Iritani Sensuke 入谷仙介. *Ōi kenkyū* 王維研究. Tokyo, 1976.

Kobayashi Taiichirō 小林太市郎. *Ōi no seigai to geijutsu* 王維の生涯と藝術. Osaka, 1944.

Teng K'uei-ying 鄧魁英. *Wang Wei shih chien-lun* 王維詩簡論. *T'ang-shih yen-chiu lun-wen chi*. Peking, 1959.

Tsuru Haruo 都留春雄. *Ōi* 王維. *Chūgoku shijin senshū* 6. Tokyo, 1958.

Tsuru Haruo et al. *Ōi shi sakuin* 王維詩索引. Kyoto, 1952.

Wagner, Marsha. *Wang Wei*. Forthcoming.

Meng Hao-jan

Bryant, Daniel. *The High T'ang Poet Meng Hao-jan: Studies in Biography and Textual History*. Diss., University of British Columbia, 1978.

Ch'en Yi-hsin 陳貽焮. *Meng Hao-jan shih-chi k'ao-pien* 孟浩然事跡考辨. *Wen-shih* 4 (1965).
———— *T'an Meng Hao-jan te yin-yi* 談孟浩然的隱逸. *T'ang-shih yen-chiu lun-wen chi.* Peking, 1959.
Frankel, Hans. *The Biographies of Meng Hao-jan.* Chinese Dynastic Histories Translations 1. Berkeley, 1961.
Hsiao Chi-tsung 蕭繼宗. *Meng Hao-jan shih-shuo* 孟浩然詩説. Taipei, 1961.
Kroll, Paul W. "The Quatrains of Meng Hao-jan." *Monumenta Serica* 31 (1974–75).
Lao Ssu-kuang 勞思完. *Lun Meng Hao-jan shih* 論孟浩然詩. *Wen-hsüeh shih-chieh* 25 (1960).
Miller, James W. "*The Poetry of Meng Hao-jan: Translations and Critical Introduction for the Western Reader.* Diss., Princeton, 1972.
Rust, Ambros. *Meng Hao-jan: sein Leben und religioses Denken nach seinen Gedichten.* Diss., Zurich, 1960.
Taniguchi Akio 谷口明夫. *Mō Kōnen jiseki kō: jōkyō ōshi o megutte* 孟浩然事跡考: 上京應試をめぐって. *Chūgoku chūsei bungaku kenkyū* 11 (1976).
Wen Yi-to 聞一多. *Meng Hao-jan* 孟浩然. *T'ang-shih tsa-lun.* Peking, 1956.
Yu Hsin-li 游信利. *Meng Hao-jan chi chien-chu* 孟浩然集箋注. Taipei, 1968.

Wang Ch'ang-ling

Bodman, Richard W. *Poetics and Prosody in Early Medieval China: A Study and Translation of Kūkai's Bunkyō hifuron.* Diss., Cornell, 1978.
Feng P'ing 馮平. *Wang Ch'ang-ling ch'i-chüeh te yi-shu t'e-se* 王昌齡七絕的藝術特色. *Kuang-ming jih-pao* 1963.2.17.
Li Kuo-sheng 李國勝. *Wang Ch'ang-ling shih chiao-chu* 王昌齡詩校注. Taipei, 1973.
T'an Yu-hsüeh 譚優學. *Wang Ch'ang-ling hsing-nien k'ao* 王昌齡行年考. Reprint. *T'ang-shih yen-chiu lun-wen chi*, vol. 3. Hong Kong, 1970.

Li Po

For a discussion of editions of Li Po's works, see Hanabusa Hideki 花房英樹, *A Concordance to the Poems of Li Po.* T'ang Civilization Reference Series 8 (Kyoto, 1957); and T'ang Ming-min 唐明敏, *Li Po chi ch'i shih chih pan-pen* 李白及其詩之版本. M.A. thesis, Kuo-li cheng-chih ta-hsüeh. Taipei, 1975 For a bibliography of secondary works, see *Li Po yen-chiu lun-wen chi* 李白研究論文集 (Peking, 1964), pp. 417–25; and *Chūgoku koten kenkyū* 16 (1968), pp. 78–84.
Chan Ying 詹鍈. *Li Po shih-wen hsi-nien* 李白詩文繫年. Peking, 1958.
Ch'i Wei-han 戚維翰. *Li Po yen-chiu* 李白研究. Taipei, 1975.
Hanabusa Hideki 花房英樹. *A Concordance to the Poems of Li Po.* T'ang Civilization Reference Series 8. Kyoto, 1957.
Ho Heng-jen 賀恒仁. *Li Po shen-shih k'ao* 李白身世考. Taipei, 1977.
Huang Hsi-kuei 黃錫珪. *Li T'ai-po nien-p'u* 李太白年譜. Peking, 1958.
Kuo Mo-jo 郭沫若. *Li Po yü Tu Fu* 李白與杜甫. Peking, 1971.
Li Po yen-chiu lun-wen chi 李白研究論文集. Peking, 1964.
Lin Keng 林庚. *Shih-jen Li Po* 詩人李白. Shanghai, 1958.
Matsuura Tomohisa 松浦友久. *Rihaku kenkyū* 李白研究. Tokyo, 1976.
Ōno Jitsunosuke 大野実之助. *Ritaihaku kenkyū* 李太白研究. Tokyo, 1959.
Waley, Arthur. *The Poetry and Career of Li Po.* London, 1950.
Wong Siu-kit. *The Genius of Li Po.* Hong Kong, 1974.

Wang Yün-hsi 王運熙 et al. *Li Po yen-chiu* 李白研究. Peking, 1962.
Yü P'ing-po 俞平伯 et al. *Li Po shih lun-ts'ung* 李白詩論叢. Hong Kong, 1962.

Kao Shih

Chan, Marie. *Kao Shih*. Boston, 1978.
Juan T'ing-yü 阮廷瑜. *Kao Ch'ang-shih shih chiao-chu* 高常侍詩校注. Taipei, 1965.
——— *Kao Ch'ang-shih Ts'en Chia-chou ch'i-jen yü shih chih p'ing-lun* 高常侍岑嘉州其人與詩之評論. *Ta-lu tsa-chih* 1968.10.
Ueno Tatsukai 上尾龍介. *Kōteki no shifū* 高適の詩風. *Kyūshu Chūgoku gakkai hō* 11 (1965).

Ts'en Shen

Chan, Marie. "The Frontier Poems of Ts'en Shen." *Journal of the American Oriental Society*, 98.4 (1978).
Li Chia-yen 李嘉言. *Ts'en shih hsi-nien* 岑詩系年. *Wen-hsüeh yi-ch'an* 3 (1956).
Nakano Miyoko 中野美代子. *Shinshin no saigai shi* 岑参の塞外詩. *Nihon Chūgoku gakkai hō* 12 (1960).
Shih Mo-ch'ing 史墨卿. *Ts'en Shen yen-chiu* 岑参研究. Taipei, 1973.
Sugaya Seigo 菅谷省吾. *Shinshin no koshi ni tsuite* 岑参の古詩について. *Shinagaku kenkyū* 24-25 (1960).
Ueno Tatsukai 上尾龍介. *Shinshin no hensai shi* 岑参の邊塞詩. *Mekada Makoto hakushi kanreki kinen Chūgokugaku ronshu* (1964).

Tu Fu

The amount of scholarship on Tu Fu is so massive and complex that it is virtually an area of study in its own right. For studies and lists of editions and commentaries on Tu Fu, see:
Hung, William. Preface to *A Concordance to the Poems of Tu Fu*. Harvard-Yenching Sinological Index Series, Supplement 14. Reprint. Taipei, 1966.
Ma T'ung-yen 馬同儼 and Chiang Ping-hsin 姜炳炘. *Tu shih pan-pen mu-lu* 杜詩版本目錄. *Tu Fu yen-chiu lun-wen chi* 杜甫研究論文集, vol. 3. Peking, 1963., pp. 350-94.
Shu Ying 叔英. *Tu Fu shih-chi te chi-chung chiao-tsao k'o-pen* 杜甫詩集的幾種較早刻本. *Tu Fu yen-chiu lun-wen chi*, vol. 3. Peking, 1963, pp. 346-49.
Ts'ao Shu-ming 曹樹銘. *Tu chi ts'ung chiao* 杜集叢校. Hong Kong, 1978.
Wan Man 萬曼. *Tu chi shu-lu* 杜集敍錄. *Tu Fu yen-chiu lun-wen chi*, vol. 3. Peking, 1963, pp. 311-45.
For a bibliography of Chinese studies on Tu Fu (mainland only), see *Tu Fu yen-chiu lun-wen chi*, vol. 1 (Peking 1962), pp. 269-73; vol. 2 (Peking, 1963), pp. 286-292; and vol. 3 (Peking, 1963), pp. 395-99. These bibliographies cover the period from 1910 until 1962. The following is a short list of some books that are important, recent, or in English:
Ch'en Yao-chi 陳瑤璣. *Tu-shih t'e-chih yüan-yüan k'ao* 杜詩特質淵源考. Taipei, 1978.
Chien Ming-yung 簡明勇. *Tu Fu ch'i-lü chien-chu* 杜甫七律研究與箋註. Taipei, 1973.
Davis, A. R. *Tu Fu*. New York, 1971.
Hawkes, David. *A Little Primer of Tu Fu*. Oxford, 1967.
Hsiao Ti-fei 蕭滌非. *Tu Fu yen-chiu* 杜甫研究, vol 1. Shantung jen-min, 1956.
Hu Ch'uan-an 胡傳安. *Shih-sheng Tu Fu tui hou-shih shih-jen te ying-hsiang* 詩聖杜甫對後世詩人的影響. Taipei, 1975.
Huang Ch'i-yüan 黃啓原. *Tu Fu shih hsü-tzu yen-chiu* 杜甫詩虛字研究. Taipei, 1977.

Hung, William. *Tu Fu, China's Greatest Poet.* Cambridge, 1952.

——— *A Concordance to the Poems of Tu Fu.* Harvard-Yenching Institute Sinological Index Series, Supplement 121 reprint. Taipei, 1966.

Kurokawa Yōichi 黒川洋一. *Toho no kenkyū* 杜甫の研究. Tokyo, 1977.

Li Tao-hsien 李道顯. *Tu Fu shih-shih yen-chiu* 杜甫詩史研究. Taipei, 1973.

Liu Chung-ho 劉中和. *Tu shih yen-chiu* 杜詩研究. Taipei, 1968.

Mei Tsu-lin and Kao Yu-kung. "Tu Fu's 'Autumn Meditations': An Exercise in Linguistic Criticism. *Harvard Journal of Asiatic Studies* 28 (1968).

Suzuki Toraō 鈴木虎雄. *Toshi* 杜詩. Tokyo, 1963.

Tu Fu yen-chiu lun-wen chi 杜甫研究論文集, Vol. 1. Peking, 1962; vols. 2-3, Peking, 1963.

Tu Fu yen-chiu tzu-liao hui-p'ien 杜甫研究資料彙編. Taipei, 1973.

Yeh Chia-ying 葉嘉瑩. *Tu Fu Ch'iu-hsing pa-shou chi-shuo* 杜甫秋興八首集説. Taipei, 1966.

Yoshikawa Kojirō 吉川幸次郎. *Toho* 杜甫, vol. 1. Tokyo, 1967.

Zach, Erwin von. *Tu Fu's Gedichte.* ed. James Hightower. Cambridge, 1952.

Yüan Chieh

Lung Kung 龍冀. *Shih-jen Yüan Chieh* 詩人元結. *Wen-hsüeh yi-ch'an* 2 (1956).

Sun Wang 孫望. *Yüan Tz'u-shan chi* 元次山集. Shanghai, 1960.

T'ang Ch'ing-min 湯擎民. *Yüan Chieh ho t'a-te tso-p'in* 元結和他的作品. *T'ang-shih yen-chiu lun-wen chi.* Peking, 1959.

Other Poets

Fukazawa Kazayuki 深澤一幸. *I Ōbutsu no kakō* 韋應物の歌行. *Chūgoku bungaku hō* 24 (1974).

Harada Kenyū 原田憲雄. *Joken shishū kyōchū* 常建詩集校注. *Jimbun rosō* 13 (1966).

——— *Kokyō zakki* 顧況雑記. *Hōkō* 8 (1958).

Ichihara Kōkichi 市原亨吉. *Chūtō shoki ni okeru kōsa no shisō ni tsuite* 中唐初期における江左の詩僧について. *Tōhō gakuhō* 28 (1958).

Juan T'ing-yü 阮廷瑜. *T'ang Huang-fu Jan shih-chi k'o pu yi hsü* 唐皇甫冉詩集可補一序. *Ta-lu tsa-chih* 1964.12.

Konishi Noboru 小西昇. *Kokyō no fūshishi* 顧況の諷刺詩. *Chūgoky bungaku ronshū* 4 (1974).

Nielson, Thomas P. *A Concordance to the Poems of Wei Ying-wu.* San Francisco, 1976.

——— *The T'ang Poet-Monk Chiao-jan.* Occasional Papers 3, Center for Asian Studies, Arizona State University, 1972.

Ono Jitsunosuke 大野実之助. *Tōdai shidan ni okeru Chōetsu* 唐代詩壇における張説. *Chūgoku koten kenkyū* 14 (1966); 15 (1967).

Pu Tung 卜冬. *Wang Chih-huan te liang-chou tz'u* 王之渙的涼州詞. *Wen-hsüeh yen-chiu* 1958.2.

Yoshikawa Kojirō 吉川幸次郎. *Chōetsu no tenki to bungaku* 張説の傳記と文学. *Tōhōgaku* 1 (1951).

MISCELLANEOUS

Bibliography

In addition to the major bibliographies of Chinese studies, the journal *Chūgoku koten kenkyū* has put out two bibliographies devoted to T'ang literature. No. 13 (1965): 82–99 covers Japanese scholarship from late 1953 until 1965. No. 20 (1973): 74–91 covers both Chinese and Japanese scholarship from 1965 until 1973.

Middle Chinese Reconstructions

The most convenient work for finding Middle Chinese reconstructions is Hugh M. Stimson's *T'ang Poetic Vocabulary* (New Haven, 1976). This work contains all the characters used in seven hundred T'ang poems, including all the *T'ang-shih san-pai-shou* 唐詩三百首 and the T'ang poems from the *T'ang-Sung shih chü-yao* 唐宋詩舉要. Stimson uses his own romanization system, which is much more convenient than the modified Karlgren system used in the *Kuang-yün sheng-hsi*. For characters not in *T'ang Poetic Vocabulary*, see Shen Chien-shih 沈兼士, *Kuang-yün sheng-hsi* 廣韻聲系. reprint (Kyoto, 1969).

Shih-hua Literature

There is no work that provides the means to find discussions on a poet in the massive and fragmentary corpus of *shih-hua* literature. However, Helmut Martin's *Index to the Ho Collection of Twenty-Eight Shih-hua* (San Francisco, 1973) provides access to the discussion of T'ang poets in that select collection. Also of use is Shen Ping-hsün's 沈炳巽 *Hsü T'ang shih-hua* 續唐詩話, reprinted in *Li-tai shih-shih ch'ang-p'ien*, series 1, ed. Yang Chia-lo 楊家駱 (Taipei, 1971). This 100-*chüan* work gathers *shih-hua* from a wide variety of sources and arranges them under the heading of individual T'ang poets.

Names and Biographical Material

Hiraoka Takeo 平岡武夫 and Ichihara Kōkichi 市原亨吉. *Tōdai no shijin* 唐代の詩人. T'ang Civilization Reference Series 4. Kyoto, 1960. Index of the poets in *Ch'üan T'ang shih*. *Tōdai no shihen* also has an index at the end of names referred to in the poems.

Hsin Wen-fang 辛文房. *T'ang ts'ai-tzu chuan* 唐才子傳: 10 *chüan*, completed in 1304. This is an important source of biographical information on many T'ang poets, though it includes much apocryphal information. Nunome Chofu's 布目潮渢 and Nakamura Takahashi's 中村喬共 *Tōzaishiten no kenkyū* 唐才子傳の研究 (Osaka, 1972) traces the sources of the material Hsin Wen-fang used.

Ogawa Tamaki 小川環樹. *Tōdai no shijin—sono tenki* 唐代の詩人—その傳記. Tokyo, 1975.

Ts'en Chung-mien 岑仲勉. *T'ang-jen hang-ti lu* 唐人行第錄. Shanghai, 1962. Index identifying or trying to identify individuals referred to in poem titles by their clan number.

Metrics, Grammar, and Poetic Usage

Chang Hsiang 張相. *Shih tz'u ch'ü yü-tz'u hui-shih* 詩詞曲語辭匯釋. Shanghai, 1962.

Wang Li 王力. *Han-yü shih-lü hsüeh* 漢語詩律學. Shanghai, 1958. Still the standard study of metrics, rhyme, and the poetic language.

Index

DATE DUE

DEC 1 4 1990		
DEC 1 8 1999		